914.4504
R

W9-BOE-897

The **Rough Guide** to

The Loire

written and researched by

James McConnachie

NEW YORK • LONDON • DELHI

www.roughguides.com

△ The keep at Châteaudun

recreated the vibrant civilization they had discovered in Italy. At the beginning of the sixteenth century, François I even brought Leonardo da Vinci, in person, to his miniature court at Amboise. When the court abandoned the Loire for Paris, in the mid-sixteenth century, the Loire slipped back into provincial obscurity.

If there's no single word for "the Loire region", it's because there's no such thing. Historically, the area is divided into separate regions, though these were replaced after the Revolution by administrative *départements* named after local rivers. Touraine became Indre-et-Loire, Anjou changed to Maine-et-Loire and the Orléanais was saddled with the name of a tiny

△ Picnic near the château of Saumur

backwater, the Loiret. Yet local people never accepted the "new" names, and in recent years tourist boards have revived the old ones. As for the region as a whole, the nearest you can get in French is "Val de Loire", meaning the classic royal stretch of the Loire valley.

Where to go

> The heartland region of Touraine, long known as "the garden of France", has the best wines, the most delicious goat's cheese and the most regal history

The Loire isn't all châteaux. If you spend plenty of down-time on the river-banks, with supplies of local cheese, fruit and wine, you'll find the Loire the most beguiling of all French regions. More active visitors can rent **canoes** and kayaks everywhere, well-marked **footpaths** run throughout the region, and **cycling** makes an excellent way to get around – rental bikes are easy to find. That said, most visitors tour by car, as relying on public transport mostly restricts you to the towns.

The heartland region of **Touraine**, long known as "the garden of France", has the best wines, the most delicious goat's cheese, the most regal history and, it's argued, the purest French accent in the land. It also has two of the finest châteaux – **Chenonceau** and **Chambord** – and by far the most developed tourist industry to match. But Touraine also takes in three of the Loire's pleasantest tributaries: the **Cher**, **Indre** and **Vienne**, each of which can be explored at a slower, more intimate pace. The attractive towns of **Blois** and **Amboise**, which have their own exceptional châteaux, make good bases for visiting the area upstream of Tours, including the wild and watery region of the **Sologne**. Downstream, around handsome **Saumur**, fascinating troglodyte dwellings have been carved out of the soft local rock. If you have just a week to spare for the region, then these are the parts to spend it in.

Of the three main cities, energetic, historic **Tours** provides the best urban base, though **Angers**, capital of Anjou, and **Orléans**, the vibrant city of the northeast, have their own urbane nineteenth-century charm. Each city has its distinctive cathedral, though none is as impressive as the three found in outlying regions: the hybrid Romanesque-Gothic cathedral of **Le Mans**, the perfectly harmonious structure of **Chartres** and giant-scale **Bourges**.

Touring the Loire without visiting any **châteaux** would be rather eccentric, and yet the sheer number of them can make choosing bewildering. Trying to pack in the maximum can quickly blunt your sensibilities, and you'll get most out of your stay by alternating château tours with visits to vineyards and gardens, enjoying long picnics and restaurant meals, and exploring the towns and the countryside on foot. The most famous châteaux usually justify the crowds they draw, but it's often wise to time your visit for lunchtime, or first and last thing.

△ St-Gatien cathedral, Tours

The River Loire

The Loire is the longest waterway in France, and is often referred to as the country's last "wild" river. Its untameable currents, shallow water and changeable channels brought an end to commercial river traffic as soon as an alternative arrived, in the form of the railway, and nowadays, the old quays remain largely forgotten except by the occasional tour boat. Dramatic floods are another feature of the river's wildness. These can swell over the banks and inundate the floodplains in a matter of hours. Thanks to hard campaigning by conservationists, plans to control the water levels of the central stretch with dams have been dropped, despite strong interest from the four nuclear power stations that use river water for their cooling systems. But for most of the year the river meanders gently past its shifting sandbanks, shaded by willows and poplars, and punctuated by long, sandy islands that shelter rich bird and animal life. More pertinently for visitors, the Loire is "wild" because its collapsing sandbanks and strong currents make it so deceptively dangerous. Swimming is illegal, though bathers can always explore the many lovely tributaries instead.

Visiting one of the lower-key sites, particularly if you have the place practically to yourself, has its own charm.

Among the A-list châteaux, **Azay-le-Rideau** and **Chenonceau** both belong exclusively to the Renaissance period, and their settings, in the middle of moat and river respectively, are very beautiful, rivalled only by the wonderful Renaissance gardens of **Villandry**. **Blois**, with its four wings representing four distinct eras, and **Amboise**, rearing cliff-like above the Loire, are extremely impressive, as is the monstrously huge **Chambord**, the triumph of François I's Renaissance. More pristinely elegant are **Valençay**, with its Napoleonic interiors, and **Cheverny**, the prime example of seventeenth-century magnificence.

Many châteaux that started life as serious military defences were turned into luxurious residences by their regal or ducal owners: good examples are **Brissac**, **Chaumont** and **Ussé**, the most fairy-tale of them all. **Langeais**, **Le Plessis-Bourré** and **Sully** are fine examples of elegant residences and strong defences combined, while other feudal fortresses have preserved their medieval feel, among them ruined **Chinon**, noble **Saumur** and the entire citadel of **Loches**. Others are more compelling for their contents than for their architecture: **Beauregard** is most famous for its portrait gallery, while at **Angers** the stark, largely ruined medieval castle houses the *Tapestry of the Apocalypse*, the greatest work of art in the entire Loire valley.

When to go

The Loire's climate is dreamily perfect. The region's situation at the centre of France makes it distinctly warmer than Britain without suffering the excessive summer heat of the south of France, and warm Atlantic air follows the Loire valley inland, creating a pleasantly temperate microclimate. Rainfall is moderate and spread throughout the year, though wet days are more frequent in the autumn months.

Spring can be surprisingly cold earlier on, and sometimes wet too, though the sunnier days and the intense green of the countryside make this one of the loveliest times of all to visit, especially from around mid-April. Be wary of coming before **Easter**, as most of the sights are only open for relatively restricted hours. **Summers** are hot but rarely sweltering. The chief drawback of visiting during **July** and especially **August** is that these months make up the high **tourist season**; in the more popular places, châteaux can get packed out by tour parties, and you'll need to book accommodation – especially if you're renting by the week – and restaurants well in advance. **June** and **September** are particularly lovely months,

△ Joan of Arc stained glass, Ste-Croix cathedral, Orléans

△ Café, Chinon

offering summery temperatures without the crowds. **Autumn** can be a
fine time to visit, especially for lovers of game and mushrooms; it's also the
season for wine fairs celebrating the harvest. Few travellers visit in **winter**.
It's not especially cold, but many sights and hotels are closed.

Average Loire monthly temperatures and rainfall

	°C	°F	rainfall/mm	rainfall/inches
Jan	4	39	49	1.9
Feb	5	41	41	1.6
March	8	46	45	1.8
April	10	50	49	1.9
May	14	57	57	2.3
June	17	63	55	2.2
July	20	68	54	2.1
Aug	19	66	53	2.1
Sept	17	63	50	2.0
Oct	13	55	62	2.4
Nov	8	46	59	2.3
Dec	6	43	54	2.1

26

things not to miss

It's not possible to see everything that the Loire valley has to offer in one trip – and we don't suggest you try. What follows is a selective and subjective taste of the region's highlights: abbeys, cathedrals, troglodyte houses, gardens, canoe trips, wine and of course châteaux – both to visit and to stay in. They're arranged in five colour-coded categories to help you find the very best things to see, do and experience. All entries have a page reference to take you straight into the guide, where you can find out more.

02 Montreuil-Bellay Page **242** • The château and church of Montreuil-Bellay form a quintessentially picturesque Loire scene, rising above the poplar-lined river meadows.

01 Villandry's gardens Page **92** • These superb gardens exactly recreate the intricate designs of the Renaissance, right down to the geometrically planned vegetable plot.

03 La Ferté-St-Aubin Page **181** • Visitors to La Ferté-St-Aubin are invited to treat it like a home – you're even allowed to try out the billiard table and sit in the armchairs.

04 Bourges Page **204** • Overshadowed by a fabulous Gothic cathedral, Bourges still preserves a powerful flavour of its medieval golden age.

05 Place Plum' Page **68** • The medieval square at the centre of old Tours is packed with café tables, and with diners and drinkers sitting out till late on summer nights.

06 Château de Blois Page **132** • The interior of the château at Blois is as colourful as its murderous history.

07 Staying in a château Page **29** • You can find chambres d'hôtes in anything from full-scale princely palaces to relatively humble turreted farmhouses.

08 Canoe and kayak trips Page **42** • The best way to get to know the River Loire is by boat, and you can hire canoes and kayaks all over the region.

09 Loches Page **115** • This small, provincial town preserves a complete medieval citadel, incorporating the eleventh-century keep and fifteenth-century *logis*. The latter contains the beautiful tomb of Agnès Sorel, the so-called Dame de Beauté.

11 Chenonceau Page **83** • The most graceful of all the Loire châteaux arches its way right across the placid River Cher.

10 Cathédrale St-Julien Page **292** • At the centre of Le Mans' giant, hybrid cathedral, the chapel vault is painted with glorious angel musicians.

12 Troglodyte houses Page **239** • Quirkiest of the region's sights are the cave houses cut into the soft stone of the riverbank escarpments – many are still inhabited, while others recreate the lifestyle of their "troglodyte" inhabitants.

13 **Montrésor** Page 121 • Set deep in the countryside of southern Touraine, Montrésor is one of the Loire's loveliest villages.

14 **Denezé-sous-Doué** Page 241 • Underneath the village of Denezé-sous-Doué, the Cave aux Sculptures is filled with mysterious, caricature-like stone figures thought to have been carved in the sixteenth century.

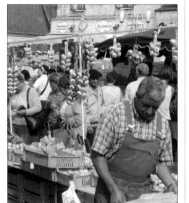

16 **Market produce** Page 31 • Every town has its lively, traditional weekly market where you can stock up on picnic provisions and local specialities.

15 **Montgeoffroy** Page 272 • Built on the eve of the Revolution, and hardly altered since, Montgeoffroy is a shrine to the vanished elegance of the ancien régime.

17 **Cycling** Page 41 • If full-on cycle-touring is too ambitious, it's easy to rent a bike and explore on day-trips. The gradients are gentle and the backroads enticing.

18 **Tapestry of the Apocalypse** Page **256** • Angers' château now guards one of the world's great medieval treasures: a hundred-metre-long tapestry depicting the Apocalypse in nightmarishly vivid colours.

19 **Chambord** Page **141** • At François I's gargantuan "hunting lodge", you can explore the whole building freely, taking in the strange double-helix staircase and the forest of chimneys above the roof terrace.

20 **Fontevraud abbey** Page **234** • The favoured abbey of the Plantagenêt family still houses their serene, polychrome tombs, including those of Eleanor of Aquitaine and her son Richard the Lionheart.

21 **Loire wildlife** Page **43** • The Loire's animal and birdlife is particularly rich in summer, when swallows and swifts swarm in the evening air, herons and egrets fish in the shallows and agile terns (pictured) hover and swoop above the rapids.

22 Loire wine Page **333** • You can visit vineyards right across the region, tasting and buying the elegant local wines direct from the growers. In Saumur and Vouvray, call in at the vast sparkling wine *caves* quarried out of the tufa.

23 Prieuré de St-Cosme Page **70** • The poet Ronsard wrote endless sonnets to his beloved roses at this priory, and is now buried among the ruins in a delightful rose garden.

24 Montsoreau and Candes-St-Martin Page **232** • If the heart of the Loire region lies anywhere, it is in these twin villages straddling the border of Touraine and the Saumurois, with their château and ancient abbey looking out across the water.

25 Chartres cathedral Page **279** • Almost all of Chartres' magnificent stained glass survives from the early thirteenth century, when the cathedral was originally built.

26 Son-et-lumière Page **36** • The biggest châteaux put on elaborate sound-and-light shows on summer evenings. The best, such as the ones at Azay-le-Rideau (pictured) and Blois, give the building a magical new perspective.

Contents

Using this Rough Guide

We've tried to make this Rough Guide a good read and easy to use. The book is divided into six main sections, and you should be able to find whatever you want in one of them.

Colour section

The front colour section offers a quick tour of the Loire region. The **introduction** aims to give you a feel for the place, with suggestions on where and when to go. Next, the author rounds up his favourite aspects of the Loire in the **things not to miss** section – whether it's great châteaux, amazing gardens or a special village. Right after this comes the Rough Guide's full **contents** list.

Basics

The basics section covers all the **pre-departure** nitty-gritty to help you plan your trip. This is where to find out which airlines fly to your destination, what paperwork you'll need, what to do about money and insurance, about Internet access, food, public transport, car rental – in fact just about every piece of **general practical information** you might need.

Guide

This is the heart of the Rough Guide, divided into user-friendly chapters. Every chapter starts with a list of **highlights** and an **introduction** that helps you to decide where to go, depending on your time and budget. Likewise, introductions to the various towns and smaller regions within each chapter should help you plan your itinerary. We start most town accounts

with information on arrival and accommodation, followed by a tour of the sights, and finally reviews of places to eat and drink, and details of nightlife. Longer accounts also have a directory of practical listings. Each chapter concludes with **public transport** details for that area.

Contexts

Read contexts to get a deeper understanding of what makes the Loire tick. We include a brief **history**, articles about **châteaux**, **wine** and **writers of the Loire**, and a detailed further reading section that reviews dozens of **books** relating to the region.

Language

The **language** section gives useful guidance for speaking French, and pulls together all the vocabulary you might need on your trip, including a comprehensive menu reader. Here you'll also find a glossary of words and terms.

Index + small print

Apart from a **full index**, which includes maps as well as places, this section covers publishing information, credits and acknowledgements, and also has our contact details in case you want to send in updates and corrections to the book – or suggestions as to how we might improve it.

Map and chapter list

Contents

Contexts

301–340

Language

343–355

Index + small print

375–384

CONTENTS

Basics

Basics

Getting there

For many travellers, getting to the Loire means flying to Paris and travelling a short distance south – Tours, in the heart of the Loire valley, is only one hour from the capital by rail, and around two hours by road. British visitors have a wider choice of the cross-Channel or Normandy ferries, the Channel Tunnel by car or Eurostar train, or direct flights from London Stansted to Tours.

Airfares vary according to season – summer and Christmas are most expensive – and whether you're travelling at weekends or midweek. Cheap fares can often be found by booking through a travel agent or flight consolidator, and there are discounted deals available to students and young people through specialist travel agents. Some of the best bargains can be found **online**.

Booking flights online

Many discount travel websites offer you the opportunity to book flight tickets and holiday packages **online**, cutting out the costs of agents and middlemen; these are worth going for, as long as you don't mind the inflexibility of non-refundable, non-changeable deals. There are some bargains to be had on auction sites too, if you're prepared to bid keenly. Almost all airlines have their own websites, offering flight tickets that can sometimes be just as cheap, and are often more flexible.

Online booking agents and general travel sites

ⓦ**www.cheapflights.co.uk** (in UK & Ireland),
ⓦ**www.cheapflights.com** (in US),
ⓦ**www.cheapflights.ca** (in Canada),
ⓦ**www.cheapflights.com.au** (in Australia). Flight deals, travel agents, plus links to other travel sites.
ⓦ**www.cheaptickets.com** Discount flight specialists (US only). Also at ☎1-888/922-8849.
ⓦ**www.ebookers.com** Efficient, easy-to-use flight finder, with competitive fares.
ⓦ**www.etn.nl/discount.htm** A hub of consolidator and discount agent links, maintained by the nonprofit European Travel Network.
ⓦ**www.expedia.co.uk** (in UK),
ⓦ**www.expedia.com** (in US),
ⓦ**www.expedia.ca** (in Canada). Discount airfares, all-airline search engine and daily deals.

ⓦ**www.flyaow.com** "Airlines of the Web" – online air travel info and reservations.
ⓦ**www.gaytravel.com** US gay travel agent, offering accommodation, cruises, tours and more. Also at ☎1-800/GAY-TRAVEL.
ⓦ**www.geocities.com/thavery2000** An extensive list of airline websites and US toll-free numbers.
ⓦ**www.kelkoo.co.uk** Useful UK-only price-comparison site, checking several sources of low-cost flights (and other goods and services) according to specific criteria.
ⓦ**www.lastminute.com** (in UK),
ⓦ**www.lastminute.com.au** (in Australia),
ⓦ**www.lastminute.co.nz** (in New Zealand). Good last-minute holiday package and flight-only deals.
ⓦ**www.opodo.co.uk** Popular and reliable source of low UK airfares. Owned by, and run in conjunction with, nine major European airlines.
ⓦ**www.priceline.co.uk** (in UK),
ⓦ**www.priceline.com** (in US). Name-your-own-price website that has deals at around forty percent off standard fares.
ⓦ**www.skyauction.com** Bookings from the US only. Auctions tickets and travel packages to destinations worldwide.
ⓦ**www.travelocity.co.uk** (in UK),
ⓦ**www.travelocity.com** (in US),
ⓦ**www.travelocity.ca** (in Canada),
ⓦ**www.zuji.com.au** (in Australia). Destination guides, hot fares and great deals for car rental, accommodation and lodging.
ⓦ**www.travelshop.com.au** Australian site offering discounted flights, packages, insurance and online bookings. Also on ☎1800/108 108.
ⓦ**travel.yahoo.com** Incorporates some Rough Guides material in its coverage of destination countries and cities across the world, with information about places to eat and sleep.

From the UK

Getting to the Loire from the UK is potentially bewildering, such is the wealth of options.

Much depends on where you're travelling from in the UK, whether you want to avoid Paris or make a short stay in the capital part of your trip, and which part of the Loire you're making for. Ryanair's direct flights from London to Tours must come near the top of the list for speed and price. If you want to bring your own car, taking a cross-Channel ferry to Le Havre or Caen allows you an enjoyable approach from the north, through Normandy, but it's considerably slower and probably more expensive than crossing by ferry or Eurotunnel to Calais and then following the motorways down past Paris. If you plan to travel via Paris, the Eurostar train is a good option, but don't ignore the possibilities of inexpensive flights.

By plane from the UK

The quickest and often the least expensive option is to take **Ryanair**'s daily direct flight from **London Stansted to Tours**. Fares rise as the plane fills up, so to get the best deals you should book as far in advance as possible. Once taxes are factored in, you might end up paying anything between around £50 and £150 for a return flight.

If you're flying **from UK regional airports**, or if the Tours flight is full or over-priced, consider **flying to Paris** and making your way south from there (see box on p.16). The best fares to Paris are on the budget airlines, Bmibaby, EasyJet and Ryanair, though again, you should book some time in advance and travel off-peak to find the real bargains – from as little as £50 if you're lucky, though £80 to £120 is more typical. Routes change frequently, but **Bmibaby** generally flies from East Midlands and Cardiff airports to Paris Charles de Gaulle (Paris CDG); **EasyJet** from Liverpool, London Luton and Newcastle to Paris CDG; and **Ryanair** from Glasgow Prestwick to Paris Beauvais airport, which is rather inconveniently situated 65km to the northwest of the city. For wider regional airport coverage, and for the occasional promotional fare, check out the routes and fares offered to Paris by the big scheduled flight carriers: Air France, bmi (formerly British Midland) and British Airways.

If you're flying on a **budget airline** it's simplest to book the ticket directly with the airline, by phone or on their website. Website addresses and contact details are given below; specialist travel agents are listed on p.12. Young people under 26 may be able to find discounted fares at agents such as STA Travel and Usit NOW.

Airlines in the UK

Air France ☏0845/359 1000,
🖳www.airfrance.com.
bmi UK ☏0870/607 0555, 🖳www.flybmi.com.
Bmibaby ☏0870/264 2229,
🖳www.bmibaby.com.
British Airways ☏0870/850 9850,
🖳www.ba.com.
EasyJet ☏0871/750 0100, 🖳www.easyjet.com.
Ryanair ☏0871/246 0000, 🖳www.ryanair.com.

By Eurostar

Travelling to the Loire **by train** means getting on the **Eurostar** at London Waterloo (or Ashford International in Kent) and whizzing through the Channel Tunnel to Paris Gare du Nord – a journey of just over two and a half hours. Unfortunately, to get an onward train from Paris to the Loire you have to transfer between the Gare du Nord and the **Gare Montparnasse** (for Angers, Chartres, Le Mans and Tours) or **Gare d'Austerlitz** (for Bourges and Orléans), which means taking a taxi or the *métro* across Paris. For tips on crossing Paris, and for details on travel from Paris to various destinations in the Loire region, see the box on p.16.

If you want to avoid the Paris interchange, there is an alternative, as long as you can be flexible about your journey time. A couple of Eurostar trains per day stop at **Lille Europe**, where after a moderate wait you can take the high-speed TGV south to Tours. The whole journey takes just under six hours, which is roughly the same as travelling via Paris, and infinitely more leisurely.

The least expensive **Eurostar ticket**, subject to availability, is the "Leisure Apex 14" (£79 return), which must be bought fourteen days in advance and include a Saturday night away. You're not allowed to change dates and there are no refunds. The ordinary "Leisure" ticket (£119 return) can be bought immediately before departure, but only if there are still seats available at this price level. Various higher-priced tickets allow increasing degrees of flexibility, and you can find yourself paying almost £300 for a last-minute, flexible ticket in high season, so it pays to book and plan ahead. If you need greater flexibility, check the various "Business" options. **First-class** tickets cost just under double the price for a bit of leather, some legroom, a newspaper and a light meal. A number of discounted seats (£59–99) are set aside on each train for **students under-26s** and **over-60s**; as with the Leisure fares, the longer you can book in advance the better your chance of securing a cheap ticket.

Eurostar tickets can be bought from travel agents or by phone or online directly from Eurostar, but for **through-ticketing** to train stations in the Loire it's better to book at mainline railway stations in Britain, through Rail Europe (℡0870/120 1606, ⊛www.raileurope.co.uk), or on the SNCF website (⊛www.sncf.com).

By car from the UK

If you're bringing a car from the UK, the quickest route is via the Channel Tunnel, using the frequent **Eurotunnel** shuttle service between the Folkestone and Calais terminals. The **car ferry** from **Dover to Calais** is slower but less expensive than Eurotunnel. Taking a ferry direct to the **Normandy** coast is a relaxing alternative, with less driving time at the end of the crossing. However, unless you take a high-speed **catamaran**, it's likely to be slower than zooming down the motorway from Calais – unless you live in the southwest of England.

Fares vary according to season, but you can expect to pay around £300 per car on Eurotunnel, possibly £50–150 less on a ferry, depending on when you travel and how many passengers there are. On ferries, **bicycles** carry at most a nominal charge in peak season. You can find compare prices and find good deals at **online agents** such as ⊛www.ferrysavers.com (℡0870/990 8492) and ⊛www.eurodrive.co.uk (℡01235/845 600).

Eurotunnel

Eurotunnel's car-carrying trains leave every fifteen minutes or so from the terminal near Folkestone (only one per hour midnight–6am). All you have to do is take the heavily signposted exit off the M20 at Junction 11A, drive up to the ticket booths to buy a ticket, wait half an hour or so and then drive straight onto one of the double-decker railway carriages. However, if you're travelling during the peak holiday periods (summer and around Easter), it's worth **booking ahead** to avoid potentially long queues, in which case you have to arrive at least thirty minutes before departure. Once aboard, you can walk around in the comfortable, garage-like chamber during the 35-minute trip.

You surface just outside Calais, and well-signposted slip-roads lead straight onto the **Paris-bound motorways**. Unless you're heading to the easternmost side of the Loire, it's simplest to take the A16 motorway via Boulogne and Amiens, which approaches Paris from the western side, but the A26/A1 via St-Omer and Arras is often just as quick, if very slightly longer. On either route, allow five hours from Calais to Tours.

Tickets are priced per car and average around £300. You can save money by booking fourteen days in advance and by travelling between 10pm and 6am, while the highest prices are charged at weekends.

Dover–Calais ferries

Sea France and **P&O Ferries** both sail from Dover to Calais at least every hour, so you can usually get away without booking ahead, though it's advisable in summer. The crossing time is one and a half hours. As for Eurotunnel, you're left with a fairly long drive south at the end of the crossing (see above).

Normandy ferries

The gentlemanly alternative is to take the long sea route to the Normandy coast. The crossing may be slow but this allows time for a meal, a stroll on deck and perhaps a film in the small cinema; the ferry companies make fairly good provision for children, too. Night crossings are even more leisurely, and you can book a cabin for around £20 per person. It's important to book in advance for the Normandy ferries.

P&O Ferries sail from Portsmouth to Le Havre (3 daily; 5hr 30min), **Brittany Ferries**

from Portsmouth to Caen (1–3 daily; 6hr), and **Transmanche ferries** from Newhaven to Dieppe (2–3 daily; 4hr). Between April and September you can save time by taking the **catamaran** service: Hoverspeed operate between Newhaven and Dieppe (April–Sept 2–3 daily; 2hr 15min), and P&O Ferries between Portsmouth and Cherbourg (May–Sept 2 daily; 2hr 45min). There are generally fewer crossings to the Normandy coast in winter.

The advantage of all these routes is the approach to the Loire region: **the drive south** is mostly along ordinary roads rather than toll-paying, petrol-guzzling motorways. You won't save all that much driving time, however: Caen is a little over three hours away from Tours, and Le Havre and Dieppe are an hour or so further; Cherbourg to Tours takes up to five hours – no faster than coming from Calais. You could plan an attractive route through the rolling Norman countryside, which is particularly appealing in the so-called Suisse Normande immediately south of Caen – where villages such as Thury-Harcourt and Pont d'Ouilly make tempting overnight stops – and in the Pays d'Auge, south of Lisieux, the home of Camembert and Livarot. Alternatively, you could push through to the cathedral towns of Le Mans or Chartres, and the fringe territory to the north of the Loire, which is covered in a dedicated chapter of the Guide, "The Northern approaches", on p.277.

There are ferry routes to Cherbourg, too, but these are less convenient for the Loire. If you're heading to the westernmost part of the region, around Anjou, consider Brittany Ferries' Portsmouth to **St-Malo** service (4–7 weekly; 8hr 45min), or Condor Ferries' Poole to St-Malo crossing, which runs from late May to the end of September via Jersey or Guernsey (1 daily; 5hr 30min).

Ferry and Eurotunnel contacts in the UK

Brittany Ferries ☎0870/901 2400, ⊛www.brittanyferries.co.uk.
Condor Ferries ☎0845/345 2000, ⊛www.condorferries.co.uk.
Eurotunnel ☎0870/535 3535, ⊛www.eurotunnel.com.
Hoverspeed ☎0870/240 8070,

⊛www.hoverspeed.com.
P&O Ferries ☎0870/520 2020, ⊛www.poferries.com.
Sea France ☎0870/571 1711, ⊛www.seafrance.com.
Transmanche Ferries ☎0870/917 1201, ⊛www.transmancheferries.com.

Travel agents in the UK

North South Travel ☎01245/608 291, ⊛www.northsouthtravel.co.uk. Friendly, competitive travel agency, offering discounted fares worldwide. Profits are used to support projects in the developing world, especially the promotion of sustainable tourism.
STA Travel ☎0870/160 0599, ⊛www.statravel.co.uk. Worldwide specialists in low-cost flights, overlands and holiday deals. Good discounts for students and under-26s.
Top Deck ☎020/7244 8000, ⊛www.topdecktravel.co.uk. Long-established agent dealing in discount flights and tours.
Trailfinders ☎020/7938 3939, ⊛www.trailfinders.com; Republic of Ireland ☎01/677 7888, ⊛www.trailfinders.ie. One of the best-informed and most efficient agents for independent travellers.
Travel Bag ☎0870/890 1456, ⊛www.travelbag.co.uk. Discount deals worldwide.
Travel Care ☎0870/112 0085, ⊛www.travelcare.co.uk. Flights, holiday deals and city breaks around the world.

Tour operators in the UK

Arblaster and Clarke Wine Tours ☎01730 893344, ⊛www.arblasterandclarke.com. Wine-and-walking and just plain wine tours of the Loire, among many other regions.
Belle France ☎01892/559 595, ⊛www.bellefrance.co.uk. Independent UK company offering cycling and walking holidays in the châteaux country around Amboise and Blois.
Headwater UK ☎01606/720 099, ⊛www.headwater.com. Walking and cycling holidays in the Loire and Berry. Sadly, no canoeing options at the time of writing, though it may be something they offer in the future.
Inntravel ☎01653/629 000, ⊛www.inntravel.co.uk. Four-day walking holidays near Chinon or along the Cher, as well as seven-day cycling tours around Chinon/Saumur or along the Cher.
Martin Randall Travel ☎020/8742 3355, ⊛www.martinrandall.com. Small-group cultural tours in the Touraine and Berry, led by an expert lecturer.

Travelling with pets from the UK

The Department for Environment, Food and Rural Affairs' (DEFRA) **Pet Travel Scheme** allows owners of cats and dogs to take them on holiday to France. For information on regulations and the necessary documentation, check online at ⓦ www.defra.gov.uk or ring the PETS helpline on ☎ 0870/241 1710.

The Wayfarers ☎ 01697/371 744, ⓦ www.thewayfarers.com. Well-established UK-based operator of guided walking holidays, with groups of a little over a dozen or so. The catalogue includes a week-long walk around Chinon and Saumur, staying in some of the nicest hotels in the region.

From Ireland

The most obvious route to the Loire from Ireland is to **fly to Paris** on Aer Lingus or Air France, and continue south from there (see box on p.16), but you can also fly **Ryanair** to London Stansted and then pick up their flight to Tours.

A much slower alternative – but it lets you bring your own car – is to take a **ferry** to the Normandy port of Cherbourg, which is around five hours' drive from the centre of the Loire region. P&O Irish Sea Ferries sail between Rosslare and Cherbourg all year round (3 weekly; 19hr) and from Dublin to Cherbourg from March to November (1 weekly; 18hr), while Irish Ferries make the crossing from Rosslare to Cherbourg between March and January (2–3 weekly; 16hr). You could also look at Brittany Ferries' summer-only route between Cork and Roscoff (1 weekly; 14hr), but there's a lengthy drive through Brittany at the end of it.

Airlines and ferry operators in Ireland

Aer Lingus ☎ 0818/365 000, ⓦ www.aerlingus.com.
Air France ☎ 01/605 0383, ⓦ www.airfrance.com.
Brittany Ferries ☎ 021/4277 801, ⓦ www.brittanyferries.ie.
Irish Ferries ☎ 1890/313131, Northern Ireland ☎ 0800/018 2211, ⓦ www.irishferries.com.
P&O Irish Sea Ferries ☎ 1800/404049, ⓦ www.poirishsea.com.
Ryanair ☎ 0818/303 030, ⓦ www.ryanair.com.

Travel agents in Ireland

Joe Walsh Tours Republic of Ireland ☎ 01/676 0991, ⓦ www.joewalshtours.ie. Long-established general budget fares and holidays agent.
Lee Travel Republic of Ireland ☎ 021/427 7111, ⓦ www.leetravel.ie. Flights and holidays worldwide.
McCarthys Travel Republic of Ireland ☎ 021/427 0127, ⓦ www.mccarthystravel.ie. General flight agent.
Rosetta Travel ☎ 028/9064 4996, ⓦ www.rosettatravel.com. Flight and holiday agent, specializing in deals direct from Belfast.
USIT Northern Ireland ☎ 028/9032 7111, ⓦ www.usitnow.com; Republic of Ireland ☎ 0818/200 020, ⓦ www.usit.ie. Specialists in student, youth and independent travel – flights, trains, study tours, TEFL, visas and more.
World Travel Centre Republic of Ireland ☎ 01/416 7007, ⓦ www.worldtravel.ie. Excellent fares to Europe and worldwide.

From the US and Canada

Getting to the Loire from anywhere in North America means **flying to Paris** and making your way on from there by road or rail – the distances are so small that it doesn't really make sense to connect on an internal flight. In fact, if you're arriving at Orly or Charles de Gaulle airports, you don't even need to travel into central Paris to pick up a high-speed train straight to the centre of the Loire valley, though you may of course want to spend time in the capital. For details of onward travel to the Loire from Paris and Paris's airports, see the box on p.16.

The widest choice of flights to Paris is offered by **Air France**, with regular, non-stop, scheduled services to Paris Charles de Gaulle airport from all over the US. From New York, there are up to eight departures a day. The big **American competitors** are usually a little less expensive, but you may have to stop off en route. The following flights, however, are non-stop to Paris: American Airlines from Dallas, Chicago, Miami and New York; Continental from Houston and New York; Delta from Atlanta,

13

Cincinnati and New York; Northwest Airlines from Detroit; and United Airlines from Chicago, Miami, San Francisco and Washington DC.

Typical midweek **fares** range from around US$500 in low season to US$1000 in high season. Flying at weekends is more expensive, and note that from New York or Washington DC you can expect to pay around US$50–200 less.

Air France and Air Canada both fly nonstop to Paris from all the major cities in **Canada**. There's little to choose between them in terms of fares. Count on CDN$1000/1600 (low/high season) from Montréal, Québec and Toronto, and CDN$1400/1900 from Vancouver.

Airlines in the US and Canada

Air Canada ☎1-888/247-2262, ⓦwww.aircanada.com.
Air France US ☎1-800/237-2747, Canada ☎1-800/667-2747, ⓦwww.airfrance.com/us.
American Airlines ☎1-800/624-6262, ⓦwww.aa.com.
Continental Airlines ☎1-800/231-0856, ⓦwww.continental.com.
Delta ☎1-800/241-4141, ⓦwww.delta.com.
Northwest Airlines ☎1-800/447-4747, ⓦwww.nwa.com.
United Airlines ☎1-800/538-2929, ⓦwww.united.com.

Travel agents in the US and Canada

Airtech ☎212/219-7000, ⓦwww.airtech.com. Standby seat broker; also deals in consolidator fares.
Educational Travel Center ☎1-800/747-5551 or 608/256-5551, ⓦwww.edtrav.com. Low-cost fares worldwide, student/youth discount offers, and Eurail passes, car rental and tours.
Flightcentre US ☎1-866/WORLD-51, ⓦwww.flightcentre.us, Canada ☎1-888/WORLD-55, ⓦwww.flightcentre.ca. Rock-bottom fares worldwide.
New Frontiers US ☎1-800/677-0720, ⓦwww.newfrontiers.com. Discount firm, specializing in travel from the US to Europe, with hotels, package deals and especially good offers to France.
STA Travel US ☎1-800/329-9537, Canada ☎1-888/427-5639, ⓦwww.statravel.com. Worldwide specialists in independent travel; also student IDs,

travel insurance, car rental, rail passes and more.
Student Flights ☎1-800/255-8000 or 480/951-1177, ⓦwww.isecard.com/studentflights. Student/youth fares, plus student IDs and European rail and bus passes.
TFI Tours ☎1-800/745-8000 or 212/736-1140, ⓦwww.lowestairprice.com. Consolidator with global fares.
Travel Avenue ☎1-800/333-3335, ⓦwww.travelavenue.com. Full-service travel agent that offers discounts in the form of rebates.
Travel Cuts US ☎1-800/592-CUTS, Canada ☎1-888/246-9762, ⓦwww.travelcuts.com. Popular, long-established student-travel organization, with worldwide offers.
Travelers Advantage ☎1-877/259-2691, ⓦwww.travelersadvantage.com. Discount travel club, with cashback deals and discounted car rental. Membership required ($1 for 3 months' trial).
Travelosophy US ☎1-800/332-2687, ⓦwww.itravelosophy.com. Good range of discounted and student fares worldwide.

Tour operators in the US and Canada

Backroads ☎1-800/GO-ACTIVE or 510/527-1555, ⓦwww.backroads.com. Biking and touring in the Loire valley, with the chance to kayak on the tranquil Cher.
Classic Journeys ☎1-800/200-3887 or 858/454-5004, ⓦwww.classicjourneys.com. Walking and cultural tours in Europe. Currently offers a seven-day tour combining walking in châteaux country with a barge trip on the canals of Burgundy.
Contiki ☎1-888/CONTIKI, ⓦwww.contiki.com. 18- to 35-year-olds-only tour operator. Their twelve-day "Best of France" tour includes a couple of days in the Loire valley.
Cosmos ☎1-800/276-1241, ⓦwww.cosmosvacations.com. Planned vacation packages with an independent focus. The tours of France all include a day or two in "châteaux country".
DuVine Adventures ☎1-888/396 5383, ⓦwww.duvine.com. Offers an independent but guide-supported six-day cycling and wine-tasting tour of Touraine.
EC Tours ☎1-800/388-0877, ⓦwww.ectours.com. California-based tour operator, offering two- to ten-day French tours taking in any or all of Paris, Normandy, Brittany and the Loire valley.
Euro-Bike & Walking Tours ☎1-800/321-6060, ⓦwww.eurobike.com. Runs cycling and walking trips in Europe, with a seven-day dedicated

cycling trip around "la Loire", and a cycling trip round the Loire, Normandy and Brittany.

Insight International Tours ☎1-800/582-8380, 🖤www.inusa.insightvacations.com. Upmarket tours by coach, with one or two options briefly taking in the Loire, along with Normandy and Brittany.

Maupintour ☎1-800/255-4266, 🖤www.maupintour.com. Features a seven-day luxury cruise along the Cher river.

National Registration Centre for Study Abroad ☎414/278 7410, 🖤www.nrcsa.com. Language courses in Amboise and Angers, as well as home-study language programmes based in Tours.

Rail Europe ☎1-877/EUROVAC, 🖤www.raileurope.com. Rail passes and advice, plus good airfares, bookings for hotels and rental cars, and flexible, multi-centre vacation packages.

From Australia and New Zealand

There are scheduled **flights** to Paris from Auckland, Brisbane, Cairns, Melbourne, Perth and Sydney, but you can find a wider range of options by flying to another European capital – usually London – and making a connection from there. The best deals from Australia or New Zealand to Europe are routed via Asia, often with a transfer or overnight stop in the airline's home city. Flights via the US are usually slightly more expensive. From Paris, you'll have to make your way overland to the Loire – all of an hour from Paris to Tours by train, or two hours in a hire car.

Fares are priced according to the French tourist seasons: the brief low season runs from early January to the end of February and through October and November; high season lasts from mid-May to the end of August and from December to early January. From Australia, you should be able to find scheduled fares to Paris for around A$2000 in low season, or A$2500 in high season. From Auckland you might pay from NZ$2200 right up to NZ$3000 in peak season.

Airlines in Australia and New Zealand

Air France Australia ☎1300/361 400, New Zealand ☎09/308 3352, 🖤www.airfrance.com.
Air India Australia ☎02/9283 4020, New Zealand

☎09/303 1301, 🖤www.airindia.com.
British Airways Australia ☎1300/767 177, New Zealand ☎0800/274 847, 🖤www.ba.com.
Cathay Pacific Australia ☎13 17 47, New Zealand ☎0508/800 454 or 09/379 0861, 🖤www.cathaypacific.com.
Garuda Indonesia Australia ☎1300/365 330 or 02/9334 9944, New Zealand ☎09/366 1862, 🖤www.garuda-indonesia.com.
JAL Japan Airlines Australia ☎02/9272 1111, New Zealand ☎09/379 9906, 🖤www.jal.com.
KLM Australia ☎1300/303 747, New Zealand ☎09/309 1782, 🖤www.klm.com.
Lufthansa Australia ☎1300/655 727, New Zealand ☎0800/945 220, 🖤www.lufthansa.com.
Malaysia Airlines Australia ☎13 26 27, New Zealand ☎0800/777 747, 🖤www.malaysia-airlines.com.
Qantas Australia ☎13 13 13, New Zealand ☎0800/808 767 or 09/357 8900, 🖤www.qantas.com.
Thai Airways Australia ☎1300/651 960, New Zealand ☎09/377 3886, 🖤www.thaiair.com.
United Airlines Australia ☎13 17 77, 🖤www.united.com.

Travel agents in Australia and New Zealand

Flight Centre Australia ☎13 31 33, 🖤www.flightcentre.com.au; New Zealand ☎0800 243 544, 🖤www.flightcentre.co.nz. Rock-bottom fares worldwide.
Holiday Shoppe New Zealand ☎0800/808 480, 🖤www.holidayshoppe.co.nz. Great deals on flights, hotels and holidays.
OTC Australia ☎1300/855 118, 🖤www.otctravel.com.au. Deals on flights, hotels and holidays.
STA Travel Australia ☎1300/733 035, New Zealand ☎0508/782 872, 🖤www.statravel.com. Worldwide specialists in low-cost flights, overlands and holiday deals. Good discounts for students and under-26s.
Student Uni Travel Australia ☎02/9232 8444, 🖤www.sut.com.au; New Zealand ☎09/379 4224, 🖤www.sut.co.nz. Great deals for students.
Trailfinders Australia ☎02/9247 7666, 🖤www.trailfinders.com.au. One of the best-informed and most efficient agents for independent travellers.
travel.com.au and **travel.co.nz** Australia ☎1300/130 482 or 02/9249 5444, 🖤www.travel.com.au; New Zealand ☎0800/468 332, 🖤www.travel.co.nz. Comprehensive online travel company, with discounted fares.

Trains to the Loire depart from the Gare Montparnasse, in the south of Paris, or the Gare d'Austerlitz, in the southeast; the station depends on your destination. You may want to pick up a **hire car** (see p.24) in Paris and head down to the Loire valley under your own steam. If so, there are three main motorway routes from Paris towards the Loire valley. For detailed **route descriptions**, check the online planner at ⊕www.viamichelin.com.

By train from central Paris

The simplest and quickest rail route is the TGV high-speed line from Paris's **Gare Montparnasse** to **Tours**, which takes a breathtaking 58 minutes. At the time of writing, a single, adult, off-peak **ticket** cost €25.80. On arrival at Tours you usually have to pick up a shuttle train from the TGV station, Tours St-Pierre-des Corps, to Tours' central station, which adds on a few minutes. From Tours you can pick up public transport to destinations all over the region, notably **Blois**, **Chinon** and **Saumur**.

Hourly trains run from the **Gare Montparnasse** to **Chartres**, and there's also a good TGV service to **Le Mans** (1hr) and **Angers** (1hr 30min), though the high-speed part of the line currently only extends as far as Le Mans. From **the Gare d'Austerlitz** there are frequent TGV departures for **Orléans** (1hr; some include a shuttle train from the suburban station at Fleury-les-Aubray to Orléans' central station), a handful of direct trains to **Bourges** (2hr) and slow, mainline SNCF trains to **Tours** (2hr 20min). Trains for **Gien** (1hr 30min–2hr) leave every couple of hours from the **Gare de Lyon**. If you're travelling from London by train, note that a couple of Eurostar trains stop at **Lille Europe** station in good time to make a connection with the TGV to Tours; for more details see p.10.

If you need **to travel between mainline stations in Paris**, allow at least an hour between arrival and departure times – a little more if you have to book your onward ticket. If you're taking the *métro*, it's useful to keep some euro coins handy for the ticket (€1.30 single at the time of writing). Note that the *métro*'s credit card ticket machines are temperamental about accepting foreign plastic. From the Gare du Nord, take *métro* line 4 (pink) signposted "Direction Porte d'Orléans" for the Gare de Montparnasse; or line 5 (orange) "Direction Place d'Italie" for the Gare d'Austerlitz.

Whichever train you catch, don't forget to **validate your ticket** (*compostez votre billet*) before you depart; just push it into the slot in the orange stamping-machines on every platform.

By car from central Paris

All three motorway routes to the Loire are fast and usually congestion-free. From Paris through to Tours, the distance is 240km, or two and a half hours, with **motorway tolls** to pay of just under €20.

The ordinary route follows the **Autoroute d'Aquitaine** (A10) south to Orléans, a distance of 127km. A second route, the **Autoroute de l'Océane** (A11) branches off the A10 some 30km out of Paris, from where it runs roughly west towards Chartres – 83km in all. From Chartres you can follow the little River Loir downstream (see p.277), or continue along the A11 as far as Le Mans and Angers. If you're making for Bourges or the eastern portion of the Loire, you could choose a third motorway route, which breaks away from the A6 just beyond Nemours, some 35km south of Paris, and becomes the **A77** to Gien.

If you want to **avoid the autoroutes**, there are three major options, two of which lead past wonderful châteaux – though bear in mind that there are plenty more ahead. The N20 runs from Paris's Porte d'Orléans direct to **Orléans** (117km); the D910 heads east from the Ponte de Sèvres to Versailles, from where the D10/N10 continues to **Chartres**; and the N7 leads southeast from Paris's Porte d'Italie to Fontainebleau and on south towards **Gien** and Sancerre.

From Paris airports

If you're arriving in Paris by air, it's possible to reach Tours and Angers without the hassle of crossing central Paris – as long as your arrival time matches up reasonably well with a **train** departure. From **Charles de Gaulle airport** there are four or five TGVs (high-speed trains) every day direct to Tours (1hr 50min), and around two TGVs daily to Angers (2hr 15min). If the train times don't match your flight, you can take the RER B suburban line to Massy Palaiseau (roughly 1hr), and connect there with reasonably frequent TGV trains to Tours and Angers. The TGV and RER stations at Massy Palaiseau are just 200m apart. If you're arriving at **Orly airport**, Massy Palaiseau is only fifteen minutes away on the RER line C2.

If you're picking up a **rental car** at Paris **Charles de Gaulle airport**, you'll have to make your way right round Paris to continue down to the Loire valley. The best bet, avoiding the route-finding nightmare of the *périphérique*, is to take the succession of *autoroutes* (A1/A3/A86/A10) that skirt the southeastern side of Paris.

Tour operators in Australia and New Zealand

France Unlimited Australia ☎03/9531 8787. All French travel arrangements, including châteaux stays and cycling tours.
French Travel Connection Australia ☎02/9966 1177, @www.frenchtravel.com.au. Everything to do with travel to and around France, including accommodation, canal boats, train travel, car rental and more. Offers a wide choice of self-guided cycle tours in the Loire, as well as a cookery class near Azay-le-Rideau.
Martin Randall Travel Australia ☎1300/559 595, @www.martinrandall.com. British company running small-group cultural tours in the Touraine and Berry, led by an expert lecturer.
Travel Notions Australia ☎02/9552 3355, @www.unitednotions.com.au/travelnotions. France specialists, and agents for leisurely "Cycling for Softies" tours, including one in western Touraine and another around the Sarthe and Mayenne valleys.

Red tape and visas

Citizens of European Union (EU) countries can travel freely in France, while those from Australia, Canada, the United States and New Zealand do not need any sort of visa to enter the country, and can stay for up to ninety days. The situation is unlikely to change, but if you're in any doubt check with your nearest French embassy or consulate before departure. A complete list of all French government websites, including embassies and consulates, can be found at @www.gksoft.com/govt/en/fr.html.

Anyone staying in France longer than three months is officially supposed to apply for a **Carte de Séjour** (see p.48), for which you'll have to show proof of income or sufficient funds, among other things. If you're an EU citizen, however, your passport is unlikely to be stamped on entry, so there is no evidence of how long you've been in the country. Even if your passport does get stamped, you can cross the border and re-enter for another ninety days legitimately.

Information, websites and maps

The French government tourist office (Maison de la France; @www.franceguide.com) gives away maps and brochures for the Loire region, some excellent, others glossy and insubstantial. Their maps and lists of campsites, hotels, festivals and so on can be handy, but much of the best material covers only one of the many official *régions* or *départements* that divide up the area – it's difficult to find information on the Loire as a whole.

Once in France, you'll find a tourist office – **Office du Tourisme** (OTSI) – in even the smallest towns and villages. Addresses, opening hours and websites are given in the Guide for all but the most minor. All staff speak English and can provide free town plans and exhaustive lists of activities, sights and accommodation, including chambres d'hôtes – in fact, about the only thing they can't do is recommend a restaurant, though you may get personal advice with a nod and a wink. Many tourist offices also produce walking maps and offer town tours.

Some towns along the Loire also have a **Maison de la Loire**, which acts as a kind of river and wildlife information and resource centre. They vary in levels of activity, but you can usually sign up for river and bird-watching walks, arrange trips in old-style river boats, and pick up lots of information on the ecology of the area. Some house small local museums as well.

French government tourist offices

This guidebook covers an area of France administered by two government *régions*, including all six *départements* of the Centre *région*, and two *départements* of the Pays-de-la-Loire *région* – namely the Maine-et-Loire and the Sarthe. Each has its own Comité Régional/Départmentale du Tourisme, or **tourist board**, listed below.

French tourist boards

Australia Level 20, 25 Bligh St, 2000 NSW, Sydney ☎02/9231 5244, @info.au@france.
Canada 1981 ave Mc Gill College Suite 490, H3A 2W9 Montréal ☎514/876 9881, @canada@franceguide.com.
Ireland 10 Suffolk St, Dublin ☎1560/235 235, @info.ie@franceguide.com.
Netherlands Prinsengracht 670, 1017 KX, Amsterdam ☎0900/112 2332, @info.nl@franceguide.com.
UK 178 Piccadilly, London W1J 9AL ☎09068/244 123, @info.uk@franceguide.com.
US 444 Madison Ave, 10022 New York ☎410/286 8310, @info.us@franceguide.com.

Regional tourist boards

Centre 37 ave de Paris, 45000 Orléans @www.visaloire.com.
Pays-de-la-Loire 1 rue de la Loire, 44266 Nantes ☎02.40.41.41.41, @www.paysdelaloire.fr.

Departmental tourist boards

Cher 5 rue de Séraucourt, 18000 Bourges ☎02.48.48.00.10, @www.berrylecher.com.
Eure-et-Loir 10 rue du Docteur Maunoury, 28002 Chartres ☎02.37.84.01.00, @www.tourisme28.com.
Indre 1 rue St Martin, 36003 Châteauroux ☎02.54.07.36.36, @http://tourisme.cyberindre.org/.
Indre-et-Loire (Touraine) 9 rue Buffon, 37000 Tours ☎02.47.31.42.52, @www.tourism-touraine.com.
Loiret (Orléanais) 8 rue d'Escures, 45000 Orléans ☎02.38.78.04.04, @www.tourismeloiret.com.
Loir-et-Cher 5 rue de la Voûte du Château, 41005 Blois ☎02.54.57.00.41, @www.chambordcountry.com.
Maine-et-Loire (Anjou) place Kennedy, 49021 Angers ☎02.41.23.51.51, @www.anjou-tourisme.com.
Sarthe 40 rue Joinville, 72000, Le Mans ☎02.43.40.22.50, @http://tourisme.sarthe.com/.

Websites

Online information is comprehensive but

shallow and often out of date. Ordinary hotels have been slow to catch on, but increasing numbers of places to stay, particularly in the higher price brackets, now have an online presence. Web addresses (or, failing that, email addresses) are given throughout the Guide. A few more general websites of particular interest or usefulness are listed below.

Tourism and recreation sites

Camping France ⊛www.campingfrance.com. Large database of French campsites, with an English-language option. Gives opening seasons and contact details, and icons indicate facilities.
France Sport ⊛www.francesport.com. Listings of all French national sports associations, both professional and participatory. Everything from skiing to surfing.
Jardins de France ⊛www.jardins-de-france.com. Association of private gardens in the Loire valley, with links and descriptions of all those open to the public.
Loire-France ⊛www.loire-france.com. French-language site dedicated to the history and culture of the entire Loire region.
Maison de la France ⊛www.franceguide.com. The English-language section of the French government tourist office website offers news, details of events, links to local and regional tourist offices, historic monuments and the like.
Monum ⊛www.monum.fr. The website of the state monuments agency, which manages many of the biggest and finest châteaux in the Loire region. Each historic building has its own expensively produced English-language pages, with details of opening hours, access and events and decicated pages for children.
Parc Naturel Régional Loire-Anjou-Touraine ⊛www.parc-loire-anjou-touraine.fr. French-language website for the regional natural park at the heart of the Loire, with contacts and details of guided walks and excursions throughout the year.
Tourist-office.org ⊛www.tourist-office.org. Database of most of France's tourist offices, listed by *région/département* and alphabetically by town.

News and information sites

Governments on the web
⊛www.gksoft.com/govt/en/fr.html. English-language portal for all French government websites, including embassies, consulates, departmental and regional authorities, political parties and state media.
Le Monde ⊛www.lemonde.fr. France's best newspaper online; French only.
La Nouvelle République

⊛www.lanouvellerepublique.fr. French-language website of the main regional newspaper covering the Loire region. Good online editorial, plus classified ads.
Yellow Pages ⊛www.pagesjaunes.fr. Online directory of French businesses, with an English-language option. Variable in its comprehensiveness and reliability.

Arts and culture sites

Festivalissimo ⊛www.festivalissimo.com. Comprehensively searchable database of festivals. French-language only.
Via France ⊛www.viafrance.com. Bilingual events database (including concerts, theatre, festivals, markets and sports) organized by category and region.

Maps

To back up the maps in the Guide, you may want to pick up free town plans or regional maps from tourist offices, but there's no substitute for a good **road map**, particularly if you're heading off down minor roads in search of chambres d'hôtes, vineyards or lesser-known châteaux.

There's no single map showing the entire area covered in this guide. In terms of detail and clarity, there's little to choose between the two best series – **Michelin**'s 1:200,000 Regional maps and **IGN**'s brown Carte Régionale 1:250,000 maps – but for coverage IGN have the edge. Both companies cover the area in two sheets (Michelin 518 *Pays de Loire* and 519 *Centre, Berry, Nivernais*; and IGN R07 *Centre* and R18 *Pays de la Loire*), but IGN's *Centre* map includes all of Touraine as well as Le Mans, Chartes and even Paris, while Michelin stops immediately west of Tours and doesn't cover the territory north of Vendôme and Orléans. For a general, single-sheet road map, GeoCenter's **Euromap** *Loire Valley* shows all but the very easternmost strip of the area covered in this Guide (Sancerre and Briare are just off the map); the 1:300,000 scale is very usable, but the smallest minor roads are missing.

Michelin also make larger-scale local maps at 1:150,000, but there's no extra detail as compared with the 1:200,000 maps, other than the addition of traditional regional names. If you're looking for really large-scale maps – for **walking**, perhaps – go for IGN's Carte de Promenade 1:100,000 series (see p.43); for serious detail check out their local maps at 1:25,000 and 1:50,000.

Map outlets

In the UK and Ireland

Blackwell's Map Centre 50 Broad St, Oxford ☎01865/793 550, ⓦmaps.blackwell.co.uk. Branches in Bristol, Cambridge, Cardiff, Leeds, Liverpool, Newcastle, Reading and Sheffield.
National Map Centre 22–24 Caxton St, London SW1 ☎020/7222 2466, ⓦwww.mapsnmc.co.uk.
National Map Centre Ireland 34 Aungier St, Dublin ☎01/476 0471, ⓦwww.mapcentre.ie.
Stanfords 12–14 Long Acre, London WC2 ☎020/7836 1321, ⓦwww.stanfords.co.uk. Also at 39 Spring Gardens, Manchester ☎0161/831 0250, and 29 Corn St, Bristol ☎0117/929 9966.
The Travel Bookshop 13–15 Blenheim Crescent, London W11 ☎020/7229 5260, ⓦwww.thetravelbookshop.co.uk.

In the US and Canada

Book Passage 51 Tamal Vista Bd, Corte Madera, CA 94925 ☎1-800/999-7909, ⓦwww.bookpassage.com.
Globe Corner Bookstore 28 Church St, Cambridge, MA 02138 ☎1-800/358-6013, ⓦwww.globecorner.com.
Longitude Books 115 W 30th St #1206, New York, NY 10001 ☎1-800/342-2164, ⓦwww.longitudebooks.com.
Travel Bug Bookstore 3065 W Broadway, Vancouver, BC, V6K 2G9 ☎604/737-1122, ⓦwww.travelbugbooks.ca.
World of Maps 1235 Wellington St, Ottawa, ON, K1Y 3A3 ☎1-800/214-8524, ⓦwww.worldofmaps.com.

In Australia and New Zealand

Map Centre ⓦwww.mapcentre.co.nz.
Mapland 372 Little Bourke St, Melbourne ☎03/9670 4383, ⓦwww.mapland.com.au.
Map Shop 6–10 Peel St, Adelaide ☎08/8231 2033, ⓦwww.mapshop.net.au.
Map World 371 Pitt St, Sydney ☎02/9261 3601, ⓦwww.mapworld.net.au. Also at 900 Hay St, Perth ☎08/9322 5733.
Map World 173 Gloucester St, Christchurch ☎0800/627 967, ⓦwww.mapworld.co.nz.

Insurance

The Loire is one of the world's safer travel destinations, but you may want to take out insurance before travelling to cover against theft, loss and flight cancellations. As for illness or injury, even though EU travellers can get most of their health needs free from the French healthcare system (see opposite for more), peripheral expenses in the event of a serious problem can add up. Before paying for a new policy, it's worth checking whether your existing home insurance or medical policies already give you cover.

If you do decide to take out separate insurance, contact a **specialist travel insurance** company, or consider the travel insurance deal we offer (see box opposite). A typical travel policy usually covers loss of baggage, tickets and – up to a certain limit – cash or cheques, as well as cancellation or curtailment of your journey. Almost all exclude so-called dangerous sports unless an extra premium is paid, though a little gentle Loire kayaking is likely to be covered under most policies. Many insurance policies can be chopped and changed to exclude coverage you don't need – for example, sickness and accident benefits can often be excluded or included at will. If you do take medical coverage, ascertain whether benefits will be paid as treatment proceeds or only after return home, and whether there is a 24-hour medical emergency number. When securing baggage cover, make sure that the per-article limit – typically under £500 – will cover your most valuable possession. If you need to make a claim, you should keep **receipts** for

Rough Guides travel insurance

Rough Guide offers its own low-cost travel insurance, especially customized for our statistically low-risk readers by a leading British broker, provided by the American International Group (AIG) and registered with the British regulatory body, GISC (the General Insurance Standards Council). There are five main Rough Guides insurance plans: **No Frills** for the bare minimum for secure travel; **Essential**, which provides decent all-round cover; **Premier** for comprehensive cover with a wide range of benefits; **Extended Stay** for cover lasting four months to a year; and **Annual multi-trip**, a cost-effective way of getting Premier cover if you travel more than once a year. For a policy quote, call the Rough Guide Insurance Line: toll-free in the UK ☏0800/015 09 06 or ☏+44 1392 314 665 from elsewhere. Alternatively, get an online quote at ⊛www.roughguides.com/insurance.

medicines and medical treatment, and in the event you have anything stolen, you must obtain an official statement from the police (called a *constat de vol*).

For details of **motor insurance**, see "Getting around", p.25.

Health

With its gentle climate, easy pace of life and world-beating healthcare system, France is one of the world's healthiest destinations. All tap-water is safe to drink and there are no nasty local maladies. No visitor requires any vaccinations.

In France, all **health services**, from a doctor's consultation to an ambulance call-out or hospital stay, incur a **charge** which you normally have to pay upfront – though doctors have been known to waive fees on an informal basis, partly to avoid paperwork. EU citizens are entitled to a refund (usually between 70 and 100 percent) of any medical and dental expenses, providing the doctor is government-registered (*un médecin conventionné*). To apply for this refund, British citizens need form **E111**, available from post offices. Non-EU visitors, including North Americans, should be sure to have adequate **medical insurance** cover – note that many ordinary policies already cover foreign travel.

Pharmacies, marked out by flashing neon green crosses – not to mention semi-nude adverts advertising cellulite treatments – are expensive in France, but well stocked and extremely efficient. For most minor ailments, the pharmacist is well qualified to dispense advice as well as remedies. Opening hours are normally the same as shops (roughly 8/9am–noon & 2/3–6pm). Cities maintain a *pharmacie de garde* that stays open 24 hours according to a rota; addresses and hours are displayed in all pharmacy windows.

For more **serious complaints**, pharmacists, tourist offices or police stations can direct you to a **doctor**, or you can always find one yourself by looking under "Médecins" in the Yellow Pages (*Pages Jaunes*). Many speak reasonably good English. Consultation fees are around €25. French doctors are enthusiastic issuers of prescriptions, which can add to the final cost of treatment, though you will be given a *Feuille de Soins* (Statement of Treatment) with little *vignette* stickers for each medicine prescribed, which you can use to claim against insurance (or by using form E111).

In serious **emergencies** you should take yourself off to the nearest Centre Hospitalier (hospital), or call an **ambulance** on ☎15. Hospital phone numbers are given in "Listings" at the end of the main city accounts in the main Guide.

Costs, money and banks

The Loire is not an expensive place to visit, at least not in northern European terms. Ease of access from London or Paris means that getting there is unlikely to be much of a financial burden, and the small distances help keep travel costs down. Accommodation and meals can be as cheap or pricey as you choose, with hotel rooms available for less than €30, and good restaurant menus for half that. That said, it's easy to splash out on luxurious château accommodation and refined gastronomy, and entry tickets to châteaux and other attractions can add up.

Costs

Typical costs might work out at €80 a day per person, based on sharing the cost of a double room (typically around €40 in a standard two-star hotel), eating a simple breakfast (€5), a good picnic lunch (€10) and a proper restaurant meal in the evening (€18), visiting a couple of châteaux, museums or other attractions (€15), and adding a little for cafés and local travel. Hiring a car will add to the cost. On a tighter **budget**, you could get by on less than €50 by staying in youth hostels, campsites or no-star hotels, and eating in more modest places.

Unless you're staying in really fancy château accommodation, **hotel prices** are remarkably standard. Budget, no-star places, much frequented by local workmen and the like, will usually charge €20–30 (❶) – scarcely more than a hostel, if shared – while double rooms in the simplest two-star provincial hotels usually cost under €40 (❷). In touristy areas, big towns, or slightly more upmarket hotels, prices for a double room creep into the €40–55 range (❸), roughly the same as most chambres d'hôtes.

Eating out is excellent value, especially at lunchtime. In the evening, you can often find three courses for under €15, and even posh places typically have a come-hither *menu* priced at under €20. Mark-ups on bottles of wine are surprisingly high, but many restaurants offer inexpensive wine by the carafe. Unless you go for simple fare, **picnic food** is relatively expensive, but the quality of pâtés, cold meats and prepared salads is high. The sting in the tail may be café costs, which can really add up.

It's hard to spend much on public **transport**, which is heavily subsidized. A train ticket from Tours to Orléans, for example, costs €15 for the ninety-minute journey. A **hire car** can cost anything from €50–100 a day, or around €250 a week, depending on the length of rental and how much you shop around; prices may be lower if you book from home. Renting a bike costs roughly €15 a day.

Admission charges to châteaux, museums and other sites can be offputting. Lazing by the river or wandering the streets is fine, but you'll have to dig into your pocket to get the best out of the Loire's châteaux, troglodyte sites and museums. Students and under-26s, as well as those over 60, can usually take advantage of **discounted entry** – bring your passport as proof of age. Children under 18 go free at state-run monuments, and most commercial attractions offer discounted entry for children, or special family tickets. If you're planning on making a lot of visits, some towns and regions offer multi-entry tickets for a number of museums and monuments (detailed in the Guide).

Currency and the exchange rate

Since January 2002, France's unit of **currency** has been the euro (€), divided into

100 cents. When speaking, locals may occasionally estimate prices in terms of francs, and cents are invariably referred to as *centimes*, but the changeover is otherwise complete. There are seven euro notes – 5, 10, 20, 50, 100, 200 and 500 – and eight different coins – 1, 2, 5, 10, 20 and 50 cents, and 1 and 2 euros.

For most of its short life, the euro has been worth roughly one US dollar. At the time of writing, however, the **exchange rate** was relatively poor for non-Euroland visitors, at €0.80 to the US dollar, €1.50 to the British pound, €0.60 to the Canadian dollar, €0.60 to the Australian dollar and €0.50 to the New Zealand dollar. For up-to-date, exact exchange rates, consult newspapers or the Currency Converter website, ⓦwww.oanda.com

Banks and exchange

Banking hours are Monday to Friday 9am to noon and 2 to 4.30pm, though larger branches may also open at lunchtime and on Saturday mornings. Smaller branches may close on Mondays, and all banks are closed on Sundays and public holidays.

If you're **changing money**, banks are the best option, though rates and commissions do vary, so shop around. Where "no commission" is advertised, the exchange rate may be disadvantageous. Avoid **bureaux de change**, especially at tourist hotspots, where commissions tend to be high and exchange rates very poor; the only benefit of these places is their long opening hours.

Credit and debit cards

By far the easiest way to access money in France is with your own **ATM card**. Most foreign bank cards will work in a French ATM/cash machine (called a *distributeur* or *point argent*), especially if they carry the Cirrus, Plus or Link symbol; on-screen instructions are given in a choice of foreign languages. Banks charge reasonable exchange rates and add a flat 1–2 percent commission to foreign cash withdrawals. Note that there is often a minimum charge, so it may be worth getting out a sizeable sum each time you use the machine.

Credit cards are accepted in all but the most inexpensive shops, hotels and restaurants. **Visa** (called *Carte Bleue* in France) is the front-runner, with MasterCard and American Express coming a distant second. Be aware that French credit cards carry a small gold-coloured chip (*puce*) on the front, which allows card-users to enter a PIN code to authorize their purchases; if you're proffered a small calculator-like machine and asked to tap in your number you'll probably need to explain that your card works differently – using the magnetic strip (*bande magnétique*) on the back and a signature. Most retailers and hoteliers in the Loire, however, are well accustomed to foreign cards. Even if this situation does arise, a little creative sign-language – or cash as backup – should resolve matters quickly.

Travellers' cheques

Travellers' cheques are of course more secure than cash. Any major brand will do. **US dollar** cheques are widely accepted in tourist areas, and cheques denominated in other major currencies are usually accepted as well. Be sure to keep the purchase agreement and a record of cheque serial numbers safe and separate from the cheques themselves. In the event that cheques are lost or stolen, the issuing company will expect you to report the loss immediately, using the emergency number given with the cheques. Most companies claim to replace lost or stolen cheques within 24 hours.

Getting around

To make the most of the Loire you'll need a car or a bike. Efficient, regular SNCF trains do serve all the main towns in the Loire as well as many of the most popular châteaux, but this limits you to the beaten track. You can also book yourself onto a coach or minibus tour from the major cities, notably Tours (see p.61), but again these only visit the major destinations. Beyond the rail network, bus services are typically infrequent (though reliable), so to get to many of the less well-known sites and villages covered in the Guide you'll need your own wheels. Hiring or bringing a car is the obvious choice, but bear in mind that the Loire is ideal cycling country. Unfortunately, the Loire itself isn't navigable by anything other than very small boats.

For advice on **cycling**, **walking** and **kayaking**, see "Outdoor Activities", on p.41. **Hitching** is unusual in this region, and you'd be unwise to rely on it for getting around; you may want to consider safety issues too, especially if travelling alone.

By car

The pros of travelling by car are evident. The main disadvantage is cost, but you also see a less attractive side of the Loire countryside from the main roads and motorways. **Car rental** costs from around €250 a week, or at least €50 a day though it can be a little less expensive if booked in advance from abroad. There are numerous agencies in all the main Loire towns, notably Tours, Blois, Orléans and Angers. Under-25s pay an extra insurance premium of upwards of €20 a day; you must still be over 21 and have driven for at least one year. OTU Voyages (☎08.20.81 .78.17, ✆www.otu.fr) can arrange car rental for drivers under 21. North Americans and Australians should note that it is very difficult to find rental cars with automatic transmission; if you can't drive a manual/stickshift vehicle, try to book an automatic well in advance and be prepared to pay for it.

Petrol/gas (*essence*) costs a little over €1 a litre for unleaded (*super sans plomb*), with a small premium for leaded four-star (*super*), while diesel (*gasoil*) costs around €0.80 a litre – figure on about $4 per gallon. **Congestion** is only a problem on the busiest summer weekends – especially around July

14, August 15 and the beginning and end of August – but you may find yourself ambling along behind lorries or caravans on the arterial roads that run alongside the Loire at any time. In any case, it's well worth planning a slow route along the lovelier minor roads.

If you're in a hurry, the **autoroute** network is fast, mostly free of traffic, and serves the main cities of the region – though at the time of writing there was still a twenty-kilometre gap between Tours and Saumur, and a fifty-kilometre hiatus along the Cher heading east of Tours towards Bourges. You have to pay tolls for the privilege of riding the *autoroute*, but any trips within the scope of this guidebook will come in under €20. For an excellent **route-planner**, check out the bilingual website, ✆www.viamichelin.com.

You're never far from a garage or a petrol station in France. If you have **mechanical difficulties**, look in the Yellow Pages (*Pages Jaunes*) of the phone book under "*Garages d'automobiles*", or "*dépannages*" for breakdowns. If you have an accident or a break-in you may need to get a report from the local police in order to make an insurance claim – contact your insurer/rental company as soon as possible to check what you should do. For motoring vocabulary, see p.345.

Car rental agencies

In Britain

Avis ☎0870/606 0100, ✆www.avis.co.uk.
Budget ☎01442/276 266,
✆www.budget.co.uk.

Europcar ☎0870/607 5000,
🖳www.europcar.co.uk.
Hertz ☎0870/844 8844, 🖳www.hertz.co.uk.
Holiday Autos ☎0870/400 0099,
🖳www.holidayautos.co.uk.
National ☎0870/536 5365,
🖳www.nationalcar.co.uk.

In Ireland

Argus Republic of Ireland ☎01/490 4444,
🖳www.argus-rentacar.com.
Avis Northern Ireland ☎028/9024 0404, Republic
of Ireland ☎021/428 1111, 🖳www.avis.ie.
Budget Republic of Ireland ☎09/0662 7711,
🖳www.budget.ie.
Europcar Northern Ireland ☎028/9442 3444,
Republic of Ireland ☎01/614 2888,
🖳www.europcar.ie.
Hertz Republic of Ireland ☎01/676 7476,
🖳www.hertz.ie.
Holiday Autos Republic of Ireland ☎01/872
9366, 🖳www.holidayautos.ie.

In North America

Alamo US ☎1-800/462-5266,
🖳www.alamo.com.
Auto Europe US and Canada ☎1-888/223-5555,
🖳www.autoeurope.com.
Avis US ☎1-800/230-4898, Canada ☎1-
800/272-5871, 🖳www.avis.com.
Budget US ☎1-800/527-0700, Canada ☎1-
800/472-3325, 🖳www.budget.com.
Europcar US & Canada ☎1-877/940 6900,
🖳www.europcar.com.
Hertz US ☎1-800/654-3131, Canada ☎1-
800/263-0600, 🖳www.hertz.com.
National ☎1-800/962-7070,
🖳www.nationalcar.com.

In Australia

Avis ☎13 63 33 or 02/9353 9000,
🖳www.avis.com.au
Budget ☎1300/362 848, 🖳www.budget.com.au
Europcar ☎1300/131 390,
🖳www.deltaeuropcar.com.au.
Hertz ☎13 30 39 or 03/9698 2555,
🖳www.hertz.com.au.
Holiday Autos ☎1300/554 432,
🖳www.holidayautos.com.au.
National ☎13 10 45, 🖳www.nationalcar.com.au.

In New Zealand

Avis ☎09/526 2847 or 0800/655 111,
🖳www.avis.co.nz.
Budget ☎09/976 2222 or ☎0800/652-227,
🖳www.budget.co.nz.
Hertz ☎0800/654 321, 🖳www.hertz.co.nz.
Holiday Autos ☎0800/144 040,
🖳www.holidayautos.co.nz.
National ☎0800/800 115 or ☎03/366-5574,
🖳www.nationalcar.co.nz.

Rules of the road

British, Irish, Australian, Canadian, New
Zealand, US and all EU **driving licences** are
valid in France. You're required to keep your
licence on you if you're driving, along with
insurance papers. Rented cars must also
have their registration document (*carte
grise*). The minimum driving age is 18 and
provisional licences are not valid.

All EU-issued **motor insurance** is now
valid in all EU countries, so there's no
requirement to upgrade your policy, though
UK drivers should note that they may only
have third-party cover while driving in
France. For a few pounds/dollars you can
buy a **green card** from your policy provider
which upgrades you to comprehensive
cover while abroad.

British drivers have to adjust the headlight dip to the right, or fit glare deflectors
that do the same job – these are sold in ferry
ports and the Eurostar terminal. You're also
supposed to carry a red triangle, spare
headlight bulbs and fit national identification
plates – "GB" etc.

French law still stipulates that unless signs
indicate otherwise you should give way to
traffic coming from the right – the notorious
priorité à droite rule. To add to the confusion, main roads are an exception, as they
now almost always have priority, shown by a
passage protégé sign of a yellow diamond
on a white background. The same sign with
a black slash indicates that vehicles coming
from your right have priority. Cars already on
roundabouts are another exception, as they
have priority over cars joining the roundabout
(from the right…). As a rule, take great care
at junctions – occasionally, older motorists
blithely expect to have priority when turning
onto a main road. *Cédez le passage* means
"Give Way", and *déviation* (in yellow) means
"diversion" – these diversions can sometimes
take you some distance out of your way on
wandering rural roads.

The **speed limit** in built-up areas is 50kph (31mph). Other limits change according to whether the conditions are wet or dry; drivers with less than two years' experience must follow the lower limit. *Autoroute* limits are 130kph (80mph), or 110kph (68mph) in the wet; urban *autoroutes* and dual carriageways with a central reservation are 110kph, or 100kph (62mph) in the wet; main roads are 90kph (55mph), or 80kph (50mph) in the wet. There are stiff fines for speeding, and they are being more rigorously enforced than in the past.

The **alcohol limit** is set low, at the EU standard of 50mg alcohol per 100ml of blood (0.05% BAC), which is just over half the UK level of 80mg, or the 80–100mg levels imposed in most US states. One glass of wine should be safely legal. Drink-driving is severely punished, and there are frequent random checks. **Seat belts** are compulsory in the back and front; children under 10 must sit in the back unless you have a rear-facing car seat.

By train

Trains in the Loire are admirably clean, reliable and inexpensive. The operator is the nationally owned SNCF, divided locally into two regional networks: TER Centre in the east, TER Pays de Loire in the west. The main line runs from Angers to Orléans, passing through Saumur, Tours and Blois, and keeping close to the Loire for much of its length. There are a number of branch lines as well, notably those radiating from Tours; unfortunately, many more minor branches now suffer from infrequent services, and occasional or total replacement by **SNCF buses**. These buses are ticketed as for trains and arrive and depart from train stations. Over and above the normal train network, two high-speed **TGV** lines connect Tours and Le Mans with Paris. TGVs are timetabled separately from normal TER trains, but connecting tickets are sold as standard.

For national **train information** you can phone (☎08.92.35.35.35, €0.34 per minute, within France only) or check online at ⊛www.sncf.com, which has an English-language option, and offers online booking. Individual **timetable** leaflets are available for each route; the display shelves at stations are usually well stocked but you can always ask if they've run out. You can also pick up a free *Guide Voyageur* for each regional network, which includes maps as well as lots of general information (in French).

Tickets can be bought online and at all train stations – given the French name of **gare SNCF** throughout the Guide. Smaller stations may be only sporadically manned, but there's always an automatic ticket machine. Before boarding, make sure to validate your ticket at the orange machine on the platform marked **compostez votre billet**, though conductors are often lenient with forgetful foreigners.

Fares are inexpensive: €15 single from Tours to Orléans, for example. Children under 12 travel for half price and under-4s travel free. Under-26s and over-60s get a 25 percent reduction, known as a **découverte** fare, on *période bleue* (blue period, or off-peak) days; you could look these up on the official SNCF calendar, as found in the *Guide Voyageur*, but staff are invariably helpful in asking your age and finding you the best tariff. The *découverte* fare also applies to any two or more people travelling together on return tickets on TGVs, or on other trains if they start their outward journey during a blue period; the same reduction applies to a group of four people travelling with a child under 12, and anyone booking a journey of more than 200km including a Saturday night away. **Bikes** travel free on most trains.

Various **rail passes** and discount cards can be bought, but you're unlikely to make enough train journeys within the Loire area to make any of these worthwhile.

By bus

On major routes trains are faster and more frequent than buses (though marginally more expensive), but where no train service exists you may have to fall back on the buses. Two kinds of bus services operate in the Loire region: **SNCF buses**, which have replaced some or all trains on many branch lines; and **public buses**, mostly run by private companies, which can be useful for local and cross-country journeys. SNCF buses are ticketed just like trains, and arrive and depart from train stations.

Timetables on ordinary public buses are usually scheduled to suit working, market and school hours. Early and end-of-school services may also be supplemented by one or two extra buses during the day on certain routes. You'll have to plan carefully; note that services can be skeletal on Sundays and during school holidays. Tickets can be bought on board public buses.

Larger towns always have a **gare routière** (bus station), often next to the gare SNCF, but many buses also call at town-centre stops. In smaller towns you can usually rely on the bus stopping at the Mairie (town hall) or market square.

Boat trips and inland waterways

First-time visitors are often surprised to find that the Loire river is no longer navigable: the most you'll get from a river **boat** on the Loire is a short cruise. The **Sarthe** and **Mayenne** rivers above Angers, however, are plied by various cruise boats, detailed in the relevant sections of the Guide.

The great **canal** networks of central France lie mostly to the east of the Loire, outside the scope of this book, but there are stretches to be explored, notably the **Canal Latéral à la Loire**, which links Briare to Sancerre before continuing upstream into Burgundy. Vestiges of the long-closed **Canal du Berry** still exist alongside the upper reaches of the Cher, but it isn't much used commercially.

For information on **canoeing** and **kayaking**, see p.42.

Accommodation

The chance to spend the night in a château is one of the great lures of the Loire region, and needn't cost the earth. If you can't afford this luxury, the region has scores of attractive, family-run hotels, and there are as many homely chambres d'hôtes – rooms in private homes rented out by the night. You can usually find a room just by turning up, but in high summer and in the period after Easter, or if you plan to stay somewhere special, it's well worth booking ahead. All hoteliers speak enough English to take a telephone booking.

Hotels

All French hotels are given official **star** ratings, but the system has more to do with size and fittings of bathrooms than with genuine quality. Most tourist hotels in the Loire are two-stars, though there is a solid foundation of no-star and one-star hotels at the budget end of the range, and a smattering of often rather chintzy three-stars at the top. The handful of four-star hotels are almost all converted châteaux deep in the countryside.

Accommodation price categories

All hotels and chambres d'hôtes in this book have been given price codes according to the following scale. The symbol indicates the price of the **least expensive double room in high season.**

Although many hotels offer a range of rooms at different prices, a range of prices (such as ❷–❺) is only given when the spectrum is especially broad, or where there are relatively few rooms in the lowest category. Prices given for dorm beds in hostels are per person per night.

❶ Under €30
❷ €30–40
❸ €40–55
❹ €55–70
❺ €70–85
❻ €85–100
❼ €100–125
❽ €125–150
❾ Over €150

At the bottom end of the scale (**❶**, or less than €30) you're likely to be in an old-fashioned, family-run **budget hotel**, often used by local workers as well as tourists, and typically above a bar or simple restaurant. Such places may be charming – with rickety wooden floors, cast-iron radiators and peeling paint on the shutters – or faintly depressing. Rooms usually have a sink (*lavabo*) in one corner, sometimes with a toilet (*WC*) behind a screen as well; bathrooms and showers (*douches*) are almost invariably found on the landing – referred to as *douche et WC dans le palier*.

For a little more money (**❷**, or around €35), you'll either find yourself in one of the relatively classy rooms offered by a simple one-star hotel, often with refreshed paintwork and a simple bathroom (*salle de bain*) added in a corner, or in one of the budget rooms at a **two-star hotel**, perhaps an old-fashioned attic room with a shared bathroom, or something modernized but spartan. In less-visited areas you can often find excellent rooms with private bathrooms in this price range, but the majority of good **tourist hotels** in the Loire fall within the next category up (**❸**, often at around €45). You can usually rely on hotels at this price to be professionally run, with night concierges, reasonably new bathrooms and decent furnishings. Rooms are typically pleasant but don't expect stylish interior design at this price level; at best, owners will have made a feature of ancient beams or fireplaces.

Prices in touristy areas, especially at swankier places with posh restaurants, can rise into the next price category (**❹**, or over €55), but you may not get much for the extra money – perhaps satellite TV and a minibar. Above this level (**❺** and up) you're definitely moving into the territory of **luxury hotels**. Some are absolutely delightful, set in historic townhouses or country châteaux and gracefully converted – real honeymoon territory – while others are aimed more at the business market. Note that relatively inexpensive rooms at the best hotels are occasionally disappointing – in a modern annexe, perhaps, or lacking the view – so be sure to ask when you book.

Many family-run hotels **close** for two or three weeks in winter. Only really out-of-the-

way places are shut in summer these days. In smaller towns and villages, hotels may also close for one or two nights a week but if you ring in advance you may be able to arrange to pick up a key, or stay on if you arrived on a previous night. Details are given in the Guide, but note that dates vary from year to year, so phone ahead to be sure.

Single rooms are rare, and it's rarer still to be offered a discount on a double room; you may, however, be offered one of a hotel's relatively inexpensive rooms. Many hotels have a few rooms with **extra beds**, on the other hand, and even if they don't they'll willingly add a bed for only a small supplement to the normal price.

The old-fashioned habit of insisting on **half-board** (*démi-pension*) has almost universally been replaced by a polite enquiry as to whether or not you'll be eating dinner at the hotel. Don't dismiss the offer: hotel restaurants are often the best in town, and the set dinners at budget hotels can be astoundingly good value. **Breakfast** is not normally included in the price of the room. Again, you'll probably be asked whether you'll be eating breakfast (*prendre le petit déjeuner*) when you check in. At roughly €5 or so, it costs scarcely more than a cup of coffee, an indifferent orange juice and a croissant in a café – and in fact you'll rarely get more than exactly that.

Hotel chains and associations

You're not likely to need them in the Loire, and they won't crop up in the listings in the Guide, but it's worth knowing that you can find a very inexpensive, basically decent room at the French budget **chain hotels**. Formule 1 (☎08.92.68.56.85, ⓦwww .hotelformule1.com), B&B (☎08.20.90.29 .29, ⓦwww.hotel-bb.com) and Premiere Classe (☎01.64.62.46.46, ⓦwww .premiereclasse.fr) have inexpensive hotels in the industrial/commercial zones of all the Loire's major cities. At Formule 1, if you reserve in advance you can let yourself in at any time of the day or night using your credit card.

Slightly more upmarket chain hotels include Ibis, Sofitel, Kyriad, Première Classe and Campanile, most of them run by the Accor group (www.accorhotels.com), which also manages the relatively swanky Mercure chain of good if businesslike hotels in Tours, Blois, Orléans, Bourges, Angers and Le Mans.

A organization to know about is **Logis de France** (01.45.84.83.84, www.logis-de-france.fr), more a French institution than an association. It markets and to some extent regulates its 3000-odd members, and its distinctive green and yellow sign showing a hearth and a map of France can be a welcome sight if you're arriving somewhere late or unexpectedly. Standards are far from uniform, and its members tend to be of the old-fashioned school of hotel-keeping – which can be either a very good or a bad thing – but you can rely on reasonable prices and cleanliness. Many *Logis* rank among the best provincial hotels in France, and are listed in the Guide. Logis de France produces a free annual guide by *région*, available from members, from the French government tourist board in your home country (see p.18), or by ordering direct by phone or online from Logis de France.

Chambres d'hôtes

Staying in **chambres d'hôtes** – "hosts' rooms", or **bed-and-breakfast** accommodation in a private home – is an excellent way to get off the beaten track and meet local people. You shouldn't expect hotel-like services such as daily changes of sheets and towels, but standards and availability have risen in recent years, and you can now find chambres d'hôtes in many towns as well as in more traditional countryside cottages or farmhouses.

The pick of the bunch are detailed in the Guide alongside hotel recommendations, but be sure to ring ahead: some proprietors may open and close from one year to the next, the best places get booked long in advance and in any case you'll often need to speak to your host to get accurate directions – many chambres d'hôtes are deep in the countryside.

Tourist offices often stock folders full of pictures and details of chambres d'hôtes in their area; if you're booking from home, a phone call will often result in a choice local recommendation. Alternatively, buy one of the official booklets published by the

national promotional agency, **Gîtes de France** (01.49.70.75.75, www.gites-de-france.fr), *Chambres et Tables d'Hôtes* or *Chambres d'Hôtes de Charme*. You can find these at international tourist board offices (see p.18) and in French bookshops and tourist offices. For the most comprehensive listings, ask for the dedicated guide for the *région* (Centre or Pays-de-la-Loire) or even the individual *département* you plan to visit, or get online – the fully searchable database is translated into English.

Costs are around €45–60 a night – equivalent to the better class of two-star hotel. By and large, standards are high, with typically simple and pleasant décor. The best chambres d'hôtes, whether historic townhouses, ancient farmhouses or mini-châteaux, are far and away the loveliest places to stay in the region: real, lovingly cared-for homes with antique furniture and exquisite period details. At the very top end of the scale, you can find chambres d'hôtes in full-blooded châteaux (see below). Prices rise steeply above €100 at this level, and the boundary between such places and hotels may be blurred.

Some proprietors also offer evening meals or **tables d'hôtes**. If you want to take advantage of this you'll usually need to let your hosts know at least a day or two in advance.

Châteaux

Accommodation in a **château** can take the form of a swish hotel or a room in a private home let out by the blue-blooded proprietor in an attempt to keep the taxman from the door. Either way, what's on offer varies as much as any other kind of accommodation.

Details of many châteaux offering accommodation are given in the Guide alongside hotels and chambres d'hôtes, but if you decide to plan your holiday around staying somewhere really special you might want to consider getting hold of a **specialist guide**. Many are listed in the standard chambres d'hôtes guide (see above), but the best guide by far is *Bienvenue au Château – Western France*, published in conjunction by the tourist boards of the Centre, Pays-de-la-Loire, Normandy, Brittany and Poitou-Charentes *régions*. Updated each year, and written in both English and French, the guide lists some 150 châteaux and manor houses which offer rooms, with drawings, brief descriptions and contact details.

Alternatively, check out *Châteaux et Hotels de France* (reservations ℡01.40.07.00.20, ℗www.chateauxhotels.com), a free guide for the whole of France, which covers posh hotels as well as châteaux; note that all of the places listed have paid for the privilege. The similar *Relais et Châteaux* association (℡08.25.32.32.32, ℗www.relaischateaux.fr) promotes a handful of luxury châteaux-hotels in the region; you can find their catalogue in tourist offices and on their website.

Youth hostels

Auberges de jeunesse (youth hostels) may be handy for lone travellers looking to save money, but people travelling in pairs or groups may as well opt for an inexpensive hotel. Prices are given per person throughout the Guide. You'll only find hostels in the larger towns – Angers, Saumur, Chinon, Tours, Amboise, Blois and Orléans – and some are in awkward locations out in the suburbs (or, in the case of Amboise and Saumur, on an island in the Loire). The big cities will also have a **Foyer des Jeunes Travailleurs**, a residential hostel aimed at young workers, though travellers can stay there too; in Tours, the Foyer is the only hostel option.

Camping

Almost every town or village in the Loire has its own municipal **camping** (campsite), usu-ally located in a pleasant spot by the nearest riverbank. Multi-starred private campsites, many with swimming pools and other facili-ties, cater to the swankier class of camper and caravanner – many of them French peo-ple from outside the region or Dutch holiday-makers. Prices at campsites vary according to facilities and whether you have a tent, a car or a caravan: count on around €5–10 per person. Most campsites stay open from March or April to the end of September or mid-October.

You'll find few opportunities for camping rough (*le camping sauvage*) in the Loire, but you could try asking at farms. Some farms have their own little official campsites any-way, signposted as **camping à la ferme**.

Gîtes and other rented accommodation

Your first port of call is likely to be **Gîtes de France** (℡01.49.70.75.75, ℗www.gites-de-france.fr), the national association promoting self-catering accommodation as well as bed-and-breakfast and camping on the farm. You can get the catalogue of **gîtes** – self-catering cottages rented by the week – from tourist boards, local tourist offices and some bookshops, or search the organiza-tion's excellent website.

For **private rentals**, British travellers should look in the classified ads in the Sunday papers. Otherwise there are hosts of online booking agencies: ℗www.frenchconnections .co.uk, ℗www.bvdirect.co.uk and ℗www .cheznous.com are well established.

Eating and drinking

The cuisine of the Loire is famously light and simple, with good-quality ingredients unmasked by complex sauces or over-fussy treatment. There's an obvious local fondness for river fish and fine mushrooms – the latter are grown all over the region – but you'll find plenty of other dishes based on the excellent local wines and local vegetables. Touraine is not called "the garden of France" for nothing... So while the Loire may not have achieved the international gastronomic profile of, say, Burgundy, you can expect to eat and drink extremely well.

The Language section of Contexts (see p.343) includes a French–English glossary which you can use as a **menu reader**. For detailed discussion of the Loire's light and incredibly varied **wines**, see p.333.

The food of the Loire

There is no such thing as traditional **Loire cuisine** for the simple reason that the Loire is not a traditional French region. Some dishes, such as *sandre au beurre blanc* (pike-perch in a butter-based sauce) and *la friture de la Loire* (small fried fish), find their way onto menus across the region, but real specialities are highly localized – the prunes of Tours, for example, or the famous green lentils of the Berry.

Freshwater fish is a firm favourite, though sadly it rarely comes from the Loire itself – in fact, if it's salmon, you can be certain that it's not, as salmon fishing has been banned for many years. If you want to eat fish fresh from the local rivers, go for **la friture**, a plate heaped high with little smelt-like *goujons* (gudgeon), *gardons* (roach) and *éperlans* (smelt), all deep-fried in a light, milky batter. Other traditional favourites include the small, herring-like *alose* (shad) and the rare *lamproie* (river lamprey), both caught in spring in long nets stretched across the river. *Brochet* (pike) and the wonderful *anguilles* (eel) – best served *en matelote*, in a heady red-wine stew – are well worth trying.

Ubiquitous on regional menus is **sandre** (pike-perch or zander), a large, white-fleshed species introduced from Eastern Europe and usually served with **beurre blanc**, a favourite regional sauce made with butter, shallots and white wine or *vinaigre d'Orléans*,

whisked into a light emulsion. Imported **salmon**, often poached in Vouvray wine or flavoured with sorrel, is still common, as is stuffed bream.

Meat is less of a speciality, though the *géline Tourangelle* (a black-feathered, corn-fed chicken from Touraine with a distinctive flavour) and *volailles de Loué* (chickens raised according to strict regulations in the Sarthe) are renowned in France. **Rillons**, great cubes of fatty pork, are tasty but rather off-putting to outsiders unless you find them sliced up and served on a green salad with goat's cheese, in which case they taste rather like particularly good *lardons* (bacon bits). You may find **rillettes** more tempting – this paste of pork mashed with lard and liver is perfect when spooned onto a bit of French bread, and both Tours and Le Mans make a fetish of it. *Andouilles* are pure pork sausages served poached and then grilled (and no relation to the Cajun smoked *andouille* or the ubiquitous French *andouillette*); those from Jargeau and Mennetou-sur-Salon are particularly renowned. In Touraine charcuteries you'll also find *pâté au biquion*, made from pork, veal and young goat's meat.

The favoured meat of the forested eastern Loire is **game**. Pheasant, guinea fowl, pigeon, duck, quails, young rabbit, venison and even wild boar are all hunted in the Sologne. You're more likely to find farmed game on restaurant menus than the real thing, even within the autumn game season, but some say the farmed stuff tastes better anyway. Game is often served in a rich sauce made from autumnal forest fruits, or **wild mushrooms** such as *girolles* (chanterelles), *cèpes* (ceps, or edible boletus) and *trompettes de la mort* (horns of plenty) – all of which thrive in the region's many forests.

Cultivated mushrooms have been big in the Loire ever since it was first discovered back in the late nineteenth century that you could grow the ordinary *champignons de Paris* in the caves that honeycomb the riverside escarpments. In recent years, some producers have experimented with **exotic mushroom** varieties such as *pleurotes* (oyster mushrooms), shiitake mushrooms and *pieds bleu*, and chefs are responding with new sauces.

The Loire valley is also superb **vegetable**-growing country. Anjou and the Orléanais are famous for horticultural research, while the gardens of Touraine produce the wonderfully sweet *haricots verts* (French beans) and leeks – known as poor man's asparagus. The sandy soil of the Sologne is ideal for the real thing, cultivated in distinctive deep rows; locals rate the fleshy white or purple-tinged variety above the smaller green asparagus. It's usually eaten simply accompanied by a vinaigrette made with local walnut oil, or a *hollandaise* sauce. Finally, from Berry, come **lentilles vertes** (green lentils), second only to those from Puy among connoisseurs; they traditionally accompany salmon, trout or oxtail.

From Anjou's orchards come greengages called *reine Claudes* after François I's queen, and the succulent Anjou pear. Tours was long famous for its **prunes**, and you'll often find them on regional menus, steeped in sweet Vouvray wine, stuffed with apricots and apples and flambéed in rum, or even served with pork. A few villages in the Saumurois have revived the tradition of *poires* or **pommes tapées** – oven-dried apples and pears, delicious with duck or poached in wine. But of all local dishes, the most famous is **tarte Tatin**, an upside-down apple tart whose fame originates in the small town of Lamotte-Beuvron, in the Sologne.

The region makes a cult of its **goat's cheese**. A local *chèvre fermier* (farm-produced goat's cheese) can be a revelation, but four named cheeses are found on most restaurant's boards. Each can be recognized by its distinctive shape: soft Ste-Maure takes the form of a long cylinder with a piece of

straw running through the middle; the richer Pouligny-St-Pierre and Valençay are pyramid-shaped; while creamier, nutty Selles-sur-Cher is flat and round, like a miniature Camembert. Sancerre has its own tiny, round, tangy *crottin de Chavignol*. *Chèvre* may be presented in any stage of readiness from a creamy, soft *frais*, often dusted with ash, to a dry, powerful *sec* that all but reeks of billy goat. **Cow's milk cheeses** are more unusual, though just south of Orléans they make the delicious Olivet bleu and Olivet cendré. Touraine even has a ewe's milk cheese: Perrusson.

The heritage industry makes a lot of noise about **fouaces** (or *fouées* in some regions), a kind of wheat bread fast-cooked in the oven, usually with goat's cheese or *rillons* as a stuffing – though Rabelais' original recipe specifies eggs, butter, spices and saffron. It's particularly popular in tourist-trap cave-restaurants in Touraine and Anjou, and can be very good in a hearty way.

Cafés and snacks

Hotel **breakfasts** are almost universally unimaginative. You'll be served a length of baguette (sometimes a croissant too) with pre-wrapped butter and jam, a glass of indifferent orange juice and a cup of filter coffee. It often comes served on a paper napkin rather than a plate; you're allowed to leave crumbs on the table. It's easy to do it yourself for a couple of euros less: *boulangeries* (bakeries) can sell you a can of orange juice along with your croissant, *pain au chocolat* or *pain aux raisins*, and in the morning you can usually find croissants in a rack on the counter at cafés and bars.

Service, tipping and the bill

The **service charge** is always included (*service compris*) in the prices listed on the menu, and you're not expected to **tip**. It's polite to round up the bill, however, and you might leave a euro coin or two if you've been particularly impressed.

To get the **bill**, attract the waiter or waitress's attention – for a man, it's always *monsieur* and never *garçon*, whatever you've learnt in school – and ask for **l'addition, s'il vous plaît**.

For **light meals** and **snacks**, cafés and bars often sell inexpensive baguette sandwiches, *tartines* (buttered half-slices of baguette) and *croques-monsieurs* (toasted sandwiches with cheese and ham). Thin, pancake-like crêpes are another option. You'll get a better and usually a healthier meal by shopping at a **charcuterie** (delicatessen), as found in every small village. These are ideal places to buy delicious **picnic food** such as pâtés, cold meats and prepared salads, though it can work out surprisingly expensive once you've added up *une tranche* (a slice) of this and *une barquette* (a carton) of that. A nearby **boulangerie-pâtisserie** will often have a selection of quiches, cakes and sweet pastries alongside the racks of narrow baguettes and the thicker, longer-lasting *pains*. For fruit and vegetables, you'll have to look for the rarer *épicerie* (grocery), or head for a supermarket.

Salons de thé (tea rooms) are mostly found in larger towns, where they are often chi-chi little places serving small savoury dishes, cakes and lots of different teas.

Restaurants

Every village has its **restaurant**, most of them serving old-fashioned French dishes perked up by local ingredients, sometimes with a dedicated menu of local specialities. **Opening hours** are short and usually inflexible, typically noon to 2pm and 7.30pm to 9pm or 9.30pm, sometimes a little later in touristy places or large towns – but don't expect to turn up outside a restaurant's stated hours and be served. Almost all restaurants are closed one day of the week, often a Monday, and often for one regular evening and one lunchtime session too; details of when a restaurant is closed are given with every review.

If it's a weekend night or you're travelling in high season, it's wise to **reserve** – phoning or calling in the same day is usually fine. Telephone numbers are given in the Guide whenever you might need them – at less touristy places this is really weekends only. Many restaurants double as hotels – don't ignore them for this reason, as the emphasis is typically on the cooking. **Children** are almost universally welcomed with an inexpensive and unpatronizing *menu enfant*.

For more glamorous, chef-concocted cuisine you'll have to book at the more expensive and formal type of restaurant, commonly found in the middle of the countryside. Livelier, more modern, **bistrot**-type places are only really found in the big towns, along with **ethnic restaurants** – mostly Indian, North African and Chinese – and traditional **brasseries**, which serve straightforward French food at all hours.

In French, a **menu** means a fixed-price set meal, which is usually the best way to eat. All restaurants have a selection of these *menus*, often starting with a bargain-priced **menu touristique** with no more than a couple of choices for each of two or three courses, and a price tag of as little as €10–15. You'll find more interesting pickings in the mid-priced *menus*, especially if there's a **menu du terroir** of regional specialities. At the top of the range you may find a multi-course **menu gastronomique** or, at the showiest places, a *menu dégustation*, which may even have a different wine served with each course. The menu itself is called *la carte*, and eating **à la carte** means you can choose from all the dishes on offer, which works out a lot more expensive.

At **lunchtime**, most restaurants offer excellent-value two- or three-course *menus* for around €10–15, or a simple, inexpensive **plat du jour** (dish of the day).

Vegetarians

Vegetarians have a hard time in French restaurants, and the Loire is no exception. If you don't eat fish you'll often have to make do with yet another omelette or tomato salad, and ordering off-menu, even for simple dishes such as these, is relatively expensive. Sympathetic restaurants may well fix you something special if you say *je suis végétarien(ne), est-ce qu'il y a quelques plats sans viande?* (I'm vegetarian, are there any non-meat dishes?), but you shouldn't rely on this. There is, however, a top-flight restaurant in Tours which offers a genuinely gastronomic, all-vegetable menu – the renowned *Jean Bardet* (see p.72).

In France, salads and often vegetables too come separately from main dishes, and cheeses come before dessert. First-timers from **North America** should note that *entrée* means an appetizer or starter – main courses are *les plats*, or *plats principals*. At the end of the meal, you'll always be offered *un café* – which means an espresso – and it's never included in the price of the *menu*.

Drinking

You can drink **water** from the tap anywhere in the Loire region, but when eating out many locals eschew it in favour of bottled mineral waters (*eau minérale*), either sparkling (*gazeuse*) or still (*eau plate*).

The vineyards of the Loire, which stretch from Sancerre in the east down to the Atlantic estuary, produce an incredible variety of **wines**, ranging from acid Muscadet to honeyed Côteaux du Layon, and from sparkling Saumur to the fruity reds of Chinon and Bourgueil. Bought wholesale from the vineyard, or in supermarkets, wine is incredibly cheap, even if it's AOC (*Appellation d'Origine Contrôlée*) – an indication of quality. You can get a decent bottle for €5, and anything above €10 is moving into more serious territory. For a full discussion of **Loire wine**, see p.333.

As for **drinking** the stuff, you'll find regional wines dominate most restaurant menus. In bars you'll be served the local plonk – just ask for *un rouge* (a glass of red) or *un blanc* (a glass of white), or even *un vin mousseux* (a sparkling wine). Not all restaurants sell wine by the glass, which is a pity, as it's an excellent way to taste. At moderately priced restaurants there's usually a **pichet** (carafe) of something local and decent on offer – you can order *un quart* (quarter litre) or *un demi* (half-litre). You'll often find a few bottles priced somewhere a little over the €10 mark. Be careful if you're drinking fine wines, however, as restaurant mark-ups can be stratospheric.

Beer (*bière*), often Kronenbourg, is popular among younger people; the standard 25cl glass of lager from the tap is ordered as *une (deux, trois) pression(s), s'il vous plaît*. **Spirits** have less of a following in the Loire than in other regions of France, partly because of the abundance of good wine, and partly because little hard liquor is produced locally, with the notable exception of the big Cointreau (triple sec) distillery just outside Angers. That said, *apéritifs* – *les apéros* in slang – are regularly drunk before a meal; *digestifs* such as Cognac and Armagnac, on the other hand, may be reserved for more special occasions.

Canned **soft drinks** are available everywhere, most commonly Coke (*Coca*), lemonade (*limonade*), Orangina (a pulpy orangeade), Lipton's (lemon- or peach-flavoured ice tea) and Minute Maid (unsweetened orange or apple juice). Otherwise you can try a gaudy-coloured *sirop*, a flavoured syrup to mix with water or lemonade: mint (*sirop de menthe*) and grenadine are popular.

In **cafés**, it's cheaper to drink at the counter (*au comptoir*) than inside, while the outdoor *terrasse* commands premium prices. Cafés serve beer, wine and hard drinks as well as **coffee**. Daytime coffee is always *un crème* – *un café au lait* is a big bowl of very milky coffee served in French homes for breakfast. After a meal you'll be offered a small, black *café* (espresso, or *un express*). You can ask for *un déca* (decaffeinated coffee). **Hot chocolate** (*chocolat chaud*) is popular in the morning, and **tea** in the afternoon. The latter comes as a glass of hot water with a bag of Lipton's-brand tea; if you want the English version, ask for milk on the side – *un peu de lait frais à part* – and add it yourself once the tea has finished brewing. **Herb teas** (*infusions* or *tisanes*) are fashionable, particularly *camomille* (camomile), *menthe* (mint), *tilleul* (lime flowers) and *verveine* (verbena).

Communications

It's easy to stay in touch while travelling in the Loire. Post offices are reliable and found everywhere, you can get online in the cities and sometimes in smaller towns too, and there's a good network of public phones. Mobile phone signal coverage is excellent, too.

Mail

Most **post offices** (*la poste*) are open Monday to Friday from 8am to around 6pm or 7pm, and Saturday from 9am to noon, though smaller post offices may keep shorter hours and close for an hour or two at lunch, and city-centre offices keep slightly longer hours.

You can buy and send a pre-paid *aérogramme* at any post office, but the easiest place to buy ordinary **stamps** is at a *tabac* (tobacconist). At the time of writing, standard prices for postcards (*cartes postales*) and letters (*lettres*) up to 20g were €0.50 for the UK and the rest of the EU, and €90 for North America, Asia, Australia and New Zealand. Postboxes are bright yellow.

You can receive letters **poste restante** – addressed to you at Poste Restante, Poste Centrale, Town x, Postcode – but most people these days use email (see p.36) instead.

Telephones

Almost all **public phones** take phonecards (*télécartes*), sold at railway stations and *tabacs* in various denominations from €5 upwards. Many call boxes also accept credit cards, but coin-operated phones are rare outside bars and cafés. Local calls from a public phone cost less than €0.10 per minute, and off-peak calls – at weekends and on weekday nights from 7pm to 8am – are thirty percent cheaper. Hotel phones usually carry a significant mark-up. If you're making a lot of calls you may save money by buying a **pre-paid phone card**. These can be used with any phone – you dial a special number and then tap in a separate code shown on the back of the card. Be warned that inexpensive pre-paid cards are occasionally unreliable.

If you're **phoning within France** you'll always need to dial the regional code first – ☎02 for all of the area covered by the Guide.

Phone numbers prefixed ☎08 are special: ☎08.00 is free-to-dial; ☎08.10 is charged at local rates, no matter where you're calling from; all other ☎08 numbers cost €0.34 per minute and can't be accessed from outside France. Mobile numbers begin ☎06. International access numbers for **phoning abroad** are shown in the box below. International off-peak hours are the same as for domestic phone calls. At peak rates, €1 gets you about five minutes to the EU countries and the US, or two minutes to Australia and New Zealand.

The easiest option for Europeans, Australians and New Zealanders is to use a **mobile phone**. If you haven't used it abroad before you'll probably need to contact your provider to get it activated for foreign use. You can enquire about the extortionate billing while you're at it; remember that you'll pay for people to call you while you're abroad. If you plan to make a lot of calls you might consider buying a French SIM card and pre-paid charge-up cards (*mobicartes*); you won't be able to receive calls on your old number, but at least you'll be able to make calls at relatively reasonable rates. Note that France operates on the European GSM standard, so **US cellphones** won't work in France unless you've got a tri-band phone.

Calling France from abroad

To make a call **to France from abroad**, use the IDD code for your country (00 or 011 in most cases) followed by the French country code (33), then the local number minus the initial "0".

From the UK, Ireland, New Zealand and Netherlands ☎00 33 (0)
From the US, Canada and Australia ☎011 33 (0)

Email

Signing up to a free **Web-based email** account such as Yahoo (ⓦwww.yahoo.com) or Hotmail (ⓦwww.hotmail.com) is the easiest way to keep in touch while you're away. The major cities in the Loire all have a number of **cyber cafés** or other Internet access points – *point internet* in French; addresses are given in the "Listings" sections at the end of the relevant city accounts in the Guide. Cyber cafés typically charge upwards of €4

an hour. Outside the big cities you may be able to get online at some post offices and even in the odd café or shop, but you shouldn't depend on it.

Laptop-users should note that French phone sockets take a non-standard plug, though you'll often find a standard RJ-11 female socket in the back of the male unit, enabling you to plug straight in. The website ⓦwww.kropla.com offers useful advice on dial tones and other potential problems.

Festivals and events

It would be hard to holiday in the Loire without coming across at least one festival. Even the tiniest villages celebrate their saint's feast day, or put on a festival dedicated to sometimes surprisingly specific items of food. Among larger festivals, there are endless wine fairs, rock, folk and classical music seasons, medieval and night markets and elaborate, after-dark son-et-lumière shows at some of the bigger châteaux. The most important festival of all, the Jour de Loire (late May or early June), celebrates the river itself, with events organized right the way along the valley.

Major festivals include the half-millennium-old celebrations for Joan of Arc's relief of the siege of Orléans (early May), Chambord's mammoth game fair (June), Saumur's horse-show spectacular (July), the rose festival of Doué-la-Fontaine (August) and Romorantin-Lanthenay's grand feast for the food of the Sologne (October) – not forgetting the classic **24 Heures du Mans'** motor race (June). Big **rock festivals** include Blois' Tous sur le Pont (late May to mid-June), the Printemps de Bourges (April) and the Aucard de Tours festival (May). Look out for the frequent programmes of **classical music** in abbeys and churches across the region, and the numerous **folk music** jamborees, such as those at Pierrefitte-sur-Sauldre (April) and Montoire-sur-le-Loir (August).

Most other festivals in the Loire region focus on food, wine, gardens or music. The **calendar of events** pp.37–39 is by no means comprehensive, and does not include certain "festivals" that run over a period of months and are really season

attractions: **Chaumont's garden festival**, for example, which attracts over 100,000 people a year, lasts from late May to late October and really counts as one of the château's attractions more than an "event". The same applies to the many horse shows and competitions organized throughout the year by the riding school in Saumur, the **Cadre Noir** (see p.229), the son-et-lumière spectacles (see below) put on by many châteaux during the summer months or the "festivals" of music and theatre set up in many big towns, notably Blois' **L'Eté Culturel**, a programme of concerts and theatre in historic settings that runs from May to September. All these events are covered in the relevant section of the Guide.

Son-et-lumière spectacles

A particular feature of the French heritage industry, and seen *par excellence* in the châteaux of the Loire is the **son-et-lumière**. The phrase literally means "sound and light" but there's no real translation. These shows are designed to turn a château into a kind of musical-historical extravaganza using elaborate sound and lighting effects, sometimes with a melodramatic voice-over or antique music, sometimes with professional actors and local townspeople in costume. The trend these days is to allow visitors to wander freely around the site admiring the various effects. At their worst, son-et-lumières are dreary affairs, a travesty of the history and architecture of an ancient building; at their best and most original they can transform the way you see a château. Children may find them equally hit and miss as well. **Starting times** usually vary according to season between about 9.30pm and 10.30pm. The list below covers all the major son-et-lumière performances.

Amboise A la Cour du Roy François ☎02.47.57.14.47, ⊛www.renaissance-amboise.com. Costumed spectacular on the high terrace in front of the château with seemingly hundreds of dancing locals and images projected onto the walls. Wed & Sat from late June to end Aug. Adults €13 (€16 in the grandstand), children aged 6–14 €7.

Azay-le-Rideau Les Imaginaires d'Azay-le-Rideau ☎02.47.45.42.04, ⊛www.monum.fr. Original and enthralling use of just light and Renaissance music, allowing you to wander freely round the château grounds. Early May to late Sept. €12 combined entry with château (€9 separately); young people aged 12–18 €5; under-12s free.

Blois Ainsi Blois Vous est Conté. ☎02.54.78.72.76. One of the best, in the atmospheric setting of the enclosed courtyard. Actors' voices tell the story of the château and its bloody history while ultra-high-tech lighting effects pick out details of the architecture. English-language version on Wednesdays. €11.50 combined ticket with château (€9.50 separately); under-12s €5 (€4.50 separately).

Bourges Les Nuits Lumière de Bourges. ☎02.48.23.02.60. Low-key but relatively sophisticated circuit of the old city, following a trail of blue streetlamps past historic buildings lit up by moving projections, while soft music plays. July & Aug daily; May, June & Sept Thurs–Sat. Free.

Chambord Les Métamorphoses de Chambord. ☎02.54.33.39.16, ⊛www.chambord.org. Free-ranging "promenade" round the château grounds, taking in clever lighting effects playing on the surface of the stone, and piped Renaissance music. July & Aug. €14 combined entry with château (€12 separately); under-18s €9 (€7 separately); under-12s free.

Chenonceau Balade Nocturne à Chenonceau. ⊛www.chenonceau.com Little more than an evening stroll in the elaborately lit-up gardens – to the tune of Corelli. No need to book. July & Aug. €5, under-7s free.

Loches Murmurailles. An unguided wander around the old city, which is transformed by historically themed light projections showing episodes from the city's history. There's also a costumed fair of jugglers and medieval dancers, with free punch on offer. July & Aug. €11, children 6–12 €6.

Major festival dates

Festival dates are notoriously changeable from one year to the next, depending on factors like Easter, when the weekend falls or the whims of the organizers. Many of the dates given below are deliberately vague, therefore, and you should always check with the local tourist office or online – websites are given where appropriate. Where festivals straddle more than one month, they are listed below under the month in which they begin.

January and February

Angers *Premiers Plans* (second half of Jan; ⊛www.premiersplans.org) – season of European directors' first films.

Montlouis-sur-Loire and around *Les Rencontres Musicales de l'Est Tourangeau* (Jan–Feb) – diverse and high-quality programme of mostly classical concerts.

March

Chalonnes-sur-Loire (first Sat of March) – festival of Anjou wines, with parades and outdoor banqueting over one weekend.

Orléans (second week of March; ⊛www.oci-piano.com) – prestigious, week-long competition for young international players of twentieth-century piano music.

Bourgueil (early/mid-March) – annual wine fair.

Vouvray (late March) – annual wine fair.

Azay-le-Rideau (late March) – annual wine fair.

Prieuré de St-Cosme, Tours *Le Printemps Musical de St-Cosme* (late March) – two weekends of chamber music.

Around Easter (variable)

Amboise (Easter weekend) – wine fair.

Selles-sur-Cher (second weekend after Easter) – annual wine fair.

Montrésor (Pentecost, ie seventh weekend after Easter) – medieval festival every even-numbered year, with night-time market, processions and dancing.

April

Saumur (April) – books and wine fair, with celebrity French authors.

Le Mans *24 Heures Motos* (mid-April; wwww.lemans.org) – Le Mans' classic 24-hour motorcycle race.

Chinon (mid-April) – wine and food fair.

Bourges *Le Printemps de Bourges* (April; ⊛www.printemps-bourges.com) – huge, week-long rock festival featuring artists such as Beck and Massive Attack (in 2003).

Pierrefitte-sur-Sauldre *Les Musicales de Sologne* (last weekend in April) – 10,000 people came in 2003 for this festival of Sologne folk music.

Orléans (29 April) – commemoration of Joan of Arc's entry into the city, followed on May 1 by celebrations of the taking of the Bastille St-Loup.

May

Orléans (May 7–8) – presentation of Joan of Arc's standard to the people of Orléans, in front of the cathedral in the evening of May 7, followed by Mass and a long procession on the morning of May 8.

Le Mans *Festival de l'Epau* (mid- to late May) – high-quality classical concerts.

Tours *Aucard de Tours* (last week of May) – big rock festival with a one-off free concert.

Tours *Florilège Vocal* (late May/early June; ⊛http://florilege.vocal.free.fr) – weekend festival of choral music.

Various locations *Jour de Loire* (late May/early June; ⊛www.jourdeloire.com) – concerts, fireworks, nature walks and boat trips along the length of the Loire, from Anjou to the Orléanais.

Blois *Tous sur le Pont* (late May to mid-June) – festival of rock and world music attracting well-respected domestic names, with small free concerts in the day.

Sully-sur-Loire (late May to late June; ⊛www.festival-sully.com) – month-long programme of classical concerts, attracting big names (Michel Béroff in 2003).

June

Amboise (early June) – marching and competing brass bands in the streets of Amboise.

Prieuré de St-Cosme, Tours *Les Journées de la*

Rose (early June) – renowned exhibition of hundreds of rose varieties.

Sancerre (early June) – the big festival for Sancerre wines.

Le Mans *24 Heures du Mans* (mid-June; ⊛www.lemans.org) – world-famous 24-hour car race.

Orléans (mid-June) – jazz festival, with concerts in the amazing setting of the Campo Santo.

La Châtonnière near Azay-le-Rideau (mid-June) – garden festival of roses and lilies.

Anjou *Festival d'Anjou* (mid-June to mid-July; ⊛www.festivaldanjou.com) – a month of plays in historic outdoor settings throughout Anjou.

Bourgueil, Langeais, Azay-le-Rideau (mid-June to Aug) – gourmet night market (Friday 6pm to midnight), visiting each of the three towns in turn.

Chambord (third weekend in June) – Europe's premier game fair. Set in the château grounds, with dogs, horns, all sorts of manufacturers' stands and hordes of hunt enthusiasts.

Saumur (last Sunday of June) – festival of military music in odd-numbered years; mask festival in even-numbered years.

Tours *Fêtes Musicales de Touraine* (late June/early July) – ten days of top-quality classical music in historic locations.

Bourges *L'Eté Culturel* (late June to late Sept) – programme of concerts and theatre.

July

Chartres (July & Aug; ⊛http://orgues.chartres.free.fr) – two-month-long organ festival and competition, with concerts every Sunday.

Angers *Festival Angers L'Été* (July & Aug) – lively two-month programme of world and French music concerts, in the lovely surroundings of the Cloître Toussaint.

Everywhere *La Fête Nationale, or Bastille Day* (14 July) – fireworks and community celebrations in every corner of France.

Le-Puy-Notre-Dame (second weekend of July) – wine and mushroom fair.

Tours *Au Nom de la Loire* (mid-July) – crazy street-theatre and performance art down by the riverbank.

Montrésor (mid-July) – dozens of painters compete to produce a locally themed work on the same day.

Tours (July 23) – garlic and basil fair on the feast day of Sainte Anne.

Saumur *Carrousel de Saumur* (late July) – three days of horse spectaculars.

Richelieu (late July) – "cape and sword" seventeenth-century weekend.

August

Northern Anjou (Aug; ⊛ http://heuresmusicales
.free.fr/) – month-long programme of classical music
in churches and château across the region.
Doué-la-Fontaine (early Aug; ⊛ www
.journeesdelarose.com) – thousands descend to see
the rose harvest arranged inside local caves.
Genillé *Festival Cosmopolite* (second week in Aug)
– two days of rock, reggae and metal, and one of
world music.
Montoire-sur-le-Loir *Folklores du Monde*
(second week in Aug) – large festival of world folk
music.
Beaulieu-sur-Layon (second weekend of Aug) –
wine and omelette fair.
Cunault *Les Heures Musicales* (mid-Aug) – week-
long feast of organ and chamber music.
Bourgueil *Fête des Vins du Val de Loire* (Aug 15)
– festival and showcase for all Loire wines.
Vouvray and Amboise (Aug 15) – wine fairs.
Thouarcé (Aug 15) – Bonnezeaux wine festival.
Chedigny (mid-Aug) – three days of blues and
gospel.
Romorantin-Lanthenay *Festival Euphonia en
Sologne* (mid-Aug to mid-Sept) – season of
classical concerts.
Sablé-sur-Sarthe (late Aug) – prestigious four-day
festival of Baroque music.
Château de Villandry *Musiques et Jardins* (late
Aug) – Baroque chamber music in the château's
gardens.
Maison de la Devinière, Seuilly (end Aug) –
Rabelaisian festival of food, music and theatrical
performances.

September

Bourges *Fête des Marais* (first weekend in Sept)
– garden and general town festival of Bourges'
marshes.

Angers *Les Accroche-Cœurs* (early Sept) – four
bizarre days of street art and theatre all over the city.
Montlouis *Jazz en Touraine* (early Sept) – major
jazz week in and around Montlouis.
Château du Rivau (mid-Sept) – pumpkin, vine
and children's fairy-tale festival.
Chartres and around (mid-Sept;
⊛ www.journees-lyriques.com) – three-day festival
of opera and classical music in historic buildings.
**Château de la Bourdaisière, Montlouis-sur-
Loire** (second week in Sept) – gardeners' tomato
festival, with tastings.
Various locations *Journées du Patrimoine* (third
weekend in Sept; ⊛ www.culture.fr) – hundreds of
historic buildings normally closed to the public open
their doors.
Orléans *Festival de Loire* (late Sept) – scores of
old-style boats descend on Orléans for a five-day
river fiesta.
Western Anjou *Marathon de la Loire* (end Sept) –
canoe race down the Loire from Gennes to
Bouchemaine.

October

Montrichard *Rendez-vous du Pain* (first weekend
of Oct) – three-day fair of bread and baking.
Loches and around *Sonates d'Automne* (early
Oct) – programme of chamber music.
Le Lion d'Angers *Mondial du Lion* (mid-Oct;
⊛ www.mondialdulion.com) – major date in the
eventing calendar, focusing on young horses.
Romorantin-Lanthenay (last weekend of Oct) –
gastronomic festival of the Sologne, attracting
20,000 people.
Azay-le Rideau (late Oct/early Nov) – weekend
apple festival.

December

Château de Brissac (first weekend of Dec) –
Christmas crafts and foods.

Opening hours and public holidays

Opening hours in provincial France are very civilized. Except in the height of summer, when tourist attractions and businesses forego the customary two-hour lunch break, everything shuts down in the middle of the day. Restaurants usually remain closed at least one night a week (often two nights in winter), and usually on the following lunchtime as well. Don't get caught out by the official closing days at state-owned museums and smaller châteaux – usually Monday or Tuesday – and remember that in cathedrals Sunday mornings are set aside for worshippers. Note too that all sights and attractions keep Sunday hours on public holidays.

Opening hours

Shop **opening hours** in France are usually Monday to Saturday 8am to noon, and 2pm to 6.30pm, though many shops, especially in rural areas, may open and close an hour later in the morning and afternoon, while shops and businesses in cities may stay open throughout the day. Sunday opening is rare, though food shops may stay open on Sunday morning and close on Monday instead. In **summer**, larger tourist offices and museums tend to stay open without interruption, and closing times are often extended by an hour or more into the evening.

Some **major châteaux** offer late-night opening once a week, or a night-time son-et-lumìere show. **Smaller museums** and **private châteaux** may only offer two short morning and afternoon sessions: from around 10am to noon, and 2pm (3pm in summer) until 5pm (or 6pm). Opening hours are given for all sights in the Guide. **Churches** and **cathedrals** are almost always open from early in the morning until dusk, or around 8pm in summer. Occasionally you'll find a rural church locked shut, but there's often a note telling you which door to knock on to get the key. Failing that, you could try to find the priest's house, or *presbytère*.

Public transport is mostly timetabled from Monday to Friday, with a slightly reduced Saturday service and very little if any action at all on *dimanches et jours fériés* (Sundays and public holidays).

Public holidays

France celebrates eleven **national holidays** (*jours fériés* or j.f.), not counting the two that fall on a Sunday anyway – Easter Sunday (*la Fête de Pâques*) and Whitsun (*Pentecôte*). Throughout the Guide, opening hours on public holidays are the same as for **Sundays,** unless detailed otherwise.

With three and sometimes four holidays, **May** is a particularly festive month. Note that if a public holiday falls on a Tuesday or a Thursday, many people *faire le pont* ("bridge it") by taking an unofficial day off on the adjacent Monday or Friday.

January 1 – le Jour de l'an
Easter Monday – Lundi de Pâques
May 1 – la Fête du travail (Labour Day)
May 8 – la Fête de la Victoire 1945 (VE Day)
40 days after Easter (May) – l'Ascension (Ascension Day)
7th Monday after Easter (mid-May to early June) – Lundi de Pentecôte (Whit Monday)
July 14 – la Fête nationale (Bastille Day)
August 15 – l'Assomption (Feast of the Assumption)
November 1 – la Toussaint (All Saints' Day)
November 11 – l'Armistice 1918 (Armistice Day)
December 25 – Noël

Outdoor activities

What it lacks in sheer adventure – there are no mountain rock-faces or white-water river-runs – the Loire makes up for in gentle walks, excursions in kayaks or old-fashioned Loire river-craft, and of course cycling expeditions. It's ideal terrain for families and older or less adrenaline-fixed travellers. If you're determined on a heart-in-mouth trip, you could always try floating over rivers and châteaux in a balloon.

Touraine's tourist board produces a particularly useful bilingual guide to activities, walks, canoe trips, riding routes and cycle rides called *Loisirs & Randonnées*, and many other *départements* publish equivalent leaflets or booklets – just ask at any tourist office. **Fishing** enthusiasts should contact tourist offices for details of local fishing clubs – the best way to get hold of the necessary licence.

Cycling

Bicycles (*vélos*) have high status in France, and cyclists are habitually treated with respect by car-drivers, café-owners and train staff alike. As long as you steer clear of the arterial main roads – national roads, marked thick red on most maps, including Michelin – you couldn't hope for better cycling terrain. The flat *levées* (dykes) running along the Loire are a classic of French **cycle-touring**, and elsewhere you'll find gradients mostly gentle and roads largely traffic-free. It's surprising how much ground you can cover in one day if you pace yourself. With a modicum of fitness, and well-judged rest stops, most people can comfortably manage a leisurely 40km a day, often much more. Every town has its cycle repair shop, and municipal authorities are building cycle lanes in many Loire cities. As for **maps**, Michelin's 1:200,000 regional series (see p.19) is perfectly adequate, though it doesn't show contours. For detail you're best off with IGN's 1:100,000 Carte de Promenade series – full details are given under "Walking" (see p.43).

Cycle routes are currently being rapidly expanded throughout the Centre *région* under the **Loire à Vélo** scheme, which aims to establish an 800-kilometre network by 2006, with a mix of dedicated cycle-paths and routes signposted along minor roads. Tourist offices have plans of the sections that have already been completed – two notable areas are the châteaux country south of Blois, and the area between Bourgueil and Chinon. Under the **Vélotel-Vélocamp-Vélogîte** scheme, a number of hotels, campsites and chambres d'hôtes in the Centre *région* have signed up to providing secure bike parks, repair facilities and free maps of cycle routes in their locale. Tourist offices can give you a special bilingual brochure on participating places.

All larger towns have at least one **bike rental** agency, detailed in the Guide, and bikes can also be rented at many hotels, campsites, tourist offices and even train stations – expect to pay around €15 a day, €10 for a half day. Theft is rare, but be aware that your rented bike is unlikely to be insured. **Mountain bikes** (*VTT* in French) are most commonly available, though a touring bike is actually more suitable for road use.

Bikes go free on many **trains** and on certain TGVs – indicated by a cycle symbol at the top of the timetable. Newer SNCF carriages have dedicated bike racks. You can take your bike on all car **ferries**, usually for free if you ring in advance. On **Eurostar** you have to dismantle the wheels, pedals and handlebars, and parcel the whole thing up in a bag of some kind if you want to take it as hand luggage, otherwise you can send it on as freight 24 hours in advance. Both these methods are free of charge.

Canoeing and kayaking

Taking a **canoe** or **kayak** out on the Loire is one of the best ways to experience the river, with its shifting sandbanks, busy bird life and of course its château-dominated vistas. On the stretch covered by this guidebook, there's no white water as such, but you should be very cautious at bridges. Particularly lovely trips can also be made on the Loire's smaller tributaries – especially the Cher, Indre, Loir and Vienne.

To go canoeing and kayaking on any of the region's rivers, including the Loire itself, contact one of the **clubs** listed in the Guide. Canoes and kayaks are usually rented out for around €8 an hour or €15 for a half-day, and you can often join a guided half-day or day-long *descente* of the river for a small surcharge. Canoe clubs are usually to be found at a "Base Nautique" near a large town, but you can get addresses from any tourist office. A useful resource is the Comité Régional du Centre de Canoë-Kayak (☎02.38.49.88.80, ⊛www.crck.org), which produces lists of canoe/kayak clubs – available at tourist offices or online.

If you're canoeing without a guide, a useful, free English-language booklet, *Canoe-kayak*, is produced by the Centre *région*, with tips on good routes and safety.

Boat trips

Sadly, the Loire is no longer used by river traffic, and indeed the only places you can take a proper river or canal cruise are up the **Mayenne** and **Sarthe** rivers, north of Angers, along the **Canal Latéral à la Loire**, north of Sancerre, or on stretches of the **Cher**. Shorter excursions in old-style Loire boats are easy to arrange, however. You can take a turn in an old-fashioned wooden *gabare* or *toue cabanée* from an ever-growing number of town quays, and many of the **Maisons de la Loire** (river and wildlife information offices) also run trips. Details of all river excursions are given in the relevant sections of the Guide.

Swimming

Swimming pools (*piscines*) are found in every town of any consequence, and privately run campsites often have elaborate pools with waterslides and other facilities. While you're not allowed to swim in the Loire – or the Cher downstream of Tours – because of the serious **dangers** of currents, whirlpools and collapsing sandbanks, many towns on the Loire's tributary **rivers** have a small artificial beach or grassy sward, often next to the municipal campsite. It's usually safe enough to swim in any of the smaller rivers, though it's sometimes hard to find a decent spot. Avoid entering the water anywhere near sand banks, especially ones that have little vegetation and are therefore likely to be newly formed and unstable. Obviously, don't swim during floods.

The safest option for swimming "in the wild" is a freshwater **lake** (*lac* or *plan d'eau*) with a dedicated, sandy beach area. Often referred to as **Bases de Loisirs**, there are many such facilities in the region, often with cafeterias and with canoes, kayaks and windsurfers for rent.

Walking

Most people think of walking in the Loire only in terms of gentle **day rambles** and indeed almost every village seems to have its sign-posted *promenade* or *randonnée*, and tourist offices can enthusiastically hand out little maps of the locale. For **short walks** – anything from two to six hours – look out for the excellent hiking **guidebooks** produced by the FFRP (Fédération Française de la Randonnée Pédestre; ⊛www.montagnes.com), including *La Touraine à pied*, *L'Anjou à pied*, *La Sarthe à pied*, *La Vallée du Loir à pied* and *La Sologne à pied*, among many others. Each details twenty or thirty walks that keep mostly to footpaths and provides good maps and route descriptions alongside. The guides are only available in French (prices vary from €8 to €12, depending on length), but it's reasonably clear what's going on even if you don't speak any; a small dictionary might prevent confusion. You can buy the guides, or smaller packs of **route cards**, in French bookshops or tourist offices.

While the Loire is not typical hiking country – there's no wilderness as such – some superb **long-distance footpaths** do extend right across the region. The foremost of these *sentiers de grande randonnée*, or **GR trails**, is the GR3, which runs along the Loire itself from Angers though to Gien. Other major trails include the GR41 from Tours along the River Cher; the GR46 from Tours to Loches along the River Indre; the GR36 from Le Mans to Saumur and south to Montreuil-Bellay; and the GR48 from Chinon up the River Vienne. Good side-trails include the GR3D through the Layon valley from Chalonnes-sur-Loire to Doué-la-Fontaine, and the GR3C from Gien through the Sologne towards Chambord. There are also a number of Country Trails or **GRPs**, including one circuit around Bourgueil, one route down the Loir from Châteaudun towards Tours, and lots of short routes through the Sologne.

The best **maps** for walking are from IGN's Carte de Promenade series, which shows contours and footpaths, and has a usable scale of 1:100,000. Three maps cover the entire area: 25 *Angers–Chinon*, 26 *Orléans–Tours* and 27 *Orléans–La Charité-sur-Loire*. IGN also publish 1:25,000 super-scale maps, but you shouldn't need this level of detail.

Riding

If you want to go **riding**, the obvious place to make for is **Saumur**, home of the famous Ecole Nationale d'Equitation (Cadre Noir) and one of the foremost areas of France for all things horsey. For details of local stables contact the Saumur tourist office (see p.225), or see the online list at L'Anjou à Cheval, ⊛http://cdte49.free.fr/. Another fine place to ride is in the ancient hunting forest of **Chambord**, where you can hire horses from the historic stables built by the Maréchal de Saxe (⊕02.54.20.31.01). But you don't have to restrict yourself to these two centres. Tourist offices all over the region can supply full lists of **Centres de Tourisme Equestre**, which may be fully fledged stables or farms where you can find instruction or pony-trekking. Costs vary considerably depending on what exactly you're doing, but for pony-trekking expect to pay a minimum of €12 an hour. A half-day can cost anything from €30 to €50.

Flights and balloon rides

At around €200 for an hour in the air, a **balloon ride** might seem expensive, but it can be an incredibly refreshing way to view a château. Trips are always just after dawn or a couple of hours before dusk, and there's usually champagne thrown in. Flights are highly weather-dependent, so you may be asked to reschedule at the last minute. A trip in a **light plane** is less romantic, but you can cover a lot more ground.

Aérocom ⊕02.54.33.55.00, ⊛www.aerocom.fr. Balloon flights from the Blois area, at €200 per person, or €175 if in a group of four or more. Children under 13 pay €150.

Au Gré des Vents ⊕02.54.46.42.40, ⊛www.au-gre-des-vents.com. Balloon trips from near Blois: Cheverny, Beauvais, Villesavin, Valençay. €180 per person, or €165 if three or more people book; children aged 12–16 €145.

France Montgolfières ⊕02.54.71.75.40 ⊛www.franceballoons.com. Balloon flights from Chenonceau, Amboise or Loches, with experienced and professional Anglo-French guides. €221 per person, or €160 booked last-minute; children under 12 €145.

Loire Valley Aviation ⊕02.54.56.16.12, ⊛www.loire-valley-aviation.com. Over-flights of châteaux in a Cessna 172 Rocket. Costs vary from €50 to €150, depending on the length of flight and whether you're in a group of two or three (maximum). Based in Blois.

Bird- and wildlife spotting

In summer, you can't fail to notice swallows and house martins darting about the roofs of the towns, and swifts wheeling high above, but if you want to see more unusual **birds** you should head for the rivers. Two species of tern – a bird like a gull built for racing – nest in the sand banks: the black-capped, red-beaked common tern and the smaller, rarer, yellow-beaked little tern; the latter has become a symbol for all Loire **wildlife**. You can often see herons and all-white egrets fishing in the shallows, little ringed plovers and sandpipers trotting about on the sand, and cormorants flying low over the water in winter. Kingfishers are rarer, but are sometimes seen on tributary waters. **Otters** are even harder to spot; the coypu, a North American water rat, is more commonly seen. Marshy areas such as the Sologne are rich in bird life: marsh harriers, reed, sedge and Sevi's warblers, bitterns, herons, and endless types of duck and grebe. The poplar plantations of the river meadows offer relatively poor pickings, but in the larger oak, birch and chestnut forests you can spot buzzards, goshawks, sparrowhawks and woodpeckers of all kinds, as well as red **deer**, roe deer and, if you're lucky, wild boar.

Trouble and the police

The Loire is a sedate, largely trouble-free place to travel. Even the cities aren't all that big, and have few of the problems associated with, for example, Paris or Marseille. Violent crime against tourists is almost unheard of, and petty theft unusual. The usual advice applies: don't carry excessive amounts of cash; be wary of pickpockets at train stations; don't leave cameras and valuables lying around in rental cars or hotel rooms; and keep a separate note of credit card and cheque numbers – and the phone numbers for cancelling them. Finally, consider taking out travel insurance (see p.20).

The **Police Nationale** deal with crime and traffic in towns, where you'll find them at the Commissariat de Police. **Gendarmes** are a separate force in charge of rural areas (and run by the Ministry of Defence). In practice you can be in trouble with either, and you can go to either for help. It's unlikely to happen, but you can be stopped, asked to produce ID and searched anywhere and at any time in France, even if you're driving.

If you are **robbed**, first check what you've lost and cancel any credit cards, if necessary. To claim on insurance you'll need to **report the theft** officially at the nearest Commissariat de Police – addresses in the main cities are given in the "Listings" at the end of the relevant city account. There you can fill out a *constat de vol*, but you probably shouldn't expect much assistance beyond this.

If you have an **driving accident** you can pretty much rely on your insurer and/or rental company to sort it out – make sure you know where the relevant accident telephone numbers are kept, and call as soon as possible. It may help if you note down as many details as you can, especially contact details for other drivers involved, and in the event of a serious problem you should get a report from the police. For minor **driving offences**, the police may turn a blind eye to foreign drivers, or they may impose an on-the-spot fine. Reckless speeding and other more serious violations will lead to you having your licence taken away, and drink-driving is taken very seriously in France (see p.26).

Drug use is as risky, as severely punished and as common in France as anywhere else in Europe. If you are **arrested** on any charge, you have the right to contact your consulate. If you're discreet, you're probably not likely to get caught, but don't expect the authorities – or your consulate – to be sympathetic just because you're on holiday.

The Loire, like the rest of western France, doesn't live up to the unfortunate national reputation for **racism**, and harassment is unlikely to be a problem. That said, black or Asian visitors may encounter various degrees of curiosity and/or suspicion. There are occasional reports of unpleasant incidents such as restaurants claiming to be fully booked, or shopkeepers with a suspicious eye, but it's no worse than anyone might find in other conservative, ethnically very uniform regions of the world. Travellers of north African or Arab appearance, on the other hand, may be unlucky enough to encounter outright hostility or excessive police interest, though once again, the Loire is relatively unproblematic. Full-on **sexual harassment** is extremely unusual, though female travellers from Anglophone countries may find ordinary male behaviour chauvinistic.

Emergency numbers

Police ☎17
Medical emergencies/ambulance ☎15
Fire brigade/paramedics ☎18
Rape crisis (*SOS Viol*) ☎08.00.05.95.95
All emergency numbers are toll-free.

Travelling with children

The Loire is a justifiably popular destination for families travelling with children. Canoeing, swimming and visits to the region's many caves, zoos and theme parks are obvious choices, and while traipsing round on a guided tour of a château and its wonderful collection of Louis XV chairs might sound like purgatory to most kids, don't underestimate the power of many châteaux to enthral. As for practicalities, there are few dangers or annoyances in the Loire, and children are welcomed in almost all restaurants and hotels – children old enough to sit reasonably still and quietly, at any rate.

Hotels charge the same rates for a room no matter who is occupying it, but you can usually save money by asking for an additional bed in a double room, often for only a small or even nominal supplement. Family rooms aren't all that common, but where they are available they may cost only a little more than a double. Most **restaurants** list an inexpensive *menu enfant*, usually with foolproof choices such as steak and chips. Younger children may be happier with an extra plate and a choice of what they can see you eating.

The cost of **entry tickets** can add up, though in state-run monuments, children under 12 go free and young people under 18 pay half price. Age limits elsewhere may vary, but tickets are almost always free for children under 4, with a discounted tariff for children under 12. You may need to carry some proof of age for children on the borderline. On SNCF **trains and buses**, children under 4 years travel free, and children between 4 and 12 pay half fares.

If you're travelling with a **baby**, be aware that most French baby foods have added sugar and salt, and the milk powders may be richer than your baby is accustomed to – soy-based milk is only available at *pharmacies*, and very expensive. Many hotels, especially the better two-stars, can provide a cot (*un lit à enfant*) in your room for a small or no charge. Disposable nappies/diapers (*couches à jeter*) are available everywhere.

Activities and sights

Tourist offices are well used to offering advice on local sights and activities that are suitable for children, and should probably be your first port of call. The tourist boards of Anjou and Touraine have co-ordinated various châteaux and other sights under the label *"Sur la piste de l'enfant Roy"* ("On the Trail of the Childe Kinge"). All the sights taking part in the scheme have special activities and leaflets for children but as yet there is little translated into English.

For details of **outdoor activities** such as swimming, kayaking, cycling and riding, see pp.41–43.

Châteaux for children

Don't rule out **château visits**. Dragging a reluctant 12-year-old round an elegant – or "boring" – eighteenth-century home is probably not a great idea, but if you pick your châteaux judiciously and prepare the ground well it can be amazing how children who are otherwise completely unengaged with history or fine buildings can seize upon a certain feature of the building or a particular historical tale. One trick is to let your charges pick their own château, perhaps from a selection of postcards. Otherwise, the following châteaux may be particularly suitable for children though it's impossible to guarantee success.

Any château with a **grand aspect**, such as those lording it over the river (Amboise, Chaumont, Chenonceau, Chinon, Montsoreau, Saumur), and those with fine **moats** (Azay-le-Rideau, Le Plessis-Bourré, Sully-sur-Loire) or medieval **towers** (Chinon, Langeais, Loches, Mehun-sur-Yèvre, Montrichard) are likely candidates. Otherwise, châteaux with **dungeons** or particularly bloody histories (Amboise, Blois, Chambord, Loches, Meung-sur-Loire) may be a good bet. **Chambord** is particularly popular for its double-spiral staircase, which has amused children for centuries, and you can take hire **boats** at Chambord, Chenonceau and Cheverny. St-Brisson and Chinon have **catapult** demonstrations in summer.

Some châteaux make a virtue of being child-friendly. **La Ferté-St-Aubin** allows children to explore the interior with complete freedom and has an "enchanted island" and miniature farm in its grounds; **Ussé** sells its connections with Sleeping Beauty hard, with a high tower stocked with fairy-tale scenes acted out by shop-window dummies; **Brézé** has a rabbit-warren of underground passages to explore; **Valençay** has a small zoo and maze; the **Château du Rivau** has fairy-tale-themed gardens. Even in otherwise adult-oriented châteaux you can sometimes find special activities or worksheets for children (though not always with English-language versions), and many guides are expert at a well-aimed joke or story designed to make children feel included. The national monuments website (⊛ www.monum.fr) includes some child-oriented pages.

Older children and **teenagers** seem to particularly go for Le Clos-Lucé, in Amboise, with its models of Leonardo da Vinci's inventions, and the tapestries of the apocalypse and the *Chant du Monde*, in Angers.

Other sights

A good choice may be to visit some of the caves in the rocky escarpments lining the rivers. The area around Saumur is particularly rich: Doué-la-Fontaine (see p.240) has "cathedral caves", a semi-underground zoo, a cave full of satirical carved figures, another used as a quarry for medieval stone coffins, and an entire cave village; the sparkling wine caves of Saumur are impressive, and older children will be able to taste the product. Just downstream of Saumur, you can see fantastical **miniature châteaux** carved out of the soft rock (see p.244). "**Troglodyte**" cave-dwellings can be seen at Trôo (see p.288), on the Loir, and at the wonderful farm-village of les Gopillières, near Azay-le-Rideau (see p.100). You can tour subterranean **mushroom farms** all over the region. Near Villandry, you can see objects being slowly "petrified" by slow-dripping cave water (see p.94).

French families are particularly keen on **zoos**. As well as the wonderful cave-zoo at Doué-la-Fontaine (see p.241), there's an large and impressive zoo at St-Aignan (see p.160). Welfare at both is generally good, but if you or your children aren't keen, you could try one of two excellent **aquariums**: one just outside Amboise (see p.82), the other near Romorantin, in the Sologne (see p.155).

You might also want to consider taking the children to Holly Park (see p.272), an outdoors-oriented activity park near Baugé, in Central Anjou; the witchcraft museum (see p.218) at Concressault, in the Haut Berry; or the **Parc Mini-Châteaux** (see p.82) near Amboise, the name of which says it all.

Travellers with disabilities

Travellers with disabilities won't encounter many difficulties peculiar to the Loire – few steep, stepped villages, for instance – but neither are there many specific concessions. Wheelchair-users, in particular, will find dedicated access is unusual anywhere outside major public institutions. Few hotels, for example, have lifts or even ramps, though many trains are now wheelchair-friendly.

To **get to France**, Eurotunnel is the simplest option if you have limited mobility, as you don't have to leave your car, while Eurostar trains have dedicated wheelchair spaces in First Class, at ordinary prices. If you're flying, note that no-frills airlines may lack the experience or resources to guarantee a smooth journey, though on paper they are obliged to offer wheelchair access to anyone who needs it. All the ferry companies have lifts to get you on and off the car deck, though you may encounter problems moving freely between decks once aboard.

Public transport in France is slowly adapting to the needs of people using wheelchairs, with ramp access available at most stations for boarding and disembarking from **trains**. Timetables show a wheelchair symbol if a train has special on board facilities, and the SNCF's free guide, the *Mémento du Voyageur à Mobilité Réduite*, is available at all stations. If in any doubt, arrive early and make yourself known to the conductor or station-attendant. **Taxi**-drivers are legally obliged to help passengers into and out of their vehicle, and to carry passengers' guide dogs. Hertz (France: ☎01.39.38.38 .38) and Europcar (France: ☎01.55.66.83 .83) can provide **rental cars** with special hand controls, if notified well in advance. You can call the main reservation centre in your own country (see pp.24–25), or the dedicated French numbers given below.

Wheelchair-users may find they have to pay a little more and prepare a little further in advance for **accommodation**, as inexpensive hotels, especially those in rural areas, rarely have lift access or even ground-floor rooms. The omnipresent Logis de France hotel federation (see p.29) has listings of hotels with special facilities, but otherwise

you should always ring in advance to find out whether a hotel is able to match your needs. Chambres d'hôtes are typically on upper floors, but you can contact Gîtes de France (see p.29) for information on places with adapted facilities.

It's hardly surprising that visits to ancient **châteaux** can be fraught with access problems. At best, wheelchair-users may be restricted to ground-floor rooms. At the major châteaux run by the national agency **Monum**, however, there are sometimes facilities for disabled visitors, and it may be possible to arrange assistance where there are not. The website ⊛www.monum.fr indicates if a site is "Access for All" or not.

Contacts for travellers with disabilities

France

APF (Association des Paralysés de France) 17 bd Auguste Blanqui, 75013 Paris ☎01.40.78.69.00, ⊛www.apf.asso.fr. National organization which can answer general enquiries and put you in touch with local offices.
Association France-Handicaps 9 rue Luce-de-Lancival, 77340 Pontault-Combault ☎ & ☎01.60.28.50.12. Produces the French-language *Guide Rousseau* (€25 plus postage) detailing access to hotels, museums and other tourist sites.

UK and Ireland

Irish Wheelchair Association Blackheath Drive, Clontarf, Dublin 3 ☎01/818 6400, ⊛www.iwa.ie. Useful information provided about travelling abroad with a wheelchair.
Tripscope Alexandra House, Albany Rd, Brentford, Middlesex TW8 0NE ☎08457/585 641, ⊛www.tripscope.org.uk. This registered charity provides a national telephone information service offering free advice on travel and transport for those with a mobility problem.

North America

Directions Unlimited 123 Green Lane, Bedford Hills, NY 10507 ☎1-800/533-5343 or 914/241-1700. Travel agency specializing in bookings for people with disabilities.

Society for the Advancement of Travelers with Handicaps (SATH) 347 5th Ave, New York, NY 10016 ☎212/447-7284, ☜www.sath.org. Non-profit educational organization with a good catalogue of publications on travel for people with disabilities.

Australia and New Zealand

ACROD (Australian Council for Rehabilitation of the Disabled) PO Box 60, Curtin ACT 2605; ☎02/6282 4333 (also TTY), ☜www.acrod.org.au. Provides lists of travel agencies and tour operators for people with disabilities.

Disabled Persons Assembly 4/173–175 Victoria St, Wellington, New Zealand ☎04/801 9100 (also TTY), ☜www.dpa.org.nz. Resource centre with lists of travel agencies and tour operators for people with disabilities.

Work and study

It's hard to find work in France unless you have a marketable skill or good local contacts. Even casual work on the grape harvest or in bars and clubs is likely to go to locals, unless you can actually sell yourself on your foreign credentials – in an Irish pub, for example. Teaching English is a relatively reliable option as there is always demand from businesspeople and those who want to work in the tourist industry. If you plan to study French, consider the many language schools in Tours, which is full of international language students in summer.

EU citizens can freely live and work in France, though officially you're supposed to pick up a **Carte de Séjour** within two months of your arrival in the country. In practice, so few EU citizens actually apply for this card that it may be more hassle than its worth to either you or the Commisariat de Police or Mairie from which it's supposed to be issued. Non-EU citizens should be much more careful to follow the rules, and will need a work permit for anything other than the most casual jobs – for information, contact the French embassy in your home country or, if already in France, the Mairie.

Finding work

If you plan to find a job in the Loire, it might be worth getting hold of the **book** Live and Work in France, by Victoria Pybus, published by Vacation Work (☜www.vacation-work.co.uk). Once **in France**, check the job offers in the regional newspaper, La Nouvelle République, which has a searchable online facility at ☜www.nr-emploi.com. Young people may be able to get help and advice in a

CIDJ, or Centre d'Information et de Documentation Jeunesse (☜www.cidj.com). The main regional office is in Orléans, 3–5 boulevard de Verdun (☜www.crij-centre.org). The national **employment agency**, the Agence Nationale pour l'Emploi (ANPE; ☜www.anpe.fr), advertises vacancies but doesn't go out of its way to help non-French citizens, especially non-French-speakers.

Wages for **fruit-picking** and the **wine harvest** are typically low, at around €7 per hour, and the work is hard – especially in the Loire when it can be wet and fairly cold at this time of year. There is much more work available apple-picking (in September) than in the late-September or early-October vendange, which is increasingly mechanized or requires skilled workers. In late summer, however, the ANPE attempts to match vineyards and orchards to workers from abroad. You can find contact details on the website, and each major city has an office. The best bet, though you'll need to speak some French and be persistent, is to get a list of vineyards from a tourist office and phone round – or, better still, do the rounds in person.

You're more likely to find work **teaching English**, though if you specifically want to find a job in the Loire region you'll probably have to forego the usual sources of TEFL jobs and ask at language schools locally: look under "Enseignement: Langues" in the local Yellow Pages (*Pages Jaunes*) directory. Offering private lessons is a competitive business. The best opportunities are probably in the big cities, especially commercial centres such as Orléans.

Language study

As the home of "the purest French in France", Touraine has a long history of teaching French as a foreign language. In summer, the international student social scene in Tours is pretty hectic; for a quieter stay, or more intensive immersion, consider Amboise or Blois. All the language schools listed below can help to arrange accommodation with local families. Course prices vary a lot (from around €250 a week), partly depending on the size of the group and the

number of hours of teaching on offer – usually either 20 or 25 hours a week.

Centre Linguistique pour Etrangers (CLE) 7 place Châteauneuf, Tours ☎02.47.64.06.19, ⓦhttp://centrelinguistique.com. Small classes of around seven students; fairly upmarket.

Eurocentres Amboise 9 Mail St-Thomas, Amboise ☎02.47.23.10.60, ⓦwww.eurocentres.com. Large, relatively inexpensive chain of language schools, offering classes of around a dozen. Amboise is a more sedate place to learn French than Tours.

Institut de Touraine 1 rue de la Grandière, Tours ☎02.47.05.76.83, ⓦwww.institut-touraine.asso.fr. Long-established language school, running classes for fifteen or so.

Tours Langues 36 rue Briçonnet, Tours ☎02.47.66.01.00, ⓦwww.langues.com. Small school right in the centre of old Tours, with relatively inexpensive classes for no more than seven students.

Univers des Langues 30 rue St-Lubin, Blois ☎02.54.56.88.46, ⓦhttp://univers-langues.com. General language school in the centre of Blois for foreigners and French students preparing exams alike. Small group classes (up to four people).

Directory

ELECTRICITY 220v, using plugs with two round pins. Transformers are best bought at home, but you can buy them in big department stores in France.

GAY AND LESBIAN TRAVELLERS France is relatively liberal as regards homosexuality, with legal consent starting at 16 and laws protecting gay couples' rights. The big cities have upfront gay communities. In rural areas, gay and lesbian couples may encounter curiosity and sometimes outright shock, but full-on prejudice or hostility is much rarer. You'll find useful contacts and listings in the excellent glossy magazine *Têtu* (ⓦwww.tetu.com), or online at ⓦwww.francetourism.com/gayguide/index.asp.

LAUNDRY *Laveries automatiques* (laundries/laundromats) are only found in the larger towns; listings are given at the end of the relevant city account. Dry-cleaning –

teinturerie or *pressing* – is a possible fallback. Most hotels dislike clients washing more than a few smalls.

SMOKING Smoking is forbidden (*fumer interdit*) in museums, châteaux and on public transport. Few restaurants have the officially required non-smoking areas.

TAX-FREE SHOPPING Visitors from outside the EU can claim tax refunds on any purchases in a single shop of over €300. Ask for the relevant forms when you buy.

TIME DIFFERENCE France is in the Central European Time Zone (GMT+1): one hour ahead of the UK, six hours ahead of Eastern Standard Time and nine hours ahead of Pacific Standard Time. France is eight hours behind all of eastern Australia and ten hours behind New Zealand from March to October (but ten hours behind *south*-eastern Australia and twelve hours behind New Zealand from

October to March). In France, and all of the EU, Daylight Saving Time (+1hr) lasts from the last Sunday of March through to the last Sunday of October, so for one week in late March and/or early April North American clocks lag an extra hour behind.

TIPPING Service is almost always included in restaurant bills, so you don't need to leave more than small change (see box on p.32). Taxi drivers and hairdressers expect around ten percent. You should only tip at the most expensive hotels; in other cases you're probably tipping the proprietor or their family. Tips for château guides are optional; you could leave a euro or two if you're particularly impressed.

TOILETS Ask for *les toilettes* or look for signs to the WC (pronounced "vay say"). If you're caught short, most bars will oblige. You'll occasionally find automated toilet booths in town centres, for which you need €0.30 in change.

WATER All tap-water is drinkable, except from taps labelled *eau non potable*.

Guide

Guide

Touraine

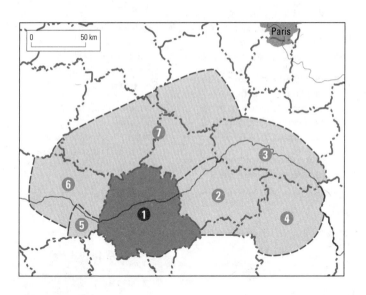

CHAPTER 1

Highlights

* **Place Plum'** Tours' ancient square is ringed round with medieval houses and packed with café tables. See p.68

* **Chenonceau** The graceful arched gallery of Chenonceau bridges the placid River Cher. See p.83

* **Villandry** At Villandry, the fabulous gardens have been recreated in a pure Renaissance style. See p.92

* **Richelieu** Richelieu's Grande Rue is the noble but melancholy remnant of the cardinal's town-planning experiment. See p.112

* **Montrésor** This utterly picturesque village has a superb Renaissance tomb in its church and fine art in its château. See p.121

* **Chapelle Ste-Radegonde** Hewn out of the tufa cliffs above Chinon, this ancient hermit's chapel shelters an extraordinary wall-painting. See p.107

* **Les Goupillières** Local cave-dwelling traditions are brought to life at this subterranean medieval farm. See p.100

* **Loches** The brutal keep and refined château of the citadel of Loches are encircled by fortified walls. See p.115

△ Bridge at Amboise

Touraine

I f the Loire valley conjures up an image of gentle rivers and exquisite châteaux, it is **Touraine**, the historic region around the cathedral city of Tours, that best matches the ideal. Touraine isn't any richer in history than neighbouring regions, or more densely populated with fine churches and châteaux, but it is somehow closer to the idea of *la France profonde* – the great French cultural myth of "deepest France". It certainly receives the most tourists of any Loire region. The writer Rabelais called Touraine the "**garden of France**", and the name still aptly describes its air of well-tended prosperity: the shallow, well-watered valleys are soft and fertile, the orchards and vineyards fruitful, and every back road takes you past carefully maintained gardens and vegetable plots. It's the perfect backdrop for the scores of pale stone châteaux that dot the landscape. Between the soft rivers, however, the plateaux are surprisingly bleak, empty of anything but farms, modest villages, vineyards and the occasional patch of ancient forest.

Although no larger than other cities in the Loire region, **Tours** stands preeminent by virtue of its history and cultural status. It was a key centre of early Christianity in France, and the favoured city of the French monarchy in the Renaissance. The Valois kings have long since departed, but Tours remains a place of government as the administrative capital of the *département* of the Indre-et-Loire – the modern bureaucratic name for Touraine. If you don't have your own transport, the city is the obvious Loire valley base, with both bus and train connections to many of the Loire's most notable châteaux.

From Tours, you can follow the course of the Loire east past the vineyards of **Vouvray** and **Montlouis-sur-Loire**, which together produce some of the region's finest white and sparkling wines, and on to **Amboise**, whose fine Renaissance château stands high on its natural battlements overlooking the Loire. A short distance south, the infinitely graceful and much-visited château of **Chenonceau** bridges the lovely Cher river, creating one of the quintessential images of idyllic Loire life.

If you're spending a lot of time in the region you might want to pick up the **Passport** (valid mid-June to mid-Oct), a leaflet that gives reductions of a euro or two off the entry tickets to many châteaux and other sites in western Touraine, especially in the Chinon region. You can pick it up free at any participating attraction, though you pay the first entry fee at the full rate. For €8 (children 7–18 €4.50), the **Carte Ambassadeur** gives access to the château at Chinon, Balzac's house at Saché and Rabelais' birthplace at La Devinière, as well as Ronsard's priory at St-Cosme and the château at Loches.

West of Tours, the north bank of the Loire sees relatively few visitors, though you can visit the grand château of **Luynes** and the dramatic, superbly furnished château at **Langeais** on the way to the wine-growing town of **Bourgueil**. To the south, the sleepy **River Indre** runs in a great arc through the heart of Touraine, lined with ruined abbeys, watermills and châteaux – none of them more beautiful than the Renaissance pearl of **Azay-le-Rideau**, mirrored in

Vendôme & Chartres▲   ▲ TGV to Paris

St-Aignan & Bourges ▶

Châteauroux ▼

the streams that flow past its walls. Nearby lie the fairy-tale château of **Ussé** and Balzac's summer writing home at **Saché**. Just short of the nearby confluence of the Loire and Cher, Renaissance gardens have been spectacularly re-created at the château **Villandry**.

The southwestern corner of Touraine is watered by the broad river **Vienne**, whose confluence with the Loire marks the border with the

Saumurois. The chief town is **Chinon**, whose ruined castle was built by Henry Plantagenêt on a cave-riddled escarpment overlooking the river. You can follow the Vienne upstream past **Tavant**, with its bright Romanesque mural paintings, and **L'Ile Bouchard**, with its ruined abbey, then up onto the plateau surrounding the goat's cheese capital, **Ste-Maure-de-Touraine**. Alternatively, head south up the River Veude to the stunning chapel at **Champigny-sur-Veude** and the weird seventeenth-century planned town of **Richelieu**.

The main draw in southern Touraine is **Loches**, a quiet provincial town at the foot of a stunning medieval citadel. If you travel beyond Loches, you'll really leave other tourists behind. To the east you can explore up the little river **Indrois**, stopping off at the half-ruined abbeys hidden in the ancient Forêt de Loches on the way to the château and abbey church at **Montrésor** – a contender for the title of prettiest little town in the region. North of the Indrois, within striking distance of the river Cher, the isolated forest château of **Montpoupon** houses a fascinating museum of hunting. The wet and wooded countryside **north of the Loire**, known as the **Gâtine Tourangelle**, sees wild boars for the most part, rather than tourists.

Information on Tours and the surrounding region can be found online at ⓦwww.tourism-touraine.com. For details of **bus** times, contact Filvert (☎02.47.47.17.18, ⓦwww.touraine-filvert.com), the operating company for the whole of Touraine.

Tours

Straddling a spit of land between the rivers Loire and Cher, the ancient cathedral city of **TOURS** has an air of quiet confidence. It may be the chief town of the Loire valley, but Tours has long had a reputation as a staid, bourgeois place, the home of lawyers and administrators rather than, say, artists or factory workers. However, the city's proximity to Paris – less than an hour away on the high-speed TGV line – has always tempered its nature, ensuring that Tours is indefinably more switched on than other French provincial cities, and in recent years an influx of smart commuters has perceptibly modified Tours' conservative feel.

On a day-to-day basis, the lively atmosphere of the centre is thanks in no small part to the student population, which is domestic through the year and international in summer. There are scores of bustling bars and cafés, an active if limited nightlife, and some fine restaurants – among the best in the region. As for culture, Tours has an excellent art gallery, some unusual museums – of wine, crafts and stained glass – and a great many fine buildings, not least of which is the glorious St-Gatien cathedral. The city's prettified old quarter is perfect for idle wandering, its fourteenth- to sixteenth-century townhouses still bearing witness to the industriousness of the bourgeoisie, which rose to power while the nobility frittered away its energy on hunting, château-building and other country pastimes.

Some history

Tours' recorded history begins with the foundation of **Caesarodunum** in the first century BC, but the city's name harks back to earlier inhabitants, the **Turones**, one of many Gaulish tribes settled in this fertile region. Tours was a

TOURS

ACCOMMODATION

Central Hôtel	E
Foyer des Jeunes Travailleurs	I
Hostel	A
Hôtel Colbert	C
Hôtel du Cygne	B
Hôtel du Manoir	J
Hôtel du Musée	D
Hôtel Regina	F
Hôtel St-Eloi	K
Hôtel de la Théâtre	G
Mon Hôtel	H

RESTAURANTS

Au Bureau	10
Chez Jean-Michel	2
Au Chien Jaune	18
Comme Autre-Fouée	12
Le Franglais	8
La Furgeotière	4
Jean Bardet	1
Au Lapin qui Fume	3
Le Petit Patrimoine	7
Le Picrocole	15
La Roche le Roy	19

BARS & CLUBS

Les 3 Orfèvres	11
Académie de la Bière	2
Le Bateau Ivre	20
L'Excalibur	9
VIP Club	14

CAFÉS

Aux Délices de Michel Colombe	16
Le Molière	17
Scarlett	5
Le Vieux Mûrier	13

Map labels:

PONT NAPOLEON

▲ Prieuré de St-Cosme

Loire

PONT WILSON

Logis des Gouverneurs château

Musée des Beaux-Arts

cathédrale St-Gatien

Hôtel Babou de la Bourdaisière

Musée de Compagnonnage

St-Julien

Musée des Vins

Hôtel Gouin

Maison de Tristan

Musée du Gemmail

Grand Théâtre

Eglise Réformée

Centre de Congrès Vinci

Préfecture

Jardin de la Préfecture

Jardin de Beaune-Semblançay

Hôtel de Ville

Gare routière

Gare SNCF

Palais de Justice

Tour de Charlemagne

Basilique St-Martin

Musée St-Martin

Tour de l'Horloge

Halles

AVENUE ANDRE MALRAUX
RUE JULES-SIMON
RUE BERNARD-PALISSY
RUE NATIONALE
RUE DES TANNEURS
RUE DU COMMERCE
BOULEVARD HEURTELOUP
BOULEVARD BERANGER
RUE MARCEAU
VIEILLE VILLE

N
0   200 m

▲ Le Mans & Saumur
▲ Pont de Fil

▶ River Cher & Loches

59

prominent centre of Christianity between the third and the eighth centuries, attracting saints and thinkers such as **St Gatien**, the first bishop of Tours, the much-loved **St Martin** (see box on p.69), who became the focus of a major cult after his death, **Gregory of Tours**, who wrote an extraordinary chronicle of world and local history in the late sixth century, and the philosopher **Alcuin of York**.

Attacks by **Vikings**, who sailed right up the Loire in the mid-ninth century, heralded a new era of conflict and insecurity. The main attraction was the wealth of the churches, and Tours was a major target. Martinopolis, the new centre that had grown up around the shrine of St Martin, was razed and then rebuilt with serious defences, leading it to be renamed Châteauneuf. The city became part of the fief of the counts of Blois and then, in 1044, fell to the Angevins. Under their aegis, a new centre, the Bourg des Arcis, grew up between Martinopolis and the old Roman centre. In the fourteenth century new city walls finally encircled the whole conurbation.

In the aftermath of the Hundred Years War, the paranoid king **Louis XI** made Tours the capital of his kingdom, attracting the artist Jean Fouquet and the composer Johannes Ockeghem to his court, and bringing silkworkers and worms from Lyon to found the **silk industry**. Mulberry trees, the favoured food of the worms, were planted all around the city and Tours boomed as a major commercial centre, dependent on the trade along the Loire. The **financiers** and merchants who bankrolled the military and courtly excesses of the monarchs from Louis XI onwards built ever finer mansions, aping the excesses of their royal and aristocratic masters by building châteaux in the countryside nearby.

Tours' **Protestant** population grew steadily from the sixteenth century, particularly among the merchant classes and workers in the 20,000-strong silk industry. When the 1685 Edict of Fontainebleau ended official toleration of Protestantism, however, thousands fled the city, trade declined, and Tours gradually became just another conservative, provincial town. Eighteenth-century works such as the construction of the axial **rue Royale** (now rue Nationale) failed to stimulate much growth, and it was only when the railway arrived in the mid-nineteenth century that the city started to prosper once more. The proud civic centrepiece of **place Jean-Jaurès** was built by the train lines and some 800m from the river – symbolically, the city had finally turned its back on the Loire.

There was brief excitement in October 1870 – when Léon Gambetta escaped the Prussian siege of Paris by hot air balloon, landing and very briefly forming the government in Tours – and again during the 1920 **Congress of Tours**, which famously split the French Left into socialist and Communist factions. During the **Second World War**, Tours was again the national capital – for three days from June 10, 1940 – as the French army fled the advancing Germans. For 48 hours the Loire became the front line, and Tours suffered incredibly destructive bombardments and firestorms. Yet the face of the modern city was mostly seriously rearranged in postwar reconstruction.

In 1959 the conservative but vastly energetic **Jean Royer** became mayor – and remained so until 1995, acquiring the nickname of *le bon roi Jean* ("Good King John"). During his "reign", **place Plumereau** and much of the **Vielle Ville** were carefully restored, and France gained the so-called *loi Royer*, a law which helped protect traditional town-centre shops from competition with out-of-town retail giants. While Tours may have failed to keep pace with the industrial successes of its neighbour, Orléans, it has found new pride, confidence and prosperity in the postwar era, and in the late 1990s, the city's development was crowned with the arrival of the **TGV** line from Paris. The first decade of the millennium has seen the city planners once more turning their attention to where it all began, on the banks of the Loire, but it may be some years yet before major works are carried out.

Arrival and information

Ryanair's daily **flights** from London arrive at Tours Val de Loire **airport**, which is very straightforward due to its tiny size. Booths for the major car-rental companies (see p.24) are found in the small waiting room on the far side of customs, next to the exit, while **taxis** wait immediately outside to take you into the centre of town for a little over €10, a journey of about twenty minutes.

The **gare routière** and **gare SNCF** are situated about 500m south of the centre, on the south side of place Général Leclerc. Most **TGV**s from Paris stop at **St-Pierre-des-Corps** station, in an industrial estate deep in the suburbs, but frequent shuttle trains (or sometimes buses) provide a link to the main central station; transferring is usually a matter of stepping off the TGV and across to an ordinary train waiting at the next platform, but if you're in any doubt just follow the crowd.

Information

On the opposite side of the square from the gare SNCF is the city's excellent **tourist office**, on the corner of rue Bernard Palissy and boulevard Heurteloup, next to the landmark Centre de CongrèsVinci (mid-April to mid-Oct Mon–Sat 8.30am–7pm, Sun 10am–12.30pm & 2.30–5pm; mid-Oct to mid-April Mon–Sat 9am–12.30pm & 1.30–6pm, Sun 10am–1pm; ℡02.47.70.37.37, ⊛www.ligeris.com). It sells a **museum pass** (*carte multi-visites*; €8) that lets you into the five city museums, including the Musée des Beaux-Arts and the Musée du Gemmail, and can give information on **château tours** (see box below).

The centre of Tours is small enough to cover on foot. For **bike rental**, contact Amster Cycles, 5 rue du Rempart, immediately east of the station (℡02.47.61.22.23), or Vélomania, 109 rue Colbert (℡02.47.05.10.11); both charge around €15 a day or a little over €50 for a week.

Château tours

It's possible to visit most of the more-visited châteaux by public transport, but if you're short of time it's worth considering a day or half-day minibus trip. A number of companies run **excursions** from Tours, and on most schedules you'll find the following châteaux: Amboise, Azay-le-Rideau, Blois, Chambord, Chenonceau, Cheverny, Clos Lucé (in Amboise), Fougères-sur-Bièvre, Langeais, Ussé and Villandry. **Ticket** prices are usually around €16 for a morning trip, taking in one or two châteaux; €23–30 for an afternoon tour – often with a third château or a wine-tasting; and €37–45 for a full-day tour. Prices do not usually include entrance fees or lunch.

Ask at tourist offices or contact the following Touraine-based **agencies** directly: Acco Dispo ℡06.82.00.64.51, ⊛www.accodispo-tours.com; Saint-Eloi Excursions ℡02.47.37.08.04, ⊛www.saint-eloi.com; Services Touristiques de Touraine ℡02.47.05.46.09; and Touraine Excursions ℡06.07.39.13.31, ⊛www.tourevasion.com. Most pick up from the tourist office in Tours or from your hotel.

Accommodation

Tours does well for inexpensive **accommodation**, with some excellent budget and two-star hotels in the area just west of the cathedral. There's less choice at the higher end of the market. It's worth booking in advance, particularly in the summer months.

Hotels

Central Hôtel 21 rue Berthelot ☎02.47.05.46.44, ⊛www.bestwesterncentralhoteltours.com. The best bet if you're determined to aim for the upper end of the market, though it's overpriced. Rooms are large and high-ceilinged, and extra beds can be added on request. Part of the Best Western chain, so service is professional but the atmosphere suffers from a largely business clientele. There's a small garden and a garage – which costs €8.50 a night. ❽

Clarion Univers 5 bd Heurteloup ☎02.47.05.37.12, ⊛www.hotel-univers-loirevalley.com. The grandest and most historic hotel in town, right opposite the town hall. The foyer is stunning, but, disappointingly, the rooms are fairly ordinary for the price (€185 for the "standard" rooms), though stuffed with all mod cons imaginable. ❾

Hôtel Colbert 78 rue Colbert ☎02.47.66.61.56, ✉hotel-colbert@club-internet.fr. Pleasant, well-furnished, family-run hotel in a good location on the restaurant strip, near the cathedral. Rooms are modern in style, with warm-coloured wallpapers, TVs and new bathrooms. Those overlooking the small garden at the back are a little more expensive than the noisier ones on the street, but double glazing means there's no problem even at the front. ❸

Hôtel du Cygne 6 rue du Cygne ☎02.47.66.66.41, ⊛http://perso.wanadoo.fr/hotelcygne.tours. Pleasantly old-fashioned and well-run hotel on a quiet street, with a delightful eighteenth-century frontage spilling over with flowers and grey shutters. The rooms are relatively unmodernized, with unattractive carpeting, but they're comfortable and preserve some of the flavour of the house, with mantelpieces, sidelamps and oddments of old-fashioned furniture. Some family rooms and smaller, inexpensive (❸) rooms on the top floor. ❹

Hôtel du Manoir 2 rue Traversière ☎02.47.05.37.37, ✆02.47.05.16.00. The situation is very pleasant, on a peaceful backstreet with a small garden and parking area out front. Inside, the feel of the nineteenth-century townhouse has been slightly spoilt by over-modernization, but the hotel is friendly, comfortable and in a good location between the cathedral and train station. ❸

Hôtel du Musée 2 place François-Sicard ☎02.47.66.63.81, ✆02.47.20.10.42. Gracefully dilapidated old hotel in a once-grand townhouse right by the cathedral and Musée des Beaux-Arts. Rooms are tatty in places, but have lots of character, with a clutter of antique or broken-down furniture and elegant canopies over the beds. One room has a small balcony overlooking the square outside, with its giant tulip tree. ❷

Hôtel Regina 2 rue Pimbert ☎02.47.05.25.36, ✆02.47.66.08.72. Friendly and well-run budget place right in the town centre, with simple, spartan, but clean rooms. Popular with backpackers, with a range of prices. More expensive rooms (❷) have showers. ❶

Hôtel St-Éloi 79 bd Béranger ☎02.47.37.67.34, ✉hotel@sainteloi.com. Excellent-value, intimate hotel run by a friendly young couple. One of the few options on the western side of town, nearer to the nightlife round place Plumereau. ❶

Hôtel du Théâtre 57 rue de la Scellerie ☎02.47.05.31.29, ✉hoteldutheatre.tours@wanadoo.fr. Charming, friendly hotel set in a tastefully restored medieval townhouse in the cathedral quarter. Ancient, exposed beams and stone walls are matched with bright paintwork, brand-new bathrooms and double glazing throughout. There are a few lower-priced, smaller rooms (❷), and three rooms with an extra single bed (❹). ❸

Mon Hôtel 40 rue de la Préfecture ☎02.47.05.67.53, ✆02.47.05.21.88. Low-budget option stacked up on three floors around an ancient, twisting staircase, with caged canaries on the ground floor. The small, ill-furnished rooms are much in need of a refit, but it's acceptable enough, and the location between the cathedral and train station is handy. ❶

Hostel and campsite

There is no campsite in Tours itself, but there is a decent camping option within striking distance of the city. Campers could also try the sites at Vouvray (see p.74) and Luynes (see p.87).

Auberge de Jeunesse du Vieux Tours 5 rue Bretonneau ☎02.47.37.81.58, ⓔtours@fuaj.org. This large, modern youth hostel has an excellent location right in the heart of the old centre, near place Plumereau. Most of the rooms are singles, but there are twenty-odd twin-bed rooms as well. Reception 8am–noon & 6–10pm. HI membership required, but you can join on the spot. €17 for the first night, €14 thereafter, breakfast included. Bicycles are hired out inexpensively, too.

Foyer des Jeunes Travailleurs 16 rue Bernard-Palissy ☎02.47.60.53.00. A fairly smart, central workers' hostel and cafeteria for under-25s. Closed Sat afternoon & Sun. €17 per night, including breakfast.

Camping Les Rives du Cher St-Avertin ☎02.47.27.27.60. Four kilometres southeast of the city, but still the nearest campsite to the centre of town, and accessible by bus #5 from place Jean-Jaurès. Closed mid-Oct to March.

The city centre

The centre of Tours fills a three-kilometre-wide strip of flat land between the Loire and its tributary, the Cher, but the city has spread far across both banks, with industrial Tours eating up the area north of the Loire. Neither river is a particular feature of the town, though there are parks on islands in both, and an attractive new footbridge leads across the Loire from the site of the old château. The city's two distinct quarters lie on either side of the axial rue Nationale, a strip of commercial no-man's-land hastily built in the aftermath of the war. The quieter of the two quarters, where most of the hotels are found, lies around the **cathedral**, while the so-called **Vielle Ville**, some 600m to the west, is more developed and more touristy, centred on picturesque place Plumereau.

Cathédrale St-Gatien

The great west towers of the **Cathédrale St-Gatien**, known locally as *la Gatienne*, are visible all over the city, rising in tier upon tier like the vision of the heavenly city they were intended to represent. Their surfaces crawl with lace-like stonework in the Flamboyant Gothic style, and even the early Renaissance belfries that cap them share the same spirit of refined exuberance. Inside, the stonework becomes more tight-lipped as it moves back in time through the fourteenth-century nave and back towards the relatively sober mid-thirteenth-century choir.

The architecture of the **choir** may be relatively restrained but its **stained-glass windows** are glorious. Inspired by St Louis' work at the Sainte Chapelle in Paris – and largely paid for by him – they form a giant band of jewelled colour under the vaults. The life of **St Martin** (see box on p.69) is shown in the second tall window right of the centre – on the final panel on the top right, you can see clearly the boat transporting his corpse along the Loire from Candes-St-Martin. Immediately right of this window, on the flat south wall of the choir, are two large windows depicting the bishops of Tours and canons of Loches; these are renowned for their unusual monochrome bands, or *grisailles*.

The choir was originally tacked onto the end of a much earlier Merovingian nave, which was in turn demolished and rebuilt a century later. You can see an awkward kink where the join was made, and in the line of the pillars on the east wall of the **north transept**. The structural problems this caused can be seen in the **rose window** of the Heavenly Jerusalem, whose perfection is spoiled by a great stone prop running through its middle. Just beyond the **south transept** stands the **tomb** of the sons of Charles VIII and Anne de Bretagne. The sarcophagus betrays the Italian origins of its sculptor, Girolamo da Fiesole, while the lifelike figures of the distressingly young princes were carved by a pupil of the great local sculptor, Michel Colombe. After the deaths of the little princes – at 3 years and at 25 days – and the accidental death of their father (see p.78), the Valois line proper came to an end, and Anne was obliged by law to marry Charles's cousin, Louis XII. Behind the tomb, a mural painting shows St Martin dividing his cloak.

A door in the north aisle leads through to the **Cloître de la Psalette** (Mon–Sat 9.30am–12.30pm & 2–6pm, Sun 2–6pm; Oct–March closes 5pm; €2.30), a cloister which has an unfinished air, what with the great foot of a flying buttress planted in the southeast corner – another attempt to solve the problem of the nave's misalignment – and the missing south arcade, which was lost when a road was driven through in 1802 by the same progressive, anticlerical prefect who destroyed the basilica of St-Martin. On the north and east sides, late Gothic is disrupted by Renaissance details, especially on the small but perfect spiral staircase, with its tightly twisting central pillar. You can climb up it to the gallery level, which leads through to the library on the cloister's west side, with its mullioned windows.

Musée des Beaux-Arts

Immediately south of the cathedral, the **Musée des Beaux-Arts**, 18 place François-Sicard (daily except Tues 9am–12.45pm & 2–6pm; free), is housed in what used to be the archbishop's palace, overshadowed by an enormous, 200-year-old cedar of Lebanon in the peaceful courtyard garden. The handsome seventeenth- and eighteenth-century building was briefly used by the provisional national government as it fled from the advancing Prussians in 1870. Today, it makes an elegant setting for a fine collection of paintings, the star attraction being the pair of works in the basement by the Italian Renaissance master Andrea **Mantegna**: the *Resurrection* and the *Agony in the Garden* (1457–9). Napoleon stole both from San Zeno, in Verona, in 1797, along with a *Crucifixion* which now hangs in the Louvre. Together, the three paintings formed the predella below the altarpiece, though the main upper section was returned to San Zeno in 1815. Even outside their proper setting, the two paintings are superb, grippingly intense in mood, the action dominated by a magical Judeo-Italian landscape. The small collection of early Italian masterpieces alongside are somewhat overshadowed, though there's a fine *Coronation of the Virgin* by Lorenzo Veneziano and two saints by Antonio Vivarini.

The visit actually begins on the **first floor** of the museum, which consists of a stately, loosely chronological progression of palatial seventeenth- and eighteenth-century rooms, each furnished and decorated to match the era of the paintings it displays. There's a lot of indifferent eighteenth-century stuff, but a few celebrity works are scattered through the collection. The **Salon Louis XV** has a flowery mythological work by François Boucher – the favourite artist of the king's lover, Mme de Pompadour – that depicts Sylvia fleeing a wolf. The small **Cabinet Rembrandt** houses Rembrandt's moody study, the *Flight into Egypt*, and opposite, **Rubens**' hasty *Virgin and Child*. Engravings of *The Five Senses* by the locally-born **Abraham Bosse** have been interpreted as full-size canvases in the handsome **Salle Louis XIII**, which is furnished with characteristically twisty-legged chairs and a gilded, polychrome fireplace, and offers a fine view of the cathedral.

Upstairs on the **second floor** are two rooms of works by local painters, and a suite that runs from eighteenth-century Neoclassicism through to contemporary works. Look out for the 1787 panorama of Tours and **Boulanger**'s portrait of a faintly corpulent Balzac. The **Salle Réaliste** has **Degas**' vibrant, hasty interpretation of the Mantegna *Crucifixion* in the Louvre, and an arresting autopsy scene by Feyer-Perrin, while the next room is named after **Monet**, who is represented by a bleak and drizzly little riverbank scene dating from 1878.

On the left of the main gate as you leave, in one of the stable buildings, there's a surprising exhibit: the stuffed remains of an elephant that caused a sensation in Tours in the early part of the twentieth century. Occasional classical **concerts** are held inside the museum; ask for details or call ☎02.47.05.68.73.

The cathedral quarter
On the north side of the cathedral, between rue Albert-Thomas and the river, just two towers remain of the medieval **château** of Tours. In 1593, the northern tower was the scene of the dramatic escape of the prince de Joinville, imprisoned here after his father, the Duc de Guise, was murdered at Blois (see box on p.135). The prince apparently out-sprinted his captors up the steps of the tower, locked the door behind him and shinned down the outer wall to freedom. You can get inside a section of the château when exhibitions are held, but there's nothing much to see otherwise. In the sixteenth-century **Logis des Gouverneurs** (Wed & Sat 2–6pm; sometimes closed during school holidays; free), just across the remnants of the city's Gallo-Roman wall, there's an exhibition on the history of Tours that gives an excellent impression of how the city has developed over the centuries, though it's depressing to see so many fine buildings that no longer exist. Opposite the château, a suspension footbridge aptly nicknamed the **Pont de Fil** (string bridge) leads across the river to the St-Symphorien quarter via the sports fields of the **Ile Aucard**.

The area behind the cathedral and museum, to the east, is good for a short stroll. There's a fine view from **place Grégoire de Tours** of the spidery buttresses supporting the cathedral's painfully thin-walled apse. Overlooking the square is the oldest wing of the **archbishop's palace**, whose end wall is a mongrel of Romanesque and eighteenth-century work, with an early sixteenth-century projecting balcony once used by clerics to address their flock.

Leading off the square, rue Général Meunier traces the line of the now-vanished Roman amphitheatre, ascending past affluent private mansions, high-walled religious institutions and the decrepit **Chapelle des Lazaristes**. From this chapel, you can continue down rue de la Porte Rouline, then left along rue des Ursulines, past the cinema Les Studios and the conservatoire, to a half-hidden muncipal garden overlooked by the tall remains of the city's **Roman walls**. Alternatively, head back down rue Manceau and through to **rue de la Psalette**, which offers a fine view of the cathedral's great north rose window, with its unfortunate buttress. On the corner of this street is the eighteenth-century house where **Balzac** set his novella *Le Curé de Tours*, a withering attack on the petit-bourgeois concerns of the provincial clergy. Half hidden by walls and foliage, the house looks just the part.

Rue Colbert and the river
From the cathedral quarter, **rue Colbert** runs west as straight as the Roman road it once was, with down-at-heel bars, ethnic restaurants and excellent little bistros competing for attention along most of its length. Heading off down to the river, **place Foire-le-Roi** recalls the fairs instituted by François I, and the old traditions, of a sort, are kept up by the all-day artisans' market on Saturdays in summer. There are some fine old half-timbered houses at the bottom end, and on the east side, at no. 8, is the handsome **Hôtel Babou de la Bourdaisière**, built for François I's finance minister in the 1520s. West of rue Voltaire, the foot of rue Colbert was widened and modernized after the destruction of the Second World War. A few historic houses survived well enough to be rebuilt, notably the house at no. 39 – now a shoe shop – where **Joan of Arc** is said to have had her suit of armour made.

Tucked away behind the corner of rue Colbert and rue Nationale hides the **Jardin de Beaune-Semblançay**, whose pretty, sixteenth-century fountain stands in front of the sad remnants of the house of Jacques de Beaune-

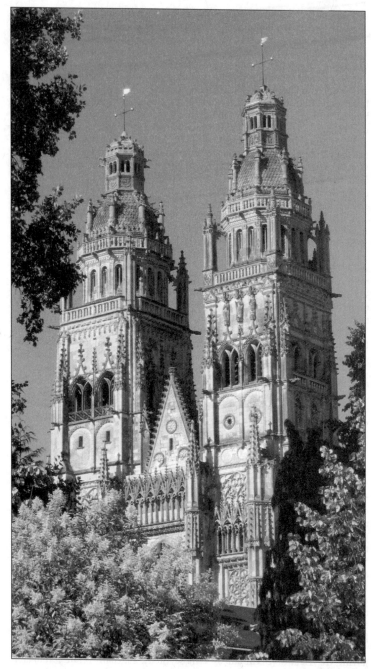

△ Towers of St-Gatien, Tours

Semblançay, François I's finance minister (see p.309). The propped-up, three-quarters ruined facade is the result of wartime shelling but it stands as an ironic testament to the financier's career, which was spent vainly attempting to fund the king's lavish court expenditure and expensive foreign military excursions with ever-dwindling royal income – and all the time creaming off the funds necessary to build this, his own fabulous Renaissance mansion. As a placard explains, the shabby garden was once a palatial complex of houses, but the only other remnant is a **chapel**, whose elegant arcade is now glazed in and serves as a lamp shop.

At the north end of rue Nationale lies the **River Loire**, its scruffy walkways overlooked by statues of Descartes and Rabelais. There are plans to develop the riverfront, but for now it's a sad place, bombed out and bereft of the roaring river trade that once filled the quays with merchandise. You can sometimes see terns wheeling and diving in the rapids formed by the arches of the **Pont Wilson**, a much-patched-up eighteenth-century bridge which locals refer to as prosaically as the Pont de Pierre, or "stone bridge". In summer, you'll see one or more old-fashioned wooden boats tied up at the jetty just downstream from the Pont Wilson; you can make an hour-long guided **river trip** aboard one of these (usually July & Aug Sat & Sun 2.30–6.30pm, but it's best to book through the tourist office first or call Alain Lacroix on ☎06.83.57.89.20; €5).

St-Julien

On the northeast corner of rue Colbert and rue Nationale stands the **église St-Julien**, which once belonged to the Benedictine abbey founded by the great chronicler and sixth-century bishop, Gregory of Tours. The heavy Romanesque tower is one of the few remnants of an older church which collapsed in a storm in 1244; the rest is a high-shouldered and slightly awkward Gothic construction. The most interesting features inside are the eleventh-century mural depicting the story of Moses, just visible from the passage above the organ, and the modern stained glass which replaced the windows destroyed when the Pont Wilson was blown up by the retreating French army in June 1944.

The old monastic buildings are home to two museums. The dry-as-dust **Musée des Vins**, at 16 rue Nationale (daily except Tues 9am–noon & 2–6pm; €2.50), is only worth visiting for its location in the barn-like twelfth-century cellars of the abbey, though if your French is up to it, there's a comprehensive display on the history, mythology and production of wine. Behind the museum, a Gallo-Roman winepress from Cheillé sits in the former cloisters of the church. The **Musée de Compagnonnage**, at 8 rue Nationale (mid-June to mid-Sept daily 9am–noon & 2–6pm; rest of year closed Tues; €4), is housed in the eleventh-century guesthouse and sixteenth-century monks' dormitory. It honours the peculiarly French cult of the artisan, displaying a bizarre miscellany of the *chefs d'œuvre*, the "masterpieces", that craftsmen had to create in order to join their craft guild as a fully-fledged *compagnon* (master craftsman). The skills are unquestionable, but many of these showpieces are breathtakingly vulgar, displaying arts as diverse as cake-making and carpentry, locksmithery and bricklaying. The guilds still exist, but membership is no longer a passport to work.

Around place Jean-Jaurès

The centre of Tours is divided by the wide, soulless modern avenue of **rue Nationale**. What you see today is the drab result of hasty reconstruction following the bombardments of 1944, but the street began life as the more prestigious rue Royale, and as rue Napoléon it was the birthplace of Balzac, in May 1799. At its tail is the huge, traffic-ridden **place Jean-Jaurès**, site of the Doric Palais de Justice, which dates from the 1840s. The grandiose **Hôtel de Ville** was

TOURAINE | Tours

67

designed at the beginning of the twentieth century by local boy Victor Laloux, with four immense caryatids supporting its balcony, each representing a river god. Laloux's talent seems to have been better suited to train stations, however, as the noble **gare SNCF**, 200m further east along busy boulevard Heurteloup, was also his design – as was Paris's world-famous Gare (now Musée) d'Orsay. The steel and glass curves of the **Centre de Congrès Vinci**, opposite the station, are the work of France's star architect, Jean Nouvel, the creator of Paris's Institut du Monde Arabe, among other buildings. Eye-catching though it is, the Vinci congress centre has proved to be something of a white elephant.

To the west of place Jean-Jaurès, a giant **flower market** takes over boulevard Béranger on Wednesdays and Saturdays, lasting from 8am into the early evening.

Around place Plumereau

One hundred metres west of rue Nationale, the **Hôtel Gouin**, at 25 rue du Commerce, has a Renaissance facade to stop you in your tracks, but the **museum** inside (daily: April–Sept 9.30am–12.30pm & 1.15–6.30pm; Oct–March 9.30am–12.30pm & 2–5.30pm; €3.50) is a dull collection of archeological oddments and the remnants of a private scientific laboratory from Chenonceau – more rich man's toys than cutting-edge research tools.

A few steps further west, the pulse of the city quickens as you approach **place Plumereau** – or place Plum' as it's known locally. The square's tightly clustered ancient houses have been carefully restored as the city's showpiece, transforming what was once a slum into a vibrant and wealthy quarter. On sunny days, the square is packed almost end to end with café tables, and students and families drink and dine out until late in the evening. To some extent, the restoration project has been the victim of its own success, as Irish pubs, pizza restaurants and international ice-cream chains shoulder their way in and the noisy party atmosphere drives out longer-term residents from the vicinity.

One of the less brash places on the square is the *Café du Vieux Mûrier*, so named for the large **mulberry tree** outside, a reminder of the days when Tours' silkworms used to feed on mulberries planted in their thousands in and around the city. Fine woodworking and slate cladding adorns the pair of medieval houses on the southeast corner of the square, while the central quartet on the southern side display elaborate brick patternwork. The handsome white stone house over on the northwest corner, with its wrought-iron balconies, is a nineteenth-century creation.

To escape the maelstrom, slip down **rue Briçonnet** into a miniature maze of quiet, ancient streets. Opposite an oddly Venetian-looking fourteenth-century house, at 41 rue Briçonnet, a passageway leads past a palm tree and an ancient outdoor staircase to the quiet and insulated **Jardin de St-Pierre-le-Puellier**. In its centre lie the dug-out ruins of a conventual church, while twin brick-and-wood tower-staircases prop up the backs of the houses on place Plumereau. Further down rue Briçonnet, at no. 16, just before the heavily modernized riverfront, is the elaborate **Maison de Tristan**. Built for a chamberlain of Louis XI in the then-fashionable style, its ornate Gothic doorway and rose-motif carvings are well worth a look.

Musée du Gemmail

Off rue Briconnet, at 7 rue du Mûrier, the **Musée du Gemmail** (April to mid-Oct Tues–Sun 10am–noon & 2–6pm; mid-Oct to March Sat & Sun 10am–noon & 2–6pm; €4.60; ⓦ www.gemmail.com) is dedicated to an obscure, locally invented modern art form that uses fragments of backlit stained glass as a medium. Although some of the works are signed by such luminaries as Raoul **Dufy**, **Modigliani** and **Picasso**, the actual execution is by professional technicians working from a design. Picasso was enamoured of the technique, and two of his works here are among the finest. The way colour is built up using layer after layer of coloured shards over a white background light, in some ways like a watercolour, is interesting, but a tackier side of the art form is seen in the reproductions of the Mona Lisa and various Gauguin paintings.

St-Martin quarter

Immediately south of place Plumereau lay the pilgrim city once known as Martinopolis after **St Martin**, a key figure in the spread of Christianity through France (see box below). There was a chapel here from the fifth century onwards, but the site reached its apotheosis with a vast Romanesque basilica, which stretched along rue des Halles from rue des Trois-Pavées-Ronds almost to place de Châteauneuf. Sadly, very little remains. Huguenot riots of 1562 severely damaged the interior, and the whole structure finally collapsed in 1797, seemingly in protest at its desecration by Revolutionary troops, who used it as a stables. Only the northern **Tour de Charlemagne** and the western clock tower now survive, but the outline of the structure is traced out in the street. The Charlemagne tower half collapsed in 1928, but was glued back together with a modern image of a cloak-rending St Martin on its south face. At its foot stands a precious carved capital, one of 140 which once graced the basilica's forest of columns.

St Martin of Tours

As a patron saint of France, **St Martin of Tours** stands in the shadow of his higher profile peers, Anne, mother of Mary, Joan of Arc, and St Denis. Yet during the first millennium the cult of St Martin was the most important in France, and it was only when St Denis was promoted by the Paris-based Capetian dynasty that St Martin's fame was eclipsed. Locally, however, St Martin still cuts quite a figure – you'll see images from his life all over the Loire valley, especially in Touraine.

The saint was born in Pannonia, in modern-day Hungary, in about 316. His father was a Roman tribune and as a young man Martin was duly sent off to do military service in Gaul. The most significant – and most often depicted – event of his life occurred at Amiens, when he met a ragged beggar at the city gates. Moved by inexplicable compassion, he cut his **cloak** in two, reached down from his horse, and gave the beggar one half. He later asked to be baptized and left the Roman army. The cloak became the most treasured relic of the Merovingian and Carolingian kings, and eventually gave its name (*capella*, in Latin) to the oratory where it was preserved – hence the English word "chapel".

After various adventures in Italy, Martin returned to Gaul in 361 to set up a monastery at Ligugé, just outside Poitiers, where he lived as a hermit. In 371 he was tricked into visiting Tours and, on arrival, was acclaimed as bishop – legend has it that he tried to hide but was revealed by honking **geese**, which became his symbol. Martin and his entourage lived just outside Tours at **Marmoutier**, a monastery built in the chalky riverside cliffs on the road to Vouvray – its remains now lie in the grounds of a private school and, sadly, can't be visited. He remained as bishop for 26 years, living a life of model simplicity, performing miracles and acquiring a reputation as the scourge of idolaters. One story tells how a group of villagers would only cut down their sacred **pine tree** if he sat in its path. The saint agreed, but as the tree fell he made the sign of the cross, miraculously deflecting it.

In around 397 or 400, while staying at **Candes** (see p.233), on the western border of Touraine, Martin fell ill and died. Monks transported his body back up the Loire to Tours in a boat – another familiar scene from the saint's iconography – where he was buried at his own request in the cemetery of the poor.

On the other side of rue Descartes, the **Basilique de St-Martin** is a sorry neo-Byzantine replacement for the original. It was erected at the end of the nineteenth century by the local architect Victor Laloux to honour the relics of St Martin, which were rediscovered in 1860 and are now housed in the crypt, which sits on the original site of the basilica's altar – hence the unusual north–south alignment of the modern church. St Martin still has a strong local following, evident from the hundreds of votive prayers carved into the walls, and the vigorous celebrations of his feast day, on November 11.

Nearby, the **Musée St-Martin**, 3 rue Rapin (mid-March to mid-Nov Wed–Sun 9.30am–12.30pm & 2–5.30pm; €2), tells the story of the saint and displays various artefacts related to him and his shrine, including a fragment of his fifth-century tomb and a copy of the huge capital under the Tour Charlemagne. From 2005, when it reopens following restoration, you will be able to access the adjacent **Cloître de St-Martin** from the museum. This single vaulted gallery is all that survives of the basilica's beautiful Renaissance cloister.

A short distance away, down rue des Halles, lies the huge, modern **Halles**, or covered market – an excellent place to browse for a picnic in the morning.

The suburbs

If you're leaving Tours on the way to the enticing countryside of Touraine, the suburbs look particularly uninspiring, a mix of bland, medium-rise apartment blocks, semi-wasteland riverbanks and endless slip roads. But a trio of unusually inspiring sites hidden away in the suburbs makes a refreshing change from the usual château itineraries. The old Le Manach **silk factory**, on the right bank of the Loire, is fascinating for its archaic but working looms, Ronsard's **Prieuré de St-Cosme** is a place of pilgrimage for poetry lovers and rose enthusiasts alike, while the huge **Grange de Meslay**, out near the airport, is a useful reminder of the ultimate source of all Touraine's wealth: the land.

Le Manach silk factory

The silkworks of **Le Manach**, at 35 quai Paul Bert, on the north bank of the Loire, east of the Pont Wilson, can only be visited on occasional tours organized by the tourist office (☏02.47.70.37.37; €11), but it's well worth enquiring, as the visit is fascinating, and unique in the region. The "factory" – which has been here since 1829 – still uses some eighty original **Jacquard looms**, some dating from the eighteenth century, on which are woven exquisite made-to-order and stock silks, brocades and velours, many of which grace the walls of restored châteaux across France. You can see the whole weaving process in action, with local artisans energetically operating the looms by hand and foot, and watch the complex and archaic processes for reeling, bobbining, warping and the like. Small cushions and other samples are sold at the end of the visit.

Prieuré de St-Cosme

In May, when the roses are in full bloom, the **Prieuré de St-Cosme**, 3km east of the centre (daily: April–Sept 9am–7pm; Oct–March 9.30am–12.30pm & 2–5pm; €3.80), is one of the loveliest and most melancholy sites in Touraine, for all that it is hemmed in by suburbs and barred off from the nearby Loire by a trunk road. Once an island priory, now a semi-ruin, it was here that **Pierre de Ronsard** – arguably France's greatest poet – was prior from 1565 until his death, in 1585. The site was a dependency of the great monastery of Marmoutier (see p.69), and vestiges of many monastic buildings survive, including the refectory, the prior's house (where you can see Ronsard's study), and half an apse, which is all that remains of the priory church. But the most affecting sight is the lovingly tended **garden of roses**, flowers which Ronsard described as having "the perfume of gods" and obsessively used as symbols of beauty – and, inevitably, decay – in his poetry. The garden has some 2000 rose bushes, and 250 varieties – including the tightly rounded, pink rose called "Pierre de Ronsard".

Occasional classical **concerts** are held between May and November, and there's a jazz festival at the end of June. On the weekend of Pentecost, in late May or early June, there's a special festival and market of roses; call ☎02.47.37.32.70 for details. To get to the Prieuré de St-Cosme by **bus**, take #7 from immediately outside the Palais de Justice, on place Jean-Jaurès, towards La Riche-Petit Plessis, getting off at the La Pléiade stop.

Sadly, you can't get inside the **château de Plessis**, but it's only 1km to the southeast, and its history has a repellent fascination. It was here that the paranoid King Louis XI immured himself – as the chronicler Philippe de Commynes put it, behind "great bars of iron in the form of a thick grating" … "with ten bowmen in the ditches to shoot at any man who dared approach the castle" – and finally died, in 1483. The brick and stone building, a rump of the original structure, is typical of the style of the era.

Grange de Meslay

As a giant barn beside the airport, the **Grange de Meslay**, 6km northeast of the centre of Tours (Easter–Oct Sat & Sun 3–6pm; €4), may not immediately seem worth the trip. But then it is no ordinary barn, and unlike the more glamorous châteaux of the Loire you'll almost certainly have the place to yourself. The last remnant of a medieval priory, now destroyed, it was built in about 1220 to store the tithes due to the abbey of Marmoutier (see p.69). The facade echoes that of a Romanesque church, but it's plainer and more rustic. Similarly, the interior uses wood where you might expect to find stone, like an agricultural version of a cathedral. Occasional classical music **concerts** and other events take place here throughout the year; call ☎02.47.29.19.29 for details, or visit the website ⓦwww.meslay.com.

To get to the Grange by bus, take #60 from place Anatole-France, on the south side of Pont Wilson, towards Petite Arche, stopping at Grange de Meslay.

Eating and drinking

The streets around **place Plumereau**, especially rue du Grand Marché, jostle with mostly overpriced cafés, bars and **bistros**, and if you're looking for pizza, pasta or steak frites, and you don't mind paying a little extra for lively atmosphere and an outside table, this is the area to head for. Most of the bar-restaurants with tables on the square serve until around midnight. On the cathedral side of rue Nationale, **rue Colbert** is lined with much less touristy bars and ethnic eateries, as well as a few good family restaurants serving regional dishes such as *rillettes*, river fish in sauces based on local wines and the famous prunes of Tours, soaked in sweet Vouvray wine.

Sugar and chocolate freaks should make a detour to **pâtisseries** like La Marotte, 3 rue du Change, and La Chocolatière, 6 rue de la Scellerie. The main **market** halls are to the west of St-Martin at the end of rue des Halles.

Cafés

Aux Délices de Michel Colombe 1 place François-Sicard. This café-bakery offers an inspiring array of chocolates and pâtisseries, including local specialities, and is open through the day. The handful of pavement tables makes for a very pleasant place to have breakfast or afternoon tea while gazing at the cathedral's towers.

Le Molière Cnr rue de la Scellerie & rue Corneille. Directly in front of the Grand Théâtre, this large Belle Époque café has faded frescoes and a relaxed atmosphere. Good for a daytime coffee or drink.

Scarlett 70 rue Colbert. Relaxed tearoom open till 7pm, serving all the varieties you could desire, as well as delicious hot chocolates and cakes. Closed Mon & Sun.

Restaurants

Au Bureau place Plumereau. One of a number of places serving pizzas and simple dishes on the square, but worth recommending for its decent *plats du jour* – like *moules frites* for around €7.50. The late-night service and happy atmosphere at the outside tables is the main draw, but don't expect anything special in terms of cuisine. Serves until 12.30am daily.

Chez Jean-Michel 123 rue Colbert ☎02.47.20.80.20. Intimate wine bar and restaurant immaculately run under the watchful eye of the proprietor, Jean-Michel, managing to be elegant and relaxed at the same time. Serves good regional dishes to go along with the excellent local wines, of which there's a large selection. *Menus* €20 and €26, with good-value lunchtime choices at €10 and €13. Closed Sat & Sun.

Au Chien Jaune 75 rue Bernard Palissy. Beautifully recreated brasserie interior, with a real *zinc* (bartop) and old posters and brass everywhere. Good if unexceptional regional cuisine and brasserie classics; very handy for the gare SNCF and tourist office. *Menus* €17–28. Closed Sun.

Comme Autre-Fouée 11 rue de la Monnaie ☎02.47.05.94.78. Something of a gimmick, in that the food is a revival of the archaic *fouace* (or *fouée*) breads praised by Rabelais. They're served hot and heavily garnished with local titbits such as hot goat's cheese or *rillettes*. Good fun, if unsophisticated. *Menus* €9–18, the latter including wine. Closed Sat eve, Sun & Mon.

Le Franglais 27 rue Colbert. Relaxed Anglo-French bar-restaurant serving up large plates of meat with chips and salad for €7–9. Closed Sun & Mon evening.

La Furgeotière 19 place Foire-le-Roi ☎02.47.66.94.75. A husband-and-wife team run this enthusiastic little restaurant. Tables are laid out on historic place Foire-le-Roi on sunny evenings while inside it's quasi-medieval, with a tiled floor, beams and lots of creamy local stone. The food is a spin on traditional French with lots of fresh ingredients from the market and some inventive flavours. *Menus* €18–46. Closed Tues & Wed.

Le Vieux Mûrier 11 place Plumereau. One of the oldest and best cafés on place Plum', with an attractive decor of rustic bric-a-brac. Serves drinks only, from 11am to around 2am. Closed Mon.

Jean Bardet 57 rue Groison ☎02.47.41.41.11, ⊛www.jeanbardet.com. Tours' top restaurant, on the north side of the Loire. Extremely sophisticated, healthy food with rare herbs and old varieties of vegetables straight from the hotel's renowned vegetable garden. *Menus* at €60, €110, €145 and an unmissable all-vegetable *menu* at €69. Worth a splurge. Closed Mon lunch, Tues lunch & Sat lunch; Nov–March also closed Mon evening & Sun evening.

Au Lapin qui Fume 90 rue Colbert ☎02.47.66.95.49. Relaxed but elegant miniature restaurant with a good, meaty menu that's half from the Loire and half from the south of France. Lots of *lapin* (rabbit) – as a terrine, as a fricassée with rosemary, as a confit leg – but it's not obligatory, as there're also dishes like fish stew with Chinon wine. Half-litres of wine at €8. *Menus* €17 and €21. Closed Mon & Sun.

Le Petit Patrimoine 58 rue Colbert ☎02.47.66.05.81. Romantic little place squeezed into an atmospheric, stone-lined streetfront site, with one or two tables out on the pavement. Serves rich, lovingly prepared Loire dishes and good Loire wines, often matching the two together. *Menus* €12.50–26. Closed Sun lunch.

Le Picrocole 28–30 rue du Grand Marché. One of the better choices among the host of commercial restaurants behind place Plumereau, with a few outside tables in the narrow, bustling street. Serves old-fashioned dishes like *andouillette* and *rillons* as well as steaks and salads. *Menus* at €11 and 16.50. Open every day.

La Roche le Roy 55 rte de St-Avertin ☎02.47.27.22.00, ⊛www.rocheleroy.com. Truly gastronomic cuisine without bank-breaking prices. Chef Alain Couturier makes a speciality of regional ingredients, and you can try wonderful dishes such as eels in white Vouvray, or in red Chinon with prunes, and veal sweetbreads with creamed morel mushrooms. The setting sounds unpromising – just off the A10 motorway bypass south, exit 22 – but the building is in fact a lovely eighteenth-century mansion, with tables set out in the garden. *Menus* €42 and €61, lunch *menu* at €29.

Nightlife and entertainment

Packed with tables and chairs, picturesque place Plumereau is *the* place to start the evening with an open-air apéritif and to finish it with a coffee. Giant Irish **pubs**, pizzerias and branded ice-cream parlours are slowly making inroads into the area, but it's easy to pick out somewhere less commercial in the busy streets around. In the cathedral quarter, the bars on rue Colbert are mostly strip-lit local affairs, but there's a decent Irish pub on the corner of place Foire-le-Roi, and the *Académie de la Bière*, just up from the cathedral at 43 rue Lavoisier, is a lively, student-friendly place, though it can be dead in summer.

Even in summer, when local students are away, the **nightclubs** just off place Plumereau fill up with backpackers, locals and language students, though things don't usually get going until past midnight. The musical diet is more good-time than cutting-edge, but you'll find good playlists and crowds at *Les 3 Orfèvres*, 6 rue des Orfèvres; *VIP Club*, 22 rue de la Monnaie; and *L'Excalibur*, in a vaulted cellar at 35 rue Briçonnet. For **gigs**, try *Le Bateau Ivre*, 146 rue Édouard-Vaillant (℡02.47.44.72.22, ⊛www.bateau-ivre.org), to the south of the gare SNCF, which attracts international reggae, world music and hip-hop acts, as well as occasionally hosting concerts of French *chanson* (entry €9–18).

For details of **classical music** concerts, ask at the tourist office, which provides a free monthly magazine of exhibitions, concerts and events in Touraine, *Détours et des nuits*. The main venues are the Grand Théâtre, 34 rue de la Scellerie (℡02.47.60.20.20), which also stages plays, opera and ballet, and the Salle Jean de Ockeghem, 15 place Châteauneuf (℡02.47.47.11.31), which runs a varied programme of recitals and concerts by local and visiting groups. Many of the best concerts are held in abbeys and churches outside the city, but good smaller venues in Tours itself include the Cloître de la Psalette (see p.64), Musée des Beaux-Arts (see p.64) and Prieuré de St-Cosme (see p.70). For **cinema**, the best venue is the Studio, rue des Ursulines (℡08.36.68.20.15, ⊛www.studiocine.com), which shows international classics in their original language, usually subtitled in French, as well as mostly arty French films.

Festivals

One of the bigger events in the festival calendar is **Au Nom de la Loire**, a festival of street-entertainers and outdoor theatricals held on the riverbank quays over the second weekend of July. In May, the rock festival **Aucard de Tours** stages concerts on the Ile Aucard, while around Pentecost (usually late May), a choral festival, **Florilège Vocal de Tours**, takes place in the Grand Théâtre on rue de la Scellerie, with a free concert at the end on place Plum'. By way of contrast, a festive **market** devoted to garlic and onions is held on place du Grand Marché on 26 July.

Listings

Airport Aéroport Tours Val de Loire ℡02.47.49.37.00, ⊛www.tours-aeroport.com. Daily flights to London Stansted on Ryanair, plus two weekly flights to Lyon on Airlinair. Ryanair's telephone number in France is ℡0892.555.666 (Mon–Fri 8am–6pm; €0.34 per minute).
Books Good selection of English-language books at La Boîte à livres de l'étranger, 2 rue du Commerce ℡02.47.05.67.29.
Car rental Avis, gare de Tours ℡02.47.20.53.27; Budget, 2 place de la Gare ℡02.47.46.22.21; Europcar, 76 rue Bernard-Palissy ℡08.25.82.50.45, airport ℡02.47.85.85.85; Hertz, 57 rue Marcel Tribut ℡02.47.75.50.00. All offer pickup/drop at Tours airport, at St-Pierre-des-

Corps TGV station or near the gare SNCF in Tours.
Email and Internet Alliance Micro, 32bis rue Briçonnet and 7ter rue de la Monnaie (Mon–Sat 9.30am–7pm), is good value. Otherwise try L'Alexandra, 106 rue du Commerce (daily 3pm–1am or 2am); and Top Communication, 68–70 rue du Grand Marché (daily 10am–10pm).
Emergencies Ambulance ℡15; Hôpital Bretonneau, 2 bd Tonnelé ℡02.47.47.47.47; late-night pharmacy, phone police (see below) for address.
Police Commisariat Générale 70–72 rue Marceau ℡02.47.60.70.69.
Taxis Groupement Taxis Radio Tours ℡02.47.20.30.40; Taxis Radio Ville de Tours ℡02.47.05.20.90.

Vouvray and the wine villages

The main reason to visit the cluster of villages around **VOUVRAY**, 10km east of Tours on the north bank, is to taste the **wines**, which range from honeyed demi-secs to brisk sparklers. The area itself is unappealing, a choked section of ribbon-strip agri-business running along the main road that joins Vouvray to neighbouring **ROCHECORBON** and **MONCONTOUR**, the whole thing squeezed between the heights of the north bank – into which the wine *caves* (cellars) are cut – and the river's edge. To get there by public transport, take the regular **bus** #61 from Tours' place Jean-Jaurès.

If you climb the escarpment behind the villages, however, everything changes. The view of the vines combing across the chalky plateau above town is intoxicating. You can follow the **Route du Vouvray** by car, or explore the footpaths signposted **Vouvray les vins**; both thread their way among the vines towards the *domaine* of individual producers, many of whom offer wines for tasting. Tourist offices can give you a map, including one with two recommended, signposted walking routes.

A name to look out for is Domaine Huët, based in Le Haut-Lieu, 1.5km northeast of Vouvray itself, where organic techniques are used. You can combine wine-tasting with a visit to the impressive, Renaissance-style terraced gardens and early sixteenth-century troglodyte chapel at the **château de Valmer** (May, June & Sept Sat & Sun 2–7pm; July & Aug Tues–Sun 2–7pm; €4), beyond Chançay, just off the D46; or visit the small museum of wine-making at the **château de Moncontour** (Easter to mid-Oct daily 10am–7pm; free). For a broad spread of Vouvray wines, especially sparkling styles, make for the co-operative **Caves des Producteurs de Vouvray**, 3km west of Vouvray's centre at 18 rue de la Vallée Coquette (daily 9.30am–12.30pm & 2–7pm), which sells the wines of around fifty small growers and offers guided tours of the large, rock-cut *caves*. For more on the wines of Vouvray, see p.333.

Two branches of a well-known Vouvray *charcuterie*, Hardouin, stand in the centre of Vouvray, on rue de la République, and on the main road; either is a good place to stock up on picnic supplies. The **tourist office**, 100m off the main road on rue Rabelais (July & Aug Mon–Sat 9.30am–1pm & 2–6.30pm; Sept–June Tues–Sat 9am–1pm; ☏02.47.52.68.73, ⊛www.vouvray.org), can provide details of exact dates, addresses of **vignerons**, and information on guided tours, but all the steep valleys leading up to the plateau are riddled with *caves*. Vouvray's lively **Foire aux Vins** takes place around August 15, with smaller-scale festivities for the tasting of the new vintage in early March, and for the *vin nouveau* in early November.

The better places to **eat** tend to be in the hotel dining rooms, though in Rochecorbon there's *L'Oubliette*, at 34 rue des Clouets (☏02.47.52.50.49), which serves good local specialities and wines in a tufa cave, with a range of *menus* starting under €20. In Vouvray itself, the *Domaine des Bidaudières*, rue du Peu Morier (☏02.47.52.66.85, ⊛www.bandb-loire-valley.com; ❼), is a delightful place to **stay**, a luxury bed-and-breakfast halfway up the escarpment, with a swimming pool. Vouvray also has a pleasant hotel with a rather grand restaurant, the *Grand Vatel*, 8 ave L. Brulé (☏02.47.52.70.32, ☏02.47.52.74.52; ❷; hotel closed March 1–15; restaurant closed Sun evening & Mon; *menus* €18–46), and a **campsite** between the Loire and the Cisse (☏02.47.52.68.81).

A single **cruise boat**, the *Saint-Martin-de-Tours*, makes fifty-minute afternoon excursions downriver to Tours most days of the week, departing from the quai de la Loire in Rochecorbon, 2km out of Tours. For timetables and reservations, contact Georges Marchand (☏02.47.52.68.88, ⊛www.chateau-croisiere.com); tickets cost €8.50.

Montlouis-sur-Loire

If you're driving on the quieter, less touristy route to Amboise and Chenonceaux, along the south side of the river, **MONTLOUIS-SUR-LOIRE** makes a pleasant place to stop. The little village huddles on the hilltop to the north of its pretty church, and like Vouvray the tufa rock is honey-combed with cool wine *caves*.

Montlouis' **wines** are similar to Vouvray's, if less well-regarded by connoisseurs – though local legend has it that men traditionally prefer them to Vouvray's somehow more feminine vintages. At any rate, a Montlouis tends to be slightly less expensive than an equivalent Vouvray, and will mature faster. The best place to sample and buy is the friendly **Cave Touristique** (April–Nov daily 10am–noon & 2–7pm), an association of lots of independent *viticulteurs* who almost always have an English-speaker on hand.

Down on the riverfront at 60 quai Albert Baillet, the **Maison de la Loire** (Tues–Sun 2–6pm; €3; ⓦ www.ville-montlouis-loire.fr/mdl/) has a small exhibition on the wildlife and ecology of the Loire. It's a good place to pick up information on walks and guided outings in the area. The festival **Jazz en Touraine** (ⓣ 02.47.50.72.70, ⓦ www.ville-montlouis-loire.fr), which takes place in and around Montlouis-sur-Loire in the second week of September, encompasses blues and world music.

If you want to stay, *Le Colombier*, 4 Grande Rue, Husseau, 4km east of the village (ⓣ 02.47.50.85.24, ⓦ www.lecolombier-loirevalley.com; ❹), has a delightful **chambres d'hôtes** in a converted dovecote. Set within its own private wood, you can visit or, preferably, stay at the **château de la Bourdaisière**, 1km south of Montlouis-sur-Loire (daily 10am–noon & 2–6pm; €6; ⓣ 02.47.45.16.31, ⓦ www.chateaulabourdaisiere.com; ❼–❾). The heart of the château was originally built in the early sixteenth century, but it has been much added to and modified over the years. It has been beautifully restored by the owners, two brothers from the princely Broglie family, with terraced gardens, atmospheric nineteenth-century interiors and a pool. The estate produces its own wine, which you can taste and buy here, and its own garden tools – the expensive kind, as sold in the Jardin du Palais Royal in Paris. You can visit the walled garden, which hothouses around five hundred varieties of tomatoes, with tastings in June and July, and a dedicated festival in September attracting foodies and garden enthusiasts alike.

Amboise and around

Twenty kilometres upstream of Tours, **AMBOISE** is a twee little riverside town trading on long-gone splendours, notably its impressive **château** and Leonardo da Vinci's peaceful residence of **Clos-Lucé**. The town draws a busy tourist trade that may detract from the quieter pleasures of strolling along the riverbank, but makes it a good destination for children – if they're unpersuaded by the bloodier elements of the château's history, they may go for the out-of-town aquarium and mini-châteaux park.

The approach from Tours along the main N152 on the north side of the river is busy but dramatic, as the bridge carries the road across the midstream Ile d'Or and head-on towards the château's magnificent facade, propped up by its mammoth towers. The D751 along the left bank, on the other hand, is quieter and has the advantage of passing through a glorious parade of plane trees just at the town limits.

AMBOISE

▲ Gare SNCF

RESTAURANTS
Chez Hippeau 2
L'Epicerie 3
Le Saint Vincent 1

Ile d'Or

N

Loire

QUAI CHARLES GUINOT

Tour des Minimes

Hôtel de Ville

Château d'Amboise

East Gate

St-Florentin

RUE FRANÇOIS I

St-Hubert

Tour Heurtault

RUE VICTOR-HUGO

Porte de l'Horloge

PLACE MICHEL DEBRE

RUE NEWTOWN

RUE MIRABEAU

Maison Enchantée

QUAI DU GENERAL-DE-GAULLE

RUE NATIONALE

QUAI DES MARAIS

RUE JOYEUSE

PLACE RICHELIEU

RUE RABELAIS

PLACE ST-DENIS

St-Denis

0   100 m

ACCOMMODATION
Le Belle Vue   C
Le Blason   G
Café des Arts   D
Le Chaptal   F
Le Choiseul   B
Hostel   A
Mme Henry   E
Le Vieux Manoir   H

Chaumont & Blois

Clos-Lucé

L'Amasse

Montlouis, Tours & Aquarium

TOURAINE | Amboise and around

▼ Pagode de Chanteloup, Chenonceau & Parc Mini-Châteaux

Arrival and information

The **gare SNCF** is on the north bank of the river, at the end of rue Jules Ferry, about 1km from the château. There are good connections to Tours and Blois. Information on Amboise and its environs, including the vineyards of the Touraine-Amboise *appellation*, is available at the **tourist office** on quai du Général-de-Gaulle, on the riverfront (April–June & Sept Mon–Sat 9.30am–1pm & 2–6.30pm, Sun 10am–1pm & 3–6pm; July & Aug Mon–Sat 9am–7pm, Sun 10am–6pm; Oct–March Mon–Sat 10am–1pm & 2–6pm, Sun 10am–1pm; ☎02.47.57.09.28, ⓦwww.amboise-valdeloire.com).

Bikes can be rented from Cycles Richard, 2 rue Nazelles, near the station (☎02.47.57.01.79), or Locacycle, on rue Jean-Jacques Rousseau (April–Oct; ☎02.47.57.00.28). **Canoes** are available from the Club de Canoë-Kayak, at the Base de l'Ile d'Or (☎02.47.23.26.52, ⓦwww.loire-aventure.com), which also runs guided trips. These are an excellent way to get to know the ecology of the Loire, and they're reasonably priced – the twenty-kilometre trip down from Chaumont (see p.152), for example, costs €20.

Accommodation

The town's **hotels** are relatively pricey and get booked up in summer some time in advance, but there are some excellent choices around town, including some lovely chambres d'hôtes. A good **campsite** can be found on the island across from the castle, the Ile d'Or (☎02.47.57.23.37), alongside the hostel.

Le Belle Vue 12 quai Charles-Guinot ☎02.47.57.02.26, ⓕ02.47.30.51.23. Long-established Logis de France three-star situated

just below the château, with comfortable, old-fashioned bedrooms. Some rooms at the front give onto a small balcony overlooking the Loire, but road noise makes this less agreeable than it might sound. Closed mid-Nov to mid-March. ❸

Le Blason 11 place Richelieu ☎02.47.23.22.41, ⓦwww.leblason.fr. Very smartly kept but homely hotel in a quiet corner of Amboise. The furnishings are modern, but unobtrusively so, and all rooms have pretty exposed beams and white walls. Triples and quads also available. ❸

Café des Arts place Michel Debré ☎02.47.57.25.04. A simple but friendly backpacker-oriented place set up behind and above a simple, inexpensive café. Rooms are clean, bright and simple – think pine bunkbeds and hard-wearing carpet. ❶

Centre Charles Péguy Ile d'Or ☎02.47.30.69.90, ⓦwww.ucrif.asso.fr. Ordinary but recently done-up hostel in a pleasant location on the midstream island, halfway across the town bridge, with a small summer swimming pool. Reception is open Mon–Fri 3–8pm, but it's best to reserve in advance. Beds cost €8.40 a night.

Le Chaptal 13 rue Chaptal ☎02.47.57.14.46. One of the few relatively low-budget options. The rooms are plain and rather spartan, and the welcome not exactly effusive, but it's perfectly decent. ❷

Château de Pintray Lussault ☎02.47.23.22.84, Ⓔmarius.rault@wanadoo.fr. Outside Amboise itself, but easy enough to find if you follow signs from Lussault, 6km downstream, towards the Aquarium de Touraine. A really delightful, blue-shuttered grand country home among the vines. Offers gorgeous chambres d'hôtes, all nineteenth-century loveliness with canopied beds and little occasional tables. ❻

Le Choiseul 36 quai Charles-Guinot ☎02.47.30.45.45, ⓦwww.le-choiseul.com. Serious elegance, set in an eighteenth-century riverside mansion almost below the château. Luxuriously furnished rooms with heavy curtains, thick carpets and fresh flowers – the best have views over the river. Open-air swimming pool in summer. Room prices range from €180 to €280. ❾

Mme Henry 3 rue Joyeuse ☎02.47.57.52.91. Two charming chambres d'hôtes in an old house hidden away behind a high wall, with views of the modest Renaissance townhouse opposite. Welcoming owners and good value. ❸

Le Vieux Manoir 13 rue Rabelais ☎02.47.30.41.27, ⓦwww.le-vieux-manoir.com. An eighteenth-century mini-manor house converted for use as a luxury bed-and-breakfast, this is the best place in town for a thoroughly romantic stay. Lovingly run by an American couple, with endless carefully chosen details of fabric and furnishing that are sometimes utterly pretty, sometimes a little chintzy. ❼–❽

The Town

The town centre has two main axes vying for lack of appeal: the busy main road that runs alongside the river, quai du Général de Gaulle/quai Charles-Guinot, and the long pedestrianized street that runs parallel to it one block in, **rue Nationale**, which is lined with cheap souvenir shops and crêperies. Things look up as soon as you approach the **château**, with the fifteenth-century **Porte de l'Horloge** guarding the entrance to **place Michel Debré**, which occupies a dramatic position under the soaring walls of the **château**. The heavy defensive lines of the buttresses smoothly transform themselves into ornately sculpted window bays as they fly upwards towards the exquisite chapelle de St-Hubert, perched incongruously above.

The château

Rising above the river like a sculpted and decorated cliff, the **château d'Amboise** (daily: Feb to mid-March 9am–noon & 1.30–5.30pm; mid-March to end March & Sept to mid-Nov 9am–6pm; April–June 9am–6.30pm; July & Aug 9am–7pm; mid-Nov to Jan 9am–noon & 2–4.45pm; €6.50) dominates the town at its feet. Once five times its present size, it was much reduced in the early nineteenth century because of lack of money to maintain it. The entrance is via the Tour Hertault, at the upper end of place Michel Debré.

In July and August, the château hosts a **son-et-lumière** spectacular at around 10pm (Wed & Sat; adults from €12, children 6–14 from €6; ⓦwww.renaissance-amboise.com), with Leonardo images projected on the walls and costumed actors prancing about to loud Renaissance-style music.

Some history

Following his marriage to Anne de Bretagne at Langeais in 1491 (see p.89), Charles VIII decided to turn the old castle of his childhood days into an extravagant and luxurious palace, adding the chapelle de St-Hubert and the Flamboyant Gothic wing that still looks down graciously on the Loire. In 1494, however, Charles left Amboise to conquer the **kingdom of Naples**, and while there he fell in love with the delights of the Italian Renaissance, writing to his brother that "you would not believe how beautiful are the gardens I have in this city, for upon my faith, it seems that they lack only Adam and Eve to make them an earthly paradise." Resolving to recreate this Eden at home, he brought back artisans from Naples – along with France's first syphilis epidemic. The work of these artists and craftsmen was an early taste of the Renaissance, provoking an appetite for Italian design which was to dominate the next century.

Charles lost Naples within a couple of years, and his ambitions for life at Amboise fared little better. In April 1498, on leaving the queen's bedchamber to watch a game of tennis, he walked through the now-destroyed **Hacquelebac gallery** where, the chronicler Philippe de Commynes observed, "everyone used to piss", and managed to hit his head on a door lintel. Nine hours later, he collapsed and died. As de Commynes pointed out, this was an ignoble end for a king who had tried to bring together at Amboise "all the beauties that he had seen . . . in France, Italy or Flanders". Sadly, much of Charles's Italianate work has been demolished, as has the wretched gallery.

Charles left the kingdom – and his wife (see p.89) – to his cousin, **Louis XII**, who spent most of his time at Blois but built a new wing at Amboise to house his nearest male relative, the young François d'Angoulême, thereby keeping him within easy reach. When he acceded to the throne as François I, he didn't forget his childhood home. He embellished the newer wing and invited Leonardo da Vinci to work in Amboise under his protection (see box on p.80). François eventually died in the château's collegiate église St-Florentin, which has long since been destroyed.

The château today is impressive, but nevertheless only a remnant of what once stood on this airy site, the greater part having been demolished in the Napoleonic era to save money on upkeep.

Visiting the château

After such a history, the château itself can seem strangely bare and empty, but the perfectly miniature **chappelle de St-Hubert**, on the south side of the terrace, is well worth lingering over. The most interesting of the carvings above its doorway depicts St-Hubert confronting the mystical vision of a deer with a cross between its horns, which converted him from a life of idle hunting to one of religious contemplation. This model of behaviour seems to have had little influence over the French monarchs, who were attracted to Amboise as much by its hunting as by anything else. Inside, the modern stained-glass windows are by the prolific twentieth-century glazier, Max Ingrand. A plaque marks the resting place of the probable remains of Leonardo da Vinci, which were discovered in the château **grounds** in the nineteenth century, on the site of the collegiate church, and transferred here.

It's worth exploring the small park a little further. Head past the château towards the **east gate**, a medieval structure which was once the château's principal entrance. On the left, running along a terrace overlooking the Loire, is the site of the famous **garden** created by the Neapolitan Pacello da Mercogliano on the orders of Charles VIII. At the time of writing there was nothing but a set of pollarded limes, but there are plans afoot to recreate the Renaissance garden, and its geometric arrangement's of imported cypresses and citrus trees.

The **château** itself is a mere fragment of the vast structure that once extended right round the ramparts. It is extremely handsome nonetheless, encapsulating all the styles of the early Renaissance. Parallel with the river is the older Charles VIII wing, while standing at right angles is the wing built by Louis XII, with its extra storey added by François I. The dormer windows of the two wings seem very similar on first glance, but a closer look reveals how the later windows have been subtly transformed under the influence of Classical ideas.

Inside, there's a fairly atmospheric progression of large rooms on the **ground floor**, hung with Aubusson tapestries and furnished in sixteenth- or seventeenth-century style, with suits of armour to offset the bare walls and floors. The **Salle des Etats** is particularly fine, its four white marble columns marching down the centre of the room, carved alternately with the symbols of France (the fleur de lys) and Brittany (the ermine's tail). The effect, offset against red brick, is impressive, though much is fanciful restoration work. The **Salle Henri II** has been attractively furnished in an attempt to recreate the feel of a royal Renaissance bedroom. The **first floor** switches abruptly in style to the stuffy, 1830s post-First Empire period, as the apartments were converted for holiday use by the last French king, Louis-Philippe. There's an anxious-looking portrait of him in the **Salle de Musique**. His descendant, the so-called **comte de Paris**, who managed to spend literally a king's inheritance before he died in 1999, set up the foundation which now owns the château.

The most exciting part of the visit comes at the end, as you climb up to the top of the **Tour des Minimes**, from where there's a fabulous panorama of the Loire. You can also see across the château's facade, and its notorious iron balcony, which played a grisly role in one of the first skirmishes in the Wars of Religion, known as the **Tumult of Amboise**. Persecuted by the Guise brothers, the powerful advisers of the sickly young king, François II, Huguenot conspirators set out for Amboise in 1560 to "rescue" their king and establish a more tolerant monarchy under their Protestant tutelage. They were ambushed by royal troops and local zealots in woods outside the town. Some were drowned in the Loire below the château, some beheaded in the grounds, and others hanged from the balcony. Descending the Tour des Minimes on its massive internal ramp, it's easy to see that it was designed for the maximum number of fully armoured men on horseback to get in and out as quickly as possible.

Clos-Lucé

Following his campaigns in Lombardy, François I decided that the best way to bring back the ideas of the Italian Renaissance was to import one of the finest exponents of the new arts. In 1516, **Leonardo da Vinci** ventured across the Alps in response to the royal invitation, and for three years before his death in 1519, he made his home at the **Clos-Lucé**, at the end of rue Victor-Hugo, five minutes' walk from the centre (daily: Jan 10am–6pm; Feb, March, Nov & Dec 9am–6pm; April–June, Sept & Oct 9am–7pm; July & Aug 9am–8pm; €6.50). Leonardo seems to have enjoyed a semi-retirement at Amboise (see box on p.80), devoting himself to inventions of varying brilliance and impracticability, and enjoying conversation with his royal patron. The house – an attractive brick mansion with Italianate details added by Charles VIII's Neapolitan craftsmen – is now a museum to Leonardo, and if you can ignore the persistent piped Renaissance music, the reconstructed interior is pleasant enough, with its suspiciously new beams and giant stone fireplaces. The **oratoire d'Anne de Bretagne**, built by Charles VIII for his new wife, is the loveliest room, a tiny chapel with a vaulted ceiling probably frescoed by Leonardo's last pupil, Francesco de Melzi. If the frescoes are by de Melzi, however, they only show how ill-equipped he was to take up his master's brushes.

Down in the basement are forty fascinating models of Leonardo's **mechanical inventions**; from the suspension bridge to the paddle-wheel boat and turbine, they are all meticulously constructed according to the inventor's plans and sketches. They are a particular hit with kids and teenagers.

Leonardo's retirement

When **Leonardo da Vinci** arrived in Amboise in 1516, it was his first visit to France, but not the first time he had worked for the French, or heard the name of Amboise. When Louis XII conquered Milan in 1500, he captured Leonardo's first patron, Duke Ludovico Sforza, and imprisoned him in France – most notoriously, in a dungeon at Loches (see p.119). During the French army's ongoing Italian campaigns, Leonardo was put to work by Charles II d'Amboise, Louis XII's governor of Milan, on military engineering schemes, and he was soon engaged on various sculptural and architectural projects as well. This work came to an end with Louis XII's renunciation of Milan in 1513, but when **François I** came to the throne, he wasted little time in tempting Leonardo away from Italy with an offer of safety and comfort at Amboise, and a fat pension of 700 gold écus a year.

Leonardo brought some of his greatest canvases with him across the Alps, probably including the **Mona Lisa** – at least, when Cardinal Louis of Aragon visited the ageing painter, in October 1517, the cardinal's secretary, Antonio de Beatis, wrote that they were shown "one of a certain Florentine lady, done from life, at the request of the late Magnificent, Giuliano de' Medici". Sadly, Leonardo seems to have done little or no painting in Amboise. The sculptor and goldsmith Benvenuto Cellini, another Italian working in France, blames François I for rarely leaving him alone: "for this reason he did not have the opportunity of putting into actual use the splendid studies which he had carried on with such devotion." An aside by de Beatis gives the more plausible explanation that "on account of a certain paralysis having seized him in the right hand one cannot expect more fine things from him" – though Leonardo was actually left-handed.

Perhaps he was simply settling into a dignified retirement, freely pursuing the unorthodox **inventions** that characterized this last period of his life. Celebrity culture makes much of these as proof of his **"universal genius"**, but in fact Leonardo's achievements were outstripped by many contemporaries, and few of his inventions were either practical or original. Their fame really rests on the fact that some seem to foretell future technologies – though Leonardo rarely worked out the actual details, as with his absurd sketch for a man-powered helicopter.

Leonardo also worked on a design for a château at Romorantin, some of the features of which may have influenced the construction of **Chambord** (see p.142), and recreated his famous mechanical lion, which took part in an elaborate masquerade at Blois. The beast apparently walked several menacing steps towards the king before its head split open to reveal the royal lilies set against a blue background.

For all this uneven output, the old man grew close to his employer, François I. Cellini heard the king say "that he believed no man had been born into the world who knew as much as Leonardo, and this not only in matters concerning sculpture, painting and architecture, but because he was a very great philosopher." A poignant anecdote relates that in the harsh winter of 1518–19, which was so cold that ice broke down an arch of Amboise's bridge, Leonardo rescued a swallow that was too frail to continue its southward migration. He kept it in his rooms at the Clos-Lucé as a companion to his decline, and died on May 2, 1519 – legend has it, in the arms of the king.

The rest of town

In summer, it's worth pausing at the **Musée de l'Hôtel de Ville**, on rue François I (July & Aug Mon–Fri & Sun 2–6pm; free), just down from place Michel Debré towards the river. The handful of little rooms hold little of note, just some busts of Leonardo and second-rate tapestries and oil paintings, but look out for the sublime fourteenth-century smiling Virgin, which used to stand under the belfry of the Porte de l'Horloge. If you've got bored kids in tow, they might be amused by the overpriced **Maison Enchantée**, 7 rue du Général Foy (July & Aug daily 10am–7pm; April–June, Sept & Oct daily 9am–noon & 2–6pm; Nov–March Tues–Sun 2–4pm; €5.40, children €4.30), which features two dozen or so ingenious little scenarios acted out by animated puppets and dolls. There's a fairground scene, a pirate ship and a kitsch version of the Nativity, but unless you're actually interested in the curious mechanical techniques, it all looks a bit old hat.

At the other end of rue Nationale, some 500m to the west of the château, the Romanesque **église St-Denis** (daily 9am–6pm) is well worth visiting, with a great view back across town to the château's battlements. The first two pairs of capitals at the westernmost end are richly carved, but the finest stonework is to be seen in two sixteenth-century works: a wonderful, polychrome Entombment group, in the corner halfway down the south aisle of the church, and the troubling figure of a drowned woman's semi-naked corpse, nearby. Local legend has it that François I himself modelled for the Christ of the Entombment, surrounded by likenesses of the Babou family of La Bourdaisière (see p.75).

Just upstream from the Pont Général Leclerc are six extraordinary brick and tufa silos, **Les Greniers de César**, with their entrance at 36 quai Charles-Guinot. Strange, almost spaceship-like constructions, they were built in the sixteenth century to store grain. The silos are usually open only to groups by appointment a month in advance, or during exhibitions, but you could chance your luck; ask at the tourist office or call ☎02.47.30.45.45.

Children in particular may enjoy investigating two unusual sculptural concessions to twentieth-century art. One is a fountain by German Surrealist **Max Ernst** showing lots of weird froggy and tortoise-like creatures spitting jets of water, which stands in front of the spot where the **market** takes place every Friday and Sunday morning, on the riverfront 50m downstream from the tourist office. The other is a large mobile by the American artist **Alexander Calder**, who lived near Saché in the 1960s (see p.101). Known as "Crimkly", it stands on the Ile d'Or, facing the château across the river.

Eating

Most of the eateries in town specialize in crêpes and overpriced snacks, and there are only a handful of decent possibilities outside the hotel **restaurants**. For a real blow-out meal, make for Pascal Bouvier's Michelin-starred dining room at the hotel *Le Choiseul* (☎02.47.30.45.45; *menus* at €46 & €80). The most enticing choice for ordinary mortals is *L'Épicerie*, 46 place Michel Debré (☎02.47.57.08.94; *menus* €10.50–35; closed Mon & Tues), which has a lovely situation overlooked by the chapelle St-Hubert, and serves good and fairly refined country cuisine; be sure to book in advance in summer. On the Ile d'Or just next to the bridge, *Le Saint Vincent*, 7 rue Commire (☎02.47.30.49.49; *menus* €18–35), has good views of the château from the dining room, and serves traditional French dishes. For something a little more lively, *Chez Hippeau*, 1 rue François I (☎02.47.57.26.30; *menus* €10–30), is a bustling brasserie next to the Hôtel de Ville, with good lunchtime *menus* and pleasant outdoor seating out back, under the walls of St-Florentin church. After around 10pm, everywhere stops serving, and Amboise is remarkably quiet after hours.

Around Amboise: Pagode de Chanteloup

If you take the main road south out of Amboise towards Bléré and Chenonceaux, and turn right just before the junction with the D31, less than 1km from the centre, you'll arrive at a long, tree-lined avenue leading to an unlikely-looking eighteenth-century **pagoda** (April Sat & Sun 10am–noon & 2–6pm; May & Sept daily 10am–6.30pm; June daily 10am–7pm; July & Aug daily 9.30am–7pm; Oct to mid-Nov Sat & Sun 10am–5pm; €6). It once belonged to the enormous but now entirely demolished château of **Chanteloup**, which was one of the largest, finest and most fashionable country houses of its eighteenth-century heyday. The pagoda's weird structure owes something to the fashion for Orientalism and something to the serene Classicism of the day, and you can climb right to the top up a skilfully constructed staircase, though you'll have to negotiate 142 narrow steps.

You can also play some addictive medieval skittle-like **games and puzzles** in the grounds, hire a **boat** on the lake (€4 for 30min) and explore the surrounding park.

Family attractions near Amboise

Just south of town on the D751 to Chenonceaux, near the Pagode de Chanteloup, the **Parc Mini-Châteaux** (daily: Jan–March & Sept–Nov 10.30am–6pm; April to mid-July and last two weeks of Aug 10am–7pm; mid-July to mid-Aug 10am–8pm; €12, children 4–15 years €7; various family tickets are available that also include entry to Aquarium, below) houses more than forty surprisingly good large-scale models of the chief Loire châteaux, made convincing by careful weathering and thousands of bonsai trees. Some are particularly large and impressive, including Loches, where they've modelled the whole citadel and all its houses, and Chinon, which you can walk right through. There's even a model TGV rattling by.

At Lussault, 6km west of Amboise towards Tours, the mammoth **Aquarium de Touraine** (same hours and ticket prices as Mini-Châteaux) boasts 10,000 fish, focusing on a special sequence of tanks featuring all the Loire species, from native bream and carp to introduced giants such as sturgeon, pike-perch and the frankly terrifying *silure*. There's also a small tropical section with turtles and alligators, and a tunnel that leads you through a large shark tank. Children can touch fish in a special tank, and watch regular piranha feeding frenzies.

For more energetic distractions, make straight for the activity park **Fantasy Forest**, in Mosnes, 11km from Amboise on the road to Chaumont-sur-Loire (daily: March & Oct–Dec 10am–6pm; April, May & Sept 10am–7pm; June–Aug 10am–8pm; ☎02.47.30.50.90, ⊛www.fantasyforest.fr). There's a go-kart luge-type affair (€8 for five descents), paintball sessions (€20), canoeing on the Loire (€20 per boat), mountain bike hire (€9 for a half-day), inflatable castles and an adventure playground for younger children (€9) and the signature activity, the "Parcours Acrobatique" (€8–20, depending on height), which involves clambering through the trees on all kinds of rope bridges, securely attached to metal wires.

Chenonceaux and around

The gentle River Cher flows so slowly and passively between the exquisite arches of the **château de Chenonceau**, 35km east of Tours, that you are almost always assured of a perfect reflection. As the nineteenth-century novelist Gustave Flaubert put it: "All is peaceful and gentle, elegant yet robust. It has calm without boredom, and melancholy without bitterness." The château is not visible from the road and you will have to pay to get even a peek. The little village of **CHENONCEAUX** (spelt with an x) is not much more than a cluster of pleasant hotels and restaurants built to serve the hordes of visitors that arrive here – the château vies with Chambord (see p.141) for the title of most-visited sight in the region, and it's a prime stop on the coach-party circuit. During summer the place teems with people, and it can become uncomfortably crowded mid-morning and mid-afternoon.

The relatively untouristed upper reaches of the Cher, including the pretty town of **Montrichard**, just 9km upriver, are covered in Chapter 2, "Blois and the Sologne" (see p.125).

Château de Chenonceau

Women always controlled the building of the **château de Chenonceau** (daily: March 16 to Sept 15 9am–7pm; Sept 16 to end Sept 9am–6.30pm; Oct 1 to Oct 15 & March 1 to March 15 9am–6pm; Oct 16 to end Oct & Feb 16 to end Feb 9am–5.30pm; Nov 1 to Nov 15 & Feb 1 to Feb 15 9am–5pm; Nov 16 to Jan 9am–4.30pm; €7.60; Ⓦwww.chenonceau.com). Catherine Briçonnet – whose husband Thomas Bohier bought the site on the proceeds of embezzling from his master, François I – hired the first architects in 1515 and had them begin building on the foundations of an old mill that stood on the granite bed of the Cher. At the same time, they destroyed the old castle belonging to the Marques, a venerable noble family which the ambitious new owners had helped along the road to financial ruin. Its moat-surrounded foundations now form a kind of island courtyard and prelude to the château. Anxious to guarantee – and advertise – their newly bought seigneurial status, the Bohiers left the corner **keep** alone, adding a few fancy windows to make it look less starkly Gothic, and engraving their initials at the base of the door. Their new château rose from the water alongside, combining in its architecture the fresh, rational ideas and Classical details of the Renaissance with the dizzy turrets and chimneys of late Gothic's courtly spirit. The Bohiers didn't have long to enjoy their ennoblement; the disgrace of the financier Jacques de Beaune-Semblançay (see p.309) brought down their son Antoine as part of a general inspection of royal accounts, and the château was given up to the Crown.

The château's most characteristic feature, the set of arches spanning the River Cher, was added later in the century by **Diane de Poitiers**, who had been given the château by her lover, Henri II. Only five years later, following the accidental death of Henri II in 1559, Diane in turn was forced to hand over the château to the indomitable **Catherine de Médicis**, Henri II's widow, in return for Chaumont (see p.152). Catherine added lots of fashionable Mannerist details, including a set of giant caryatids on the entrance facade; these now stand in the park. But her most important contribution was to build on top of the bridge. Laid out as three smoothly horizontal storeys, this section of the building has shaken off the febrile, more vertically oriented Gothic air that still clings to the main body of the château. The more you look, the more different the two parts seem, although they are separated by hardly more than fifty years, and both could be called Renaissance.

After a long period of disuse, one **Mme Dupin** brought fashionable life of the eighteenth century to this gorgeous residence, along with her guests Voltaire, Montesquieu and Rousseau, whom she had hired as tutor to her son and who became, according to his own account, "fat as a monk" during his stay. Saved by her local charitable works, Mme Dupin continued to live here until after the Revolution, château and owner slipping into old age together. Restoration back to the sixteenth-century designs – which involved removing many of Catherine de Médicis' additions – was completed by another woman, **Mme Pelouze**, in the late nineteenth century. The château is now a profitable business, owned and run by the Menier family firm, of chocolate fame.

The interior

Inside, the château is surprising small, with four main rooms set either side of a central corridor on all three floors, but there's a huge array of arresting tapestries, chimneys, ceilings, floors and furniture on show. The surprisingly good collection of **paintings** includes works by or attributed to Veronese, Tintoretto, Coreggio, Murillo and Rubens, among others, as well as a number of portraits of the château's female owners, which helps to flesh out the history. Many of the tiled floors are original.

As soon as you step inside the château, it's obvious that this is no rambling medieval building. The layout is symmetrical and logical, with two main rooms on either side of a central hall with a beautiful Renaissance ceiling, its stone vaults strangely offset in a zigzag pattern. On the ground floor, the tapestry-hung **Guards' Room**, on the left, leads through to the modest chapel, and on to Catherine de Médicis' green-velvet-lined **study** and **Diane de Poitiers' bedroom**, with its fine chimney created by the great Mannerist sculptor, Jean Goujon. On the other side of the hall, the impressive **François I room** features two contrasting images of the goddess Diana; one is in fact a portrait of Diane de Poitiers, attributed to Primaticcio, while the other represents a relatively aristocratic Gabrielle d'Estrées. In the same room is Zurbarán's superb *Archimedes*. Mme Dupin's winsome portrait hangs in the **Louis XIV room**, next door, giving an impression only slightly more composed than when the philosopher Jean-Jacques Rousseau first met her: "her arms were uncovered, her hair was loose, her peignoir in disarray. . . it quite turned my poor head." Rigaud's portrait of Louis XIV was apparently given by the king as a souvenir of his own visit. Down the steps, the vaulted **kitchens**, conveniently positioned just above the water level, are well worth a look.

The section of the château that spans the Cher is relatively empty. The seemingly incongruous checkerboard flooring of the elegant **long gallery** is in fact true to the Renaissance design, though potted plants have replaced the Classical statues which Louis XIV carried off to Versailles. Catherine de Médicis used to hold wild parties here, all naked nymphs and Italian fireworks. She intended the door on the far side to continue into another building on the south bank, but the project was never begun, and these days the gallery gives onto quiet, wooded gardens. In 1940, the Cher briefly formed the boundary between occupied and "free" France. The current proprietors, who rode out Nazi occupation, like to make out that the château's gallery was much used as an escape route. Given that their adjacent farm quartered a German garrison, it would have been a risky place to cross.

Being both straight, and inside the main building, the carved stone **staircase** is another piece typical of Renaissance design. The first and second floors are usually much quieter than the lower floors so there's more space to admire unique decorative details such as the seventeenth-century window-frame in the **César de Vendôme room**, supported by two carved caryatids, and the moving ceiling in the **bedroom of Louise de Lorraine**, which mourns Louise's murdered husband Henri III in black paint picked out with painted tears and the couple's intertwined initials. She lived out her widowhood at Chenonceau, always dressed in the white of royal mourning.

The grounds

Something of the quiet spirit of Mme Dupin's twilight years can be felt if you visit her dilapidated **tomb**, which stands on lion's foot pedestals in the woods on the far bank of the Cher (you are given a token for re-entry when you leave by the gallery's end door). Inscribed upon it is a dedication to the Virtues, to Genius and to the Graces. The **gardens** on the near bank were the scene of wild celebrations for the marriage of the Dauphin François II and Mary Stuart, Queen of Scots, in 1558. Court ladies dressed in rustic style stood at the foot of every tree waving ribbons, and, as the newlyweds crossed the bridge, fireworks went off – a first for France – and thirty cannon fired from the quay, causing so much smoke and flame that, according to a captain of the guard, "the very water seemed to burn." At Catherine's last party, in June 1577, Henri III and his favourites arrived dressed as women, while Catherine's infamous ladies in waiting, known as the "Flying Squadron", are said to have appeared half naked, with their hair flowing. The story certainly fits the popular image of Catherine's court as a den of vice, a legend much put about by Huguenot detractors.

Various outbuildings allow you to escape the crowds. The immaculately restored **farm courtyard** can be visited freely, along with its huge flower and vegetable garden, and the **stables** (€3) now house a collection of waxworks acting out various historical scenes associated with the château. Adults may find the figures interesting for their meticulously recreated clothes, which show off some of the precious textiles worn by sixteenth-century aristocrats, but it's too worthy for most children.

In July and August, as part of the **Nocturne à Chenonceau**, the gardens and château are lit up between 10pm and 11.30pm, with atmosphere provided by Corelli's chamber music played through speakers. The exterior-only evening ticket costs €5. Also in the summer months, you can take **boats** out onto the Cher.

Practicalities

The tiny village of Chenonceaux has been almost entirely taken over by a handful of comfortable **hotels**, any of which would make a good base for exploring further up the Cher, though there's nothing much to see between forays. All of them are on rue du Docteur-Bretonneau, within easy reach of the château and the **gare SNCF** – which has decent train connections to Tours and up the Cher towards Bourges. The *Hôtel du Roy* at no. 9 (T02.47.23.90.17, F02.47.23.89.81; ❸) is relatively inexpensive; while *La Roseraie*, at no. 7 (T02.47.23.90.09, Wwww.charminghotel.com; ❸), is very welcoming, with good food, extensive grounds and a swimming pool. At no. 6, *Le Bon Laboureur* (T02.47.23.90.02, Wwww.amboise.com/laboureur; ❹) is the most luxurious option, with an award-winning restaurant. For **camping**, the municipal site (T02.47.23.90.13; closed Oct–March) is located between the railway line and the river.

Around Chenonceaux: Prieuré de St-Jean-du-Grais

The road from Tours to Chenonceaux on the left bank of the Cher, the N76, passes through a number of small riverside towns. Three kilometres south of one of the prettier of them, **Azay-sur-Cher**, 18km east of Tours, is the crumbling old priory complex of **ST-JEAN-DU-GRAIS** (April to mid-June Sat & Sun 10am–6pm; mid-June to Sept daily 10am–6pm; €4.50), whose stone buildings date back to the twelfth century, though they were damaged and in some cases dismantled altogether after being sold off by the Revolutionary authorities. Of the church, only the bell tower remains, a sturdy construction capped by a curiously stunted and weathered stone spire. Beside it stand various shells of monastic buildings – some with vestiges of stonework, arches, pillars and the like – which you can visit on the guided tour.

The north bank west of Tours

The north bank of the Loire, to the west of Tours, is often neglected. The honey-pot châteaux lie mostly on the south side of the river, and once you're on the main road west it's easy to speed past towards Saumur and Anjou. But the elegant private château at **Luynes** and the strange Gallo-Roman tower of **Cinq-Mars-la-Pile** have their own low-key appeal, and even if the main focus of your visit lies to the south it would be well worth making a foray across the river to the splendidly furnished and quintessentially late-medieval château at **Langeais**. Further west, at the limits of Touraine, the attractive market town of **Bourgueil** makes for a pleasant stop, with its ancient abbey and opportunities to buy the excellent local wine. Deep in the verdant country north of Bourgueil, **Gizeux** is worth visiting for its château's wall-paintings and its church's Renaissance tombs.

If you don't have your own transport, you can visit Cinq-Mars-la-Pile and Langeais by **train**, while Luynes is on Tours' excellent suburban **bus** network. The distances mean that it's possible to visit some of the châteaux by **bicycle**, perhaps returning to Tours via Villandry (see p.92). You'd have to be fairly committed to make it round via the bridge at Langeais in a day – a round trip of just under 50km – but you could easily take the train one way. The main N152 road along the riverbank *levée* can be easily avoided for almost all of its length.

Luynes and around

Roughly 1km back from the river and 11km west of Tours, the small town of **LUYNES** nestles under the cliff-like walls of its lofty **château** (April–Sept daily 10am–6pm; €8), which is buttressed by an imposing row of four round towers. In 1619, the château became the ducal home of Charles d'Albret, a favourite of the young Louis XIII, and has remained in the family ever since. As it stands today, the building is an unsettling jumble of styles, its courtyard enclosed by a grim thirteenth-century curtain wall that faces the refined residential wing, itself split into a romantic, brick-built section dating from the 1460s and an elegant, late-seventeenth century wing. The longevity of the Luynes' ownership is palpable if you take the guided tour of the interior, which is richly furnished with the aristocratic apparatus of the last four centuries: family portraits and photographs, weapons, hunting trophies and fine furnishings. Down on the main square, the fifteenth-century wooden-beamed **market hall** dominates place des Halles.

Frequent **buses** (line #55) make the journey out from Tours. On the edge of town, there's a municipal **campsite** (☎02.47.55.60.85; closed mid-Sept to April). For local accommodation, head a couple of kilometres north of town along the D49, following the signposts to the **chambres d'hôtes** at *Le Moulin Hodoux* (☎02.47.55.76.27, ⓦhttp://moulinhodoux.free.fr; ❹), set in a converted watermill on the peaceful little Bresme river, with a small swimming pool and a pretty garden.

If you're in the mood for further exploration, two minor sights lie close at hand. A short detour 3km west along the road signposted to St-Etienne-de-Chigny will take you to **LE VIEUX-BOURG**, where the **church** is a perfectly preserved mid-sixteenth-century construction. The tie-beams of the timber roof are spewed from the mouths of carved monsters, while the east window features a gorgeous stained-glass Crucifixion. Two kilometres northeast of Luynes, off the road towards Fondettes, you can follow a fragment of the course of a **Gallo-Roman aqueduct** along a signposted lane. A handful of tall stone piers, some with brick-lined arches intact, are all that is left of a structure that once carried water from a nearby spring all the way to the Roman town of Caesarodunum, now Tours.

Cinq-Mars-la-Pile

The main road west follows the Loire embankment as far as **CINQ-MARS-LA-PILE**, 18km from Tours, where the Tours–Angers railway line crosses to the northern bank. If you're coming into town by road from Tours, you pass close by the strange *pile* (pillar) from which the town gets its name just before you enter the city limits. Rising roughly thirty perfectly square metres from base to top, or exactly one hundred Roman feet, the brick tower is probably a Gallo-Roman memorial from the second century, though it lacks any inscriptions or the statue niche found in similar structures in southern France. The monumental banality of its construction, adorned only by a few crumbling geometric patterns on the upper part – the turrets are later additions – only adds to the enigma of why it was built. The other part of the town's name, Cinq-Mars, is probably a corruption of St-Médard, the name of the largely Romanesque **church**, which is capped by an octagonal stone spire.

In summer, you can walk around the overgrown ruins of the **château** (April–June & mid-Sept to Oct Sat & Sun 11am–6pm; July to mid-Sept daily except Tues 11am–8pm; €2.30), which consists of two crumbling stumps of twelfth-century towers, with a couple of vaulted ceilings. The present state of decay dates from the treason of Henri Ruzé d'Effiat, the marquis of Cinq-Mars and another of Louis XIII's favourites, who supported Gaston d'Orléans' bid to overthrow Cardinal Richelieu in 1642. As the Loches-born writer Alfred de Vigny describes in his novel, *Cinq-Mars*, d'Effiat was beheaded and his château rendered uninhabitable. You can **stay** in two chambres d'hôtes in a low outbuilding (☎02.47.96.40.49, ⓔchateau-cinq-mars@wanadoo.fr; ❹); they're not especially romantic, but the artist-owner is welcoming.

Langeais

LANGEAIS, 23km west of Tours, is utterly dominated by its forbidding château, which rises up sheer at the end of the town's main street. Otherwise, the small town is peaceful but fairly insipid, though a few fifteenth-century houses are dotted about the centre, notably one immediately opposite the château's drawbridge. Even if you're not stopping in Langeais, it's worth taking a good look at the bridge over the Loire, a 1930s construction whose bizarre concrete towers are intended to mimic the château.

North of Langeais lies the beautifully wooded *landes* country of **Castelvalérie**; the tourist office (see p.89) can provide recommendations of signposted walks and horse-riding centres.

The château

Any hints of luxury and welcome provided by the elegant windows of the **château** (daily: April to mid-July & mid-Aug to mid-Oct 9.30am–6.30pm; mid-July to mid-Aug 9.30am–8pm; mid-Oct to March 10am–5.30pm; €6.50) are obliterated by the combined effect of drawbridge, stone walls and massive towers. The most extraordinary feature of the exterior is the *chemin-de-ronde*, or guard-walk, which smoothly wraps its way round the topmost level of the walls, resting on perfect stone machicolations. On closer inspection, the war-like impression is moderated by subtle details: between each machicolation is a carved trefoil, and the sheer regularity of the structure puts it in a different league from the average medieval fortress built higgledy-piggledy for war.

The château is sometimes described as one of the first stirrings of a new architectural age. It was the work of one **Jean Bourré**, who as a bourgeois lawyer in the service of Louis XI, was himself a sign of the new era. He built numerous châteaux, including Le Plessis-Bourré, in Anjou (see p.269), but Langeais was particularly important as it was done by the king's command, and it had the power to stop potential incursions up the Loire by the Bretons. This threat ended with Charles VIII and Anne de Bretagne's marriage in December 1491, which was celebrated at Langeais (see box opposite).

If you're tired of the bare rooms or misplaced eighteenth-century furnishings of so many châteaux, Langeais is a relief: for once, the furnishings are mostly fifteenth century, to match the building, even if the other decorations are mostly reconstructions. The château is owned by the Institut de France, the wealthy and powerful state foundation which encompasses the Académie Française, among other august bodies. When it was bequeathed the château by the nineteenth-century collector Jacques Siegfried, it also took over his unrivalled and exceptionally valuable **collection of furniture**. This creates a lived-in impression that's rare even in châteaux a century or two younger. There are fascinating tapestries, some rare paintings and polychrome Madonnas, cots and beds, and a number of imposing *chaires*, or seigneurial thrones.

The **Crucifixion room** takes its name from a tapestry of the Crucifixion from the workshop of Rogier van der Weyden; nearby hangs a fine tapestry taken from the église St-Saturnin in Tours. The best is saved for the huge **marriage chamber**, whose centrepiece is Anne's gilded and bejewelled **wedding coffer**. Figures of the apostles, as well as the wise and foolish virgins, are depicted on the lid, while the main body is carved with a miniature Annunciation – an ironic choice, with hindsight, as none of Charles and Anne's four children survived them, thus bringing the Valois dynasty to an end. A diptych of the couple portrays them looking less than joyous at their union, while on the walls is a set of tapestries showing seven of the "Nine Prow Knights", models of chivalric virtue drawn from the Bible, antiquity and early Christianity. The upper-floor **chapel room** – which isn't in fact a chapel though it has a marvellous, church-like wooden ceiling – has a wax-work recreation of the royal wedding, along with piped music and a commentary. From here you can access the **guard-walk**, which you can follow all the way round the château – as long as you're not put off by the dizzy views over the rooftops and out to the river. In summer, swarms of swallows and house martins take up residence, swooping and darting around the machicolations.

The marriage of Anne de Bretagne

On December 6, 1491, a deal was made at the château de Langeais which secured the future of the French kingdom and finally brought to an end the independence of Brittany: **Charles VIII** married **Anne, duchess of Brittany**. The ceremony was conducted under tight security, and the couple travelled separately to Langeais under cover of night.

Secrecy was necessary because of the marriage's enormous significance and its shady political circumstances. Anne was technically already married to **Maximilian**, the Habsburg emperor, who ruled over Austria, the Netherlands, Franche-Comté, Alsace and parts of Burgundy. If he were to inherit Anne's Breton lands, the French kingdom would be all but surrounded by an implacable enemy. Mindful of the threat, France invaded Brittany in December 1488, and by June 1491 Anne was besieged at Rennes. When the city finally fell in October, Anne was forced to give up either her duchy or her marriage to Maximilian. She chose the latter, and Pope Innocent VIII granted her a dispensation annulling her unconsummated marriage to Maximilian (she was only 15). For his part, Charles was already engaged to Maximilian's daughter, Margaret of Austria. Unusually, the couple seem to have been deeply in love – Margaret is known to have wept on hearing of Charles's marriage, and kept his portrait with her until she died – but political necessity prevailed.

The marriage stipulated that Charles would not become duke of Brittany, but it was the end of the duchy's independence anyway, as if Charles were to die before Anne, she would be obliged to marry his successor. Having apparently secured his future, Charles decided to create a fabulous new home for Anne in Amboise (see p.78).

The **gardens** are overlooked by the grim remnants of a **keep**, one of the first of Foulque Nerra's strategic constructions. Built in around 1000 – which makes it one of the earliest of its kind in France – the tower marks Foulque's determination not to relinquish the territories he had wrested from the counts of Blois, who held the rest of Touraine. His grip may not have been as strong as he thought: a contemporary recounts him trying to win back the castle in 1038.

Practicalities

The **gare SNCF**, which has good connections to Tours, Saumur and Angers, is practically in the middle of town. The **tourist office** is next door on place du 14 Juillet (July & Aug Mon–Sat 9.30am–7pm, Sun 10am–12.30pm & 3.30–6pm; rest of year Mon–Sat 9.30am–12.30pm & 2.30–6pm, Sun 10am–12.30pm; ℡02.47.96.58.22, ⓦwww.tourisme-langeais.com).

Langeais is a peaceful place to overnight, and it has a pleasant, thoroughly old-fashioned three-star **hotel**, the *Errard-Hosten*, 2 rue Gambetta (℡02.47.96.82.12, ⓦwww.errard.com; ❹), which offers spacious rooms as an adjunct to its excellent **restaurant** (*menus* €26 & €45). There's also a decent, two-star Logis de France hotel, *La Duchesse Anne* (℡02.47.96.82.03; ❹), which has a relatively inexpensive, but good restaurant. Best of all, there's the *Anne de Bretagne*, 27 rue Anne de Bretagne (℡02.47.96.08.52; ❸), which offers some genuinely exceptional **chambres d'hôtes** in a beautifully restored early nineteenth-century home almost under the walls of the château. For a really refined place to stay, head 16km north along the D57 to the fifteenth-century *Vieux Château d'Hommes*, just outside the village of Hommes (℡02.47.24.95.13, ⓦwww.le-vieux-chateau-de-hommes.com; ❻), where the rooms are in a converted barn in the grounds of the moated château. The attractive municipal **campsite** is 1km from town, off the main road to Tours (☎02.47.96.85.80; closed mid-Sept to May).

Bourgueil

Until the Revolution, the wine town of **BOURGUEIL**, 45km west of Tours on the north bank of the Loire, lay just outside the boundaries of Touraine. It now falls within the *département* of the Indre-et-Loire, Touraine's modern replacement, and for the visitor it is inextricably linked with Chinon, 18km to the south, as the two are great rivals for the title of the producer of the greatest red **wine** in the Loire region. You can taste and buy the wines at the **Maison des Vins**, 18 place de l'Eglise (mid-May to mid-Sept Tues–Sat 10am–12.30pm & 3–7pm; mid-Sept to mid-May Fri 2–6pm, Sat 10am–noon & 2–6pm; free), which is owned and run by local winegrowers; they can also recommend individual *caves* to visit.

The town itself is surprisingly sleepy, though it comes to life on Tuesday mornings, as the network of narrow streets and little squares off the central rue du Commerce fill up with **market** stalls selling local produce – lots of garlic – inexpensive clothing, hunting gear and the like. The chief sights in the handsome old town centre are the large **covered market** on place des Halles and the adjacent church on place de l'Eglise, **St-Germain**, which was over-restored in the nineteenth century but has an unusual Angevin-style choir running the entire width of the nave and aisles. But the showpiece is the ancient **Abbaye de Bourgueil**, which lies at the foot of rue de Tours, on the eastern edge of the town. Unfortunately, the more impressive thirteenth- to seventeenth-century section is occupied by nuns, and can't be visited, but the eighteenth-century wing, with its fine staircase, has been converted into a modest municipal **museum** of folk traditions (April–June, Sept & Oct Sat & Sun 2–6pm; July & Aug Mon & Thurs–Sun 2–6pm; €5), and the town cinema. Just outside town, in the northeastern suburb of Sablons, off the road to Restigné, the **Musée Van Oeveren** (July & Aug Tues–Sat 2–6pm; €6) shows off the owner's aggressive collection of fencing and duelling weapons and ephemera.

Bourgueil's main **festival** is the Fête du Vin du Val de Loire, which attracts some fifty winegrowers on August 15; on the third Tuesday in July the town celebrates garlic; and on the third Tuesday in October chestnuts are honoured. An evening "gourmet market", with stalls selling wines and hot and cold local specialities, arrives in Bourgueil on the third weekend of July and August.

Practicalities

The **tourist office**, 16 place de l'Eglise (mid-May to mid-Sept Mon 3–5.30pm, Tues–Sat 9am–12.30pm & 2.30–6.30pm, Sun 10am–12.30pm; mid-Sept to mid-May Tues–Sat 9am–12.30pm & 2.30–6pm; ☎02.47.97.91.39, ⓦwww.ot-bourgueil.fr), can give advice on visiting the surrounding region, including the handful of **Boule de Fort** clubs, where you can watch or join in the Angevin version of bowls, which is played on a curved, wooden floor.

The best two **hotels** lie cheek by jowl on the narrow rue de Tours, just a few steps from the covered market. The ageing but comfortably bourgeois *Ecu de France*, 9 rue de Tours (☎02.47.97.70.18, ⓔecu-de-france@wanadoo.fr; ❷), occupies a handsome old post-house, and has attractive, old-fashioned rooms with boxed-off shower units in the corner. Next door, *Le Faisan Doré*, 5 rue de Tours (☎02.47.97.72.44, ⓕ02.47.97.95.64; ❷), is more working-class in tone, with a bar and an admirably inexpensive evening *menu*; there are cheap, rather mean rooms in an annexe out back, and more expensive rooms in the main building, the latter newly done up with wood-effect floors and decent furnishings. Both hotels have good restaurants, and serve lunch or dinner at street-side tables.

For somewhere really special to stay, make for the *Château des Réaux* (☎02.47.95.14.40, ℮reaux@club-internet.fr; ➏–➒), on a backroad between the towns of Chouzé-sur-Loire and Port-Boulet, 5km from Bourgueil. The château's adorable hodge-podge of styles dates back to the Renaissance, and the whole thing is surrounded by a moat and well-tended but informal gardens. The rooms are delightfully romantic and unprecious – though make sure you ask for one in the main body of the château – and the welcome is warm and genuine – you can even help yourself to drinks at the bar.

If you don't want to eat at one of Bourgueil's hotel **restaurants**, try the *Moulin Bleu*, 7 rte du Moulin Bleu, 2km out of town on the road to St-Nicolas-de-Bourgueil (☎02.47.97.73.13; *menus* from €17; closed Tues evening & Wed), which serves lots of good, winey regional specialities, and has a lovely rural situation.

Gizeux

North of Bourgueil, you can follow the course of the little river Changeon upstream through heavily wooded, sparsely populated backcountry to the tranquil village of **GIZEUX**, 13km away. At the end of a long avenue of giant plane trees, the **château** (May–Sept Mon–Sat 10am–6pm, Sun 2–6pm; €6; ⓦwww.gizeux.free.fr) extends like a game of dominoes around its grassy grounds, each wing dating from a different epoch. A resident theatre company arrives every summer – offering children's workshops and classics of French theatre presented as a walkabout on Friday and Saturday evenings – and there's always an exhibition of dolls of some kind, but the main reason for English-speakers to visit is to see two remarkable sets of **wall-paintings**.

The core of the château was built in the sixteenth century by the **du Bellay** family – from the Plessis-Macé branch (see p.268), rather than that of the poet Joachim. In the 1590s, Marie de Yvetôt, the wife of René du Bellay, commissioned an unknown artist to decorate the wooden panelling of the central **salon**, and the result still graces the walls in its original, unrestored state. Colourful floral designs compete with biblical and mythological *grisailles*, set against an ancient terracotta floor scattered with threadbare chairs from the eras of Louis XIII, Louis XIV and Louis XV. Roughly one hundred years later, one Anne de la Frézollière bought the château from the daughters of the du Bellay family, which had no male heirs, and ordered a rival decoration for the **long gallery**. She offered the blank walls to pupils from the painting school at Fontainebleau, who set about practising views of great French châteaux. Initially, the result is hilariously cack-handed, with châteaux such as Chambord rendered with amazingly bad proportions (and suspiciously identical dogs), but as you progress down the gallery the work becomes more assured.

A signposted circuit offers a four-kilometre **walk** around the village, passing the château and the adjacent **église Notre-Dame**, where you can see the white marble **tomb** effigies of René du Bellay and his severe-looking wife Marie, kneeling in the south transept in prayer. It's one of the finest works of the Tourangeau sculptor Nicolas Guillain, and strangely affecting if you've just admired the Du Bellays' home improvements at the château. Across in the north transept, the superficially similar tomb of Martin du Bellay and his wife Louise de Savennières was sculpted less than twenty years later, but the style of the stonework, and the costumes, is already quite different.

If you're approaching from Bourgueil, you can visit a working, seventeenth-century watermill on the way. Turn off after 8km at a signpost for the **Moulin Scée** (Tues–Sun: May, June & first 2 weeks of Sept 1.30pm, 3pm & 4.30pm;

July & Aug 10am, 11.30am, 2.30pm & 4pm; free), then drive 1km along a rural backroad. The charming – but monolingual – miller will happily show you round, and demonstrate the process by which he makes flour for discerning local *boulangeries*.

The northern half of the circular GRP **footpath**, the Côteaux de Bourgueil, encompasses the whole Changeon valley; walking the complete northern route from Bourgeuil to Gizeux and back would be an ambitious full-day expedition, taking you through undulating woodland and past the occasional hamlet. The FFRP's walking guide, *La Touraine à pied* (see Basics, p.42) outlines a shorter, three-hour circuit around Continvoir, 2km east of Bourgueil, taking you through beautiful, lightly wooded countryside.

Villandry

Even if gardens aren't your thing, those at the **château de Villandry** are definitely worth a visit – and the château itself is a beautifully restored Renaissance gem. Even getting there can be a pleasure, as Villandry is a superb cycle ride from Tours, 13km east along the Cher.

The château

The **château de Villandry** (gardens daily: May–Sept 9am–7.30pm, rest of year till dusk; château daily: mid-Feb to April & Oct to mid-Nov 9am–dusk, May–Sept 9am–6pm; €7.50 château and gardens, €5 gardens only; Ⓦ www.chateauvillandry.com) is one of the highlights of the region, so if you want to explore in peace, arrive early, late or at lunchtime.

The château was erected in the 1530s by one of François I's royal financiers, **Jean le Breton**. Like so many of the court's banker-accountants, Le Breton was eager to legitimize his new status – and launder his fortune – so he purchased and then knocked down the twelfth-century château des Colombiers (see box opposite), preserving only the feudal keep as a symbol of his arrival as an aristocrat. Le Breton's Renaissance structure still abuts this keep, arranged around three sides of a *cour d'honneur*, the fourth wing having been demolished in the eighteenth century, at the same time as the apparently Renaissance details around the windows and dormers were recarved. The square towers closing off the courtyard, which look more like eighteenth-century work, are actually an extremely novel part of Le Breton's original scheme – by the time that Le Breton began building here, the court had quit the Loire valley for Fontainebleau, and the sober architecture of Paris and its Ile-de-France region was in the ascendant.

Little is known about the original design of the gardens, as they were totally remodelled in the nineteenth century in the then-fashionable style of an English country park. In 1906, however, the château was bought by an American heiress, Ann Coleman, whose husband, **Joachim Carvallo**, a Spanish doctor, decided to recreate a French garden in the grandest and most historically accurate style.

The gardens

Carvallo's research led him to believe that gardens were as much symbolical as ornamental or practical, so at the topmost level, very much in the elevated Classical spirit, is the **water garden**, a large pond surrounded by neat lawns and carefully trained lime trees. Water flows down from it through a small canal that runs underneath the walls of the old keep and fills the château's moat. Next down, at the level of the château itself, the **ornamental garden** "serves as an extension of the salon", according to Carvallo. It reflects the middle state of the human condition, poised between divine rationality and base animal desires. Four geometrical arrangements of immaculately trimmed box hedges symbolize different kinds of love: tender, passionate, fickle and tragic – the dark green of the box enflamed by red flowers in summer. At the top end of this section are three crosses – Maltese, Languedoc and Basque – while another box garden on the opposite side of the canal acts as a less successful allegory of music.

The highlight, spread out across 12,500 square metres of perfectly flat ground, is the **potager**, or Renaissance kitchen garden. Symbolically and physically, it may be the lowest and most vulgar part of the gardens, but it is the most fascinating. Carrots, cabbages and aubergines are arranged into intricate patterns, while rose bowers and miniature box hedges form a kind of frame. Even in winter, there is almost always something to see, as the entire area is replanted twice a year. Sadly, the vegetables are not sold for consumption, but when the beds are thinned out in the summer months you can sometimes find tomatoes, aubergines, peppers and the like in a box in one corner of the garden – just leave a coin for the gardeners' annual dinner. Other vegetables are simply mulched. Up close, keen amateurs can admire rare and beautifully presented varieties, while city-bred kids may get a kick out of trying simply to work out which vegetable is which – placards provide a key. At the far end of the garden, overlooked by the squat tower of the village church, beautiful vine-shaded paths give onto the medieval **herb garden** and the **maze**. Just beyond, there's a children's playground.

There are various **festivals** throughout the year, notably the *potager* weekend, in early September, with lots of workshops and demonstrations, and the Nuits des Mille Feux, on the first weekend of July, when the gardens are lit by hundreds of candles at night.

The last days of Henry Plantagenêt

By the summer of 1189, **Henry II**, king of England and ruler of the great Angevin empire, was old, fat and suffering from a severe anal abscess, but he hadn't lost his appetite for fighting. His son, Richard the Lionheart, had joined forces with his arch-enemy, the French king Philippe-Auguste, and their combined armies had captured Le Mans, Henry's beloved birthplace. Henry watched as the city burned, cursing God "thou hast vilely taken away the city I loved best on earth ... I will pay thee back as best I can." The French armies pursued Henry as he fled south towards his castle of Chinon (see p.102). They captured Tours on the way, leaving Henry nowhere to hide. Philippe-Auguste summoned Henry to a conference at Colombiers, modern **Villandry**, and demanded that he do homage to the French king for all his territories on the Continent. Further, Richard was to be confirmed as heir, and would be allowed to marry his betrothed, Alais – who had become Henry's mistress. Henry could hardly remain upright on his horse but refused to dismount. As he agreed to submit to the terms, and bent forward to give his son the kiss of peace, he whispered, "God grant that I may not die till I have had a fitting revenge on you." He was then carried back to **Chinon**, where he plotted vengeance even as he lay dying. But when he learned that his youngest son, John, had also joined the rebellion, Henry turned his face to the wall saying, "I care no more for myself nor for aught in this world." Hours later, he died in delirious agony, shouting over and over, "Shame, shame on a vanquished king."

The interior

It's worth paying the extra to visit the **château**, if only for the unmissable turret-top view over the gardens and out to the confluence of the Loire and Cher. Inside, the château is the epitome of eighteenth-century elegance, Carvallo having decided that restoring Renaissance standards of comfort wouldn't make for an ideal home. The **dining room** suggests the transition from inside to outdoors, with its Provençal marble fountain and bizarre terracotta stove, and windows looking onto the ornamental garden. The nearby staircase is an eighteenth-century addition, replacing the unfashionably medieval spiral staircase which used to stand in the *cour d'honneur*. The views over the gardens improve on the first floor, from the exquisite bedrooms. The **long gallery** is lined with the Carvallos' collection of Spanish paintings, many of them distressingly religiose, and it leads to a stunning **Mudejar ceiling**, which was brought to Villandry from a fifteenth-century palace in Toledo and painstakingly reassembled. On first sight, the intricate arabesques and geometric patterns in gilded and coloured wood are pure Moorish work, but Spanish Christian motifs recur, notably the scallops – the symbol of St James of Compostela – that frame each corner.

Les Grottes Pétrifiantes de Savonnières

The unprepossessing entrance to the **Grottes Pétrifiantes de Savonnières** lies on the main road to Tours, 1km east of Villandry (Feb & March daily 9.30am–noon & 2–5.30pm; April–Sept daily 9am–6.30pm; Oct to mid-Dec Tues, Wed & Fri–Sun 9.30am–noon & 2–5.30pm; €5.20; Ⓦwww.grottes-savonnieres.com). These so-called caves are in fact abandoned medieval quarries, though the slow trickle of water through calcite has formed plenty of natural stalactites and stalagmites, some of them moderately impressive. The owners have turned the process to commercial use, producing an amazingly kitsch array of petrified objects by leaving dolls and pots and little statuettes exposed to the flow, all of which are for sale in the shop. It gets a little chilly during the forty-plus-minute tour, which takes you some distance through the underground tunnels, so bring a coat or jumper.

Practicalities

To **get to Villandry**, in summer you can take a **minibus** directly from Tours (Ⓣ02.47.70.37.37); the service leaves from the tourist office at 10am and 2.30pm and costs €16 return. There are two attractive places to **stay** nearby, both with small swimming pools. The *Château du Vau*, 6km east of Villandry, between Savonnières and Ballan-Miré (Ⓣ02.47.67.84.04, Ⓦwww.chez.com/chateauduvau; ➏) is a large private château set in its own grounds, with five guest rooms. On the edge of Savonnières, the *Prieuré des Granges*, 15 rue des Fontaines (Ⓣ02.47.50.09.67, Ⓦwww.prieuredesgranges.com; ➐), is a rambling old priory, with half a dozen discreet rooms, some of which give onto private gardens.

Just past Villandry, 1km down the D121 towards Druye, an upmarket farmhouse **restaurant**, the *Domaine de la Giraudière* (Ⓣ02.47.50.08.60; *menus* from €13; closed mid-Nov to mid-March), throngs with families enjoying meals in the courtyard on summer evenings. The food is honest home-cooked fare, with the farm's own goat's cheese featuring prominently.

Azay-le-Rideau

Even without its château, the quiet village of **AZAY-LE-RIDEAU**, 27km southwest of Tours, would bask in its serene setting, complete with an old mill by the bridge and an ancient church. On its little island in the Indre, the château is one of the loveliest in the entire Loire region: perfect turreted early Renaissance, pure in style down to the blood-red paint of its window frames. The village's apparently odd name needs some explanation: *rideau* doesn't actually mean "curtain", but derives from the Ridel family, who occupied a minor fortress at Azay in the thirteenth century. In fact, the village was known for centuries as Azay-le-Brûlé ("the burnt"), after the Dauphin Charles smoked out a Burgundian garrison here in 1418.

Arrival and information

Trains from Tours call at Azay-le-Rideau on their way to Chinon roughly every two hours (some services are replaced by SNCF buses). Cyclists should pick up the SNCF's useful leaflet, *Autour du Train* (ⓦ www.autourdutrain .asso.fr); it gives timetable information and recommends a thirty-kilometre one-way route, stopping off at Villandry on the way between Tours and Azay-le-Rideau. The **gare SNCF** is awkwardly situated a fifteen-minute walk west of the centre, along ave Riché.

Azay's **tourist office** sits just off the main rue Nationale, on place de l'Europe (May, June & Sept Mon–Sat 9am–1pm & 2–6pm, Sun 10am–1pm & 2–5pm; July & Aug Mon–Sat 9am–7pm, Sun 10am–6pm; Oct–April Mon–Sat 9am–1pm & 2–6pm; ☎02.47.45.44.40, ⓦ www.ot-paysazaylerideau.com). The **bus stop** is on the main road, immediately beside it, while the village's main square, **place de la République**, is just behind. You can rent **bikes** from Cycles Leprovost, 13 rue Carnot (☎02.47.45.40.94), or from the Maison des Jeunes, Parc du Sabot (☎02.47.45.30.12), which in summer also hires out

AZAY-LE-RIDEAU

ACCOMMODATION
Le Clos Philippa	D
Le Grand Monarque	A
Hôtel de Biencourt	E
Manoir de la Rémonière	F
M et Mme Sarrazin	C
Les Trois Lys	B

RESTAURANTS
L' Aigle d'Or	1
Les Grottes	4
La Ridelloise	3
La Salamandre	2

canoes for short trips on the Indre. An overpriced **Internet café** and snack shop, *Le Petit Gousier*, 12 rue Balzac (€2 for 15min), can be found just off the main square.

Accommodation

Azay-le-Rideau has a trio of pleasant **hotels**, budget, mid-range and fairly expensive, clustered round its main square, as well as two excellent chambres d'hôtes and a fantastic château offering accommodation. The nearest **campsite**, *Camping du Sabot* (☎02.47.45.42.72; closed Nov–March), lies upstream from the château, signposted off the D84 to Saché.

Le Clos Philippa 10 rue de Pineau ☎02.47.45.26.49. Delightful chambres d'hôtes in an old, L-shaped house a few steps away from the château. Rooms are large and well appointed with tiled floors or floorboards, water decanters by the beds and lots of swags of good French fabrics giving an antique feel. ❹

Le Grand Monarque 3 place de la République ☎02.47.45.40.08, ⓦ www.legrandmonarque.com. The poshest hotel in the village, a solid three-star with a traditional, slightly formal atmosphere and handsome, attractively furnished rooms with "historic" touches such as beams and exposed stone walls. A pleasant walled garden makes a good place for breakfast. Closed mid-Dec to Jan. ❺–❾

Hôtel de Biencourt 7 rue Balzac ☎02.47.45.20.75, ⓔ biencourt@infonie.fr. This attractive and unpretentious two-star hotel has a great location on a quiet side-street leading down from the market square to the church and château. The actual building is eighteenth-century – in lovely white stone, with charming red shutters – but the interiors are largely modernized, and furnished in a mixture of styles. The nicest rooms are in the old school building at the end of the little garden. A handful of inexpensive rooms (❷) come with showers only, and there's a big family room under the roof. Closed mid-Nov to Feb. ❹

Manoir de la Rémonière 1km from Azay on the opposite side of the Indre, on the road to Saché ☎02.47.45.24.88. The best option by far if you can afford it. Once the château's fifteenth-century hunting lodge, it now does bed and breakfast, with some atmospheric and slightly ramshackle rooms in the main building, and less interesting ones in the outbuildings. Has a small, unheated outdoor pool. ❻–❼

M et Mme Sarrazin 9 chemin des Caves Mecquelines ☎02.47.45.31.25, ⓔ sarrazin .alaincathy@wanadoo.fr. The friendly young owners offer a rare chance to actually sleep in a troglodyte room, in a quiet location just out of the village, on the D84 heading east. There are two rooms, both adorable: one is small and cosy, with a hollowed-out bedchamber off the living room, a miniature kitchenette and a wonderful hacked-out bathroom deep in the rock; the other (❹) is large and retro in style, with a big central fireplace, a proper kitchen, a mezzanine level for the main bed and spare beds for an extra two people. ❸

Les Trois Lys 2 rue du Château ☎02.47.45.20.36, ⓦ www.lecheval-rouge.com. The only budget option, though it isn't in fact all that inexpensive. Acceptable, but in need of a refit. ❷

The château

The romantic hero of Balzac's novel *Le Lys dans la Vallée* described Azay-le-Rideau's **château** (daily: April–June & Sept 9.30am–6pm; July & Aug 9.30am–7pm; Oct–March 10am–12.30pm & 2–5.30pm; €5.50; ⓦ www.monum.fr) as "a diamond cut with facets, set in the Indre, and mounted on piles hidden by flowers". The flowers may have been tidied away in the last century and a half but "diamond" remains exactly the right word: Azay really is the most precious and captivating of all the Loire's châteaux – and the one requiring the most minute examination if you want to discover its true value. The setting in the waters of the Indre remains as exquisite as when Balzac saw it, the famous reflection now fringed by the mature trees of landscaped gardens. You'll have to pay the entrance fee if you want to have a good look at the outside, as the château is hidden away behind high walls and a leafy driveway.

Begun in 1518, Azay was one of the very first truly Renaissance châteaux to be built in France, an expression of the new wealth, power and cultural ambition of the merchants and bankers of Tours who surrounded Louis XII and François I. Azay's builder, **Gilles Berthelot**, was one of four powerful *trésoriers* of France. He was also a close relation of Jacques de Beaune-Semblançay, the great banker behind François I's overspending, and a cousin of Catherine Briçonnet, the *grande dame* of the château de Chenonceau, which predates Azay by just five years. In an atmosphere of fierce rivalry for cultivated extravagance, Berthelot threw up his château as fast as he could, famously getting his team of mason Etienne Rousseau, sculptor Pierre Maupoint and carpenter Jacques Thoreau – all Frenchmen, despite the Italian influences in their designs – to work literally day and night. Even so, Azay wasn't finished before Berthelot and his cronies fell from favour in the huge corruption scandal of 1527 (see p.309), and what stands today is probably only half a château. It's likely that the original plan would have been for four identical wings enclosing a courtyard, and you can still see a rough edge where work stopped in 1527, when Berthelot fled for Metz.

The **courtyard** is dominated by the great open **staircase**, a structure as important as the feudal towers of earlier châteaux in defining the status of the *seigneur*. It even looks like a tower in reverse, a space carved out of the main body of the château, with flat, lace-like encrustations of stone carving defining the space behind. The balustrades on the first- and third-floor levels of the staircase bear the emblems of François I and his wife, the salamander and the ermine, while delicately carved Classical motifs crawl over the creamy stone. The loggia-like pairs of the staircase's window arches are particularly Italian in inspiration. There is one anomaly: the large tower on the right as you approach the courtyard was added in the mid-nineteenth century, replacing an incongruous-looking medieval tower that Berthelot never got round to demolishing.

You don't need to know anything about architecture to love the **southern facade** of the château: it's breathtakingly pretty, rising out of a broad, pool-like stretch of the slow-moving Indre. It's striking in its perfect symmetry, each corner finished off by an *échauguette* tower daintily suspended just above the water level, each row of windows defined by a neat horizontal string course and delicate pilasters pointing up to the dormers in the roof, and the whole facade drawn together by the noble windows of the central axis. A guard-walk runs all the way round the topmost level, but it's hardly a fortification: the machicolations look suspiciously like a Classical cornice.

The **interior**, dolled up with the usual miscellany of period and reproduction furnishings and tapestries of all eras, doesn't add much to the experience, but the grand staircase is worth seeing close up. The medallions of the kings and queens of France on the first flight are nineteenth-century additions, while those in the loggia above date from the sixteenth century, depicting kings, philosophers and possibly Gilles Berthelot and his Blésoise wife Philippe Lesbahy. The ground floor was refitted by the **Marquis de Biencourt**, the château's owner in the nineteenth century, with the obligatory library and billiard room. The **gardens** are another of Biencourt's additions, fashionably styled as an English landscaped park.

Azay's **nocturnal spectacle**, Les Imaginaires d'Azay-le-Rideau (May, June & Sept Fri–Sun from 9.30pm; July daily from 10.30pm; Aug daily from 10pm; €9, or €12 with daytime château entry), is one of the best in the region. Elaborate lighting effects transform the château with beautiful patterns that, not incidentally, illustrate the geometric principles behind its architecture. You can wander freely round the grounds admiring the spectacle from all angles, all the while being serenaded by loudspeakers hidden behind bushes.

St-Symphorien

Relatively few visitors make the effort to visit the **église St-Symphorien** (daily 9am–7pm), though it's right next to the château and its western front is adorned with one of the strangest and most compelling bits of stonework in the region, a rare survival of the **Carolingian renaissance** of the ninth century. High above the main door, two rows of strange, doll-like statues stand impassively below triangular patches of lozenge-shaped stones that seem to mimic roofs. The whole thing looks like a facade within a facade, but sadly, the lower row of figures was rudely cut through by a window in the thirteenth century, when the current church was built. The crossed halo of the central figure in the upper row indicates Christ, but the identities of the other statues are disputed. Curiously, the saints on Christ's left have halos, while the figures on the right – perhaps disciples of St-Symphorien – have none. The nave aisle on the left of the main facade, with its beautiful wide door, was added in 1578.

Eating and drinking

For something simple, *La Salamandre*, a simple **restaurant** and pizzeria with a terrace overlooking the main square, is reliable enough, but you'd do much better at *La Ridelloise*, 24 rue Nationale (☎02.47.45.46.53; *menus* €11–23), which has a pleasant stone-and-beams setting matched with a family atmosphere and inexpensive but decent cooking. For a really special meal out, especially in summer, make for *L'Aigle d'Or*, 10 ave Adélaïde Riché (☎02.47.45.24.58; *menus* €26–58; closed Wed & Sun evening), which serves elegant and sometimes inspired cuisine in its delightful garden, shaded by a catalpa tree; lots of dishes come in sauces of local wine, and bottles are reasonably priced. At *Les Grottes*, 23ter rue de Pineau (☎02.47.45.21.04; *menus* €21–37; closed Thurs), you can eat good regional specialities in a troglodyte cave carved out of the rock, but it's touristy and slightly overpriced.

Around Azay-le-Rideau

I found infinite love written in the long ribbon of water streaming in the sun between two green banks, in the rows of poplars adorning this vale of love with their flickering lacework, in the oak trees rising between the vineyards on the ever-changing slopes that the river rounds off, and in the shadowy horizons shifting athwart each other.

Honoré de Balzac, *Le Lys dans la Vallée*

Around Azay-le-Rideau, the shy **River Indre** lies concealed for the most part by thickets of willows and poplars, or hidden in the middle of wide water meadows that soak up the regular floods. You'll only actually see the river when you cross it, which you can do at Azay-le-Rideau, or downstream at marshy **Marnay** where there's a giant museum of motor vehicles. The gardens at nearby **La Chatonnière** make the most of the well-watered, sunny climate. Southwest of Marnay, the Indre makes a dogleg and begins to parallel the line of the Loire, less than a kilometre away. The broad, shared floodplain is overlooked to the south by the wooded heights of the Forêt de Chinon (see p.108), at the edge of which stands the fairy-tale **château d'Ussé** and the village of **Rivarennes**, where a rustic technique for drying pears is still practised. Upstream of Azay-le-Rideau, you can visit the cave-village of **Les**

Goupillières on the way to another Indre bridge at Saché, where Balzac had his summer writing retreat. Nearby, a tiny, willow-rich tributary valley conceals the village of Villaines-les-Rochers, a miniature centre for basket-weaving.

Downstream of Azay-le-Rideau

Four kilometres from Azay-le-Rideau, just off the D57 which runs west along the right bank of the Indre, lie the exceptional **gardens** at **LA CHATON-NIERE** (April–Oct 10am–7pm; €5; ⓦ www.lachatonniere.com). The setting alone – in a fold of the valley, under the shadow of a private Renaissance château – is gorgeous, while the gardens themselves are a showpiece for French-style design. Master gardener Ahmed Azéronal has developed nine gardens (so far) since 1995, all following carefully considered themes. Among the most enticing are the Jardin de l'Elégance, set around lawns with statues and ponds; the Jardin des Sens, with hundreds of tea roses; the Jardin de l'Abondance, a *potager* of endless varieties of vegetables beautifully presented in a leaf-shaped area; and the Jardin des Sciences, made up of medicinal herbs. Behind it all are six hectares of wildflowers appropriately named the Jardin de l'Exuberance.

If you continue 2km to Lignières-de-Touraine, then turn back towards the Indre on the D7 for 3km, you'll reach **MARNAY** and the **Musée Maurice Defresne** (daily: Feb, March & Nov 9.15am–6pm; April–Oct 9.15am–7pm; €10; ⓦ www.musee-dufresne.com). This absolutely giant collection of motorized vehicles, especially tractors, was brought together by M. Dufresne himself, a successful local manufacturer of tractor trailers and dealer in agricultural implements. There are endless tractors, of course, but also scooters, cars, planes and motorized ploughs, plus a British double-decker bus, Blériot's 1909 plane, a working turbine watermill and even a Revolution-era guillotine. It's magical or interminable, according to your point of view – there always seem to be local grandads showing their grandchildren round, but you probably need to be something of a petrol-head to really enjoy it, or get a shiver of nostalgia when you see a 1930s Massey-Ferguson.

Three kilometres further down the D7 on the road to Rigny-Ussé, the inhabitants of the pretty village of **RIVARENNES** have revived a bizarre local speciality, "hammered pears". An old barn houses the tiny, co-operatively run **Musée des Poires Tapées** (April–Sept daily except Mon 10am–12.30pm & 2–6.30pm; €2.50), where you can find out how the pears are traditionally dried in ovens and "tapped" to check their moisture content. A video describes how the technique died out in the 1930s but was successfully revived in the late 1980s, and you can taste and buy the actual product – it's amazing cooked with duck, or steeped in wine and sugar.

Rigny-Ussé

With its shimmering white towers and terraced gardens, the **château d'Ussé** (daily: mid-Feb to March & Oct to mid-Nov 10am–noon & 2–5.30pm; April–Sept 9.30am–6.30pm; grounds and outbuildings €3; guided tour €9.80; ⓦ www.tourisme.fr/usse) is the quintessence of a fairy-tale castle – so much so that it's supposed to have inspired Charles Perrault's classic retelling of the **Sleeping Beauty** myth, *La Belle au bois dormant*. The château lies on the edge of the village of **RIGNY-USSÉ**, 14km west of Azay-le-Rideau, as the Indre approaches its confluence with the Loire.

The exterior is beautiful, a late-fifteenth-century vision of white turrets and machicolations largely built by Antoine de Bueil, comte de Sancerre, who married the illegitmate daughter of Charles VII and Agnès Sorel (see p.118). The inner courtyard was once closed by a fourth wing, demolished in the seventeenth century to improve the picturesque view.

Going inside for the **guided tour** isn't half as compelling as you'd expect, and hardly worth the high entrance fee. You are shown the Oriental collections of a nineteenth-century duc de Blacas, the ancestor of the present proprietors, then the old chapel, now fitted out as an aristocratic drawing room full of tapestries and furnishings from across the centuries, the kitchens and a long, tapestry-lined eighteenth-century gallery. The highlights are the iron-balustraded staircase designed by François Mansard, the King's Bedchamber on the first floor, with its eighteenth-century wall-hangings of Tours silk, and the choice furnishings – notably the Mazarin-style desk inlaid with lemon wood, in the old chapel, and the Boulle desk in red tortoiseshell and brass, in the bedchamber.

It wouldn't hurt to skip the tour of the interior, as you can still take in the **gardens** designed by Le Nôtre, and the tall **round tower** whose theatrical attic rooms are populated by dressed-up dummies illustrating the story of Sleeping Beauty – a hit with some younger children. You also get to see the loveliest feature of all, the Renaissance **chapel** in the grounds, shaded by ancient cedars.

Practicalities

The **village** is little more than a few houses stretching along the road, but there's a very welcoming family-run hotel, *Le Clos d'Ussé* (☎ & ☏02.47.95.55.47; ❶–❸), which offers just eight simple, old-fashioned rooms, including some inexpensive ones with shared bathrooms; the hotel restaurant is inexpensive and homely. Set in a tranquil, wooded fold of the valley behind the château, the *Domaine de la Juranvillerie*, 15 rue des Fougères (☎02.47.95.57.85, ✉dm.cutini@wanadoo.fr; ❸), is a charming little group of cottages, one housing a simple, attractive **chambre d'hôtes** with a bedroom upstairs and a dining room below (the medieval-themed table d'hôte costs €18); the friendly owners are enthusiastic naturalists and can advise on walks in the Forêt de Chinon. To get there, take the D7 east of Ussé and turn right after about 2km at the signpost; it lies just beyond the ruined abbey of **Turpenay**.

La Vallée Troglodytique des Goupillières

As the D84 backroad passes out of Azay-le-Rideau, heading east, it's overshadowed on the left by low, creamy cliffs riddled with **caves** used as storehouses, wine *caves* and even homes – one of which offers chambres d'hôtes (see p.96). These chambers are the modern-day remnants of the region's fascinating *troglodyte* (cave-dwelling) traditions, which can be explored at the fascinating complex of **LES GOUPILLIERES**, 3km from Azay-le-Rideau (April–Nov Mon–Fri 10am–7pm, Sat & Sun 2–7pm; €4).

The "troglodyte valley" is actually a paddock-like area depressed five or six metres below the level of the surrounding farmland, its outer edges burrowed away to create cave farmhouses, cave barns, cave grain silos and even a cave rabbit-hutch. The whole "village" was hacked out of the soft tufa rock by hand, over hundreds of years, new rooms and dwellings being added – or rather subtracted – as need arose. It was gradually abandoned around a hundred years ago, but has been rediscovered and re-excavated by a knowledgeable local family, who now run the guided tours with infectious enthusiasm. They also keep goats, hens, ducks, geese and even pot-bellied pigs, making the site feel almost like a well-tended, working farm rather than some sort of sterile archeological dig. In one of the more ancient caves you can see the niches used for silkworm production, the silk being sold at Tours. Another was used in medieval times as a refuge from marauding bands of mercenaries and soldiers; as you're shown the false tunnel leading to a murder-hole, and the real tunnel plunging deeper underground to a chamber big enough for all the village and its animals, the insecurity of peasant life is shockingly brought home.

Saché

Continuing east from Les Goupillières on the D84, you pass the hamlet of **LA SABLONNIERE**. Just to the north, on top of a hill surrounded by vines, with beautiful views of the Indre valley, was the last *atelier* of **Alexander Calder**, sculptor of mobiles and "stabiles". Calder also worked at **La Chevrière**, just down the slope to the east.

One of the artist's toy-like mobiles decorates the main square of **SACHÉ**, 8km from Azay-le-Rideau. However, it is **Honoré de Balzac** rather than Calder who draws the pilgrims to Saché, as the writer often stayed at the small château, describing it as "a melancholy abode full of harmonies". He sought peace and inspiration here, though complaining that "there's no peace living in a château. People come to visit and you have to dress at a particular time. Provincial people find it very odd that anyone should want to miss dinner in order to pursue an idea." He nevertheless managed to write several of his 91 novels at Saché, notably *Le Père Goriot* and *Le Lys dans la Vallée*. The sixteenth- and seventeenth-century manor house has been turned into the **Musée Balzac** (daily: April–Sept 9am–7pm; Oct–March 9.30am–12.30pm & 2–5.30pm; €3.80, grounds only €1.50), with lots of imprints, caricatures and bits of manuscripts. The most compelling rooms are those decorated in full, florid nineteenth-century style, preserved or restored exactly as they were when Balzac stayed here. The vestibule is heavy with the sound of a grand-father clock, the dining room thickly carpeted and painted with lurid, mint-green walls, and the walls of the *salon* decorated imperial-style with swags of painted cloth apparently hanging from lion's-face medallions. Upstairs, in Balzac's writing room and bedroom, a crucifix hangs over his cot-like bed; adjacent, his writing desk stands next to the window and the view across the valley.

Villaines-les-Rochers

Six kilometres south of Azay-le-Rideau is the troglodyte village of **VIL-LAINES-LES-ROCHERS**, famous for its wickerwork co-operative, set up in 1849 by the local curate to keep the village economically sustainable. It's a weird place, tucked into a secretive, enclosed valley bristling with pollarded willows, and there are now seventy-odd *vanneries* (wicker workshops) in and around the village – wickerwork signs seem to hang from every house. You can visit the **Musée de la Vannerie** (May–Sept daily except Mon 2.30–6.30pm; €2.50), which has surprisingly interesting exhibitions on the theme of wick-erwork and willow, and buy baskets, chairs and so forth from the **Coopérative de Vannerie**, 1 rue de la Cheneillère (July & Aug daily 9am–7pm; Sept–June Mon–Sat 9am–noon & 2–7pm, Sun 10am–noon & 2–7pm; ⓦ www.vanner-ie.com), or at one of the many *vanneries* dotted around the village. Many are dug into the rock, providing the perfect humid conditions for keeping the wil-low supple.

Chinon

You could be forgiven for thinking that **CHINON**, 52km southwest of Tours, was still a Plantagenêt fief. More than 100,000 tourists visit each year, ten times the local population, and an unusual proportion of them are English. The physical attractions are obvious – the ruined castle, the medieval streets, the situation on the banks of the smooth Vienne, the excellent local vineyards – but many Chinonais believe that something deeper is at work, an abiding sense that Chinon, for all its quintessential provincial Frenchness, is in some way part of the English patrimony. Increasingly, it actually is: scores of the fine old manor houses in the countryside round Chinon now belong to English people, both holiday-makers and permanent residents.

Arrival and information

The train line from Tours and Azay-le-Rideau passes through the beautiful, thickly wooded Forêt de Chinon before terminating at Chinon's **gare SNCF**, which lies to the east of the town. From here, ave Pierre Labussière and rue du 11-Novembre lead to the **gare routière** on the large place Jeanne-d'Arc, ten minutes' walk away, at the eastern edge of the old town. Keep heading west, either along the riverbank or across place Mirabeau into rue Rabelais, and you'll soon reach the old quarter. The **tourist office** is on place d'Hofheim, off the central rue Jean-Jacques Rousseau (May–Sept daily 10am–7pm; Oct–April Mon–Sat 10am–noon & 2–6pm; ☎02.47.93.17.85, ⓦwww.chinon.com), and can provide addresses of local vineyards where you can taste Chinon's famous red wine. If you plan to visit a number of sights in the region, consider buying the Carte Ambassadeur (see box on p.55).

An antiques and flea market takes place every third Sunday of the month, while regular **market day** is Thursday. Just beside the campsite, Confluence Chinon Canoë-Kayak (☎06.84.94.74.69) hires out **canoes** and kayaks in July and August, and runs half-day and full-day guided trips. **Bathing** in the Vienne near Chinon is discouraged, as it's potentially dangerous due to collapsing sandbanks and freak currents.

Accommodation

Chinon has an excellent selection of **hotels**, and there are some enticing **châteaux** offering accommodation in the countryside around. For a full list of chambres d'hôtes, including châteaux, contact the tourist office. The **campsite**, *Camping de l'Ile Auger* (☎02.47.93.08.35; closed mid-Oct to mid-March), overlooks the old town and château from the south bank of the Vienne.

Château de Coulaine Beaumont-en-Véron, 6km from Chinon ☎02.47.93.01.27. Superb late-medieval château with an oversized tower, and three simple chambres d'hôtes. The owners make excellent wines and there's a large park to stroll in. Closed mid-Nov to mid-March. ❹

Château de Danzay Near Avoine, 5km north of Chinon ☎02.47.58.46.86, ⓔdanzay@lenet.fr. This miniature medieval castle could almost be a large farmhouse poshed up with a turret and Renaissance windows. As a hotel, it's a real hideaway gem. There are only seven rooms, with stone walls, huge fireplaces, four-poster beds tucked under the roof beams and lots of luxurious little touches. Outside there's a heated swimming pool and expensively manicured gardens. Prices begin at just under €200. ❾

Chris' Hôtel 12 quai Jeanne d'Arc ☎02.47.93.36.92, ⓦwww.hotels-france.com/chris. Decent but unexceptional two-star hotel on the large market square on the eastern edge of town. Rooms are slightly fussy in feel, but well kept and light filled, and there's a garden behind. ❸

Hôtel Agnès Sorel 4 quai Pasteur ☎02.47.93.04.37, ⓦwww.agnes-sorel.com. The

CHINON

ACCOMMODATION
Hôtel Agnès Sorel   A
Hôtel Diderot   B
Hôtel de France   C
Chris 'Hôtel   F
Le Tennessee   D
La Treille   E

RESTAURANTS
Les Années 30   1
La Bonne France   5
Café des Arts   3
La Maison Rouge   2
Au Plaisir Gourmand 4

collégiale
St-Mexme

Lycée
St-Mexme

St-Étienne

Sous-
Préfecture

RUE PITOCHE

RUE DIDEROT

RUE DE BUFFON

RUE HOCHE

RUE JULES ROULLEAU

RUE RONSARD

RUE DU 11-NOVEMBRE

PLACE
JEANNE D'ARC

Statue of
Joan of Arc

RUE PHILIPPE DE COMMINES

RUE MARCEAU

RUE DU JEU DE PAUME

Tourist office

RUE JEAN-JACQUES ROUSSEAU

RUE DE LA LAMPROIE

RUE RABELAIS

QUAI JEANNE D'ARC

Île de Tours

Caves
Painctes

Musée
du Vin

Hôtel
de Ville

PLACE
DE LA
FONTAINE

RUE VOLTAIRE

RUE ÉMILE HÉBERT

PLACE DU
GÉNÉRAL
DE GAULLE

Statue of
Rabelais

RUE DU COMMERCE

QUAI DE L'ÎLE SONNANTE

RUE DU GRENIER À SEL

RUE HAUTE SAINT MARTIN

RUE DU PUITS DES BANCS

Écho

RUE DU CHÂTEAU

Tour Coudray
château
Logis Royal

Tour de
l'Horloge

Musée des Amis
du Vieux Chinon

RUE HAUTE SAINT MAURICE

St-Maurice

RUE PARMENTIER

PLACE DE
LA VICTOIRE
DE VERDUN

QUAI CHARLES VII

QUAI DANTON

QUAI TOURS

Vienne

Camping de
l'île Auger

AVENUE FRANÇOIS MITTERRAND

Maison de
la Rivière

QUAI PASTEUR

▲ Tours

N

0   100 m

103

hotel's situation down by the main road along the riverbank, at the western edge of the old town, lacks atmosphere and is awkward for the train station, but it's very clean and welcoming inside. The two more expensive rooms in the annexe (**⑥**) have nice balconies overlooking a little courtyard, while other rooms are modern but reasonably tasteful. Bikes are rented to all-comers for €14 per day. **❸**

Hôtel Diderot 7 rue Diderot ☏02.47.93.18.87, ⓦwww.hoteldiderot.com. Solidly bourgeois hotel hidden away in a venerable townhouse in the quiet, historic streets just east of St-Mexme church. Has some grand old rooms with antique furnishings in the main building, and some brighter modern ones in the annexe, which fronts pretty floral terraces. Old-fashioned welcome. **❸–❹**

Hôtel de France 47–49 place du Général de Gaulle ☏02.47.93.33.91, ⓔelmachinon@aol.com. The historic town-centre hotel, with wrought-iron balconies overlooking the leafy main square. Best Western welcomes you on the doormat, but five hundred years of hotel history still manage to cut through the corporate sheen, and the standards are very high. Rooms are attractive and cosy, with big comfy beds, beams and exposed stone walls, and only the occasional bit of cheap repro wood to spoil the effect. More expensive rooms (**⑤**) have a partial view of the château. **❹**

Manoir de la Tesserie Le Vieux Bourg, Cravant-les-Côteaux, 9km from Chinon ☏02.47.93.39.96, ⓔjparisis@free.fr. Two top-class chambres d'hôtes in a lovely fifteenth-century manor house at the edge of the village, with private grounds and a small swimming pool. **⑤**

Le Tennessee 11 rue Voltaire ☏02.47.93.02.85. Three basic but acceptable rooms tucked away on the second floor above a Tex-Mex bar and restaurant. Good if you're on a budget, as it's right in the centre of the old town. **❷**

La Treille 4 place Jeanne d'Arc ☏02.47.93.07.71. Tiny, spartan and full of character: this is one of the most best budget hotels in the region. A handful of clean and very simply decorated rooms – wood-effect lino, white walls, old shutters – are shoe-horned onto the first floor of this ancient building. Below is a friendly local bar and restaurant run by a husband-and-wife team; *monsieur* looks after the cooking (see review on p.108). Book well in advance, as there are just four rooms. **❶–❷**

The Town

The spectacular line of towers and ramparts rearing up on the high ridge behind town look as if they must enclose one of the best of this region's châteaux, but almost all is ruined within, the result of centuries of neglect and Richelieu's borrowing of ready-dressed masonry for his own nearby château (see p.112). Still, there's a dramatic history to ponder among the ruins, and a fine view of the grey walls and roofs of the medieval town below, crammed in between the heights of the cliffs and the broad River Vienne.

The château

A fortress of one kind or another existed at Chinon from the Stone Age, but it was under the overlordship of **Henri Plantagenêt**, who became king of England as Henry II, that the heart of the medieval **château** was built. Chinon became the setting for the most tragic events of Henry's life. It was from here that his son Henry, the "Young King", fled to the court of the French king Louis VII, an act which kickstarted the rebellion of Henry's wife **Eleanor of Aquitaine** (see box on p.235) and their younger son Richard the Lionheart. When Henry crushed the rebels in 1174, he is thought to have imprisoned Eleanor at Chinon. Fifteen years later, the wheel had turned: defeated by the unholy alliance of Louis VII's son Philippe-Auguste and his own son Richard, Henry died at Chinon in 1189 (see box on p.93). It didn't take long for Richard to fall out with his French ally, and local legend claims that he breathed his last in Chinon after being wounded in a battle in 1199, though he was probably dead on arrival. The Plantagenêt lands passed to Henry's youngest son, John, who presided over the final humiliation: after a year's siege in 1204–05, Philippe Auguste finally took the castle and put an end to Plantagenêt rule over Touraine and Anjou.

Today, the **château** (daily: April–Sept 9am–7pm; Oct–March 9.30–11.30am & 2–5.30pm; €4.60) is little more than a ring of tumbledown walls and broken

The miracle at Chinon

During the Lenten fast of 1429, the Dauphin Charles was sequestered at Chinon, one of the few strongholds left to him by the English in the disastrous aftermath of Agincourt. It was a bleak time for the French cause, but everything changed at a stroke with the arrival of a peasant girl from Lorraine, **Joan of Arc**, who somehow talked her way into meeting Charles. The usual story, repeated everywhere, is that Charles's courtiers set up a test by concealing him anonymously among the assembled nobles, but Joan miraculously picked him out straight away. It sounds more like a conjuring trick than an epoch-changing miracle and turns out to be based only on an eyewitness report that "when the king learned that she was approaching, he withdrew behind the others, but Joan recognized him perfectly, bowed to him and spoke to him for some minutes." Another tale claims that Joan revealed herself as Charles's illegitimate half-sister, and revealed details of a dream he'd had about his own legitimacy – but this is just royalist fantasy.

Joan herself told a different and far more powerful story. Interrogated in prison, she claimed that the king received a sign that made him believe in her. Under pressure from her inquisitors, she revealed that the sign was "beautiful, honourable and good", and later confessed that an angel appeared – a real one that "stepped on the ground" and "entered the room by the door" – and gave a golden crown to the archbishop of Reims, who in turn gave it to Charles. Perhaps she was talking about herself. In any case, the symbolism could hardly have been clearer, and it wasn't lost on Charles, who finally set about recovering his kingdom. For more on Joan, see the box on p.174.

towers. The relatively intact **Logis Royal** contains a few rooms filled with a couple of Flemish tapestries – one showing the famous recognition scene (see box above) – and a model of the château before it was destroyed. On its outer wall, at first-floor level, a large fireplace under a stone hood gives away the original site of the **grande salle**, the setting for the famous encounter between **Joan of Arc** and the Dauphin Charles, later Charles VII. If you look closely you can see the remains of a door just to the right; behind it you can trace a line of holes in the front wall of the *logis* which were once used to support a passage that led directly from the king's bedroom.

Of more tangible interest is the **Tour Coudray**, over to the west, covered with intricate thirteenth-century graffiti carved by imprisoned Knights Templar, who awaited burning here after their dangerously wealthy and powerful quasi-monastic order was smashed by Philippe IV "le Bel", in 1307. Underneath lie dungeons and an ice house. To the east, over the main gate, the intact, fourteenth-century **Tour de l'Horloge** houses an eccentric little museum of Joan-related odds and ends.

The echo

If you take the road leading north behind the château, then turn down the small, seemingly private lane that doubles back alongside the Clos de l'Echo vineyard, you'll come to a small, overgrown vantage point after about 200m, signalled by what must be the oddest road sign in France – "**ICI L'écho**" – pointing through a hedge roughly in the direction of the high walls of the château. Try it: your voice comes back bright and hard off the château's walls.

Local tradition uses the timing of the echo to deliver a misogynistic rhyme: "Les femmes de Chinon sont-elles fidèles?", you ask – "ELLES?", the echo replies. "Oui, les femmes de Chinon", you confirm – and back comes the riposte, "NON!" ("Are the women of Chinon faithful?"; "THEM?"; "Yes, the women of Chinon"; "NO!")

The last weekend of July and the first weekend of August bring a touristy **medieval fair** to the château's grounds, with costumed reconstructions of battles, olde-fayre snacks and the like, and in August there's an evening son-et-lumière, **Les Nocturnes Insolites** (Tues–Fri from 10pm; €9.50), with costumed actors playing out scenes at various points among the ruins.

Rue Voltaire to the river

The heart of town is **place du Général de Gaulle**, overlooked by the town hall and set out with café tables under the false acacias. At its foot is the river and the town's proud statue of local hero **Rabelais** (see p.329), while at the top end is **place de la Fontaine** – named after a cast-iron statue of the three Graces – which gives onto steep stone stairs leading up to the château.

Leading east, **rue Voltaire** is lined with half-timbered and sculpted townhouses – look out for nos. 10 and 12, which date from the fifteenth century, and the old salt-storage house at no. 20. It's best to skip the tacky wine- and barrel-making museum, the Musée du Vin, with its second-rate animated coopers, but the tour of the so-called **Caves Peinctes**, just off rue Voltaire (July to mid-Sept Tues–Sun 10.30am, 3pm, 4.30pm & 6pm; €3) is moderately diverting, though the paintings suggested by the name are long vanished, if they ever existed – no one's sure. There's little inside now except a dark tunnel, a fountain lined with two thousand empty bottles and a huge, hollowed-out space used for local weddings and the functions of the local wine guild, but you get a glass of wine at the end of the tour.

At the end of rue Voltaire, beyond a series of beautiful fourteenth- and fifteenth-century houses, is the lovingly kept **Musée des Amis du Vieux Chinon**, 44 rue Haute St-Maurice (April–Sept daily 10.30am–12.30pm & 2–6pm; €2.60), where the Etats Généraux met in 1428 to raise the funds for Joan of Arc's mission of reconquest. The highlights of the museum's small collection are the **Chape de St-Mexme**, a chasuble-like Sassanid garment with a design of multiple leopards that was probably spoil from the Crusades, and a powerful bas-relief of the Crucifixion from the eleventh-century, with Christ's head framed by images of the sun and moon. Stairs lead up to a vaulted upper room where Delacroix's portrait of a fruity-looking Rabelais looks down on a collection of nineteenth-century faïence from Langeais.

Ancient **rue Haute St-Maurice** passes below the walls of the château's *logis* as it gradually slopes its way down towards the river. Just set back from the riverbank, at the western limits of town, the **Maison de la Rivière**, 2 quai Minster (April–June, Sept & Oct Tues–Fri 10am–12.30pm & 2–5.30pm, Sat & Sun 2–5pm; July & Aug Tues–Fri 10am–12.30pm & 2–6.30pm, Sat & Sun 3–6pm; €4; ☎02.47.93.21.34) celebrates the once-thriving Loire shipping industry with lots of detailed models of the many kinds of strange, narrow sailboats and steamships, and a full-size cutaway *fûtreau* built by a local craftsman. On weekend afternoons in summer, you can even take a 45-minute trip on a traditional *fûtreau* or *toue* (€6), and staff lead regular guided nature walks.

St-Mexme and the Chapelle Ste-Radegonde

The eastern side of town is much quieter and less touristy. **Rue Jean-Jacques-Rousseau**, with more half-timbered houses, leads past the tourist office and the **église St-Etienne**, a fifteenth-century affair with a beautiful Flamboyant Gothic portal, on its way to the **collégiale St-Mexme**. Only the west tower and a half-shell of the nave remains of what was once an important Romanesque church, and it's only just possible to make out heavily weathered geometric and floral patterns, and what may be a figure of Christ. Rue Hoche runs down to the river at place Jeanne d'Arc, an expanse of tarmac designed in the nineteenth century to accommodate the **weekly market**, which still takes place here on Thursdays, with delicious fresh food stalls open till midday and lots of less enticing stands selling cheap clothing, accordion music, hunting hats and the like right through the day. The square is dominated by an extraordinary equestrian **sculpture of Joan of Arc** in mid-battle charge, all flying hooves, sword and standard, which was given to the town by its sculptor, Jules Roulleau, in 1893.

Evidence of Chinon's renowned sunny micro-climate can be seen on the north side of the square, where one of Chinon's many palm trees flourishes behind the high walls of the odd-looking Lycée St-Mexme. A lane, rue Pitoche, leads east past this school, climbing slowly and then contouring along the cliffs past numerous **troglodyte dwellings**, some of which are still inhabited. After a kilometre or so the path peters out at the **chapelle Ste-Radegonde**, a rock-cut church which is part of a complex of cave dwellings once occupied by hermits. Sainte Radegonde was a sixth-century German princess who renounced the world and her husband – probably not a great sacrifice, since he eventually murdered her brother – in order to devote her life to God. The chapel's guardian has lived in the troglodyte house next door for nearly thirty years and often takes visitors into the chapel and caves behind – check with the tourist office in advance, or ask politely. High on one wall of the chapel, a captivating **painting** depicts a horseback cortege of regal figures, probably the Plantagenêt royal family. It's uncertain whether it celebrates the marriage of King John in 1200 or marks the end of **Eleanor of Aquitaine**'s captivity in Chinon (see box on p.235). The leading figure is probably Henry II, followed by his wife Eleanor (crowned, centre) and their daughter Jeanne, followed in turn by their sons Richard the Lionheart (receiving a falcon, which may symbolize his succession to the duchy of Aquitaine) and John Lackland. Dated to the end of the twelfth century, it may be the only contemporary portrait of Eleanor in the world – not counting the effigy on her tomb in Fontevraud.

Eating and drinking

There aren't as many **restaurants** in Chinon as you might expect. Some have gone for the touristy medieval theme in a big way, but if you choose carefully you can find an excellent and not overpriced meal.

Les Années 30 78 rue Voltaire ☏02.47.93.37.18. Tiny, cosy restaurant with a bar in the corner in the old-fashioned way. Meals are reliably good, with one or two more adventurous dishes. *Menus* at €23 and €36. Closed Wed.

La Bonne France 2 place de la Victoire de Verdun ☏02.47.98.01.34. Something of a local secret, tucked away on a tiny old square just behind the bridge. Offers four good-value *menus* at €14, themed according to different French regions – there's one for Touraine – and has a few tables out on the square. There's also an excellent value weekday lunch *menu* at €9 and an evening *menu* at €22. Closed Tues.

Café des Arts place du Général de Gaulle. The food isn't anything special – salads and brasserie fare, mostly – but it's a pleasant place to have a drink or a simple meal out on the square.

La Maison Rouge 38 rue Voltaire. Hearty, meaty cuisine, served in pleasantly ancient surroundings, though it feels touristy. The "Assiettes Rabelaisiennes" (€14.50) feature regional specialities; otherwise, lunch *menus* begin at €12. There's lots of good local wine, too: you can have it by the glass for around €3, or buy a half-litre *pichet* of ordinary Chinon red for €7.50.

Au Plaisir Gourmand 2 rue Parmentier, off quai Charles VII ☏02.47.93.20.48. The nearest thing Chinon has to a true gastronomic restaurant, with a classically trained chef giving fresh local ingredients the real treatment. The atmosphere can be formal, however, with a single over-dressed dining room. *Menus* at €27 and €39. Closed Mon, Tues lunch & Sun evening.

La Treille 4 place Jeanne d'Arc ☏02.47.93.07.71. Utterly old-fashioned hotel restaurant with wooden tables and a sparse but homely decor. The speciality is wild plants, and you may find your salad laced with flower petals and herb-like leaves. Otherwise the cooking is careful and traditional, with excellent set *menus* at €20 and €30 and reasonably priced Chinon wines. Closed Wed, and Thurs evening.

The Chinonais

The countryside around Chinon, the **Chinonais**, was made famous by Rabelais as the setting for the Picrocholine wars of his satirical epic, *Gargantua*. It's the epitome of a Loire landscape: north of Chinon lies the ancient **Forêt de Chinon** while to the west is the soft **Pays du Véron**, a rural angle of land squeezed between the Loire and Vienne. Over on the southern bank of the Vienne lies the rich countryside made mythical by **Rabelais**, whose birthplace you can visit at **La Devinière**. But the main sights of the Chinonais lie to the east, up the Vienne, whose northern bank rises to low tufa cliffs riddled with caves, some of them still used as wine cellars, storage rooms or even houses. The ruined churches at **Tavant**, with its Romanesque wall-paintings, and **L'Ile Bouchard** may draw you upstream, and you could continue up the peaceful **Manse** valley towards the relatively bleak plateau of **Ste-Maure-de-Touraine**, which divides the western and eastern parts of southern Touraine. Just north of Ste-Maure, the impressive church at **Ste-Catherine-de-Fierbois** is a little-known stop on the Joan of Arc circuit.

Forêt de Chinon and Pays du Véron

Northeast of Chinon, the elevated terrain of the *landes* is covered by the ancient **Forêt de Chinon**, crisscrossed by roads and forest alleys that make for delightful cycling or walking – the GR3 long-distance footpath runs right through from Chinon to Azay-le-Rideau (see p.95). Even the rail route from Azay is superb. If you want to **stay** in the area, there's a good chambres d'hôtes near Rigny-Ussé (see p.100).

To the west, the tranquil **Pays du Véron** feels like the softly beating heart of the Loire landscape. It's an especially lovely corner of the region, characterized in the east by gently sloping fields, vineyards and pine trees, and in the west by flat meadows leading down to the water, fringed by hedgerows of oak and ash as well as the ubiquitous willows and poplars. Unfortunately, this rural idyll is somewhat overshadowed by the nuclear power station just upstream near **Avoine**, a nightmarish vision of futuristic 1960s design.

The Maison Rabelais at La Devinière

The sixteenth-century monk, doctor, humanist, *bon viveur* and writer **François Rabelais** was probably born at his family's manor farm of **La Devinière**, 6km southwest of Chinon. Local tradition holds that he was born on the road from Chinon, however, and Rabelais' most famous and work, the very loosely autobiographical *Gargantua*, suggests he was actually born in a nearby willow grove – but then, it also famously claims that Gargantua entered the world clamouring for wine, "climbing through the diaphragm to a point above the shoulders where this vein divides in two, he took the left fork and came out by the left ear. As soon as he was born he cried out, not like other children: 'Mies! Mies!' but 'Drink! Drink! Drink!'" (see p.329)

The manor house itself is modest, fitting Rabelais' father's station as a lawyer in Chinon, and the main attraction is inside, where there's an excellent but dry museum (daily: April–Sept 9.30am–7pm; Oct–March 9.30am–12.30pm & 2–5pm; €3.80) dedicated to the writer's life and works. You'll need to speak French to get the most out of the exhibits, or be familiar with *Gargantua* and *Pantagruel*, as the museum is dominated by old texts, plus a few portraits and engravings, and a couple of roughly reconstructed rooms. The countryside around is beautiful, the gentle slopes lined with vines, and true Rabelais enthusiasts will want to imagine it as Grandgousier's monstrously inflated kingdom. The château of Le Coudray-Montpensier, on the other side of the valley beyond Seuilly, is private and cannot be visited.

Tavant

The more attractive road east of Chinon runs along the rocky right bank of the Vienne, but the southern route, along the flat D760, has the advantage of passing through **TAVANT**, 16m from Chinon. Roughly 100m back from the main road, a little jewel-box of a church, **St-Nicolas** (March–Nov Wed–Sun 10am–12.30pm & 1.30–6pm, closed first Sun of every month; €3), shelters an extraordinary collection of **Romanesque wall-paintings** in its **crypt** that ranks among the finest in Europe. It's an extraordinary claustrophobic space, thick with four pairs of columns, whose vault is almost entirely covered with 27 early twelfth-century images. Many scenes show a subtle mastery of captured movement. Two of the most enigmatic figures frame the entrance, both holding lilies; they're clearly important, as the finely sculpted capitals below indicate, but their identities remain obscure. In fact, it's unsure why this crypt should have been so richly painted at all, as it hasn't been identified with any major relic cult or tomb – though the chapel was associated with a priory, whose remnants survive on the other side of the main road.

It's thought that the entire structure, inside and out, would once have been painted in bright colours, but today just fragments of mid-twelfth-century paintings survive in the upper church, as well as a giant figure of Christ in Majesty on the half-dome of the apse. Fine stone carving remains on the west portal, however, and on the capitals of the crossing, where griffons are matched with sirens, two-bodied monsters and a tree with a serpent. If the chapel isn't open when you arrive, ask for the guardian at the nearby Mairie.

L'Ile-Bouchard

The island referred to in the name of **L'ILE BOUCHARD**, 18km east of Chinon, turns out to be a bland car park of a square encircled by two branches of the river Vienne. The more interesting features of this little town lie on either bank. Roughly 500m south of the island centre lies the melancholy ruin of the **Prieuré St-Léonard**. The apse is all that's left of an eleventh-century priory church, standing in a grassy enclosure under a practical little modern roof and looking like a broken-down theatrical backdrop. The astonishing stonework is remarkably well preserved, however, especially the lovingly sculpted scenes from the life of Christ, clearly visible on both sides of the capitals. The gate is always open to visitors and you may well be joined by the site's guardian, who lives in an adjacent house and gives out explanatory leaflets.

On the north side of the river, in the village-like centre of town, the little **église St-Gilles** was the scene of a meticulously documented miracle that took place over six days in December 1947, when the Virgin and the Angel Gabriel repeatedly appeared to four local schoolgirls, one of whom, now a retired teacher, still lives in the village. The Virgin apparently commanded the girls to pray for France – to be rescued from Communism, according to local

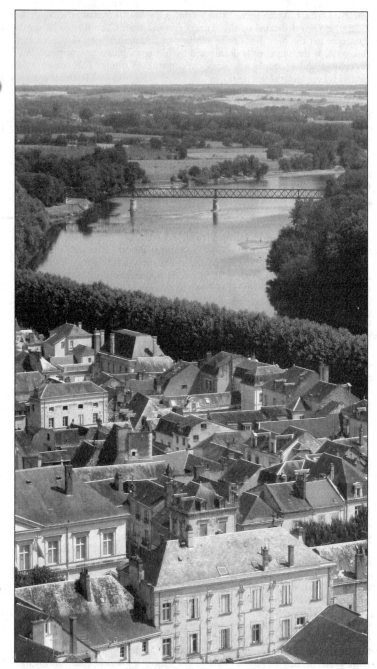

△ The old town and the Vienne, Chinon

interpretation – and to build a special golden grotto of an Annunciation scene, a triumph of kitsch that now stands in the north aisle of the church, the focus of veneration by scores of pilgrims every day.

Practicalities

A couple of places on the fringes of town offer pleasant **chambres d'hôtes**. On the road in from Ste-Maure-de-Touraine, the *Moulin de Saussaye* (℡02.47.58.50.44; ❸) has simple, inexpensive rooms dotted around the old farm and watermill buildings, but the main draw is the simple but excellent farm **restaurant** (open weekends and occasional extra evenings in summer – ring to check; *menus* for under €20), serving fresh duck and chicken dishes straight from the farm in a very welcoming, homely atmosphere. Halfway up the wooded bluff to the south of town – follow the signs off the road to Champigny-sur-Veude for about 1km – the *Château de la Commanderie* (℡02.47.58.63.13, ⊛www.lacommanderie.com; ❹) is set in a grand old house with an appealingly rustic atmosphere created by exposed stone walls and floorboards; the friendly owners also do a table d'hôte (€25) on reservation.

The island at the centre of L'Ile Bouchard has a good **restaurant**, *L'Auberge de l'Ile* (℡02.47.58.51.07; *menus* from €23; closed Tues & Wed, Jan & Feb), though the dining room is unprepossessing, despite the river view.

The lower Manse valley

The bosky, mill-lined **Manse valley**, which slopes away from the Vienne at L'Ile Bouchard towards the plateau of Ste-Maure, is one of the more bucolic corners of Touraine, its gentle rises populated by sleepy villages, woods and tiny vineyards. The attractive village of **CRISSAY-SUR-MANSE**, 8km from L'Ile Bouchard, is dotted with medieval and Renaissance mansions built in more energetic days and now occupied by wealthy refugees from the cities. Behind high walls you can just see the remains of the château which once belonged to the wealthy Turpin-de-Crissé family, while the church at the bottom end of the village has some beautiful Flamboyant Gothic windows.

On the western side of the village, at the junction with the C2 to Crouzilles, a signposted road threads 2km north across the undulating countryside to **ROCHES-TRANCHELLION**, where you can explore the ruins of an early sixteenth-century **collegiate church** – look for the steps leading up beside a farmhouse with hundreds of exotic caged birds in the courtyard. The west front preserves some fine Renaissance chisel-work.

The hamlet of **CROUZILLES**, 3km east of L'Ile Bouchard, close to the Vienne, has a very simple but welcoming bar-tabac-auberge next to the church, *Au Bon Accueil* (℡02.47.58.58.11; ❷), which serves inexpensive, meaty, traditional meals (*menus* €14–22) and has some clean, modern **rooms** upstairs (❷–❸).

Ste-Maure-de-Touraine

For most visitors, **STE-MAURE-DE-TOURAINE**, 18km east of L'Ile Bouchard, means little more than a roadside stop on the thundering N10 highway, though Ste-Maure-de-Touraine is also the quality-controlled name of one of the region's best-known **goat's cheeses**, distinguished by its flattened cylindrical shape and the straw running down the middle. There is a small, reasonably attractive old centre on the hill above the road, with an old covered market sporting seventeenth-century carved doors, a small château housing a museum of local history and a heavily restored church. If you want to look round the modest local **museum** (€3.80) – there's a tasting of local wine and goat's cheese at the end – or visit the Romanesque **crypt** of the church, you have to ask for an accompanied visit at the **tourist office**, next door to the château (Mon–Sat 10.30am–noon & 2.30–4.30pm; ☎02.47.65.66.20). Staff can also give advice on visiting local **goat farms**.

An infrequent **bus** service (line #H) makes the trip from Tours via Ste-Catherine-de-Fierbois. There's little reason to stop at any of the string of **hotels** lining the main road, but some 4km west of Ste-Maure-de-Touraine, near Noyant-de-Touraine, the fifteenth-century *Château de Brou* (☎02.47.65.80.80, ⓦwww.chateau-de-brou.fr; from €100) is worth going out of your way for. It has been converted into a romantic and very luxurious three-star hotel, set at the end of a long drive among 100 hectares of wooded grounds. Each of the dozen rooms is beautifully and very carefully decorated with bright, chintzy fabrics, and furnishings that range from the old and handsome to the plain eccentric.

The **Manse valley** (see p.111) continues southeast beyond Ste-Maure-de-Touraine. If you're heading east towards Loches, consider travelling via the troglodyte village of **Les Côteaux**. A delightful back road, the C3, passes neat vegetable plots, grazing goats, tumbledown cave cottages and endless poplar trees on its way to the village of **Sepmes**, 7km southeast of Ste-Maure-de-Touraine.

Ste-Catherine-de-Fierbois

Seven kilometres north of Ste-Maure-de-Touraine, the fifteenth-century church at **STE-CATHERINE-DE-FIERBOIS** is bizarrely impressive for such an inconsequential little village. The first chapel here is supposed to have been established by Charles Martel after his historic defeat of a Moorish army in 732, a battle that turned the tide of the Moors' northward thrust from Spain. Seven hundred years later, **Joan of Arc** (see box on p.174) slept at the chapel and heard three Masses the following morning – St Catherine was especially precious to her as one of her "voices" – before continuing to Chinon. Two months later Joan ordered her aides to return to collect a sword "marked with five crosses" that she assured them would be hidden behind the altar – probably left there as a votive offering by a soldier. It became one of her most powerful symbols, but was shattered and lost – the legend goes – when Joan beat a prostitute with it after the defeated attack on Paris.

The size and importance of the existing **church** is entirely due to an archbishop of Tours who acted for Joan at her rehabilitation trial, and erected this church in her memory. The wide vault is eye-catching, and fine scraps of Flamboyant Gothic carving decorate the doors on either side of the altar, but the *pièce de résistance* is the west front – or it will be once the authorities have completed a typically thorough "restoration" at some point in 2005 or 2006.

Once you've looked at the **statue of Joan** in the square and the adjacent **Maison du Dauphin**, built in around 1415, there's nothing else to do except have a meal or a drink at the homely *Auberge Jeanne d'Arc* (☎02.47.65.68.61; *menus* €15–30; closed Mon). If you're moving on towards Chinon, take the back roads via St-Epain (the D101) and down the Manse valley (the D21).

Richelieu and around

RICHELIEU, 24km south of Chinon, is an extraordinary place. If it wasn't for the ambitions of Cardinal Richelieu, it would look more like what it really is, a small, provincial town of no particular pretensions, but in the 1630s, the Cardinal decided to celebrate his new status as a top-rank nobleman by creating what the brown-nosing poet La Fontaine was to call "the most beautiful village in the universe", with a château to match. He rushed the initial work through in less than a dozen years and then ran out of steam.

The nexus of town is the perfectly symmetrical **Grande Rue**, lined with 28 noble townhouses. Although they are almost identical inside and out, the houses were actually put up by individual speculators attracted by – or armtwisted into supporting – the Cardinal's scheme, and willing to follow the exact building specifications of his architect, Jacques Lemercier. Several have plaques outside with brief biographies of their original owners. No. 15, named after one Louis Barbier, houses the little **Musée du Chat** (daily 2–5pm; €4). Even if you're not interested in modern cartoon-caricatures of Richelieu's fourteen cats (which apparently went everywhere with him), or cat-related stamps, books and objects, or even the four real moggies that haunt the house, it's well worth visiting for the chance to look round the almost untouched interior, which preserves the stipulated layout. A sixteen-metre-long central passage, which has its obligatory "large room with a fireplace" on one side and "kitchen with a cellar and pantry" on the other, leads through to a 56-metre-long garden.

The Grande Rue terminates at each end in a perfectly quadrangular square closed by a grand gate. The more impressive of the two is the southern square, **place du Grand Marché**, framed on either side by a huge **covered market**, whose high roof is supported by a fantastically timbered chestnut-and-oak frame, and the **church**, built in a frigid but nevertheless awe-inspiring version of the Baroque style. The roads that run east and west off the square, rue de Loudun and rue des Halles, apparently end in two more gates, but one of them is actually a blind as it backs onto the little river Mable. The northern square, **place des Religieuses**, is more modest, its pollarded plane trees and parking spaces frowned over by former conventual buildings.

The layout of the old town still fits within a perfect grid, surrounded by a high walls and a moat, but sadly only the two squares and the Grande Rue are really grand, the rest of the town's houses only having been built in succeeding centuries. The greatest tragedy to befall Richelieu's modest tourist industry, however, is the loss of its **château**, whose absence is as palpable as a missing limb as you pass through the impressive **Porte de Châtellerault**, at the southern end of the Grande Rue, across the circular place du Cardinal and into a huge and empty park. Built at the same time as the town, the château was absolutely vast, only rivalled in scale and ambition by Louis XIV's Versailles, which was begun some thirty years later. Its disappearance is the result of Richelieu's heirs selling it off in the aftermath of the Revolution to a contractor who used it as a stone quarry – an ironic end, as much had originally been built with stone robbed from Chinon's château. You can see reproductions of engravings of the château in the tourist office, or get a dim sense of what it must have been like if you enter the 480-hectare **park** (daily: April–Oct 10am–7pm; Nov–March 9am–5pm; €2), where a single pavillion, the "**Dôme**", and part of the Orangerie survive. The rest of the park is given up to avenues of trees and meadows, with a deer-hunting forest behind. Bizarrely, the whole thing belongs to the University of Paris. In summer, you can hire **boats** (April–Oct; €2.30/hr) and splash about on the remnants of the canal.

Practicalities

The skeletal school bus service runs during term time only, so you'll need your own **transport** to get around the Richelais. The helpful **tourist office**, 6 Grande Rue (April to mid-May & Oct Mon–Sat 9am–12.30pm & 2–5.30pm; mid-May to Sept Mon–Sat 9am–12.30pm & 2–6pm; Nov–March Mon, Tues

& Thurs–Sat 9am–12.30pm & 2–5.30pm; ☎02.47.58.13.62, ⓦwww.cc-pays-de-richelieu.fr), can provide lots of information on Richelieu and the country around, and produces an excellent free booklet in English, *Round and About the City of the Cardinal*.

Richelieu has some amazing **chambres d'hôtes**. In the middle of the Grande Rue, the *Maison Louis Barbier*, at no. 15 (☎02.47.58.19.23; ❺), provides a taste of seventeenth-century fine living, with two beautiful ground-floor rooms featuring original decor and four-poster beds. *La Maison*, 6 rue Henri Proust (☎ & ☏ 02.47.58.29.40, ⓦwww.lamaisondemichele.com; ❻), is a beautifully decorated early nineteenth-century house with spacious, high-ceilinged rooms with polished wood floors set around a grand old staircase and hall, and a large garden behind. Four kilometres northeast of Richelieu, just outside Chaveignes, the grand, sixteenth-century *Château de la Vrillaye* (☎02.47.58.24.40, ⓦwww.chateaudelavrillaye.com; ❺/❻) offers two beautifully appointed rooms looking out on the park and private vineyard, and use of a pool and tennis courts.

The long-standing town **hotel**, *Le Puits Doré*, 24 place du Marché (☎02.47.58.16.02, ⓔkiengat@wanadoo.fr; ❸), occupies a prominent corner of the main square; the rooms are generally decent, with some old features, while the ones under the roof beams are pretty; the **restaurant** serves traditional bourgeois fare. A reliable alternative for an evening meal is the *Auberge Le Cardinal*, 3 rue des Ecluses (☎02.47.58.18.57; *menus* from €12), facing the park gates.

Champigny-sur-Veude

Like Richelieu, 7km south, **CHAMPIGNY-SUR-VEUDE** is missing its château, which was destroyed on the orders of the Cardinal himself – as popular legend would have it, he wanted to ensure nothing competed with his own palace. Running alongside the main road, the old château walls still guard substantial sixteenth-century *communs* and the oversized white stone buttresses and steeply pitched roof of the **chapelle St-Louis** (May–Sept 10am–noon & 2–6pm; €3), which possesses some of the finest Renaissance **stained-glass windows** in France. The chapel's architecture is an odd mix of Gothic and Renaissance, but the windows follow a purer, later style, having been fitted by local master glaziers in the latter half of the sixteenth century. The uppermost tier depicts scenes from the Passion and Resurrection, the middle row follows the life of St Louis and the lower level acts as a portrait gallery for the Bourbon-Montpensier family, who owned the château. The highlight is the apse, filled with a staggering Crucifixion scene of three powerfully muscular figures set against a deep blue sky.

The obvious way to visit Champigny-sur-Veude is to stop off on the way from Chinon to Richelieu, but on weekend afternoons in July and August a refitted old **steam train** (☎02.47.58.12.97; €6 return) makes the journey from Ligré, halfway between Champigny and Chinon, to Richelieu. If you're coming from Chinon you'll have to walk or cycle to Ligré, a distance of some 7km, but if you're based in Richelieu you can take the earlier of the two trains, stop off at Champigny, have a quick look around (there's usually an hour and a quarter between trains) and take the later train back to Richelieu. Check exact times first, however, as they may be subject to change.

Château du Rivau

Their shape is perfectly medieval, but the white-stone towers and conical turrets of the **château du Rivau** (June–Sept daily 1–7pm; May & Oct Sat & Sun

2–7pm; €6; ⓦ www.chateaudurivau.com), 11km north of Richelieu, have had such a good clean-up that they look almost new. All this effort has been to provide a suitable backdrop for the **gardens**, which have been developed as a whimsical attraction in recent years.

The ambitions of the project are obvious as soon as you walk past the lavender knot garden, through the gates and into the ancient *basse cour*, which is lorded over by a high gatehouse keep and filled by the **potager de Gargantua**, in which giant vegetables are brought on through late summer and autumn. Beyond lies the austerely medieval château, which is plain and empty inside. The main attraction is the **garden**, which features an arbour of climbing roses, an orchard and a fantastical forested area littered with modern sculptures such as giant wooden legs apparently running through the forest, little gardeners entirely made of terracotta pots and lovers' benches watched over by poetic quotations. One corner is devoted to children, with gnomes, toadstools and fairy-tale creatures hiding among the shrubs. On the first weekend of July, costumed elves and goblins invade the grounds to entertain younger visitors.

South and east of Richelieu

The hilltop village of **FAYE-LA-VINEUSE**, 7km south of Richelieu, once had a population of over 10,000 and stood behind high walls like a medieval Tuscan town. The walls are gone, but the village still has a handsome setting, with a number of fine old houses in the narrow streets of the village centre. The chief relic of grander days is the twelfth-century **collégiale St-Georges**, which has some fascinating carved capitals in its large crypt.

Deep in the countryside some 20km east of Richelieu, the twelfth- to fifteenth-century **Abbaye de St-Michel** at **BOIS-AUBRY**, 3km southeast of Luzé, is largely a romantic ruin, though a dramatic fifty-metre-high belfry and a serenely vaulted Romanesque chapterhouse still stand, along with various Gothic fragments. Monks returned in 1978 to set up a small community, and they now offer ten simple **chambres d'hôtes** (ⓣ02.47.58.34.48, ⓦ http://perso.wanadoo.fr/boisaubry/abba-acceuil.html; ❷), equipped with bunk beds, which attract occasional overnight visitors and Christians on retreat.

Loches

LOCHES is the obvious place to head for in the southeastern part of Touraine. Its walled **citadel** is by far the most impressive of the Loire valley fortresses, with its unbreached ramparts and the Renaissance houses below still partly enclosed by the outer wall of the medieval town. Tours is only an hour away by bus or train, but Loches makes for a quiet, relatively untouristy base for exploring the Cher valley, or the much lesser-known country along the Indre and Indrois rivers.

Arrival, information and accommodation

From Tours, trains and buses alike arrive at the **gare SNCF** on the east side of the Indre, just up from place de la Marne, where the **tourist office** is housed in a little wooden chalet (July & Aug daily 9.30am–7pm; Sept–June Mon–Sat 9am–12.30pm & 2–6pm; ⓣ02.47.91.82.82, ⓦ www.lochesentouraine.com).

Accommodation

Most visitors to Loches come on day-trips, so the **accommodation** options are fairly limited. Loches' three-star **campsite**, *Camping La Citadelle* (☎02.47.59.05.91, ⓦwww.lacitadelle.com; closed mid-Oct to mid-March), is situated between two branches of the Indre, by the swimming pool and stadium, looking up at the east side of the citadel.

Hôtel de Beaulieu 3 rue Foulques Nerra, Beaulieu-les-Loches ☎02.47.91.60.80. Charming, tumbledown sixteenth-century house right next to the abbey, with just nine plain old rooms. It's an independent-spirited place, and often closed in the afternoons, so be sure to ring in advance. ❷

Hôtel de France 6 rue Picois, near the Porte Picois ☎02.47.59.00.32, ⓕ02.47.59.28.66. Friendly and old-fashioned post-house hotel with a

handsomely restored entrance hall and a small courtyard with parking out back. The bedrooms are relatively simple, but clean and well-maintained. Closed Sun evening & Mon, except in July and Aug. ❸

Hôtel George Sand 37 rue Quintefol ☎02.47.59.39.74, ⓔgsandhotel@compuserve.com. A fifteenth-century coaching inn, though much rebuilt, sitting between the eastern ramparts of the citadel and the Indre. It has three stars, so the facilities are very good – the best rooms are at the back, looking onto the river. ❺

La Tour Saint-Antoine 2 rue des Moulins

℡02.47.59.01.06, ℻02.47.59.13.80. Looks like a large, tourist-oriented hotel from the outside, with lots of flags fluttering over the large, roadside restaurant, but the welcome is warm when you arrive and the simple rooms are good value. ❷

The lower town

The isolated, sixteenth-century **Tour St-Antoine** stands sentinel over the wide, central **place de la Marne**, at the foot of the old town. Everything looks dull and modern down here, but things quickly get better, as Loches' onion-skin-like layout means that as you penetrate each layer of town walls the buildings get more and more impressive.

From the place de la Marne, rue de la République slopes up to the tiny **place du Blé**, where the town's two main cafés face each other across the square. Just to one side, a secretive, tunnel-like gateway leads under one of the town's two surviving fifteenth-century towers, the **Porte Picois**, and into the old town proper. This is a tiny area, but very attractive, with narrow cobbled streets falling away from the main axis of rue du Château and the Grande Rue. On market days (Wednesday and Saturday mornings), these streets thrum with locals shopping for fruit, vegetables and lots of local produce, notably goat's cheeses, pâtés and the like.

A number of the old town's Renaissance mansions are worth a closer look. The tall, Renaissance **Hôtel de Ville**, abutting the inner side of the Porte Picois, was built under François I and still has his distinctive salamander symbol carved over its windows. Over on rue du Château, check out the curious scene of an archer confronting a centaur carved high on the end wall of the so-called **House of the Centaur**, and the beautiful Italiante details on the facade of the adjacent **Chancellerie**. The latter houses a good exhibition on the history of Loches (daily: April, May, Sept & Oct 10am–12.30pm & 2.30–5pm; June–Aug 10am–6pm; free), with lots of engravings and old town plans, with explanations in English. Rue du Château continues up to the mighty twelfth-century gatehouse known as the **Porte Royale**, the main entrance to the citadel, while the Grande Rue slopes down to the **Porte des Cordeliers**, down by the River Indre.

The citadel

Turn left just after the Porte Royale for the **Musée Lansyer** (Jan–March & Oct–Dec Mon–Sat 10am–1pm & 2–5pm; April–Sept daily 10am–12.30pm & 2–6.30pm; €4.30), which occupies the house of local nineteenth-century landscape painter Emmanuel Lansyer. Despite briefly studying under Gustave Courbet – too briefly, perhaps – his paintings are nothing to write home about, but there are some pleasant local landscapes and the museum's rooms are attractively decorated in period style.

A few steps beyond lies the **collégiale de St-Ours**, whose distinctively eccentric roof-line looks like the spiny back of a prehistoric animal, with its two octagonal stone pyramids, called *dubes*, lined up between a pair of relatively conventional spires. In essence it's a Romanesque structure, built in the eleventh and twelfth centuries as a kind of private chapel for the counts of Anjou, but it has one or two extremely early Gothic features, notably the Plantagenêt vault of the porch. Inside the porch, the west portal is elaborately carved with all manner of humans, animals and monstrous figures, and preserves traces of its original bright paint. Look out for the allegories of the seven

Liberal Arts on the outer arch, under the figures of the Virgin Mary and the Magi. In the nave, the hollow octagonal vaults grab most of the attention, with their strange, fish-scale-like decoration on the triangular pendentives. Otherwise, there are a handful of ornately sculpted capitals to examine, as well as the stoup, or basin for holy water, which was once a Gallo-Roman altar.

For six weeks in the sumer you can follow the "Murmurailles" night-time **son-et-lumière** circuit around the citadel, watching the fancy light projections and the performers acting out historical scenes (Fri & Sat: last two weeks of July 10.15pm, Aug 9.45pm; €11, children 6–12 years €6).

The Logis Royal

The northern end of the citadel is occupied by the **Logis Royal**, or royal lodgings, of Charles VII and his three successors (daily: Jan–March & Oct–Dec 9.30am–5pm; April–Sept 9am–7pm; €3.80, €5.10 including the donjon). It has two distinct halves, similar at first glance, but separated by a century in which the medieval need for defence began to give way to a more courtly, luxurious lifestyle. The first section, the **Vieux Logis**, was built in the late fourteenth century as a kind of pleasure palace for the Dauphin Charles and his official mistress, Agnès Sorel, who had the good luck to be the owner of the manor at Beauté-sur-Marne as well as Loches, giving her the title of "La dame de Beauté" (the Lady of Beauty). A copy of Charles's portrait by Fouquet can be seen in the antechamber to the **Grande Salle**, where the Dauphin met the second woman of importance in his life between June 3 and June 5, 1429 – Joan of Arc, who came here victorious from Orléans to give the defeatist Dauphin another pep talk about coronations. The chamber today has been dressed in late medieval style, with a bare terracotta floor under the roof beams, and various weapons, chests and tapestries against the pale stone walls.

Agnès was buried at the adjacent collégiale de St-Ours, but her shining white **tomb** now lies in the first room of the second part of the *logis*, the **late-fifteenth-century wing**, a beautiful recumbent figure tenderly watched over by angels. The alabaster is rather more pristine than it should be, as it had to be restored after anticlerical Revolutionary soldiers mistook her for a saint – an easy error to make. Around it hang two copies of portraits by which you can judge her famous beauty. One depicts her as a regal Madonna, surrounded by strange red cherubs, while the other shows her more intimately, in drabber garb; bizarrely, her bared breast – in both pictures – was no artist's fantasy, but a courtly trend set by Agnès herself.

The **triptych** that dominates the next room is no copy, but an original work of 1485 painted for the Chartreuse du Liget (see p.120) by an unknown artist working within the School of Tours. It's a brilliantly coloured and splendidly composed Crucifixion scene with a strong Flemish influence. Beyond lie the two rooms of Anne de Bretagne's **oratory**, whose every surface is carved with Franciscan knotted tassels and the stylized ermines' tails of Brittany, the homeland of Charles VIII's wife (see box on p.89). Originally, they would have been painted gold and silver against a blue background.

The donjon

From the Logis Royal, cobbled streets overlooked by handsome townhouses wind through to the far end of the elevated citadel, where the **donjon** (same hours as Logis Royal; €3.80, €5.10 including Logis Royal), begun by Foulque Nerra, the eleventh-century count of Anjou, stands in grim ruin. Vertiginous gantry stairways climb up through the empty shell of the massive **keep** to its very top, but the main interest lies in the dungeons and lesser towers.

After the Logis du Gouverneur, which now houses the ticket office, you come to the **Tour Ronde**, built under Louis XI to provide a platform for artillery. It also served as a prison for Louis XI's adviser, Cardinal Balue, though the most dungeon-like room, underneath, was probably used for storing grain. Instead, Balue was kept locked up in a wooden cage (a reproduction hangs over the courtyard outside) in one of the upper rooms, perhaps the extraordinary **graffiti chamber** on the second floor, which is decorated with an enigmatic series of deeply-carved, soldier-like figures apparently wearing top-hats, which are linked together almost all the way round the walls like a paper chain. There's also a small but elaborate altar-cum-shrine. It's not known when either was carved – perhaps the thirteenth century, or even earlier.

From the courtyard, steps lead down into the bowels of the **Martelet**, which became the home of a more famous prisoner: Ludovico "Il Moro" Sforza, Duke of Milan, patron of Leonardo da Vinci and captive of Louis XII. In the four years he was imprisoned here, he found time to decorate his cave-like cell with ruddy wall-paintings that are still faintly visible, though nothing like as impressive as they once were, to judge by the reconstructed drawing on the plaque. The dungeons peter out into quarried-out galleries which produced the stone for the keep.

Beaulieu-les-Loches

The ancient suburb-village of **Beaulieu-les-Loches** is a little-visited place, despite being only 1km from the centre of Loches, on the other side of the Indre. Its parish church is built into the ruins of the **Abbaye de la Trinité**, a Benedictine abbey church built to house the bones of Foulque Nerra, the dreaded count of Anjou who also established the keep at Loches. A twelfth-century belfry still towers over the ruins of the Romanesque nave, which was damaged by fire in the fourteenth and fifteenth centuries. The monks simply rebuilt, using stones from the original, creating the stark Gothic church that now seems to prop up the ruins. You can take a stroll round the back of the whole structure, catching glimpses of some Romanesque chapels and the wonderful stone carving on the gable of the ruined north transept, which seems to depict a hunting scene.

Eating and drinking

For a drink or a simple **meal**, either of the café-brasseries on the central place du Blé makes an excellent choice: *Le Bistrot du Balto* is an informal, locally patronized affair with football on the TV and a good *plat du jour*, while *Le Grand Café des Arts* is a larger, slightly more elaborate place with a long brasserie menu. Over in Beaulieu-les-Loches, there's an inexpensive but excellent little bistro right next door to the abbey, *L'Estaminet* (*menus* €8–12; closed Mon). In the old town of Loches, *Cak'T*, 6 Grande Rue, offers all kinds of teas, coffees and cakes in a bright, homely setting.

For something more elaborate make for the hotel-restaurant at the *George Sand*, 37 rue Quintefol (*menus* €17–44), which can be patchy but is usually very good, and has a lovely, sunny dining terrace overlooking a weir on an arm of the River Indre. The restaurant at the *Hôtel de France*, 6 rue Picois (*menus* €15–43), is formal but the cooking is both classy and interesting, with lots of regional specialities. The best option of all is to stock up at the superb **market**, held in the winding streets just above the château gate on Wednesday and Saturday mornings.

The Lochois

For once, the most interesting sights in the **Lochois**, the region around Loches, don't lie along the river. In a modest way, the **River Indre** is certainly pretty, dotted with watermills and old villages, but you're better off making forays into the remnants of the ancient **Forêt de Loches**, which covers the modest uplands between the Indre and Indrois, immediately east of town. Here you'll find a quartet of monastic buildings. On the far side of the forest, astride the little River Indrois, **Montrésor** is famously one of the prettiest villages in the Loire region, with its still-inhabited château and Renaissance church. North and east lies sparsely populated land that has only partially been reclaimed from the forest. Bizarrely, the one-horse hamlet of **Nouans-les-Fontaines** is the guardian of a rare fifteenth-century masterpiece, which hangs in its church; the **château de Montpoupon**, isolated in a woodland clearing to the north, possesses a less surprising attraction – a museum dedicated to hunting.

The Forêt de Loches

Only a remnant survives of the **Forêt Domaniale de Loches**, but it's still a large and forbidding swathe of ancient woodland, and seems to close in on the D760 as it motors east from Beaulieu-les-Loches. The presence of a quartet of half-ruined religious buildings only adds to the forest's brooding feel. The first you come to as you head east from Loches is the bizarre circular chapel of **St-Jean-du-Liget**, standing in a wheat field surrounded by forest, roughly 300m off the main road. The beautiful series of wall-paintings inside depicts scenes from the life of Christ, along with a Tree of Jesse and various saints. They date from around 1180, though the chapel itself may be even older.

To get inside to see them, you may need to call in first at the **Chartreuse du Liget**, 1km further along the road, with its incongruous eighteenth-century gateway topped by a bas-relief of the dynamic, cross-wielding figure of St Bruno, the founder of the strict Carthusian order. The *chartreuse*, or charterhouse, was founded by Henry II Plantagenêt in order to atone for the murder of Thomas Becket, but almost nothing remains of the original abbey church, just a pile of ruins surrounded by eighteenth-century outbuildings, now in private hands. If you want to have a proper look round, or visit St-Jean-du-Liget, you need to ask the owner, and purchase a small explanatory leaflet (€0.30): knock at the door on the left of the main building, indicated by a small plaque (official hours are daily 8am–6pm, but there's not always anybody there, so it's best to ring in advance on ☏02.47.92.60.02).

Another kilometre up the road, another clearing in the woods shelters **La Corroierie**, a collection of fifteenth-century buildings that once sheltered the lay brothers attached to the charterhouse. The distance between the two foundations emphasized the strict sequestration of the hardcore Carthusians proper. Again, the complex is privately owned, but you can usually have a poke around the remnants of a twelfth-century church without anyone objecting, and explanatory panels have been set up for the purpose. Look out for the fresco of the Crucifixion, and the remains of a watermill.

The last of the quartet, the **Prieuré de Grandmont-Villiers**, sits at the end of a long farm track that leaves the main road opposite the turning to Chemillé-sur-Indrois, roughly 2km beyond the Chartreuse du Liget. The priory was another of the institutions set up by Henry II in his sudden outpouring of religious remorse, and for once it's still in use as a religious foundation.

Its new occupiers follow the strict and little-known Grandmont rule, an austere Augustinian monastic order established in the eleventh century, suppressed under Louis XV and, somewhat bizarrely, revived in 1979. They follow hermit-like principles of living, which seem admirably suited to this backwoods area: the three brothers live a humble, withdrawn life, scratching out an existence by raising chickens and livestock, and growing vegetables. One of them is always on public duty, however, and will happily, if quietly, show you round the roughly rebuilt church and the cloister buildings, which incorporate lots of ancient fragments of stonework, notably a fine Renaissance window in the priory itself.

If you want to **walk** or **cycle** in the forest, contact the tourist office at Loches (see p.115), which can supply details of signposted routes.

Montrésor and around

The name of this utterly picturesque village, 19km east of Loches, says it all. In modern French, **MONTRESOR** means "my treasure", and once you've passed through the forbidding Forêt de Loches, turned down into the hidden valley of the Indrois and discovered the picture-postcard château rising above the river meadows, you'll feel as if you've discovered something really precious. What's more, Montrésor harbours a collection of art works quite disproportionate to its size and significance. Disappointingly, the real etymology of the name probably stems from the Latinate "Mont Thesauri".

Montrésor is unlucky enough to have been officially classified as one of "The Most Beautiful Villages in France", but it doesn't seem to have affected it in the slightest, nor brought hordes of tourists. There's just one café, one *tabac* and the inevitable hairdresser's salon, though admittedly the antiques shop and jeweller's are probably concessions to out-of-town visitors. One of the nicest things to do is take the short, signposted **circular walk** that runs along the Grande Rue, across the footbridge at the west end of the village, then through the meadows beside the River Indrois – from where there's a fabulous view of the village panorama – then across the pretty, nineteenth-century iron footbridge and back up into the village below the church. On the way round the Grande Rue, make a short detour to the **Halle des Cardeux**, a seventeenth-century covered market with a handsome timber roof.

Like so many others in the region, the **château** (April–Nov daily 10am–noon & 2–6pm; €6) dates back to Foulque Nerra, the belligerent eleventh-century count of Anjou, but its earliest visible parts are the curtain wall and stumps of towers built by Henry II Plantagenêt in the late twelfth century in a vain attempt to save his French dependencies from the French king, Philippe-Auguste (see box on p.305). The château's main wing, however, was put up at the end of the fifteenth century by the magnificently named Ymbert de Bastarnay, who, as an adviser to Louis XI, Charles VIII, Louis XII and François I, must have been some political operator. He built the château in the middle part of his career, before the First Renaissance had really got going, so it preserves a basically late medieval look. **Inside**, however, it's perfect nineteenth century, the work of a Polish emigré called Xavier Branicki, who bought the estate in 1849 and made all the latest improvements. His descendants still own the château, and they'll either give you an excellent guided tour or allow you to wander around freely, taking in the just-as-he-left-it feel, with its grand-scale, dusty furnishings, heavy wallpapers and lots of Polish artworks and hunting trophies. Sadly, if the painting of *Christ and the Woman Taken in Adultery* is indeed by Veronese, it's not his best.

The **collégiale** (9am–7pm) now acts as the parish church, but it was originally built for one purpose: to sanctify the remains of the family of Ymbert de Bastarnay. His **tomb** still stands at the western end of the nave, a pale alabaster figure lying in prayer on a sombre black slab, accompanied by his wife and son. The tomb was broken up in the Revolution and only reassembled in 1875, but the amazing realism of details such as the pillows and the painfully aged face of Ymbert make it easy to agree with the tentative attribution to Jean Goujon, the premier sculptor of the French Renaissance. The church itself took just over twenty years to build, beginning in 1519, a period which saw the flowering of the First Renaissance. The basic concept, therefore, is Flamboyant Gothic, but Renaissance details such as the frieze above the west portal intrude insistently. The original **stained-glass window** at the east end shows three scenes from the Passion. Don't miss the amusingly carved misericords of the choir stalls, or the mawkish Annunciation by the great seventeenth-century painter **Philippe de Champaigne** in the north chapel.

Practicalities

The helpful **tourist office**, on the central Grande Rue (April–June, Sept & Oct daily 10am–noon & 2–6pm; July & Aug daily 10am–7pm; Nov–March Mon–Fri 10am–noon & 2–6pm; ☎02.47.92.70.71, ⓦwww.montresor-village.com), can provide lots of information on chambres d'hôtes and other attractions in the area. There's no hotel in Montrésor, and just one **restaurant**, the relaxed and very friendly *Café de la Ville*, 29 Grande Rue, which has outdoor tables and a good *menu* of fish and traditional meat dishes, with two courses for €17, or €28 for the full *menu* with wine. At Genillé, 12km to the northwest, the *Relais Agnès Sorel*, 6 place Agnès Sorel (☎02.47.59.50.17; *menus* €27 & €34; closed Sun evening & Mon), has three simple **rooms** (➋–➌) above its excellent **restaurant**, which serves delicate, inventive cuisine.

Three kilometres northwest of Montrésor, there's **camping** at **CHEMILLE-SUR-INDROIS**, where an artificial lake has been developed with a small beach for swimming, and pedalos and kayaks are hired out. There are two campsites, private and municipal, so there's plenty of space; the more attractive one is the private *Camping du Lac* (☎02.47.92.77.83; closed Oct–March). On the opposite side of the lake, the *Moulin de Chaudé* **restaurant** (☎02.47.92.71.31; *menus* €15–32; closed Mon) has a wood-fired grill and a pleasant outdoor terrace.

Nouans-les-Fontaines

The hamlet of **NOUANS-LES-FONTAINES**, 10km east of Montrésor, is scarcely more than an isolated crossroads in the middle of undulating fields, a junction for the main D760 to Loches and the D675 that cuts razor-straight across the countryside between the Cher and the wetlands of the Brenne. As such, its parish **church** (daily 8am–8pm) is an unlikely repository for one of France's greatest fifteenth-century paintings, but it makes the experience of viewing it all the richer. Jean Fouquet's wonderful **altarpiece** is usually referred to as a Pietà, and the central focus is indeed on the heart-rending figure of Mary kneeling beside her son's body, but it's also closely related to the Entombment scenes so popular in France, with the familiar bearded and be-hatted figures of Nicodemus and Joseph of Arimathea seen lowering Jesus's slim, muscular body onto a winding sheet. The painting was probably cut down at some stage in its life, only adding to the incredible, almost claustrophobic intimacy of the scene. The frame is further crowded by two kneeling donors. The white-surpliced man is usually identified as one Jean Bernard, a bishop of

Tours, though another theory claims that it may be the great Jacques Cœur of Bourges (see p.210), based on the presence of the watching figure of St James (St Jacques). Be sure to bring a two-euro coin to illuminate the panel behind its over-sized, bullet-proof glass case.

The rest of the church is fairly dull, and there's nothing to see or do in the village, unless you decide to have a meal at the family-run **restaurant** – only in France would a village this small have a fancy restaurant – *Le Lion d'Or*, which offers *menus* from €18 all the way up to €47.

Montpoupon

The woodland setting of the **château de Montpoupon** (Feb, March & Oct–Dec Sat & Sun 10am–noon & 2–4pm; April–June & Sept daily 10am–noon & 2–6pm; July & Aug daily 10am–6pm; closed Jan; €6.50, Ⓦ www.montpoupon.com), which lords it over a sudden forest clearing some 24km northeast of Loches, betrays its entire *raison d'être*. Hunting has always been the passion of its owners, and it's now the theme of an intriguing museum that's well worth a visit even if you're no supporter.

The site is an ancient one, well defended on a rise set in a small valley, but the current structure dates mostly from the thirteenth to fifteenth centuries. Tall, crenellated, circular towers prop up the noble *logis*, whose mullioned windows were opened up in around 1460, and the whole site is encircled by the remains of a curtain wall, guarded by an impressive gatehouse that is the most recent structure of all, dating from 1500. The historic owners, the de Prie family, sold the estate in 1763 to the marquis de Tristan, whose heirs split the 1200-hectare forested estate from the château. The latter was bought by one Jean Baptiste de la Motte Saint Pierre, whose descendant, the elderly Mlle de le Motte St-Pierre, still lives here. It's her nephew, a Parisian art dealer, who has created the **museum of hunting** in the stables and out-buildings.

You'll need quite an appetite to get round it all. You begin with a collection of carts and carriages, then the *pigeonnier* (see p.147), with its original turning mechanism for inspecting the pigeonholes, then the **Logis de Veneur**, the huntsman's lodge, which houses a reconstruction of a real saddlery that ceased to be used in 1997 and was transported here lock, stock and barrel, as well as the nineteenth-century living quarters of a chief huntsman which gives a strong impression of an almost but not quite vanished world of traditions and techniques. On the opposite side of the courtyard are scores of watercolours, photographs, hunting costumes, hunting instruments, and hunt-inspired Hermès scarves – Hermès was originally a saddler. Finally, there's a taxider-mist's studio, a reconstruction of a gamekeeper's home and full-size models of horses in their stables.

Hunting continues to be a theme **inside the château**, which you can see on hourly guided visits. There's a stag theme in the tiled flooring of the entrance hall, a light made out of an old hunting shop sign and a fine series of seventeenth-century Beauvais tapesties. But the furnishings are mostly elegant antiques, which the guide describes in some detail. Look out for the antique bathroom in the tower, off the so-called marshal's bedroom. The tour ends in the kitchens, which were supplied with electricity as early as 1870 – almost a hundred years before the nearby village of Céré-la-Ronde.

The friendly *Auberge du Château*, just 200m away (☎02.47.94.25.53; *menus* €12–15; closed Mon & Tues evening), provides a very huntsman-like setting for a solid meal – or a lighter *plat du jour*, with dishes like steaks, omelettes and salads available for around €8.

Travel details

TOURAINE | Travel details

Trains

Tours to: Amboise (18 daily; 20min); Azay-le-
Rideau (7 daily; 30min); Blois (18 daily; 40min);
Bourges (12 daily; 1hr 40min); Chartres (usually
requires change; 4–6 daily; 2hr 10min–3hr
20min); Chenonceaux (6 daily; 35min); Chinon (7
daily; 45min); Cinq-Mars-la-Pile (4 daily; 20min);
Langeais (8 daily; 25min); Le Mans (7 daily; 1hr);
Loches (2 daily; 1hr); Montlouis (6 daily; 15min);
Montrichard (10 daily; 30min); Orléans (12–18
daily; 1hr–1hr 30min); Saumur (12 daily; 45min);
Vendôme (11 daily; 30min–1hr).

Buses

Chinon to: Azay-le-Rideau (2 daily; 1hr); Langeais
(2 daily; 1hr); Port-Boulet (for Saumur; 2–3 daily;
15min); Richelieu (2–3 daily; 40min).
Tours to: Amboise (7 daily; 50min); Azay-le-
Rideau (2 daily; 50min); Chartres (2 daily; 1hr
40min); Chinon (2 daily; 1hr 10min); Loches (12
daily; 40min); Luynes (18 daily; 30min);
Richelieu (1–4 daily; 1hr 50min); Ste-Maure-de-
Touraine (4–6 daily; 50min); Vouvray (16 daily;
20min).

Blois and the Sologne

CHAPTER 2

Highlights

* **The château de Blois** The breathtaking architecture of this royal château spans centuries, while its history is stained with a notorious royal murder. See p.132

* **Au Rendez-Vous des Pêcheurs, Blois** Serious about its cooking but unpretentious, this restaurant is a great place to go for that top-priced menu. See p.139

* **Cycling between châteaux** A network of cycle routes connects Blois with the many fine châteaux that stud the wooded country to the south. See p.140

* **Château de Chambord** A behemoth of a Renaissance palace set in miles of game-rich woodlands, Chambord is the most kingly château of them all. See p.141

* **Château de Cheverny** Gleaming white in its carefully manicured park, Cheverny is the ultimate expression of the French nobility's opulence. See p.148

* **The Sologne** Walking or cycling are the best ways to explore the pine woods and wetlands of the Sologne. See p.153

* **St-Aignan** The prettiest of the little towns on the River Cher, with a crumbling château, a fascinating church and some friendly and unpretentious places to eat and stay. See p.160

△ Château de Cheverny

Blois and the Sologne

The low-lying country between the rivers **Loire** and **Cher**, south of the ancient city of Blois, palpably hasn't pulled itself away from its feudal past – even if the Revolution replaced the region's historic name, the Blésois, with the more businesslike Loir-et-Cher. The area is still dominated by swathes of ancient forest, much of it set aside for hunting, while scores of pristine châteaux stand in strong contrast to the relatively unimpressive villages and hamlets that dot the backroads.

Unlike its neighbours on the Loire, Tours and Orléans, **Blois** has never really made the leap from provincial capital to fully fledged modern city. It does, however, contain one of the most fascinating châteaux in France, standing on a rocky pedestal in the heart of the city, and the presence of significant numbers of tourists means that there are plenty of good restaurants and bars. Blois' modest size means it's easy to escape into the countryside. The southern hinterland of the city has long been famous for its game, making this prime territory for aristocrats looking to build a country residence. As a consequence, the area is studded with fine châteaux, and two in particular are ranked among the finest palaces in Europe: mammoth **Chambord** and refined **Cheverny**, two white-stone gems set in the green of their extensive private parks.

A little further south and east of Blois lies the forested, watery and wildlife-rich area known as the **Sologne**. Châteaux are thicker on the ground here than anywhere else in the region, but they're almost all definitively closed to the hoi polloi. The best way to visit the area is on foot or by bicycle, or by spending a night in a country hotel, sampling the renowned cuisine, with its rich, seasonal flavours of local forest mushrooms, game, stewed hare, freshwater fish and asparagus.

Even compared with the other gentle tributaries of the Loire, the slow-flowing **River Cher** seems unusually placid. Physically, the effect is largely created by the canalization of the river, which extends downstream from Noyers-sur-Cher, where the man-made Canal de Berry ends. In tourist terms, the valley's tranquillity is partly enforced by the château de Chenonceau, in Touraine (see p.83), whose arched bridge seems to act as a kind of weir for tourists – the coach parties just don't get upstream. The towns along this middle stretch of the Cher are relatively unassuming, though **Montrichard** and **St-Aignan** make attractive bases for a few days' stay. Most visitors come for St-

Aignan's **zoo**, or to see the great château of **Valençay**, a short distance south of the Cher, which combines Renaissance ambition with cool Classical elegance.

Train lines run along the Loire and the Cher, with a third branch connecting Valençay with Romorantin-Lanthenay and Salbris, in the Sologne. **Public transport** elsewhere in the region is sparse, with just a handful of infrequent buses run by Transports du Loir et Cher (℡02.54.58.55.55, ⓦwww .tlcinfo.net).

Blois

The small but historic city of **BLOIS**, on the Loire 53km east of Tours, is entirely dominated by its château. As a favoured residence of the sixteenth-century Valois kings, it is one of the most fascinating châteaux of them all, and one of the most exciting to visit, with its airy esplanade, dramatic courtyard and gaudily painted rooms steeped in bloody events.

The city, pleasant though it is, comes a distant second. While it flourished briefly under Louis XII, who had his court here, Blois has long been over-shadowed by its larger neighbours, Tours and Orléans; mercifully, it feels much less devoted to tourism than smaller, rival château-towns such as Amboise or Saumur. There are few sights of particular interest other than the château and the excellent Musée de l'Objet, but it's fun to explore on foot: narrow roads wind up the steep inclines, hidden squares shelter cafés, restaurants and fine old townhouses, and flights of steps cut down to the river, which is spanned by one of the Loire's most handsome bridges.

Arrival, information and accommodation

Blois is compact and easy to get around on foot: avenue Jean-Laigret is the main street leading east from the **gare SNCF** to place Victor-Hugo and the château, and past it to the town centre. The **gare routière** is directly in front of the gare SNCF, with buses leaving three times a day (at most) for Cheverny and Chambord. The **tourist office**, on rue de la Voûte du Château, the château esplanade (May–Sept Mon 10am–7pm, Tues–Sat 9am–7pm, Sun 10am–7pm; Oct–April Mon–Sat 9am–12.30pm & 2–6pm, Sun 9.30am–12.30pm; ℡02.54.90.41.41, ⓦwww.loiredeschateaux.com), organizes hotel rooms for a small fee and can provide information on day coach tours of Chambord and Cheverny.

There's a good range of inexpensive and decent **hotels** in Blois, but nothing that will sweep you off your feet.

Hotels

Hôtel du Bellay 12 rue des Minimes ℡02.54.78.23.62, ⓦhttp://hoteldubellay.free.fr/. Homely budget option. The twelve cosy little rooms are tightly packed on two floors up a steep little staircase. Rooms are well worn but clean, and much cheered up with floral wallpaper, pictures of local sights and the odd wooden beam. Overlooks the town centre from the top of the hill. ❶

Hôtel de France et de Guise 3 rue Gallois ℡02.54.78.00.53, Ⓔhoteldefranceetguise@free.fr. Grand old hotel on a busy road just below the château. Formerly the Guises' townhouse, though

the now-outdated modernization largely hides the evidence. Some rooms have balconies with views of the château loggia, but they're all comfortable. ❸

Mercure 28 quai St-Jean ℡02.54.56.66.66, Ⓔh1621@accor-hotels.com. No character whatso-ever, but it certainly offers *tout confort* – all mod cons, including a pool. Overlooks the river to the east of the town centre. ❼

Le Monarch 61 rue Porte Chartraine ℡02.54.78.02.35, Ⓔlemonarque@free.fr. Professional and energetically managed hotel with rooms cheerfully renovated in a modern style, with

BLOIS

ACCOMMODATION

À la Ville de Tours	G
Hôtel du Bellay	C
Hôtel de France et de Guise	D
Mercure	A
Le Monarch	B
St-Jacques	E
Le Savoie	F

RESTAURANTS

Les Banquettes Rouges	7
Le Castelet	6
La Garbure	5
L'Orangerie du Château	4
La Palmeraie	1
Au Rendez-Vous des Pêcheurs	8

BARS

Le Loch Ness	3
Le St-James	2

131

lots of bright yellow paint and blue curtains. Usefully located at the top end of town. ❸

St-Jacques 7 rue Ducoux ☎02.54.78.04.15, ℻02.54.78.33.05. Plain and institutional, but also inexpensive, well-maintained and near the train station. ❷

Le Savoie 6 rue du Ducoux ☎02.54.74.32.21, ✉hotel.le.savoie@wanadoo.fr. Unexceptional but likeable hotel near the train station, with reasonably pretty little rooms. Run by a friendly

young couple. ❸

À la Ville de Tours 2 place de la Grève ☎02.54.78.07.86, ℻02.54.56.87.33. Small, discreet family hotel set in a quiet quarter of town, with eight decent rooms. A few rooms look out across the square and the main road towards the river, while the darker ones at the back give onto an internal courtyard. The restaurant below serves homely cuisine, and the owners like to offer full- or half-pension. ❷

Hostel and campsite

Auberge de Jeunesse Les Grouets 18 rue de l'Hôtel-Pasquier ☎02.54.78.27.21, ✉blois@fuaj.org. Five kilometres downstream from Blois, between the Forêt de Blois and the river. Bus #4 runs on average every 45min, so you'll probably need wheels. Closed mid-Nov to Feb. €7.80.

Camping des Châteaux Lac de Loire Vineuil ☎02.54.78.82.05. On the south bank of the river, 4km from the town centre. Bus #57 (stop "Mairie Vineuil") runs only three times daily, but the campsite offers bike rental. Windsurfers, jet-skis and canoes can be hired from the adjoining water-sports base.

The château

You can glimpse different angles of the **château de Blois** (daily: April–June, Sept & Oct 9am–6pm; July & Aug 9am–7pm; Nov–March 9am–12.30pm & 2–5.30pm; €6) from all over town, but the best view is from inside the extra-ordinary inner courtyard – for which you have to pay the entrance fee. You can also get into the courtyard as part of the evening **son-et-lumière** show (see box opposite), which evocatively conjures up the château's history, but it would be a shame to miss the garishly decorated interior of the château. The two-hour, guided **visite insolite** (July & Aug daily at 3pm; English-language tour sometimes available on request, call ☎02.54.90.33.32; €7) explores parts of the château not normally seen, such as the roof and cellars, and the foundations of the medieval towers.

Some history

Blois' château began life as the powerful fortress base of the warring **counts of Blois**, the great rivals of the counts of Anjou, but by 1391 it had passed into the hands of Louis d'Orléans, brother of the mad king Charles VI. The Orléans family didn't have much luck with their acquisition. In 1407, Louis d'Orléans was assassinated in Paris by henchmen of the Burgundian duke Jean Sans Peur. His widow retired to Blois, where she died of grief a year later, while their son, the poet-duke **Charles d'Orléans**, was imprisoned in England following the French defeat at Agincourt in 1415 – where he wrote poetry as the self-styled "Scholar of Melancholy" – and was only ransomed 25 years later. When Charles returned to Blois, he established a fine library and organized poetry competitions that drew the brilliant and notorious **François Villon**, another poet-jailbird (see p.325), who was awarded a pension. At the age of 68, Charles finally had a son, Louis. He did a turn in prison too, at Bourges, but then unexpectedly came to the throne in 1498 as **Louis XII**, following the sudden death of his cousin Charles VIII at Amboise. The luck of the Orléans family seemed to have turned.

Louis XII made Blois his main residence, knocking down the outmoded feudal towers inherited from his father and building a fine new lodging with trendy Italianate details for Anne de Bretagne, the wife he inherited from his cousin along with the kingdom. The chronicler Jean d'Auton wrote in 1506 that "there they passed the time in great joy and pleasure, for the king was very healthy and in good spirits, and all his country was happy and at peace, with wealth abounding." But Louis failed to produce a male heir, and when he died in 1515 he bequeathed throne and château to his second cousin, **François I**, who had married his daughter Claude. François lost no time in rebuilding the château's north wing in an up-to-date style that was even more indebted to the Italian Renaissance. François eventually received the Habsburg emperor Charles V here – a triumph of diplomacy, as the last time Charles had visited Blois was to be betrothed to Claude de France, now François' wife.

Unlike most Loire châteaux, Blois continued to remain an important royal residence throughout the sixteenth century, partly due to **Catherine de Médicis**' fondness for it. Catherine's son François II and his wife Mary Stuart ruled largely from Blois, and her younger sons Charles IX and Henri III continued to use it for hunting and festivals. But Blois' most significant moment in French history came when it was twice the venue for the French parliament (unlike its English equivalent, it convened wherever the court was to be found). The session of 1588, called to halt the Wars of Religion, culminated in the notorious assassinations of the **Guise brothers** (see box on p.135), on the orders of Henri III.

The religious conflicts ended with the accession of Henri IV. After his death, his widow, **Marie de Médicis**, was briefly consigned to house arrest at the château by her son, Louis XIII, but she escaped down the outer wall on the night of February 21, 1619. Louis later assigned the château, along with the titles of duc d'Orléans and comte de Blois, to his brother Gaston, who set about construction of an entirely new palace following the designs of the great architect François Mansart. Luckily, Gaston only succeeded in rebuilding the west wing before the birth of a son and heir to his brother made him reconsider the state of his fortunes – he had been spending heavily on his hobbies of clock-collecting, boating on the Loire and growing tobacco and tomatoes. Gaston died in the apartments of the François I wing in 1660, and thereafter the château lapsed into obscurity, barely surviving its use as an army barracks in the early nineteenth century. In the 1840s, following the politically fashionable "rediscovery" of the romance of French royal history, architect **Félix Duban** set about the radical restoration works still visible today.

Blois' son-et-lumière

The **son-et-lumière** at the château of Blois is one of the best in the region, making the most of the enclosed courtyard setting. Crowds gather outside as dusk falls, before being let into the main courtyard. The beginning of the show is the best bit, as clever lighting effects really bring the chiselwork and the disparate architectural styles of the château to life, and a booming actor's voice recounts the story of its construction. The elaborate historical music-and-lighting show that follows is by turns kitsch, exciting and downright tacky, but the finale, following the duc de Guise step by step towards his murder, is dramatic – it was actually here, after all, that he was killed.

The show takes place just after dark on summer evenings (mid-April to mid-Sept), which means 10.15pm from mid-April to May, 10.30pm in June and July, 10pm in August and 9.30pm in the first half of September. **Tickets** (€9.50, or €11.50 including château entrance) can be booked in advance at the tourist office or by calling ☎02.54.78.72.76, though you can usually just turn up at the gate. The show is presented in English on Wednesdays.

Visiting the château

From the plateau-like esplanade in front of the château, you step through the little door to the right of the glamorous equestrian statue of Louis XII – a nineteenth-century copy – under the crowned porcupine that was Louis' emblem, through the ticket office and into the main **courtyard**, where you are confronted with an extraordinary clash of four architectural styles, only slightly muted by time. Tucked away in one corner is the plain stone of the Gothic **Salle des Etats**, the thirteenth-century manorial assembly hall, while the Flamboyant Gothic **Louis XII wing** is easily identified by the use of brick, the windows and doors dressed with stone and a few borrowed Italianate details. The graceful lines and inspired Renaissance stonework of the northern **François I wing** are interrupted by a giant spiral staircase, one of the last flowerings of the French medieval tradition before the fashion for straight, internal stairs took hold. As Balzac put it, the stone is "cut like a piece of Chinese ivory". Architecturally speaking, one of the most radical features of this wing is its giant sculpted cornice that almost conceals the dormer windows in the roof. The Classical designs tentatively introduced by Louis and François reach their apotheosis on the western side, in the **Gaston d'Orléans wing**, designed by François Mansart in the 1630s.

Salle des Etats

Signposts point you to the oldest and most dramatic part of the building first. The vast Grande Salle was built in the early thirteenth century by Thibaud VI, comte de Blois, just before the château passed out of the hands of his family. The room is usually called **Salle des Etats**, after the French parliament, the Etats-Généraux, was summoned here by Henri III in 1576 and again in 1588, to debate the religious crisis enveloping the kingdom. In 1588, when the king gave his opening speech to some five hundred representatives of the three "estates" of clergy, nobility and gentry, the walls would have been decked with rich tapestries; these days, the vaults, pillars and fireplaces are a riot of golds, reds and blues dating from architect Félix Duban's mid-nineteenth-century efforts to turn the empty château into a showcase for sixteenth-century decorative motifs. The paint wasn't long dry when revolutionaries were tried here for conspiring to assassinate Napoleon III, a year before the Paris Commune of 1870.

François I wing

A door leads through to the **François I wing**, where an **archeological museum** on the ground floor displays original stonework from the staircase and dormer windows, as well as carved details rescued from other châteaux. The collection shows how badly tufa stone weathers over time, and how much of the stonework you see today must therefore be completely "restored". The upper floors, while mostly empty, are enlivened by the rich colours of Duban's bold reinvention of the interiors – to call it a restoration would be pushing it, though his work is at least loosely faithful to the original decorative spirit. François I's salamander emblem recurs ostentatiously, along with the ermine and ermines' tails of his wife, Claude de France, duchess of Brittany. The interior is surprisingly narrow, with just two flanking rows of rooms separated by an astonishingly thick wall – this was in fact the original outer wall of the château before François I tacked the **Façade des Loges** to the outside.

The **first-floor** suite belonged to Henri III's notorious mother, Catherine de Médicis. The rooms are got up in extraordinarily vivid golds, reds and blues, but the most striking chamber is the *cabinet*, or **study** – the only room in the

château to have preserved its original decor. According to Alexandre Dumas'
novel, *La Reine Margot*, Catherine kept poison in the hidden cupboards that
lurk behind four of the study's 237 carved wooden panels, but these are actually fairly standard accoutrements in the Italian-inspired *studiolo* – *cabinet* in
French – a private room for contemplation, study and safe storage of fine art.
You can see the concealed foot pedals in the skirting that spring open the
cubby-holes, which are usually left open to display Renaissance objets d'art.

Stairs lead up through the thickness of the internal wall to the **second floor**,
the province of Catherine's son, Henri III, with more fabulously colourful neo-
Renaissance decoration. It was in the **royal bedroom**, now graced by a reconstructed four-poster bed, that the duc de Guise was hacked to death by the king's
assassins (see box below). As Flaubert noticed, the king's oratory lies just two
doors away, "a coincidence not unusual in itself but which strikes one forcibly
here, in a man whose sensuality was stimulated by religion and whose cruelty was
whetted by fear". A large adjoining room displays nineteenth-century paintings
of the Guise murder, including two full-length portraits of a suitably effete Henri
III and a duc de Guise who looks as if he could have fought off Henri's gang of
murderous *mignons* with one hand tied behind his back.

The murder of the duc de Guise

In 1588, the French parliament convened in Blois' medieval Grande Salle. **Henri III**
opened proceedings by attacking "the unbounded ambitions of certain subjects".
No one had any doubt who he meant. The powerful **Henri, duc de Guise**, and his
brother, the Cardinal of Lorraine, were the populist leaders of the ultra-Catholic **Holy
League**, which claimed to defend the faith against Protestantism and the king's
weak, compromising policies. Back in 1560, it was Guise who was the target of the
Huguenot rebels at Amboise (see p.79), and Guise who was most diligent in the exe-
cutions that followed. In the quarter-century since the Tumult, France had fallen into
open civil war, with Protestants and Leaguers alike raising armies to fight each other
and, on occasion, the king.

The conflict became known as the **War of the Three Henrys**, with Henri, duc de
Guise, Henri III and the Protestant Henri de Navarre as leaders of the main factions.
The king decided that the only solution was to get rid of Guise, who was rumoured
to be setting himself up as heir to the throne on the basis of his family's claimed
descent from Charlemagne. Guise was secretly receiving money from Philip II of
Spain.

At dinner on December 22, the duke found a note on a napkin warning him of the
threat to his life. Contemptuously, he scribbled on it, "they wouldn't dare", and
retired to spend the night with the beautiful Catherine de Beaune-Semblançay. Early
the following morning, while waiting for a meeting to begin in the **Salle du Conseil**,
Guise received a message from the king asking him to attend him in the nearby
Vieux Cabinet (now destroyed). To get there, Guise had to pass through the **royal
bedroom**, which lay just the other side of the thick partition wall of the château;
there he was set upon by the king's loyal bodyguard, the **Forty-Five**. He received a
stab wound in the neck but fought on, fending off his attackers "like a wounded bull"
– the noise of their feet could be clearly heard on the floor below. When he finally
succumbed, he cried out "God have mercy!" and fell to the ground. Legend has it
that the king came through to deliver a contemptuous kick to his rival's body, commenting, "My God, he looks even bigger dead than alive". Guise's brother, the cardinal, was murdered soon after, and both bodies were burned in secret.

The royal family didn't have long to enjoy their newly asserted mastery of the kingdom. Catherine de Médicis died at Blois just ten days after the murders, and the
Guises were avenged a year later when a monk assassinated the king.

Few visitors bother to penetrate inside the severe **Gaston d'Orléans wing**, but it's well worth having a look at Mansart's breathtaking internal staircase, with its framed trompe-l'oeil cupola. A seventeenth-century painting in the adjacent, fifteenth-century **chapelle St-Calais** shows Gaston, along with his brother Louis XIII, adoring the holy sacrament. The chapel is sadly over-restored, though there's a fine Gothic vault given the full technicolour Duban treatment, and some interesting 1950s stained-glass windows by the prolific Max Ingrand. A gap alongside the chapel allows you to walk through to a terrace known as the **Perche aux Bretons**, after the lodgings of Anne de Bretagne's bodyguard of a hundred Breton gentlemen, which once stood on this spot. At the edge of the ramparts, the **Tour du Foix** is one of the few visible vestiges of the thirteenth-century château of the counts of Blois. From the terrace there are excellent views over the city.

Louis XII wing

Back in the main courtyard, the **Louis XII wing** is relatively disappointing on the inside, for all that it bears witness to Blois' heyday. The ground floor houses an undistinguished **Musée des Beaux-Arts**, with a few sixteenth-century paintings, a lot of nineteenth-century sculptures and a collection of tapestries, one of which, from the Parisian Gobelins workshop, shows the château as it appeared in the early eighteenth century.

The rest of the city

The twists and turns, hills and stairs of the city centre make it a confusing place to walk around, though the area is in fact very small. The higher ground forms a horseshoe shape around the **place de la Résistance**, which lies at the north end of the main town bridge, the **Pont Jacques Gabriel**. On the west side of the horseshoe, the **château** perches above the abbey church of **St-Nicolas** and the river, while the **cathédrale St-Louis** stands on the eastern slopes above the winding streets of the old **Quartier du Puits Châtel**, where Blois' limited nightlife is to be found.

Around the château

For all its attractive airiness, there's little to do on the château's esplanade except wander around with an ice cream – unless you plan on taking a half-hour cart-horse-and-carriage tour (April–Oct 2–6pm; €5) or visiting the tourist office. In July and August, however, a local produce **market** takes place every Thursday afternoon.

The tall building at the far end from the château is the less-than-magical **Maison de la Magie** (daily: April–June & Sept 10am–noon & 2–6pm; July & Aug 10am–6.30pm; €7.50). Children are unlikely to be convinced by the rather shoddy optical illusions inside, still less the stuffy room dedicated to local impresario, Robert-Houdin, but the afternoon magic shows are in mime, so at least there's no need to understand French. Younger children may want to catch the mechanical dragons stretching their golden necks through the front windows, on the hour. Steps lead down from here to the pleasant **place Louis XII**, centred round the rump of a fifteenth-century fountain that survived the artillery storm of June 1940.

From the square, you can continue down to the river, or take rue Anne de Bretagne west to the **Musée d'Histoire Naturelle** (Mon–Fri 9am–noon & 2–6pm; €2.40). Instructive dioramas explain various regional environments and the birds and animals that live in them, but children aren't likely to find it very exciting, still less the dusty **Musée d'Art Religieux** (Tues–Sat 2–6pm; free) – all shabby mitres and gilt reliquaries – that occupies the same building. **Rue St-Lubin**, home of Blois' better bistro-restaurants, heads west of place Louis XII towards the **église St-Nicolas** (daily 9am–6.30pm), which once belonged to the Benedictine abbey of St-Laumer. It's very bare inside, but the choir is a handsome example of the Romanesque style, and there's a fine cupola over the crossing. The abbey buildings alongside were rebuilt in the seventeenth century, following the destruction of the old monastery by rampaging Huguenots.

Turning back north, **rue des Fossés du Château** climbs round under the Gaston d'Orléans wing of the château before ending up at place Victor Hugo, where there's a small public garden ringed by traffic and overlooked by the Baroque **église St-Vincent**. The modest greenery is a pleasant reminder of the fabulous Renaissance gardens designed by Pacello Mercogliano that once stood here, but the main reason to come is to look up at the extraordinary **Façade des Loges**, the masterpiece of François I's château, modelled on a loggia of the Vatican designed by Bramante and Raphael – François had met Pope Leo X while campaigning in Italy. Rising smoothly from the natural rock that led the counts of Blois to build their fortress here in the first place, it stretches like a great Italianate cliff from the old Salle des Etats on the left to one of the surviving medieval towers on the right, smoothly wrapping itself round before coming up short against the relatively brutal Gaston d'Orléans wing. A covered bridge once led across from here to the raised garden terraces. Rue de la Voûte du Château leads back up to the esplanade.

The cathedral quarter

The cafés on **place de la Résistance** are popular on summer evenings, though the real action goes on in the atmospheric streets immediately east, in the **Quartier du Puits Châtel**. A number of medieval houses survive here, particular on rue des Juifs, where the old ghetto lay, on rue Vauvert and rue Pierre de Blois. At the east end of the handsome **place St-Louis**, the **Maison des Acrobates** is a particular fine half-timbered construction decorated with sculpted tumbling figures.

The **cathédrale St-Louis** (daily 7.30am–6pm), at the west end of the square, rests on Carolingian foundations and leans against a weighty bell tower. The lowest storey of the tower is twelfth century, while the top was only completed in the mid-sixteenth century. Surprisingly, the Gothic body of the cathedral actually postdates the tower. The interior is fairly bare; indeed some of the stone blocks above the nave arcade are still blind, waiting for the sculptor's chisel. The crypt contains the bones of St-Solenne, a bishop of Chartres who died at Blois, but the most interesting feature is the modern **stained-glass windows**, completed in 2003 by the Dutch artist Jan Dibbets working in collaboration with a French glassmaker. They follow a careful programme of colour symbolism, adorned with biblical tags in Latin.

Leading off place St-Louis, rue du Palais traverses above the town centre, passing the long stairs at the head of rue Denis Papin and leading into rue St-Honoré. At no. 8, the elaborate **Hôtel Alluye**, the private house of the royal treasurer Florimond Robertet, is a rare survival of Blois' golden years under Louis XII. At the top of the hill, the twelfth-century **Tour Beauvoir**, on rue des Cordeliers (Easter–June, Sept & Oct Sat & Sun 2.30–6pm; July & Aug daily 3–7pm; €3) was the town prison until the end of World War II. Various exhibitions are held inside, but the main reason to come is for the view from the top.

Pont Jacques Gabriel and St-Saturnin

The highly distinctive angular humpback of the **Pont Jacques Gabriel** dates from 1724, though as the monument at the bridge's apex explains, it has been partially destroyed many times – unusually, because of warfare rather than flooding. The last demolition job protected the retreat of the German army in 1944. The suburb on the far side of the city, the **Quartier de Vienne**, is home to the **église St-Saturnin**, whose Flamboyant Gothic west portal dates from the time of Anne de Bretagne, who commissioned it. The cloister-like structure alongside is in fact an unusual walled cemetery from the era of François I, now used to show off the **Musée Lapidaire** (April–June, Sept & Oct Sat & Sun 2–5pm; July & Aug daily 2–5pm; free with château entrance ticket), a collection of sculptural fragments gathered from the rubble after the bombardments of 1940.

Musée de l'Objet

It's well worth slogging uphill to the unusual **Musée de l'Objet**, set back from the town centre at 6 rue Franciade (mid-May to mid-Sept Tues–Sun 1.30–6.30pm; mid-Sept to mid-May Sat & Sun 1.30–6.30pm; €4). The museum celebrates conceptual sculpture, and most of the works here have been made using found objects rather than traditional materials. The entrance sets the tone: hanging from the ceiling of the staircase, a forest of hammers gradually morphs into handbags – a work entitled *Passage André Breton* (1996), by Jean-Jacques Lebel. The two long, spacious galleries are filled with similarly witty or alarming artworks and installations, including some by major figures in modern art: **Christo** is represented by a disturbing wrapped mannequin, while the conceptual artist **Joseph Kosuth** has a piece called *Leaning Glass* (1965), which is exactly that. Other pieces are simpler fun, including *Le Couple de Damas* (1986), a life-size couple dancing on a kitsch bit of carpet cut out in the shape of a tiger skin, by the French group Présence Panchounette, and the random plunks and twangs of Joe Jones's *Guitare* (1973), which emanate from a guitar randomly strummed by a dangling, jerking plectrum.

Haras National

A solid bet for horse lovers, or maybe children, is the **Haras National**, 62 ave Maunory (mid-March to May & Oct Mon–Fri 2.30pm, Sat 2.30pm & 4pm; June & Sept Mon–Sat 2.30pm & 4pm; July & Aug Mon–Sat 10.30am, 2.30pm, 3.30pm & 4.30pm, Sun 10.30am & 3pm; €6), one of 23 studs distributed around the country. It's odd to find a stud so close to the centre of town, especially as there's no field for the forty-odd stallions to gallop around in. The reason is quite simple: the horses are all here for breeding only – as becomes clear when you are shown the extraordinary leather horse used to goad the stallions into doing their bit for artificial insemination.

Elsewhere there's a horse shower and solarium – for drying, not tanning up – a working saddlery, a vet's room, an old stables full of carriages and a smithy where you can sometimes see the blacksmiths at work. As for the stallions, they're an impressively virile lot, best seen exercising on the little sandy circuit on the front lawn. In the second set of stables you are shown the stud's much-loved carthorses, including four massive **Percherons**, a breed which gets its name from La Perche, the region just north of Le Mans. Astonishingly, these horses can weigh up to 1000kg. The ninety-minute visits are always guided, and usually in French – though you're given an excellent English leaflet.

Eating, drinking and entertainment

Most of Blois' traditional **restaurants** can be found on or around rue St-Lubin, between the château and the river. On the east side of town, there's a cluster of bars and eateries in the Quartier du Puits Châtel; the delightful little square at the end of rue Vauvert, in particular, has a number of crêperies and pizzerias with tables set out under an Indian bean tree, and from here alleyways cut through to rue de la Foulerie, the best place for ethnic food – Portuguese, Moroccan and Indian – and late-night **bars**. The cocktail bar *Le St-James*, at 50 rue de la Foulerie, with its little square behind, is a good bet late on weekend nights, while *Le Loch Ness*, a Beamish-serving "pub" nearby at 7 rue des Juifs, is perennially popular.

A new **music festival**, Tous sur le Pont, got started in 2003 with an impressive line-up of domestic, international and local acts, ranging from Rita Mitsouko through to Juliette Greco and Manu Dibango. Gigs took place in locations all over the city, including the château and the Jardins de l'Evêche, and the festival looks set to become a yearly event, beginning in the last week of June and carrying through to mid-July; ask at the tourist office for information and tickets.

Restaurants

Les Banquettes Rouges 16 rue des Trois Marchands ☏02.54.78.74.92. Serves unusually adventurous food in a pretty lemon-yellow dining room with the red bench-seats of its name. You'll find dishes like pork ribs with honey and lime, or herb-stuffed squid on the €18.50 and €24.50 *menus*. Service is very proper but the modern bistro atmosphere is more relaxing than usual. Closed Mon & Sun.

Le Castelet 40 rue St-Lubin ☏02.54.74.66.09. Specializes in homely Loire cuisine, using regional produce such as Sologne honey and *andouilles* from Vouvray, matched with local wines. Very enjoyable, as long as you don't expect anything too elaborate. A few tables sit out on the adjacent side-street. Closed Wed & Sun.

La Garbure 36 rue St-Lubin ☏02.54.74.32.89. Good specialities from the Périgord and Gascogne regions for around €15, including the speciality, *garbure*, a typically hearty sausage, duck and vegetable stew. Friendly and unpretentious, but rather touristy. In fine weather, outside tables sit across from those of *Le Castelet*. Closed Wed, Thurs lunch & Sat lunch.

L'Orangerie du Château 1 ave Jean-Laigret ☏02.54.78.05.36. The well-heeled flock to this posh restaurant, which offers seriously refined regional cuisine, though the atmosphere can suffer from the group banqueting factor, with over-fussy service. Dining rooms are spread across various wings and levels, the best one being in the echoey vaulted chamber to one side. There are *menus* for less than €30, though you'll do better picking one in the €40–65 range. Closed Mon lunch, Wed & Sun evenings.

La Palmeraie 44 rue de la Foulerie. A good alternative to the usual trad French, with decent couscous and tagines from around €12, and the usual souk-like decor.

Au Rendez-Vous des Pêcheurs 27 rue Foix ☏02.54.74.67.48. Unquestionably the best gastronomic restaurant in town, with an impeccable, fresh, uncluttered dining room, and elaborate fish dishes on the eight-course €64 *menu découverte*. There is a come-hither €24 *menu* (not served Sat eve), but it doesn't show the chef at his best. Closed Mon lunch & Sun, and 3 weeks in Aug.

Listings

Bike rental Cycles Leblond, 44 levée des Tuileries (☏02.54.74.30.13); Holiday Bikes, 7 rue du Dr Desfray (May–Aug only; ☏02.54.56.07.73).

Boat trips The Observatoire Loire, 4 rue Vauvert (☏02.54.56.09.24), offers two-hour excursions on an old-style *fûtreau* sailboat with a guided commentary (in French) on river wildlife; book tickets at the observatory itself or through the Blois tourist office. They also run guided nature walks. It helps if you speak French, but some guides can get by in English.

Canoes and kayaks Between June and September you can hire canoes from the Base de

Loisirs in Vineuil, 1km upstream from the town centre on the southern bank, and paddle about in perfect safety in the calm water behind the barrage.

Email and Internet Le Troisième Monde, 39 ave Jean Laigret, near the train station (Mon–Sat 11am–10pm).

Emergencies Ambulance ☏15; Centre Hospitalier de Blois, Mail Pierre Charlot ☏02.54.55.66.33; late-night pharmacy, phone police (see below) for address.

Police 42 quai St-Jean ☏02.54.55.17.99.

Taxis ☏02.54.78.07.55.

Blésois châteaux

Some of the finest **châteaux** in the whole Loire region are clustered on the left bank of the Loire, in the historic **Blésois region** – now known prosaically as the *département* of the Loir-et-Cher. The location – within easy reach of Blois, on the edge of the semi-wilderness of the Sologne – explains the attraction for château-builders: this is prime hunting territory. Even the greatest château of them all, **Chambord**, started life as a hunting lodge, and it still sits within its own dedicated game reserve, the **Domaine de Chambord**, while elegant, aristocratic **château de Cheverny** still maintains a pack of hounds.

These days, the châteaux themselves are the bait. Chambord alone attracts around 750,000 visitors each year, and while few sights in Europe compete in that league, both Cheverny and noble **Chaumont**, perched on its terrace above the Loire, rank among the loveliest and hence busiest châteaux in the entire Loire region. But with its woods and quiet backroads, the area doesn't feel crowded, and you could even find yourself alone in smaller châteaux such as **Villesavin**, **Troussay** and **Fougères-sur-Bièvre**. Even the **château de Beauregard**, with its extraordinary portrait gallery, sees surprisingly few visitors.

Public transport in the area is very poor, with even the main routes served by only a couple of commuter buses a day, which means timings are less than helpful for sightseeing. Note, however, that the local bus company TLC (☎02.54.58.55.55, ⊛www.tlcinfo.net) runs **coach trips** to Chambord and Cheverny, with morning and lunchtime departures from Blois' gare SNCF (mid-May to Aug; €10). Check exact times when you buy your ticket from the tourist office. Staff may also be able to find places on a chartered taxi or minibus tour.

The best option is **cycling**, as a new three-hundred-kilometre-long network of tranquil cycle routes and dedicated cycle paths takes advantage of the mostly flat forest alleys and wooded backroads. The only section of the route not complete at the time of writing was along the traffic-ridden highway heading southeast out of Blois. Bikes can be rented in Blois (see p.139) and many of the smaller towns in this chapter, while tourist offices and some hotels stock a free map of the cycle network, *Le Pays des Châteaux à Vélo*. If you want to **walk**, you're best off following one of the area's excellent GR footpaths (see box on p.154).

Château de Beauregard

The little-visited **château de Beauregard** (Feb 8 to end March, Oct, Nov & Dec 20 to Jan 3 daily except Wed 9.30–noon & 2–5pm; April–June & Sept daily 9.30am–noon & 2–6.30pm; July & Aug daily 9.30am–6.30pm; €6.50) lies in the Forêt de Russy, an easy seven-kilometre cycle ride south of Blois, on the D956 to Contres. It's a satisfying château to visit, as there are only a handful of rooms open to the public, and three of them are especially magnificent.

Beauregard's existence is owed to the efforts of a family of butchers from Blois, the Doulcets, to outgrow their humble origins. The first owner of the fief, Jean Doulcet, was ennobled by Louis d'Orléans in 1455, but it was left to his son to erect the first château, and the building as it stands today was largely rebuilt by Jean du Thier, a humanist and friend of Ronsard, in the 1550s. In the seventeenth century, the new owner, Paul Ardier, modified it again, adding the facade facing the garden and the long gallery. The result is sober and serene, very much at ease in its manicured park.

The highlight of the château is a richly decorated **portrait gallery**, its walls entirely panelled with 327 paintings of kings, queens and great nobles. They're hardly the finest paintings in the region, but the overall impression is staggering, and in any case the original object would have been to edify and amaze, rather than to display fine art. Few of the portraits can have been done from life, but many are probably good likenesses nonetheless, as they would have been copied from well-known images where possible. If you've spent any time in the region, it can be rewarding to put faces to names – there's Jean de Berry, the duc de Sully and all of France's kings from Philippe VI (1328–50), who precipitated the Hundred Years War, to Louis XIII (1610–43), who occupied the throne when the gallery was created. In among the French notables are various European celebrities, from the Habsburg Emperor Charles V to Francis Drake and Anne Boleyn. Emperors, kings, nobles and executed wives alike are all given equal billing – except for Louis XIII, whose portrait takes up the space of nine others. The floor of blue-and-white Delft tiling – unfortunately partly covered by protective carpeting – depicts Louis' army on the march.

On the other side of the partition wall, the **southern gallery** is lined with fine old furnishings, including some impressive sixteenth- and seventeenth-century pieces. At the gallery's far end, the **Chamber of Bells** was installed by Jean du Thier. It's a little wood-scented oaken cube of a study, every surface painted, gilt or carved in the finest humanist tradition of the *studiolo*. No effort has been spared to create the right atmosphere of high-flown artistic brilliance, held to be most conducive to study and reflection. The painted panels show the proper activities for the Renaissance man, from music to hunting and warfare, and from farming and sculpture to, apparently, tennis.

The grounds slope down towards the River Beuvron, and it's well worth taking a stroll at least as far as the sunken **Jardin des Portraits**, a Renaissance-influenced creation by contemporary landscaper Gilles Clément, who was responsible for Paris's futuristic Parc André Citroën. It could be better tended, but the garden's formal arrangement – by colour of flower and foliage – is fascinating. Elsewhere in the grounds you'll find an alley of cyclamens, and cedars on the picnic lawns beside a pretty, reed-fringed lake. A garden festival is held here every year in early April.

Château de Chambord

The gargantuan **château de Chambord** (daily: April–Sept 9am–6.15pm; Oct–March 9am–5.15pm; €7; ⓦ www.chambord.org) has always inspired extravagant comparisons. The writer Châteaubriand thought it "like a woman whose hair had been blown about by the wind", while Touraine-born novelist Alfred de Vigny felt "as if an Oriental djinn, compelled by the power of some wonderful lamp, had snatched it away … from some country of the sun to conceal it in mistier lands". Henry James wrote more prosaically that "the whole thing was monstrous … the exaggeration of an exaggeration".

François I's "hunting lodge" is certainly one of the most bizarre and magnificent commissions of its age. Its patron's principal object – to outshine the Holy Roman Emperor Charles V – would, he claimed, leave him renowned as "one of the greatest builders in the universe". And yet for most of its life the château has stood empty and forgotten, a wilderness of stone surrounded by thick forest contained behind a giant wall. The cold, draughty size of the château made it unpopular as an actual residence – François I himself stayed there for some forty days during his 32-year reign – and Chambord's role in history is slight.

Leonardo's posthumous masterpiece?

The authorities in charge of looking after **Chambord** are desperate to attribute its plan to international superstar and marketing dream **Leonardo da Vinci**, even though he died four months before building began, in 1519. Their arguments come down to "it's so good it must be by him", backed up by cherry-picking in his notebooks for similar bits of design – a spiral staircase under a cupola here, a square-shaped palace with corner towers there and a single sketch of a curious staircase with four separate ramps climbing round a square well.

It is true that Leonardo had a close relationship with François I at Amboise (see p.80), and he certainly made sketches of an ideal city to be built near Romorantin, in the south of the Sologne, though little came of these plans. It's likely, however, that Chambord's design was by an obscure Italian architect called **Domenico da Cortona**, and that it was perfected by the French master masons supervising construction – not to mention the 1800 workmen who laboured and all too often died at the marshy site, plagued by mosquitoes and fever. Leonardo may have had at least some input. He made a note that he had met da Cortona, so they probably discussed their king's projects – perhaps Leonardo even suggested refinements.

The most brilliant architectural idea at Chambord, the **double-spiral staircase**, may in fact be due to the great Italian architect Giuliano da Sangallo. He is thought to have taught da Cortona in Italy, and is known to have created a double-spiral staircase at the Pozzo di San Patrizio in Orvieto – used by donkeys to bring up water from the well. Another Chambord curiosity, the belfry-like **lanterns** that top the conical roofs, may be François I's own idea. After his disastrous defeat at the **Battle of Pavia**, in 1525, the king was taken prisoner and held at the Carthusian monastery near the city, where he wrote to his mother, "All is lost save my honour and my life". It would seem odd to commemorate such humiliation, even if François did think his honour intact, but there's no doubt that Chambord's roofscape, completed in the 1530s, bears a striking resemblance to the Charterhouse of Pavia.

Before you even get close, the sheer scale of the palace is awe-inspiring. There are over 440 rooms and 85 staircases, and a petrified forest of 365 chimneys runs wild on the roof. In architectural terms, the mixture of styles is as outrageous as the size. François I wanted to establish prestigious Italian Renaissance art forms in France, and he certainly used Italian architects, but the labour would have been supplied by French masons. So the massive round towers with their conical tops, and the explosion of chimneys, pinnacles and turrets on the roof bring to mind Flamboyant Gothic, but Italianate Classical details also proliferate, notably the niches decorated with shell-like domes, and the distinctive, diamond-shaped panels of Anjou slate done up to look like marble. An eighteenth-century survey counted eight hundred different capitals atop the many columns and pilasters, each a unique variation on one of the Classical orders.

Whoever the genius behind Chambord may be (see box above), the design is pure Renaissance: rational, symmetrical and designed to express a single idea – the central power of its owner. Four hallways run crossways through the central keep, at the heart of which the great staircase rises up in two unconnected spirals before opening out into the great lantern tower, which draws together the confusion on the roof like a glorious crown.

The summer **events** and festivals calendar is a busy one, with night-time lighting displays, guided walks and wildlife-stalking in the forest, costumed tours for children and classical concerts, among other attractions. Check the main website at ⓦ www.chambord.org for details.

The donjon, staircase and roof terrace

Chambord's design may be ingenious but it's not very practical, what with its confusing four-way symmetry and double-spiral staircase. Marguerite de Navarre used to complain to her brother François I that she was always getting lost when he wasn't there to help her. These days, a free leaflet helps explain the basics. It's worth bearing in mind that when you get on the great staircase you come off it on the same side of the château as you got on – just one level up or down.

On each floor, the **donjon**, or keep, is divided up into four separate apartments grouped round the four corner towers. At the heart of the building is a cavernous cross-shaped stone atrium. Two giant earthenware stoves can be seen here, decorated with the coat of arms of the notorious Maréchal de Saxe, victor of Fontenoy, who ordered them in a vain attempt to heat what served briefly as his home. At the centre of the atrium is the famous **staircase**. Children love to play on it, entranced by the fact that you can catch glimpses of other people on the second, interwinding flight, but never actually catch them up. It's not a modern fascination – Anne d'Orléans, known as "La Grande Mademoiselle", recalled that she used to play on the stairs with her father, Gaston d'Orléans: "he came down as I went up, and laughed aloud to see me run, thinking as I did to catch him." A good place to admire the structure is from the bottom of the narrow central well, accessible at the ground-floor level.

The great staircase ends at the roof level, sheltered by the stunning glazed space of the **lantern tower**, which then continues on skyward through a series of fantastical tiers, culminating in a gilded fleur-de-lis topped by a slender cross. The stairs give onto the **roof terrace**, Chambord's crazed highlight, where you can wander freely in the middle of a forest of chimneys, balconies, turrets, balustrades, finials, dormer windows and steeply pitched slate roofs. You can also eyeball the endlessly inventive Renaissance stonework and look across at the single-spiral staircase towers that serve the château's side wings, slender versions of their parent at Blois. Beyond the château walls, moated lawns give way to the trim woodland of the surrounding park and the forested scrub of the Sologne.

The apartments

A number of rooms on the ground and first floors were fitted out by **Louis XIV**, one of the few French monarchs grand enough not to be dwarfed by the château – in fact, one of the few to spend any time here at all. Louis commissioned his architect Jules Hardouin-Mansart to complete the chapel and west wing, and made a number of autumn hunting trips here with his court. In 1670, the assembled nobles were famously entertained by the première of Molière's *Le Bourgeois Gentilhomme*.

As reconstructed today, the most interesting Louis XIV-era rooms are in the grand position at the front of the château's first floor, in the wing running between the north and west towers. The **Salle de Compagnie**, in the very centre of the facade, has one of the only pieces of original pre-Revolutionary furniture left in the château, a giant console table with a limestone top that is said to have been used for the embalming of the Maréchal de Saxe. The adjacent **Salle du Roi** has been sumptuously renovated as Louis XIV's bedchamber. The king's valet's room is preserved in the tower room alongside, the simple camp bed visible through an original wood-and-glass partition uncomfortably reminiscent of a shop-front.

The first floor of the south tower is taken up by the **eighteenth-century apartments** installed by the marquis de Polignac, the château's governor in the last years before the Revolution. The marquis made the château habitable by lowering ceilings, constructing wooden floors, building small fireplaces within the larger ones, and cladding the walls in panelling and ornate wall-coverings – the latter at their (reproduced) best in the **Laurel** and **Indian chambers**.

On the opposite side of the vestibule, the east tower apartments are occupied by the **Musée du duc de Bordeaux**, dedicated to the man better known as Henri, comte de Chambord, the last serious pretender to the French throne (see box below). The large collection of miniature copper artillery pieces gathered in one of the rooms was used for the count's military training, though as Henry James noted sniffily, "I wondered, if he should take it into his head to fire off his little canon, how much harm the comte de Chambord would do." You can spot the occasional French monarchist fanatic on pilgrimage, but to anyone else the museum is exceedingly dull, a sad collection of portraits, busts, sentimental knick-knacks and oppressive furnishings.

Most people miss out the **second floor** altogether, but it's worth stepping off the staircase at least for the nobly coffered ceilings that vault over the vestibules. The half-empty apartment rooms house a rambling **Musée de la Chasse**. Even if you're not a hunting enthusiast, you can find some beautiful paintings and engravings of animals among the guns and glorificatory paintings, and you get a good sense of the emptiness and chilly silence that has so long been Chambord's lot. The finest exhibits are two superb seventeenth-century tapestry cycles, kept in the north tower suite. One set depicts Diana, goddess of the hunt; another, based on cartoons by Lebrun, tells the story of Meleager, the heroic huntsman from Ovid's *Metamorphoses*.

The last Bourbon

At his birth in September 1820, Henri, duc de Bordeaux, was acclaimed as the **enfant du miracle**, the "miracle child", as France thought it had seen the last of the Bourbons following the death of his father early the same year. There were enough loyalists left in the country to buy the child the **Château de Chambord**, the money having been raised by public subscription. Even more surprising than Henri's birth is the fact that he claimed the throne at all. The Bourbons had already been kicked out of France twice: in the Revolution and again when Henri's grandfather Charles X was chased from the throne in the Three Glorious Days of July 1830, to be replaced with his cousin, Louis-Philippe.

Henri's mother, Marie-Caroline de Bourbon-Sicile, was a vociferous "legitimist" – that is she supported the Bourbon claim rather than the "Orléanist" claim of Louis-Philippe's supporters – and she brought up her child in the old, pig-headed Bourbon way. Despite his unassuming new title of **comte de Chambord**, it was expected that Henri would reclaim his rightful throne – the child's collection of miniature artillery, now exhibited at the château, was intended as more than a plaything. After the fall of Napoleon III, in 1871, a conservative, royalist government took control of the National Assembly, and overtures were made to the count to return to Paris as Henri V. Everyone assumed he would take up the throne.

But with characteristic Bourbon arrogance, Henri released what has become known as the **White Flag Manifesto** of 5 July 1871, probably written while he spent his only three nights at Chambord. He claimed that he couldn't relinquish the Bourbon's white flag – "the standard of Henri IV, of François I and of Joan of Arc ... which floated over my cradle and will shade my tomb" – in favour of the Republican *tricolore*. What he meant was that he wouldn't submit to the Crown being awarded him by the National Assembly, rather than being due to him by God. As his final refusal letter of October 1873 admitted, "I do not want to be the legitimate king of the Revolution."

The side wings

François I's apartments were installed in the **east wing** in the early 1540s, served by their own separate tower staircase. The intimate sequence of inter-locking rooms may be largely bare and empty, but it gives a surprisingly good sense of a lived-in space. The highlights are the bedchamber, fitted out with Renaissance-style furnishings, and the light-filled *studiolo*, or private study, with its delicate coffered and vaulted roof inscribed with the royal fleur-de-lis and François' own flaming salamander emblem. You can also see panels from two wonderful series of tapestries known as *Les Chasses du roi François* ("King François' hunt"), most woven in the seventeenth century.

The **west wing** of the keep, accessed by another tower staircase, is almost entirely filled by the airy **chapel**. Each rib of the broad vault rests on twin columns, according to the latest fashion of the 1540s.

The stables

The **stables** just south of the château were turned into barracks by the **Maréchal de Saxe**, who was given Chambord to live in by Louis XV, in thanks for the great victory at Fontenoy, during the War of the Austrian Succession. They housed the marshal's riotous-living private army, which stayed with Saxe during his 1748–50 sojourn, before he tired of the château's unhealthily marshy atmosphere. The buildings are now ruined, but an open-air **equestrian show** (May, June & Sept Mon–Fri 11.45am, Sat & Sun 11.45am & 4pm; July & Aug daily 11.45am & 5pm; €7.50; ⓦ www.chambord-horse-show.fr) uses the site for displays of trick riding, with costumed riders.

Practicalities

An infrequent **bus** service (1–3 daily) serves Chambord from Blois, dropping you off right in front of the château. You can rent **bikes** and **boats** from the jetty where the Cosson passes alongside the main facade of the château; bikes cost €8 for two hours, rowboats around €10–20 per hour, depending on the number of people.

Accommodation in the village of **CHAMBORD** itself can be found opposite the château (and beside the cafeterias and postcard stalls) at the *Hôtel du Grand St-Michel* (ⓣ 02.54.20.31.31, ⓕ 02.54.20.36.40; ❹). Taking in the sight of Chambord after the crowds have left is very satisfying, and the more expensive rooms (❺) have direct views of the château, but the hotel is distinctly scruffy. Ten kilometres east, at Crouy-sur-Cosson, there are chambres d'hôtes at the *Moulin de Crouy*, 3 rte de Cordellerie (ⓣ 02.54.87.56.19, ⓦ http://lemoulindecrouy.com; ❸), an ivy-clad watermill set in large gardens, with a swimming pool.

The Domaine de Chambord and around

In 1528, the traveller Andrea Navagero wrote that in the forests near Blois was a deer so marvellous that no one would hunt it, indeed "every respect is paid to it, such as one would show to a wonder of the world." Much of the forest has disappeared since then, but a well-protected game reserve, the **Domaine de Chambord**, survives behind its 32km of wall. Wild boar roam freely, and badgers, foxes, hares, rabbits and even wild sheep live in the forest, though red deer are still the beasts you're most likely to spot, along with circling buzzards. Regional information is available online at ⓦ www.chambordcountry.com.

Only two areas of the reserve are open for free exploration: the strip along-side the Cosson as it flows towards Blois, and the area west of the road to Muides-sur-Loire, where there are four circular routes along signposted paths.

You can get around easily enough on foot, or rent a **bike** from the boat jetty next to the château de Chambord. To get deeper into the forest you'll have to sign up in advance for a **guided excursion**, such as the five-hour cycle ride (€30, lunch included), or four-hour dawn nature walk (€24, with breakfast), or the more expensive trips exploring the reserve in a 4WD or on horseback. A free leaflet available at the château gives details (French-language only, but all staff speak English and can help), or you can call ☏02.54.50.50.00.

St-Dyé-sur-Loire

The materials used for building Chambord almost all arrived at the tiny riverside port of **ST-DYE-SUR-LOIRE**, 3km from Chambord (with a dedicated cycle path connecting the two). These days the riverside quays are mere embankments, but they make for a delightful place to stroll, especially at sunset when the sandbanks teem with birds. The friendly **Maison de la Loire**, 73 rue Nationale (Mon 10am–noon, Tues–Fri 10am–noon & 2–6pm, Sun 2–6pm; ☏02.54.81.68.07), has a small exhibition on the port and the building of Chambord, as well as lots of information on the natural history of the river (€2.50). Staff can organize inexpensive bird-watching trips and half-day canoe trips down from St-Laurent.

A rather swanky **hotel**, the *Manoir Bel Air* (☏02.54.81.60.1; ❸), stands at the eastern end of the village; the rooms at the back have great river views, and there's a good riverside restaurant, but it can feel unfriendly and oversized. You're better off at M and Mme Bonnefoy's extremely friendly, antique-furnished **chambres d'hôtes**, 102 rue Nationale, at the western end of the village (☏02.54.81.60.01; ❹); their back gate gives onto a path that runs down a field and right onto the riverbank. Opposite the church, the whimsical delicatessen-cum-**restaurant** *La Bourriche aux Appetits* (☏02.54.81.65.25; *menus* at €24/39; closed Mon–Thurs) is a charming place to dine on fresh, inventive fish dishes and terrines.

Bracieux

There's not a lot to **BRACIEUX**, a pleasant little town just beyond the southern wall of the Domaine de Chambord, but it makes a good base for visiting the surrounding châteaux, especially by bike. On Thursday mornings (and Sunday mornings in summer), a market gathers under the ancient covered *halle*, which is the town's main sight.

There are two **hotels**: the decent *Hôtel du Cygne* (☏02.54.46.41.07, ☎02.54.46.04.87; ❸), and the *Hôtel de la Bonnheure*, 9 rue René Masson (☏02.54.46.41.57, ☎02.54.46.05.90; ❸), which has a good range of rooms and apartments set around floral gardens. Both rent bikes to guests for a moderate price. Bracieux also has a large, three-star **campsite** (☏02.54.46.41.84; closed mid-Oct to mid-April) with a summer-only pool and the option to rent chalets (around €40 for up to six people). At the edge of the village, where the Chambord and Blois roads split, there's a top-flight **restaurant**, *Le Relais de Bracieux* (☏02.54.46.41.22; *menus* €38–120; closed Tues & Wed), with a strong emphasis on local, seasonal produce – you might find a *croustillante* of Loire eels in Orléans vinegar, wild boar with spiced vegetables or hare fillet with juniper berries.

Château de Villesavin

Despite its prime location midway between Chambord and Cheverny, many visitors hurry past the graceful **château de Villesavin**, set back from the road

3km west of Bracieux (mid-Feb to May, Oct & Nov daily 10am–noon & 2–7pm; June–Sept daily 10am–7pm; Dec Mon–Fri 10am–noon & 2–6pm; guided tour €7.30, grounds only €5.80). In terms of bang for your buck, the entry ticket is definitely expensive for what's on offer – a modest, low-slung set of white-stone buildings arranged around three sides of a courtyard – but as an antidote to the bombast of its neighbours, Villesavin is perfect. You'll need your own transport to get here.

The present structure is the work of **Jean le Breton**, who shared François I's defeat and imprisonment at the Battle of Pavia in 1525. On his return from Italy, Le Breton was rewarded with the task of managing the payments for the construction of Chambord, and he found time to build his own château nearby, starting construction in 1527 and finishing it only ten years later – having begun work at Villandry (see p.92) in the meantime. Legend has it that Villesavin was built with materials or funds earmarked for Chambord, but all that's really known is that many of the Italianate architectural ideas, and probably some of the craftsmen, were borrowed from the giant building site down the road.

Despite Le Breton's links with Chambord, in many ways Villesavin is closer in spirit to the Roman "Villa Savinus" that may once have stood at this spot. Over and above the obviously Classical details, the arrangement of the low-level buildings round a courtyard gives off a distinct whiff of Rome, suggesting refined but practical country living. There's even a statue of the goddess Diana in the centre of the facade, while the **chapel** is relegated to a side wing; inside, the walls and vaults are entirely painted in still-bright colours, with a fine sixteenth-century wall-painting of the Flagellation.

The outbuildings on the far side of the chapel house a bizarre museum dedicated to nineteenth-century marital garb, but persevere as far as the giant **dovecot** (see box below), its 1500 pigeonholes still accessible by a ladder turning around a central spindle. From here you can walk round to the plainer southern facade of the château.

The guided tour of the **interior** is only moderately interesting, and usually in French only. This is, after all, a real home rather than a museum, lived in today by the comte and comtesse de Sparre. The only room in the château that preserves its sixteenth-century form is the kitchen, with its blackened beams and roasting spit in the huge fireplace. The rest of the rooms are graceful and airy eighteenth-century work, though the current owners are slowly returning some of the windows to their original Renaissance shape.

For a lunch stop, the *Bistro d'Arian*, in the village of Pont d'Arian, 1km south, is a traditional but friendly **restaurant** serving excellent *cuisine du terroir* – well-cooked food using lots of local produce.

Pigeon pest

One of the triumphs of the French Revolution was dismantling the dovecotes that once belonged to every château. These **colombiers** or *pigeonniers* were an important status symbol for the nobility, as the number of doves or pigeons that each *seigneur* was allowed to keep was in direct proportion to his land holding: the larger the dovecote, the larger the estate. An important château might be home to a thousand or more doves, which would descend on new-sown fields like a plague of locusts. Barred by law from hunting even vermin, peasants were powerless to protect their crops. Meanwhile, the birds' droppings were sold on as a valuable fertilizer.

Château de Cheverny

Fourteen kilometres southeast of Blois, the **château de Cheverny** (daily: April–June & Sept 9.15am–6.15pm; July & Aug 9.15am–6.45pm; Oct–March 9.30am–noon & 2.15–5/5.30pm; ⓦ www.chateau-cheverny.fr; €6.10) is the perfect seventeenth-century château. Built largely in the 1620s and early 1630s and never altered, it presents an immaculate picture of symmetry, harmony and the aristocratic good life – descendants of the first owners still own, live in and go hunting from Cheverny today. The stone from which it is built – from Bourré on the River Cher (see p.159) – lightens with age, and the château gleams like a great white brick in its acres of rolling parkland.

The **Hurault** family have been the *seigneurs* of a château here since 1510, but the story of the present building begins infamously a hundred years later, when one Henri Hurault was visiting the court of Henri IV. The legend goes that as he left the king's chamber, he caught a glimpse in a mirror of the king making the sign of a cuckold's horns behind his head. He galloped home in a jealous rage to Cheverny, where he surprised his wife in bed with her lover. After murdering the lover in the garden, he forced his wife to choose death by poison or pistol shot. She chose the bottle rather than the bullet, leaving Henri free to marry again. His second wife, Marguerite, masterminded the building of the new château while her husband was an officer of Louis XIII's court.

For once, the old building was entirely expunged, and Marguerite took advantage of the clean sheet by building an entirely new kind of structure: purist, Classical and restrained. Cheverny's **architecture** seems unrelated to the feudal fortress, a new departure for a Loire château, but there are telltale throwbacks. In particular, the little room and steep roof that top off the central staircase block make it look rather like a tower, and the side pavilions could almost be corner turrets.

Since the château was first built, the Huraults have proved a tenacious lot. In 1764 they were forced to sell the château to Jean-Nicolas Dufort-de-Saint-Leu – who wanted to retire to a modest country retreat in order to put a cap on his outrageous spending at Versailles – but a descendant of the family, the marquis de Vibraye, managed to buy it back under the restored Bourbon king, Charles X. The current owner, one Charles-Antoine Droulhet de Sigalas, now styles himself marquis de Hurault de Vibraye, to underline the historic connection. He lives on the second floor with his wife and three children, whose photos litter pianos and occasional tables throughout the château.

The interior

The château's **interior** decoration has only been added to, never destroyed, and the extravagant display of paintings, furniture, tapestries and armour against the gilded, sculpted and carved walls and ceilings is almost overwhelming. The most precious objects are hard to pick out from the sumptuous whole, but the highlight must be the work of the painter Jean Monier. His cack-handed but charming painted wall panels in the **dining room** tell stories from *Don Quixote*, while the beams and panels of the **Arms Room**, on the first floor immediately above, are awash with mottoes and flowers, and the golden chimneypiece shows his version of the *death of Adonis*. On the opposite side of the room, a seventeenth-century tapestry from the Parisian Gobelins workshop is extraordinary for its vibrant and unfaded colours. In the **King's Bedroom**, just beyond, the colours are yet more astonishing, with

△ François I staircase, Château de Blois

paintings by Monier of Perseus and Andromeda adorning almost every surface, four fabulously intricate tapestries on the walls and an original gilded and silk-hung sixteenth-century bed.

On the other side of the central staircase, the **Private Apartments** are more modest and far more congenial. They were in use until 1985, and give a rare glimpse of a contemporary château's elegant decor. By way of contrast, on the ground floor immediately below, the **Great Drawing Room** has a typically cluttered nineteenth-century feel, overstocked with Louis XIV chairs and other scraps of precious furniture. It is, however, hung with some very fine portraits, including an excellent Mignard effort over the fireplace showing Henri Hurault's grandson's wife, and a set depicting Louis XIII along with his wife, his brother Gaston d'Orléans and his niece Anne, Mlle de Montpensier. Between the windows on the north side of the room hangs a gorgeous portrait of Henri Hurtault's daughter Elisabeth, whom Mlle de Montpensier described as having "admirable hands and the loveliest elbow I have ever seen", among other more conventional compliments. On either side of the mirror opposite the chimneypiece are two remarkable pictures: one shows Cosimo de' Medici, future grand duke of Florence, and is attributed to **Titian**; the other is from the school of Raphael. But the most treasured paintings are in the **gallery** beyond, where the three small, sixteenth-century Hurault family portraits above the door are by François I's court painter, **François Clouet**.

The outbuildings and grounds

The rear facade of the château is very different from the front, with its projecting towers and dressed stone windows and edges biting into the plainly rendered walls in what became the classic Louis XIII style. The low building at the far end of the lawns is the **Orangery**, built by the Duforts, no doubt as part of their penny-pinching regime.

Given its situation on the edge of the Sologne, the château has always been a centre for hunting with dogs. Near the main entrance, the **trophy room** holds around two thousand sets of antlers. The **kennels** alongside house a hundred lithe hunting hounds – a cross between foxhound and Poitevin – that mill and loll about while they wait for the next stag. If you can stomach it, feeding time (5pm) is something to be seen, the dogs obediently waiting for permission before tearing into their meat. Cheverny's hunt culls around thirty animals a year, a figure set by the National Forestry Office.

You can explore the elegant **grounds** on foot, or take a sedate, hour-long tour by golf-buggy and boat (April to mid-Nov; €10.80 including château entry).

Tintin in the Loire

Some visitors to Cheverny find the château oddly familiar. If they do, it's probably because Hergé used it as the model for Marlinspike Hall (Moulinsart in French), the ancestral home of Tintin's nautical friend, **Captain Haddock**. The only change Hergé made was to remove the large outer pavilions from his drawings.

The connection is milked dry in the slick exhibition, **Les Secrets de Moulinsart**, housed in the outbuilding next to the main gate (daily 9.30am–6.45pm; adults €10.50 with château ticket, children aged 7–14 €6.20 with château ticket), which retells various Tintin stories in rooms dressed up in the style of the cartoon, enlivened by audio-visual effects and film clips.

Practicalities

Cheverny's small but very helpful **tourist office**, 12 rue de Chêne des Dames (daily: March–Oct 11am–7pm; Nov–Feb 2–6pm; ☎02.54.79.95.63), is on the main road 50m along from the château gates. **Bikes** can be rented from the cycle shop on place de la Maire (☎02.54.79.95.63), in **COUR CHEVERNY**, Cheverny's larger neighbour, 1km away. Most people come by car, but there is a **bus** service connecting Cheverny to Blois and Romorantin, which runs three times daily in each direction.

You can **stay** at Cour-Cheverny's well-maintained and good-value two-star, the *Hôtel des Trois Marchands* (☎02.54.79.96.44, ⓦwww.hoteldes3marchands .com; ❸; closed March); the hotel restaurant is elegant and rather smart, or there's the inexpensive bar and grill next door. Set back from the road to Fougères-sur-Bièvre in its own park, a couple of kilometres out of town, the three-star *Château de Breuil* (☎02.54.44.20.20, ⓔbreuil@chateauxhotels.com; ❽; closed Jan–March) is distinctly classy, with elegant, period-furnished bedrooms. Right opposite the château entrance, the **restaurant** *Le Pichet* (☎02.54.79.97.23; *menus* €17–27) does decent regional fare, with brasserie dishes and drinks served on the terrace in fine weather.

The surrounding countryside is packed with good **chambres d'hôtes**. The following are among the nicest, but Cheverny's tourist office can supply a more complete list. Six kilometres from Cheverny, near Chitenay, *Le Clos Bigot* (☎02.54.44.21.28, ⓔclos.bigot@wanadoo.fr; ❸) is a picturesque collection of old buildings built round a courtyard, with rooms in the dovecote; nearby, just off the road between Cormeray and Cellettes, M et Mme Calonne offer rooms at the modest but attractive *Château de la Coque* (☎02.54.70.33.92; ❹). At Contres, 10km south of Cheverny, *La Rabouillère*, chemin de Marçon (☎02.54.79.05.14, ⓦwww.larabouillere.com; ❹), is a half-timbered farmhouse with four cosy and freshly decorated rooms; while the grand house of *Le Saint Michel*, 22 rue de Bel Air (☎02.54.44.12.84, ⓦwww.lestmichel.com; ❺), in the village of Les Montils, 8km north of Fougères-sur-Bièvre, has large, handsome rooms that aim at an aristocratic, nineteenth-century style, though they lack the real antique furnishings.

Château de Troussay

Three kilometres from Cheverny, on the road to Cormeray, the **château de Troussay** (April–June & Sept daily 10.30am–12.30pm & 2–6pm; July & Aug Mon & Wed–Sun 10am–6.30pm, Tues 10am–10pm; Oct Sat & Sun 10.30am–12.30pm & 2–5.30pm; €4.60) is a little gem. It was originally built in the fifteenth century as a *gentilhommière*, or country manor, the noble details round chimneys and windows added only in the sixteenth century. In fact, some oddments of sculpture only found their way onto the facade after 1828, when the historian Louis de Saussaye rescued various bits of decoration from dilapidated châteaux in the region.

More purloined fragments can be seen on the French-language guided tour of the interior, notably the stained-glass windows from the Guises' *hôtel* in Blois and the delicately carved but heavy **oratory door**, a rare survival from the demolished château de Bury, arguably the first Renaissance château of them all. In all, the interior is handsome rather than spectacular, as fits the setting.

As is normal in a minor château, the *communs*, or outbuildings, run right up to the main front of the house, forming a large sandy yard – Troussay was more than half a farm for much of its life. The links are acknowledged in a small exhibition on Sologne life in part of the old stables, which displays lots of old photos and agricultural implements, with meticulous homespun explanations (in French). A little room is entirely devoted to doing the laundry, but most curious is the section on dog carts, used in the Sologne by everyone from schoolchildren to the postman.

Château de Fougères-sur-Bièvre

The proudly defensive **château de Fougères-sur-Bièvre** (mid-May to mid-Sept daily 9.30am–noon & 2–6pm; mid-Sept to mid-May daily except Tues 10am–noon & 2–4.30pm; €4) lies in the village of the same name, 10km southwest of Cheverny. The château was built in 1470 by Louis XI's chancellor, the aptly named Pierre de Refuge, who was clearly sceptical about long-term peace: unlike its more luxurious contemporaries this is a veritable fortress, turned tightly in on itself.

The inner **courtyard** is the most attractive feature. Spindly towers buttress the walls, little slate roofs crowded between and on top of them, and a long arcaded gallery runs the length of one side as far as the **chapel**, which housed a millwheel for most of the nineteenth century. Two decorated door lintels survive from Pierre de Refuge's day, but the rest of the stonework is plain. Inside, you can scurry freely about the many corridors, rooms and spiral staircases, even clambering under the oak-framed roof and strolling along the **guard-walk**, and there are rarely other visitors to interfere with the medieval fantasy. Unfortunately, the château's more recent history as a mill and later a hostel means almost nothing survives apart from the bare walls, ceilings and fireplaces. Various exhibits along the way explain medieval building techniques, but you'll need fairly good French to appreciate the explanations.

Château de Chaumont

When Catherine de Médicis forced her rival, Diane de Poitiers, to hand over Chenonceau (see p.83) in return for the **château de Chaumont** (daily: April & late Sept 10.30am–5.30pm; May to mid-Sept 9.30am–6.30pm; Oct–March 10am–12.30pm & 1.30–5pm; €6.10; grounds open daily 9.30am–dusk; free), Diane is thought to have had the worst of the deal. You can't help feeling Diane could hardly complain. Sitting on a low hilltop overlooking the Loire, 20km downstream from Blois, the château occupies one of the finest bits of real estate in the region. To get to the château you can take one of the frequent **trains** from Blois or Tours, get off at Onzain and stroll across the Loire – no more than a thirty-minute walk.

The original fortress on the site was destroyed by Louis XI in revenge for the part its owner, Pierre d'Amboise, played in the "League of Public Weal", an alliance of powerful nobles against the ever-increasing power of the monarch. But Pierre found his way back into the king's favour, and with his son Charles I, he was able to build much of the quintessentially medieval castle – complete with machicolated round towers, moat and drawbridge – that stands today. Under Louis XII, Pierre's grandson **Charles II d'Amboise** was sent to Milan as governor of the newly won French territories, where he became the patron of Leonardo da Vinci. With his uncle, the powerful Cardinal Georges d'Amboise, he was one of the first to import the fashionable ideas of the Italian Renaissance into France. His interlaced initials, as Charles de Chaumont, are repeated along the odd frieze that runs in a band across the exterior walls, alternating with what looks like a thorny, steaming dung heap but is supposed to signify *chaud mont* ("hot hill") – though the château's name actually comes from *chauve*, meaning bald, a reference to the woods cleared from the hilltop in order to build the original castle. More letter Cs appear on the elaborately alle-gorical plaque that overlooks the drawbridge, above the heads of two naked savages holding the family coat of arms. The building works were completed by **Diane de Poitiers**, who arrived in 1559, just nine years after Catherine de Médicis bought the château from the Amboise family.

The interior

Proto-Renaissance design is more obvious in the courtyard, which today forms three sides of a square, the fourth side having been demolished in 1739 to improve the views over the river, which are spectacular. Inside the château, the heavy nineteenth-century decor of the ground-floor rooms dates from the ownership of **Marie Say**, daughter of the millionaire sugar baron Constant Say, and her husband **Amédée de Broglie**, who together lived here in grand style until the bottom fell out of the sugar market and the château was sold to the French state in 1938.

A few rooms on the **first floor** have been remodelled in Renaissance style. The large council chamber is floored with seventeenth-century majolica tiles, its walls adorned with wonderfully busy sixteenth-century tapestries showing the gods of each of the seven planets known to exist at the time. Sadly, the stunning series of tapestries commissioned by Charles II to depict Petrarch's Triumphs – Time, Youth, Love, Eternity – are now kept in the Cleveland Museum of Art.

The grounds

The Broglie family also transformed the 21-hectare landscaped **park** into the fashionable English style – all rolling lawns and tall trees, no fussy French flower-beds – and built the remarkable Belle Époque **stables**, with their porce-lain troughs and elegant electric lamps for the benefit of the horses at a time before the château itself was wired, let alone the rest of the country. A corner of the château grounds now plays host to an annual **Festival des Jardins** (mid-May to mid-Oct daily 9.30am–8.30pm; €8, or €11 with château entry), a huge affair which shows off the extravagant efforts of scores of contemporary garden designers.

On weekends in summer, you can secure the best view of the château from the deck of a traditional Loire boat. Book in advance with the Association Millière Raboton (☎06.88.76.57.14, ✆m.raboton@wanadoo.fr), whose scheduled **boat trips** (March–June & Oct 2.30pm; July–Sept dawn, 3pm, 5pm & 7pm; €10–15) leave from the quay immediately below the château, and last roughly an hour and a half.

The Sologne

Depending on the weather and the season, the **Sologne** can be one of the most dismal areas in France, a damp, flat, featureless bog that earns its soubriquet

The **Sologne** isn't an official French region, but instead spreads across three admin-istrative *départements*: the Loir-et-Cher, the region's heartland, to the west: the Cher, to the east; and the Loiret, to the north. Only the western area that falls with-in the Loir-et-Cher *département* is covered in this section. The eastern and northern fringes of the region are covered elsewhere in the guide, where you'll find accounts of **Aubigny-sur-Nère** (see p.218) and the area around **La Ferté-St-Aubin** (see p.181), with its rambling château and nearby nature reserve.

Walking in the Sologne

There are over 1000km of signposted **footpaths** in the Sologne, many accessible by bicycle, and tourist offices in most towns and villages can provide maps, along with details of horse-riding and bike rental. Two *grandes randonnées*, or national walking routes, lead through the Sologne, both variants of the main GR3 along the Loire – which turns a little inland south of Blois, passing close to the château de Beauregard before forking at rue de Meneuil, 5km northwest of the château de Villesavin. The northern **GR3C** runs through Chambord and east, mostly along forest roads, to Thoury and La Ferté-St-Cyr, where it rejoins the southern branch, the **GR31**, which has taken a more attractive route through Bracieux and along footpaths through the southern part of the Forêt de Chambord. From La Ferté-St-Cyr you can continue on the wooded GR3C east towards Ménéstreau-en-Villette (see p.182), divert southeast on the GR31 towards La Ferté-Beauharnais and Lamotte-Beuvron, where it turns south, or take the **GRP** (*grande randonnée de pays*) **Vallée des Rois** north towards Cléry-St-André, in the Orléanais (see p.184). A number of other GRP side-routes allow you to make circular walks.

The best **map** for all these routes is IGN 3615, *Sologne*. If you can follow French, the walkers' guidebook *La Sologne à Pied* (€7.50) details some twenty walks lasting from two to six hours – even if you don't speak French you can just follow the route maps. If you're exploring the Sologne during the **hunting season** (Oct 1–March 1), don't stray from the marked paths; there are endless stories of people being accidentally shot.

of *triste* ("sad") *Sologne*. But at other times its forests, lakes, ponds and marshes have a quiet magic – in summer when the heather is in bloom and the ponds are full of water lilies, or in early autumn when locals go hunting for wild mushrooms, apricot-scented *chanterelles* and flavour-rich *cèpes*. Wild boar and deer roam here, not to mention the ducks, geese, quails and pheasants which far outweigh the small human population.

The Sologne remains the refuge of the French aristocracy, along with the descendants of rich industrialists who bought land and built châteaux here in the latter part of the nineteenth century. Hunting is the thing, not tourism, and much of the Sologne is out of bounds or simply physically impenetrable. This conservative culture means that it's a frustrating region to visit: most châteaux are cached in forests at the end of long, barred drives – Sologne estates are unusually large by French standards.

One of the few private châteaux to open its doors to visitors is the romantic **château de Moulin**, built in the handsome red brick typical of the region. Nearby, the large but exceedingly dull town of **Romorantin–Lanthenay** acts as something of an unofficial regional capital, but to get the best of the Sologne you'll have to head into the countryside, either to a country hotel like the one at **La Ferté-Imbault**, or out to a wilderness area such as the **Pays des Etangs**, around the little village of **St-Viâtre**.

Romorantin-Lanthenay

Forty kilometres south of Blois, **ROMORANTIN-LANTHENAY** is a French byword for stick-in-the-mud provincial dullness. Even the old Renault/Matra factory which sustained the town for so long is finally closing its doors, leaving almost ten percent of Romorantin's inhabitants out of work. But it remains the biggest town in the Sologne, and there are a couple of good hotel-restaurants if you choose to base yourself in the area. The best time to visit is in the last weekend in October, during the **Journées**

Gastronomiques food festival, when hundreds of street stalls tempt you with traditional and novel dishes centred on game, wild mushrooms, apples and pumpkins.

The Town

Romorantin made a bid for stardom in the early sixteenth century, when Leonardo da Vinci drew up plans for a utopian city to be called Romolontino, or "little Rome", but his sketches were never realized, or at least they only took shape further north, at the château of Chambord (see box on p.141). Today, Romorantin has just two sights of local interest. The **Musée de Sologne**, housed in the old mills astride the River Sauldre, just below the town centre (June–Aug Mon & Wed–Sat 10am–6pm, Sun 2–6pm; Sept–May Mon & Wed–Sat 10am–noon & 2–6pm, Sun 2–6pm; €4.50; ⓦwww.museedesologne.com), is large and surprisingly glossy, with elaborately presented exhibits on the history, ecology and traditions of the area. But unless you read French, or you're particularly interested in brickworks, gamekeeping and local biscuit products, it's unlikely to enthrall. The **Musée Matra**, at 17 rue des Capucins, on the north side of the main road bridging the Sauldre (Mon & Wed–Fri 9am–noon & 2–6pm, Sat & Sun 10am–noon & 2–6pm; €4.50, or €7.62 with Musée de Sologne), shows off the Matra and Renault cars that were built at the factory on the site. There's a smattering of flashy racing cars, and a proud but less exciting display of the Renault Espace people-carrier, the most recent – and last – product of the factory.

You're better off at the huge, child-friendly Aliotis **aquarium** (Feb daily 11am–6pm; March & Oct daily 1.30–6pm; April–June & Sept daily 10am–6.30pm; July & Aug daily 10am–7.30pm; Nov–Jan Wed & Sun 1.30–6pm; €10, children aged 3–14 €7; ⓦwww.aliotis.com), 5km outside Romorantin, on the road to Salbris. It has displays of huge local fish like the graceful sturgeon and hideous *silure*, as well as exotic species such as a three-metre bull-shark, giant turtles, a seventy-year-old, hundred-kilo crocodile and a tank containing around a thousand piranhas. There are lots of activities for children, including panning for snail shells and semi-precious stones in a shallow pool, guddling for carp in a hands-on tank, taking pedalos out on the river (€3), petting the goats and other farm animals in the little park – and feeding the shark.

Practicalities

For information on walking routes in the Sologne, as well as bike hire, contact the **tourist office** on the main square, place de la Paix (Mon 10am–12.15pm & 2–6.30pm, Tues–Sat 8.45am–12.15pm & 1.30–6.30pm; July & Aug also Sun 10am–noon; ☏02.54.76.43.89, ⓦwww.tourisme-romorantin.com). The tourist office can also put you in touch with the Romorantin-based organization Sologne Nature Environnement (☏02.54.76.27.18, ⓔsne@free.fr), which runs guided walks and nature-spotting expeditions right through the year.

If you fancy a splurge, head for the *Grand Hôtel du Lion d'Or*, 69 rue G.-Clemenceau (☏02.54.94.15.15, ⓦwww.hotel-liondor.fr; ❼), an old manor house, with a fabulous courtyard garden, sixteen well-appointed **rooms** and a stellar **restaurant** (meals over €75) where the chef is known for his use of organic ingredients and, sometimes, medieval spices; if you've never had frogs' legs in a seventeenth-century variety of wild garlic, this is the place to try it. *Le Colombier*, 18 place du Vieux-Marché (☏02.54.76.12.76), is friendly and quiet, and serves Solognot specialities in its small restaurant (*menus* at €17 & €23; closed Mon, Sat lunch & Sun evening).

La Ferté-Imbault

One of the most impressive but definitively closed châteaux in the Sologne lies at the eastern edge of the village of **LA FERTE-IMBAULT**, 18km east of Romorantin. Surrounded by stables and well-tended lawns, the noble, red-brick pile looks extremely moneyed. It should be – the château's estates once stretched across some 10,000 hectares, roughly twenty times the French average. The village is pleasant to stroll around, with the remains of a Romanesque chapel standing among the pretty brick houses and floral displays of the little island of St-Taurin, and picnic tables on the banks of the River Sauldre.

There's a good traditional **hotel** on the main square, the *Auberge à la Tête de Lard*, 13 place des Tilleuls (T02.54.96.22.32, Wwww.aubergealatetedelard.com; **❸**), which has pleasant, quiet rooms and a good restaurant (*menus* €16–46; closed Mon, Tues lunch & Sun eve), and rents out mountain bikes to guests.

Château du Moulin and around

Built almost entirely of brick, surrounded by water, and standing in romantic isolation at the end of a long avenue of oak trees, the **château du Moulin** (daily except Wed 10am–12.30pm & 2–6.30pm; €6.50) is the quintessential Sologne château. It lies just outside the village of Lassay-sur-Croisne, 10km west of Romorantin-Lanthenay, and is still occupied by its elderly owner, Mme de Marchéville, whose family bought it off the du Moulins in 1901.

The original builder, local *seigneur* Philippe du Moulin, earned the right to set himself up as a nobleman with a fortified château after saving Charles VIII's life at the 1495 Battle of Fornovo, the unpleasant coda to the king's Italian campaigns. Only the main keep and the wide, low corner tower date from the original fifteenth-century fortifications, the rest of the defences having been cleared to leave a kind of open, moated courtyard, though the gatehouse block of tall, narrow towers was subsequently rebuilt. The château's brickwork is striking, curving smoothly around the various towers, the pink tint offset by an inlaid lozenge pattern in dark grey and the window frames of white tufa stone. It's the same style made popular by Louis XII at Blois and elsewhere, but seems more natural here in the Sologne, where even the humblest houses are built of local brick.

Guided visits of the **interior** take place roughly every half-hour, and last around 45 minutes; if it's not too busy staff should be able to lay on an English-language tour. You're shown a series of half a dozen rooms in the main keep section, all beautifully furnished by the father-in-law of the current proprietor, one Louis de Marchéville. He also installed a clever central-heating system, the radiators disguised as traditional iron chimney-backs. The main **salle d'apparat** is one of the highlights, with the chestnut ceiling painted in the seventeenth century and the small polychrome statue of St Catherine, from the school of the great Tourangeau sculptor Michel Colombe. Upstairs, Mme de Marchéville's own bedroom is entirely furnished with seventeenth-century pieces. On the second floor, the **chambre de Philippe du Moulin** contains two extremely rare bits of fabric: the bedcover is actually made from fabric removed from the walls of the Ste-Chappelle in Paris, while the strange tapestry on the wall dates from the fourteenth century, in the semi-abstract patchwork style of Bergamo.

Locature de la Straize

To see how the other half lived, make for the nearby **Locature de la Straize** (April–Oct: Sat & Sun 10–11.30am & 3–6pm; Mon, Wed & Thurs call

ⓣ02.54.83.82.89 to make an appointment; €4). The owner, who lives in an adjacent house, has reconstructed this sixteenth-century *locature* (farm-workers' cottage, in Sologne dialect) as it would have been lived in until the early part of the twentieth century: the barn on one side of the partition wall, and the simple one-room accommodation on the other. Sitting on the edge of marshy fields and woodland, it's a rather moving contrast to the usual round of châteaux. Monsieur Picard has also collected an array of Solognot items in the barn next to his own house, creating a private **museum** of old clothing, tools and items in use in daily life, many of them from his own family. The hamlet of La Straize lies just a couple of kilometres west of the château du Moulin, but to get there you'll have to drive for some 6km until you get onto the road between Gy-en-Sologne and Soings-en-Sologne, which it lies halfway between.

The Pays des Etangs

If you had to pinpoint the Sologne's marshy heart, it would lie in the area immediately southeast of the village of **ST-VIATRE**, which is some 30km northeast of Romorantin-Lanthenay. Known as the **Pays des Etangs**, or "land of little lakes", this is the Sologne at its dampest. Birdwatchers can spot great crested and black-necked grebes, marsh harriers, and endless types of ducks, with the chance to see ospreys in September, and cranes in October and November. You may even hear bitterns in spring, and black and whiskered terns nest on the water lilies. For information on the many walks in the area, or to learn about Sologne pond life, call in on the **Maison des Etangs** (mid-June to mid-Sept 10am–noon & 2–6pm; rest of year call ⓣ02.54.88.93.20), which occupies a half-timbered house in the centre of St-Viâtre.

One of the best ways to see the area is by **bicycle** along the **route des Etangs**, which forms a 21km triangle between St-Viâtre, the village of Marcilly-en-Gault, some 7km southwest, and the Etang de Marcilly, a small lake 2km south of the little town of **LA FERTE-BEAUHARNAIS**. You pass endless lakes and ponds along the route, with lots of offshoot paths to explore for picnicking or bird-watching. Bikes can be hired at Camping de la Varenne (ⓣ02.54.83.68.52; closed Oct–Easter) at **NEUNG-SUR-BEUVRON**, a tiny Sologne town 4km west of La Ferté-Beauharnais.

A pleasant **walking route** circles the muddy little Néant, a wooded stream just north of St-Viâtre. From the village, take the D123 towards Chaumont-sur-Tharonne and stop after 3km at Ste-Marie farm. From here a rough tarmac farm road heads east, passing the farm of St-Loup, where the odd brick structure used to house the relics of St-Loup, a local saint with reputed healing powers. The road follows the north bank of the Néant for some 4km, ending at the junction with the D49. Turn right at this main road, crossing the Néant, and then turn right again a short distance beyond the bridge at the signpost for the GR31 footpath. You then follow this footpath back along the south side of the Néant to the D123, ending up a few hundred metres south of where you started. The whole circuit from Ste-Marie is about 8km long.

If you're looking for somewhere to **stay** in the area, the *Auberge de la Chichone*, 6 place de l'Eglise (ⓣ02.55.88.91.33, ⓕ02.54.96.18.06; ❸), is right in the middle of St-Viâtre, next to the church, and has just half a dozen simple rooms in rustic Solognot style; its **restaurant** (*menus* €15–30; closed Tues evening & Wed) is similarly old-fashioned, but good. Alternatively, make the pilgrimage 15km northeast to the modest town of **LAMOTTE-BEUVRON**, where the large, well-to-do *Hôtel Tatin*, 5 ave de Vierzon (ⓣ02.54.88.00.03, ⓦwww.hotel-tatin.com; ❹; closed first week in Aug), is the original home of tarte Tatin – supposedly created by accident by the Tatin sisters, who once ran the hotel – and serves it all day long. It's some way to go for an upside-down apple tart, but the restaurant is pretty good across the board, with refined *menus* in the €20–30 range.

The middle reaches of the Cher

The middle reaches of the **Cher** are its sleepy heart, defined here as the stretch of river bordering the Sologne, falling within the government *département* of the Loir-et-Cher. While this part of the Cher lacks the historical and architectural glamour of the Touraine, to the west, or Blésois, to the north, the little towns and villages along the way have a relaxed, backwater feel. The two main centres are **Montrichard** and **St-Aignan**, both with handsome châteaux lording it over the town – though Montrichard's is ruined and St-Aignan's closed to visitors – and both with man-made **beaches** where you can swim. Near Montrichard you can make forays to low-key sights such as the decrepit château of **Le Gué-Péan**, the Gallo-Roman ruins at **Thésée-la-Romaine** and the mushroom and silkworm caves at **Bourré**, while just outside St-Aignan there's a large and professionally run **zoo**.

The exquisitely refined château of **Valençay** technically lies in the department of the Indre, but it's only a short excursion south of the Cher, close to the goat's-cheese-producing town of **Selles-sur-Cher**. If you're continuing upstream all the way to Bourges, you might want to stop off at the medieval town of **Mennetou-sur-Cher**. Beyond Mennetou, the river enters the Cher *département* at the industrial town of Vierzon, which is of no interest to visitors.

Public transport is relatively good, with **trains** serving all the towns along the Cher, from Tours and Chenonceaux, through to Montrichard, St-Aignan and on to Vierzon and Bourges.

Montrichard

In many ways just a laid-back market town on the banks of the Cher, **MONT-RICHARD** also happens to have a full complement of medieval and Renaissance buildings, plus a hilltop **castle**, of which just the keep remains after Henri IV broke down the rest of the defences. Between mid-July and mid-August costumed medieval spectacles (daily at 2.30pm & 4.30pm) make the most of the fortress's situation, but it's well worth climbing up at any time of year for the view over the Cher. Various buildings on the way up to the keep contain the lovingly tended but rather dull town **museum** (March & April Sat & Sun 10am–noon & 2–6pm; May–Sept daily same hours; €5), which is divided into worthy sections on local archeology and history, paleontology, milling and bizarrely, the archeology of the Sahara.

Montrichard's Romanesque **church** was where the disabled 12-year-old princess, Jeanne de Valois, who would never be able to have children, married her cousin, Louis, duc d'Orléans, in 1476. Louis subsequently became king after the unlikely death of Charles VIII at Amboise, and politics dictated that he marry Charles VIII's widow, Anne de Bretagne. Poor Jeanne was divorced and sent off to govern Bourges, where she turned to religion, founding a new religious order. She eventually took the veil herself – though she wore her nun's habit under her clothes.

In summer, canoes, pedalos and **kayaks** can be hired (☎02.54.32.11.84; closed mid-Sept to May) at the pleasant artificial **beach** on the opposite bank of the

Cher – and it's possible to paddle as far as Chenonceau, 7km downstream. For those feeling less energetic, the *Léonard de Vinci*, a miniature **cruise-boat**, makes ninety-minute trips upstream to Bourré (see below) and back, leaving from the main jetty (April–June, Sept & Oct Sat & Sun 3pm & 5pm; July & Aug daily 3pm & 5pm; ☎02.54.75.41.53; €9). You can also visit the **caves Monmousseau** (April to mid-Nov daily 10am–6pm), a ten-minute walk east of town along the route de Vierzon, where racks of bottles of sparkling wine line the quarried-out cellars; there's the usual tasting at the end of the tour.

Practicalities

Montrichard's **tourist office** is in the Maison Ave Maria, 1 rue du Pont (April–Sept Mon–Sat 9am–noon & 2–6pm, Sun 10am–noon; ☎02.54.32.05.10, ⊛www.montrichard.fr), an ancient house with saints and beasties sculpted down its beams. The only enticing **hotel** is *La Tête Noir*, 24 rue de Tours (☎02.54.32.05.55, ℻02.54.32.78.37; ❸), with its terrace on the river, but the *Hôtel de la Gare* (☎02.54.32.04.36; ❷), beside the station, is inexpensive and decent enough. The atmospheric *Manoir de la Salle du Roc*, 69 rte de Vierzon (☎02.54.32.73.54, ℻02.54.32.47.90; ❺), offers grand **chambres d'hôtes** set in an ancient manor house above the main road leading east from Montrichard towards Bourré. More upmarket still, if not quite as romantic, is the sixteenth-century, three-star *Château de la Ménaudière*, 3km from Montrichard on the D115 towards Amboise (☎01.47.20.18.27, ⊛www.chateauxcountry.com; ❼), a tall, elegant building set in its own grounds, with an outdoor heated swimming pool and a classy restaurant. Montrichard also has a municipal **campsite**, *L'Étourneau* (☎02.54.32.10.16; closed mid-Sept to May), on the banks of the Cher. Decent **meals** can be had at *Les Tuffeaux*, a brasserie on Montrichard's main square, place Barthélémy Gilbert.

Bourré

Three kilometres to the east of Montrichard, the hills around **BOURRÉ** are riddled with enormous, cave-like quarries, dug deep to get at the famous château-building stone that gets whiter as it weathers. Some of the caves are now used to cultivate mushrooms – big business in the Loire – a peculiar process that you can witness at the **Caves Champignonnières**, 40 rte des Roches (French-language guided tours daily: March–June & Sept at 10am, 11am & hourly 2–5pm; July & Aug also 1pm & 6pm; Oct & Nov 11am, 3pm & 4pm; €5.50). You won't see any bulk growing here, but rather boutique, showpiece production of *pleurotes* (oyster mushrooms), *pieds bleus* and shiitakes, as well as a few common field agarics – known in France as *champignons de Paris*. A second tour (€5.50 or €9.50 for both tours) takes you to a "subterranean city" sculpted in recent years as a tourist attraction, and impressive enough in its way. An excellent shop sells mushrooms, including rare varieties, and mushroom products. At the bottom of the hill, you can visit troglodyte houses and a seventeenth-century silkworm-breeding farm deep in the caves at **La Magnanerie**, 4 chemin de la Croix-Bardin (guided tours, usually in French only: April–Sept Mon & Thurs–Sun at 11am, 3pm, 4pm & 5pm; €3.20).

Thésée-la-Romaine and château du Gué-Péan

Ten kilometres upstream of Montrichard, the village of **THESEE-LA-ROMAINE** gets its name from the Roman ruins that now stand alongside the D176 highway, 1km short of the village. As you approach along the riverbank road, you'll see a large sward of grass broken up by trenches, gravel paths and stony lines of walling, the remains of the second-century Gallo-Roman potters' community of Tasciaca, known locally as **Les Maselles** (Easter–June Sat & Sun 2–6pm; July to mid-Sept daily except Tues 10am–12.30pm & 2–6.30pm; €4). There's little to see at the site itself, though one section of fortified wall still stands impressively high and smooth, the grey stone offset by narrow bands of brick. Most of the finds – figurines, coins and lots of pots and jars – are displayed in the **Musée Archéologique**, in the Mairie at Thésée (Easter–June Sat & Sun 2–6pm; July & Aug daily except Tues 2–6.30pm; €2, or €4 with entry to ruins), which is set among extensive gardens.

The privately owned **château du Gué-Péan** (guided tour only: July & Aug 10.30am–12.30pm & 2–6.30pm; €5) is hidden away in the wooded backcountry 4km north of Thésée, accessed by a lane running east of Monthou-sur-Cher – which is in fact set back 2km from the river. It's protected by a medieval-style moat and four mismatched pepper-pot towers, but the inner court dates from the sixteenth century, built by one François Alaman, a royal official who designed and managed the gorgeous diplomatic spectacle known as the Field of the Cloth of Gold, when Henry VIII of England encountered François I. The rooms you visit on the tour of the interior don't harbour any particular surprises – fine sticks of Louis XV and Louis XVI furniture – but this is definitely one of those secretive châteaux where you can fantasize about living the life of a *châtelain*.

St-Aignan and around

ST-AIGNAN, 15km upstream of Montrichard, presents an extremely picturesque face to the world – as long as you're approaching from the right direction. Seen from the opposite bank of the Cher, the town appears to nestle snugly at the foot of its outsized Romanesque church and château, which lines the top of a minor escarpment like a great wall of mismatched windows, chimneys and decorated brick- and stonework. Meanwhile, the modern town leads a workaday life on the high ground behind, centred around **place du Président Wilson**, a large car park which is transformed into a **market** every Saturday morning.

Planted in the very centre of town, just up from the river off the axis of rue Constant Ragot, the solid stone buttresses of the **collégiale de St-Aignan** (Mon–Sat 9am–7pm, Sun 1–7pm) rise sturdily from the steep ground. The approaches are charming: up the slope from the river, or down the steps that lead from the château straight up to the west portal. Inside, the lofty nave is closed off by an airy, three-storey apse adorned with carved capitals – unfortunately most of them nineteenth-century recreations. A leaflet points you towards the half-dozen twelfth-century originals – note the many-headed monster on the north side of the ambulatory, and the fighting rams over on the south side. The unusually tall eleventh-century **crypt** is renowned for its remarkably preserved, brightly coloured **wall-paintings**. The most striking of these is found on the half-dome vault of the central chapel, a late twelfth-century *Christ in Majesty*. On either side are two very different works dating from the fifteenth century, with captions flowing from the mouths of the protagonists like a comic strip. The large *Last Judgement* on the facing wall is later still, from the sixteenth century, while the oldest wall-paintings, hidden in the deeper recesses of the crypt, show scenes from the legend of Saint Gilles.

The **château** belongs to the wealthy marquis de la Roche-Aymon, a big forestry landowner, and it's closed to the public. You're allowed to wander round the outside, though crossing the main courtyard may feel a bit like trespassing. A flight of 144 steps climbs from the collégiale to a grand gravelled terrace enclosed on one side by the L-shape of the Renaissance *logis*, and on the other by the remnants of the eleventh-century fortress. The delightful, harmonious sixteenth-century facade of the *logis* makes a powerful contrast with the mongrel appearance of the château as seen from below, its dressed white stone, decorated dormer windows and stone-crossed window frames recalling the finest creations of the First Renaissance. The octagonal **staircase tower**, however, is a confused nineteenth-century addition, marring the François I effect with anachronistic *œil-de-bœuf* windows and a Chambord-like pepper-grinder lantern perched on the top.

The far corner of the terrace leads through to a great **view** of the river, and you can continue down the steep steps of the Degrés des Trois Gloirieuses to place du 8 Mai 1945, opposite the bridge. Alternatively, take the chestnut-lined Fossés du Château round towards the Hôtel de Ville, at the top end of rue Constant Ragot. For information on local Côteaux du Cher wines, the **Maison du Vin** (July & Aug daily 10am–noon & 3–6pm; Sept–June Tues & Thurs 8am–noon), on place Wilson, is open for tastings and sales.

The midstream **Ile des Trois Evêques** is used as a picnic area and informal beach, though swimming in the Cher is officially banned. However, there are indoor and outdoor **swimming pools** over on the downstream side of island (outdoor pool open July & Aug Mon 1–7pm, Tues–Sun 11am–7.30pm; €2.60), and you can windsurf, canoe and sail on the lake a couple of kilometres upstream; boats and windsurfers are rented out at the **Base Nautique des Couflons**, near Seigy (daily 9am–8pm; ☎02.54.75.44.90), which also organizes guided descents of the Cher and Sauldre by raft or canoe.

Practicalities

The **tourist office**, 60 rue Constant Ragot (May, June & Sept Mon–Sat 9.30am–12.30pm & 2–6pm, Sun 10am–noon; July & Aug Mon–Sat 9.30am–12.30pm & 2–6.30pm, Sun 10am–noon & 3–6pm; Oct–April Mon–Sat 10am–12.30pm & 2–6pm; ☎02.54.75.22.85, ✉st-aignan@wanadoo .fr), is just off place Wilson, in the upper part of town. The only two **hotels** are both down beside the river, on either side of the bridge: the *Hôtel du Moulin*, 7 rue Novilliers (☎02.54.75.15.54; ❶; closed Sun), is a fairly basic but clean and friendly place above a bar; while *Le Grand Hôtel St-Aignan*, 7–9 quai J.-J.-Delorme (☎02.54.75.18.04, ✉grand.hotel.st.aignan@wanadoo.fr; ❶–❸; Nov–March restaurant closed Sun evening, Mon & Tues lunch), is a hushed, well-furnished affair, with a good restaurant (*menus* €15–32.50). Alternatively, chambres d'hôtes can be found at *Le Sousmont*, 66 rue Maurice-Berteaux (☎02.54.75.24.35; ❸); the situation on the main one-way road into town from the north is a bit noisy, but the inside is immaculately kept, with lots of charming nineteenth-century features, and the welcome is warm, with breakfast served in the flower-filled garden on fine days. St-Aignan has an excellent **campsite** on the bank of the river near Seigy, the *Camping des Cochards* (☎02.54.75.15.59; closed mid-Oct to March).

For an alternative to the hotel **restaurants**, two relaxed places make use of the tree-shaded place de la Paix, just across from the collégiale, on the far side of rue Ragot: the extremely welcoming *L'Amarena* (☎02.54.75.47.98, closed Mon lunch) serves inexpensive Italian food and pizzas, and has outside tables; while *Chez Constant* (☎02.54.75.10.75; *menus* at €11 & €16; closed Mon & Tues) serves up generous portions of regional specialities in an atmospheric old bar with a restaurant section at the back. For a **drink**, try *Chez Daniel*, 2 rue du Four, a combined wine bar and tearoom just off the place de la Paix.

Zoo Parc Beauval

Unless you've just arrived in the region, you'll hardly have escaped the advertising for the **Zoo Parc Beauval** (daily: mid-March to Oct 9am–dusk; Nov to mid-March 10am–dusk; €13; ⊛www.zoobeauval.com), 4km to the south of St-Aignan on the D675. Despite the superficial commercialism, the zoo is spacious and attractive, with sumptuous flower-beds giving way to little streams and islanded lakes. The space given to the animals is adequate – most live in artificial mini-habitats rather than cages – and the zoo is part of various European programmes for breeding threatened species in captivity, so there are always babies to admire. Alongside the open-air enclosures for deer, giraffes, zebras, big cats, camels, bears and the like, there's a big monkey house, a vivarium and an Australian-themed hothouse with kangaroos and kookaburras in the adjacent enclosure. Seats at the two **spectacles** (frequent shows daily from April to mid-Nov) – performing seals and a raptor display – are included in the ticket price, and the **petting zoo** in the far corner goes down very well with smaller children.

Selles-sur-Cher

Since work began on converting the château at **SELLES-SUR-CHER**, 15km upstream of St-Aignan, into a luxury hotel, the main reason to visit has disappeared, unless you're bent on buying the famous local goat's cheese from a local shop. But Selles-sur-Cher remains a pleasant market town, centred on a wide square set some 50m back from the river, with the former abbey church of **St-Eusice** at its centre. The church's apse is Romanesque – don't miss the carved frieze on the outside – but over-restored, while the nave dates from the fourteenth century, though its vault was demolished by Huguenots in 1562 and has been replaced by a wooden structure that's visibly too light for the columns supporting it. The rough stone coffin of the saint lies on an altar in the crypt, surrounded by votive marble plaques and their modern equivalent – votive postcards.

Around the back of the church, the Hôtel de Ville incorporates the small **Musée du Val de Cher** (June to mid-Sept Tues–Sun 10am–noon & 2.30–5/6pm; €3.15), which uses small scenes acted out by dummies to explain various local phenomena, including the old laundry boats that were once moored on the river and the techniques used to make goat's cheese. The museum also allows access to the seventeenth-century cloister. A grassy embankment runs along the pleasant **riverfront** from the bridge towards the **château**, a grand combination of medieval fortifications and seventeenth-century luxury, the latter built in brick by Pierre-Philippe de Béthune, the brother of the duc de Sully (see p.194). Unfortunately, it's barricaded over while works take place converting it into a hotel, which is set to open in late 2005 or early 2006.

Joan of Arc may have stayed here in 1430, but the decor at the *Hôtel du Lion d'Or*, 14 place de la Paix (℡02.54.97.40.83, ℻02.54.97.72.36; ❸), currently owes a lot more to the 1980s, with large but unappealing **rooms** arranged motel-like off a first-floor terrace at the back; there's a gorgeous 300-year-old wisteria, however, and a fairly good **restaurant** below (*menus* €20 lunch and €30 evenings), with café chairs spread out onto the main square. At any rate, it's the only option in town while works at the château continue. For something more romantic, the tumbledown *Château de Chémery*, 8km north of Selles-sur-Cher (℡02.54.71.82.77, ✉chateaudechemery@libertysurf.fr; ❹), offers ramshackle, antique-furnished rooms giving onto the moat or the inner court of the castle; you can reserve the table d'hôte (€19) in advance.

Château de Valençay

Fifteen kilometres south of Selles-sur-Cher, the **château de Valençay** (daily: April–June, Sept & Oct 9.30am–6pm; July & Aug 9.30am–7.30pm; €8.50; Ⓦ www.chateau-valencay.com) is an isolated tourist destination in the otherwise almost completely unvisited *département* of the Indre. Architecturally, it's an overgrown mongrel of a château, but none the less beautiful for the mix of styles. The little turrets of the Renaissance keep clash with the enormous, bell-like tower pavilions, which jar in turn with the serene Neoclassical inner court, but the ensemble – all built of the palest tufa stone and capped by roofs of deep grey slate – is refined and impressive, set among handsome classical gardens. The mid-sixteenth-century wings were originally built to show off the enormous wealth of the d'Etampes family, but the lasting impression of a visit to the château today is the imperial legacy of a later owner, the great diplomat **Talleyrand** – famously described by his master Napoleon as "shit in a silk stocking".

An extraordinary political operator and survivor, Talleyrand owes his greatest fame to his post as Napoleon's foreign minister. A bishop before the Revolution, with a reputation for having the most desirable mistresses, he proposed the nationalization of church property, renounced his bishopric, escaped to America during the Terror, backed Napoleon, negotiated the imperial capitulation and then represented the restored Bourbons at the Congress of Vienna. One of his tasks for the emperor was keeping **Ferdinand VII of Spain** entertained at Valençay after the king had been forced to abdicate in favour of Napoleon's brother Joseph. Napoleon advised Talleyrand that "if you had a theatre at Valençay, and could arrange for actors to play there, it wouldn't be a bad idea." Talleyrand quickly had a stage built, which still exists here today, along with seventeen original stage sets. Six years after Ferdinand's arrival, the Treaty of Valençay, signed in the château in 1813, put an end to his enforced holiday and gave him back his Spanish throne. Talleyrand eventually fell from grace under the Bourbons, and retired to his château with his lover, the duchesse de Dino, who happened to be his nephew's wife. Together, they would entertain and politically seduce their guests with the help of elaborately structured dinners prepared by Marie-Antoine de Carême, the originator of French *grande cuisine*.

The **interior** dates from Talleyrand's glory days, and is consequently largely First Empire: elaborately embroidered chairs, Chinese vases, ornate inlays to all the tables, faux-Egyptian details, finicky clocks and chandeliers. A single discordant note is struck by the leg-brace and shoe displayed in a glass cabinet along with Talleyrand's uniforms – the statesman's deformed foot was concealed in every painting of the man, including the one displayed in the portrait gallery that runs the length of the graceful Neoclassical wing.

The château **park** (same hours as above; €1.50) keeps a small collection of unhappy-looking camels, zebras, llamas and goats, and there's a small, imaginative **maze** for which you'll need to understand some French in order to work out the riddling passwords that open the various doors – or ask for the answers at the ticket office. Theatricals take place in the courtyard or kitchens of the château roughly every hour (April–June, Sept & Oct Sat & Sun only; mid-July to Aug daily), with costumed actors replaying fanciful scenes from Talleyrand's time.

About 200m from the château gates, on the long straight road leading north of town, a **car museum** (daily 10am–12.30pm & 1.30–6pm; €2.30) houses an excellent collection of sixty-odd mostly prewar cars, though there are a few more recent vehicles, such as a covetable 1970s Renault Alpine, built for rallying. The **memorial** on top of the hill, at the edge of the forest, commemorates the wartime dead of F-section, known in the UK as the Special Operations Executive, whose mission was to aid and equip the French Resistance. It was here that the first spy's parachute drop took place, on the night of May 5, 1941.

Once you've seen the château, the car museum and the war memorial you've about exhausted the possibilities of Valençay. If you do decide to stay on, the nicer of the two **hotels** is the *Lion d'Or*, place de la Halle (T & P02.54.00.09.20; ③), a very simple provincial hotel on the main square, opposite the grain market. For something to **eat**, the best bet is *La Renaissance*, an informal restaurant which does pizza and reasonable-value *assiettes* of cold meats and salad for around €10.

To get to Valençay by public transport, you can take the **train** from Orléans (change at Salbris), passing through Romorantin-Lanthenay. It's also possible to join the branch line that runs along the Cher at Gièvres, but there's often a longish wait for a connection. An infrequent **bus** service connects with Blois.

Mennetou-sur-Cher

There's little of interest on the river upstream of Selles-sur-Cher, but if you're making your way to Bourges you might want to stop off at the miniature medieval town of **MENNETOU-SUR-CHER**, 15km west of Vierzon. The steep, pedestrianized, cobbled streets running between the fortified gates are perfect for a relaxed stroll, but the pride with which the town markets its local speciality, *andouillette à la ficelle* – a sausage of pig's intestine with a string running through the middle – gives a clue as to the shortage of actual things to see and do. Once you've visited the Flamboyant Gothic **église St-Urbain**, near the thirteenth-century Porte d'en Bas, and wandered the length of the **Grande Rue** between the half-ruined Porte du Nord and the Porte Bonne Nouvelle, admiring the half-dozen fifteenth- and sixteenth-century houses, there's little left to do except cross the busy N76 road and the Canal du Berry that runs alongside it, then walk 100m down to a grassy sward shaded by weeping willows. You can **picnic** and **swim** in the Cher here, and there's a playground for children. The municipal **campsite** (T02.54.98.11.02; closed mid-Sept to April) is just downstream, with a swimming pool.

Travel details

Trains

Blois to: Amboise (17 daily; 20min); Beaugency (20 daily; 25min); Meung-sur-Loire (20 daily; 35min); Onzain (for Chaumont; 17 daily; 10min); Orléans (22–26 daily; 40min); Tours (18 daily; 40min).
Valençay to: Montrichard (change at Gièvres; 3 daily; 1hr 30min); Romorantin-Lanthenay (6 daily; 35min); Tours (change at Gièvres; 3 daily; 2hr–2hr 30min).

Buses

Blois to: Bracieux (2–3 daily; 45min); Chambord (1–3 daily; 45min); Cour-Cheverny (3 daily; 35min); Romorantin-Lanthenay (3 daily; 1hr); St-Aignan (2–3 daily; 1hr 10min); Vendôme (2–3 daily; 1hr); Valençay (3 daily; 1hr 30min); Vierzon (3 daily; 2hr).
Romorantin-Lanthenay to: Mennetou-sur-Cher (5 daily; 20min); Vierzon (5 daily; 40min).

The Orléanais

CHAPTER 3

Highlights

✳ **Rue de Bourgogne, Orléans** Lively bars and relaxed restaurants line Orléans' old Roman road, the rue de Bourgogne. See p.179

✳ **La Ferté-St-Aubin** You're free to sit in the armchairs, play the piano and generally imagine yourself the châtelain at this Sologne château. See p.181

✳ **Beaugency** This medieval town is one of the most attractive places to stay anywhere on the banks of the Loire. See p.185

✳ **Talcy** A foray north onto the plain of the Beauce brings you to the château where Cassandre, the muse of the poet Ronsard, lived. See p.188

✳ **St-Benoît-sur-Loire** The mortal remains of St Benedict brought pilgrims in their thousands to this handsome stone abbey. See p.192

✳ **Sully-sur-Loire** With its strong towers, deep moat and powerful overlord, Sully is the quintessential medieval castle. See p.193

✳ **Château des Pêcheurs** The aristocratic obsession with angling is all too evident at this eccentric château. See p.198

✳ **Briare** An extraordinary Belle-Époque aqueduct carries a canal high over the Loire itself. You can cross it on foot or on a canal-boat cruise. See p.198

△ Summer flowers at Château de Sully

3

The Orléanais

I
n the great years of the French monarchy, the **Orléanais** had the misfortune to fall between two poles of royal power: Touraine and the Ile-de-
France. The region's career started well, as the heartland or "navel" of
druidic power in the centuries before the Roman conquest, and it was
later thrust into prominence as the home fief of the Capetian dynasty, which
ruled France from the tenth to the fourteenth centuries. In the last millennium, however, the Orléanais has gently lapsed into provincial irrelevance.
Even the modern name for it, the *département* of the Loiret, refers to a tiny
stream, in contrast to neighbours glowing under the relatively noble names
of the Cher and the Seine-et-Marne. This has always been, and remains, a
wealthy region, but the sense of departed grandeur is even stronger here than
in the rest of the Loire valley: the châteaux seem quieter and more abandoned, and the churches, forests and abbeys palpably more ancient. On the
left bank, south of the Loire, lies the low-lying marshy woodland of the
Sologne (covered in Chapter 2, see p.153). On the right bank, the dull flat
arable fields of the Beauce stretch away to the northwest, towards Chartres,
while the great, dark swathe of the Forêt d'Orléans looms on the northeast.
As a tourist destination, the Orléanais is an acquired taste – and relatively few
tourists make the effort.

The cathedral city of **Orléans** has a very different feel. Enterprising and
upbeat, it seems more oriented towards Paris and the future than to the river
and the history that flows through it. But the city's past does bind it firmly to
the region, especially in the person of Joan of Arc, the "Maid of Orléans", who
is celebrated in the magnificent cathedral. Some excellent town museums and
a relaxed restaurant and nightlife scene make the city all the more appealing.
Directly south of Orléans, but included in this chapter as an obvious day-trip
from the city, is the charming brick-built château at **La Ferté-St-Aubin**, on
the northern fringe of the Sologne.

Downriver of Orléans, the small, pretty towns of **Meung–sur–Loire** and
Beaugency huddle on the bank of the Loire within a few kilometres of each
other, each with its historic château in the very centre of town. Meung's
château is the more interesting of the two to visit, but Beaugency is a more
attractive place to stay, with its cobbled medieval squares and excellent hotels.
Interesting side-trips can be made to the **château de Talcy**, with its poetic
links, and the royal abbey church at **Cléry-St-André**.

Upriver from Orléans, the north bank is shadowed by the giant **Forêt
d'Orléans**, a good place to explore on a bike, or pass through on the way to
the **château de Chamerolles'** perfume museum. One fifteen-kilometre
stretch of the Loire is particularly fascinating: you can visit a jewel box of a

Carolingian oratory at **Germigny-des-Près**, a major Romanesque abbey church at **St-Benoît-sur-Loire** and a muscular château at **Sully-sur-Loire**. A little further south, the brick-built château and town of **Gien** are often held to mark the end of the Loire valley proper, but it's worth persevering as far as **Briare**, where the Canal Latéral crosses the river on an exquisite nineteenth-century aqueduct. Near Gien, the châteaux at **St-Brisson** and **La Bussière** – one devoted to medieval artillery, the other to fishing – are quirky and little-visited destinations.

Online **information** on the *département* of the Loiret can be found at Ⓦ www.tourismloiret.com. Rapides du Val-de-Loire (☎02.38.53.94.75, Ⓦ www.rvl-info.com) operate almost all the area's **buses**, though services are only frequent enough to be useful downstream of Orléans – an area which is better served by the train anyway.

Orléans

ORLÉANS is the northernmost city on the Loire, sitting at the apex of a huge arc in the river as it switches direction and starts to flow southwest. Its proximity to Paris, just over 100km away, has always shaped this ancient city. Goods and passengers sailing up the Loire would disembark at Orléans for the journey to the capital and, despite the city being hundreds of kilometres inland, it developed as an important port – in 1663 the poet La Fontaine was surprised to see a "miniature Constantinople". The city's glory may have faded along with the fortunes of the river, but in recent years high-speed motorway and rail links to Paris have underpinned an economic renaissance. Orléans is now one of the fastest growing cities in France, with a population of around a quarter of a million and an unemployment rate of around six percent – unusually low by French standards.

ACCOMMODATION

Le Brin de Zinc	D
Hostel	I
Hôtel de l'Abeille	C
Hôtel des Cèdres	B
Hôtel Charles Sanglier	E
Hôtel Marguerite	H
Hôtel de Paris	A
Hôtel du Sauvage	F
Jackotel	G

0   100m

ORLÉANS

RESTAURANTS

Les Antiquaires	11	La Mangeoire	8	La Petite Marmite	2
La Chancellerie	1	Noé	5	Le Viking	7
Les Fagots	9	La Petite Folie	6		

BARS & CLUBS

L'Arrozoir	4
Le Club	1
Le Ka	10
Paxton's Head	3

Parc Floral de la Source & La Ferté St-Aubin

All this energy translates into a vibrant, exciting city to visit, its new-found municipal pride vigorously expressed in a lively restaurant and nightlife scene, redevelopment of the riverside quays and new, ultra-modern trams – a perfect foil to the handsome eighteenth- and nineteenth-century streets. For once, there's no château and historic sights are relatively thin on the ground – even the **cathedral** somehow lacks a soul and the giant **église St-Aignan** is semi-ruined – but the streets of the old city are fascinating to explore, and there are two excellent museums: the **Musée des Beaux-Arts**, with an unusually good collection of paintings, and the **Hôtel Cabu**, with a strange display of third-century animal sculptures. One of the best times to visit is May 8 (**Joan of Arc Day**), when the city is filled with parades, fireworks and a medieval fair.

Some history

Despite a rich early history – of being a centre of revolt against Julius Caesar in 52 BC (for which it was burnt to the ground), besieged by Attila the Hun in the mid-fifth century, elevated to the position of temporary capital of the Frankish kingdom in 498 and becoming a hotbed of Manicheanism in the eleventh century (a heresy for which the cathedral's canons were burnt) – one event alone has defined Orléans. In 1429, the city was under siege by an English army eager to capture what was then the key to the Loire valley and

THE ORLÉANAIS | Orléans

Meung-sur-Loire & Beaugency

& St-Jean-de-Braye

the last remaining territories of the Dauphin. On April 29, **Joan of Arc** (see box on p.174) relieved the siege by fighting her way through to the now-vanished Porte de Bourgogne, an event considered to be the turning point in the Hundred Years War.

A brief period of resurgence, during which a number of fine Renaissance mansions were built, was followed by the devastation of the sixteenth-century Wars of Religion, which affected Orléans particularly severely as a centre of Protestant learning. After the peace of the Edict of Nantes, however, the city prospered on the back of wheat from the Beauce to the north, wool from the Sologne to the south and timber from the Forêt d'Orléans to the east, while the **river trade** swelled with domestic and imported goods, especially muscovado sugar from the Caribbean. All this wealth and activity came to an abrupt end with the arrival of the railways, which rendered river transport suddenly redundant. Six months of occupation by Prussian troops in 1870–71 set the seal on the city's decline, and the German bombardments of June 1940 only completed the humiliation, destroying a large part of the city centre. Since World War II, however, Orléans has vigorously reasserted itself, developing major engineering and "cosmo-ceuticals" industries in the hinterland, and making great strides in rebuilding what is once more a proud and thriving city.

Arrival, information and accommodation

The **gare SNCF** leads straight into the modern shopping centre on place d'Arc, which fronts onto a huge swathe of busy roads; the old city centre lies on the far side of the traffic, accessed by the pedestrian bridge that leads to rue de la République. On foot, count on ten to fifteen minutes to the cathedral; if you're heading towards the western side of the old city, it might be worth taking **tram A** from place d'Arc to place du Général de Gaulle, but it's not far to walk. The **gare routière**, on rue Marcel-Proust, is 200m back from the tourist office, also on rue Marcel-Proust, on the corner of rue Albert-1er.

The main **tourist office**, 6 rue Albert-1er (Mon 10am–1pm & 2–6.30pm, Tues–Sat 9am–1pm & 2–6.30pm; closes 5.30pm in winter; ℡02.38.24.05.05), is just across the road which runs alongside the shopping centre, and there's another branch near the cathedral, at 6 rue Jeanne d'Arc (April–Oct Mon 2–6pm, Tues–Sun 10am–6pm; Nov–March Tues–Sat 2–6pm, Sun 10am–noon). If you speak French, the website ⓦwww.orleanscity.com is good for information on city events, while the main city portal, ⓦwww.ville-orleans.fr is mostly translated into English.

Accommodation in Orléans is mostly uninspiring, but a few central two-stars stand out from the rest.

Hotels

Le Brin de Zinc 62 rue Ste-Catherine ℡02.38.53.88.77. The bar of the busy brasserie below acts as reception, where you are given a key and sent round to the back door on a seedy back alley. Things get rather better inside, as the rooms have been done up fairly recently in a simple, modern style. Price and location are good. ❷

Hôtel de l'Abeille 64 rue Alsace Lorraine ℡02.38.53.54.87. This thirty-room hotel has been in the same family for a century. The handsome Belle Epoque exterior and the reception area are very promising, but the rambling interior hasn't quite recovered from a stint as a much cheaper hotel, with some alarmingly bright paintwork and worn-out fittings. Most of the rooms are modern and comfortable, however, and the rest are being freshly done up in a rustic style. Stands on the corner of the pedestrianized shopping street of rue de la République – convenient for the station. ❸

Hôtel des Cèdres 17 rue Maréchal Foch ℡02.38.62.22.92, ⓦwww.hoteldescedres.com. Welcoming three-star with a garden, in a peaceful street just outside the ring road encircling the old town. A good option for families, as the rooms are fairly spacious and a number of them have cots and communicating doors, and there's garaged parking for an extra €6. All rooms were being entirely renovated at the time of writing, and look set to be smartly decorated. ❹

Hôtel Charles Sanglier 8 rue Charles-Sanglier ☎02.38.53.38.50, ⓕ02.38.81.24.07. One of the few really central options, so tends to get fully booked up. On the down side, the modern building is unprepossessing, and the rooms are small – most have plastic shower units tucked away in the corner behind a screen. On the positive side, this is a well-maintained and comfortable hotel, with a friendly atmosphere and well-furnished rooms. ❷

Hôtel Marguerite 14 place du Vieux-Marché ☎02.38.53.74.32, ⓔhotel.marguerite@wanadoo.fr. Central, friendly and very well run. The large, immaculate rooms have been recently repainted in cheery colours, with comfortable, if slightly aseptic, modern furnishings. ❸

Hôtel de Paris 29 Faubourg-Bannier ☎02.38.53.39.58. Old-fashioned but clean rooms above a very ordinary bar, just behind the train station. Noisy wooden stairs and floors, and very basic fittings, but the management is extremely helpful and prices are low. ❶

Hôtel du Sauvage 71 rue de Bourgogne ☎02.38.62.42.39, ⓕ02.38.77.17.59. Traditional and distinctly faded hotel in the quiet area behind the cathedral. The old, timbered rooms are let down by ugly modern furnishings. ❷

Jackotel 18 place du Cloître-St-Aignan ☎02.38.54.48.48, ⓕ02.38.77.17.59. Peaceful location overlooking the church of St-Aignan across a shaded square, in a quiet corner of the old town southeast of the cathedral. The decor is faintly offputting, in an anonymous 1980s style that needs updating, but the rooms are at least large and clean. ❸

Hostel and campsite

Camping Gaston Marchand Chemin de la Roche, St-Jean-de-la-Ruelle ☎02.38.88.39.39. The municipal campsite, and the closest to Orléans, 5km away out on the Blois road, beside the Loire; bus #26, stop "Petite Espère". Closed mid-Oct to March.

Auberge de Jeunesse d'Orléans 1 bd de la Motte Sanguin ☎02.38.53.60.06, ⓔasse.crjs@libertysurf.fr. Clean but institutional-feeling hostel with good kitchen facilities, just south of the eastern foot of rue de Bourgogne, in a park by the river. Ten minutes' walk from the cathedral, or take bus #4 or #8 from the bus and train stations, stop "Pont Bourgogne". HI membership accepted, or you can join on the spot for €10.70, or €15.25 for over-25s. Reception Mon–Sat 8am–9pm, Sun 9–11am & 5–7pm.

The City

Joan turns up all over town, most notably on horseback in the centre of the **place du Martroi**, the pedestrianized square at the heart of the commercial end of town. The square lies at the foot of **rue de la République**, which runs due north to the gare SNCF, standing just set back from the main axis of **rue Jeanne d'Arc**, which runs east to the cathedral. Just to the north of the cathedral lie the modern **Musée des Beaux-Arts** and the Renaissance **Hôtel de Ville**, while the **old city** lies to the south, sloping down from the long, narrow **rue de Bourgogne** – where Orléans' main restaurant and nightlife is to be found – to the **river**, whose quays are sadly mostly given over to high-speed traffic.

The cathedral

The grand nineteenth-century avenue of rue Jeanne d'Arc marches arrow-straight up to the giant doors of the **cathédrale Ste-Croix** (daily 9.15am–6.45pm), where Joan celebrated her victory over the English. The uniformly Gothic structure actually dates from well after her death, as Huguenot iconoclasts destroyed the transepts in 1568, and in 1601 Henri IV inaugurated a rebuilding programme that lasted until the nineteenth century. The lofty towers of the west front, which culminate in a delicate stone palisade like a crown of thorns, were barely complete in time for the Revolution, while the skeletal spire wasn't finished until 1858.

△ Statue of Joan of Arc at Hôtel Groslot, Orléans

The Maid of Orléans

In 1429, during the **Hundred Years War** between England and France, a 17-year-old peasant girl in men's clothing somehow talked her way into meeting the heir to the French throne. She persuaded him to reconquer his kingdom, roused his army to the crucial victory at Orléans and guided him to his coronation. Less than three years later she was captured in battle, tried as a heretic and burnt at the stake. It took another 491 years for **Joan of Arc** – now nationalist heroine, feminist icon and Witness of the Faith – to be made a saint.

Everything Joan accomplished seems to have been through her own formidable charisma, and with the help of mysterious, angelic "voices", which accompanied her until her death. She first heard them in around 1425 – three years after both the **Dauphin** (the heir to the French throne) Charles and Henry VI of England had declared themselves king of France – describing their sound as "sweet and low and beautiful". Joan understood that these voices brought a message directly from God, instructing her to go to the Dauphin and help him win back his kingdom. Her belief was ardent enough to convince almost everyone she met too, a process that finally ushered her into the presence of Charles at **Chinon**, in 1429.

No one knows what exactly happened at Chinon (see box on p.105), but it was enough to convince Charles that he was the legitimate heir to the French throne. Charles's supposed weakness, and the allegations of his bastardy, were not, as is often alleged, the obstacle. Instead, it was the 1420 **Treaty of Troyes**, a document of questionable legality in which Charles VI had disinherited his son in favour of Henry V of England. Joan's arrival, and the sign she brought, made the Dauphin believe that God was on his side and, whatever the legal arguments, in late medieval eyes that made him the rightful king.

And yet his kingdom hung by a thread. The strategic city of **Orléans**, just upstream from Chinon, was besieged by the English, and barely held by Charles's most heroic captain, **Jean Dunois**, the "Bastard of Orléans" (see p.284). Joan's role in the week-long battle that lifted the siege, in early May 1429, was probably slighter than is usually claimed, but her standard and sheer conviction certainly inspired the troops to victory. **Meung-sur-Loire** and **Beaugency** fell to the French in June and July, and on July 17 Charles was crowned at Reims, with Joan at his side.

For Joan, the turning point came in September, when her attack on English-held Paris failed. Charles, now looking for diplomatic solutions, disbanded the main army, leaving Joan to fight with a few hundred ill-supplied troops. On May 23 of the following year, after a disastrous winter campaign, Joan was captured by Burgundian troops at Compiègne. She was ransomed by the English, who turned her over to a hostile inquisitorial court in Rouen, a town they controlled.

The record of Joan's five-month **trial** survives, complete with her own defence. She comes across as spirited, precise and full of integrity, even as her interrogators tried to trap her into proving herself a heretic by claiming she had spoken to God through his angels. "I saw them with my bodily eyes as well as I see you", she protested, "and when they left me I wept, and I would have had them take me with them too." Along with her outrageous adoption of male clothing – she never explained it, only saying that it was "at the command of God and his angels" – this claim was enough to condemn her.

Joan's sentence was enacted on **May 30, 1431**, in the marketplace at Rouen, the fire being built some distance from her so that death would be slow. Joan asked for a crucifix to be brought to her and, as she burned, called out the same word over and again: "Jesus!" "Everyone present could hear it", her executioner reported, "almost all wept with pity."

Inside, slender stone columns extend without capitals in a single vertical sweep from the cathedral floor to the vault: impressive but oddly unmoving. Joan's canonization in 1920 is marked by a garish monumental altar next to the north transept, supported by two jagged and golden leopards that represent the English. The highlight is the late nineteenth-century **stained-glass window** sequence in the nave, which tells the usual romanticized version of Joan's life story (see box opposite) in a series of readable, cartoon-like images. Starting from the north transept and working back to the west doors, we see: Joan the shepherdess hearing voices; Joan finding the king in the crowd at Chinon; the miracle of the angel at Chinon; and Joan carrying her standard triumphantly into Orléans. Moving across the nave to the south aisle: the thanksgiving at Ste-Croix; Charles VII's coronation at Reims; Joan "rendered by treachery into the hands of the English"; Joan in prison; and Joan burnt at the stake. *L'Anglois perfide* ("perfidious Albion"), gets a rough ride, while the role of the Burgundians in her capture and the French clergy in her trial is rather skated over.

Before you move on from the cathedral, note the two innocuous-looking statues at either end of the cathedral square. On the north side, *La Beauce* depicts the flat, agricultural region north of Orléans in the form of a buxom woman holding golden ears of wheat; on the south side *La Loire* is shown as an idealized young woman with a bounteous skirtful of fruits.

Musée des Beaux-Arts

You are largely spared the Maid in the cavernous **Musée des Beaux-Arts**, opposite the Hôtel de Ville (Tues–Sat 10am–12.15pm & 1.30–6pm, Sun 1.30–6pm; €3), which spreads across five floors. There's plenty of second-rate stuff, but lurking among it are a number of works that make this one of the best regional art museums in France – well worth a rainy or even a sunny afternoon. The museum regularly stages good temporary exhibitions too – the tourist office has details.

The main **French collection** occupies the first floor, arranged either side of the central staircase. The more interesting seventeenth-century works are on the right of the stairs, beyond a huge room lorded over by the *Four Church Fathers*, depicted in alarmingly Mannerist style by Martin Fréminet (1567–1619). Both these and Claude Deruet's *Four Elements*, displayed in the hexagonal room just beyond, once hung in the château de Richelieu. While apparently devoted to the four elements as seasons, Deruet's quartet actually glorifies the family of Louis XIII: the king, his wife Anne of Austria, his brother Gaston d'Orléans and the cardinal himself can be spotted presiding over lavish festivities. Next door, in room 3, the highlight is the Le Nain brothers' dream-like and compelling *Bacchus Discovering Ariane on Naxos* (c.1635), where the young god discovers Ariadne after she has cried herself to sleep following the departure of Theseus.

Eighteenth-century works occupy the rooms on the left of the staircase, notably the exquisite collection of **pastel portraits** in room 8. Jean-Baptiste Perronneau, a leading exponent of the art, who often visited Orléans, is represented by a number of subtle and refined pieces, but the gems are Maurice Quentin de la Tour's *Portrait of a Young Negro* (1751), and Chardin's irresistible *Self-portrait with Spectacles*, from 1773.

The two mezzanine levels immediately below offer an alluring taste of **French nineteenth-century art**. The dog-legged corridor of the upper level runs past a large collection of works by the Romantic painter Léon Cogniet (1794–1880): look out for the horror expressed in his studies for *The Massacre* *of the Innocents*, and in Delacroix's *Head of an Old Woman*, but otherwise speed your way down to the large chamber on the lower mezzanine level. Here, **Realism** takes over, set against walls painted blood-red and stacked with canvases in proper nineteenth-century style. Two works by Orléans-born artists dominate the room: the melodramatic *The Fire* (1850), by Alexandre Antigna, and *The Apotheosis of the Rabble* (1885), by Maurice Boutet de Monvel – an artist better known for his 1896 comic-book version of the life of Joan of Arc.

Twentieth-century art lurks in the basement. The big names are Gauguin, with a still life called *Fête Gloanec* (1888), Picasso, with *Woman's Head with a Collar* (1926), and Tamara de Lempicka, with an iconic painting of a fashionable skier entitled *Saint-Moritz* (1929), but the works with local connections are just as rewarding. A small inner chamber has a number of African-influenced sculptures by Henri Gaudier-Brzeska (1891–1915), who was born just outside Orléans at St-Jean-de-Braye (see p.180), and a number of works devoted to the poet and literary figure Max Jacob, who lived in nearby St-Benoît (see p.192) for many years.

Foreign art, mainly Flemish and Italian sixteenth- and seventeenth-century works, is banished to the second floor, where the highlights are Coreggio's renowned *Holy Family* (1522), a work of incredible tenderness, and Velázquez's overwrought *St Thomas* (1620), an early painting influenced by Caravaggio that shows the apostle hearing the news of Christ's resurrection.

Hôtel Groslot and Campo Santo

Opposite the cathedral and museum, on the other side of place d'Étape, the fancy, red-brick **Hôtel Groslot** (July–Sept Mon–Fri & Sun 9am–7pm, Sat 5–8pm; Oct–June Mon–Fri & Sun 10am–noon & 2–6pm; free) is thought to be the work of the sixteenth-century architect Jacques Androuet du Cerceau. It's now part of the Hôtel de Ville, and used for civic ceremonies including marriages, which explains why it's usually closed to visits on Saturdays. Joan appears in the courtyard, this time in pensive mood, with her skirt dented by twentieth-century bullets – the statue is actually by the daughter of Louis-Philippe, the last king of France. Inside, you can wander through the plush, neo-medieval reception rooms, where the mayors are listed back to 1569.

On the other, rather desolate side of the Musée des Beaux-Arts, the **Campo Santo**, off rue Fernand Rabier (daily: April–Sept 7.30am–8pm; Oct–March 8am–5.30pm; free), was the town's main cemetery until just before the Revolution. It's a weird, hidden-away space, a blank square of green surrounded on three sides by pearly-white arcades that date from the fifteenth century. It comes to life during the town's jazz festival at the end of June, when it's used for concerts. The nearby **Ancien Évêché**, 100m down rue Dupanloup, was built for the bishops of Orléans in the 1640s; there's a fine view of the cathedral's apse from the stately garden at the back.

Rue Jeanne d'Arc and around

Handsome rue Jeanne d'Arc was largely built on the back of voluntary donations from the people of Orléans, who in 1825 managed to raise 400,000 gold francs within mere days to pay for it. The area to the north was heavily damaged by German bombing in 1940, though the centrepiece **place du Martroi** has been handsomely rebuilt round the equestrian statue of Joan by the sculptor Denis Foyatier, who was born at La Bussière (see p.198) in 1793. Joan's armoured appearance is in line with the nineteenth-century fashion for a warlike Maid; copper-green friezes round the base depict scenes from her life. North of the square, rue de la République is the main commercial and shopping drag, continuing across the busy ring road to the station via a pedestrian bridge.

The narrow streets to the south of rue Jeanne d'Arc are more enticing, with a number of Renaissance mansions to admire. The facade of the **Hôtel d Créneaux**, 32 rue Ste-Catherine, is particularly fine, while the **Maison d Ducerceau**, at 6 rue Ducerceau, the continuation of rue Ste-Catherine, is a considered Classical structure. Like the Hôtel Groslot, it is thought to be by the architect Jacques Androuet du Cerceau, famous for his meticulous aerial drawings of Loire châteaux. The design of the ornate **Hôtel Cabu**, square Abbé-Desnoyers, off rue Ste-Catherine (May, June & Sept Tues–Sun 1.30–6pm; July & Aug Mon 1.30–6pm, Tues–Sun 10am–noon & 1.30–6pm; Oct–April Wed, Sat & Sun 1.30–6pm; same ticket as Musée des Beaux-Arts), is also attributed to Du Cerceau. Inside, the **historical and archeological museum** houses the extraordinary **Treasure of Neuvy-en-Sullias**, a collection of bronze animals and figurines found near Orléans in 1861. The cache was probably buried in the second half of the third century AD to protect it from marauding Germanic invaders, or possibly from being melted down for coinage at a time of rampant inflation. The words inscribed on the base of the glorious, naturalistic horse sculpture states that it is an offering to the god Rudiobo, while the bronzes of wild boars are more stylized and may be symbols of war or the priesthood. Discovered in the locality of the Forest of the Carnutes, where Celtic druids gathered for their annual shindig, it's possible that the collection represents the last flourishing of Celtic religion at the end of the Gallo-Roman period. The floors above house various medieval oddments and Joan-related pieces, as well as exhibits on the history of Orléans.

At the end of rue Jeanne d'Arc, beside the funky tram stops on place Général de Gaulle, stands the semi-timbered **Maison de Jeanne d'Arc** (May–Oct Tues–Sun 10am–12.15pm & 1.30–6pm; €2). It's a disappointing place to visit: the house turns out to be a 1960s reconstruction, and the main exhibit is a fairly dull set of diorama models of the siege of Orléans, with recorded commentaries in French or English. Otherwise there are just a few Joan-related plates, books and engravings. A short distance from Joan's house, the **Centre Charles Péguy**, 11 rue Tabour (daily 1.30–6pm; free), houses a rather dry celebration of the life and work of Charles Péguy (1873–1914), a Christian Socialist writer from Orléans. The building itself is more interesting, an early sixteenth-century mansion that only reveals its richly sculpted heart once you've penetrated to the inner courtyard.

The old city

The scattered vestiges of the **old city** lie between **rue de Bourgogne**, the Gallo-Roman thoroughfare, and the river. The modern **Préfecture** at 9 rue de Bourgogne, was built on the site of the Roman forum; in the basement, a spartan civic reception room provides odd surroundings for an excavated first-century dwelling – or bits of it – and the walls of a ninth-century church. It's not a site as such, but you could ask the receptionist if you want to have a look. Across the street is the **Salles des Thèses**, all that remains of the medieval university of Orléans where the hardline Reformation theologian Calvin studied Roman law. A short distance further west on rue de Bourgogne, the circular Greek revival-style **Protestant chapel** dates from the 1830s.

Between the Préfecture and the river, the attractive narrow streets of the old city are disrupted by the former **Dessaux vinegar works**, one building of which was designed by Gustave Eiffel. Orléans' vinegar-making traditions go back some six hundred years – to the times when wine would go off during the journey up the Loire – but since the Dessaux factory closed down in 1983, only one traditional vinegar-maker remains in the city, the Maison Martin-Pouret. (The factory is out in the suburb of Fleury-les-Aubrais, but you can buy bottles of their vinegar and mustard all over town.) Until recently, the Dessaux quarter was semi-derelict, but renovation and rebuilding works are finally going ahead as part of a grand municipal scheme to bring the entire riverside quarter back to life with blocks of flats and a large student residence. On the corner of rue des Africains and rue de la Folie, a plaque marks the house of Joan's brother and companion-in-arms.

Part of the **Gallo-Roman city wall**, which marked the eastern limits of the ancient city, can be seen on rue de la Tour Neuve near rue Edouard Fournier and again in the base of the **Tour Blanche**, just south, which is occasionally used for exhibitions by the city council's archeological department. To the east of rue de la Tour Neuve lies the fifteenth-century **église St-Aignan**, begun by Charles VII and hugely extended by Louis XI; astonishingly, what you see is only the choir and transepts, the nave having been destroyed by Huguenots in 1567. Peaceful place du Cloître St-Aignan, on the north side of the church, was once the site of the monastic cloisters. If you're here in high summer, don't miss seeing the remarkable eleventh-century **crypt** (July & Aug daily 2–6pm; or contact the tourist office), which was built in the early eleventh century to house the relics of St Aignan, an early bishop of Orléans who legendarily saved the city from the warriors of Attila the Hun in 451. In the 1950s, beautiful polychrome capitals were discovered inset into the fifteenth-century walls, but the tomb itself is even more impressive, a great stone chamber with four holes through which pilgrims could catch a glimpse of the precious relics.

West of the Quartier Dessaux, the transformation of the riverside area is at its most complete at the all-new **place de la Loire**, which slopes down to the river from a nine-screen cinema complex, its flagstones inset with a pattern that's supposed to suggest waves.

Eating, drinking and nightlife

There are one or two good places to eat on and around the place du Martroi, but rue de Bourgogne is where it's at for both **restaurants** and **nightlife**. You can choose from among French, Spanish, North African, Middle Eastern and Indian cuisines, all at reasonable prices. For buying your own provisions there are the covered **market halls** on place du Châtelet, near the river.

Restaurants

Les Antiquaires 2 & 4 rue au Lin ☎02.38.53.63.48. Run by one of the master chefs of France, this is Orléans' best restaurant and must be booked in advance. Lobster consommé, wild turbot with girolle mushrooms and a pike-perch steak are some of its delights, served in an old-fashioned, formal dining room. The excellent €35 *menu* (not available Sat evening or Sun) includes wine, otherwise there are *menus* at €39 and €56. Closed Sun evening, Mon & first three weeks of Aug.

Le Brin de Zinc 62 rue Ste-Catherine. Bustling bistro just off place du Martroi. The outside tables are packed with a noisy crowd tucking into huge pots of mussels (€10–12) and giant desserts.

La Chancellerie 95 rue Royale, cnr place Martroi ☎02.38.53.57.54. Customers in the upmarket restaurant section get starched white tablecloths – even outside – and a distinctly classy €32.50 *menu*, but the café-brasserie is a good place for a drink on the square, with a fair lunch *menu* for around €14.

Les Fagots 32 rue du Poirier ☎02.38.62.22.79. Wonderfully convivial place that looks like it has been crammed into someone's grandmother's kitchen, albeit a grandmother with a mania for collecting coffeepots. Excellent grilled meats done on the griddle in one corner of the room. Main courses around €12–14. Closed Sun & Mon.

La Mangeoire 28 rue du Poirier ☎02.38.68.15.38. A real local secret: homely, brightly lit bistro packed full of locals enjoying straightforward pasta, salads and French standards, with starters at €5 and mains at a little over €10. Closed Sun.

Noé 195 rue de Bourgogne 5t02.38.53.44.09. Relaxed café-style bistro with a chintzy decor of yellowing posters and dusty old bottles. The food is reasonably priced, with a *menu* at €14, but a bit hit-and-miss: best stick to the classics.

La Petite Folie 223 rue de Bourgogne ☎02.38.53.39.87. From the new wave of designer bar-restaurants, full of trendy twenty- and thirty-somethings having a drink with friends or a light meal. The food is actually very good: fresh and healthy with lots of zingy, unconventional combinations. You might find asparagus flan, chicken with sauce Canadienne, then strawberry soup with wine – all for around €20. Closed Sun.

La Petite Marmite 178 rue de Bourgogne

☎02.38.54.23.83. The most highly regarded restaurant on this busy street mixes the homely with the deeply trendy: the owner presides over the warm, bustling, rustic interior with Almódovar-esque cool. The excellent €18 *menu du terroir* features local products such as Jargeau *andouille* and guineafowl from the Sologne, and there are more expensive *menus* as well. Booking essential. Mon–Fri open evenings only, Sat & Sun open lunchtime and evening.

Le Viking 233 rue de Bourgogne ☎02.38.53.12.21. Oddball mix of fancily upmarket and relaxed in a camp kind of way, with candelabras on the pink-clothed tables. The food is similarly surprising: trad French *menus* (from €17.50) and luxurious cheese- or fish-based galettes (€12–17). Closed Sun.

Bars and clubs

L'Arrozoir 224 rue de Bourgogne. One of the classier venues on the rue de Bourgogne strip, with restaurant service at lunchtime and from 6 till 10.30pm and a busy but laid-back bar carrying through till 3am on weekend nights. Closed Mon & Sun.

Le Club 266 rue de Bourgogne. Musty cellar club-bar with a tiny dance floor overlooked by a little mezzanine seating level. The friendlier choice if you're out late at the weekend and want to push on past 2am or have a dance – otherwise don't bother. Entry €10 with a drink.

Le Ka Place du Châtelet. The only proper club in the town centre, but it's not the coolest of venues – what's with the weird Egyptian theme? – or the

friendliest – girls may find themselves having to avoid lechy townies. Open daily 10.30pm–5am, but only gets going late. €5 entry, or €8 with a drink.

Paxton's Head 264–266 rue de Bourgogne. English pub with a club in the cellars that's popular with a twenty-something crowd, with occasional live music. Tues–Sat 3pm–3am.

Le Zig 108 ave du Loiret, beside the Pont du Loiret on the main road to Olivet. Orléans' best club, and worth making the journey out of town for – though only on Friday and Saturday after 1am. Plays R&B, funk or club classics – depending on the night – to a relatively sophisticated crowd. Taxi essential. € 9 with one drink.

Festivals

The **Fête de Jeanne d'Arc** is a series of period-costume parades held on April 29, May 1 and May 7–8, with the big set-pieces occurring in front of the cathedral on the night of May 7 and morning of the May 8. The **Festival de Jazz d'Orléans** (Ⓦwww.ville-orleans.fr/orleansjazz) is held right through June, culminating in concerts held in the Campo Santo. In the second week of August, the **Imagined Images** festival (Ⓦwww.images-imaginees.org) displays open-air cinema at various places in town, with theatricals in the Campo Santo. In September 2003, a new **Loire Festival** was held with five days of concerts and shows, many held on old boats moored by the Châtelet quay, and café and restaurants on a terrace built out over the river; it is hoped that it will become an annual event.

Listings

Bike rental The closest outlet to the town centre is in Olivet, a suburb in the south of Orléans (take tram #A to the stop Victor Hugo and walk): Kit Loisirs, 1720 rue Marcel Belot ☎02.38.63.44.34, Ⓦwww.kitloisirs.com. Hires out good road bikes

as well as mountain bikes.

Car rental Avis, 13 rue Sansonnières ☎02.38.62.27.04; Budget, 5 rue Sansonnières ☎02.38.54.54.30; Europcar, 81 rue A.-Dessaux ☎02.38.73.00.40.

Cinemas Le Select, 45 rue Jeanne-d'Arc, often shows good art-house movies in the original language (☎08.92.68.69.25); the new nine-screen cinema in the La Charpenterie complex on place de la Loire, Cinema Multiplex Pathé, 45 rue des Halles (☎08.92.68.69.25), sometimes shows v.o. versions of Hollywood blockbusters.

Email and internet Access available at Bizznet, 256 rue de Bourgogne (Mon–Fri 9am–8pm, Sat 10am–6pm), and Cyberodysseus, 32 rue du Colombier (Mon–Wed 9am–9pm, Thurs–Sat 9am–1am), just north of place du Martroi.

Emergencies Ambulance ☎15; police ☎17; Centre Hospitalier, 1 rue Porte-Madeleine ☎02.38.51.44.44.

Police 63 rue du Faubourg-St-Jean ☎02.38.24.30.00.

Taxis Taxi Radio d'Orléans ☎02.38.53.11.11.

Around Orléans

If you're spending more than a couple of days in **Orléans**, two sights in the outer suburbs may well draw you out of the city. Even if you're just passing through, the **Parc Floral** at Orléans-la-Source makes a good stop-off on the way south into the Sologne, and you could call in at the Fonderie Bollée at **St-Jean-de-Braye** on your way upstream towards Gien.

The overgrown village of **La Ferté-St-Aubin** is only 21km south of Orléans, but the distinctive red brick of its low buildings is distinctively *Solognote* – from the backwoods region of the Sologne (most of which is covered in Chapter 2; see p.153). Most visitors come on day-trips from Orléans, to visit the château, lunch in one of the restaurants in and around town and maybe have a walk in the nearby Domaine du Ciran. The trio make for an excellent day out, especially for children, and all are accessible on **public transport**.

Parc Floral de la Source

Orléans expanded rapidly after World War II, and in 1959 the suburb of **Orléans-la-Source** was created to take some of the pressure off the city. The grounds of the château de la Source (which now belongs to Orléans' campus university and doesn't have anything much to offer the visitor) have been transformed into the enormous **Parc Floral de la Source** (daily: April to mid-Nov 9am–6pm; mid-Nov to March 2–5pm; €3.60, or €6 with hothouses; Ⓦwww.parcfloral-lasource.fr), where you can wander among endless gardens of roses, irises and rhododendrons, visit the wonderful butterfly-house, and look at the principal source of the Loiret – which turns out to be a rather unimpressive stream, for all that it inspired the name of the château (*source* means "spring") and of the entire *département* of the Loiret.

To get to the park **by car**, take the Pont du Maréchal Joffre, heading south along the N20 towards Bourges, and then follow the signs for the Parc Floral. It's much more fun, however, to take the spanking-new **tram A** from place de Gaulle towards Hôpital de la Source, getting off at Université-Parc Floral.

St-Jean-de-Braye

The village of **ST-JEAN-DE-BRAYE**, where sculptor Henri Gaudier-Brzeska was born in 1891, is now a suburb of the city. Most visitors are businesspeople on their way to the giant cosmetics factory, which employs around 1800 people and manufactures almost all **Christian Dior**'s perfumes and make-up. There are no guided visits, however, so the few tourists that come to St-Jean are those who have heard about the **Fonderie Bollée** (Fri–Sun 2–6pm; €3), a working bell foundry where generations of the same family of bellwrights have used traditional techniques since the 1840s – and before then the Bollées were itinerant bell-makers. Even if you don't speak French, it's well worth seeing the workshops and museum, though bear in mind that the foundry isn't in action on Saturdays and Sundays, or in the month of August. To make an excursion of it, take the path that runs along the Canal d'Orléans to the pretty village of **COMBLEUX** – count on around one hour one-way.

To get to the Fonderie, take **bus** #4 from the gare SNCF stop or bus #27 from the riverside quai du Châtelet, getting off at St-Loup. **By car**, it's easiest to follow the river west and turn off at the signs.

La Ferté-St-Aubin and around

The privately owned **château de la Ferté-St-Aubin** (mid-Feb to mid-Nov daily 10am–7pm; €7, children aged 4–15 €4.50; ⓦwww.chateau-ferte-st-aubin.com) lies at the north end of the village, set back from the busy N20 road behind its own moat and meadow. From the outside, it's one of the warmest and most enticing of all Loire châteaux, the combination of salmon-coloured brick, creamy limestone and dark roof slates almost irresistible, especially as the place is well worn at the edges.

The approach is adorable: you cross a meadow and a moat, passing through a stone gate flanked by two doll-sized turrets, with *œil-de-bœuf* windows peering out of their hat-like roofs. The **stable** buildings stand symmetrically on either side, marked by seventeenth-century terracotta horses' heads rearing under the central pediments – the block on the right is now used for exhibitions, but the left-hand row still stables the proprietor's horses.

The main château building in front is far less well ordered, falling down in three step-like wings of very unequal sizes: the smallest section, known as the **petit château**, dates from the late sixteenth century, while the **grand logis** to the right was completed in the 1630s. The interior is a surprise: this is a nineteenth-century-style home, and you are invited to treat it as such. You can wander freely into almost every room, playing billiards or the piano, picking up the old telephone, sitting on the worn armchairs or washing your hands in a porcelain sink; only the rather fancier **grand salon**, with its *boiseries* painted with views of the château and its antique furnishings, is cordoned off. The none-too-tidy **attic** floor is chaotically full of bits and pieces, as a good attic should be: there are roomfuls of antique children's toys and artisans' tools and dummies apparently ironing the laundry, and a section where an old *épicerie* (grocer's shop) has been set up just as it was when it closed – lock, stock and barrel transferred here.

Roughly every hour there are demonstrations down in the **kitchens** of how to make madeleine cakes – the sweet spongy biscuit that so inspired Proust. The charismatic cook is part of the husband-and-wife team that looks after the château, and she gives a fascinating tour of the old kitchens as she works. The show ends with a tasting.

At the rear of the château, also enclosed by the moat, is the so-called **Enchanted Island**. This really is a magical place for younger children, a patch of wooded ground cleverly set up with lots of games that encourage imaginative play: there's a fort with sponge balls supplied for storming it, a Wendy house on stilts, little cabins with models acting out fairy-tales, a play farm with tools for digging, a kitchen hut, a play *épicerie*, rabbits in hutches, chickens in runs and goats running wild everywhere. Older children and adults can explore the reconstructed 1930s **station** building adjacent. You're free to clamber aboard the original *Compagnie des Wagons Lits* (Orient Express) carriages pulled up outside, still complete with their old-fashioned buffet and sleeper cars.

Practicalities

The **gare SNCF** is roughly 200m southwest of the main square, with around nine trains arriving daily from Orléans and continuing south to Vierzon and Bourges. Buses are geared to commuters, heading into Orléans in the mornings, and returning in the afternoons only – useless for day-trips. The **tourist office**, rue des Jardins (April–Sept Tues–Sat 9.30am–12.30pm & 2.30–6.30pm, Sun 10am–noon; Oct–March Tues–Sat 9.30am–noon & 3–5pm; ☎02.38.64.67.93), can advise on travelling deeper into the Sologne.

Oddly enough, there's no hotel in La Ferté-St-Aubin, but if you plan to **stay** there are a number of chambres d'hôtes in the vicinity. Olivier and Camille Cadel, 15 chemin de Bethléem (☎02.38.76.90.70; ❸), have simple rooms on the wooded edge of the hamlet of **MENESTREAU-EN-VILLETTE**, 6km from La Ferté, and there's a very special option at *La Ferme des Foucault* (☎38.76.94.41; ❹), isolated at the end of a long, wooded farm road, with luxuriously appointed rooms under the roof beams and books in English scattered everywhere; to get there turn off at the signpost on the D64, halfway between Marcilly-en-Villette and Sennely. Another level of luxury up, the *Château les Muids*, 5km south of La Ferté on the main N20 (☎02.38.64.65.14, ⓦwww.chateau-les-muids.com; ❺), is a handsome eighteenth-century brick château with its own extensive grounds; the rooms are nicely furnished but the ones at the front suffer from road noise. La Ferté's municipal **campsite** (☎02.38.76.55.90; closed Oct–March) is tucked away on the banks of the Cosson, on the opposite side of the N20 road from the château.

For **eating**, a good, inexpensive option is the *Auberge Solognote*, at 50 rue des Poulies (closed Tues evening & Wed), behind the covered market on La Ferté's main square, where you can join local workmen in a simple lunchtime *formule* for €7.50, or pay a little more for steaks, salads or slightly more elaborate *menus*. On the main road 100m from the château, the *Ecu de France*, 6 rue du Général Leclerc (☎02.38.64.69.22; *menus* €15–35; closed Tues evening & Wed), serves traditional French food in a very rustic, hunting-lodge-style dining room. *Le Relais*, on the main square at Ménestreau-en-Villette (☎02.38.76.97.40; *menus* €30–50; closed Tues eve, Wed & Sun eve), has a similar feel, with its fireplace and boar's head, but the carefully prepared seasonal dishes are distinctly upper-class and rather expensive unless you go for the €15 weekday lunch *menu*. *La Grenouillère*, on the edge of the village of Chaumont-sur-Tharonne, 12km south of La Ferté-St-Aubin along the D922 (☎02.54.88.50.71), features excellent innovative cooking on the €30 evening *menu*, and has outside seating in summer.

Domaine du Ciran

Six kilometres east of La Ferté-St-Aubin, just off the D108 and halfway between Ménestreau-en-Villette and Marcilly-en-Villette, the **Domaine du Ciran** (daily 9/10am–sunset; €5; ⓦwww.domaineduciran.com) is a small nature reserve covering a number of Sologne environments: sandy pine forest, heathland, meadows and the inevitable marshy *étangs* (large ponds). There's a five-kilometre signposted circular walk for which you should count on at least two hours to allow for diversions to various bird-hides, though two shortcuts allow you to reduce the length of the walk to 3 or 4km. No hunting has been allowed here since 1977, when the miniature château and its attached estate were bought by a private association, so the butterfly- and bird-life – especially herons and ducks – is wonderfully rich, and you may well catch a glimpse of wild deer. The best time to come is before dusk, when you've also got the best chance of coming across wild boar – they're not very threatening unless they're with their babies, but shouldn't be approached.

Camping (May–Sept) is allowed in a small field near the *gîtes* used by visiting groups of schoolchildren.

Downriver from Orléans

Heading downriver from Orléans towards Blois, the D951 is much the more attractive road, set just back from the main floodplain on the left bank. The northern routes on the opposite bank are pretty depressing; whether you take the A10 motorway or the busy N152 highway, the success of the region's light industry is all too visible. If you're visiting either of the main towns described in this section, **Meung-sur-Loire** and **Beaugency**, it makes sense to approach from the south – crossing Beaugency's 23-arch bridge is a particular treat, and you can call in at the giant basilica at **Cléry St-André** on the way. West of Beaugency, the **château de Talcy** actually lies in the Loir-et-Cher *département*, centred on Blois, but is included here as an excursion.

Between four and six **buses** daily make the trip from Orléans to Beaugency on route #9, passing Meung-sur-Loire, but the **train** service is much more regular, as both towns lie on the main line to Blois and Tours. For Cléry-St-André and Talcy you'll need your own transport.

Meung-sur-Loire

Fourteen kilometres southwest of Orléans, **MEUNG-SUR-LOIRE** is an agreeable place to spend half a day visiting the château and wandering around the small walled town. A gateway off the central place du Martroi leads up to the **château de Meung** (mid-Feb to Nov daily 10am–noon & 2–7pm; Dec to mid-Feb Sat & Sun 2–6pm; €7.20), surprisingly well hidden behind the church and a screen of trees. It remained in the hands of the bishops of Orléans from its construction in the twelfth century right up to the Revolution, the connection made immediately evident when you see the ruined fortifications linking château and church. Since the Revolution, it has passed through seven or eight private hands, acquiring an unkempt feel.

Inside and out, Meung is really two very different châteaux in one. On the side facing the church and the old drawbridge, the château looks grimly defensive with its thirteenth-century pepperpot towers, while the far side, facing the park, presents a much warmer face to the world, its eighteenth-century windows framed by salmon-pink stucco. You can explore the older part on your own, even climbing up under the roof, where the owners have tried to spice things up by laying out a few ghostly surprises. It's a shame that most of this pleasantly shambolic section of the building was remodelled in the nineteenth century, and little sense of the building's history remains. On the guided tour, you get to visit the more impressive eighteenth-century wing, where the bishops entertained their guests in relative comfort. The furnishings date from the epoch, but were actually brought here by more recent owners, so there's little to distinguish them from those you might find in secular houses of the same period: fine stucco ceilings face parquet flooring heavy with old polish, and the rooms are filled with upright chairs, graceful sideboards and old mirrors.

The final part of the guided tour is far and away the most popular, especially with children, as you descend into the chilly, deep **cellars**, where criminals condemned by the episcopal courts were imprisoned. The most famous of the detainees was the poet François Villon – murderer, thief and originator of the much-quoted line "*Mais où sont les neiges d'antan?*" ("But where are the snows

Literary Meung

Meung has accumulated a number of literary associations over the years. Over seven hundred years ago one Jean Chopinel – or **Jean de Meun** in the old spelling – added 18,000 lines to the already 4000-line-long *Roman de la Rose* (see p.324), written half a century earlier in 1225 by Guillaume de Lorris, from the town of the same name in the nearby Forêt d'Orléans. Inspired by the philosophical spirit of the times, De Meun transformed De Lorris's exquisite, allegorical poem into a finely argued disquisition on the nature of love, and the resulting *roman* inspired generations of European writers, Chaucer among them. Poet **François Villon** was imprisoned in the château in 1461 (see below), while somewhat more recently the town featured in the works of **Georges Simenon** – his fictional hero, **Maigret**, takes his holidays here.

of yesteryear?"). His writings indicate that he was imprisoned in the bottom of a well, outside the main body of the château, and the guide will show you an appalling chamber sunk into the ground of the gardens. Villon was imprisoned at the château between May and October 1461, which seems a relatively short time until you actually look down into the dank prison.

The rest of the town is perfect for an afternoon stroll, but there's little to detain you. Just next to the château gates, the thirteenth-century **église St-Lyphard** is renowned among architectural historians for the unusual trefoil-shaped floorplan of its choir. You can wander down from the square to the plane-tree-lined riverfront, where the bridge makes its way across the Loire, overlooked by a statue of Jean de Meun (see box above). For a longer walk, a signposted route traces the little streams known as **les mauves** as they flow through town, taking you along stony backstreets and past the medieval town gate, the Porte d'Amont.

Practicalities

The **gare SNCF** has good connections by train to Blois and Orléans. If you really want to **stay**, there's only one hotel in town, the *Auberge St-Jacques*, 60 rue du Général de Gaulle (☎02.38.44.30.39, ☎02.38.45.17.02; ❷); the rooms are plain and decent, but the situation on the main *route nationale* is offputting – ask for a room at the back. You'd be much better off at *La Mouche de l'Abeille*, which offers three chambres d'hôtes – two with wonderful river views – in an attractive old house on the riverbank (☎02.38.44.34.36, ⓦwww.chambres-hotes-loire.com; ❹). For something to **eat**, head straight for the *Café du Commerce* on the main place du Martroi (closed Mon), an energetic, family-run café-brasserie serving the standards, with a usually good *plat du jour* for around €8.

Cléry St-André

Cléry St-André, 6km east of Meung, is only distinguished by its enormous **basilica**, which dwarfs the square at the centre of the tiny town. The church owes its surprising size and significance first to Notre Dame de Cléry – whose pint-sized, thirteenth-century statue in oak is still worshipped here, standing on the main altar – and secondly to **Louis XI**, who rebuilt a church destroyed by the English in the Hundred Years War. This act of piety was brought on by Louis' defeat of the English at Dieppe in 1443, one of the battles that helped bring the war to a close, and a victory the king attributed to the assistance of the Virgin. Between 1465 and 1483, Louis came here regularly to pray, as depicted by the moving effigy on his **tomb**, which stands at a slant by the north door. He is one of only three French kings not to be buried at St-Denis, just outside Paris. The present stone tomb actually dates from the reign of Louis XIII, the original having been destroyed by Huguenots in the Wars of Religion.

The fifteenth-century church building has suffered over the centuries, but still stands as a wonderfully bright example of late Gothic architecture. One of the finest details is the crawling sculpture over the portal into the **sacristy** (hours vary, but usually open summer 3–6pm), where you can admire the fifteenth-century wooden panelling, and take a spiral staircase up to **Louis XI's private oratory**, with its little window for watching the Mass. You can also visit a Neogothic chapel housing the tombs of the Dunois Longueville family (see p.284), the chapterhouse and the impressive chapelle de St-Jacques, built in the sixteenth century by two brothers from Brittany – hence the Breton ermine's tail emblem carved all over its walls.

The bells in the tower occasionally ring out the carillon de Vendôme (see box on p.186).

Beaugency

Six kilometres downstream of Meung along the Loire, the small town of **BEAUGENCY** survives almost intact behind its medieval walls, the atmosphere of genteel charm only ruffled by the lively Saturday market. While there's not a great deal to see – the château is only notable for its worthy museum of local life – the tightly packed streets, all built in local Beauce limestone, and the riverside quays make this one of the prettiest of all Loire towns, and the excellent choice of hotels makes it an appealing base for a night or two.

Arrival, information and accommodation

The **gare SNCF**, on place de la Gare, is five minutes' walk from the central place du Docteur Hyvernaud, where you'll find the small **tourist office**, beside the Hôtel de Ville (Mon–Sat 9.30am–12.30pm & 2.30–6pm; May–Sept also Sun 10am–noon; ☎02.38.44.54.42, ⓦ www.ville-beaugency.fr).

Hotels

Le Bout du Pont ☎02.38.46.41.95, ⓔ jgue@club-internet.fr. Good chambres d'hôtes in an old house located literally at the other end of the bridge. One room has great views across the river, the others are quieter, overlooking the garden at the back, with a cluttered, nineteenth-century-style decor. ❸

Hostellerie de l'Ecu de Bretagne 5 rue de la Maille d'Or ☎02.38.44.67.60, ⓦ www.ecu-de-bretagne.fr. A classic old coaching inn beside the pleasant place du Martroi. Run in the good old French manner, marrying the graciously formal with the warm and welcoming. The rooms are well furnished and scrupulously maintained, and there's an inexpensive annexe (❷) just down the street with simple, perfectly acceptable rooms but no reception – you are given a key. Closed Sun evening mid-Nov to March. ❸

Hôtel de l'Abbaye 2 quai de l'Abbaye ☎02.38.44.67.35, ⓕ02.38.44.87.92. The setting in a seventeenth-century abbey makes this one of the most interesting hotels in the region. The grand staircase, huge corridors and ancient wooden doorframes preserve the monastic feel, but the actual bedrooms inside are a more miscellaneous bunch: all are fairly luxurious, but some are more characterful than others, the best having high ceilings, original features and views of the river – try asking for room no. 7. ❺–❼

Hôtel de la Sologne 6 place St-Firmin ☎02.38.44.50.27, ⓦ www.hoteldelasologne.com. Delightful little stony-fronted, cream-shuttered hotel on the nicest of Beaugency's squares. Sixteen rooms in all, four of them with views of the Tour de César, others set round the little internal courtyard with its glazed-over breakfast area. The bright, modern rooms are extremely comfortable, with elegant wallpaper and furnishings that would not disgrace a much more expensive hotel; prices depend on the size. Closed Dec 20–Jan 15. ❸–❹

Hôtel des Vieux Fossés 4 rue des Vieux-Fossés ☎02.38.44.51.65, ⓔ chpouradier@wanadoo.fr.

Central and inexpensive, with twelve very simple but clean rooms, three of them with shared bathrooms in the corridor. ❶–❷

Le Relais des Templiers 68 rue du Pont ☎02.38.44.53.78, ⓦhttp://relais-templiers.actu-anet.com. Intimate and enthusiastically run family hotel in a fine old building at the bottom end of town, close to the little stream that runs along the rue du Rû. Rooms are modern but tastefully furnished, and the best ones on the top floor are

tucked away under atmospherically exposed rafters. ❸.

La Tonnellerie 12 rue des Eaux Bleues, Tavers ⓦwww.tonelri.com. Three kilometres southwest along the main N152, in the little village of Tavers, this luxury hotel is set in a vine-covered building round a peaceful garden courtyard. The rooms are very swish, and the hotel has all the facilities you could think of, including a classy restaurant and a pool, but the prices are rather high. ❽

Hostel and campsite

Auberge de Jeunesse de Beaugency 152 rte de Châteaudun, Vernon ☎02.38.44.61.31, ⓔbeaugency@fuaj.org. A decent and really quite attractive HI hostel located 2km north off the main Orléans–Blois road from the east side of town. HI membership required, but you can

join on the spot. Beds cost €9.30 a night. Closed Jan.

Camping Municipal du Val de Flux ☎02.38.44.50.39. One of the best around, making the best of its perfect riverside location on the opposite bank from town. Closed Oct–Easter.

The Town

The old town squeezes inside what remains of the medieval walls, clustered around a handful of central squares. At the top end of town, **place du Martroi** is broad and handsome, but relatively uninteresting, its Romanesque priory church of **St-Etienne** sadly over-restored and used for exhibitions. Rue du Martroi leads off slightly downhill towards the **Tour de l'Horloge**, the old town gate, surmounted by its clock. The road leading through the tower gateway takes you to the tree-shaded **place du Docteur Hyvernaud**, presided over by the exquisite Renaissance **Hôtel de Ville**, a bizarrely proportioned structure with a curious carved frieze between the ground and first-floor levels. Inside, the main council chamber is graced by eight superb **tapestries** from the era of Louis XIII, but you'll have to ask at the tourist office (on the same square) to be allowed inside to have a look – which somehow makes it more fun. The four tapestries on the left as you enter describe pagan traditions of sacrifice, while the slightly larger set on the opposite wall illustrates the four continents as perceived in the seventeenth century: a turbaned woman for the Americas; a bare-breasted, white-looking woman for Africa; Queen Anne of Austria, covered in a mantle of fleurs de lys, for Europe; and a mystical-looking woman for Asia.

The Dauphin's bells

Before Joan of Arc steeled him to fight for his kingdom and his coronation, the lands controlled by the Dauphin Charles were meagre indeed. A contemporary rhyme tells the litany of his possessions:

Mes amis que reste-t-il	O my friends, what land is there
A ce dauphin si gentil?	Left to this young prince and heir?
Orléans, Beaugency,	Orléans, Beaugency,
Notre-Dame de Cléry,	Our Lady of Cléry,
Vendôme, Vendôme.	Vendôme, Vendôme.

The poem was set to music, and the tune – known as the **carillon de Vendôme** – is now rung out three times daily by the bells at Beaugency and hourly at Vendôme. It's fun scrabbling to work out how the words fit the tune in time – it helps if you know that the first "Vendôme" runs straight on from "Cléry" and the second "Vendôme" gets four syllables.

In 1152, the **Council of Beaugency** met in the abbey church of Notre-Dame to settle what turned out to be one of the most crucial questions in French history: could Eleanor of Aquitaine legally be divorced from Louis VII of France? The argument was based on the technical principle of consanguinity, and the council's decision, that that the couple were indeed too closely related, freed Eleanor to marry the up-and-coming Henry Plantagenêt – even though he was in fact even more closely related. Henri already controlled Normandy, Maine, Anjou and Touraine, and when he went on to become Henry II of England, Eleanor's huge land-holdings in southwest France fell under the sway of the English Crown. The ensuing struggles between the French and English kings over their claims to these territories – and to the French throne itself – lasted for interminable years, acquiring the name of the Hundred Years War.

The more interesting part of town lies down towards the river. Narrow rue du Traîneau runs below the market square to the lovely **place St-Firmin**, where a statue of Joan of Arc is overshadowed by the **Clocher St-Firmin**, a belfry tower whose carillon rings out a well-known tune (see box opposite) at a few minutes past 8am, noon and 7pm. The square slopes down towards the massive shell of the eleventh-century **Tour César**, the brutal keep of the old château, only pierced by a few empty, anachronistic windows. On the downhill side of the tower lies **place Dunois**, bordered on one side by the rather grim, fifteenth-century **château Dunois**, which Joan of Arc's companion in arms Dunois, the so-called Bastard of Orléans (see p.284), acquired by marriage. You can take a peek at the courtyard without anyone minding – passing under the sign that has read "Quartier des Détenus" since the château was used as a debtor's prison – but it is plain enough, with a narrow staircase tower and a few sixteenth-century windows. You can only visit the interior as part of a guided tour of the **local history museum** which occupies it (daily except Tues 10am, 11am, 2pm, 3pm, 4pm; June–Aug also 5pm; €3.40), which is stultifying or illuminating, depending on your appetite for folk arcana. There's Gallo-Roman glassware, a collection of chasubles and liturgical objects, a set of encyclopedias rescued from the abbey, dozens of lace caps, a giant nineteenth-century keyed bass bugle called an ophicleide and a large display of nineteenth-century dolls and toys that, sadly, you're not allowed to play with. The only obvious remnant of Dunois' day is the tiny **oratory**, whose domed roof is frescoed with coats of arms, one of them showing Dunois' "bend sinister" – a left-sloping bar set across three fleurs de lys, indicating illegitimate royal descent.

Place Dunois is completed by the rather severe Romanesque abbey church of **Notre-Dame**, the venue for the Council of Beaugency in 1152 (see box above). Inside, the superb wooden vault was installed in the mid-seventeenth century by the monks themselves – canons from the fraternity of Ste-Geneviève – but the most striking feature of the interior is the modern stained glass, which uses bold colours for symbolic effect, best seen in the choir, where Our Lady herself reigns pre-eminent in blue.

At the foot of place Dunois, a short, sloping alley runs down under an archway to **rue du Pont**; a left turn takes you some 300m to the pretty little **rue du Rû**, a narrow, flower-lined street with a little rivulet of a town stream flowing down the middle. A right turn takes you straight to the **river**. During the Hundred Years War, the **bridge** here was the only crossing between Orléans and Blois, making Beaugency a constant battleground – Joan of Arc "liberated" the town on her way to Orléans in 1429, in company with Dunois. Remarkably, the 26-arch medieval structure still stands, and from the parapet

ACCOMMODATION

Le Bout du Pont	F
Hostellerie de l'Ecu de Bretagne	B
Hôtel de l'Abbaye	D
Hôtel de la Sologne	C
Hôtel des Vieux Fossés	E
Le Relais des Templiers	A

RESTAURANTS

La Crep'zeria	2
Le Petit Bateau	1
Le Relais du Château	3

BEAUGENCY

there's an excellent view of the keep and church towers rising above the leafy ranks of plane trees lining the quays. The large seventeenth-century building immediately upstream is what remains of the **abbey**, now a luxury hotel (see p.185).

Eating and drinking

The best **restaurants** in town are almost all on rue du Pont. Pick of the bunch for its carefully prepared traditional French dishes is *Le Petit Bateau*, at no. 54 (☎02.38.44.56.38; *menus* €21–31; closed Sun evening & Mon), which has an upmarket but unpretentious atmosphere, with big beams running between exposed stone walls and a floral terrace. One step down in terms of gastronomic pretensions is *Le Relais du Château*, just short of the bridge at no. 8 (☎02.38.44.55.10; *menus* €12.50–28; closed Wed & Thurs lunch), which serves reliable but somewhat homelier dishes. *La Crep'zeria*, 32 rue du Pont (closed Mon, Sat & Sun lunch), has fairly ordinary pizzas, salads and crêpes, but the sun-trap terrace is good for relaxed outdoor dining. Even if you're not staying at the hotel, do consider the excellent restaurant at *L'Ecu de Bretagne* (see p.185), which has a deserved local reputation for using lots of fresh and home-made produce.

Château de Talcy

Fifteen kilometres west of Beaugency, the **château de Talcy** (April & Sept daily except Tues 9.30am–12.30pm & 2–6pm; May & June daily 9.30am–12.30pm & 2–6pm; July & Aug Mon–Fri 9.30am–12.30pm & 2–6pm, Sat & Sun 9.30am–6pm; Oct–March daily except Tues 10am–12.30pm &

2–4.30pm; €4.60) is one of the few features in the otherwise featureless plain of the Petite Beauce, which stretches between the rivers *le* Loir and *la* Loire. The landscape seems particularly bleak along the D917 from Beaugency to Josnes, where stretches of straight road carve their way across scarcely undulating wheat fields, passing endless rows of pylons running north from the nuclear power station at St-Laurent-des-Eaux.

Talcy began life as a kind of fortified farmhouse, a role hinted at by the forbidding entry gate with its machicolations under the roof. Once you've penetrated to the cobbled courtyard, however, the château's nobler incarnation is revealed in the shape of the arcaded Renaissance wing added by the Florentine financier Bernardo Salviati, who bought the château in 1517, bringing along his daughter Cassandra – she who inspired Ronsard's groundbreaking sonnet sequence, *Les Amours de Cassandre*.

The numerous eighteenth-century windows that carve up the walls hint at what lies within: *ancien régime* furnished elegance. Horticulturalists will love the extensive **gardens**, which present endless varieties of fruit trees, many of them rare varieties little seen since the eighteenth century, and many shaped in arcane variations on the art of pruning. The huge dovecote with 1500 pigeonholes (see box on p.147) is also worth seeing.

Upriver from Orléans

East of Orléans, the ancient **Forêt d'Orléans** arcs its way along the right bank of the Loire, wrapping itself over the watershed that divides the Loire from the Seine basin. You can tour the forest roads by bike or car, and the villages of **Ingrannes** and **Lorris** make useful bases for an extended visit. Beyond the forest lie the grain-growing plains of the Beauce, to the northwest, and the green fields of the Gâtinais, to the northeast. The **château de Chamerolles**, with its gardens and perfume museum, makes a good destination on the forest's northern side.

Following the **Loire** upstream from Orléans, the greatest of the châteaux are left behind, along with the majority of the region's summer visitors, but there are some fascinating places to visit, notably the Romanesque abbey at **St-Benoît-sur-Loire** and the nearby Carolingian oratory at **Germigny-des-Près**, which bear witness to the region's venerable Christian roots. Further upstream, **Sully-sur-Loire** is a superb example of a moated castle, while the town of **Gien** has a fine setting, its brick-built château and church gazing down on an ancient, many-arched town bridge. Even more spectacular is the bridge at **Briare**, where an extravagant aqueduct crosses high above the Loire itself.

Bus route #3 passes through all the riverside towns covered in this section on its way between Orléans and Gien, but it is aimed squarely at commuter traffic, with only three or four services a day (one or two on Sundays), one of which leaves Orléans very early in the morning, while the others depart in the late afternoon. No buses or trains serve the Forêt d'Orléans.

Forêt d'Orléans

The great swathe of woodland – one of the largest in France – that makes up the **Forêt d'Orléans** is one of the ancient places of France, one of the last remnants of the great wood. The druids are thought to have held their conventions here, at what Caesar called the navel of France. The forest is criss-crossed with arrow-straight roads and woodland tracks but unless you're travelling with bikes strapped to the top of a car, or you're a determined hiker, it can be difficult to get the best out of this area. There are few destinations as such, and the majority of visitors seem to be local retired people who drive out in the afternoons, find a spot on one of the many benches that supervise the forest crossroads and watch the world drive by.

Ingrannes and around

One of the most peaceful ways to appreciate the forest flora is to arrive for one of the Sunday opening days of the **Arboretum des Grandes Bruyères** (April–Nov Sun 10am–6pm; closed Easter Sun, Pentecost Sun, 4th Sun in July & 2nd Sun in Aug; €8; ☎02.38.57.12.61), 1km outside the attractively soporific little village of **INGRANNES**, in the central part of the forest 9km north of Fay-aux-Loges, along a signposted side-road. The arboretum is really a huge woodland garden on the fringes of the forest, presided over by Scots pines and carpeted with heathers, with the occasional frog-rich pond or exotic tree, and wonderful clumps of magnolias and old roses scattered throughout. The charming owner-gardener, the comtesse de la Rochefoucauld, will happily swap tips (in exquisite English) and cuttings. Near Ingrannes, you can bathe, **camp** (☎02.38.59.35.77; closed Nov–March) and rent canoes and pedalos at the **Etang de la Vallée**, a lake just off the road to the extremely pretty village of **COMBREUX**, which lies on the Canal d'Orléans.

The obvious way to have lunch is to find a quiet forest clearing off the main road and make a **picnic**, but there's an excellent alternative at *Le Chêne Vert*, place de l'Eglise (☎02.38.57.11.97; closed Mon, Thurs evening & Sun evening), a splendidly rustic **restaurant** on the village green at Ingrannes. At Combreux there's an idyllic, twenty-room country **hotel**, the *Auberge de Combreux*, 34 rte de Gatinais (☎02.38.46.89.89, ⓦwww.auberge-de-combreux.fr; ❹), with ivy on the walls, a swimming pool in the garden and a good but fairly expensive restaurant (*menus* at €18 in the week, otherwise around €30); guests can hire bikes.

Lorris

The small town of **LORRIS**, 18km northeast of Sully-sur-Loire, sells itself as the "Capital of the Forest of Orléans", though poetry enthusiasts may know it better as the birthplace of Guillaume de Lorris, the original author of the thirteenth-century *Roman de la Rose* (see box on p.324). The town is moderately appealing, with its ancient covered market and cluster of old-fashioned squares, and it's certainly a useful base for getting into the forest.

In town, you can visit the surprisingly imposing church of **Notre-Dame de Lorris**, a transitional Gothic structure with a really wonderful early sixteenth-century organ; the quirky little **Ecomusée Georges Lemoine** (accessed from the tourist office, see below for hours; free), which traces the life and work of a jeweller working in Lorris in the 1940s; and the excellent **Musée de la Résistance** (Mon & Wed–Sat 10am–noon & 2–6pm, Sun 2–6pm; €5), which is admirably well-presented, with models of Resistance fighters sending coded radio signals, and lots of old cartoons, photos and propaganda posters, though you'll need to read French to get the best out of the local history.

Giant stands of oak and even sequoias can be seen in the vicinity of the **Carrefour de la Résistance** – named after a group of *maquisards* encircled and shot here – a woodland crossroads 10km south of town, in the heart of the forest; ask at the **tourist office**, 2 rue des Halles (June–Aug Mon–Sat 9am–noon & 2–6pm, Sun 10am–noon & 3–5pm; Sept–May Mon–Sat 9am–noon &

2–6pm; ☎02.38.94.81.42, ✉otsi.lorris@wanadoo.fr), for more precise directions and a map. From the crossroads, a signposted botanical walk leads off through the forest for 3km towards the **Etang du Ravoir**, a long forest lake that has become home to one of the few pairs of ospreys breeding in France. A special bird-hide has been built to tell the story of the so-called "fishing eagle", and if you're lucky there's even a chance to see ospreys nesting, or better still, dive-bombing the lake – though only in summer months; call the forestry office, the O.N.F., for details of how to get to the hide on ☎02.38.65.47.00. Alternatively, make for the **Etang des Bois**, 5km west of town along the D88, where there's a pleasant artificial **beach** shaded by pines, with a sandy roped-off swimming area, and pedalos, canoes and windsurfers for rent. You can **camp** on one side of the lake (☎02.38.92.32.00; closed Nov–March).

There are no **buses** to or from Lorris, so you'll need your own transport to get there. For getting around the area, **bikes** can be hired at Garage Delaveau, rte de Gien (☎02.38.92.40.02), 2km away from Lorris's town centre, in the light-industry zone. There's a single **hotel** in town, the *Hôtel-Restaurant du Sauvage* (☎02.38.92.43.79; ❸; closed Fri, Sun, Feb & 2 weeks in Oct), a typically sleepy provincial hotel with decent enough rooms but a stronger emphasis on the restaurant, with refined French cuisine for upwards of €20.

Château de Chamerolles

On the northern side of the Forêt d'Orléans, 35km northeast of Orléans, the **château de Chamerolles** (Feb, March & Oct–Dec daily except Tues 10am–noon & 2–5pm; April–June & Sept daily except Tues 10am–6pm; July & Aug daily 10am–6pm; €4.90, or €7.80 combined ticket with the château de Sully – see p.193) is a sedate, Sunday-afternoon-outing kind of place. The château's moat, drawbridge and pepper-pot towers, its Renaissance windows and arcade, and the perfect lozenge patterns set into its brickwork are delightful, but the main attractions of the visit are the **Promenade des Parfums**, a museum of perfume, and the **gardens**, beautifully restored by the current owners – the *département* of the Loiret.

The château was the work of one Lancelot 1er du Lac (named after the legendary Arthurian knight but sadly, no relation), who rose to the position of governor of Orléans under Louis XII, in the early years of the sixteenth century. In the south wing, a suite of rooms presents various French interiors from the sixteenth century to the present day, with an emphasis on objects related to the *toilette* – bathing, personal grooming and the use of scent. Each room has a "press-and-sniff" button with a recreation of a typical perfume of the era. Up on the first floor, under the rafters, there's a huge array of 300-odd nineteenth- and twentieth-century perfumes and perfume bottles. It isn't as extensive as the racks of contemporary scents on sale in the **shop**, which are cleverly arranged by type rather than by brand. A little drawbridge leads out of the back of the château to the formal **gardens**, a large terrace of geometrically arranged herbs, flowers and fruit and veg, while the château's flank sets off a contrasting, "English-style" landscaped garden set around a reed- and iris-fringed lake.

There is an infrequent **bus** service from Orléans to Chilleurs-aux-Bois, but you'd have to walk the last 3km, so the trip only really makes sense by car – though cyclists can work out some great routes along the quieter forest roads.

Orléans to Germigny-des-Prés

There's little to detain you immediately upstream of Orléans. Taking the left bank, you pass the pleasant town of **JARGEAU**, locally renowned for its largely twelfth-century church and its *andouilles* and *andouillettes* – perfumed and delicious sausages made with pork and tripe. The right-bank route takes in **CHATEAUNEUF-SUR-LOIRE**, where the remnants of a seventeenth-century château overlook a rhododendron garden, and the old stable buildings house a rather good **Musée de la Marine de Loire** (daily except Tues: April–Oct 10am–6pm; Nov–March 2–6pm; €3.50), which tells the story of the old Loire mariners and their boats.

Heading upstream along the right bank, the little D60 is a much more pleasant road than the main D952 to Gien. Five kilometres out of Châteauneuf, the village of **GERMIGNY-DES-PRÈS** is home to an outwardly unassuming **church** (daily: April–Oct 8.30am–7pm; Nov–March 8.30am–5pm) that incorporates one of the oldest buildings in France at its east end. The tiny, perfectly formed **oratory** is one of the few structures surviving anywhere from the Carolingian Renaissance. It was built in 806 for Theodulf, who was one of Charlemagne's counsellors as well as bishop of Orléans and abbot of St-Benoît (see opposite). The apparently Arabic horseshoe arches actually reflect Theodulf's Spanish-Visigothic origins, while the chapel itself is a typically Carolingian design, rationally planned in the shape of a Greek cross. The original structure only lacks its western apse, which was replaced by a long nave in the fifteenth century, although it was also damaged in the nineteenth century by too-perfect restoration work. Still, the unique gold and silver mosaic on the dome of the eastern chapel preserves all its rare beauty. Long covered by distemper, it was only discovered by accident in the middle of the nineteenth century when children were found playing with coloured glass cubes in the church. Unusually, the mosaic represents the Ark of the Covenant, the biblical Jewish repository for the tablets of the Ten Commandments. The decision not to depict Christ in Majesty or the Virgin Mary, as was more common, may reflect Charlemagne's opposition to the cult of images.

St-Benoit-sur-Loire and around

Thirty-five kilometres upstream of Orléans, **ST-BENOÎT-SUR-LOIRE** derives its name and its considerable fame from a daring grave-robbery. In around 672, a group of monks from the **abbaye de Fleury** returned home from a raid on Monte Cassino in Lombard-occupied Italy with the remains of St Benedict (Saint Benoît), the sixth-century founder of the reforming Benedictine order. The presence of the relics secured a prestigious future for the abbey, and over the course of the next 1100 years, its abbots included many familiar names from French and Loire history – a de la Trémoïlle, from the Château de Sully (see p.193); Cardinal Louis II of Guise, who was murdered in the château at Blois (see box on p.135); and the great Cardinal Richelieu, who received the title of abbot as a political reward in 1621. For all its importance, the abbey stagnated as often as it flourished, and its population had dwindled to ten monks at the time of the Revolution, after which it was abandoned and dismantled. The church itself survived, and Benedictine monks returned in 1944. The community now numbers forty brothers, who observe the original Rule and can be heard singing Gregorian chant at the daily midday Mass (11am on Sunday). They earn their keep by producing some nine tonnes of sweets a year, as well as selling enamel paintings.

Built in warm, cream-coloured stone between 1020 and 1218, the present **church** (daily 6.30am–10pm; ⓦ www.abbaye-fleury.com) dates from the abbey's greatest epoch. The oldest and most imposing part, the **porch tower**, illustrates St John's vision of the New Jerusalem in Revelation – foursquare, with twelve foundations and three open gates on each side. The fantastically sculpted capitals of the heavy pillars are alive with acanthus leaves, birds and exotic animals. Three of them depict scenes from the Apocalypse, with the horsemen clearly visible, while another shows Mary's flight into Egypt on a donkey.

The **interior** exemplifies the serene simplicity of the Romanesque style, though the vaults of the nave – the last section to be built – are just starting to point upwards in the half-way-to-Gothic style known as Transitional. A fascinating capital in the north aisle just before the choir shows St Benedict rolling in thorns to mortify his flesh and distract himself from the temptations of a prostitute. The light-filled **choir** is split into two levels divided by a wall pierced with tiny Roman windows for viewing the relics: above, a marble mosaic of possible Roman origin covers the chancel floor; below, in the ancient **crypt**, the relics of St Benedict lie buried at the very root of the church's forest of columns and arches, in a modern reliquary designed by a monk from Solesmes (see p.297). You can leave by the **north door**, where an unfinished Romanesque frieze, discovered only in 1996, shows the progress of sculpture from blind block of stone to finished work. On the outside of the north portal, a frieze under the figure of Christ Teaching depicts the translation of the relics of St Benedict – here shown as bones being thrown willy-nilly into a sack.

Practicalities

The tiny **town** has little to offer other than a stroll around the old houses beside the quays, but visiting the abbey late in the evening might be appealing enough to make you want to stay a night. The **tourist office**, 44 rue Orléanaise (March–Oct Mon 2.30–6pm, Tues & Thurs–Sat 9am–noon & 2.30–6pm, Wed 9am–noon; Nov–Feb Tues, Thurs & Fri 9am–noon & 2.30–5pm, Sat 9am–noon; ☏02.38.35.79.00, ✉otstbenoitsurloire-maisonmaxjacob@wanadoo.fr), occupies the house that once belonged to **Max Jacob**, the fashionable Montmartre-based poet who converted to Judaism and retired to St-Benoît. Jacob was interned in 1944 in the camp at Drancy, where he died, and there's a small (free) memorial exhibition to him above the tourist office. **Bikes** can be hired from Racing Cart, rte du Vieux Chemin (Mon & Thurs–Sun 10am–noon & 2–8pm; ☏02.38.35.76.46).

If you decide to stay, there are only two **hotels**: the *Labrador*, 7 place St-André (☏02.38.35.74.38, ⓦwww.hoteldulabrador.fr; ❹), a comfortable but heavily modernized place right next to the abbey with a good restaurant (*menus* €16–42); and the basic *La Madeleine*, 65 rue Orléanaise (☏02.38.35.71.15; ❶; closed Jan), on the high street, which has its own simple restaurant. Alternatively, Mme Bouin, 6 chemin de la Borde (☏02.38.35.70.53, ⓦwww.france-bonjour.com/la-borde; ❸), runs comfortable **chambres d'hôtes** in a modern farmhouse situated 2km from town, just off the D148 towards Ste-Scholastique; bikes can be hired and there's a table d'hôte on request.

Sully-sur-Loire

SULLY-SUR-LOIRE lies on the south bank of the Loire, 8km southeast of St-Benoît. The tiny town is an innocuous modern affair almost entirely rebuilt after the war, but the **château** that stands between town and river is a peach (daily: April–Sept 10am–6pm; Oct–Dec, Feb & March 10am–noon & 2–5pm; closed Jan; €3.40; guided visits only). Rising massively out of its wide moat, it's a picture-book castle, still complete with pointy-capped towers, machicolations and drawbridge despite savage wartime bombing that twice destroyed the nearby Loire bridge. **Children** may particularly enjoy the visit, as they can follow a historical treasure trail round the château (July & Aug only), opening coffers to find key words and filling in answers in a little booklet in English, and then dress up in chain-mail armour and clamber on a horse in the dedicated Chivalry Room.

The original Sully family achieved brief fame under Maurice de Sully, the builder of Notre-Dame de Paris, but the male Sully line came to an abrupt end in the Hundred Years War, the domain passing by marriage to Georges de la Trémoïlle, an extravagantly tall, wealthy and fat man who had a new fortified château built here in 1400. As one of Charles VII's favourites – he bankrolled the Dauphin's campaign – de la Trémoïlle infuriated **Joan of Arc** by encouraging the Dauphin to pursue a pacifying, diplomatic solution to the wars. After Joan's failure to liberate Paris in 1430, de la Trémoïlle attempted to ground her by virtually imprisoning her in the castle. She escaped, but was captured less than two months later at the disastrous battle of Compiègne. Three years later, an assassination attempt on de la Trémoïlle failed only because the sword failed to pierce his corpulent flesh. The castle changed hands in 1602, this time being snapped up by Henri IV's hyperactive minister, Maximilien de Béthune, duc de Sully, who added the moat and park, and pushed out the riverbank to protect his glorious creation from the vagaries of the Loire. After Henri's death, the arrogant minister – known as **Le Grand Sully** – was forced into retirement, which he spent writing his memoirs at Sully. In the eighteenth century young Voltaire, exiled from Paris for libellous political verse, spent time at the château, sharpening his wit in the company of the society figures with whom the duc de Sully of the time liked to surround himself. At the end of the century, the penultimate duke backed the Revolution and saved his château by partially dismantling the towers of the keep – potent symbols of feudalism. The last duke died without heir in 1807.

The **interior** is slowly being restored in a variety of styles by its owners, the *département* of the Loiret, but many rooms are still sparsely furnished. The giant **Lower Great Hall** is adorned by an unusually beautiful series of **tapestries** depicting the story of Psyche, woven in the reign of Henri IV. A spiral staircase and guard-walk lead to the **Great Garret**, a vast chamber lined with fifteen-metre-high, 600-year-old oak rafters. The absence of any trusses or tie beams is astonishing, and makes the rows of arching beams look like the ribs of some giant's sternum. Elsewhere in the château, other rooms have been completely restored to flesh out the château's history: you can see eighteenth-century chambers in the Louis XV wing (which is actually a faux-medieval reconstruction after a fire in 1918) and Sully's apartments in the Petit Château, which was heavily renovated in the nineteenth century.

The bridges of Sully-sur-Loire

Sully hasn't had much luck with its **bridges**. The earliest – washed away by a great flood in 1363 – was thought to have been an exceptionally long-lived Roman structure, but recent archeological digs have shown that it was actually built in around 1000. Even so, it had been by far the longest-surviving bridge at this site. After its destruction, boats and ferries were the only means of crossing at Sully for almost five hundred years, until a toll bridge was built in 1836. Optimistically constructed in oak, it didn't survive the flood of 1856, but was rebuilt and continued to be used until the local authorities completed a magnificent suspension bridge in 1933. Partially blown up by the retreating French army in June 1940, it was mended in 1943 and used until definitively destroyed by American aerial bombing in 1944. Yet another bridge was built immediately after the war, but succumbed to the pressure of ice in the big Loire freeze of January 1985. Today's structure is ugly but tough, built in heavily reinforced concrete.

Practicalities

The **train station**, on the Bourges–Etampes line, is ten minutes' walk from the centre of the village, where the **tourist office** can be found on place de Gaulle (May–Sept Mon–Sat 9.30am–12.30pm & 2–7pm, Sun 10.30am–1pm; Oct–April Mon–Sat 9.30am–noon & 2.30–6.30pm; ☎02.38.36.23.70, ⓔ ot.sully.sur.loire@wanadoo.fr). **Bikes** are a good way to explore – especially if you're headed north into the Forêt d'Orléans (see p.189) – and can be hired from Cycles Venon, at 8 rue du Maréchal Foch, just behind the post office (☎02.38.36.24.78).

Two decent **hotels** can be found near the central marketplace. The *Hôtel de la Tour* (☎02.38.36.21.72, ⓕ02.38.36.37.63; ❸) is rather stuffily furnished, and the reception is the bar downstairs, but it's comfortable, and the two rooms in the tower are good fun. The *Hostellerie du Grand Sully*, 10 boulevard du Champ-de-Foire (☎02.38.36.27.56, ⓕ02.38.36.44.54; ❸), is a very reliable choice with a good restaurant (*menus* from €25; closed Sun evening & Mon). The **camping municipal** (☎02.38.36.23.93; closed Nov–April) has a great riverside location, practically in the grounds of the château.

For **eating** out, *Côtes et Jardin*, at 8 rue du Grand Sully (☎02.38.36.35.89; €11 lunchtime *menu*, otherwise under €20; closed Sun evening, Tues evening, Wed & last 2 weeks in Sept), serves exceptionally good-value, high-class French cuisine; it's easy to find – look for the town's sole-surviving Renaissance mansion, on the road to the château.

Sully's **International Music Festival** (ⓦ www.festival-sully.com) runs right through June, featuring classical concerts held in a huge marquee in the grounds of the château.

Gien

On the right bank of the river, 23km upstream of Sully-sur-Loire, **GIEN** had the life bombed and burned out of it between 15 and 17 July 1940, when the rapidly advancing Germans caught up with the French army – for once not retreating fast enough. The damage was extensive, but a freak rainstorm saved most of the fifteenth-century **château**, and a postwar reconstruction in the local glazed brick has recreated some sense of the town's former fifteenth-century quaintness. Unfortunately, Gien's hotels reflect the existence of its thriving manufacturing industry – which includes a major toilet-roll manufacturer and a Japanese perfume factory – rather than tourism, so the choice is mostly uninspiring.

The sixteenth-century stone **bridge** spanning the river still offers excellent views of Gien's medieval-style mass, with the château towering above town next to the modern church. Looking downstream, the four great cooling towers of the nuclear power station at Dampierre-en-Burly (see p.314), can also be seen, emitting tell-tale clouds of water vapour. An alarm siren is tested on the first Wednesday of every month, though it's not clear what the *Giennois* could do if it went off – local wits advise making for the wine cellars with a corkscrew.

The château and church

The red brick of the **château**, inset with grey bricks in elaborate checkerboard and lozenge patterns, owes something to the local styles and materials of the Sologne (see p.153), a region to the west rich in clay but poor in stone, and something to the elegant, proto-Renaissance style elaborated under Louis XI. The royal influence is hardly surprising, as the château was built by Louis' daughter, Anne de Beaujeu. As the elder sister of the young Charles VIII, Anne became the precarious regent of France during her brother's strife-ridden minority. Building the château was practically a retirement hobby, as by the time she began it, in 1494, Charles had married and assumed full control of the kingdom. Some two hundred years later, in 1652, another great female regent arrived, when Anne of Austria sheltered in Gien with her young son and charge Louis XIV during the revolts against taxation known as the *Frondes*.

Little survives of the château's original interior, and the entire building has now been turned over to the **Musée International de la Chasse et de la Nature** (daily: June–Sept 9am–6pm; Oct–May 9am–noon & 2–6pm; €5.50), an appropriate theme for Gien, caught as it is between the Sologne and the Forêt d'Orléans, both rich hunting grounds. In fact, the countless exhibits venerating *la chasse* – hunting horns, tapestries, exquisite watercolours of horseback hunts, beautifully crafted guns, falconers' gear, noble oil portraits of dogs – rather outweigh *la nature*. If you're put off by the thought of a hunting museum, you might remind yourself of the deep significance of hunting in the French psyche: one of the great material gains of the Revolution was the right of ordinary people to hunt – a right zealously exercised today, particularly in the Sologne.

That said, the two topmost rooms are just grisly, the first adorned with five hundred-odd pairs of antlers, all shot by the prolifically murderous Hettier de Boislambert – most impressive is the extraordinary wall of antelope and gazelle horns from Africa, twisted and curved and pointed in every conceivable shape – and the second displaying the hairier trophy collection of François de Grossouvre, featuring three entire leopards, two large buffalo heads and one gnu. The museum also hosts special exhibitions – some, such as that of animal sculpture, will be of more interest to nature and animal lovers than hunters.

Next door to the château, the **église Ste-Jeanne d'Arc** was entirely rebuilt in the 1950s, only the massive stone bell tower having survived the war. Inside, Max Ingrand's fiery stained-glass windows recall the destruction of the old church, while Gien *faïencerie* makes up much of the religious artwork.

Musée de la Faïencerie

Like Nevers, further south on the Loire, Gien is well known in France for its faïence, or majolica, a technique of enamelling earthenware to produce fine china which came to Gien from Faenza via the rather roundabout route of England – one Thomas Hall introduced the technique in 1812. Gien lacks its own unique style, copying instead the blue patterns of Nevers and Italian-type multicoloured designs. A good half of the wares are now produced using a "chromographic" method similar to printing, rather than hand-painted in the traditional manner. A large factory still operates in Gien, employing over two hundred people, and you can buy the ordinary tableware in the **factory shop** on place de la Victoire, 1km west of the château and bridge (Mon–Sat 9am–noon & 2–6pm), and the hand-worked, arty stuff either in the shops found all over town, or direct from the **Musée de la Faïencerie** (Jan & Feb Mon–Sat 2–6pm, Sun 9am–noon & 2–6pm; March–Dec Mon–Sat 9am–noon & 2–6pm, Sun 10am–noon & 2–6pm; €4), which is immediately adjacent to the factory shop. The museum is housed in the cellars of the old workshops, and displays the more extravagant plates, vases and gee-gaws produced over the last 180-odd years, ranging from exquisitely worked vases to some oversized and monstrously pretentious objets d'art. A video shows current fabrication techniques, which you may be able to see for real in the **factory** (by appointment only; closed July, Aug & Dec; ☎02.38.67.89.99), though tours are supposed to be reserved for groups only.

Practicalities

The **tourist office** is on the central place Jean Jaurès (June & Sept Mon–Sat 9am–noon & 2–7pm; July & Aug Mon–Sat 9am–noon & 2–7pm, Sun 10am–noon; Oct–May Mon–Sat 9.30am–noon & 2–6pm; ☎02.38.67.25.28, Ⓦwww.gien.fr), while the **gare SNCF** is a good 2km back from the old centre, at the end of ave de la République – not that you're likely to use it, as the only line runs south to Briare, Cosne and Nevers and north to Montargis. **Bus** #3, which runs between Briare and Orléans, stops at place Leclerc, at the north end of the bridge.

The best of Gien's **hotels** is *La Poularde*, 13 quai de Nice (☎02.38.67.36.05, Ⓕ02.38.38.18.78; ❸), on the way out of town on the road to Briare, which has rooms looking out onto the river and an excellent restaurant (*menus* €16–51). If it's full, you could try the rather ugly, modern *Sanotel*, 21 quai de Sully, on the south bank of the river facing town (☎02.38.67.61.46, Ⓕ02.38.67.13.01; ❸), which is just about redeemed by its riverside location and views, and has some inexpensive rooms facing away from the river (❷); or the *Hôtel des Alpes*, 20 rue Victor Hugo (☎02.38.67.21.67; ❶), a decent enough one-star in the town centre. The town **campsite**, *Camping Touristique de Gien* (☎02.38.67.12.50, Ⓦwww.camping-gien.com), has a swimming pool, and stands just back from the so-called Gien beach, a wide sandy strip bordering the river on the south bank of town.

For an alternative to the **restaurant** at *La Poularde* (see above), make for the small strip of good eating places on quai Lenoir, by the bridge; *Le Regency*, at no. 12 (☎02.38.67.04.96; closed Sun evening, Wed & first two weeks in July), is a good choice, with carefully prepared fish dishes.

Château des Pêcheurs

Twelve kilometres northeast of Gien is a château dedicated to another of the Sologne's favourite activities – fishing. The so-called **château des Pêcheurs** at **La Bussière** (April–June & Sept to mid-Nov Mon & Wed–Sun 10am–noon & 2–6pm; July & Aug daily 10am–6pm; €6) is moored on the edge of its enormous, six-hectare fishpond, connected by a bridge to its large **gardens**, which were originally designed by Le Nôtre, the landscaper of Versailles. Initially a fortress, the château was turned into a luxurious residence at the beginning of the seventeenth century, but only the gateway and one pepperpot tower are recognizably medieval. Like Gien, the brick construction is typical of the Sologne. The impressive scale of the outbuildings is explained by the château's strategic location on the old trading route from Paris to the south, and to the vast taxes on grain imposed on its feudal lands.

Guided tours are available, but you're free to wander around, soaking up the exquisitely genteel atmosphere evoked by the handsome, largely nineteenth-century furnishings and the eccentrically huge collection of **freshwater fishing** memorabilia bequeathed by comte Henri de Chasseval, whose widow lives in an apartment in one of the outbuildings. Paintings, models, stuffed fish, engravings, flies and rods are scattered throughout the house, while a huge coelacanth, a giant prehistoric relic of a fish discovered in the Comoros Islands, lurks in a formaldehyde tank in the basement, next to the well-preserved kitchens and laundry. Keen gardeners can explore the elaborate **potager**, or formal vegetable garden, packed with flowers, herbs, vegetables and fruit trees.

Château de St-Brisson

On the south side of the Loire, halfway between Gien and Briare, medieval weaponry is the theme at the **château de St-Brisson** (April–Nov daily except Wed 10am–noon & 2–6pm; €3.50), which is energetically run by the local village. In summer, costumed demonstrations (June & mid-Aug to Sept Sun 3.30pm & 4.30pm; July to mid-Aug daily except Wed 3.30pm; €2.30) of three different kinds of catapults and one small cannon are given in the moat. The château also hosts contemporary art exhibitions and occasional jazz and classical **concerts**, both of which help to make up for the rather unattractive mix of styles (twelfth- to seventeenth-century) of the building itself. You can take guided tours of the interior, which is fairly ordinary for the most part, though the salon is rather fine, with its huge beams painted with the coats of arms of some of St-Brisson's owners.

If you're looking for somewhere quiet to **stay**, the *Auberge Chez Huguette*, 7 rue du Bizoir (☎02.38.36.70.10; ❷), is welcoming and relaxed, with a good, inexpensive restaurant serving local produce.

Briare

The small town of **BRIARE**, 10km from Gien on the Orléans–Nevers road and the Paris–Nevers rail line, centres on its Belle Époque iron aqueduct, the **Pont Canal**, linking the Canal de Briare to the north with the Canal Lateral à la Loire, which runs south to the Saône. The design of the Pont Canal came from the workshops of Gustav Eiffel (of Tower fame), but parts of the canal scheme date back to the early seventeenth century, when internal waterways linking the Mediterranean, Atlantic and Channel coasts were devised. Poised high above the Loire, you can walk along the aqueduct's extraordinary 625-

metre span, with its wrought-iron crested lamps and railings, hopefully without a cruise boat spoiling the effect.

At the far end of town, the tiny **Maison des Deux Marines** (daily: March–May & Oct 2–6pm; June–Sept 10am–12.30pm & 2–6.30pm; €4.50) is dedicated to the rival boatmen who plied the Loire and the Canal Lateral. Just across the street, the modest **Musée de la Mosaïque et des Emaux** (daily: Feb–May & Oct–Dec 2–6pm; June–Sept 10am–6.30pm; €4) has a small collection of reproduction and contemporary mosaics made using locally manufactured tiles – Briare's wares adorn sites as prestigious and varied as the mosque at Medina and Paris's RER stations.

The **tourist office** is at 1 place Charles-de-Gaulle (daily 10am–noon & 2–5pm; ☎02.38.31.24.51) and can provide details of canoe rental as well as maps of footpaths, towpaths and locks. If you want to cross the Pont Canal in a **boat**, the simplest option is to reserve a place on the ninety-minute cruise run by Bateaux Touristiques (July & Aug daily 3.15pm; April–June & Sept Sun only 3.15pm; €6.40, children under 15 €4.20; ☎02.38.37.12.75, ⓦwww.bateaux-touristiques.com). The same company also offers various canal trips and lunch/dinner excursions. Renting your own **canal boat** is an expensive business, at upwards of €400 just for a weekend in the summer months, but you don't need a licence; contact Charmes et Nautiques, Port de Plaisance, Briare (☎02.38.31.28.73, ⓦwww.charmes-nautiques.com).

For **accommodation**, the modern *Hôtel le Canal*, 19 rue du Pont-Canal (☎02.38.31.24.24, ⓔauberge-du-pont-canal@wanadoo.fr; ❷), is appealingly situated right next to the Pont Canal.

Travel details

Trains	Buses
Orléans to: Beaugency (15 daily; 20min); Blois (22–26 daily; 40min); Bourges (9 daily; 1hr–1hr 40min); La Ferté-St-Aubin (13 daily; 15–25min); Meung-sur-Loire (15 daily; 15min); Paris (at least hourly; 1hr); Romorantin-Lanthenay (change at Salbris; 7 daily; 1hr 30min); Tours (12–18 daily; 1hr–1hr 30min).	**Orléans** to: Beaugency (4–6 daily; 45min); Briare (1 daily; 2hr 20min); Chartres (9 daily; 1hr 10min–1hr 45min); Germigny-des-Près (3 daily; 1hr); Gien (3 daily; 1hr 50min); Meung-sur-Loire (8 daily; 35min); St-Benoît-sur-Loire (3 daily; 1hr); Sully-sur-Loire (2–3 daily; 45min–1hr 20min).

The Haut Berry

CHAPTER 4

Highlights

* **Cathédrale St-Etienne, Bourges** The early Gothic cathedral at Bourges is one of the most dramatic buildings in France, its immense scale set off by intensely coloured stained glass. See p.207

* **Palais de Jacques-Cœur, Bourges** The refined mansion of the late-medieval financier Jacques-Cœur has endless quirks, from its owners' statues apparently looking out of an outside window, to its internal steamroom. See p.209

* **Les Bonnets Rouges, Bourges** You can stay in the heart of Bourges' atmospheric medieval quarter at this ancient, picturesque chambres d'hôtes. See p.207

* **Mehun-sur-Yèvre** Melancholy, broken towers are all that remain of the beloved château of the duc de Berry. See p.214

* **La Borne** Scores of potters have settled in the backwater village of La Borne, and many have open studios where you can view and buy their wares. See p.216

* **Sancerre rouge** The dry white wine of Sancerre is one of France's best-loved wines, but the excellent and unusual red is rarely seen outside the region. See p.218

Canoe trip from St-Satur A canoe trip is the best way to get to know the river, and the stretch near Sancerre is particularly lovely. See p.219

△ Palais de Jacques-Cœur, Bourges

The Haut Berry

A mong French people, the historic region of the **Berry** is a byword for backwater obscurity. The region's roots are resolutely peasant, encompassing a strong local tradition of sorcery and a deliciously humble cuisine based on green lentils, potatoes, goat's cheese and nuts. In geographical terms, the Berry is something of a no-man's land. It lies at the very heart of France, cut off from the Loire by the semi-wilderness of the Sologne and the rolling hills of the Sancerrois. The region has been divided in two since the twelfth century, when the Lower, or Bas Berry, was part of the Plantagenêt empire, while the Upper, or **Haut Berry**, remained one of the key possessions of the French Crown. During the Revolution, the historic division was institutionalized with new *département* names: the *département* of the Cher corresponds with the Haut Berry, as covered in this chapter, while the Bas Berry became the *département* of the Indre – a relatively dull region to the southwest which lies outside the scope of this book.

The Berry's principal attraction is the ancient cathedral city of **Bourges**, the de facto capital of the kingdom under the Dauphin Charles in the fifteenth century. It boasts two of the finest medieval buildings in France: the fascinating **Palais de Jacques-Cœur** and the awesome **cathédrale St-Etienne**. Nearby, the old town of **Mehun-sur-Yèvre** preserves a moving ruin, one of the last vestiges of the late medieval palaces of the powerful duc de Berry. The little-known vineyards of **Reuilly** and **Quincy** lie close at hand, as well as the amazing Romanesque wall-paintings at **Brinay**. After Bourges, the Haut Berry's main sight is the hilltop town of **Sancerre**, which presides over a sweeping bend of the Loire and endless vine-combed hillsides. More accurately, it's Sancerre's excellent **wine** that is the main draw, as there's not a lot to see and do in the area, for all its beauty.

West of Sancerre and north of Bourges, in the deeply rural country known as the **Pays Fort**, things are quieter still. The region is hemmed in by slopes of the Sancerrois to the south and the damp forests of the **Sologne Berrichonne**, to the west – the inspiration for Alain Fournier's classic Solognot novel, *Le Grand Meaulnes*. Fournier himself was born in **La Chapelle-d'Angillon**, one of three small towns that punctuate the old road from Bourges to Paris, along with **Aubigny-sur-Nère** and **Argent-sur Sauldre**. All three have modest château museums to visit, but the more interesting sights lie deeper in the Pays Fort: the potters' village of **La Borne** and the **château de Maupas**, with its huge collection of fine china plates, testify to the region's history of ceramic production, while the children's museum of sorcery just outside **Concressault** draws on murkier local traditions.

There is a good **train** service between Bourges and Mehun-sur-Yèvre, but the only practical way to get around the rest of the Haut Berry is by **car**. The few bus routes in the Pays Fort and Sancerrois are closely tied to the timetables of commuters or school students.

Bourges

The attractive medieval city of **BOURGES** feels oddly remote, a deeply provincial city isolated on the flat plain of the Berry, stranded at the geographic centre of France. It lies some distance from the Loire valley proper – both Blois and Orléans are around 120km away – but the city's historical links with surrounding regions are strong, and the presence of one of the finest and largest Gothic cathedrals in France, rising gloriously out of the handsome medieval quarter, provides reason enough for making a detour. Bourges also offers an impressive late medieval mansion, the Palais de Jacques-Cœur, a remarkably successful outdoor sound-and-light show on summer evenings and an excellent programme of festivals and events. Sadly, the citizens of Bourges aren't called "Bourgeois" but instead, "Berruyer".

Some history

You might not think it from its modest size today, but Bourges was intimately connected with the French monarchy through much of the Middle Ages. On

Christmas Day in 1137, the coronation of Louis VII was solemnized in the cathedral, along with that of his new queen, **Eleanor of Aquitaine** (see box on p.235), who only ten days before had inherited the vast duchy of Aquitaine from her father. When Eleanor remarried, fifteen years later, her husband Henry II gained control over her extensive lands and Bourges became an isolated outpost of the French kingdom, the only royal territory south of the Loire. Henry's Plantagenêt empire didn't outlast him, however, and under Philippe-Auguste, Bourges once more became the chief city of an important duchy. From the 1190s, new walls were built, and the city commissioned an avant-garde **cathedral** in the radical new Gothic style.

By the mid-fourteenth century, Bourges had become a wealthy mercantile centre, despite the endless warfare provoked by marauding English armies. In 1360, the city and the duchy of the Berry were granted to **Jean de France**, a highly cultivated grandson of the French king, Jean le Bon. As the **duc de Berry** (see box on p.208), he was reluctantly drawn into politics in the 1390s when his nephew Charles VI began to suffer bouts of insanity – famously, Charles was convinced that he was made of glass and would break unless iron rods were inserted in his clothing. The king's three uncles, the dukes of Anjou, Berry and Burgundy, were forced to act as co-regents. Inevitably, they fell out, and when Louis d'Anjou was assassinated in 1407, Jean found himself at the head of the anti-Burgundian cause. Within five years, the Burgundians briefly had Bourges under siege, and soon after, in 1415, Henry V of England spectacularly won the battle of **Agincourt**. Jean de Berry is supposed to have died from despair in the aftermath of the French defeat.

Jean de France's successor as duc de Berry was the disinherited Dauphin Charles, later **Charles VII**, who took refuge in the city. All of northern France had fallen under the English heel, while most of the south of France lay in the hands of the Duke of Burgundy. Charles's rump kingdom consisted of little more than Berry and the Loire valley, causing the English to dub him "the little king of Bourges". It looked as if it would take a miracle to win back the kingdom – which duly arrived in the shape of Joan of Arc. A lesser-known figure behind Charles's dramatic comeback was the eminent **Jacques Cœur**, a pioneering merchant, arms-dealer, taxman and financier who controlled and supplemented the royal finances from his palace at Bourges.

Charles turned his back on Bourges after his coronation, and in 1487, a **fire** destroyed as much as half the city. Subsequent French monarchs were more interested in the fine hunting grounds of the Loire valley or the metropolitan attractions of Paris, and apart from a brief flourish of rebuilding in the early Renaissance, Bourges has languished as an ordinary provincial city, albeit a wealthy one, for most of the last half-millennium – though Napoleon III established France's central **armaments industry** here in 1861, a trade which thrives to this day.

Arrival, information and accommodation

The **gare SNCF** lies 1km to the north of the old city centre, at the end of ave Jean Jaurès and its continuation, ave Henri Laudier, while the **gare routière** stands just west of the city, beyond boulevard Juranville, on rue du Prado. The **tourist office**, at 21 rue Victor-Hugo, is just round the corner from the south facade of the cathedral (April–Sept Mon–Sat 9am–7pm, Sun 10am–7pm; Oct–March Mon–Sat 9am–6pm, Sun 2–5pm; ☎02.48.23.02.60, ⓦwww.bourgestourisme.com); there is also a regional tourist office at 5 rue de Séraucourt (Mon–Fri 9am–12.30pm & 1.30–5pm; ☎02.48.48.00.10,

W www.berrylecher.com). To hire a **bike**, you'll have to make your way to the cycle shop Narcy, 31 ave Max Dormoy (☎02.48.70.90.28), ten minutes' walk from the city centre.

Most **accommodation** in Bourges fails to make the best of the old city. The only really attractive, central option is the *Bonnets Rouges* chambres d'hôtes, but there are a number of decent hotels.

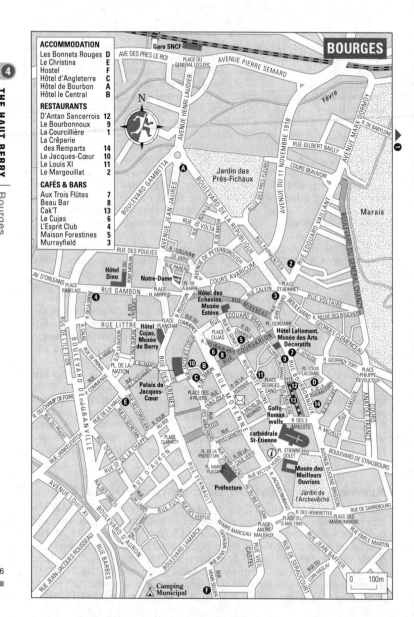

BOURGES

ACCOMMODATION
Les Bonnets Rouges   D
Le Christina   E
Hostel   F
Hôtel d'Angleterre   C
Hôtel de Bourbon   A
Hôtel le Central   B

RESTAURANTS
D'Antan Sancerrois   12
Le Bourbonnoux   9
La Courcillière   1
La Crêperie
 des Remparts   14
Le Jacques-Cœur   10
Le Louis XI   11
Le Margouillat   2

CAFÉS & BARS
Aux Trois Flûtes   7
Beau Bar   8
Cak'T   13
Le Cujas   6
L'Esprit Club   4
Maison Forestines   5
Murrayfield   3

0   100m

Hotels and chambres d'hôtes

Les Bonnets Rouges 3 rue de la Thaumassière ☎02.48.65.79.92, ⊛http://bonnets-rouges .bourges.net. Five characterful chambres d'hôtes, furnished with antiques dating from the last two centuries and decorated in a handsome, old-fashioned style, are set in a beautiful seventeenth-century house built around a tiny, hidden courtyard. The rooftop rooms have splendid views of the cathedral. ❹

Le Christina 5 rue de la Halle ☎02.48.70.56.50, ⊛www.le-christina.com. The modern, plain, six-storey exterior is uninspiring, but inside you'll find a friendly, professionally run hotel with seventy rooms, so it's likely to have space if others are full. The rooms are cheerfully and freshly decorated, though the inexpensive ones (with showers rather than baths) are quite small, and those at the back are a little dark. The larger rooms come with baths and air conditioning. In all, good value and close to the old centre, but not very characterful. ❸–❹

Hôtel d'Angleterre 1 place des Quatre-Piliers ☎02.48.24.68.51, ⊛www.bestwestern.fr/hotel-dangleterre. This is the old, traditional town-centre hotel, in an excellent location right by the Palais de Jacques-Cœur. The atmosphere is an odd mixture of old-fashioned, slightly shabby charm and the professional three-star standards of the Best Western conglomerate, to which it now belongs. The inexpensive rooms are very small for the price, however, while the more expensive ones aren't all that special, given the extra you're paying. ❺–❻

Hôtel de Bourbon bd de la République ☎02.48.70.70.00, ⊛www.alpha-hotellerie.com. This, the poshest hotel in Bourges, has been partially built in the ruins of seventeenth-century abbey, with an extraordinary-looking but rather expensive restaurant created out of the chapel. The rooms don't make much of the ancient building, however: they're standard luxury hotel-chain fare, all plush carpets, minibars and over-dressed modern furniture. The location isn't great, either, on a busy road between the old centre and the train station. ❻

Hôtel le Central 6 rue du Docteur Témoin ☎02.48.24.10.25. Tiny, inexpensive and old-fashioned rooms with creaky, soft beds. Above a friendly bar just off the central rue Moyenne. ❶

Hostel and campsite

Auberge de Jeunesse Jacques-Cœur 22 rue Henri-Sellier ☎02.48.24.58.09, ⓔbourges@fuaj.org. Hostel located a short way southwest of the centre, overlooking the River Auron. Bus #1 to "Val d'Auron", stop "Condé"; or a 10min walk from the cathedral or gare routière. Daily 8am–noon & 5–10pm; closed mid-Dec to mid-Jan. HI membership required, but you can join on the spot.

Camping Municipal de Bourges 26 bd de l'Industrie ☎02.48.20.16.85. Decently sized site located south of the HI hostel. Bus #6 from place Cujas, stop "Joffre", or a 10min walk from the gare routière. Closed mid-Nov to mid-March.

The City

The centre of Bourges sits on a low hill rising from the marshes of the River Yèvre. The main axial street, **rue Moyenne**, runs south–north between the cathedral, at the top end, and the Palais de Jacques-Cœur, at the bottom, with the narrow streets of the small medieval quarter falling away on either side.

The cathedral

Despite its huge size, the **cathédrale St-Etienne** (daily: April–Sept 8.30am–7.15pm; Oct–March 9am–5.45pm; free) looks almost delicate from the outside, the smooth lines of its paper-thin nave walls supported by a regular, skeleton-like structure of flying buttresses. The cathedral owes its size to the importance of the archbishops of Bourges, who as primates of Aquitaine oversaw a vast territory stretching across central and southern France, while its design owes much to Paris's Notre-Dame, though it incorporates improvements such as the astonishing height of the inner aisles. Like Chartres cathedral, St-Etienne is one of the great achievements of the High Gothic style, which dominated the first quarter of the thirteenth century.

The façade of the west front, unlike the rest of the cathedral, is something of a hotch-potch of styles. The exquisitely narrow nave is dramatically pierced by the

Grand Housteau, a rose window created under Jean de Berry. The taller tower on the left, the **Tour de Beurre**, had to be rebuilt after the original collapsed on New Year's Eve 1506. At the lowest level, five great **portals** yawn open, reflecting the five-aisle design inside. The sculpture of the tympanum above the central door could engross you for hours with its tableau of the Last Judgement; thirteenth-century imagination has been given full rein in the depiction of the devils, complete with snakes' tails and winged bottoms and faces appearing from below the waist, symbolic of the soul in the service of sinful appetites. One of these damned souls in a cauldron appears to be wearing a bishop's mitre. It's fascinating to compare the style of the carving on the west portals with the earlier stonework of the inner **north** and **south portals**, which were incorporated from the earlier Romanesque cathedral, and date mostly from the 1160s.

The interior's best feature is its magnificent **stained glass**. There are geometric designs in the main body of the cathedral, but the most glorious windows, with astonishing deep colours, are on the lower level behind the **choir**. They were all created between 1215 and 1225, in the first phase of building. Working upwards from the bottom left pane, you can follow the stories of the Prodigal Son, the Rich Man and Lazarus, Joseph – you can spot him by his coat of many colours – the Virgin, the Good Samaritan, Christ's Crucifixion, the Last Judgement and

The duc de Berry

At the age of 20, **Jean de Berry** (1340–1416), the third son of Jean II le Bon, was granted the duchies of Berry and Auvergne. He made **Bourges** his capital, creating a miniature court that could vie in magnificence with those of his three brothers – Charles, who would become Charles V, Philippe le Hardi of Burgundy and Louis d'Anjou. All three brothers were renowned as much for their artistic patronage as for their wealth and power. Jean de Berry must have been especially lavish in his spending, as when he died – legendarily of a broken heart after the defeat at Agincourt – there was too little ready money left to pay for his funeral.

During his lifetime, the duke built new châteaux all over France and amassed a vast collection of objets d'art, including twenty rubies, one of which is said to have weighed 240 carats. In Bourges, he commissioned his master architect, Guy de Dammartin, to remodel the cathedral's facade, to build a fine new palace and to construct a Sainte Chapelle in homage to the original in Paris. He built another new château at **Mehun-sur-Yèvre**, where he kept a zoo of exotic animals that included ostriches, camels and a pet bear called Martin – the bear was the duke's personal emblem. Palace, château, zoo and Sainte Chapelle have all been largely destroyed, and all that remains intact – though dispersed – is Jean de Berry's fabulous **library**.

Chief among the hundreds of precious manuscripts it contained were the gorgeously illuminated "books of hours", or prayer-book calendars, and most exquisite among these was the celebrated **Très Riches Heures du Duc de Berry**. Painted by the Flemish Limbourg brothers in the International Gothic style, it is one of the finest illuminated manuscripts ever created – the swansong of the era before the invention of printing – and contains detailed, contemporary depictions of medieval châteaux. Jean de Berry himself is seen feasting in the illustration for the month of January, while the month of September is represented by **Saumur** (see p.227) at its chivalric best, its sheer walls and tall towers culminating in a glorious encrustation of machicolations and finials. The illustration for the first Sunday of Lent depicts the sweeping, delicately sculpted towers of Mehun-sur-Yèvre (see p.214). Today, the manuscript is kept in the Musée Condé, at Chantilly, outside Paris, and is far too precious and fragile to be viewed by anyone other than serious scholars. Art books full of reproductions are easy to find, however (see p.322), and you can view the complete work online at ⊛www.christusrex.org/www2/berry/.

the Apocalypse. On either side of the central absidal chapel, polychrome figures kneel in prayer; these are **Jean de Berry** and his wife, their fleur-de-lys cloaks advertising their royal connections. The bodies were carved by Jean de Cambrai, a Flemish sculptor working for Jean de Berry in the 1400s, but the heads are nineteenth-century recreations following a drawing by Holbein.

On the north side of the nave aisle, just before the ambulatory, the **chapelle Jacques-Cœur** has a wonderful mid-fifteenth century stained-glass window. At the western end of the nave, the painted decoration of the fascinating **astronomical clock** celebrates the wedding of Charles VII, who married Marie d'Anjou here on April 22, 1422. Above looms the giant, oak-built, seventeenth-century **organ**, which thunders out for Mass (Sundays at 11am) and at occasional concerts.

The Tour de Beurre and crypt

On the far side of the nave aisle is the door to the **Tour de Beurre** (daily: May & June 9.30am–12.15pm & 2–6pm; July & Aug 9.30am–6.15pm; Sept–April 9.30am–12.15pm & 2–5.15pm; tours roughly every 1hr; €5.50, or €8.50 with Palais de Jacques-Cœur), which you can climb unsupervised for fantastic views over the old city, the marshes and the countryside beyond. The same ticket allows you to join a guided tour of the **crypt**, where you can see the puggish but impressive alabaster statue of Jean de Berry. It is one of the few remaining parts of his original, elaborate tomb, alongside a few pieces at the Louvre and the Musée du Berry (see p.210). A small bear, symbol of strength, lies asleep at the duke's feet. Alongside are rare fragments of the cathedral's original rood screen, which survived the Protestant siege of 1562 but not the modernizers of the mid-eighteenth century. At the centre of the crypt you'll find a wonderful polychrome *Entombment*, dating from the 1530s, while behind it lie the dark vestiges of the old Romanesque crypt, where the relics of St Etienne were kept, until the Revolution.

Around the cathedral

Next to the cathedral, on place E.-Dolet, the **Musée des Meilleurs Ouvriers de France** (Tues–Sat 10am–noon & 2–6pm, Sun 2–6pm; free) displays show-off pieces by French artisans in what was once the archbishop's palace. The theme changes each year; recent exhibitions have featured glass-blowing, woodwork and pastry-making. Behind lies the **Jardin de l'Archevêché**, formal gardens that are perfect for a stroll, offering good views of the fifteenth-century chapels whose weird octagonal spires rise up from the cathedral's apse.

Admirers of Jean de Berry can walk down rue Victor Hugo and across rue Ducrot to the **Préfecture**, which incorporates fragments of the **ducal palace**, including a couple of windows on the facade. If you ask politely at reception (Mon–Fri 8am–6pm), you may be allowed inside to see the two main remnants: the **salle d'apparat**, on the ground floor, and the council chamber up on the second floor, where there's a famous but over-zealously restored chimneypiece known as the **cheminée aux Ours** after the delightful, miniature carved bears – Jean de Berry's mascot – that cavort across it.

Palais de Jacques-Cœur

The **Palais de Jacques-Cœur** (daily: May & June 9.30am–12.15pm & 2–6.30pm; July & Aug 9am–1pm & 2–7pm; Sept–April 9.30am–12.15pm & 2–5.30pm; guided tours every 30min–1hr, depending on the season; €6.10) was the most luxurious and futuristic house built in the region during the fifteenth century, even incorporating a steamroom. It was the head office, stock exchange, dealing rooms and home of Jacques Cœur, a medieval magnate with a remarkable life story. Born in Bourges in around 1400, he started out working for his father, supplying luxury goods to the court, and quickly built up a lucrative portfolio of royal offices. After a successful expedition to the Near East in 1432, he imported spices, furs, exotic textiles, jewels, wine, salt and weapons from all over the Mediterranean. By the late 1440s, he was rich enough to finance Charles VII's military campaigns, but was denounced as a traitor at the height of his power, and arrested. After successfully escaping to the Vatican, he died leading a naval expedition against the Turks in 1456.

The building itself reflects the flamboyance and energy of its owner, starting with the fake windows on the facade of the entrance pavilion, from which two whimsical sculpted figures look down into the street. The inner **courtyard** is dominated by the staircase tower elegantly sculpted with bas-reliefs of everyday characters, including two thought to depict Jacques-Cœur and his wife. The arcaded galleries on either side were designed to facilitate socializing and business deals.

Inside, there are hardly any furnishings, but much of the decoration of the house's stonework recalls the man who had it built. There are numerous hearts (for *cœur*) and scallop shells (for *coquilles St-Jacques*), along with inscriptions of Jacques-Cœur's mottos: "dire, faire, taire de ma joie" ("speak, act, be silent of my joy") and "à vaillant riens impossible" ("nothing is impossible for the brave"). Above the door of a first-floor bedchamber there's a wonderful sculpture of a galéasse in full sail, with a reconstruction of the **tomb of Jean de Berry** nearby. But the finest piece of original decoration lies on the second floor, where angels fill the starry spaces between the ribs of the vaults of the **chapel**.

Musée du Berry

A flight of stone steps leads down beside the Palais de Jacques-Cœur to rue des Arènes and the sixteenth-century **Hôtel Cujas**, a classic Loire structure with its pale, carved stone window frames and little *échauguette* wall-towers. Inside, the **Musée du Berry** (Mon & Wed–Sat 10am–noon & 2–6pm, Sun 2–6pm; free) would be just another moderately interesting local history museum if it wasn't for its precious collection of **pleurants**. These cloaked, cowled, weeping figures are only a little over a foot high, but they're among the most precious pieces of French medieval sculpture. They were commissioned by Charles VII in around 1450, from the sculptors Etienne Bobillet and Paul de Mosselman, to complete the tomb of Jean de Berry for Bourges' Sainte-Chapelle, which was demolished in 1757. Almost half of the forty-odd figures have been lost. Of the survivors, apart from the ten examples here, one graces the New York Met, there's a pair in the Louvre, another in the château de la Verrerie (see p.218) and another in Paris's Musée Rodin – the sculptor paid 6000 francs for a single example shortly before his death.

Other sections of the museum display collections of Etruscan bronzes and Roman funerary monuments, bearing witness to Bourges's ancient roots, while a thorough exhibition on the theme of old-fashioned rural life occupies the first floor, testimony to the region's strong peasant traditions.

Hôtel Lallemant

At the foot of rue Bourbonnoux stands the impressive **Hôtel Lallemant**, an Italianate private mansion begun by a cloth merchant called Jean Lallemant in 1494, and finished by his two sons – both also called Jean – in 1520. After a stint in the nineteenth century as a primary school for poor girls, it now hous-

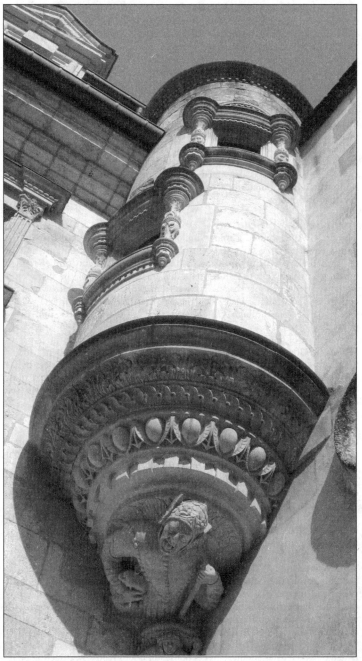

△ Cul-de-lampe at Hôtel Lallemant, Bourges

es the **Musée des Arts Décoratifs** (Tues–Sat 10am–noon & 2–6pm, Sun 2–6pm; free), an exquisite museum of paintings, tapestries, furniture and objets d'art, including works by the Berrichon artist Jean Boucher (1575–1633) in the **Salon Bleu**. Each room is decorated and furnished in the style of a different era, covering the heyday of French elegance, from the sixteenth through to the nineteenth centuries. At the top of the stairs, the tiny **oratory** is a miniature masterpiece, its coffered ceiling carved with obscure alchemical symbols that include flaming spheres, an eagle on a skull and cavorting dolphins.

Even if you don't visit the museum, you can take the tunnel-like staircase through to the **inner courtyard**, a delightful stony enclosure replete with little towers, sculpted windows and stone medallions. Take a close look at the *cul-de-lampe* at the base of the small corner tower, which is carved with the grotesque, scaly figure of a merman. On the opposite, higher-level side of the courtyard, the loggia is decorated with seventeenth-century frescoes whose ruinous state says something about the difference between the Italian climate and that of Bourges.

The rest of the old city

The fire of 1487 caused a minor building boom, and the old city is dotted with a few handsome survivors from this era. Sloping down from the apse of the cathedral, **rue Bourbonnoux** is lined with ancient and timber-framed buildings, its cobblestones and restaurants making it one of the city's most attractive streets. A short distance down from the cathedral, a narrow passage cuts in to a picturesque back alley, the **Promenade des Remparts**, which gets its name from the high, crumbling remains of the **Gallo-Roman ramparts** that hem it in.

At the foot of rue Borbonnoux, just beyond the Hôtel Lallemant (see p.210) lies **place Gordaine**, the old market square, ringed by half-timbered townhouses and informal café-restaurants. The pedestrianized shopping street of rue Coursalon runs west from here towards the leafy open space of **place Cujas**. You can peek at the much-restored arcades of a former **convent** on rue Mirebeau, immediately north, but the more impressive building is the adjacent **Hôtel des Échevins**, off rue Edouard Branly. The main body of the *hôtel* was built in 1489, its facade half-obscured by an extraordinary octagonal staircase tower whose four storeys are picked out in restrained bas-reliefs that mimic Flamboyant Gothic arches. An elegantly arcaded Classical wing runs at right angles. Inside, the **Musée Estève** (Mon & Wed–Sat 10am–noon & 2–6pm, Sun 2–6pm; free) is dedicated to highly coloured, mostly abstract paintings and tapestries created by the locally-born artist Maurice Estève, who died in 2001.

A few steps west, along rue Mirebeau, lie half-timbered houses, a convent where Calvin studied and, at the end, the pleasant **place Notre-Dame**, with its sixteenth-century church. Just beyond that, on rue Gambon, stands the **Hôtel-Dieu**, a late medieval hospice building with a restored chapel.

The Marais

Just 200m from the cathedral, a great boggy swathe of allotments, canals, fishponds and meadows stretches away to the northeast. Known as **Les Marais** ("the marshes"), this is where Bourges's bourgeois residents get in touch with their peasant roots, raising vegetables for the dinner table, fishing and exercising their hunting dogs. A sign on a toolshed sums up the spirit of the place: *"liberté, santé, tranquillité"* (liberty, health, tranquillity). The Marais may be half-tamed by sluice gates and little dykes but it still floods regularly, attracting plentiful wildlife of a modest kind – ducks, moorhens, dragonflies and various pond-dwelling creatures. A good circuit of about an hour's duration leads north from the gate just east of place Philippe Devoucoux, winding through the heart of the Marais and exiting via rue de Babylone, from where it's a twenty-minute walk back to the centre. It's hard to get very lost, as the towers of the cathedral offer a constant reference point.

Eating and drinking

Bourges's main centre for **eating** is along rue Bourbonnoux, which runs between place Gordaine and the cathedral – place Gordaine itself is attractively medieval but mostly good for pizzas. For tea and pâtisseries, head straight to *Cak'T* (daily 3–7pm), a charming, lace-tablecloth kind of place set in a stunning vaulted chamber; it's hidden away behind rue Bourbonnoux, on the promenade des Ramparts. Alternatively, there's a small tearoom by the counter of the excellent pâtisserie *Aux Trois Flûtes*, on the corner of rues Joyeuse and Bourbonnoux (closed Mon). For chocolates and the local sweet speciality of *fourrées au praliné* try the imposing *Maison Forestines*, on place Cujas.

Popular late-night **drinking** venues include the inevitable "pub" – this time Scottish – *Murrayfield*, 11 rue Jean Girard, just off place Gordaine. *L'Esprit Club*, 81 rue Gambon (closed Sun), is a studenty cybercafé five minutes northwest of rue Moyenne, with occasional DJ nights and live gigs. On warm nights, make for place Cujas, where you'll find the café-bars *Beau Bar* and *Le Cujas*.

Restaurants

D'Antan Sancerrois 50 rue Bourbonnoux ☎02.48.65.96.26. Good and occasionally imaginative local cuisine with interesting specials on the blackboard. The dining room is rather odd – high-ceilinged and with a faintly 1980s style – but that needn't put you off. A la carte mains from €10–13. Closed Sun & Mon lunch.

Le Bourbonnoux 44 rue Bourbonnoux ☎02.48.24.14.76. This friendly basement restaurant has a good range of inexpensive *menus* (€12–30), with dishes ranging from well-cooked classics to some more ambitious regional specialities. Closed Sat lunch & Fri, also closed Sun evening Nov–Easter.

La Courcillière rue de Babylone ☎02.48.24.41.91. Given its situation deep among the allotments and tiny canals of the *marais* – a good 1.5km from the old centre – this feels almost like a country restaurant, with its outdoor terrace shaded by pollarded willows. The food is meaty and unpretentious, with lots of fish dishes, steaks and a rôtisserie. *Menus* at €15, €20 & €25. Closed Tues evening, Wed, & Sun evening.

La Crêperie des Remparts 59 rue Bourbonnoux ☎02.48.24.55.44. Cosy, rustic-looking crêperie

with a better-than-usual range of crêpes, galettes and salads – and a magnificent, two-person fishy fondue Bretagne (€46; order in advance). Closed Sun & Mon lunch.

Le Jacques-Cœur 3 place Jacques-Cœur ☎02.48.70.12.72. This restaurant has a solid local reputation as one of Bourges' best, though it's mostly out-of-town visitors that dine here, attracted by the medieval decor of leaded lights and roof beams, with heavy red and gold accents in the colour scheme. The food is very good, if towards the more formal and traditional end of the spectrum. *Menus* €24–60. Closed Sun evening & Mon.

Le Louis XI 11 rue Porte Jaune ☎02.48.70.92.14. Serves impeccable steaks and char-grilled meats in a small, informal dining room crammed with tables and chairs. Steaks from €12, *menus* €9–23. Closed Sun.

Le Margouillat 53 rue Edouard Vaillant ☎02.48.24.08.13. For a complete change, this friendly, fun bistro offers delicious food from Réunion such as giant prawns or pork and beans served with hot dips, plus delicious tropical desserts and cocktails. *Menus* €13–19. Closed Mon lunch, Sat lunch & Sun.

Festivals and Les Nuits Lumière

Bourges's **music festival** programme is impressive. **Les Printemps de Bourges** (ⓦwww.printemps-bourges.com) features hundreds of contemporary music acts, from new rock groups to big-name rappers, and lasts for one week during the French Easter holidays. More esoteric are the **Festival**

Synthèse, an electronic and acoustic music bash during the first week of June, and **Un Eté à Bourges** (late June to late Sept), a line-up of free, outdoor performances of anything from local organ music to Chinese jazz.

In the summer months, you can follow a circuit through the streets of the old city between imaginatively lit-up landmark buildings, called **Les Nuits Lumière de Bourges**. Historically themed moving slide shows are projected onto the walls of various Renaissance and medieval mansions, while atmospheric lute and choral music plays. Even if it doesn't sound like your kind of thing, the circuit is remarkably well done, and the strange blue streetlights that indicate the route are decidedly eerie. The show begins at sundown every day in July and August, and on Thursdays, Fridays and Saturdays in May, June and September.

West of Bourges

Two waterways lead west of Bourges, the placid river **Yèvre** and the **Canal de Berry**. Both leave the Berry region just downstream of the largely featureless industrial town of Vierzon, which straddles the Cher some 30km west of Bourges. Vierzon really doesn't repay a visit – indeed there's nothing much to detain you until Mennetou-sur-Cher, another 15km west (see p.164) – but close to Bourges there's a trio of rather recherché attractions: the ruined château of the duc de Berry at **Mehun-sur-Yèvre**, the Romanesque wall-paintings at **Brinay** and the isolated vineyards of **Reuilly** and **Quincy**.

Mehun-sur-Yèvre

The château at **MEHUN-SUR-YEVRE**, a quiet market town 17km west of Bourges, was once to Bourges what Versailles is to Paris – the favourite country seat of the court. It was the extravagant home of the duc de Berry, and frequently used by Charles VII, who died here of starvation in 1461 – some say he was unable to feed himself because of lockjaw, others that it was through a perfectly justifiable fear of being poisoned by the agents of his rebellious son, Louis XI.

A lightning strike in 1555 largely ruined the **château**, but it's still an evocative, if melancholy, stopping place on the trail of the duc de Berry. Two towers stand among the ruinous foundations, one relatively intact – though the famous picture in the *Très Riches Heures du Duc de Berry* (see box on p.208) shows that it was once half as tall again, capped by an elaborate superstructure. Fragments of original stonework, including some apostles' heads that may be the work of Jean de Berry's Flemish sculptor Jean de Cambrai and a few bits of the six-metre-tall tower-top statue, can be seen in the small **museum** inside (May, June & Sept Tues–Sun 2–6pm; July & Aug daily 10am–noon & 2–6pm; Oct–April Sat & Sun 2–6pm; €4.55 combined ticket with Pôle de la Porcelaine – see below). You can climb to the top of the **tower**, which stands 40m above the town and the meadows to the south where the duke had his world-beating library and zoo of exotic beasts.

Below the château, the flashily presented **Pôle de la Porcelaine** (same hours and ticket as château) displays excellent and exhaustive collections of local fine china, and can book you on a guided tour of the Pillivuyt porcelain factory, which lies on the far side of the Canal de Berry. Between museum and factory lie the **Jardins du Duc de Berry**, a kind of municipal park made up of interconnected islands in the muddy river Yèvre. The town itself is fairly pretty but quickly exhausted, its main features being a pair of gate-towers, the

Porte de l'Horloge, and the **collégiale Notre-Dame**, a barn-like church with an unusual horseshoe-shaped choir, some dramatic modern stained glass and a set of nineteenth-century frescoes of Joan of Arc, who rested at Mehun with Charles VII in the extraordinary year of 1429 (see box on p.174).

Brinay

Halfway between Mehun-sur-Yèvre and Vierzon, on the south bank of the Cher, the modest Romanesque church at tiny **BRINAY** conceals one of the most complete sequences of twelfth-century **wall-paintings** found anywhere in France. Scenes from the life of Christ run right round the walls of the sanctuary, though interestingly, there's no Crucifixion scene, as this topic didn't become popular until the thirteenth century. Around the inside of the almost-horseshoe arch that divides the nave from the sanctuary, you can just make out the labours of the months – look out for February, warming his hands at a fire, and the grape-crushers of September.

If you want to overnight in the area, look no further than the two prettily furnished **chambres d'hôtes** at the *Château de Brinay* (℡02.48.51.38.31, ⓦ www.chateaudebrinay.fr.st; ❹), a substantial old pile set in quiet grounds between the church and the main road, with a swimming pool.

Reuilly and Quincy

Twenty-five kilometres west of Bourges, the village of **REUILLY** would be as sleepy as any in the Bas Berry – it just falls within the *département* of the Indre, on the edge of the flat plains of the Champagne Berrichonne – if it wasn't for a recent fashion for the minuscule local wine *appellation*. Buoyed by this unexpected fame, the **tourist office** (Tues–Sun: mid-June to Sept 10am–noon & 3–7pm; Oct to mid-June 10am–noon & 2–6pm; ℡02.54.49.24.94, ⓦ www.ot-reuilly.fr) now runs a tiny wine museum and local art gallery. Staff can point you in the direction of local wine-producers, as well as various private châteaux in the vicinity, some of which open their doors to the hoi polloi in July and August. The most interesting local sight is the village **church**, which has a characteristic *passage Berrichon* – a passageway leading behind the pillars of the nave to the transepts – and a claustrophobic ancient crypt that dates back to the Carolingian era. Fifteen kilometres northeast of Reuilly, the wines of **QUINCY** are a serious rival. There's nothing much to see in the village, but it's easy to hunt down producers' *caves* if you follow the signs. Most are open Monday to Friday, some on Saturday too.

On the road leading out of Reuilly towards the little **gare SNCF** – with good connections to Orléans – the friendly *Hôtel des Trois Cepages* (℡02.54.49.26.90; ❸) has plain, bright, modern **rooms** and a homely restaurant.

The Pays Fort and Sancerrois

The main D940 trunk road flies arrow-straight due north of Bourges towards the bridge over the Loire at Gien (see p.195), the ancient gateway to Paris. As it goes, it effectively divides the gently undulating pastures of the **Pays Fort**, to the east, from the low-lying forests and reedy *étangs* of the **Sologne Berrichonne**, to the west. Both are deeply rural areas, relatively unused to outsiders and correspondingly welcoming. Sights are low key or even eccentric – one route recommended by local tourist offices takes you round granaries with pyramid-shaped roofs – but there's a satisfying sense of having stepped well off the beaten track. The most interesting attractions are the potteries of **La Borne**, near **Henrichemont**, and the châteaux of **Maupas**, **La Chapelle d'Anguillon** and **La Verrerie**, while the old town of **Aubigny-sur-Nère** is handsome, if uneventful.

To the southeast, the slopes become steeper, and cows and sheep are replaced by the more valuable vines of the **Sancerrois** – the region around the picturesque hilltop town of **Sancerre**. For more information on the entire area, you can look online at ⓦwww.pays-sancerre-sologne.com, or ask for the detailed brochure at any local tourist office.

Henrichemont and around

You don't have to travel far from Bourges towards Sancerre before the land begins to undulate, with trees foresting the ridgetops and vines striating the slopes. **Menetou-Salon**, 20km north of Bourges, is the hub of its own well-regarded *Appellation d'Origine Contrôlée* wine region, while down in the valley, 9km north, squats **HENRICHEMONT**, the area's principal town. The most interesting feature is the perfectly symmetrical layout conceived by Henri IV's loyal administrator, the duc de Sully (see p.194), as the centrepiece for the independent principality of Boisbelle, which he bought in 1605. Sadly, the model Renaissance town he envisaged never came to fruition, and only a couple of fairly indifferent mansion houses were ever built round the broad market square. The town is otherwise resolutely ordinary.

A more rewarding excursion is to the potters' village of **LA BORNE**, strung out along a wooded ridge 4km southeast of Henrichemont. La Borne has been known for its rough stoneware since the seventeenth century, but in the post-war period it has become a centre for artistic and experimental pottery, attracting scores of artisans from all over France and beyond, almost all of whom keep open house for visitors and potential customers – just follow the signs and knock on doors. There are three more formal exhibition spaces: the excellent **Musée Vassil Ivanoff** (Easter–Sept Mon & Wed–Sun 2–7pm; €2.30), which showcases the sensual creations of the Bulgarian master potter who invigorated La Borne's contemporary pottery scene when he arrived here in 1946; the **Musée de la Poterie**, which archives La Borne's traditional pottery (Easter to mid-Nov Sat & Sun 3–7pm; also open Mon–Fri 3–7pm during school holidays; €3; ⓦwww.la-borne.com/museepot); and the **Centre de Création Céramique** (March–June & Sept–Dec Sat & Sun 3–7pm; July & Aug daily 3–7pm; free), which exhibits and sells the works of some of the fifty-odd potters who live and work in and around the village. The range of foods at *L'Epicerie*, the central village grocery and deli, says a lot about the village's "alternative" traditions; you can get drinks and snacks at the tearoom here, as well as a reasonably priced "*menu surprise*" – it's usually excellent.

From La Borne, the D46 winds down for 8km through beautiful woodland to **MOROGUES**, the main wine-growers' village in the Menetou-Salon *appellation* (see Contexts, p.338). There are plenty of opportunities to taste and buy wine, while 1km beyond the village is the **château de Maupas** (Easter–Sept daily 2–7pm; €6.50), an attractive mishmash of local brickwork from La Borne and older stone turrets. In the nineteenth century the château was heavily restored, inside and out, by an ancestor of the current marquis who was close to the so-called comte de Chambord (see box on p.144). The guided tour takes in lots of fussily decorated rooms filled with fine furnishings and valuable objets d'art, but the highlight of the visit is the extraordinary two-storey display of almost 900 eighteenth- and nineteenth-century china plates which lines the grand staircase.

La fête étrange

There is much dispute as to where the magical party in **Alain Fournier's novel** *Le Grand Meaulnes* was set, despite the fact that it was clearly an imaginary mixture of many places. Fournier was born in La Chapelle-d'Angillon, and spent much of his childhood there, but went to school in Epineuil-le-Fleurial (the Ste-Agathe of the novel), well south of Bourges. It was at Epineuil that Jean-Gabriel Albicocco shot his film of the book, and the village elementary school now houses a small museum. But the "domain with no name" where the *fête étrange* takes place is certainly in the Sologne: "In the whole of the Sologne," Fournier wrote, "it would have been hard to find a more desolate spot."

Lovers of the magical early twentieth-century novel, *Le Grand Meaulnes* (see p.331), may want to make the pilgrimage to **LA CHAPELLE-D'ANGILLON**, 11km north of Henrichemont on the main road to Gien, as it was here that author "Alain-Fournier" was born – as plain Henri Fournier – in 1886. Sadly, there's nothing much to see, and the Alain-Fournier museum in the **château** (Sun 9am–noon & 2–6pm; €8; ⓦ www.chateau-angillon.com) is of little interest to non-French speakers. You might, however, want to pay the rather steep entry fee to see the beautiful Renaissance gallery once used for the *jeu de paume* – an early kind of royal tennis – or the eccentric but rather lovely Albanian museum deposited here by King Léka I.

Aubigny-sur-Nère

AUBIGNY-SUR-NERE, 14km north of La Chapelle-d'Angillon, makes much of its connections with the **Stuarts**, hosting a grand Franco-Scottish festival in mid-July. These aren't the royal Stuarts, however, but the descendants of one John Stuart who helped Charles VII reclaim his throne in the fifteenth century and was granted the territory as reward. Curiously, a distant relative, Louise de Kerouaille, was one of the many mistresses of Charles II, last Stuart king of England, and was granted the château at Aubigny by Louis XIV in return for her services as a spy.

The town is fairly picturesque, dotted with half-timbered and stone houses, especially along **rue du Prieuré**, the broad and bustling main street. At the top end of the street stands the **église St-Martin** (Easter–Nov Mon–Thurs 2–6pm, Fri–Sun 10.30am–6pm), a rather fine early sixteenth-century Gothic church with a beautiful stained-glass window of the life of St Martin; sadly, the **château** at the bottom end has barely survived transformation into the local Mairie. Inside the château, you can visit two small **museums** (July to mid-Sept daily 2.30–7pm; rest of year Sun 2.30–6pm; €3), dedicated to the Franco-Scottish "Auld Alliance" and to the works of a minor local writer, Marguerite Audoux, but both are rather dull.

Practicalities

The **tourist office** at Aubigny-sur-Nère is in a half-timbered old house next to the church, at 1 rue de l'Eglise (May–Sept Mon–Fri 9.30am–12.30pm & 2–7pm, Sat 9am–12.30pm & 2.30–7pm, Sun 10am–12.30pm & 2.30–5.30pm; Oct–April closes 1hr earlier; ⓣ02.48.58.40.20). The town has a pair of attractive **hotels**, both on the fringe of the old centre: the *Auberge de la Fontaine*, 2 ave du Général-Leclerc, on the road to Bourges (ⓣ02.48.58.02.59, ⓕ02.48.58.36.80; ❸), is friendly and comfortable, with large, well-appointed rooms; *La Chaumière*, 2 rue Paul Lasnier, on the road to Sancerre (ⓣ02.48.58.04.01, ⓦ www.hotel-restaurant-la-chaumiere.com; ❹), is set in an old, smartly renovated house with warm decor. Both hotels have good, moderately priced **restaurants**; alternatively, you could try the relatively funky *Bien Aller* at 3 rue des Dames (☎02.48.58.03.92; two courses for €15), a good-value bistro with some interesting variations on the usual trad fare marked up on its specials board.

Around Aubigny-sur-Nère

The rather plain village of **ARGENT-SUR-SAULDRE**, 9km north of Aubigny, has lost its château, but the grand old outbuildings have been turned into the **Musée des Métiers et Traditions de France** (mid-April to mid-Oct Mon–Thurs 2–5.45pm, Fri–Sun 10–11.30am & 2–6pm; €3). The museum uses old looms, bizarre machines for making brooms and clogs and a display about the production of weathercocks to create a nostalgic meander through eighteenth- and nineteenth-century country crafts and trades. A comfortable hotel directly opposite the château, the *Relais de la Poste* (☎02.48.81.53.90, ℗02.48.73.30.62; ❸; closed Sun), makes for a good place to stop over, and has a decent restaurant. If you want to dip a toe into the Sologne, try *La Solognote*, Grande Rue, Brinon-sur-Sauldre (☎02.48.58.50.29, ℗02.48.58.56.00; ❹; closes occasionally for holidays, so ring in advance), a charming country hotel in a deeply rustic village 16km west of Argent-sur-Sauldre.

Eleven kilometres east of Aubigny, along the D21, is the **Musée de la Sorcellerie** (April, May & Oct daily 10am–6pm; June–Sept 10am–7pm; €5.50; ⓦwww.musee-sorcellerie.fr), a witchcraft museum just outside **CONCRESSAULT**. It's a bit over the top with its animated reconstructions of witchcraft trials, but kids will have fun, and some of the prints and paintings of legendary witches are interesting.

Louise de Keroualle, the owner of the château d'Aubigny, was also proprietor of the much lovelier **château de la Verrerie**, on the river Nère 11km upstream of Aubigny (March–May & Sept to mid-Nov Mon & Wed–Sun 10am–6pm; June–Aug daily 10am–6pm; €7, park only €4), though her descendants sold it in 1841 to the de Vogüe family, who now run it as a tourist attraction and luxury chambres d'hôtes. The setting is beautiful, with two wings half enclosing a courtyard and a slope of sward that descends to the banks of the lake. The southern wing has a fine Renaissance arcade, but the chief draw is the elaborately frescoed chapel. The gorgeously furnished **chambres d'hôtes** (☎02.48.81.51.60, ℗02.48.58.21.25; ❾) are in the grand style, with exquisitely old-fashioned but luxurious bathrooms. Prices start at around €150, climbing to over €300 for the top suite, with its study in the ancient tower. The restaurant in the gatehouse is chintzy but attractively so, and offers reliable evening meals for around €30, with wine.

Sancerre and St-Satur

At the easternmost edge of the Loire region – and its highest point at a dizzy 342m – is **SANCERRE**, a name better known in wine circles than on tourist circuits. Apart from eating and drinking – the preoccupation of most visitors – there are few particular sights or attractions in the town itself, but the countryside around is certainly picturesque: seen from the south, the vision of Sancerre huddling at the top of its steep, round hill, with vineyards furrowing the hillsides all around could almost be Tuscany. Endless *caves* offer tastings of the local **wine**. The dry whites, made from the Sauvignon Blanc grape, are by far the best known, but don't ignore the unusual and extremely appealing reds, which are light in colour but rich in earthy, spicy flavours. Well suited to the wines is the local **crottin de Chavignol**, an *appellation contrôlée* goat's cheese named after a neighbouring village.

Sancerre wine tours

Unusually, Sancerre wines aren't allowed to carry the name of an individual vineyard, as most are owned by a number of different producers, each in possession of a small, precious "parcel" of land. Instead, most wines are sold under the producer's name or, in exceptional cases, are given an individual *cuvée* name that just may give away the identity of the vineyard it came from, but only to those in the know. If you want to seek out good local vineyards, you're best off with a guide, and the friendly, informative **Aronde Sancerroise**, at 4 rue de la Tour, just off the central Nouvelle Place (Mon–Fri 10.30am–12.30pm & 2.30–6.30pm, but closed during wine tours; ☎02.48.78.05.72), offers excellent half-day minibus **tours** (4–8 people; €228). If you just want to buy, there are also free, informative tastings on the spot – but no swallowing is allowed.

If you want to do it yourself, the tourist office (see p.220) can supply a list of over three hundred **vignerons** in the immediate area – or check out the website ⓦwww.vins-centre-loire.com. Wine outlets in Sancerre itself belong to the most famous names – Mellot, Vacheron – and have mark-ups to match, but most *vignerons* outside town are small-scale, traditional winemakers and welcome visitors every day except Sunday – some, on Sundays too. There are particularly rich pickings in the cluster of villages between Sancerre and Crézancy-en-Sancerre, 11km southwest. For a particular recommendation, make for the **Dauny** *cave*, in Champtin (daily 8am–8pm; ☎02.48.79.05.75); this family has been making excellent organic wines for three generations, including the rarer, pale red Sancerre. For a lesser-known buy, it's well worth exploring the neighbouring areas of Menetou-Salon and Pouilly-Fumé.

The counts of Sancerre long presided over the town. Most distinguished among them was Jean de Bueil, known as the "Scourge of the English" for his military successes under Charles VII in the early fifteenth century – exploits he later fictionalized in his classic account of the war, *Le Jouvencel*. During the Wars of Religion, the increasingly powerful merchants and townspeople sided with the Protestant cause, and it took a six-month siege in 1573 to bring them to heel. Later religious infidelities led to the old château being almost completely destroyed, and today only the **Tour des Fiefs** remains, ruinous at the apex of the hill. Frustratingly, the tower is rarely open for visits, so strollers will have to be content with the views from the **rampart walks** which ring the old town, or a visit to the simple **church of Notre-Dame**, on place du Beffroi. The adjacent **belfry tower** is a relatively mighty structure built by the city's merchants in the late fifteenth century as an expression of their civic pride; sadly, it lacks its original spire.

St-Satur

The two chief sights of **ST-SATUR**, the village at the foot of the hill below Sancerre, are the Gothic **abbey church**, which once belonged to the monks who first planted vines at Sancerre, and the 430-metre-long curving **viaduct**, which has been open to walkers since the railway shut down in 1968. There are a couple of good hotels in town (see p.220), but the main reason to visit is to take a guided **kayak trip** with Loire Nature Découverte, quai de Loire, down beside the campsite (April–Oct 7.30am–9pm; ☎02.48.78.00.34). The owner, Yvan Thibaudat, is something of a naturalist, and his guided half- or full-day expeditions (€14/20 per person) are fascinating. You are usually driven upstream and then float back down through the **Réserve Naturelle du Val de Loire**, a nature reserve created along a twenty-kilometre corridor of little islands and sandbanks that is particularly rich and diverse in wildlife. To get to the shop, turn left just before the Pont de St-Thibault, which bridges the Loire, following signs to the campsite. Just beyond the campsite there's a huge, heated, open-air **swimming pool**, Les Godilles (July & Aug 11am–7pm).

Practicalities

Sancerre's **tourist office** is in the modern building at the centre of the Nouvelle Place (daily: June–Sept 10am–6pm; Oct–May 10am–12.30pm & 2.30–5.30pm; ☎02.48.54.08.21, ⓦwww.sancerre.net/otsi). To visit the vineyards you'll need your own **transport**, though SNCF runs a bus service four times daily from Sancerre through St-Satur and across the river to Cosne-sur-Loire, in time to meet the train to Gien.

The choice of **hotels** in Sancerre itself is rather disappointing. *Le Saint-Martin*, 10 rue St-Martin (☎02.48.54.21.11, ⓕ02.48.54.17.50; ❸), is central and pleasant enough, but needs a refit inside, while *Le Panoramic*, Rempart des Augustins (☎02.48.54.22.44, ⓔpanoramicotel@wanadoo.fr; ❸–❹), may have a fine view and an excellent outdoor swimming pool but it's otherwise disagreeably modern, and the rooms with a view are expensive. Luckily, there are two charming **chambres d'hôtes**: *Le Logis du Grillon*, 3 rue du Chantre (☎02.48.78.09.45; ❸), has four pretty, spotless little rooms, while the friendly *La Belle Epoque* on rue St-André (☎02.48.78.00.04; ❸) offers a single large, beamed room stuffed with antiques. If you want a really good hotel you'll have to descend to St-Thibault, the riverside quarter of St-Satur, which sits at the bottom of the hill below Sancerre. The large rooms at the *Hôtel de la Loire*, 2 quai de la Loire (☎02.48.78.22.22, ⓦwww.hotel-de-la-loire.com; ❺), are scrupulously maintained and beautifully furnished in an array of antique styles, while the five simple, clean bedrooms above the welcoming *Auberge de St-Thibault*, 37 rue J. Combes (☎02.48.78.04.10; ❶), a block away from the river, are exceptional value. The large, well-equipped three-star **campsite** *René Foltzer* (☎02.48.54.04.67; closed Oct–April) is 200m north of the bridge, on the St-Satur side of the river.

It's worth booking ahead at either of Sancerre's two best traditional **restaurants**: *La Pomme d'Or*, 1 rue de la Panneterie (☎02.48.54.13.30; closed Tues & Wed eve), is the local favourite, serving local river-fish dishes in delicate sauces, and good Charolais steaks; the elegant *La Tour*, 31 Nouvelle Place (☎02.48.54.00.81), is more formal, with a heavy-beamed and carpeted dining room. Both offer excellent *menus* starting at around €15 and good wine lists. Alternatively, the *Auberge Joseph Mellot*, Nouvelle Place (☎02.48.54.20.53; closed Sun & Tues eves, & Wed), serves good, simple meals designed to complement its own top-notch wines, while *La Collina*, 10 place du Connétable (closed Sept & Dec), is a surprisingly good Italian trattoria, though the pizzas are starter-sized. If you don't mind driving, consider making the three-kilometre trip out to Chavignol, where the *La Côte des Monts Damnés* (☎02.48.54.01.72; closed Sun evening, Tues evening & Wed) is aiming at a Michelin star, but remains friendly and excellent value, with *menus* in the €20–40 range and a superb wine list.

Travel details

Trains	Buses
Bourges to: Mehun-sur-Yèvre (14 daily; 10min); Orléans (9 daily; 1hr–1hr 40min); Tours (12 daily; 1hr 40min).	**Sancerre** to: Bourges (1–3 daily; 1hr 15min); Cosne-sur-Loire (for Gien; 3–4 daily; 15min).

5

The Saumurois

CHAPTER 5

Highlights

✳ **Carrousel de Saumur** Saumur's cavalry traditions entirely take over the town during this festival of old-fashioned military muscle, held in late July. See p.225

✳ **Saumur Brut** Matured inside vast cave-cellars, the sparkling wines of Saumur are a serious rival to Champagne's. See p.230

✳ **Candes-St-Martin** This historic village at the confluence of the Loire and Vienne preserves an ancient and beautiful collegiate church. See p.233

✳ **The Plantagenêt tombs** The graceful tombs of the Plantagenêts, kings of England and dukes of Anjou, lie in melancholy splendour in the giant Romanesque abbey of Fontevraud. See p.237

✳ **Dénezé-sous-Doué** Discovered in a cave in 1950, Dénezé's satirical sixteenth-century carvings are weirdly compelling. See p.241

✳ **Zoo de Doué** The zoo at Doué-la-Fontaine has a bizarre but humane setting in an old quarry filled with semi-tropical plants. See p.241

✳ **Montreuil-Bellay** With its picture-book castle rising above the poplar-lined River Thouet, Montreuil-Bellay is one of the prettiest small towns in the Loire region. See p.242

✳ **Bed-and-breakfast in a cave** Spend a night in a "troglodyte" cave-house at *Les Bateliers*, in the pretty village of Cunault. See p.245

△ Riverbank and château, Saumur

5

The Saumurois

The stretch of the Loire valley between Chinon and Angers is known as the **Saumurois** after its chief town, Saumur. The gentle slopes of the south bank are clothed in patches of woodland and sunny vineyards, while across the water the rich meadows watered by the River Authion are given over to grazing and market gardens. The main east–west route, the D952, lies on the north bank, sweeping along the raised embankment of the *grande levée*, a flood wall first raised by Henry II Plantagenêt in the twelfth century. It's a grand road, but all the sights covered in this chapter lie on the prettier, quieter south bank. Here you'll find one of the sweetest of all Loire regions; less grand than Touraine, maybe, but equally fascinating.

Historically and administratively, the Saumurois is no more than an enclave of greater Anjou – even the chief local town, **Saumur**, is a deeply provincial place compared to the regional capital Angers, though its haughty château, proud cavalry traditions and classy sparkling wines give it status well beyond its size.

To the **east of Saumur**, on the border with Touraine, lie the twin villages of **Montsoreau** and **Candes-St-Martin**. The pair present very different faces to the world, the former with its noble château, the latter with its ancient church dedicated to the local patron, St Martin. A few kilometres inland is the great Romanesque abbey of **Fontevraud**, where the medieval tombs of the Plantagenêt royal family are one of the highlights of the whole Loire region. Heading **west of Saumur** towards Angers, still on the south bank, you can visit the sleepy villages of **Trèves** and **Cunault**, the latter with another remarkable Romanesque church.

But the most fascinating local sights are **troglodyte dwellings** – homes gouged out of the soft tufa rock – of which there are more in this region than anywhere else in France. It's reckoned that in the twelfth century half the local population lived underground. Today, some of the rock dwellings have surprising uses – nearly two-thirds of France's mushroom cultivation originates in Saumurois caves, while others have been turned into "*troglo*" bars and restaurants. The region around **Doué-la-Fontaine** is particularly rich in bizarre troglodyte attractions, ranging from cathedral-like quarries and underground farmhouses to a cavern sculpted with satirical human figures in the sixteenth century. Close by, the picturesque château-town of **Montreuil-Bellay** stands astride the River Thouet at the southern bounds of the region. From here you can make forays to see the Girdle of the Virgin at **Le Puy-Notre-Dame**, or the rock-cut passages underneath the **château de Brézé**.

Saumur

Of all the comfortably bourgeois towns along the Loire, **SAUMUR** is the most genteel, with its graceful château, elegant sparkling wines and 250-year association with the military. The town is still the home of the aristocratic French Cavalry Academy and its successor, the Armoured Corps Academy, and you can sometimes see uniformed officers strolling about, though the tanks are mostly kept out at the military camp near Fontevraud. Once you've seen the château and the sparkling wine *caves*, and strolled along the river quays, there isn't a tremendous amount to do, but Saumur makes a pleasant base for exploring the delightful countryside to the west, or foraging east towards Touraine.

Saumur reached its chivalric apogee under **King René** (see box on p.255), and later achieved notoriety as a Protestant stronghold in the late sixteenth and early seventeenth century – a horrified Louise de Bourbon, abbess of Fontevraud, called the town a "second Geneva", a potential rival to Calvin's Swiss power-base. Henri IV's governor of Saumur, the "Protestant Pope" **Philippe Duplessis-Mornay**, helped draft the Edict of Nantes, which granted religious tolerance, and founded Saumur's **Académie Protestante**, whose students, scholars and publishers underpinned a miniature economic and cultural boom – the academy's riding school attracted co-religionists from as far away as England and Holland. When the Edict of Nantes was revoked in 1685, causing the departure of the Protestant population, the town was only saved from ruin by the river trade. In 1767, the government minister Choiseul brought the national riding school, the **Ecole d'Equitation**, to Saumur; it was extended in 1824 and renamed the Ecole Royale de Cavalerie. Meanwhile, the merchant classes grew wealthy on the back of the town's textile industry. Balzac's vicious satire on Saumur's mid-nineteenth-century bourgeois-provincial society, *Eugénie Grandet*, dented the town's reputation, but the heroic defence of the Loire in 1940 (see box on p.229) helped salvage civic pride. Today, the thriving wine, equine and tourist industries provide solid foundations for Saumur's evident prosperity.

Moving on from Saumur to Angers, you can either take the train or one of three buses: #5 along the south bank; #11 along the north bank; or #10 inland via Beaufort-en-Vallée (see p.273). Heading east, the train runs along the north bank to Tours. Connecting buses to Chinon usually meet some of these trains at Le Port Boulet, on the Loire 13km north of Chinon, but check locally as timetables may change.

Arrival and information

Arriving at the **gare SNCF**, you'll find yourself on the north bank of the Loire: turn right onto ave David d'Angers and either take bus #A to the centre or cross the bridge to the island on foot. From the island the old **Pont Cessart** leads across to the main part of the town on the south bank, where you'll find the **gare routière**, a couple of blocks west of the bridge on place St-Nicolas, and the **tourist office**, next to the bridge on place de la Bilange (mid-May to mid-Oct Mon–Sat 9.15am–7pm, Sun 10.30am–5.30pm; mid-Oct to mid-May Mon–Sat 9.15am–12.30pm & 2–6pm, Sun 10am–noon; ☏02.41.40.20.60, ⓦwww.saumur-tourisme.com).

The **old quarter** lies between the château and the Hôtel de Ville, an unmistakeable landmark on the riverbank a few steps east of the Pont Cessart. **Internet** access is available at Welcome Services Copy, 20 rue du Portail Louis, Config Système, 9 rue de la Petite Bilange, and at the *Hôtel Cristal* (see p.226).

Festivals and river trips

The famous **Carrousel de Saumur** takes place in the last two weekends of July on the huge place du Chardonnet, a swathe of open grand overlooked by the old Ecole de Cavalerie, which has been used for knights' tournaments since the eleventh century. The Carrousel usually features some kind of horse-dance spectacle and a drive-by from the tank museum, as well as the main presentation by the elite Cadre Noir riding school; tickets are best purchased well in advance through the tourist office (see above). In late May, the Ecole Nationale d'Equitation (see p.229) invites foreign riding schools to perform, while the second weekend of October sees **Les Musicales du Cadre Noir**, a horse show set to classical music. A **military band festival** takes place in late June (odd-numbered years only), with contingents from all over the world invited to blow and stamp and wheel about.

In summer, you can take **river trips** aboard the *Saumur-Loire* (mid-June to mid-Sept daily; departures hourly 2.30–5.30pm; €7), departing from quai Lucien Gautier, opposite the tourist office. The town tours in a horse-drawn *calèche* or *petit train touristique* are less worthwhile. **Canoes and kayaks** can be hired from the Base de Loisirs de Millocheau, on the riverfront in St-Hilaire-St-Florent, the suburb immediately west of the centre (July & Aug daily; May, June & Sept Sat & Sun; ☏02.41.50.62.72).

Accommodation

Accommodation in Saumur is mostly upmarket and attractive, if pricey. The **campsite** is crowded in summer, but has a good location on the Ile d'Offard, next to the youth hostel.

Hotels and chambres d'hôtes

Anne d'Anjou 32 quai Mayaud ☏ 02.41.67.30.30, ⓦ www.hotel-anneanjou.com. This rather grand hotel is set in a listed eighteenth-century building with a magnificent, sweeping staircase. The location, on the main road along the riverfront, is usefully central, and the hotel offers a wide range of attractively decorated and good-sized rooms, some with views up to the château. The garden restaurant, *Les Ménestrels* (see p.231), is one of the poshest in Saumur. ❺–❾

La Bouère-Salée rue Grange-Couronne ☏ 02.41.67.38.85, ⓦ www.ifrance.com/labouere. This delightful, good-value bed-and-breakfast occupies a handsome nineteenth-century townhouse. The only drawback is the inconvenient location, 300m north of the train station off rue des Maraîchers. ❹

Hôtel Cristal 10–12 place de la République ☏ 02.41.51.09.54, ⓦ www.cristal-hotel.fr. One

of the nicest hotels in town, with river or château views from most rooms and very friendly proprietors. Bike hire and Internet access available. ❸

Hôtel de Londres 48 rue d'Orléans ☏ 02.41.51.23.98, ⓦ www.lelondres.com. This comfortable old town-centre hotel has been sprucely done up in pale lemon and terracotta, but preserves some older features such as a lovely, iron-balustraded staircase. In tone, it's a welcoming mixture of modern and old-fashioned. Offers secure private parking. ❸

Hôtel St-Pierre 3 rue Haute-St-Pierre ☏ 02.41.50.33.00, ⓦ www.saintpierresaumur.com. Aims at a hushed, prestigious atmosphere with its plush decor, ancient beams and stone spiral staircase, but the rooms are a little overpriced and over-fussy for some tastes. Nevertheless, a very comfortable, reliable address. ❼

RESTAURANTS
Auberge St-Pierre	2
Auberge Reine de Sicile	1
Les Délices du Château	5
L'Escargot	6
Les Forges de St-Pierre	3
Les Ménestrels	4

ACCOMMODATION
Anne d'Anjou	F
La Bouère-Salée	A
Hostel	B
Hôtel Cristal	C
Hôtel de Londres	D
Hôtel St-Pierre	E
Le Volney	G

Le Volney 1 rue Volney ☏02.41.51.25.41, ⓦwww.le-volney.com. This budget hotel lies just south of the centre. It's simple enough, but clean and newly redecorated throughout, and the man-agement is very friendly. A few inexpensive but cosy little rooms with shared bathrooms are tucked away under the roof, and there are a cou-ple of larger family rooms too. ❶–❸

Hostel and campsite

Centre International de Séjour ave de Verden, Ile d'Offard ☏02.41.40.30.00, ⓕ02.41.67.37.81. Large hostel at the east end of the island with laundry facilities, views of the château and use of the swimming pool at the campsite next door. Reception 9am–noon & 2–7pm. Boat and bike rental available. Closed Nov–Feb.

Camping municipal ave de Verden, Ile d'Offard ☏02.41.40.30.00, ⓕ02.41.67.37.81. This big, well-run site is next door to the hostel. There's a heated pool, and you can sometimes swim in the Bras des Sept Voies – the minor, northern channel of the Loire. It's potentially dangerous, however, so seek local advice before taking a dip.

The Town

The main attraction of central Saumur is, of course, its **château**, though you might spend an hour or two exploring the tiny old quarter, as described by Balzac in *Eugénie Grandet* (see p.330), and strolling along the **river esplanade**. Sadly, the historic cavalry school, the Ecole d'Application de l'Arme Blindée et de Cavalerie, is closed to visits, but a trio of churches, each from a different epoch, is worth visiting. After touring the château, however, most visitors head out into the suburbs (see p.228) where, unusually, some of the town's most interesting sights are found.

The château

Set high above town, Saumur's airy white fantasy of a **château** (daily: June–Aug 9.30am–6pm; Sept–May 10am–1pm & 2–5.30pm; closed Tues Nov–March & Mon in Jan; €2, €6 with entry to museums), may seem oddly familiar, but then its famous depiction in *Les Très Riches Heures du Duc de Berry* (see box on p.208), the most celebrated of all the medieval books of hours, is reproduced all over the region. It was largely built in the latter half of the four-teenth century by Louis I, duc d'Anjou, who wanted to compete with his brothers Jean, duc de Berry, and Charles V. The threat of marauding bands of English soldiers made the masons work flat out – they weren't even allowed to stop for feast days. After the death of René d'Anjou (see p.255) in 1480, own-ership of the château passed over to the French Crown, after which it fell into gradual decline, being used variously as an arsenal, a prison and a munitions store. Its serenely impregnable image took a knock in April 2001, when a huge chunk of the star-shaped outer fortifications added by Philippe Duplessis-Mornay collapsed down the hill towards the river. The château itself is built on more solid ground.

On the cheaper ticket, you can climb down to the dungeons and up into the watchtower – which has an extraordinary double-spiral staircase – but it's worth paying the extra to enter the former royal apartments, which are given over to a pair of museums. The **Musée des Arts Décoratifs** houses an impressive collection of European china, as well as some superb fifteenth-century tapestries. One pair, from Tournai, shows knights fighting savages in the first scene, then happily socializing with their hairy brethren in the second. The long tapestry series in the following room tells the story of St-Florent, a local Roman soldier who worked miracles in the fourth century. Even if you're not particularly interested in horses, the **Musée du Cheval**, in the attic of the château, is worth seeing. Starting with a horse skeleton it progresses through the evolution of bridles and stirrups over the centuries, culminating with a diverse collection of elaborate, lovingly worked saddles from Tibet, Morocco, Mexico and all over the world.

The lower town

The oldest, most atmospheric part of town is centred on **place St-Pierre**, the ancient crossroads at the heart of town. A pair of half-timbered houses survives from the sixteenth century, one of which has a facade carved with lifelike figures. **Rue Fourrier** and the streets leading south of **rue Dacier** are dotted with houses dating from the sixteenth century and earlier; on rue des Païens, the **Tour Grénetière** survives from the early fifteenth-century town walls. The **église St-Pierre**, off rue Haute St-Pierre (9am–noon & 2–5pm), hides behind a Counter-Reformation facade built as part of the church's efforts to overawe Saumur's persistently Protestant population. Its unusual half-Gothic, half-Romanesque interior is more subdued, though the choir stalls are exuberantly carved and the sixteenth-century tapestry sequence depicting the life of St Peter is richly coloured.

The **riverside quays** once stood outside the town walls, and hummed with river trade; these days, cars are the only traffic, though you can stroll along the slipway below the embankments when the river isn't in flood. The partly sixteenth-century **Hôtel de Ville**, on quai Lucien Gautier, dominates the river frontage. Next door, you can try Saumur's sparkling wines at the **Maison du Vin** (April–Sept Mon 2–7pm, Tues–Sat 9.30am–1pm & 2–7pm, Sun 9.30am–1pm; Oct–March Tues–Sat 10am–1pm & 3–6.30pm; Ⓦwww.interloire.com). Staff can also provide addresses of wine-growers and *caves* to visit, and help you find your way to the sparkling wine cellars of St-Hilaire-St-Florent (see p.230).

Two of Saumur's most interesting sights, both churches, lie on the fringes of the old town. Down by the public gardens south of the château, Saumur's oldest church, **Notre-Dame de Nantilly** (9am–6pm), houses a fine tapestry collection dating mostly from the sixteenth and seventeenth centuries. The church itself is beautiful in a severe, Romanesque way, its daringly wide tunnel vault supported by four-metre-thick walls. Don't miss the statue of Our Lady herself, carved in wood in the twelfth century and now tucked away in the right transept.

Notre-Dame des Ardilliers, down by the river on the eastern edge of town (daily 8am–noon & 2–6.30pm) was founded at the site of a spring – now dry – where a statue of the Pietà was miraculously discovered in the fifteenth century. The church was dedicated by Louis XIV, and is a typically grandiose Baroque affair dominated by the tremendous dome of its rotunda, which had to be rebuilt after the bombings of June 1940. The adjacent Oratory buildings once belonged to a theological college created to fight the battle of dogma with the Protestant academy in the town proper; they now shelter a small community of nuns, the Communauté Jeanne Delanoue, a home for retired clergymen and a Catholic school for girls.

The suburbs

Some of Saumur's biggest attractions lie out in the suburbs, particularly in and around the *commune* of **St-Hilaire-St-Florent**, 2km west of the centre and separated from Saumur proper by the little river Thouet. The great **sparkling wine caves** are here, along with the distinguished **Ecole Nationale d'Equitation**, the national riding school. Closer to hand, but also on the western side of the Thouet, the undistinguished suburb of **Bagneux** is the surprise home of one of France's most impressive dolmens, while the semi-industrial southeastern quarter of town houses the **Musée des Blindés**, a gargantuan tank museum.

Musée des Blindés

Even if you're not a military buff, there's something awesome about the giant collection of old tanks at the **Musée des Blindés**, at 1043 route de Fontevraud, 3km south of the town centre (daily: May–Sept 9.30am–6.30pm; Oct–April 10am–5pm; €5.50; Ⓦ www.musee-des-blindes.asso.fr). Walking through the huge, hangar-like space it's possible to grasp the evolution of the beast from the glorified armoured cars produced by Panhard and Renault in World War I to the highly technical behemoth of a killing machine that is the modern French army's Leclerc tank. In between you'll stumble over swarms of tanks, howitzers and other bits of armour, their strong and weak points explained by bilingual placards. The World War II section could make up a division on its own, and there's a moment of real frisson when you spot the lethal Panzer, which so harried the French army in 1940.

The museum is well signposted for motorists; alternatively, **bus** #C towards "Chemin Vert" and bus #A pass close by; both leave from rue Franklin Roosevelt at the junction with rue Dacier and rue Beaurepaire in Saumur.

Ecole Nationale d'Equitation

The region's horsey roots extend right back to the Arab thoroughbreds introduced by Richard the Lionheart, but the **Ecole Nationale d'Equitation**, 4km from the town centre, just outside St-Hilaire-St-Florent, was only created in 1972. This distinctly aristocratic institution exists to train up the cream of French horsemen and -women and has to some extent taken on the mantle of the old Ecole de Cavalerie, though most of the forty-odd Ecuyers du Cadre Noir – the black-clad riding instructors – are now civilians. Even the evocatively named Colonel de la Porte du Treil, the current chief of the school, turns out to be a colonel in the *gendarmerie* only.

June 1940: the cadets of Saumur

On the night of June 18, 1940, towns and cities all along the Loire were declaring themselves "open" to the invading German armies. As the local populations retreated into their troglodyte caves and cellars, much as they would have done in medieval times, refugees streamed south across the river. On the radio, Pétain was calling for an armistice, and de Gaulle was making his first rebellious broadcasts from London. In Saumur, Colonel Daniel Michon, the commandant of the Ecole de Cavalerie, received the order to withdraw south, but he decided to apply it to the horses only, addressing his students with the stirring words: "Gentlemen, for the school it is a mission of sacrifice. France is depending on you." Guns were set up on the town bandstand and at the river crossings, and for three days, Saumur's two thousand cadets and instructors held a forty-kilometre stretch of the Loire against the Germans, repulsing wave after wave of boat attacks. De Gaulle called it the first act of the Resistance, but it could also be called the last chivalric battle fought on French soil – by strange chance, the 18,000 attacking troops belonged to the deeply aristocratic 1st Cavalry Division, from the elite Hanoverian Panzer school.

The fighting was fierce but hopelessly unequal, and by late evening on June 21 the Germans had occupied the heights around the château. Saumur was outflanked and no longer defensible. News came through that Pétain had signed the armistice, and the surviving cadets either retreated on bicycles towards Fontevraud or surrendered to the occupying troops. Most of the captives – who almost alone in the French army had won the respect of their opponents – were quickly released and force-marched into the Unoccupied Zone, saluted by German troops and cheered by French crowds as they went.

The school (April–Sept Tues–Sat 9.30–11am & 2–4pm; €6.50 for morning visits, €4.50 afternoons) offers excellent guided **tours** of the whole massive complex (only the longer morning tours allow you to watch a training session as well). You can see the state-of-the-art tack room, saddlery and veterinary hospital, and endless rows of stables whose hot and cold showers and equine sun beds service some four hundred blue-blooded horses. The Cadre Noir's displays of dressage, anachronistic battle manoeuvres and the secret-recipe trick jumps – *courbette*, *croupade* and *cabriole* – are regular events at the school's stadium-sized show ring. The tourist office in Saumur has programme details, or you can check online at ⓦwww.cadrenoir.tm.fr.

To **get there** by public transport take bus #B from the south end of rue Franklin Roosevelt to the "Alouette" stop, then continue down the route de Marson, turning right at the signpost; it's about ten to fifteen minutes' walk. If your enthusiasm for horses won't wait, take yourself off to the **Petit Souper** riding school, 500m short of the Ecole Nationale d'Equitation, where an hour's instruction at any level costs €20 – or €9 for a half-hour on a Shetland pony for tots. Book at least one day in advance on ☏02.41.50.29.90.

Sparkling wine cellars

The main D561 leading west from Saumur towards Gennes passes through the suburban *commune* of **St-Hilaire-St-Florent**. The central stretch of the road, along rue Ackerman and rue Leopold Palustre, is lined with the impressive entrances to the cellars of Saumur's most prestigious makers of sparkling wine. Choosing between Ackerman-Laurance, Bouvet-Ladubay, Langlois-Château, Gratien & Meyer, Louis de Grenelle and Veuve Amiot is a matter of personal taste, and possibly a question of opening hours, though most are open all day every day throughout the warmer months (generally 10am–6pm, though most close for a couple of hours at lunchtime out of season). All offer the chance to see spectacular cellars carved out of the soft rock, lined with millions of bottles undergoing the obligatory second fermentation. You might be persuaded by Veuve Amiot's free tour (currently the only one that doesn't charge), Ackerman-Laurance's eighteen-metre-high underground chamber or Bouvet-Ladubay's impressive "underground cathedral" and contemporary art gallery.

To get there by public transport, take **bus** #B from rue Franklin Roosevelt to the "Senatorerie" stop. Alternatively, make for the **Caves Coopératives** at St-Cyr-en-Bourg (☏02.41.53.06.08), a short train hop south of Saumur and near the station, where there are kilometres of cellars.

For more on sparkling wines, see Contexts, p.339.

The Dolmen de Bagneux

Take the main road south of town towards Montreuil-Bellay, the N147, and after just over 2km you'll come to the dispiriting suburb of **BAGNEUX**. Persevere a little, however – take the rue du Dolmen which leads left past the Mairie – and you'll be well rewarded. The **Dolmen de Bagneux** (mid-June to mid-Sept daily 9am–7pm; mid-Sept to mid-June Mon, Tues & Thurs–Sun 9am–7pm; €3; ⓦwww.saumur-dolmen.com), squatting incongruously in the garden of the friendly but ordinary bar at no. 56, is the chief among the cluster of megalithic tombs found in the region downstream of Saumur. The owner jokingly calls it his "garden shed"; in fact, it's one of the largest and best-preserved such monuments in Europe, a 23-metre, 500-tonne rectangle of gravestone-like slabs capped by an enormous roof of three flat stones. Sadly, the smattering of archeological finds have been carried off to various museums.

Eating and drinking

Saumur's choice of good **restaurants** isn't quite as extensive as you'd hope, but there are several reasonably inexpensive places around place St-Pierre, many of which offer a chance to enjoy a glass of sparkling Saumur brut at an outside table. Almost everything closes up fairly early, and there's nothing much to do after hours except seek out a café or "pub" that's still serving. The area around place St-Pierre is the best bet; alternatively, try the bar of the *Hôtel Cristal*, down on the riverfront.

Auberge Reine de Sicile 71 rue Waldeck-Rousseau, Ile d'Offard. ℡02.41.67.30.48. Over the bridge, on the Ile d'Offard, this handsome restaurant stands next to the medieval home of King René's mother, the queen of Sicily. The dining room is atmospherically ancient and the food is delicious, with fish dishes grilled in front of you in the old chimneyplace. Try the *matelote d'anguilles* – eel stew. Closed Mon, Sat lunch & Sun evening, and for the last three weeks in Aug.

Auberge St-Pierre 6 place St-Pierre ℡02.41.51.26.25. This bustling brasserie-restaurant has outside tables, a good choice of *menus* starting at around €10, and a long list of excellent, inexpensive Saumur wines. Perfect for an informal evening meal. Usually closed Sun evening & Mon, except sometimes in July & Aug.

Les Délices du Château Château esplanade ℡02.41.67.65.60. The location alone, up on the high ground right next to the château, makes this a good place for a special treat. Serves *haute cuisine*, specializing in elegant fish dishes in local wine sauces, with views and prices to match. The offshoot *L'Orangeraie* is a tearoom and brasserie

with more down-to-earth dishes. Closed Mon, Tues evening & Sun.

L'Escargot 30 rue du Maréchal Leclerc ℡02.41.51.20.88. A courteously old-fashioned place serving good regional fish and mushroom dishes on *menus* from €10 to €22.50. It sometimes feels as if you're eating in someone's rather formal family dining room, which makes for a hushed atmosphere that you will either love or hate. Closed Sun evening & Wed, and mid-Aug to Sept.

Les Forges de St-Pierre 1 place St-Pierre ℡02.41.38.21.79. Specializing in grilled meat, this is another of the busy, slightly touristy but ultimately enjoyable restaurants on the atmospheric old place St-Pierre. Closed Tues evening & Sun.

Les Ménéstrels At the *Hôtel Anne d'Anjou*, 32 quai Mayaud ℡02.41.67.71.10. Saumur's best place for serious, formal gastronomy, though the stone walls and exposed beams add a note of rustic relaxation. Most locals say it has the edge over *Les Délices du Château*, and it's usually less touristy, unless the hotel has a tour party staying. The set lunch *menu* is a bargain at €19, but expect to pay at least twice that for an evening meal.

East of Saumur

East of Saumur, the sunny microclimate and rocky soil provides the ideal conditions for making red wine, which is produced locally under the renowned *appellation* of Saumur-Champigny (see Contexts, p.337). You can find wine-growers' caves in the pretty villages of **Parnay** and **Turquant**, both of which are utterly typical of the Saumurois. Set well back from the Loire's floodplain in the shelter of the tufa escarpment, the sandy stone walls of their ancient houses are hardly distinguishable from the surrounding natural rock. On the cliff-tops behind, traditional *moulins caviers* – windmills built on cone-shaped stone platforms – stand out against the sky, though few still turn. Behind them, the mild vine-covered slopes stretch away to the south, with apple orchards around **Le Val-Hulin**. A little further upstream, handsome **Montsoreau** is more substantial, its slate-roofed houses spreading out in the shadow of the tall, tufa-built château. Montsoreau's immediate neighbour, the picturesque village of **Candes–St-Martin**, overlooks the confluence of the Loire and Vienne. Its ancient church, and the giant abbey at **Fontevraud**, just inland, are two of the most palpably historic places in the whole Loire region.

Two **buses** serve all the towns along the riverbank as far as Montsoreau, where they turn inland to Fontevraud: the #S1 (2–4 daily) leaves from Saumur's gare routière, while Voyages Augereau's coach leaves from place St-Nicolas (4–6 daily). You'll be much more independent with a car or bicycle.

Parnay to Turquant

At **PARNAY**, 7km upstream from Saumur, a tiny valley cuts into the escarpment at right angles to the river. Lined with gardens and orchards – some tenderly cultivated, others romantically abandoned – it's a lovely place to stroll, and you can taste and buy local wines at the troglodyte caves of the **château du Marconnay**, 75 rte de Saumur, Parnay (April to mid-Nov Tues–Sat 10am–6pm, Sun 2–6pm; mid-Nov to March call ☎02.41.51.46.89; €3). A couple of kilometres further on, in **LE VAL–HULIN**, you can find the last producer of the once-common Saumurois dried apple – known as the *pomme tapée*, as each apple, after drying, is given a little expert tap to check its readiness. You can tour one of the workshops at **Le Troglo des Pommes Tapées** (Easter–June & Sept to mid-Nov Sat & Sun 10am–noon & 2.30–6pm; July & Aug Tues–Sun 2.30–6pm; €4.60), where you are taken through the apple drying and tapping process before finishing with a tasting.

TURQUANT, a few hundred metres beyond Le Val-Hulin, is the starting point for a **sentier d'interprétation**, a fascinating two-hour circular walk around the village following signposts set up by the Parc Naturel Régional Loire-Anjou-Touraine (see box opposite). Turquant also has two very appealing **accommodation** options. The rooms at the beautiful, fifteenth-century *Demeure de la Vignole*, 3 impasse Marguerite d'Anjou, Turquant (☎02.41.53.67.00, ⓦhttp://demeure-vignole.com; ⑤), have roof beams, warm stone walls and black and white tiled floors; there's even a troglodyte room set into the adjoining tufa cliffs, for which you pay a modest supplement. In the centre of the village, the relatively basic but still charming chambres d'hôtes at *Le Balcon Bleu*, 2 rue des Martyrs, Turquant (☎02.41.38.10.31, ⓔturquant@chez.com; ②) are set around a small courtyard garden; two of the rooms (③) have kitchen facilities.

Montsoreau

Montsoreau (Feb–April & Oct to mid-Nov 2–6pm; May–Sept daily 10am–7pm; €7.50; ⓦwww.chateau-montsoreau.com) is one of the most photogenic châteaux of them all, its north side rising cliff-like almost straight out of the river, while presenting a more elaborately decorated face to the sun on the other. It was built in the 1450s by Jean de Chambes, one of Charles VII's cronies, and added to piecemeal in succeeding centuries. The most obvious later feature is the Renaissance staircase tower, with its exquisitely sculpted bas-relief panels showing the devices of the Chambes family – "je le ferai" (I will do it) – and various allegorical scenes of Italian inspiration.

The château has been recently turned into an elaborately presented and child-friendly **museum**. There are over a dozen rooms of strategically lit models, video projections and slide shows backed by ambient music and French-language commentaries (a translation is available). On the ground floor is an exhibition on the history of the Loire and its role as a trading route, using some beautiful models of old river-boats. The first-floor rooms tell the story of the château itself, including its most famous incarnation as the setting for Alexandre Dumas' novel *La Dame de Montsoreau*. The upper rooms house a miscellany of excellent exhibitions on local windmills, wind-vane designs,

Parc Naturel Régional Loire-Anjou-Touraine

The boundaries of the **Parc Naturel Régional Loire-Anjou-Touraine** are wide, extending down both sides of the Loire from Villandry west to St-Georges-des-Sept-Voies, as well as north towards Beaufort-en-Vallée and south to Montreuil-Bellay – which roughly matches the area covered in this chapter, plus a good chunk of western Touraine. Given the dense local population this is no fenced-off nature reserve or wilderness park, more a locally designated area of particular natural beauty. The **Maison du Parc**, in the centre of Montsoreau, behind the château (T02.41.53.66.00, Wwww.parc-loire-anjou-touraine.fr) can provide information on the park's most interesting activities for visitors, including fascinating nature walks led by experts and the circuits known as "Sentiers d'Interpretation" – short, sign-posted walks of a couple of hours' duration that take you past bilingual information points describing local flora, fauna and traditions. There are two delightful four-kilometre walks in the Saumurois: one starts outside the collégiale at **Le Puy-Notre-Dame** and takes you round the vineyards, while the other begins in the centre of **Turquant** and takes you past troglodyte caves, orchards and woods, as well as through the vines. More are planned.

troglodyte caves and so on, but the real treat is the panoramic view from the open-air **battlements**, right at the top.

A major local attraction is the **Champignonnière de Saut aux Loups** (daily: March–June & Sept to mid-Nov 10am–12.30pm & 2–6.30pm; July & Aug 10am–6.30pm; €4.20; Wwww.sautauxloups.fr.st), where the traditional troglodyte housefronts conceal vast, underground mushroom-growing caves. You'll be offered a tour (in English if they're not too busy) followed by the chance to eat rather expensive *menus* featuring *galipettes* – giant, oven-cooked mushrooms garnished with goat's cheese, *rillettes* and other tasty morsels.

Practicalities

The welcoming and well-run *Hôtel le Bussy*, 4 rue Jehanne d'Arc (T02.41.38.11.11, F02.41.38.18.10; ❹), has just twelve rooms and an enviable situation right behind the château. The best **restaurant** in town is the *Diane de Meridor*, 12 quai Philippe-de-Commines (T02.41.51.71.76), which serves classic regional specialities with a good-value lunch *menu* at €13. The *Aigue-Marine*, a boat moored to the riverbank at the east end of town, is a fun place to eat, though the food is pretty simple and it's often closed outside the peak summer season.

Candes-St-Martin

The ancient village of **CANDES-ST-MARTIN** gets the second half of its name from the great Tourangeau saint, St Martin (see box on p.69), who died here in around 400 while trying to settle a dispute between squabbling monks. This is a beautiful corner of the region, the village set under a rocky bluff overlooking the confluence of the Loire and Vienne. Discreet plaques point out the village's many handsome old buildings, though they're often hidden behind high walls – notably the fifteenth-century Château Vieux and seventeenth-century Château Neuf, once the summer residences of the archbishops of Tours. You won't need help finding the **collégiale**, however, which stands squarely at the centre of the village and whose elaborately sculpted **porch** is one of the greatest architectural delights of the Loire. Unusually, the porch is oriented to the north in order to welcome the many pilgrims who would have arrived by water; inside, ranks of statues stand resplendent in polychrome paint, enclosed by a tent-like vault which springs dramatically from a slender central pillar. It was under scaffolding and closed to visitors at the time of writing – nearly a million euros have been spent on restoration so far – but work should be completed during 2005.

Inside the church proper, the **nave** feels incredibly spacious, a sensation created by the cool, pale stone walls and lofty, dome-like Plantagenêt vault. The nave is taller than was originally planned for, a fact given away by the oddly placed statuettes of saints, which were originally carved to mark the point at which the ribs of the vault would spring away from their supporting columns, but now hover awkwardly some distance below. The oldest part of the church, though heavily restored, is the **chapelle St-Martin**, on the left of the choir, where you can trace the life of the saint in nineteenth-century stained-glass windows.

Don't miss the view of the confluence from the hilltop just southwest of the village – the road is helpfully signposted "**Panorama**". Down below, you can explore the remnants of the old quays. The risk of collapsing sandbanks makes **bathing** in the Loire genuinely dangerous, but you may see locals swimming quite happily from a well-established sandy island, accessible from the bridge some 500m upstream. If so, you might think it safe enough to join them.

Practicalities

Right beside the church, in a building apparently falling apart with age, the *Auberge de la Route d'Or*, place de l'Eglise (☏02.47.95.81.10; closed Tues evening & Wed), is an excellent **restaurant** for local specialities like *alose* (shad) and *anguilles* (eels); service is relaxed and the atmosphere is unstuffy, and there are outside tables on the square in summer. If you're looking for somewhere to **stay**, *La Fontaine*, 14 rte de Compostelle, on the main road just before Montsoreau (☏02.47.95.83.66), offers simple but pleasant chambres d'hôtes, some with views straight onto the river. On the high ground behind Candes-St-Martin, *Les Sarments*, 15 rue Trochet (☏02.47.95.93.40, ⊛http://lessarments.free.fr; ❸), has similarly plain but attractive rooms, and there's a good view from the terrace.

Fontevraud

At the heart of the stunning Romanesque complex of the **abbaye de Fontevraud**, 13km southeast of Saumur and 5km inland from Montsoreau, are the tombs of the Plantagenêt royal family, eerily lifelike works of funereal art that powerfully evoke the historical bonds between England and France. The tiny village of **FONTEVRAUD-L'ABBAYE** seems to hover at the abbey gates, servicing the hordes of visitors that arrive here with a single hotel and a handful of café-restaurants and gift shops.

Some history

Fontevraud was first established in around 1100 by an ascetic hermit-preacher, **Robert d'Arbrissel**, who had previously lived in a kind of woodland commune with both male and female followers. Gradually, the beds of leaves were replaced by huts and then by stone buildings, but unusually the institution remained both nunnery and monastery. When d'Arbrissel died he declared that his successor should always be a woman – a deeply unconventional move that on the one hand rejected the commonplace medieval notion that women were innately sinful, and on the other allowed the monks to profit spiritually from the humiliation of serving under an abbess. During the course of the twelfth century, the patronage of the counts of Anjou enabled the creation of the giant Romanesque complex that can be seen today.

Eleanor of Aquitaine, the woman described in Shakespeare's *King John* as a "cankered grandam" and a "monstrous injurer of heaven and earth", was born in Poitiers in 1122, the granddaughter of the troubadour-duke, Guillaume IX. Her crime was to have behaved with the same vigour and fierce independence as the great male rulers of her age. At the age of 15, Alienor, as she is called in French, inherited the duchy of Aquitaine, which then covered most of southwestern France. Soon after, she married Louis VII, king of France. It was not a successful union – the cultivated, beautiful southern heiress being ill-matched with her monkish husband from the relatively boorish north. In 1147, Eleanor scandalized contemporaries by accompanying Louis on the disastrous Second Crusade, during which it is thought she embarked on a brief affair with her urbane uncle, Raymond of Toulouse.

Back in Paris, a disillusioned Eleanor met and fell in love with the fiery, volatile Henry Plantagenêt, the son of Geoffroi le Bel, count of Anjou, and Matilda, titular queen of England. By 1152, she had persuaded the Council of Beaugency (see box on p.187) to annul her marriage, and eight weeks later, Henry Plantagenêt arrived in Poitiers for his wedding. The marriage caused alarm throughout Europe as it united Aquitaine with the Plantagenêt lands of Normandy, Anjou, Maine and Touraine, creating a huge new power bloc across western France. The following year Henry inherited the English throne from his mother, and became Henry II.

Eleanor spent much of the next twenty years alternately travelling through and governing the Plantagenêt domains, both as regent for Henry – while he was away on one of his frequent wars against Louis and his allies – and as ruler of Aquitaine in her own right. She gave birth to eight children, and all three elder boys inherited their mother's independence of spirit; the youngest, John, turned out a little different, perhaps because he was sent away to Fontevraud to be educated by the nuns. By the late 1160s, Henry was tiring of his now middle-aged wife and began publicly flaunting a new lover, causing Eleanor to return in fury to her own Aquitaine. Meanwhile, troubling was brewing between Henry and his sons, who were demanding autonomy in ruling their apportioned lands, much to Henry's displeasure. The crisis came in the aftermath of Henry's murder of Thomas Becket, when the whole family assembled at Chinon at Christmas 1172. In March, the eldest – Henry, the "Young King" – suddenly fled to Louis VII in Paris, seeking a more generous overlord. Geoffrey and Richard too sided with the French king, and it seems that even Eleanor plotted with her first husband against her second. Henry fought back with characteristic speed and fury, however, fighting and burning his way through Touraine, seizing Eleanor at Poitiers and dragging her north to captivity, first in Chinon and then in Salisbury.

By the time Henry died in 1189 (see box on p.93), Eleanor had been a prisoner for sixteen years. Despite being almost 70 years old, she travelled to Navarre to find a bride for her son Richard the Lionheart – Bérengère of Navarre (see p.295) – presented her at Messina, in Sicily, where the troops were gathering for the Third Crusade, and then travelled back by way of Rome. By 1194, however, Eleanor's energy had finally abated, and she retired to Fontevraud as a royal guest of the nuns. Here she buried her son Richard – killed by an arrow in 1199 – and watched the Plantagenêt empire crumble under the assaults of Philippe-Auguste, the formidable new French king. She died in 1204, at the then extraordinary age of 82, honoured and hated in equal measure, but incontrovertibly one of the greatest women of her age.

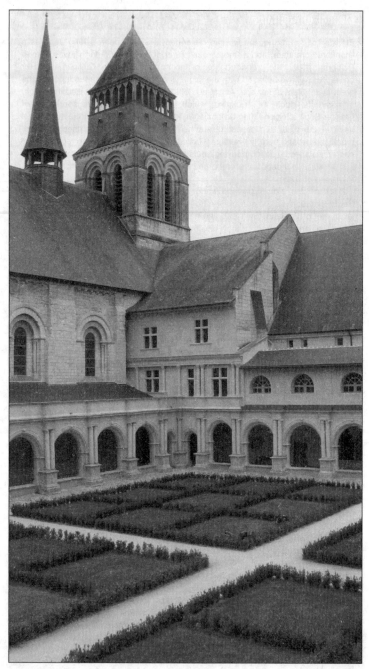

△ Cloister, Fontevraud

Typically, the abbesses were members of the Angevin aristocracy. Matilda, the second of the line, was the aunt of **Henry II Plantagenêt**, count of Anjou, who visited Fontevraud in 1154 shortly before sailing to England for his coronation. His son John, later king of England, even lived here for five years as a child, and when Henry died at Chinon in 1189, Fontevraud was the obvious choice for his burial – though it seems to have been against his wishes. Henry's widow, **Eleanor of Aquitaine** (see box on p.235), lived out the last decade of her life at Fontevraud, and was on hand to organize the creation of a second tomb for her son **Richard the Lionheart**, who died in 1199. When the tombs of the two kings were joined by Eleanor's own, probably shortly after her death in 1204, a royal necropolis seemed to be under construction. Ironically, even as the Plantagenêt line was being celebrated in funereal art, King John was losing all his continental lands to his Capetian suzerain, Philippe-Auguste – who was extending and redesigning his own royal burial complex at St-Denis, near Paris.

The abbey declined in the wake of the Plantagenêts' fall from power, but was periodically revived by unusually committed and industrious abbesses, most notably by the aristocratic **Bourbon abbesses**, beginning with Renée de Bourbon in the early sixteenth century and culminating in the rule of Louise de Bourbon Lavedan and her successor, Jeanne-Baptiste de Bourbon, who died in 1670. In the latest period the rules were applied with renewed strictness, and the (men's) monastery surrounded by a deep moat, with two hawthorn hedges for good measure. This barrier apparently wasn't sufficient to prevent incursions, however, as stone walls had to be added two years later. The nuns were finally sent away by the revolutionaries in 1792, after which Fontevraud was used as a prison until 1963. Since 1975 the site has been occupied by the **Centre Culturel de l'Ouest** (CCO), an important centre for medieval archaeology that has been a thorough if sometimes over-zealous restorer of Fontevraud – the entire complex now gleams with newly cut tufa stone and well-tended gardens.

The abbey complex

The buildings of the **abbaye de Fontevraud** (daily: June–Sept 9am–6.30pm; April, May & Oct 10am–6pm; Nov–March 10am–5.30pm; €5.50) cover a large area, as they were originally built to house and segregate not only nuns and monks but also the sick, lepers and repentant prostitutes, and were repeatedly extended at high points in the abbey's long history. The English-language guided tours (mid-June to Aug; roughly four times daily) are excellent, but you're free to explore on your own.

The **Plantagenêt tombs** lie in the serene and spacious abbey church: Henry II flanks his wife Eleanor of Aquitaine – her notorious youthful beauty preserved in painted stone, her hands clasping an open book – while at their feet are Richard the Lionheart and Isabelle of Angoulême, the widow of King John, whose tomb (the only one in wood, rather than stone) joined the other three in 1254. The tombs may originally have lain in the last bay of the nave, next to the northwest pillar, but were moved about in 1504 and again in 1638 to allow the whole community to worship in the nave – at which time two effigies of Joan, Henry's daughter, and her son, Raymond VII of Toulouse, were replaced by more conveniently shaped kneeling figures. Ten days after Louis XVI was guillotined in 1793, the tombs were broken open and damaged, but they at least survived decapitation. A worse fate almost befell the Plantagenêts in the nineteenth century, when Queen Victoria successfully lobbied Empress Eugénie to give them up to Westminster Abbey; luckily, the Franco-Prussian war intervened.

The **abbey church** itself is an enormous building ninety metres long, its Romanesque bones unobscured by fanciful decoration. Powerful pillars support the early twelfth-century choir, while the nave, completed some fifty years later, is even more majestic, with its sequence of strangely dome-like Angevin vaults. The southern gallery of the **Grand-Moûtier**, the glorious cloister adjoining the church, was begun on Gothic precepts, but masons with experience of the new Italianate style were gradually brought in, and by the time the other three wings were built, beginning in 1540, Classical principles had fully taken root.

An exquisitely carved doorway leads through to the vaulted **chapterhouse**, decorated with intense sixteenth-century wall-paintings by the Angevin artist Thomas Pot, to which most of the Bourbon abbesses later had their portraits added. Nearby you can visit the community room, where the nuns worked on handicrafts, the vaulted cells of the noviciate and the **refectory**, on the opposite side of the cloisters to the church. The last is an impressively vast space with distended Gothic vaulting surmounting Romanesque walls. A beautiful Renaissance staircase leads up to the **dormitory**, a seventy-metre-long space arched over by vast roof beams.

All the cooking for the religious community, which would have numbered several hundred, was done in the bizarre-looking twelfth-century **kitchen**, an octagonal structure bristling with 21 spiky chimneys and a foiled, fish-scale-like roof. The design is virtually a unique survival, though it does recall the cone-shaped bays of St-Ours, in Loches (see p.117). Elsewhere in the complex, you can explore the infirmaries, the leper-house **prieuré de St-Lazare**, the **St-Benoît hospital** – where there's a beautiful fragment of an early thirteenth-century, sculpted Last Judgement – and lots of restored rooms sometimes used for art exhibitions or concerts. An exhibition on medieval gardens gives useful background on the extensive and meticulously recreated **gardens**, which include flower, medicinal and vegetable areas.

Practicalities

Unless you have a car or bicycle, **getting to Fontevraud** is a matter of catching the bus run by Voyages Augereau from place St-Nicolas in Saumur (4–6 daily; 30min); services aren't frequent, so get an up-to-date timetable from the tourist office or gare routière. Fontevraud has its own little **tourist office**, allée Ste-Catherine (May Tues–Sat 9.30am–12.30pm & 2–6pm, Sun 10.30am–12.30pm & 2.30–5.30pm; June–Aug Tues–Sat 9.30am–12.30pm & 1.30–7pm, Sun 10.30am–12.30pm & 2.30–5.30pm; Sept Tues–Sat 9.30am–12.30pm & 1.30–7pm; ☎02.41.51.79.45), where staff can advise on visiting Fontevraud's other churches and chapels, and suggest some good routes for walks. For details of the frequent concerts, lectures, art exhibitions and theatre programmes at the abbey, contact the Centre Culturel de l'Ouest directly (☎02.41.51.73.52, ⓦwww.abbaye-fontevraud.com), or ask at the tourist office.

The most enticing **place to stay** is the *Prieuré St-Lazare* (☎02.41.51.73.16, ⓦwww.hotelfp-fontevraud.com; ❸). It's actually within the abbey complex, though sadly the rooms are more like a modern hotel's than a monastic cell; there's also a posh restaurant, inexpensive brasserie and tearoom. In the village, *La Croix Blanche* (☎02.41.51.71.11, ⓔla_croix_blanche@hotmail.com; ❸) is an old-fashioned and slightly frumpy hotel, but clean and welcoming. Both have rather proper – and rather expensive – **restaurants**. Three kilometres north of Fontevraud, just off the main road to Montsoreau, is the *Domaine de Mestre* (☎02.41.51.71.90, ⓦwww.dauge-fontevraud.com; ❹), a handsome old farmhouse complex that has been converted into an artisanal soap factory and chambres d'hôtes; the rooms are charming in a rustic, nineteenth-century way, and there's a good table d'hôte most evenings.

Doué-la-Fontaine and around

The outwardly unremarkable town of **Doué-la-Fontaine** owes its local fame to a quirk of geology. It lies on a bed of *falun* limestone (see box below) that has produced a number of fascinatingly weird "troglodyte" cave sites and a reputation for growing fabulous roses – some seven million are exported from here every year, making up over half of France's annual production. The caves may be dramatic, but the town is stranded in a flat and deeply rural corner of France that feels an awfully long way from the sophistications of Saumur, let alone Tours or Paris.

Doué and the region around it are best visited on a day-trip, but there's no train and only a thin **bus** service between Saumur and Doué (2–4 daily). In any case you'll need wheels to get around between the various sights, so if you don't have a car think about renting a bicycle in Saumur and making a long day of it.

Tufa and falun

The beguiling milk-and-honey colour of the towns and villages of the Loire comes from the region's classic stone: *tuffeau*, or **tufa** in English. It's a kind of pale, soft, creamy limestone that you can sink a thumbnail into, and easily quarried. From prehistory right up to modern times, local people used to burrow into the long escarpments that run parallel to the rivers, creating hobbit-like tunnel homes and at the same time quarrying stone for building houses in the valley. The **"troglodyte" cave-dwellings** were warm in winter, cool in summer, weatherproof and easily defensible. Many have now been abandoned or turned into garages, wine cellars or chicken coops, but they are increasingly being renovated and restored. It's even possible to stay at a few hotels and chambres d'hôtes that offer troglodyte rooms, the nicest being at Azay-le-Rideau (see p.96) and Cunault (see p.245). The harder varieties of tufa, as found around Bourré, on the Cher (see p.159), were used for the great châteaux and churches of the Loire, and the demand for this stone also created hundreds of kilometres of cave-like quarry tunnels. Many are now used for giant, commercial mushroom farms, especially in the Saumurois, and you can tour smaller, tourist-oriented versions throughout the region.

Doué-la-Fontaine, just south of Saumur, has a different geology. It stands on a great plateau of **falun** (soft shellstone), another type of limestone but with a deeper, more golden colour. It is packed with tiny shell fossils and you can scrape it away with a fingernail almost as if it were compacted sand. Unlike tufa, *falun* lies flat, so the people of Doué were forced to quarry straight down into the bedrock. Over generations, cave-villages were created, the houses ringing the edge of shallow, arena-like depressions. It's estimated that as much as two-thirds of the population around Doué once lived underground, which sounds barbaric until you see how neat and effective these cave-houses actually are. Excess stone could be broken up and used to lime the fields, reducing the soil's natural acidity. Where *falun* was quarried commercially, the premium on grazing and farmland round Doué meant that the quarrymen tried to keep the roof intact. They first created a narrow trench and then gradually cut the stone away underneath, leaving the region pockmarked with giant, gourd-shaped quarries whose size you'd never guess from the narrow opening above.

Doué-la-Fontaine

If you were just passing through **DOUE-LA-FONTAINE**, 13km southwest of Saumur, you might not give it a second glance. There's no château, only a ruined Carolingian house and the shell of a Romanesque collegiate church, and the three central squares – place du Champ de Foire, place Vénard and place des Fontaines – fail to make much of an impression. But two lovely rose gardens, a pair of peculiar quarries, a museum of old shops and a quite wonderful zoo make Doué an enjoyable place to visit. Unusually, all the sights lie on the outskirts of town. Doué's thriving rose industry really flourishes during the **Journées de la Rose** (second week of July; 9.30am–8pm; €7; ⓦwww.journeesdelarose.com), a five-day festival of rose-growing held in giant cave-galleries. Some 100,000 prize specimens are presented, making a vivid spectacle.

The **tourist office** is at 30 place des Fontaines (July & Aug daily 9.30am–12.30pm & 2–6.30pm; April–June & Sept Tues–Sat 9am–12.30pm & 2–5.30pm; Oct–March Mon 9.30am–12.30pm, Tues & Fri 9.30am–12.30pm & 2–5.30pm; ⓣ02.41.59.20.49, ⓔtourisme.doue.la.fontaine@wanadoo.fr). There are two plain but acceptable hotels, both on place du Champ de Foire, but it's hard to think why you'd choose to stay at either. Both have **restaurants**: the *Hôtel de France* is the more enticing – the decor may be horrendous but the food is good and prices moderate. If you want to eat in a "troglo" restaurant, make for *Le Caveau*, 4 place du Champ de Foire (ⓣ02.41.59.98.28; mid-Sept to Easter closed Mon–Fri), where the €19 *menu* allows you to try the traditional *galipettes* (giant mushrooms) and *fouaces* (a kind of medieval pitta bread); it's rather touristy, but good fun.

La Cave aux Sarcophages

Hidden away just inside the ring road, near the exit roundabout for Montreuil-Bellay, is the eeriest of Doué's strange troglodyte attractions, **La Cave aux Sarcophages**, at 1 rue Croix Mordret (April to mid-Sept 10am–noon & 2–7pm; €4). Between the sixth and ninth centuries, stone coffins were quarried here on an almost industrial scale. The attraction of a stone sarcophagus was a powerful one for a Merovingian aristocrat, as the composition of the *falun* rock (see box on p.239) made it ideally suited for preserving flesh as long as possible – an important factor if you're expecting bodily resurrection at an imminent Last Judgement. It's estimated that over 30,000 such coffins were extracted from an area of some 11,000 square metres, though you're only shown a few areas where broken sarcophagi were left in situ. There's not, therefore, a lot to see, though there's something spooky about the whole idea, and the **guided tour** (in English if there are no French groups waiting, in which case you're given a translation) is extremely informative, describing how the caves were transformed into hiding places in later, more troubled times.

Les Perrières

The most dramatic of Doué's troglodyte sites is the "*caves cathédrales*" at **Les Perrières**, 545 rue des Perrières (May to mid-Sept Tues–Sun 10am–noon & 2–7pm; €4), signposted off the ring road on the way into town from Saumur. This is a classic scooped-out quarry site on the traditional pattern (see box on p.239), so there's nothing to see in particular apart from the flowers and plants that grow profusely all around, but as you walk through the long underground chambers, 20m high in places, you'll feel suitably ant-like and insignificant. Occasional lamp-lit tours take place on Tuesday evenings (contact the tourist office for information). Doué has another similar complex, cleverly used as the town dump.

Zoo de Doué

Even if you wouldn't normally visit a zoo, you might think about calling in at the **Zoo de Doué** (mid-Feb to April & Oct to mid-Nov 10am–6pm; May–Sept 9am–7pm; €13, children aged 3–10 €8; ⓦ www.zoodoue.fr). It makes brilliant use of a warm, sheltered situation in one of the region's complexes of *falun* quarries, and endless streams and bamboo thickets conspire to create a powerful Lost Eden feel. If you have reservations about animal captivity, console yourself with the thought that the zoo is committed to a major conservation scheme for endangered species, and the animals are at least constrained by natural rock instead of bars. Bears occupy a rocky hollow, leopards cruise about in a kind of stone gulch, giraffes poke their heads above the top of their quarry pit and pythons and anacondas slumber in dark, steamy tunnels. Various animal feeding times are advertised throughout the day. To get there, follow the signs west out of town towards Cholet, along the D960; the zoo is at the very edge of town, almost 3km from the centre.

Nearby, just off the road to Cholet, **Les Chemins de la Rose** (May–Sept daily 9.30am–7pm; €5.50) is a very English-style garden, filled with some ten thousand rose bushes featuring over eight hundred varieties.

Troglodyte sites north of Doué-la-Fontaine

A particularly fascinating trio of troglodyte sites lies just north of Doué-la-Fontaine. At **ROCHEMENIER**, 6km north, you can tour the **Village Troglodytique** (April–Oct daily 9.30am–7pm; Nov, Feb & March Sat & Sun 2–6pm; €4; ⓦ http://perso.club-internet.fr/troglody). This was a complete troglodyte village, used by a group of ordinary farming families until a hundred years ago. You can see their barns, cowsheds and cellars, with old farm implements on display, and the living quarters, complete with windows, beds, ovens and all the accoutrements of farm life. The most fascinating chambers are the communal ones, particularly the large village hall, whose walls are scored with pick marks to prevent echoes, and the extraordinary subterranean chapel with its mock Gothic arches. If your French isn't up to the optional guided tour, buy the excellent, inexpensive booklet in English, which fills in all the details of daily life. One hundred metres along the main road, you can sample a €19 *menu* of "heritage" fare – mushrooms followed by traditional *fouaces* breads stuffed with *rillettes* and goat's cheese – in troglodyte surroundings at *Les Caves de la Genevraie* (⓽02.41.59.34.22; July & Aug closed Mon, Sept–June closed Mon–Fri).

Just 2km north of Rochemenier, on the D69 between Doué and Gennes, **DÉNEZÉ-SOUS-DOUÉ** is the site of the bizarre **Cave aux Sculptures** (Tues–Sun: April & May 2–6pm; June–Aug 10am–7pm; Sept 10am–6pm; €3.80). Housed under a protective concrete roof, the walls of the cavern are lined with a host of naïve and cartoon-like statuettes which mock religion, morality, the state and the ruling class. The cave was only rediscovered in 1950, so the exact origin and meanings of the sculptures are obscure, but current thinking attributes them to a sixteenth-century quasi-Masonic sect. If your French is up to it, the guardian can point out figures thought to represent François I and Catherine de Médicis.

There's another troglodyte farming hamlet at **La Fosse des Forges** (Feb & Nov Sat & Sun 2–6pm; March–May & Oct 10.30am–12.30pm & 2–6pm;

June–Sept 9.30am–7pm; €4.50). The site isn't as substantial as Rochemenier's, but it's run with dedication by the owner, who plans to retire to his own troglodyte house here. You'll need French to make the most of his tour, but everything is pointed out with delightful enthusiasm, from eel traps to chimneys and traditional feather dusters. To get there, take the tiny D214 out of Doué-la-Fontaine to the tiny village of **FORGES**, 4km north, and follow the signs for 1km.

Montreuil-Bellay

Approached from the north, **MONTREUIL-BELLAY**, 18km south of Saumur, presents one of the most idyllic views in the region. On the far side of the old stone bridge across the Thouet, the château rises up like the very model of a medieval castle, its giant chapel, sturdy fortifications and whimsical turrets looming high above feathery ranks of poplars that sway and stir in constant motion on the banks of the river.

As is clear from its imposingly elevated situation, the **château** (April–Oct Mon & Wed–Sun 10am–noon & 2–5.30pm; guided tour €7, grounds only €3.50) began life as a defensive fortress, one of many built by the aggressive Foulques Nerra, an eleventh-century count of Anjou. Most of the present structure, however, dates from the fifteenth century, under the d'Harcourt family. The guided tour (usually in French only) of the main body of the d'Harcourts' château, the **Château Neuf**, takes you through a succession of late-medieval rooms sumptuously decorated at various points between the fifteenth and twentieth centuries, as well as the giant kitchens. You may be shown the two superimposed d'Harcourt **family chapels** – the lower of which was gorgeously frescoed in the 1480s, with angels making music in the sky-blue vaulting and a large Crucifixion filling one wall – but they are often closed to visitors except those on group tours; you could try asking. You're sure, however, to be shown the seventeenth-century bedroom of the beautiful but rebellious **duchesse de Longueville**, who was exiled here between 1652 and 1654, and the furnishings and religious objets d'art collected by the late Mme Augustine de Grandmaison. But the château's proudest treasure is the elaborately studded **marriage coffer** of Marguerite de Valois, "la reine Margot", which dates from her later-annulled marriage to Henri IV. At the end of the tour you are shown the vaulted **cellars**, where you can taste (and buy) the wines made by the current owners. The "grounds only" ticket allows you to explore the **canons' lodgings**, a curious quartet of diminutive towers with roofs like witches' hats. Each had a private wine cellar and steam bath inside – surprising amenities for monk's cells.

The barn-like Gothic **collégiale** is visited separately from the château (daily 8.30am–7pm) – on Sunday mornings you can even see the parishioners trooping across the drawbridge to Mass. Note the black funereal band halfway up the wall, which displays the coats of arms of the château's various deceased owners. The **town** preserves substantial vestiges of its medieval walls, notably a powerful gatehouse, but the most appealing place to wander is down beside the **River Thouet**, where paths and a pontoon bridge lead to some idyllic picnic spots. In summer, you can rent canoes and pedalos too.

Practicalities

Bus #9 provides a skeletal service to Doué-la-Fontaine, with just three buses daily. The **tourist office**, place du Concorde (March & Oct Mon–Fri 9.30am–12.30pm & 2–5.30pm; April–June & second half of Sept Tues–Sat

9.30am–12.30pm & 2–6pm, Sun 10.30am–12.30pm & 2.30–5.30pm; July & Aug Mon–Sat 9.30am–12.30pm & 2–7pm, Sun 10.30am–12.30pm & 1.30–5.30pm; 1–14 Sept Mon–Sat 9.30am–12.30pm & 2–6pm; ℡02.41.52.32.39, ✉office-de-tourisme@ville-montreuil-bellay.fr) can provide lots of information on the town's historic buildings.

There are just two **hotels**, but both of them are good. The *Relais du Berry*, 96 rue Nationale (℡02.41.53.10.10; ❸) has a relaxing, spacious feel, with a refurbished older wing and a modern annexe offering smart rooms with château views; the *Splendid' Hôtel*, 139 rue du Docteur-Gaudrez (℡02.41.53.10.00, Ⓦwww.splendid-hotel.fr; ❷), is relatively inexpensive and old-fashioned. Guests at both can use the heated pool and sauna facilities at the *Relais*. The *Demeure des Petits Augustins*, place des Augustins (℡02.41.52.33.88, ✉moniqueguezenecbb@minitel.net; ❹) is run by a local history enthusiast and offers three antique-furnished **chambres d'hôtes** in a gorgeous, vine-covered, seventeenth-century townhouse.

The *Splendid' Hôtel* has a generally decent if sometimes hit-and-miss **restaurant**. For more eating options, try the *Auberge des Isles* (℡02.41.50.37.37), which does simple grills and salads at an attractive location down on the riverbank; or the rather more formal *Hostellerie St-Jean*, 432 rue Nationale (℡02.41.52.30.41; closed Sun evening and Mon), where you'll find elegant and traditional cooking. The comfortable, three-star **campsite**, *Camping Les Nobis* (℡02.41.38.72.88, ✉camping.les.nobis@aol.com; closed Oct–Easter) has a good location beside the Thouet and a swimming pool.

Le Coudray-Macouard and the château de Brézé

Eight kilometres north of Montreuil-Bellay, on the road to Saumur, the village of **LE COUDRAY-MACOUARD** is another contender for the title of the region's prettiest village. An attractive, twelfth-century chapel and the sixteenth-century **Seigneurie du Bois** are the chief monuments, but just wandering about the medieval streets is enjoyable enough, especially in summer, when there's usually a serious attempt at the local "village in bloom" prize under way.

The **château de Brézé**, 7km west of Le-Coudray-Macouard (daily: March to mid-Nov 10am–6.30pm; €6.70), is outwardly impressive enough: a typically noble sixteenth-century château built in creamy-white tufa with an unusually deep dry moat. The interior décor is very refined, but what goes on underground is the main point of the visit. Just over a kilometre of tunnels was hacked out of the soft rock beneath the château in the medieval era; the stone was used for building, and the tunnels for defence and grain storage. A guide will take you on a tour round the many chambers, staircases, storerooms and passages. The largest chamber is used to stage a melodramatic sound-and-light show, with images of troglodyte sites projected onto the walls while spooky music plays.

Le Puy-Notre-Dame and around

The tiny village of **LE PUY-NOTRE-DAME**, 6km west of Montreuil-Bellay, is dwarfed by the **collégiale Notre-Dame**, a church whose bizarre size is explained by its position on the pilgrim route to Santiago de Compostela and by its possession of a great medieval relic: the **Girdle of the Virgin**. Pregnant women in particular may want to pay their respects to the jewelled reliquary –

the *ceinture* is supposed to help childbirth, and was borrowed at various times by Anne de Bretagne (see box on p.89) and Anne of Austria, the mother of Louis XIV. The church itself is an airy, pale-walled space under a lofty Angevin vault. Look out for the choir stalls, riotously carved in the sixteenth century.

A signpost beside the collégiale signals the beginning of a two-hour **circular walk** through the woods and vineyards south of the village, one of a number set up in the region by the Parc Naturel Régional Loire-Anjou-Touraine (see box on p.233). At the edge of the village is a small museum of silk-making, **La Soie Vivante** (mid-May to Oct Tues–Sat 10am–noon & 2–6pm, Mon & Sun 2–6pm; €4), based around two working Jacquard looms and various silk-related paraphernalia. It's modest enough, but an interesting reminder of this almost-vanished local industry.

At **SANZIERS**, 3km southeast of Le Puy, you can visit the **Cave Champignonnière de St-Maur** (daily: March–Oct 10am–6pm; €4), another underground mushroom farm-cum-troglodyte attraction. The sixteenth-century quarry site is moderately impressive, and there's a rather good demonstration (though in French only) of how various rustic quarry tools were once used, as well as tastings of the proprietor's wines and, of course, his mushrooms.

If you want **to stay**, the enterprising owner of the silk museum runs a friendly and efficient **chambres d'hôtes** operation, *Le Chai de la Paleine* (T02.41.38.28.25, Wwww.relais-du-bien-etre.com; ④). The *Château Tour Grise*, rue des Ducs d'Aquitaine (T02.41.38.82.42, Ephilippe.gourdon@latourgrise.com; ③), is a more attractive option, its two stone-walled and heavily-beamed rooms set in the converted outbuildings of an organic wine-maker's manor house, overlooking a courtyard garden.

West of Saumur

Once you're free of the clutches of the suburbs of Saumur, the riverside **D751** becomes one of the loveliest roads in the whole Loire region, squeezed between the escarpment and the south bank of the river. Drivers and cyclists with time on their hands can potter along this delightful backroad, passing miniature meadows and diminutive vegetable plots shaded by poplars and willows, while all the heavier, Angers-bound traffic rushes along the trunk road on the opposite bank.

If you don't have transport you could catch **bus** #5 from Saumur towards Angers, but the service is very infrequent (2–4 daily), especially outside school terms, so check the timetables carefully before committing yourself. You'd do better to hire a bicycle in Saumur.

Chenehutte and Trèves

Just beyond the suburban conurbation of St-Hilaire-St-Florent, a warren of tufa caves has been made over into a tourist attraction, the **Musée de Champignon** and **Parc Miniature Pierre et Lumière** (mid-Feb to mid-Nov daily 10am–7pm; €11.50 for both tours, €6.50 for one only; Wwww.musee-du-champignon.com). You can visit either attraction separately, or both together. If you haven't seen mushrooms growing underground, the former is worth trying, but the *parc miniature* is more impressive, an underground collection of scale models of Loire châteaux and cities, all of them cunningly sculpted out of the soft rock. There's a good Fontevraud measuring about 2m square.

Eight kilometres out of Saumur, at **CHENEHUTTE-LES-TUFFEAUX**, the sixteenth-century priory atop the cliff has been turned into the luxury *Le Prieuré* **hotel** (☎02.41.67.90.14, ✉prieure@grandesetapes.fr; ❼). If you want to stay here, make sure to book one of the actual priory rooms – Hilton meets King Arthur in style – rather than the modern pavilions in the grounds.

A couple of kilometres further down the road, the higgledy-piggledy **église St-Aubin** in the pretty hamlet of **TREVES** hides a wonderfully carved porphyry font and the effigy of one Robert le Maczon, a companion of Joan of Arc, who built the adjacent **keep**, now ruined.

Cunault

The pot of gold at the end of the D751 is the giant **église Notre-Dame** at **CUNAULT**, 12km west of Saumur, a Romanesque pilgrimage church overlooking a beguiling bend in the Loire. The powerful, eleventh-century **belfry** is the earliest such tower in Anjou. From the western portal, with its sculpted Virgin and Flamboyant Gothic window, you can gaze in one magnificently untrammelled line down the nave to the high altar. Romanesque imagination is given free rein in the sculpture of the hundreds of capitals, with demons vomiting forth the column beneath them or supporting the vault above, Atlas-like, on their arched backs. Other capitals are more restrained: simple but elegant representations of the traditional acanthus leaf. The curving **ambulatory**, where hundreds of pilgrims would once have filed around the sanctuary, is filled with light. Tucked away on its south side is the extraordinary thirteenth-century **chasse de St-Maxenceul**, a reliquary chest carved from a single block of walnut with scenes of Christ, the Virgin and the apostles. On the north side, look out for an awkward but strangely moving early sixteenth-century **pietà** in polychrome stone. If you can time your visit for **Gregorian Mass** (chanted by a visiting choir every Sunday at 11.15am) or one of the summer **concerts** (July & Aug: Sun at 5pm) or **organ recitals** (May: Sun at 5pm), so much the better.

The ancient, stony **village** is tiny but still manages to show off a handsome Renaissance priory and a private **château** (closed to visitors), built in a rambling, mongrel mixture of architectural styles, mostly in the nineteenth century. The **chambres d'hôtes** *Les Bateliers*, 28 rue de Beauregard (☎06.67.18.66.73, ⊛http:bateliers.chez.tiscali.fr; ❸) offers a rare chance to stay in a cave room; the two ordinary rooms are attractive enough, but try to book the "troglodyte" suite (❹), a beautiful vaulted chamber with a sunny terrace outside and a kitchen within.

Gennes

Just over a kilometre beyond Cunault, **GENNES** is best known for its **Roman amphitheatre**, signposted off the D70 on the way southwest out of town (April–June Sun 3–6.30pm; July & Aug Mon–Fri & Sun 10am–6.30pm; €3); if you speak French the guided tour is interesting, but there's little to see apart from a sunken, sandy circle surrounded by broken-down stone seats. More rewarding is the view from the **monument to the cadets of Saumur** (see box on p.229), perched high on the hilltop beside the ruined church of **St-Eusèbe**. The back lanes immediately inland are worth exploring for the concentration of Megalithic **dolmens and menhirs**, but you'll need a good map to track down more than a handful; tourist offices can help – try the Saumur or Angers branches (see p.225 and p.254).

A distinctive suspension bridge, built immediately after World War II, leads across to the north bank, where the village of **LES ROSIERS-SUR-LOIRE** is distinguished by a curious Renaissance bell tower rising high above the main square. The village's charm is, however, spoilt by the trunk road.

Travel details

Trains

Saumur to: Angers (14 daily; 20–30min); Tours (12 daily; 45min).

Buses

Doué-la-Fontaine to: Angers (4–6 daily; 1hr); Montreuil-Bellay (3 daily; 40min); Saumur (2–4 daily; 30min).
Saumur to: Angers via the south bank (2–4 daily; 1hr 30min); Angers via the north bank (4 daily; 1hr–1hr 30min); Fontevraud (4–6 daily; 35min); Le Mans (1–2 daily; 2hr).

Central Anjou

CHAPTER 6

Highlights

✳ **The Tapestry of the Apocalypse** Housed in the château d'Angers, this medieval masterpiece depicts the unfolding of the Apocalypse in one hundred metres of vivid, woven colour. **See p.256**

✳ **Château du Plessis-Bourré** Inside this belligerent-looking moated castle is a fascinating ceiling dating back to the fifteenth century, painted with alchemical symbols and riddles. **See p.269**

✳ **Château de Montgeoffroy** There's a *Marie Celeste* feel to this eighteenth-century château, built and decorated just before the Revolution and scarcely touched since. **See p.272**

✳ **The Layon valley** The sunny microclimate of the Côteaux du Layon allows the local wine-growers to produce some of France's finest sweet white wines. **See p.264**

✳ **Château de Brissac** The tour of this extravagant seventeenth-century château offers a taste of aristocratic opulence; you can even stay in some of the originally furnished rooms. **See p.266**

✳ **Les Tonnelles, Béhuard** Les Tonnelles is one of Anjou's finest gastronomic restaurants, and also its best located, on the holy island of Béhuard. **See p.263**

✳ **Au Cabernet d'Anjou, Le Thoureil** This ancient mariners' bar has a lovely terrace overlooking the Loire – a great place for drinks at sunset. **See p.268**

△ Gatehouse at Le Plessis-Bourré

6

Central Anjou

njou is much the most diverse of the Loire's regions, unsure whether to face west towards the sea or inland up the "royal Loire". Historically, it is linked with its eastern neighbours far more than with Brittany to the west – the counts of Anjou ruled Touraine in the eleventh century, and the two regions formed the heart of the Plantagenêt empire some two hundred years later. And yet Anjou has a remarkably different feel from other Loire valley regions. Dark, rugged schist replaces pale, creamy stone as the favoured building material, the horizons seem to widen and there's the faintest tang of sea salt in the air – a sensation that grows stronger as you travel west. This chapter covers only **central Anjou**, the heartland of the region in the vicinity of Angers. The southeastern pocket, known historically as the Saumurois, is covered separately in chapter 5.

Anjou's capital, **Angers**, is a spruce cathedral town with a single unmissable highlight, the Tapestry of the Apocalypse, housed in the city's ruined château. You could happily spend a few days visiting the city's other churches and museums, and enjoying its modest but upbeat nightlife. Otherwise, Anjou's superb vineyards are likely to lure you out into the countryside. Lazing around the Loire and its tributaries between visits to wine-makers and châteaux can fill a good summer week around Angers, as long as you have your own transport – otherwise it's a two-buses-a-day problem, or no buses at all. Worthy exceptions are the vineyards at **Savennières**, which you can reach by train, and **St-Aubin-de-Luigne**, where you can rent rowing boats during the summer. If you want to explore the beguiling villages and gentle wine valleys of the **Layon** and **Aubance**, you'll definitely need a car or bicycle.

Anjou has more **châteaux** than any other Loire region, but most are in private hands and can't be visited. Among the few which can, **Le Plessis-Bourré** looks like a true castle, complete with moat and drawbridge, while **Le Plessis-Macé**, retains only its outbuildings, though even these are very grand. Both are isolated in the watery countryside north of Angers. **Serrant**, south of Angers, and **Brissac**, in the Aubance valley, are seventeenth-century giants, their architecture as extravagant as their furnishings. East of Angers, the perfectly preserved interiors of **Montgeoffroy** offer a window on a more charming, eighteenth-century vision of aristocratic life. By contrast, René d'Anjou's château at **Baugé**, to the northeast, is an empty shell, albeit recently filled with a hi-tech historical museum, but the fascinating and little-visited town around it makes a worthy destination, and you could spend a few days exploring the forested countryside.

From mid-June to mid-July, the **Festival d'Anjou** (Ⓦ www.festivaldanjou .com) brings churches, châteaux and concert halls together for a programme of theatre and musical events.

Segré

Châteauneuf-sur-Sarthe

M A I N E -

Le Lion d'Angers

Le Plessis-Bourré 🏛

E T - L O I R E

Le Plessis-Macé 🏛

Montreuil-Juigné

◀ Nantes

Angers

St-Barthélemy-d'Anjou

Authion

🏛 Serrant   Bouchemaine

Les Ponts-de-Cé

Trélazé

St-Georges-sur-Loire

La Pointe

Loire

St-Saturnin

Savennières

Béhuard

Coutures

Chalonnes-sur-Loire

Corniche Angevine

Rochefort-sur-Loire

Brissac-Quincé 🏛

Aubance

La Haie-Longue

St-Aubin-de-Lugné

Layon

Beaulieu-sur-Layon

Rablay-sur-Layon

Faye-d'Anjou

Bonnezeaux

Thouarcé

Martigné-Briand

Chemillé

Aubigné-sur-Layon

Lys

Layon

▼ Cholet

Angers

As capital of the historic region of Anjou, the city of **ANGERS** (pronounced *on*-jay) maintains a certain proud distance from its neighbours – the city isn't quite on the Loire river and neither does it exactly fall within the classic Loire region. Yet Angers looks very much like a Loire town, with its ruined château gazing down on the broad River Maine and its abandoned quays recalling the long-vanished river trade. Although larger than Tours and Orléans in terms of population, the city feels homely and provincial, overshadowed by the great Breton capital of Nantes, 75km west.

On the surface, Angers is a handsome, largely nineteenth-century place – Henry James, offended by the newness of its buildings, called it "stupidly and vulgarly modernized". Even if the old quarter has mostly vanished, the town centre and medieval suburb of **La Doutre**, just across the river, retain some fine old townhouses and churches, and the **cathédrale St-Maurice** is a superb example of the twelfth-century Angevin style. Unusually, two of the city's most compelling attractions are tapestries. One is ancient – the breath-taking **Tapestry of the Apocalypse**, kept in the ruined château; the other modern – the similarly apocalyptic **Chant du Monde**, housed in a twelfth-century hospital. In the evenings, a youthful population and the presence of two major universities help drive a relaxed **bar** and **restaurant** scene.

Some history

Angers gets its name from a Celtic tribe, the **Andecavi**, but only really took shape under the Romans, as Juliomagus. "Barbarian" invasions threatened the city for much of its early life, culminating in destructive Viking raids in the mid-ninth century. Only under the warlike **counts of Anjou**, who took control from the tenth century, was the city made truly secure – in fact, their efforts ensured that it became the power-base of a miniature empire. Under the prolific castle builder, **Foulque Nerra**, the "Black Falcon" (987–1040), the Angevins managed to subdue both the Saumurois and Touraine, and were only prevented from making further conquests by the obduracy of the counts of Blois. Later generations enlarged their territories by marriage rather than warfare – Count Foulques V brought the Maine region, to the north, within the family fief, while his son, **Geoffroi "Plantagenêt"** – so-called because he habitually planted a sprig of broom (*genêt*) in his headgear – wed Matilda of England, daughter of Henry I, in 1128, gaining control of Normandy. Geoffroi's son, Henri, pulled off an even bigger coup by marrying Eleanor of Aquitaine in 1152, thereby effectively taking over her vast dominions in southwestern France (see box on p.235). Just two years later he became Henry II of England. Angers grew rapidly in the brief Plantagenêt heyday, even if its overlords actually preferred to live elsewhere.

After the Plantagenêt collapse, the city passed into the hands of the French royal family. As regent, Louis IX's mother, Blanche de Castille, had the city encircled by giant **fortifications** from 1230, the walls being completed in just ten years in the face of the waxing power of an independent Brittany. Monasteries grew in the shelter of the walls, and Angers' life as a major **university town** began with the founding of a school of law in 1244. In the mid-fourteenth century, the French king Jean le Bon granted Anjou as a semi-autonomous appanage to his son Louis who, as the first **duc d'Anjou**, set about raising the status of his new city with commissions for new château buildings and for a great tapestry series depicting the apocalypse. Louis' grandson, René d'Anjou (see box on p.255), made further improvements, establishing Angers as a thriving artistic and mercantile centre. It continued to flourish into the sixteenth century and beyond, the city's now greatly expanded **university** attracting two of Renaissance France's greatest writers: the satirist Rabelais, from Chinon, and the poet Joachim du Bellay, from western Anjou.

In the 1790s, the Catholic and fiercely anti-revolutionary armies of the Vendée helped throw the entire region into turmoil, but like so many Loire towns, it was the arrival of the railways in the mid-nineteenth century that most affected the city, as the port trade slowly dwindled and died. In 1875 a major **Catholic university** was established immediately west of the city centre. Today, the 10,000 students at "*la Catho*" still make up a powerful presence in the city, along with their 16,000 rivals at the modern, public Université d'Angers, founded in 1971 on the opposite bank of the River Maine. Meanwhile, the Institut National d'Horticulture, or INH, turns out hundreds of plant experts each year, many of them bound for highly technical jobs in Anjou's thriving horticulture industry.

Arrival and information

The **gare SNCF** is south of the centre, about a ten-minute walk from the château. Bus #6 (#25 on Sun) makes the journey to the tourist office and château, while buses #1and #16 will take you to the central place du Ralliement; a flat-rate **bus** ticket, which you can buy on board, costs €1. The **gare routière** is down by the river, just past the Pont de Verdun on place Molière.

The main **tourist office** is on place Kennedy, facing the château (May Mon–Sat 9am–6pm, Sun 10am–6pm; June–Sept Mon–Sat 9am–7pm, Sun 10am–6pm; Oct–April Mon 2–6pm, Tues–Sat 9am–6pm, Sun 10am–1pm; ☎02.41.23.50.00, Ⓦwww.angers-tourisme.com). You can buy a **museum pass** (€8), which allows access to the tapestries as well as the city's museums and galleries. Useful **online** information can be found at the city's official website, Ⓦwww.ville-angers.fr.

Accommodation

Angers' thriving commercial life pulls in a steady business clientele, so there's rarely a problem finding somewhere to stay. Charming city-centre hotels, especially those at the budget end of the scale, are in shorter supply, however, so it's worth booking ahead.

Hotels

Hôtel d'Anjou 1 bd Foch ☎02.41.88.24.82, Ⓦwww.hoteldanjou.fr. Part of the Best Western chain, but not overwhelmingly large or commercial, with just over fifty rooms. The prices guarantee a largely business clientele, but its central location makes it a useful option for visitors too. ❻

Hôtel du Centre 12 rue St-Laud ☎02.41.87.45.07. Battered but cheerful rooms above a central bar on a pedestrianized street, though noisy night-time chatter from the street is a drawback in front-facing rooms. ❶

Hôtel Continental 12–14 rue Louis de Romain ☎02.41.86.94.94, Ⓔle.continental@wanadoo.fr. This well-equipped and well-run hotel offers good service and a bright pastel decor. The location on a quiet street just off place Ralliement is good, but note that it can get busy during the week with a business clientele. ❸

Hôtel des Lices 25 rue des Lices

☎02.41.87.44.10. The setting is very genteel, in a balustraded townhouse on an elegant town-centre street, but the prices are a bargain and the welcome genuine. Rooms are clean and modern. Closed first half of Aug. ❷

Hôtel du Mail 8 rue des Ursules ☎02.41.25.05.25, Ⓔhotedumailangers@yahoo.fr. Old-fashioned and extremely attractive two-star set in a seventeenth-century building with a courtyard. The two dozen rooms are tastefully done in fresh, bright colours and the location in a quiet corner of the centre is excellent. Parking is available for a small extra charge. ❸

Hôtel St-Julien 9 place du Ralliement ☎02.41.88.41.62, Ⓦwww.destination-anjou.com/saintjulien. Large hotel right in the centre of the city, offering a good spread of over-modernized but perfectly acceptable rooms. Some of the prettier little rooms under the roof have views over town. ❸

Hostels and campsite

Centre d'Accueil du Lac de Maine 49 ave du Lac de Maine ☎02.41.22.32.10, Ⓦwww.lacde-maine.fr. Rather swish hostel-style accommodation, complete with extensive sports facilities, a 20min ride southwest of the town; bus #6 (bus #11 7.30pm–midnight, bus #26 on Sun) either from the train station or bd Générale-de-Gaulle. Private rooms €24.20, dorms €9.95. You can rent canoes at the Base Nautique in the complex. There's also a campsite here (see below).

Camping du Lac de Maine ave du Lac de Maine ☎02.41.73.05.03, Ⓕ02.41.73.02.20. Sandy campsite next to a lake off the D111 south of the city centre; it's reachable on bus #6 (bus #11 7.30pm–midnight, bus #26 on Sun). Closed Dec–Feb.

Foyer Darwin 3 rue Darwin ☎02.41.22.61.20, Ⓔcontact@foyerdarwin.com. Inexpensive young workers' hostel twenty minutes' walk west of La Doutre, near the Belle-Beille campus; take bus #6 or #8.

The city centre

The city centre slopes gently down to the bank of the Maine, circumscribed to the south and east by a series of wide, busy boulevards which follow the line of the old city walls, demolished on Napoleon's orders in 1807. The heart of Angers is the nineteenth-century, Neoclassical **place du Ralliement**, with the two stucco-fronted and now pedestrianized avenues of **rue Lenepveu** and **rue St-Laud**, just to the north, forming the city's main axes. Medieval Angers lies immediately west, where the **château** guards the main bridge across the Maine, the **Pont de la Basse-Chaine**, and the **cathédrale St-Maurice** towers above the wide river quays.

The château

The **château** (daily: May–Aug 9.30am–6.30pm; Sept–April 10am–5.30pm; €5.50) is a formidable early medieval fortress whose air of impregnability is accentuated by the darkness of the western Anjou schist from which it's built, offset by pale bands of tufa. The kilometre-long curtain wall is buttressed by seventeen circular towers – once crowned by pepper-pot roofs – that grip the rock below. You can stroll round the length of these ramparts, looking down on the town, the château gardens first created under René d'Anjou (see box below) and the waters of the Maine. In the centre of the château enclosure are a few heavily restored remnants of the **great palace** of the counts of Anjou: the chapel was built in about 1410 by Louis II and Yolande d'Aragon, as were the adjacent royal apartments, to which René d'Anjou added a vaulted gallery in 1450. Both were bombed in World War II, but have since been reconstructed. They are now used for occasional tapestry exhibitions.

Anjou's last king

As claimant to the thrones of Naples, Sicily and Jerusalem, as well as ruler of the duchy of Anjou in the mid-fifteenth century, **Le Bon Roi René** (Good King René) styled himself a king rather than a duke, though he never succeeded in actually controlling any part of his royal patrimony. René twice failed to conquer Naples, but at least his claim was convincing, as it had been directly bequeathed to Louis I of Anjou, his grandfather. The nominal title of King of Jerusalem, by contrast, had simply been bought by an ancestor, Charles I of Anjou, in 1277. The only coronation René attended was that of his friend Charles VII, in 1429, with Joan of Arc alongside (see box on p.174).

But René's court, which moved between Angers, Baugé and Saumur – as well as up the Loire and then down the Rhône to Provence – was certainly regal. Chivalric ideals were celebrated in elaborate festivals and pageants in which René himself cut a splendid figure, dressed in black armour and riding a black-coated horse emblazoned with the insignia of his Order of the Crescent Moon. His motto was "burning desire", and he wrote a classic of romance literature, *Le Livre du Cœur d'amour épris*.

It was the swansong of the Middle Ages, and didn't last. René had no sons and was too poor to supply his daughter with an adequate dowry. Princesse Marguerite was eventually married off to Henry VI of England, but after years of interminable English warfare she fled back to France, where Louis XI offered her protection in exchange for Anjou and Touraine. She agreed, effectively bringing Anjou's autonomy to an end.

The Tapestry of the Apocalypse

The **Tapestry of the Apocalypse** was woven between 1373 and 1382 for Louis I of Anjou; it was originally 140m long, of which 100m now survives. From the start, it was treated as a masterpiece, and only brought out to decorate the cathedral of Angers on major festival days. It takes as its text John's vision of the Apocalypse, as described in the Book of Revelation, recreating the saint's vision in seventy stunningly rendered, nightmarish scenes. If you're dressed for a hot summer day, be warned that air conditioning keeps the temperature inside low.

The sheer grandeur of the conception is overwhelming, but the tapestry's horrifying brilliance lies in its details: the skeletal face of the horseman Death, the minutely observed clothing of the servants of God fighting the Dragon, and the flowers and mountains and trees that form a disturbingly naturalistic backdrop. Perhaps even more impressive are the colours: rich golds, greens and blues woven on alternating deep red and dark blue ground. Amazing as they are, the original colours were even more vivid – as you can see if you buy the handy English-language booklet (€5.50), which contains photographs of the tapestry's unfaded reverse side. Astonishingly, this is no chaotic tangle of wool ends, as would be normal for a tapestry, but a perfectly finished mirror image of the front which remained hidden and pristinely preserved behind the tapestry's back lining until it was removed for repair in 1981.

If you plan to follow the story right through, the booklet comes in handy but a Bible would be even better. In brief: the Day of Judgement is signalled by the breaking of the seven seals – note the four horsemen – and the seven angels blowing their trumpets. As the battle of Armageddon rages, Satan – first depicted as a seven-headed red dragon, then as the seven-headed lion-like Beast – marks his earthly followers. The holy forces retaliate by breaking the seven vials of plagues, whereupon the Whore of Babylon appears mounted on the Beast. She is challenged by the Word of God, seen riding a galloping horse, who chases the hordes of Satan into the lake of fire, allowing the establishment of the heavenly Jerusalem.

You'll need a drink after all that, and handily enough you can head straight out of the château and into the **Maison du Vin de l'Anjou**, 5bis place Kennedy (March–Dec Tues–Sat 9am–1pm & 3–6.30pm, Sun 9am–1pm), where the very professional and helpful staff will offer you wine to taste before you buy, and provide lists of wine-growers to visit.

Cathédrale St-Maurice

The most dramatic approach to the **cathédrale St-Maurice** is via the quayside, from where a long flight of steps leads straight up to the mid-twelfth-century portal – which shows another version of the Apocalypse. Built in the 1150s and 1160s, the cathedral exemplifies the Plantagenêt style – in fact, it's probably the earliest example in France of this influential architectural development in which the keystones of the vault are raised above the level of the ordinary wall arches, creating a dome-like effect. The three aisle-less bays of the nave span a distance of over 16m, the lofty Plantagenêt or Angevin vaulting creating structural strength as well as a faintly Byzantine feel.

The earliest stained glass, in the north wall of the nave, is late twelfth or early thirteenth-century; the window depicting the Virgin and Child is especially famous for its design and rich colours. In the choir, one window is dedicated to Thomas Becket, murdered on the orders of Henry Plantagenêt. The fifteenth-century rose windows in the transepts are impressive, with Christ's earthly suffering, in the north transept, facing Christ in Glory to the south –

note the red and blue of his robe, inspired by the Tapestry of the Apocalypse. The stone carving on the capitals and the supports for the gallery are beautiful, but the cathedral is over-zealously furnished with a grandiose high altar and pulpit and a set of tapestries that can't compete with Angers' other woven treasures.

If the river damp is getting into your bones, you could always light a candle to **St Maurice**, who is traditionally invoked against gout and cramps. His sainthood dates from his captaincy of the largely Christian Theban Legion, which was massacred in the late third century for refusing to sacrifice to the old Roman gods.

Galerie David d'Angers and Musée des Beaux-Arts

Angers' most famous son took the name of his home city as a *nom de plume*. **David d'Angers** (1788–1856) was the premier sculptor of the post-Napoleonic era, and his works seem to grace every major public building in the country, most notably the frieze of Paris's Panthéon. In Angers, his statue of St Cecilia adorns the cathedral chancel, but his best works are exhibited in the **Galerie David d'Angers**, a space dramatically created by glassing over the ruins of a thirteenth-century church, the **église Toussaint** (mid-June to mid-Sept daily 9.30am–6.30pm; mid-Sept to mid-June Tues–Sun 10am–noon & 2–6pm; €2). The sculptor was a prime activist in mid-nineteenth-century republican struggles and a close friend of many great Romantic artists and thinkers of the time, many of whom are celebrated here in busts or bronze medallions. You can also visit the adjacent **cloister**, a smoothly arcaded space.

The **Musée des Beaux-Arts**, at 10 rue du Musée (mid-June to mid-Sept daily 9.30am–6.30pm; mid-Sept to mid-June Tues–Sun 10am–noon & 2–6pm; €2), is housed in the **Logis Barrault**, a proudly decorated mansion built by a wealthy late fifteenth-century mayor. Years of extensive restoration have cleaned up – and in some places entirely remade – the Flamboyant Gothic stone carving, and the museum inside reopened in 2004. Eighteenth- and nineteenth-century paintings dominate the collection, with works by Watteau, Chardin and Fragonard, as well as Ingres' operatic *Paolo et Francesca* – the same subject depicted by Rodin in *The Kiss* – and a small collection devoted to Boucher's *Génie des Arts*. You'll also find Lorenzo Lippi's beautiful *La Femme au Masque*, and a room devoted to the history of Angers.

The rest of town

In front of the cathedral, on place Ste-Croix, is the town's favourite carpentry detail, the unlikely genitals of one of the carved characters on the medieval **Maison d'Adam**. A block north, **rue de l'Oisellerie** is lined with carved, half-timbered houses that were once bird-shops (*oiselleries*). A few steps further west, **place du Ralliement** is the hub of modern Angers and the site of the nineteenth-century **Théâtre Municipal**.

The main shopping street is **rue Lenepveu**, whose main sight is the **Hôtel Pincé**, at no. 32. The mansion's facade crawls with Italianate decoration, while inside is the collection of the **Musée Pincé** (mid-June to mid-Sept daily 9.30am–6.30pm; mid-Sept to mid-June Tues–Sun 10am–noon & 2–6pm; €2), a mixed bag of antiquities, mostly ceramics from Greece, China and Japan. The staircase is a beautiful piece of Renaissance craftsmanship, however, as is the medallioned stone roof on the first floor.

If the cathedral hasn't sated your appetite for Angevin vaulting, make for the **église St-Serge**, on ave Mairie-Talet, north of the centre (Mon–Sat 9am–7pm, Sun 2–6pm; free). Formerly part of an abbey – you can visit the chapter room, cloister and refectory – it is now enclosed within the university grounds. Inside the church, a superb early Gothic choir rises from the slenderest of columns. Close by is the verdant and relaxing **Jardin des Plantes** (8am–dusk; free).

La Doutre

The district facing the château from across the river is known as **La Doutre**, from the French *d'outre Maine*, which simply means "the other side of the Maine". Like Paris's Left Bank, it's the focus of the city's student life and has a relatively relaxed, downbeat feel; similarly, it preserves a few mansions and houses dating from the medieval period. The riverfront is dominated by the elite **ENSAM**, the Ecole Nationale des Arts et Métiers, which hot-houses the cream of the region's students.

Abbaye de Ronceray and la Trinité

Fronting onto La Doutre's central square, place de la Laiterie, the **Abbaye de Ronceray** was founded by Foulques Nerra in the early eleventh century, but its ancient buildings are now occupied by one of France's elite *grandes écoles*, training the leading students of aerospace technology. The abbey church hosts art exhibitions, and it's worth visiting just to see the Romanesque galleries of the old abbey.

Inside the twelfth-century **église de la Trinité**, an exquisite Renaissance wooden spiral staircase fails to mask a great piece of medieval bodging – the corner wall is bent around the adjacent abbey. The high vaulting of the nave is unusual, the ribs of the middle section meeting inside a stone ring offset by a tiny dome behind, which gives a delightful effect like a suspended spider's web. Perhaps the design was too ambitious, as a significant twist in the line of the roof has developed over the course of the centuries.

Musée Jean Lurçat et de la Tapisserie Contemporaine

In the north of the area, a short way from the Pont de la Haute-Chaine (about fifteen minutes' walk from the château), the **Hôpital St-Jean**, at 4 boulevard Arago, was built by Henry Plantagenêt in 1174 as a hospital for the poor, a function it continued to fulfil until 1854. With its airy Angevin vault springing energetically from two perfect rows of columns, it makes a dramatic setting for the **Musée Jean Lurçat et de la Tapisserie Contemporaine** (mid-June to mid-Sept daily 9.30am–6.30pm; mid-Sept to mid-June Tues–Sun 10am–noon & 2–6pm; €3.50), which contains the city's great twentieth-century tapestry, **Le Chant du Monde**. The tapestry sequence was designed by Jean Lurçat in 1957 in response to Angers' Tapestry of the Apocalypse, though he died nine years later before its completion (the artist's own commentary is available in English). It hangs in a vast vaulted space, the original ward for the sick, or Salle des Malades. The first four tapestries deal with "La Grande Menace", the threat of nuclear war: first the bomb itself; then "Hiroshima Man", flayed and burnt, with the broken symbols of various world religions seemingly falling away from him; then the collective massacre of the "Great Charnel House"; and finally the last dying rose falling with the post-Holocaust ash through black space – the "End of Everything". From then on, the tapestries celebrate the joys of life: "Man in Glory in Peace", "Water and Fire", "Champagne" ("that blissful ejaculation", according to Lurçat); "Conquest of Space", "Poetry" and "Sacred Ornaments". Modern tapestry is an unfamiliar art, and at first Lurçat's use of stark, bright colours on a heavy black ground can be overwhelming – or even uncomfortably reminiscent of a heavy metal T-shirt. The Romanesque **cloisters** at the back are also worth a peek.

There are more modern tapestries in the adjoining building, where a significant collection has been built up around the donation by Lurçat's widow of several of his paintings, ceramics and tapestries. Among the most interesting works are the abstract, almost three-dimensional tapestries of Thomas Gleb, who died in Angers in 1991. If you want to explore Angers' contemporary tapestry micro-industry further, the neighbouring **Centre Régional d'Art Textile**, 3 boulevard Daviers (Mon–Fri 10am–noon & 2–4pm), can put you in touch with artists at three local *ateliers* and let you know where to find private exhibitions.

The suburbs

The château de Pignerolle, in the satellite village of **ST-BARTHELÉMY D'ANJOU**, 4km east of Angers (signposted off the N147), is home to the **Espace Européen de la Communication** (April–Nov daily 10am–12.30pm & 2.30–6pm; Nov–March Sat 2.30–6pm, Sun 10am–12.30pm & 2.30–6.30pm; €7; Ⓦ www.museecommunication.org), a typically histrionic French science and technology museum. It's quite good fun, with everything from Leonardo's helicopter drawings to German submarines brought into play, and fantastical scenes of the future, but don't expect to come out much the wiser.

For something completely different, you could go on a guided tour around the **Distillerie Cointreau**, just off the ring road between Angers and St-Barthelemy d'Anjou, where the famous orange liqueur has been distilled since the mid-nineteenth century (tours May, June, Sept & Oct Mon–Sat at 10.30am & 3pm, Sun also 4.30pm; July & Aug daily at 10.30am, 2.30pm, 3.30pm & 4.30pm; Nov, Dec & Feb–April Mon–Sat at 3pm, Sun also 4.30pm; call ☎02.41.31.50.50 for times of tours in English; €5.50; take bus #7 from boulevard Maréchal Foch). You'll learn a lot about the Cointreau brothers and how marvellous the drink is, a little bit about distilling techniques and very little about the recipe – which isn't quite as secret as Cointreau like to make out, if the number of rival brands of *triple sec* is anything to go by. You get a little sip of a cocktail at the end, but the highlight is definitely the rows of gleaming copper stills.

The **Musée de l'Ardoise** (July to mid-Sept Tues–Sun 2–6pm; mid-Sept to Nov & mid-Feb to June Sun 2–6pm; €5.40; Ⓦ www.multimania.com/museeardoise) is rather lost in the industrial satellite village of **TRELAZE**, 2km southeast of the centre. It's not a museum as such, rather a demonstration of traditional slate-mining techniques by former miners, on the site of an open-cast slate mine which still produces some of the finest-quality slate in the world. It helps if you understand a little French, but just watching a sexagenarian split a giant block of stone into millimetre-perfect, size-graded slates using a big wooden hammer and a pair of outsize clogs is fairly astounding, even if you don't get the commentary. If your French is up to it, you could even arrange to visit the mine proper: call ☎02.41.96.70.70.

Eating

Angers' energetic and lively atmosphere spills over into its **restaurant** scene, which is varied and forward-looking. You can find traditional Angevin dishes, but you're by no means restricted to them.

La Cantina 9 rue de l'Oisellerie ☎02.41.87.36.34. Relaxed café-bistro serving rich dishes from south-western France such as *magret de canard* (duck steak). It's good value for lunch, with straight-forward fish and meat *plats* and salads for around €10. Closed Sun lunch and Mon & Tues evening.

Les Caves du Ralliement 9 place du Ralliement ☎02.41.88.47.77. Busy brasserie underneath the *Provence Caffè* (see below). Good for inexpensive *moules* or *steak frites* with a beer, or perhaps eel stew with a glass of wine. You can sit in the sun-shine at an outside table on the square. Closed Mon evening.

Le Grandgousier 7 rue St-Laud ☎02.41.87.81.47. Serves traditional regional dishes complemented by local wines. A good-value €14 *menu* is served before 9.30pm (Mon–Fri only), and there's also a good €24 *menu* which includes glasses of three different Anjou wines. Closed Sun.

Le Magasin 48 rue de la Parcheminerie ☎02.41.81.05.89. Trendy restaurant serving excellent modern Mediterranean food to a bright young crowd in a 1970s-retro dining room. All starters at €4.90; all mains at €11.90. Open until midnight; closed Sun.

Papagayo 44 bd Ayrault ☎02.41.87.03.35. Friendly bar-bistro near the university campus, with a great atmosphere in term-time and a kitsch little conservatory room for summer. Serves decent brasserie food, with a good lunchtime *menu* at €9 and *plats* for around €13 in the evening. Closed Sun & Mon evening.

Le Petit Mâchon 43 rue Bressigny ☎02.41.86.01.13. Low-priced local wines and inexpensive *andouillettes* and other regional delicacies. Closed Sat lunch & Sun.

Provence Caffè 9 place du Ralliement ☎02.41.87.44.15. Classic French food with an emphasis on fish and rich, Mediterranean flavours. The rather formal service and the seriousness of the food is offset by a very Provençal Van Gogh colour scheme. Expect to pay around €30, without wine. Closed Mon, Sun & three weeks in Aug.

La Rose d'Or 21 rue Delâge ☎02.41.88.38.38. Old-fashioned restaurant with ambitious gastro-nomic regional cuisine – the entrecôte, for instance, comes in a lovingly prepared Bourgueil sauce using wine from the chef's own vineyard. *Menus* from €18.50. Closed Sun evening & Mon.

Le Soufflerie 8 place du Pilori ☎02.41.87.45.32. Popular café specializing in soufflés, both large and savoury (at around €9) and small and sweet (around €6). Closed Sun, Mon & first half of Aug.

Drinking and nightlife

In the daytime, you can sample Anjou wines in the Maison du Vin de l'Anjou (see p.256). For evening drinking, make for the lively, late-opening **bars** around rue St-Laud: *Bar du Centre*, below *Hôtel du Centre*, is usually full of young Angevins, and there's a cluster of popular Irish-type places at the bottom end of the road, around place Romain. Just beyond the square, at 23 rue du Mail, *Safari* (closed Mon) is a trendy, slightly Afro-themed bar with a trendy twenty-something clientele and DJs playing funk and hip-hop at weekends. Two small, laid-back places can be found a short way down towards the river on rue de la Parcheminerie: *Au Jacare*, at 46bis, plays electro and jazz; while two doors down, *Ti Bazar* does good snacks (oysters in winter) in the early evening, then gets loud and busy towards midnight. Over in **La Doutre**, the *Sun Café*, 3bis bd Henri Arnauld, is one of the nicer student bars – though don't bother coming during the summer vacation – while *La Descente de la Marine*, at 28 quai des Carmes, is an old-time bar with a strong nautical flavour, attracting lots of students and young people who come down for an outdoor, early evening *apéro* on the quay.

Later on, *Le V.I.P. Café*, 5 rue Montaubon (closed Sun), is a friendly, relative-ly upmarket venue, with DJ nights alternating with gigs. Among the full-on **clubs**, *Le Boléro*, 38 rue St-Laud, is popular and central, with a relaxed, pop-kitsch music policy, while *Le Mid'Star*, 25 quai Félix Faure, is the biggest and best-known clubbing venue, playing a lot of R&B and house. For something more esoteric, check out the gigs, games and debates at *Le Carpe Diem*, a "café-philosophe" at 15 rue St-Maurille (☎02.41.87.50.47; closed Sun). *Chabada*, 56 bd du Doyenné, in the Monplaisir quarter just north of St-Serge (take a taxi) puts on live music; to find out about concerts, go to the FNAC music store on rue Lenepveu or check online at ⓦ www.lechabada.com.

Festivals

At the end of May, the **Tour de Scènes** festival brings rock and world music acts to the squares and quais of the city centre for four days of concerts. The **Festival Angers l'Eté** features excellent jazz and world music gigs in the atmospheric Cloître Toussaint, the cloisters behind the Galerie David d'Angers, on Tuesday and Thursday evenings throughout July and August; you can book tickets in advance through the tourist office, which also sells same-day tickets (fine days only) from noon. In early September, the festival **Les Accroche Cœurs** brings a host of theatrical companies, musicians and street-performers for three days of surreal entertainment.

Listings

Bike rental A desk in the tourist office rents bikes and mountain bikes for €11 a day. Otherwise, try Anjou Bike Center, in the nearby riverside hamlet of Blaison-Gohier (☎02.41.57.10.52, ⓦwww.anjou-bike-center.com).

Boats Numerous companies rent out canoes and run guided kayak trips on the five rivers in the vicinity of Angers. Try: Anjou Loisirs, Base de Loisirs à Notre-Dame du Marillais, St-Florent-le-Veil (on the Èvre; ☎02.41.70.56.78); Canoe Kayak Club d'Angers, 75 ave du lac de Maine (on the Maine and Lac de Maine; ☎02.41.72.07.04, ⓦwww.ckca.fr.st); Club Nautique d'Écouflant, rue de l'île St-Aubin, Écouflant (Sarthe, Mayenne, Loir, Maine; ☎02.41.34.56.38, ⓦwww.kayakecouflant.com); and Louet Evasion, Camping de Chalonnes-sur-Loire (Èvre and Loire; ☎02.41.74.91.48). The tourist office has details of more sedate trips on sightseeing boats.

Car rental ADA, place de la Gare ☎02.41.20.06.66; Autop, 30 rue Denis-Papin ☎02.41.88.54.44; Europcar, 3 ave Turpinde Crissé ☎02.41.87.87.10; Hertz, 14 rue Denis-Papin ☎2.41.88.15.16.

Cinemas The multi-screen Gaumont-Colisée, bd Foch, and Les 400 Coups, rue Claveau, are most likely to show undubbed (*version originale*, or "v.o.") foreign films.

Email and Internet You can get online at 8 rue Plantagenêt, near Les Halles; 37 rue Bressigny, near bd Foch; 25 rue de la Roë, just east of place

de la République; and 55 rue Beaurepaire, in La Doutre.

Emergencies Ambulance ☎15; Centre Hospitalier, 1 ave de l'Hôtel-Dieu ☎02.41.35.36.37.

Festivals During July and Aug, jazz and world music concerts are held on Tuesdays and Thursdays in the Cloître Toussaint as part of the Angers L'Été festival (programme details and tickets from tourist office). The Festival d'Anjou is a prestigious theatre festival using châteaux throughout the Maine-et-Loire *département* as venues from late to mid-July (details on ☎02.41.88.14.14, ⓦwww.festivaldanjou.com). There's also a three-day festival of street theatre in early September, Les Accroche Cœurs (programme details from tourist office).

Laundries 9 place Hérault; 17 rue Marceau; 15 rue Plantagnêt; 5 place de la Visitation.

Market A number of markets are held throughout the city from Tuesday to Saturday, including a flower market on place Leclerc on Saturday – Anjou is a major flower-growing region – and an organic produce market on rue St-Laud on Saturday.

Pharmacies For details of late-night pharmacies, phone the police on ☎02.41.47.75.22.

Police Commissariat, 15 rue Dupetit-Thouars ☎02.41.57.52.00.

Taxis Accueil Taxi Radio ☎02.41.73.98.20; Allo Anjou Taxi ☎02.41.87.65.00.

South of Angers

There's no particular historical or geographical integrity to the area immediately south of Angers. Most of the sights included in this section lie within the parallel valleys of the **Layon** and **Aubance**, modest streams that flow northwest towards Angers on the left bank of the Loire, watering sunny, gently undulating country thick with vines. There are a number of gentle attractions, plus the massive **château de Brissac**, but the real draw is **wine**. You can tour the vineyards of the sweet white wine *appellations* of Côteaux du Layon, Quarts de Chaume and Bonnezeaux. By contrast, **Savennières**, on the north bank of the Loire, is an outpost of excellence for dry white wine. Just north of here, you can take in a second sixteenth-century giant, the **château de Serrant**, and the pilgrim island of **Béhuard**, with its sanctuary devoted to Mary.

The whole swathe of Anjou to the south of Angers is really car- or cycle-touring territory, though you can get to Brissac-Quincé in the Aubance valley by **bus** #9 from Angers.

Château de Serrant

The **château de Serrant** lies 15km southwest of Angers, 2km short of **ST-GEORGES-SUR-LOIRE** (guided tour only: April–June, Sept & Oct daily 9.45am–noon & 2–5.15pm; July & Aug daily 10am–5.15pm; Nov & Dec Wed–Sun 10–11.30am & 2–3.30pm; €9). From the outside, it's a domineering rather than a graceful structure, its walls built in the striking Angevin combination of purply-brown schist but edged with creamy tufa, while heavy, bell-shaped slate cupolas press down on the massive corner towers. If you don't have your own transport, you could take one of the **buses** (lines #7 and #18) from Angers to St-Georges-sur-Loire, and double back on foot to the château.

Construction was begun in 1539 but the château was added to, discreetly for the most part, up until the eighteenth century. In 1759 it was sold to an Irishman, Francis Walsh, to whom Louis XV had given the title Count of Serrant as a reward for Walsh's help against the old enemy, the English – Walsh had provided the ship for Bonnie Prince Charlie to return to Scotland for the 1745 uprising. The Walsh family married into the ancient La Trémoïlle clan, whose descendants – via a Belgian offshoot – still own the château.

The massive rooms are packed with the trappings of old wealth, but the guide's endless cataloguing of the tapestries, paintings and furniture shouldn't put you off appreciating some real gems, including a complete first edition of Diderot's *Encyclopédie*. Much of the decor dates from the late nineteenth and early twentieth centuries, but it's tastefully done, and you are also shown the Renaissance staircase, the sombre private chapel designed by Hardouin Mansard, a bedroom prepared for Napoleon (who only stopped here for a couple of hours) and the vaulted kitchens.

The north bank of the Loire west of Angers

If you leave Angers via La Doutre and the north bank of the River Maine, you'll quickly pick up signs to the D111 and **BOUCHEMAINE**, an old river port just short of the mouth (*bouche*) of the Maine, some 10km from Angers. Suburban **bus** line #6 provides a regular service from Angers. There are a couple of good **restaurants**, nicely positioned down on the quayside, the most atmospheric being *Le Noë Inondable* (closed Sun), an old-fashioned Loire mariners' bar with a bright conservatory dining room added on; the food is simple but good – inexpensive steaks and fish dishes.

Roughly a kilometre downstream, **LA POINTE** lies at the actual confluence with the Loire – from here on west, the Loire attains majestic proportions in all but the driest months. It's a good place to picnic, beside the broad quays with their stone groins projecting into the wide waterway. Alternatively, try the lovingly prepared fish dishes at *La Terrasse* **restaurant**, place Ruzebouc (☎02.41.77.11.96; closed Sun), which has a good lunch *menu* (€15.50;

evenings from €22) and a big view. Plain but decent **rooms** are available at the adjacent *Hôtel Ancre de Marine* (☎02.41.77.14.46; ❸). **Canoes** and **kayaks** can be hired inexpensively from the very professional Club Nautique de Bouchemaine (☎02.41.77.22.35), just off the road between Bouchemaine and La Pointe; you can also book long, guided descents of the Loire.

Savennières

Seven kilometres downstream of Bouchemaine, on the north bank of the Loire, the comfortable village of **SAVENNIERES** is best known as an *appellation* with a huge reputation for dry whites – in fact it's regarded as one of the very few truly first-class Loire wines (see p.336). Typically, the actual area of production is tiny, with vines spread across just three hills on the fringes of the village, but the quality is exceptional. An excellent place to taste and buy is at the **Domaine du Closel**, Château des Vaults, 1 place du Mail (Mon–Sat 9am–6pm; free; Ⓦwww.savennieres-closel.com), where *madame* is a true enthusiast who speaks English and runs her estate on organic principles. Other *vignerons* can be found both in and around the village. It's also worth a look at the extremely ancient **église St-Pierre**, right in the centre. The oldest parts – best seen in the fishbone patterning of the brick on the west front – date from as far back as the tenth century. The south portal probably received its geometrical patterns some hundred years later, while the Romanesque apse is a relative latecomer, dating from the twelfth century.

If money is no object, head roughly 2km east of town towards Epiré and turn off at signs to the elite vineyard of **Coulée de Serrant** (Mon–Sat 9am–noon & 2–6pm; free; Ⓦwww.coulee-de-serrant.com), where the Chenin Blanc vines flourish in an unusually steep, well-protected and sunny micro-valley. Sadly, the tiny size of the appellation – just 7ha, all under the one proprietor – means that you can't taste unless you promise to buy. If you do, expect to pay a minimum of around €40 per bottle for the most recent vintage, and many times that for older wines.

Béhuard

The D106 south of Savennières takes you underneath the TGV line, across the first of a pair of Loire bridges and straight onto **BEHUARD**, a peaceful, verdant, mid-stream island with a tiny village hidden away among its poplar trees. The secretive feel is emphasized by the ban on motor traffic in the village – you have to park your car and walk a few yards. At the centre of things is the pilgrim church of **Notre-Dame**, perched on a rock to avoid the frequent floods. It's a lovably eccentric structure, built in the 1470s on the orders of Louis XI, the nephew of René d'Anjou (see box on p.255). Loire mariners have come here for centuries to pray to the Virgin for protection, and her principal statue now occupies a niche halfway up the north wall of the sanctuary, covered by an embroidered mantle. The beautifully carved misericords inside date back to Louis XI's time.

Nearby, an open-air pilgrim church occupies a large field – signalled by a giant Calvary neatly framed by two Lombardy poplars. There are plentiful opportunities for **walking** by the river (bathing is dangerous and illegal) and on paths between gardens and orchards. For a real treat, book in at the superb **restaurant**, *Les Tonnelles* (☎02.41.72.21.50; closed Sun evening & Mon), which has a beautifully restrained, contemporary dining room and a lovely outside terrace under vines. The menu is highly seasonal, but expect a lot of perfect fish and shellfish dishes; the €23 lunch *menu* is fantastic value, or you can spend anything up to €100 for the evening *menu dégustation*, which comes with selected wines.

The Layon valley

Heading south from the bridge over the Loire at Béhuard, after 3km you come to a small town called **ROCHEFORT-SUR-LOIRE** – it actually lies on a parallel branch of the river known as the **Louet**. There's little to see other than the very ruined **château de St–Offrange**, though a lively market takes place on Wednesday mornings, and you can **swim** and hire **canoes** and **pedalos** from a pleasant sandy "beach" on the north bank of the Louet, right next to the bridge. West of Rochefort, the D751 climbs steeply to the top of the **Corniche Angevine**, a surprisingly steep bluff that rears up alongside the banks of the Louet for some 9km. There's a fine view from the road: the southern slopes are lined with vines, while to the north you can look out across green meadows to the Loire's main channel.

At **LA HAIE LONGUE**, 3km west, you can turn down off the Corniche into the vine-covered **Layon valley**, one of the region's warmest and most enticing corners, dotted with curious *moulins à cavier* – hut-like windmills built on conical-shaped stone platforms. The valley has an unusually sunny microclimate, a factor that the local *vignerons* rely on to create their famous **Côteaux du Layon** wines (see Contexts, p.337), which need hefty doses of summer sunshine as well as autumnal "noble rot" to produce their honeyed flavour. You can stop off at lots of small, attractive villages, and wine-growers advertise tastings on roadside hoardings everywhere.

St-Aubin-de-Luigné and Chaume

The handsome, schist-built manor houses of **ST-AUBIN-DE-LUIGNÉ**, 3km southeast of La Haie Longue, are gathered in a relatively steep fold of the hills, making for a very picturesque scene. The best view is from the **Moulin Guérin**, a former windmill turned viewing tower rising up from the vine-covered hills overlooking the village. In summer, old-fashioned wooden **rowboats** can be rented inexpensively for dabbling in the waters of the Layon (May to mid-June Sun 2–7pm; mid-June to mid-Sept daily 2–7pm; ☎02.41.78.52.98). For a **restaurant** meal, try *Le Clézio*, 9 place de l'Eglise (☎02.41.78.33.15; closed Sun evening, Mon, & Tues evening), which serves good, simple Angevin cuisine. Wine-growers can be found all over the village, but committed wine buyers should also make for the elite **Quarts de Chaume** *appellation*, which covers a minuscule area between St-Aubin and Beaulieu-sur-Layon, with just half a dozen wine-growers. Even in a less well-regarded year, a bottle of this stuff will cost upwards of €20, about double the price of an "ordinary" Côteaux du Layon.

Beaulieu-sur-Layon to Thouarcé

At **BEAULIEU-SUR-LAYON**, the **église Notre-Dame de l'Assomption**, on rue de la Mairie a few steps away from the newer church in the main square, is in fact just the choir section of a once larger twelfth-century church. It's a curious, beautiful structure; inside, the half-dome of its apse preserves a naïve but moving Christ in Majesty surrounded by the symbols of the evangelists.

Pretty **RABLAY-SUR-LAYON**, 2km south of Beaulieu, has reinvented itself as an art and craft village, with a sizeable population of local artisans who exhibit at the **Centre Artisanat**, place du Mail (April–June & Sept–Nov Wed & Fri–Sun 2.30–6.30pm; July & Aug Tues–Sun 2.30–6.30pm; Dec Tues–Sun 2.30–6.30pm; free), alongside works by French and international artists. There's a pleasant picnic spot in the centre of the village, beside the Layon.

THOUARCE, 9km upstream of Rablay-sur-Layon, is the largest village within the *appellation* of **Bonnezeaux**, which produces some of the best sweet wines in the world. It's only slightly larger than its *grand cru* rival, Quarts de Chaume, but there are a dozen or so producers, so you can sample freely before you buy. Thouarcé has a dedicated wine festival at the beginning of August, and two good **restaurants** make it an excellent stopping place at any time: *Le Relais de Bonnezeaux*, just off the road between Thouarcé and the village of Bonnezeaux (℡02.41.54.08.33, 🅦www.relais.bonnezeaux.com; closed Mon, Tues evening & Sun), is the place to go for gastronomic food, with a lovely situation in a modernized country train station overlooking the steep, vine-combed slopes and an excellent range of *menus* from around €20 to €50 – the more expensive *menus* come with carefully selected wines. The friendly, vine-covered *Auberge du Cheval Blanc*, on place du Prieuré, Thouarcé (℡02.41.54.04.40; closed evenings on Mon, Thurs & Sun), offers a wide choice of less inventive but nevertheless delicious dishes, with an emphasis on fish in sauces.

Martigné-Briand and Aubigné-sur-Layon
The cruelly dilapidated state of the **château** (guided tours only: April–June, Sept & Oct Tues–Sat 2–5pm; July & Aug Tues–Sun 10am–noon & 2–6pm; €3; 🅦www.chez.com/chateaumartigne) at **MARTIGNE-BRIAND**, 7km southeast of Thouarcé, is the result of its location on the borders of the Vendée, a conservative region which rose up in favour of the monarchy in the wake of the Revolution. The château was the first true Renaissance château in Anjou, but was burnt and partially dismantled by Revolutionary troops in 1793 and today presents a stark, though rather lovely face to the world. An enthusiastic local association runs guided tours. Martigné-Briand was not only a political boundary: a natural, geological frontier signals the beginning of the **Saumurois** (covered in chapter 5), as the more steeply undulating, schist-formed hills of the western Massif Armoricain, centred around Brittany, change into the gentler limestone slopes of the Paris basin. It's very easy to see the divide, as slate-roofed Angevin houses constructed in drab-coloured schist give way to the paler, limestone-built, tiled-roof homes typical of the central Loire valley.

Just 3km from Martigné-Briand, on the southern bank of the river, honey-coloured **AUBIGNE-SUR-LAYON** usually makes a strenuous effort in the national "village in bloom" competition, with appealing results. Short, signposted walking circuits show off the priory, the old lime kiln, the washhouse and other modest local sights, but the main attraction is the **église St-Denis**, with its eleventh-century nave, twelfth-century choir and eighteenth-century *trompe l'œil* wall-paintings in the transepts. A good place to sample the local Côteaux du Layon wines is at the **château d'Aubigné**, which lies at the end of a short driveway that leads under the fortified gatehouse beside the church's west end; the actual château is ruined, but the wines – sweet and sparkling – are excellent. The friendly *Layon Blues Café*, on the main rue Nationale, can supply sandwiches and simple **brasserie** meals.

Layon valley practicalities
The most enjoyable way to explore the Layon valley is by **bicycle**, and it's close enough to be feasible as a long day-trip from Angers; the only alternative is to drive, as public transport is sparse. There's a maximum of three buses a day up the Layon from Angers (lines #17 and #24), though on some days there are no services at all; there are slightly more frequent buses on line #6, which connects Angers with Rochefort-sur-Loire and St-Aubin-de-Luigné.

For information on the valley, the largest and most helpful **tourist office** is in Beaulieu-sur-Layon, on the main rue St-Vincent (June–Aug Mon–Sat 10am–noon & 2–6pm, Sun 10am–1pm; Sept–May Mon–Fri 2–5pm; ℡02.41.78.65.07). Ask for the excellent map of circular walks in the Layon valley: *Côteaux et Villages en Layon* (€3.80). Otherwise, look online at ⓦwww.layon.org.

The best of the half-dozen **hotels** in the area is the welcoming *Grand Hôtel*, 30 rue René Gasnier, Rochefort-sur-Loire (℡02.41.78.80.46, ⓦwww.le-grand-hotel.net; ❷), a pleasantly old-fashioned place with a decent restaurant. Failing that, try *Le Castel* in Brissac-Quincé (see opposite) or the simple, family-friendly **hostel** (℡02.41.78.65.07; Mon–Fri only; €10 per person per night) run by the tourist office in Beaulieu-sur-Layon, which offers private two- to four-bed rooms during the week. Among the most attractive chambres d'hôtes in the region are the very peaceful *Domaine de l'Etang*, 3km from Martigné-Briand on the road to Thouarcé (℡02.41.59.92.31, ⓦwww.domaine-etang.com; ❹); the guest rooms have been converted from an old stable block at the end of the large garden, and there's a swimming pool. Another good option is *Au Logis de la Brunetière*, Faye d'Anjou (℡02.41.54.16.24; ❸), which has three welcoming rooms set in a picturesque Angevin farmhouse. Rochefort has an excellent, well-equipped **campsite**, *St-Offrange*, route de Savennières (℡02.41.78.82.11; closed Oct–April), while St-Aubin-de-Luigné has a slightly more modest municipal site (℡02.41.78.33.28; closed Oct–April) and Thouarcé has the pleasant *Camping de l'Ecluse*, rue des 3 Ponts (℡02.41.54.14.36; closed mid-Oct to mid-April).

The Aubance valley

The **Aubance valley** begins just northwest of Doué-la-Fontaine, in the Saumurois (see p.239), and the river flows for some 30km through delightful, bucolic countryside before joining the Loire close to Angers. The **château de Brissac** is the main draw, but if you do want to explore the area in depth, call in at the tourist offices in Angers or Brissac-Quincé and pick up a copy of the excellent map, *Boucle Aubance Brissac* (€3.80), which details twenty-odd walking tours lasting from ninety minutes to six hours. Every minor château, windmill, *cabane de vigne* (old-fashioned vine-growers' hut), church and viewpoint in the area is clearly marked.

If you've got young children in tow, the **Parc de Loisirs de l'Etang**, near St-Saturnin, 3km from Brissac-Quincé (May & June Wed–Sun 11am–7pm; July & Aug Tues–Sun 11am–7pm; €2), makes an obvious destination. It's basically a giant playground, with a few extra activities (€1 supplement), most notably the big but gentle waterslide and horse-drawn carriage and donkey rides.

Brissac-Quincé

Twenty kilometres southeast of Angers, **BRISSAC-QUINCÉ** is dominated by its tall, weighty and altogether rather overweening château, known as the **château de Brissac** (guided tours only: April–June & mid-Sept to Oct daily except Tues 10am–noon & 2.15–5.15pm; July to mid-Sept daily 10.15am–12.15pm & 2.20–5.45pm; €8; ⓦwww.chateau-brissac.fr) after the line of dukes who have owned it since 1502. The village itself is rather sleepy, except during the Thursday morning market, but it's pleasant enough, and does very nicely out of two local wine *appellations*. Apart from the château, the chief sight in the village is the Renaissance **église St-Vincent**, named after the patron saint of wine-growers, which has a fine set of stained-glass windows.

The **château** lies just down the hill from the centre, looking like an ugly duckling frozen halfway through its transformation into a swan. On the main west front, two round towers survive from an earlier, fifteenth-century fortress, with the château's ill-proportioned seventeenth-century facade awkwardly wedged in between them. Under the original rebuilding plan, the old fortified towers were to be pulled down, but the death of duc Charles II in 1621 brought the project to a standstill. In the latter half of the nineteenth century, the brilliant marriage of the eleventh duke to Jeanne Say, from the giant sugar company now known as Beguin-Say, provided the funds for lots of improvements, notably laying out the grounds as an English park. The twelfth duke did just as well with May Schneider, the heiress of the great French steel dynasty. The marquis de Brissac, son of the thirteenth duke, married a ballerina, and now lives on site, managing the château's thriving tourist business and its **vineyard**, which has been here since 1515. You can buy a separate wine-tasting ticket (€3), which also allows you to stroll around the large park, along the forest path, round the *étang* and down beside the banks of the Aubance.

If you want to see the **interior**, the guided tour is obligatory. Thankfully, you're spared all 303 rooms and are only shown the most impressive, many of which have sumptuous ceilings. You're taken round the dining room, with its painted "marble" musician's gallery, up the superb Louis XIII staircase to the seventeenth-century bedchambers, then along the Grand Gallery and "hunting chambers", with their sixteenth-century tapestries, and into the Gothic chapel and the not-so-miniature private opera house up on the second floor – one of Jeanne Say's little modifications. On the way round, the guide points out the most fabulously expensive of the endless cabinets, wardrobes and bits of china, as well as portraits ranging from seventeenth-century oils to present-day photos.

Practicalities

The **tourist office**, 8 place de la République (mid-April to Sept Mon–Sat 10am–12.30pm & 2–6pm, Sun 10am–1pm; Oct to mid-April Mon–Wed & Fri 2–5pm, Thurs 9.30am–12.30pm & 2–5pm; ☏02.41.92.21.50, ⓦwww.brissac-tourisme.asso.fr), can provide detailed information on touring the Aubance valley.

If you want to **stay**, the only hotel in Brissac-Quincé is *Le Castel*, 1 rue Louis-Moron (☏02.41.91.24.74, ⓦwww.destination-anjou.com/castel; ❹), beside the bridge over the Aubance. It's modern in style, but spick and span, with extra-large, comfortable beds. The most luxurious option is to stay at the château itself, which offers some of the most amazing – and expensive – **chambres d'hôtes** (ⓦwww.brissac.net; ❾) you'll find anywhere: for around €400 you can stay in a real seventeenth-century room, as shown to visitors, with genuine period furnishings – the Louis XIII room even has a bathroom on the far side of a secret door. Just down the road in St-Melaine-sur-Aubance, 4km northwest, the *Logis de l'Appartenance* (☏02.41.45.27.44; ❸) offers some very attractive chambres d'hôtes, set in a modernized sixteenth-century farmhouse with a small tower and a swimming pool.

If you're looking for a **restaurant** meal, try *Le Haut Tertre*, 1 place du Tertre (☏02.41.91.79.95; closed Mon evening, Thurs evening & Sun), a contemporary bistro-style place in an old setting, with a reasonably priced *menu* of grilled meats, salads and fish dishes. *Le Clémenceau*, 21 rue de la Marne (☏02.41.91.22.01; closed Sun evening & Mon), is similarly priced but with a more traditional, regional *menu*, and has outside seating in summer.

North of the Aubance lies a delightful swathe of undulating farmland speckled with orchards and patches of woodland. Much of this is limestone territory, and very similar in ambience to the neighbouring Saumurois (covered in chapter 5). Dolmens, ruined windmills and private châteaux – some sporadically open to visitors in the summer months – dot the landscape here and there, but oddly enough the two most captivating sights are both underground contemporary art sites.

Just outside **ST-GEORGES-DES-SEPT-VOIES**, 11km east of Brissac-Quincé, is the bizarre **Hélice Terrestre de l'Orbière** (daily: May–Sept 11am–8pm; Oct–April 2–6pm; €4). Until his death in 1996, artist Jacques Wasminski gouged out a series of curling, interweaving tunnels in the soft tufa, sculpting their inner surfaces with elaborate, swirling geometric patterns that sometimes recall Mayan stonework, and sometimes the creepy biomorphic passageways of the film *Alien*. Children, in particular, love exploring this mind-expanding, whole-body artwork, especially the spherical chamber which echoes any sound you make with bell-like resonance.

At the **Manoir de la Caillère**, 3km west on the edge of the village of **COUTURES**, artist Richard Rak exhibits and sells his work in a set of rather tamer tufa caves. There's a touch of Surrealism in his collage-style paintings, which use found objects, terracotta pieces, bits of paper and feathers, as well as traditional paint. M Rak lives right next door in a troglodyte house, so if the gate is open – as it usually is when he's at home – then the gallery is too. There's no entry fee, but you could leave a couple of euros as a tip; if you want to buy, the cost can run into thousands.

For a special lunch stop or sunset drink, make for **Le Thoureil**, where *Au Cabernet d'Anjou*, on place de l'Eglise, is a 300-year-old mariners' bar complete with a vaguely nautical and deeply atmospheric interior and a wonderful sunny terrace overlooking the river. Hearty meals are served at lunchtime and in the evening, or you can just sit back with an inexpensive glass of Côteaux du Layon.

North of Angers

Immediately **north of Angers**, the rivers Sarthe, Mayenne and Loir converge in a boggy mess of water and pastureland. It's not a particularly enticing area – unless you head further upstream into the peaceful, green valleys of the Loir and Sarthe (see chapter 7) – but the châteaux of **Le Plessis-Bourré** and **Le Plessis-Macé** make for interesting excursions from Angers, or a good diversion if you're approaching from the north. You'll need your own transport to get to both. The wooded plateau of northeastern Anjou is even shorter on highlights, though the ancient market town of **Baugé** is a good stopping place for its château and relic of the True Cross, and **bus** connections to Le Mans, Saumur and Angers make it a feasible destination if you're using public transport. West of the Mayenne, in the agricultural northwest of Anjou, you'll find little of note except the peaceful, green countryside, though you can walk or take a cruise along the river itself.

Château du Plessis-Macé

The graceful, low-slung buildings of **Le Plessis-Macé**, just off the main northbound N162, 14km out of Angers (guided tours only: April–June, Sept & Oct Wed–Sun 1.30–5.30pm; July & Aug daily 10.30–6.30pm; €5), are scarcely grand enough to be called a château, and in fact they were originally only the *communs*, or outbuildings, of the larger fortress which now lies next to them in flinty ruins. This early fortress was built in the twelfth century by one du Plessis to protect the Angevin capital from the Bretons, on the one hand, and the counts of Blois, on the other. The elaborate, pale-coloured tufa stonework that still projects above the dark schist walls is mid-fifteenth-century work, dating from the same era as the similarly elaborate windows, doors and gables of the habitable part of the château. It's this later part of the château – built by Louis de Beaumont, a chamberlain of Charles VII and a cousin of the original Plessis family – that is visited today.

The obligatory **guided tour** is in French, but there's an English-language leaflet that helps with translation, and if the guides aren't too busy you may get your own tour in English. The main doorway leads under a fulsomely corniced **balcony** – from an architectural point of view, the highlight of the château. It was originally a kind of bridge between kitchen and *logis*, and the carved tufa has been exceptionally well preserved by the overhanging roof. Much of the **interior** was remodelled in the mid-nineteenth century by the Walsh family of Serrant (see p.262), who bought the château from an uncle of the great Angevin poet Joachim du Bellay (see p.327) in the 1680s. The decor may not be original, therefore, but there's lots of fine furniture, ranging from Louis XIII chairs to Charles X cabinets and eighteenth-century tapestries. The **chapel**, at the end of the tour, is dominated by an elaborately carved fifteenth-century tribune.

Château du Plessis-Bourré

Confusingly, the château at **Le Plessis-Bourré**, 17km north of Angers between the Sarthe and Mayenne rivers (guided tours only: Feb, March, Oct & Nov daily except Wed 2–6pm; April–June & Sept Mon, Tues & Fri–Sun 10am–noon & 2–6pm, Thurs 2–6pm; July & Aug daily 10am–6pm; €7.50, ⓦ www.plessis-bourre.com), has nothing to do with the du Plessis who built the nearby château du Plessis-Macé. The name derives instead from the old French word for a palisade, or fortress, allied with the surname of Jean Bourré, the powerful fifteenth-century treasurer of France who built it. It took just five years to built, work ending in 1473, but Bourré's haste is explainable less by defensive urgency than by his own mania for building – he was also responsible for the great château at Langeais, among many others. The château may look as if it still expects an attack across its vast moat, spanned by an arched bridge with a still-functioning drawbridge, but the large, decorated windows herald a new, more luxurious era. This château was built to receive important visitors, among them Louis XI and Charles VIII, and it is suitably flamboyant.

The first three rooms on the ground floor are a surprise, beautifully decorated and furnished in the Louis XVI, XV and Régence styles respectively, but things revert to type in the huge Gothic Salle du Parlement, with its earthenware-tiled floor and massive sculpted fireplace. The highlight of the tour comes in the Salle des Gardes, just above, where the original, deeply coffered ceiling stems from Bourré's fashionable interest in alchemy. Every inch is painted with allegorical scenes: sixteen panels depict alchemical symbols such as the phoenix, the pregnant siren and the donkey singing Mass, while eight cartoon-like paintings come with morals attached – look out for "Chicheface", the hungry wolf that only eats faithful woman; its victim is supposed to be Jean Bourré's wife. You leave via the 36-metre-long library, with its collection of fans, and the serene chapelle Ste-Anne.

△ Gates, Montgeoffroy

Baugé and around

The largely flat and heavily wooded northeastern corner of Anjou has its modest capital in **BAUGE**, 36km east of Angers. Unless you arrive on a market day (Monday afternoon and Saturday morning), the town may not look all that inviting at first glance, with its Neoclassical court building, contemporary town hall and fifteenth-century château glaring at each other across the gravel expanse of the place de l'Europe as if engaged in a Mexican standoff. But explore a little further and you'll discover the remnants of a rather lovely fifteenth-century town, especially along rue de la Girouardière and rue Basse, and around the ancient **place du Marché**, where you'll find a number of venerable houses.

The opportunities for hunting in the local forests weren't lost on the dukes of Anjou, who transformed one of Foulque Nerra's eleventh-century keeps into a relatively luxurious château. The single wing that you see today is all that remains of the **château de Baugé** on place de l'Europe (daily: May to mid-Sept 10am–6pm; mid-Sept to mid-Nov 2–6pm; Ⓦ www.chateau-bauge.com; €8), the dreamy chivalric castle built by René d'Anjou (see box on p.255) in the 1450s. The exterior preserves a glimmer of former grandeur, its biscuit-coloured stone offset by the pale tufa of the cross-shaped windows, and its main staircase tower ennobled by a carved Gothic portal. Sadly, there's little left of the interior other than the palm-tree vault at the top of the newel of the great staircase, and the original beamed ceilings. As if to compensate, the insides have been transformed into an audio-visual experience dedicated to the life of "Good King René" – the walls are lit up with chivalric projections and video reconstructions of battles, while dramatic music plays.

The dusty old **museum** of local art and history that used to occupy the château is being transferred to the **Hôtel Dieu**, just north of the château along place du 8 Mai and rue Anne de Mélun. Established in 1639, this huge charitable hospital was mostly complete by the end of the seventeenth century, and it is due to reopen as a museum, hopefully in 2005. The highlight should be the **apothecary's stores**, which have been preserved intact since 1675, along with all its beautiful jars of unguents, spices and medicinal potions. Ask at the château or tourist office for details.

If you follow rue du Mail down from the château, crossing the nineteenth-century axis of rue Victor Hugo, and then bearing right along rue de la Girouardière, you'll come to the **Hospice de la Girouardière**, a religious institution founded in 1783 to look after incurables. Ring on the doorbell (Mon & Wed–Sun 2.30–4.15pm; free) and a nun – they now look after the mentally handicapped – will take you through to a room off the hospice's modern chapel, where the **Vraie Croix d'Anjou** is displayed in a heavily fortified safe-cabinet. The faithful still come here in large numbers to seek spiritual inspiration from this unusually large fragment of the True Cross – one of the pieces unearthed in Jerusalem in the fourth century and brought back to France by a Crusader in the thirteenth century – but more secular-minded visitors may be more astonished by its fourteenth-century decoration, encrusted with rubies and sapphires and adorned with two heartbreaking miniature figures of Jesus on the Cross, made from solid gold. The relic has had a curious afterlife. It was adopted by René d'Anjou as the symbol of the region, and later became known as the Cross of Lorraine after his marriage to Isabelle of Lorraine. Its two-armed shape was adopted as the symbol of the French Resistance in World War II.

Le Vieil Baugé and Pontigné

Five villages in the **Baugeois**, the countryside around Baugé, are locally famous for their churches' tall, octagonal steeples, added in the eighteenth century to sturdy Romanesque towers and given an extraordinary quarter-turn twist – an effect that adds a very distinctive *je ne sais quoi*. Two of the most distinctive are within walking distance of Baugé. **LE VIEIL BAUGE**, 2km southwest of Baugé, was the site of an important battle that pitted the French and their Scots allies against the English in 1421; the result was the first setback for England in the wake of their great victory at Agincourt, just six years earlier. The dramatic (and accidental) lean of the church's steeple makes it look quite extraordinary, and the church inside is no less interesting, with its airy early twelfth-century choir and sixteenth-century transept.

The twist on the steeple of the **église St-Denis** at **PONTIGNE**, 5km east up the River Couasnon, is particularly extreme, while the chapels of the transept are home to some captivating early thirteenth-century **wall-paintings** – art historians have dubbed the unknown artist "the Master of the Big Feet", and it's easy to see why. If you're heading out from Baugé, stop off just over halfway by the sign for the **Dolmen de la Pierre Couverte**, an ancient megalith reached by a pretty path through the woods. Two kilometres south of Pontigné lies the **Forêt Domaniale de Chandelais**, an ancient forest traced by motorable and eminently cyclable avenues.

If you've got bored kids in tow, you could take them off to **Holly Park**, 5km west of Baugé on the edge of **ECHEMIRE**. It's a miniature theme park with a kind of canoeing aqua-rollercoaster, as well as a normal rollercoaster and other funfair attractions. Opening hours outside the central summer months are complex and highly variable (July & Aug usually 10.45am–6.45pm), so check at the tourist office in advance or call ☎02.41.89.70.25.

Practicalities

The **tourist office** is inside the château (mid-June to mid-Sept daily 10am–12.30pm & 1.30–6.30pm; mid-Sept to mid-June Mon–Sat 11.30am–12.30pm & 1.30–6pm; ☎02.41.89.18.07, ⓦwww.tourisme-bauge.fr.st). Baugé would make a peaceful place to overnight. The best **hotel** is the *Boule d'Or*, in the centre of town at 4 rue du Cygne (☎02.41.89.82.12, Ⓕ02.41.89.06.07; ❸; restaurant closed Sun evening & Mon), a comfortable, old-fashioned two-star in the Logis de France stable. Failing that you could try the *Grand Turc*, 9 ave Jeanne d'Arc (☎02.41.89.10.36; ❶), a no-frills no-star mostly used by itinerant workers, but clean and friendly enough. Both have **restaurants** catering perfectly to their clientele. If you've got transport, you could head out to *Le Logis de Poëllier*, in Poëllier, off the D211 south of Echemiré, 7km west of Baugé (☎02.41.89.20.56, ⓦhttp://poellier.free.fr; ❸), an attractive *gîte* and chambres d'hôtes complex created in the genteel tufa buildings of a sixteenth-century farmhouse; a hearty table d'hôte is available on request. The municipal **campsite** (☎02.41.89.14.79; closed mid-Sept to mid-May) is on chemin du Pont des Fées, beside the River Couasnon, 300m from the centre; there's a heated **swimming pool** next to it.

Château de Montgeoffroy and around

Perfectly preserved down to its last exquisitely aristocratic decorative detail, the **château de Montgeoffroy** – just outside the village of **MAZE**, 22km west of Angers – is the swansong of the ancien régime (guided tour only: mid-March to mid-June & mid-Sept to mid-Nov 9.30am–noon & 2.30–6.30pm; mid-June to mid-Sept 9.30am–6.30pm; €8.50). The approach road sets the tone: through finely wrought iron gates and up a long drive that seems to lead straight into the large, handsome windows at the centre of the main facade. It's at once imposing and tasteful.

The property has been in the possession of the Contades family since 1676, but the present château was built between 1772 and 1776, on the eve of the Revolution, drawing heavily on local peasant labour and craftsmanship – a factor that may have helped save it. It was the brainchild of **Louis–Georges–Erasme de Contades**, a field marshal of France who had carried the crown for Louis XVI's coronation and was looking to spend a luxurious retirement in the country. The Revolution may have spoiled his plans, but he refused to emigrate, finally succumbing to an apoplexy in 1795 at the age of 92. The marshal's architects decided to preserve two sixteenth-century towers at the edges of the outbuildings, bearing witness to the Contades' feudal origins, but the central wing is a perfect, elegant and utterly coherent specimen of the Louis XVI style. The interior is painted entirely in subtly different shades of cool greys and blues, with warm parquet flooring throughout and light streaming through the French windows. The furniture, too, almost all dates from the early 1770s, as testified by the detailed record books kept during the building work.

The **guided tour** (usually in French, but English tours may be available on request) begins with the two main suites on the ground floor, each admirably designed for gracious living. The **salon d'hiver** (winter room) faces north and is relatively small and easily heated, while the **salon d'été** (summer room) looks south onto the sunny courtyard. The oval **dining room** is superb, draped with warm fabrics, lined with muted grey *boiseries* (wood panelling) and heated by a florid-looking porcelain stove. The tour continues outside with the Ste-Catherine **chapel** – another sixteenth-century survival, with carved, painted bosses on the Angevin vaults and a fine stained-glass window – and the copper-pot-lined **kitchen**. The latter is particularly interesting as it had the only original tap in the château, all the rest of the water being brought by servants. Finally there are the spacious stables, notably the polygonal **tack room**, pungent with the smell of horses and leather, its walls lined with saddles, bridles and whips.

Beaufort-en-Vallée

At **BEAUFORT-EN-VALLEE**, 6km west of Mazé, the outrageously over-sized and over-sculpted **église Notre-Dame** was commissioned by Jeanne de Laval after the death of her husband, René d'Anjou, in 1480. The nave and northern transept date from this era, as well as the bell tower, which was completed in 1542; the rest is pure nineteenth-century Gothic fantasy. The stained glass from this later epoch is particularly extravagant, created by Parisian glassmaker Edouard Didron.

South of Beaufort lies the rich horticultural land of the Authion valley; at **Les Rosiers-sur-Loire** (see p.245), 11km south of Beaufort, you can cross the Loire into the heartland of the **Saumurois** (covered in Chapter 5).

Travel details

Trains	Buses
Angers to: Le Mans (17 daily; 40min–1hr 20min); Saumur (14 daily; 20–30min); Savennières (3–5 daily; 10min); Tours (12 daily; 1hr–1hr 30min).	**Angers** to: Baugé via Beaufort-en-Vallée (3 daily; 1hr 15min–1hr 30min); Bouchemaine/La Pointe (every 40min; 25min); Brissac-Quincé (5–7 daily; 30min); Doué-la-Fontaine (4–6 daily; 1hr);

Rochefort-sur-Loire (4–5 daily; 40min); Saumur via Gennes (1–4 daily; 1hr 30min); St-Aubin-de-Luigné (4–5 daily; 45min); St-Georges-sur-Loire (for Serrant; 5–7 daily; 40min); Thouarcé via the Layon valley (up to 3 daily; 50min).

Baugé to: Angers via Beaufort-en-Vallée (3 daily; 1hr 15min–1hr 30min); Le Mans (2 daily; 1hr 15min); Saumur (2 daily; 45min).

7

The northern approaches

CHAPTER 7

Highlights

* **Chartres cathedral** The jewel of France's Gothic cathedrals is set in the plain of the Beauce, halfway to Paris but within easy striking distance of the Loire. See p.279

* **Châteaudun** A proud late medieval château towers above the Loir at this sleepy provincial town. See p.284

* **Trôo** The tufa escarpment overlooking the Loir at Trôo is riddled with cave-houses, in one of which you can even stay. See p.288

* **Le Mans' old quarter** The medieval quarter spreads along a low ridge, with the fabulous cathédrale St-Julien at its highest point. See p.292

* **Mulsanne straight** Heading south from Le Mans towards Tours, the main road follows the 24-hour race track for an exhilarating stretch. See p.294

* **Picnicking by the river** The sleepy River Sarthe is perfect for riverbank picnics. See p.295

* **Saints de Solesmes** The abbey church at Solesmes, on the banks of the Sarthe, contains two superb sixteenth-century sculpture groups. See p.297

△ Ronsard's motto, La Possonnière

7

The northern approaches

H eading south from Normandy or the Paris region, most visitors hurtle through the quiet, deeply rural country north of the Loire on their way to the Loire valley proper. This is, after all, a great swathe of undistin-guished agricultural land, stretching from the grain-growing plains of the **Beauce**, on the eastern side, watered by the **River Loir**, to the pastureland and orchards of the **Maine** to the west, drained by the **Sarthe**. Those who linger, however, will discover a quietly rewarding back-country that is best explored by imitating one of the sleepy rivers and meandering slowly south towards the Loire. As for the region's two magnificent cathedrals, in the cities of **Chartres** and **Le Mans**, they are well worth visiting even if you're not approaching from the north.

Famously, Chartres is visible for miles around, rising up above the flat fields of the Beauce like an image from a Flemish landscape painting. South of the city, the Loir – a tributary of the Loire – passes through two attractive provincial towns: **Châteaudun**, famous for its château, and **Vendôme**, chiefly known for its canals and its Gothic church. Downstream from Vendôme, the Loir is practically lined with picturesque villages. Many, such as **Lavardin** and **Montoire-sur-le-Loir**, are graced by ancient churches preserving Romanesque wall-paintings. The riverbank village of **Trôo** is fascinating for its "troglodyte" cave-houses, while further downriver lie the poet Ronsard's manor house at **La Possonnière** and the giant Renaissance château at **Le Lude**.

Over to the west, if the famous race track of the "24 Heures" can't persuade you to stop in **Le Mans**, the city's historic quarter and magnificent cathedral might. Heading south down the River Sarthe towards Anjou, you can have your pick of pretty villages – **Asnières-sur-Vègre**, **Juigné-sur-Sarthe** and **St-Denis-d'Anjou** – or stop off at the pottery museum at **Malicorne-sur-Sarthe**. Most beguiling of all is the thriving monastery at **Solesmes**, where you can hear Gregorian chant and see the sixteenth-century sculptures known as the "saints de Solesmes".

Chartres

When King Philippe-Auguste visited **Chartres** to mediate between Church and townsfolk after the riots of October 1210, the cathedral chapter noted that

"he did not wish to stay any longer in the city but, so as to avoid the blasphemous citizens, stayed here only for one hour and hastened to return." Chartres' modern visitors – bussed in to see the famous cathedral and bussed straight out again – often stay little longer, which is a great pity. One of the world's most astounding buildings, the cathedral is best experienced early or late in the day, when low sun transmits the stained-glass colours to the interior stone and the quiet scattering of people leaves the acoustics unconfused. The little town at the cathedral's feet has its own, more modest charms.

Arrival, information and accommodation

If you're travelling down to the Loire by **train**, services run from Paris's Gare du Montparnasse at least every hour on weekdays, but note that there are slightly fewer trains at weekends, especially on Sundays; the journey takes roughly one hour. From the **gare SNCF**, it's less than ten minutes' walk to the cathedral and **tourist office** (April–Sept Mon–Sat 9am–7pm, Sun 9.30am–5.30pm; Oct–March Mon–Sat 10am–6pm, Sun 10am–1pm & 2.30–4.30pm; ☎02.37.18.26.26). The latter can supply free maps and help with accommodation.

Among Chartres' handful of **hotels**, *Le Grand Monarque*, 22 place des Epars (☎02.37.21.00.72, ⓦwww.bw-grand-monarque.com; ❼), is something of an institution, and by far the swishest in town. Otherwise, the tiny *Chêne Fleuri*, 14 rue de la Porte Morard (☎02.37.35.25.70; ❷), is hidden away in the nicest part of town, down by the old ramshackle houses and streets along the river Eure. The rest of the hotels are uninspiring, but the modern two-star *Bœuf Couronné*, 15 place Châtelet (☎02.37.21.72.13; ❸), is decent enough, and has some inexpensive rooms without bathrooms (❶). The clean, modern **youth hostel**, *Auberge de Jeunesse de Chartres*, 23 ave Neigre (☎02.37.34.27.64; €10.50) is found up on the opposite bank of the river, fifteen minutes' walk from the cathedral. The **campsite**, *Camping des Bords de l'Eure*, is down beside the river at 9 rue de Launay (☎02.37.28.79.43; closed Oct–March).

The cathedral

Built between 1194 and 1260, the **cathedral** (daily: Jan–April & Nov–Dec 8.30am–7.30pm; May–Oct 8am–8pm; free) was one of the quickest ever constructed and, as a result, preserves a uniquely harmonious design. An earlier, Romanesque structure burnt down in 1194, but the church's holiest relic – the **Sancta Camisia**, supposed to have been the robe Mary wore when she gave birth to Jesus – was discovered three days later, miraculously unharmed. It was a sign that the Virgin wanted her church lavishly rebuilt – at least, so said the canny medieval fundraisers.

The astounding size of the cathedral is entirely owed to the presence of the Sancta Camisia. In the medieval heyday of the **pilgrimage to Santiago de Compostela**, hordes of pilgrims on their way south to Spain would stop here to venerate the relic. The church needed to accommodate them with a sizeable crypt which they could shuffle round, taking their turn to view and honour the relic, and with a nave large enough to sleep in – the sloping floor evident today allowed for it to be washed down more easily. The Sancta Camisia still exists, though after many years on open display it was recently rolled up and put into storage. It may yet be restored to the cathedral.

The geometry of Chartres is unique in being almost unaltered since its consecration, and virtually all of the **stained glass** is original thirteenth-century work. Many of the windows in the nave were donated by craft guilds and merchants, whose symbols can often be seen in the bottommost pane. Some of the stories fit the donors' work, such as the carpenters' window showing Noah's ark. The largely twelfth-century "**Blue Virgin**" window, in the first bay beyond the south transept, is venerated by art-lovers and worshippers alike.

Chartres may be the best-preserved Gothic cathedral in Europe, but if a group of medieval pilgrims suddenly found themselves here they would be deeply dismayed. The paint and gilt work that once brought the portal sculptures to life has vanished, while the walls have lost the whitewash that so well reflected the vivid colours of the stained-glass windows. Worse still, the high altar has been brought down into the body of the church, among the hoi polloi, and chairs cover up the thirteenth-century **labyrinth** on the floor of the nave (except on Fridays between April and October, when you can trace its two-hundred-metre-long route all the way to the centre).

The cathedral's **stonework** is captivating, particularly the **choir screen**, which curves around the ambulatory, depicting scenes from the lives of Christ and the Virgin. Its sculptor, Jehan de Beauce, was also responsible for the design of the Flamboyant Gothic north spire. Outside, hosts of sculpted figures stand

△ Twin spires, Chartres

Cathedral tours

One of the best ways to appreciate the detail of the Cathédrale Notre-Dame is to join one of Malcolm Miller's **guided tours** (April–Nov Mon–Sat noon & 2.45pm; days and times vary in winter; ☎02.37.28.15.58; €11.20), starting just inside the west door. His is no ordinary patter, but a guided lecture by someone who has studied Chartres for decades, with fascinating digressions into the significance of the building's symbols, shapes and numbers.

like guardians at each **entrance portal**. Like the south tower and spire which abuts it, the mid-twelfth century **Royal Portal** actually survives from the earlier Romanesque church, and it's interesting to compare its highly stylized figures with the more naturalistic sculptures on the north and south porches, completed half a century later.

You have to pay extra to visit the crypt and treasury, though these are relatively unimpressive. Crowds permitting, it's worth climbing the **north tower** (Mon–Sat 9am–12.30pm & 2–4.30pm, Sun 2–4.30pm; May–Aug open until 5.30pm; €4) for its bird's-eye view of the sculptures and structure of the cathedral. There are **gardens** at the back from where you can contemplate the innovative flying buttresses.

The rest of town

Though the cathedral is the main attraction, a wander round the town of Chartres has its rewards. Occasional exhibitions of modern and ancient stained glass are displayed in a medieval wine and grain store, now the **Centre International du Vitrail**, at 5 rue du Cardinal-Pie on the north side of the cathedral (Mon–Fri 9.30am–12.30pm & 1.30–6pm, Sat & Sun 10am–12.30pm & 2.30–6pm; €4; ⑩www.centre-vitrail.org). The **Musée des Beaux-Arts** (May–Oct Mon & Wed–Sat 10am–noon & 2–6pm, Sun 2–6pm; Nov–April Mon & Wed–Sat 10am–noon & 2–5pm, Sun 2–6pm; €2.45), in the former episcopal palace just north of the cathedral, has some beautiful tapestries, a room full of works by the French Fauvist Maurice de **Vlaminck** and an excellent *Sainte Lucie* by the Spanish Baroque painter **Zurbarán**. There are good temporary exhibitions, too.

Behind the museum, rue Chantault leads past old townhouses to the **River Eure** and Pont du Massacre. You can follow this reedy stream, lined with ancient wash-houses, upstream via rue du Massacre on the right bank. The cathedral appears from time to time through the trees. Closer at hand, on the left bank, is the Romanesque church of **St-André**, now used for art exhibitions, jazz concerts and so on.

A left turn at the end of rue de la Tannerie, then third right, will bring you to one of Chartres' more eccentric tourist attractions. The **Maison Picassiette**, at 22 rue du Repos (April–Oct Mon & Wed–Sat 10am–noon & 2–6pm, Sun 2–6pm; €2.40), was entirely decorated with mosaics by a local road-mender and later cemetery-caretaker, Raymond Isidore. Working between 1938 and 1962, two years before he died, Isidore used bits of broken pottery and glass to create a strange yet moving example of Christian Naïve art –"I took the things that other people threw away", as he put it.

Back at the end of rue de la Tannerie, the bridge over the river brings you back to the **medieval town**, where you wander about spotting little details such as the sixteenth-century carved salmon that decorates a house at the eastern end of place de la Poissonnerie. A large **food market** takes place on place

Billard and rue des Changes on Saturday morning, and there's a **flower market** on place du Cygne (Tues, Thurs & Sat).

At the edge of the old town, on the junction of boulevard de la Résistance and rue Collin-d'Arleville, stands a memorial to **Jean Moulin**, Prefect of Chartres until he was sacked by the Vichy government in 1942. When the Germans occupied the town in 1940, Moulin refused to sign a document claiming that Senegalese soldiers in the French army were responsible for Nazi atrocities. He later became de Gaulle's number-one man on the ground, co-ordinating the Resistance, but died at the hands of Klaus Barbie in 1943, on his way to a concentration camp in Germany.

Eating and drinking

For a snack, the friendly *Café Serpente* is usefully located at 2 Cloître-Notre-Dame, opposite the south side of the cathedral. It's tatty inside, but the food is decent enough, and served all day. For a proper **restaurant** meal, try *Le Pichet*, 19 rue de Cheval Blanc, almost under the northwest spire (☎02.37.21.08.35; closed Mon, Wed, Tues evening & Sun evening), or the slightly upmarket *L'Estocade*, 1 rue de la Porte Guillaume (☎02.37.34.27.17; closed Mon & Nov–April), which has a lovely situation down by the River Eure; you can get two simple but excellent courses for under €15 next door at *Le Boujou*, *L'Estocade*'s bistro section. The *St-Hilaire*, 11 rue du Pont St-Hilaire (☎02.37.30.97.57; closed Mon lunch, Sat lunch & Sun), serves classy but inexpensive regional cuisine (*menus* €15–30) in a homely little upstairs dining room.

The Loir

Source d'argent toute pleine,
Dont le beau cours eternal
Fuit pour enrichir la plaine
De mon païs paternel.

> *A la source du Loir*, from *Le quatriesme livre des odes* (1550), Pierre de Ronsard

The poet Ronsard, who was born and buried beside the **Loir**, described it as "a full, silver stream whose beautiful course forever flows, enriching the plains of my native land." It is indeed one of the loveliest of the Loire's tributaries, like a junior version of its big sister – typically placid but prone to moody floods, its largely untamed banks lined with willow, alder and poplar trees, and dotted here and there with fishermen and punt-like wooden boats.

The river starts its course a few kilometres west of Chartres and flows roughly south, passing below the walls of the great castle at **Châteaudun** on its way into the Loir-et-Cher *département*. At **Vendôme**, one of the few decent-sized towns in the northern Loire, with a superb Gothic church, the river turns west. This, the **Vendômois** region, is one of the Loir's loveliest stretches, flowing past scattered vineyards, ruined castles and frescoed Romanesque churches around **Lavardin** and **Montoire-sur-le-Loir**, then on past the troglodyte village of **Trôo**, towards Ronsard's birthplace at **La Possonnière**. Continuing west, it forms a dividing line between the forests of northern Touraine and the rich, hedgerow-lined fields of Normandy as it enters the *département* of the Sarthe. In this downstream stretch, the chief sight is the giant Renaissance château at **Le Lude**. Finally, the river pours itself into the Sarthe and then the Maine, immediately north of Angers and just a few kilometres upstream of the Loire.

Châteaudun

The name of **CHATEAUDUN**, 44km south of Chartres, comes from two words that both mean fortress (Latin *castellum* and Celtic *dunum*), which rather underlines the fact that the town's château is the main thing to see – a beacon of interest in the middle of the dull, grain-growing plateau of the Beauce. It's also easy to visit by train, as it's on the main SNCF line (not the high-speed TGV line) between Tours and Paris–Austerlitz.

The château

The large, late medieval **château** (daily: April–June, Sept & Oct 10am–12.30pm & 2–6pm; July & Aug 10am–7pm; Nov–March 10am–12.30pm & 2–5pm; €6.10, or €7 with Musée Municipal) lies at the western end of town. Its rough keep and two wings jammed together at right-angles give it a half-finished, bastardized look, which suits both its history and the name of its most famous resident – Jean Dunois, the "**Bastard of Orléans**", who built the shorter of the two wings and its attached chapel. Dunois was Charles VII's ablest military captain, the companion of Joan of Arc and the chief instrument in the "liberation" of France from the English between the 1420s and 1450s. As the son of Louis d'Orléans and nephew of Charles VI, he was always destined to be powerful, but his illegitimacy meant that his titles and possessions had to be won as much by merit as breeding. Châteaudun was a gift from his older brother, the poet Charles d'Orléans (see p.132), while Beaugency (see p.185) came as part of his wife's dowry.

The longer of the two wings was built by Dunois' grandson, François II, **duc de Longueville**, in the 1510s. Scarcely fifty years separate it from the earlier work, but its architecture betrays a subtle but seismic shift in French taste. Dunois' elegant staircase, in the angle of the two wings, uses an ecclesiastical, Flamboyant Gothic vocabulary, while Longueville's larger staircase, although outwardly similar, is carved inside with delicate Classical motifs culled from the Italian Renaissance – the first time these had been applied anywhere in the Loire valley. A much starker counterpoint is provided by the massive, brooding presence of the **Great Tower**, built by Thibaud V, comte de Blois, in 1170.

The **interior** retains plenty of original giant roof beams and fireplaces, but the fifty-odd sixteenth- and seventeenth-century **tapestries** have only been hung here in recent years. The best of them follow wonderfully bold designs by the early seventeenth-century French painter Simon Vouet. But the most interesting part of the visit is to the **Ste-Chapelle**, built by Dunois in the 1450s and 1460s. Skeins of stone seem to hang between the painted ribs of the vault, light floods in from the generous Gothic windows, and statues line the walls. The Madonna and Child immediately left of the altar is late fourteenth century, while the others were mostly commissioned at the time the chapel was built. The armoured, laurel-crowned figure positioned a little lower than the others, third in on the right-hand side, is thought to be Dunois himself. All would once have been painted in bright colours, and a splendidly colourful wall-painting of the Last Judgement fills the wall of the southern chapel. The **Great Tower**, with its massive, bell-shaped chambers, can only be visited on the optional guided tour (2–3 daily; free).

The rest of town

The new town, rebuilt after a disastrous fire in 1723, occupies a small grid of streets on top of a promontory on the left bank of the Loir. At its centre lies **place du 18 Octobre**, an old-fashioned market square lined with trees and little shops and overlooked by the eighteenth-century Hôtel de Ville. The fountain at the centre celebrates the first clean water to be pumped up from the Loir, in 1860. Immediately north of the square is the **Musée Municipal**, at 3 rue Toufaire (April–June & Sept Mon & Wed–Sun 9.30am–noon & 1.30–6pm; July & Aug daily 9.30am–6.30pm; Oct–March Mon & Wed–Sun 9.30am–noon & 1.30–5pm; €3.50, or €7 with château), a charmingly random collection of local curiosities, minor paintings, porcelain and archeological tit-bits. The highlights are a mock-up of a typical "Beauceron" peasant interior, and the fabulous collection of bright and exotic birds hand-stuffed by a local marquis in the nineteenth century.

The western end of town, between the château and the sixteenth-century abbey church of **La Madeleine**, survived the great fire, so there are plenty of handsome fifteenth- to seventeenth-century houses to admire, especially on the cobbled **rue St-Lubin**, which descends steeply towards the river. The two hundred steps of the **passage St-Pierre** provide a picturesque route down to the Loir, leading from the château car park down to **rue des Fouleries** which runs right along the riverbank, below the town walls. A picnic spot in the mid-dle of the Loir offers a fine view of the château's cliff-like northern facade. Halfway along rue des Fouleries lies the entrance to the **Grottes du Foulon** (April & May daily 2–6pm; June–Sept daily 10am–noon & 2–6pm; Oct–March Sat & Sun 2–6pm; €5; ⓦ www.grottes-du-foulon.net), a large, naturally formed cave chamber. You'll need to speak French to get much out of the obligatory guided tour, on which the guide shows how the millions of flint geodes that stud the roof can be cracked open to reveal chalcedony, opal and quartz. The tour concludes with an amateurish sound-and-light show telling the story of Châteaudun's 1723 fire. In July and August you can rent **canoes and kayaks** from the shop immediately opposite.

Practicalities

The **gare SNCF**, with connections to Tours, Paris and Chartres, is a good ten minutes' walk northeast of the centre, on boulevard Grindelle. The central **tourist office** is opposite the museum, at 1 rue de Luynes (July & Aug Mon–Sat 9am–noon & 2–6pm, Sun 10am–noon; Sept–June Tues–Sat 9am–noon & 2–6pm; ☎02.37.45.22.46, ⓦwww.ville-chateaudun.com). If you want to **stay**, the best bet is the clean, welcoming two-star *St-Louis*, 41 rue de la République (☎02.37.45.00.01; ❸), which has a good situation roughly 200m east of the main square. For a **restaurant** meal, the *Arnaudière*, 4 rue St-Lubin (☎02.37.45.98.98; closed Sun evening & Mon), has an atmospheric decor of old beams and stone walls, and serves delicious, traditional cuisine – expect to pay at least €30 a head. For something simpler, try *Le Commerce* (closed Mon), a friendly brasserie on place du 18 Octobre.

Vendôme

VENDOME, 33km northwest of Blois, is a watery, ancient place, surrounded by two branches of the Loir and criss-crossed by miniature canals. The south bank is overlooked by the ruined castle atop its high rocky cliff, while a size-able modern town spreads to the north. The old centre islanded between the two is the main draw, however, a likeably old-fashioned town that preserves some fine old buildings, notably the **église de la Trinité**, a Flamboyant Gothic church that's cathedral-like in its ambition.

Originally part of the county of Anjou, both town and château were bought by the Bourbon family in 1371. Vendôme became a hotbed of ultra-

Catholicism during the sixteenth-century Wars of Religion, a crime for which it was pillaged and partially burned by the forces of none other than **Henri IV**, the town's own erstwhile duke. Other than being the birthplace of **Rochambeau**, the hero of American independence at the battle of Yorktown, Vendôme failed to distinguish itself in succeeding centuries. In the postwar era, the town has transformed itself into a thriving industrial centre for electronics and white goods.

The Town

The old town is centred on **place St-Martin**, a piazza-like space which echoes every hour to the musical chimes of its fifteenth-century bell tower (see box on p.186). Immediately to the east, you can't miss the exuberant Flamboyant Gothic facade of the **église de la Trinité**, which was probably conceived by Jehan de Beauce, the master of Chartres cathedral, in the early sixteenth century. The church originally belonged to a major Benedictine abbey founded in 1032 by the count of Anjou, Geoffroy Martel. He legendarily saw three burning spears fall from the sky into a spring at the spot, and brought two precious relics to his new church: the arm of St George and the *Sainte Larme*, a crystal-encased tear supposed to have been shed by Christ on the tomb of Lazarus. Their presence attracted thousands of pilgrims, and the resulting wealth allowed the church to be continually added to and rebuilt. As a result, practically every medieval architectural style is represented, ranging from the Romanesque transepts and belfry, to the tall, narrow Rayonnant choir and Flamboyant facade. The most beautiful stained-glass window is the mid-twelfth-century **Majesté Notre Dame**, in the chapel behind the high altar.

The abbey buildings were converted into a military barracks under Napoleon, but in recent years have become the home of the **Musée de Vendôme** (April–Oct Mon & Wed–Sun 10am–noon & 2–6pm; Nov–March Mon & Wed–Sat 10am–noon & 2–6pm; €2.80), a large but basically modest museum of folk crafts and local art works – chief among which are the animated metal sculptures by local twentieth-century artist Louis Leygue. Adjacent to the museum entrance is the **chapterhouse** (open access), in which you can still see a huge eleventh-century wall-painting depicting the Supper at Emmaus and Jesus's miraculous fishing episode, among other less visible scenes.

Rue du Change, the ancient and now pedestrianized high street, runs north past the gate of the watery **Parc Ronsard**, which is surrounded by canalized offshoots of the Loir. The park is overlooked to the north by the largely seventeenth-century **Hôtel de Ville**, once the austere **Collège des Oratoriens**, as attended – and profoundly loathed – by the novelist Honoré de Balzac. "A fat little boy with chubby cheeks and a red face", he was visited just twice in six years by his mother, and frequently punished for naughtiness by being locked up under the stairs. "Without books", he wrote, "this system of punishment would have totally brutalized me." You can peek inside the handsome courtyard during office hours. The park also looks onto a fifteenth-century manor, the **Hôtel du Saillant**, now the tourist office and a medieval washhouse from the same era, as well as some massive plane trees planted in the mid-eighteenth century. On the east side of rue du Change, opposite the park entrance, you can take a sedate **boat tour** round town (July & Aug daily 2.30–7pm; €4), admiring the elaborate floral displays set up each year by the town hall.

Remnants of the medieval town walls still stand on the banks of the Loir. The **Porte St-Georges**, a fifteenth-century fortified gateway, lies at the southernmost end of rue Poterie, which runs 200m west of the parallel rue du Change.

The thirteenth-century **Tour de l'Islette** can best be seen by turning off rue du Change at its northern end, opposite the Romanesque **chapelle St-Jacques**, and following rue du Puits to a footbridge across the northern branch of the Loir. From here you can turn south at place de la Liberté down rue Antoine de Bourbon – passing the thirteenth-century **Porte d'Eau**, which supplied Vendôme's mills and tanneries with water – and finally turning right to cross the Loir again and approach the Trinité church from behind its apse.

It's a steep climb up to the broken remnants of the **château** (daily 9am–7pm; free); continue south along rue du Change past place St-Martin, then cross the Loir on rue St-Bié and follow the rampe du Château up and round. The castle was originally run by the quasi-monastic Knights Templar as a wayfaring sanctuary for pilgrims but fell steadily into ruin from the sixteenth century onwards. Today there's nothing much to see other than ruined towers and a fine view across town.

Practicalities

The **tourist office** is housed in the Hôtel du Saillant, 47 rue Poterie (April–June & Sept Mon–Sat 9.30am–12.30pm & 2–6pm, Sun 9.30am–12.30pm; July & Aug Mon–Sat 9.30am–12.30pm & 2–6pm; Oct–March Mon–Sat 10am–12.30pm & 2–6pm; ☎02.54.77.05.07, ⓦwww.tourisme.fr/vendome), and in summer there's also an information point on the rue du Change (July & Aug daily 2–7pm). The **gare SNCF** lies a good ten minutes' walk north of the centre on rue Darreau, off faubourg Chartrain, but you're more likely to arrive at the high-speed **gare TGV** 5km northwest of town, which is connected by shuttle buses to the central place de la Liberté. If you want to hire **bikes** to explore the Loir valley, make for Huger Cycles, 59 faubourg Chartrain (☎02.54.77.19.38), north of rue du Change.

There's one attractive, central **place to stay**, the *Auberge de la Madeleine*, 6 place de la Madeleine (☎02.54.77.20.79; ❷), an old-fashioned hotel on a pretty square at the north end of rue Poterie. It has a good traditional **restaurant** (closed Wed), with *menus* from €15. For simpler, more modern cuisine, try *Le Vieux Moulin*, 21 rue du Change (closed Mon), a brasserie with great outdoor seating overlooking a weir (summer only). Local speciality **chocolates**, called Saintes Larmes, are sold at the *confiserie* at 9 place St-Martin.

The Vendômois

The stretch of the Loir downstream of Vendôme, as far as La Chartre, all falls within the northern part of the *département* of the Loir-et-Cher, an area known traditionally as the **Vendômois**. This is the heart of the Loir valley: green, sedate and relaxing, the river lined with cave-houses and cave-cellars cut into the tufa escarpment (see box on p.239). You'll need your own wheels to get about, and cycling is particularly rewarding as the distances and gradients are both small. For comprehensive local information on the area, including addresses of local chambres d'hôtes, contact the tourist office in Vendôme (see above), or check online at ⓦwww.loir-valley.com.

The pretty, peaceful village of **THORÉ-LA-ROCHETTE**, 9km west of Vendôme, is typical of this stretch of the Loir valley, its rock-cut *caves* used to store the wines of the surrounding Côteaux du Vendômois, a minor local *appellation*. In summer, a single-carriage 1950s **tourist train** (June & Sept 1–15 Sat & Sun 2.25pm; July & Aug Sat 2.25pm, Sun 9.30am, 2.25pm & 5.30pm; €10, children under 16 €7.50; ☎02.54.72.80.82) runs three-hour trips down to Trôo and back, along a leafy stretch of line.

Lavardin and Montoire-sur-le-Loir

Crammed into a verdant side-valley 19km west of Vendôme, the tiny village of **LAVARDIN** is absurdly pretty. The ruined walls of its medieval château, which once guarded the border between the Plantagenêt lands and the northern holdings of the Capetian kings of France, cascade down from a hilltop promontory towards the old stone houses of the village. A beautiful and surprisingly large Romanesque church, the **église St-Genest**, lies at the heart of the village, preserving some wonderful, rust-coloured twelfth- to fourteenth-century wall-paintings in its choir. Down beside the river, a very friendly and atmospheric **restaurant**, the *Relais d'Antan* (℡02.54.86.61.33; closed Mon & Tues; *menus* at €25 & €33), showcases the excellent and imaginative cuisine of its chef-owner.

On the opposite, north bank of the Loir, just under 2km away, **MONTOIRE-SUR-LE-LOIR** is a modest market town with two unusual claims to fame. It was at the train station here that Pétain met Hitler in October 1940 to agree the Vichy's government's official policy of collaboration, an event remembered by a modest exhibition on the spot. Nowadays, the town is celebrated for its week-long festival of world and folk music, the **Festival International de Montoire**, which attracts hundreds of artists and thousands of spectators in mid-August, with a giant parade on August 15. During the rest of the year, the museum **Musikenfete**, just off place Clemenceau (Tues–Sat: March–Sept 10am–noon & 2–6pm; Oct–Dec 2–6pm; €6.10), shows off scores of unusual instruments from around the world, some of which you can play, accompanied by videos of musicians playing them. Close by, on the broad, horse-chestnut-lined market square is the **tourist office**, at 16 place Clemenceau (April–Sept Mon–Sat 10am–noon & 3–7pm, Sun 11am–1pm; Oct–March Tues–Sat 10am–noon & 3–5pm; ℡02.54.85.23.30, ⓔmontoire@tourisme.cc), which can provide you with a key to the **chapelle St-Gilles** (same hours as tourist office; €2.50), a Romanesque chapel with three bold eleventh-century paintings of Christ covering its half-dome vaults. To get to the chapel, take rue Ronsard south off place Clemenceau, and turn right immediately after the bridge. For accommodation and food, make for the *Hôtel du Cheval Rouge*, 1 place Foch (℡02.54.85.07.05; ❸; closed mid-Nov to mid-Dec), a genteel, old-fashioned **hotel-restaurant** with an emphasis on the latter role. It also offers some bargain-priced rooms (❶) with shared bathrooms.

Trôo

Seven kilometres downstream of Montoire, the "troglodyte" village of **TROO** (pronounced to rhyme with "no") rises gently in a series of rocky tiers from the north bank of the river. The hilltop is capped by the **collégiale St-Martin**, an imposing Gothic structure, but the real interest lies in the relatively lowly houses of the village itself, spread out along two main transverse lanes, the rue Basse and the rue Haute, which are connected by steep stone stairways. Most of the houses are, in fact, caves – even the ones with conventional facades communicate behind with an elaborate network of some 14km of tunnels that riddles the hillside from top to bottom. During the Middle Ages, when it's thought that most of the caves were cut, the rich would have lived on the upper levels, and the poor down at the bottom.

Beside a stairway joining rues Basse and Haute, in the very centre of the village, is the **Cave des Amis de Trôo** (hours vary, but generally mid-March to mid-Nov Mon–Fri 2–7pm, Sat & Sun 10am–7pm; €2.50, or €4 with Cave Yuccas). This is a good place to start exploring, as it houses an exhibition on the geology of the area, the orchids and subtropical plants that grow here, the local folk traditions and the bat population – seventeen of France's thirty species can be found in and around Trôo. Even if you don't speak French, there's plenty to be gleaned. At the time of writing, the local association were hoping to get permission to run tours of the **caforts**, the seven underground levels of tunnels that lace the hillside beneath. Just above, the delightful **Cave Yuccas** (same hours and price as Cave des Amis), so called because yucca plants grow abundantly against the sunny, south-facing rock, has been done up as a traditional troglodyte house, complete with chimneys and a bread oven, and furnished with old-fashioned tables, chairs and beds. There are various curiosities elsewhere in the village, including the **Grotte Pétrifiante** – a cave-spring that quickly coats any objects left there in limestone – the old bakery and a much-venerated statue of St Gabriel, but the most enjoyable thing to do is test the dramatic echo inside the **puits qui parle**, or "talking well", which is found at the top of the village, 100m beyond the collégiale. On the opposite side of the river, the **église St-Jacques-des-Guérets** shelters twelfth-century wall-paintings.

The most characterful **accommodation** option is run by Barbara and Bernard Savaete (℡02.54.72.50.34, ✉bandbcave@minitel.net; ❸), who let out a troglodyte room right in the heart of the village. For something more elegant, there are antique-furnished bedrooms at the *Château de la Voute* (℡02.54.72.52.52, 🌐www.chateaudelavoute.com; ❼), a large eighteenth-century house overlooked by two medieval towers, situated towards the foot of the village. At the east end of the village, on the road out towards Montoire, is the *Auberge Ste-Catherine*, carrefour Ste-Catherine (℡02.54.72.51.23; ❶; closed Jan), a friendly, family-run hotel in a venerable tufa-built house. It offers half a dozen simple and inexpensive rooms, and well-cooked French classics in a stone-vaulted dining room (*menus* from €15; closed Sun evening & Mon). *Le Petit Relais*, next to the collégiale, is an attractive if touristy **restaurant** offering a *menu du jour* for under €20 and bottles of local cider.

La Possonnière

In 1524, the poet **Pierre de Ronsard** (see p.328) was born at the manor house of **La Possonnière**, 11km west of Trôo (late March to mid-Nov Mon & Wed–Sun 10am–2pm; €3.50). The main building is a refined, early-fifteenth-century gentleman's residence commissioned by Ronsard's father. The other side of the L-shaped courtyard is formed by a miniature tufa cliff into which "troglodyte" rooms have been dug out, with elaborate doorways adorned with inscriptions in French or Latin describing their use. The main house also wears its literary credentials on its sleeves, its doors and windows captioned with quirky epigrams and the family emblem of a flaming rose bush – a typically Renaissance visual pun on *roses ardentes* (burning roses) – "Rons-ard" for short. The interior (late March to June & Sept to mid-Nov Mon & Fri–Sun 2–6pm; July & Aug daily 10am–7pm; €5) can only be visited on a guided tour, which is usually available in English. There's not much to see inside, though a museum dedicated to the poet is planned.

Ronsard asked to be buried on the **Ile Verte**, the midstream "green island" at Couture-sur-Loir, 1km north. His wish was only honoured for a few years, however, as his body was later exhumed and transferred to the Prieuré de St-Cosme, near Tours (see p.70). The island remains a peaceful place to sit or stroll.

Le Lude

Strategically situated at the ancient border between Touraine, Anjou and the Maine – Le Mans, Tours and Saumur are all less than 50km distant – is the mighty château of **Le Lude** (April–Sept daily 10am–12.30pm & 2–6pm; guided tours afternoons only; closed Wed in April, May & Sept; gardens €4.60, château €6; [@]www.lelude.com). The shape is basically medieval, a central keep defended by four belligerent, machicolated corner towers whose rough-hewn, thirteenth-century foundations are still exposed in the deep, dry moat. The decoration, however, is pure early Renaissance, dating from the 1520s. The windows are outlined in finely carved tufa, the walls studded with Classical medallions, and the towers joined by arcaded terraces topped by balustrades. All this was the work of **Jean Gendrot**, architect to Jacques de Daillon, who presumably developed his tastes while serving in François I's Italian wars. The last of the Daillon family died in 1685, and the château fell slowly into disuse until 1751, when it was bought by Joseph Duvelaër, a merchant who had made his fortune in the East Indies. He bequeathed it to his niece, Françoise Butler, who squeezed the supremely Classical **Louis XVI facade** between the towers of the east front in 1787, just before the Revolution.

Françoise Butler's aristocratic descendants still occupy the château, which gives the guided tour of the **interior** (often available in English on request; afternoons only) a voyeuristic frisson – there are family photos everywhere. The stony **vestibule** is the only complete Renaissance room, though many original painted wall panels and beams were uncovered in the nineteenth century. Similarly, the exceptional **Oratory** – actually, an Italian-inspired *studiolo*, or room intended for private study, meditation and storage of fine art – was only discovered in 1853, its walls entirely painted with representations of Old Testament stories and its vaulted ceiling covered in birds, flowers and nymph-like figures. Both are early sixteenth century, the ceiling probably from the school of Primaticcio, the great decorative artist behind François I's palace at Fontainebleau. Many of the other rooms visited on the tour preserve elegant Louis XVI decorative schemes, or are nineteenth-century reconstructions packed with old Flemish tapestries and antique furnishings.

Even if you don't join a tour of the interior, you can explore the passageways that link both sides of the moat underneath the château, and the extensive terraced **gardens**, which fall away towards the Loir. On the first weekend in June, a large **garden festival** takes over château and grounds. Thousands of plants are on sale or display, and there are various workshops – for which you'll need excellent French.

The adjacent village of **LE LUDE** is rather dull, but there are plenty of shops for stocking up on picnic supplies. Alternatively, the hotel-**restaurant** *La Renaissance*, 2 ave de la Libération, on the road out towards La Flèche ([@]02.43.94.63.10; closed Sun evening & Mon), offers generally rather fancy fare, as well as a good, inexpensive *menu du jour*.

Le Mans

LE MANS, the historic capital of the Maine region, is taken over by car fanatics in the middle of June for the famous 24-hour race, but during the rest of the year it's a fascinating and unusually peaceful place to visit. As a large, industrial and traditionally left-wing city, its atmosphere could hardly be more different from bourgeois Tours, 80km to the south, but the two cities share a passion for *rillettes*, a kind of potted pork meat, as well as a good deal of history: Le Mans was the favourite home of the Plantagenêt family, the counts of Anjou, Touraine and Maine. The old quarter, in the shadow of the magnificent cathedral, is unusually well preserved, while outside town you can visit the serene Cistercian abbey of Epau and, of course, the race track.

ACCOMMODATION
Chantecler D
Levasseur B
Première Classe A
Select E
Hostel C

RESTAURANTS
Auberge des 7 Plats 1
Le Flambadou 3
Le Fontainebleau 2
Le Grenier à Sel 4

Chartres & Paris

LE MANS

0   200 m

Tours & Racing Circuits ▼

Arrival, information and accommodation

The hub of modern Le Mans is the **place de la République**, with its assortment of Belle Epoque facades and fountains and more modern office blocks. Bus #16 runs between here and the **gare SNCF** via ave Général-Leclerc, where the **gare routière** is located. The **tourist office**, on rue de l'Étoile (Mon–Sat 9am–6pm, Sun 10am–noon, July & Aug also Sun 2–6pm; ☎02.43.28.17.22, ⊛www.ville-lemans.fr), lies a couple of minutes' walk east of place de la République. **Bikes** can be rented from Top Team, on place St-Pierre, in the old town.

Unless your visit coincides with one of the big racing events during April, June or September (see p.294), you should be able to find **accommodation** easily without having to book, though disappointingly, there's nothing in the old town.

Hotels

Hôtel Chantecler 50 rue de la Pelouse ☎02.43.14.40.00, ⊛www.hotel-chantecler.com. This quiet, independent three-star is very professionally run, but friendly nonetheless. The rooms are modern but well fitted-out, and parking is available. ❹

Hôtel Levasseur 5–7 bd René Levasseur ☎02.43.39.61.61, ℗02.43.39.61.65. This two-star hotel has a good location just off place de la République, but it's rather rambling inside, and the rooms feel a bit functional. Closed Aug. ❸

Hôtel de Rennes 43 bd de la Gare ☎02.43.24.86.40, ℗02.43.87.02.95. This simple, inexpensive hotel right next to the station has been done up in bright colours and cheery pastels, and is spotlessly kept. Inexpensive rooms with shared bathrooms are available, and all rooms are double-glazed. ❷

Hôtel Select 13 rue du Père-Mersenne, off ave du Général-Leclerc ☎02.43.24.17.74. This small hotel is pretty basic, with little sinks behind screens and grubby floral wallpaper, but the price is right. ❶

Première Classe 40 rue du Vert-Galant ☎02.43.24.47.24, ℗02.43.24.58.41. This anonymous and business-like chain hotel isn't really aimed at tourists, but it's central, comfortable and reasonable value, so makes a good fall-back option. ❷

Hostel

Le Flore 23 rue Maupertuis ☎02.43.81.27.55. A clean and modern HI hostel, quite close to the centre. Take ave du Général-de-Gaulle from place de la République, continue along ave Bollée; rue Maupertuis is the third on the left.

The City

The modern centre of Le Mans is **place de la République**, bordered by a mixture of Belle Epoque buildings and more modern office blocks, and the Baroque bulk of the **église de la Visitation**. Almost all the sights lie inside the beautiful **old quarter**, on the raised ground immediately west of the cathedral.

Cathédrale St-Julien

At the crown of the old town is the immense **cathédrale St-Julien**, on cobbled place du Grente (daily: late June to late Sept 8am–7pm; late Sept to late June 8am–noon & 2–6pm; free). The approach from the east, up the steps from **place du Jet d'Eau** and past the forest of flying buttresses that props up the incredibly tall Gothic choir, is undeniably dramatic. The older half of the cathedral, the nave, was only just completed when Geoffroi le Bel – the count of Maine and Anjou who wore a sprig of *genêt* (broom) in his hat, hence Plantagenêt – married Matilda, daughter of Henry I of England, in 1129, thus founding the Plantagenêt line. The cathedral is one of the greatest

Romanesque structures in France, in both scale and decorative ingenuity. According to Rodin, the sculpted figures of the south porch were rivalled only by those at Chartres cathedral and the Parthenon in Athens, though they are now sadly weathered. The archaic lozenge patterns of the **west front** date right back to the 1050s, when the nave was begun, but the most ancient stone of all is propped up against the southwest corner, a strangely anthropomorphic, pink-tinted **menhir** that may be a last remnant of a prehistoric sacred site at this spot. Local tradition would have you put your fingers in the holes for good luck.

Inside, for all the power and measured beauty of the Romanesque structure, it's impossible not to be drawn towards the High Gothic choir. At the transept, there's a vertiginous leap up to the 34-metre-high thirteenth-century vault. The whole choir is filled with coloured light filtering through the stained-glass windows, but the brightest colours are found in the **chapelle de la Vierge**, at the easternmost end of the choir, where the stunning vault is painted with angels singing, dancing and playing medieval musical instruments, set against a lustrous red background. The **sacristy**, on the south side of the ambulatory, is worth seeing for its single central column, which seems to fountain out into the vault above.

The city centre

The **old town** lies on a hill above the River Sarthe to the north of the central place de la République. Its medieval streets, a hotchpotch of intricate Renaissance stonework, medieval half-timbering, sculpted pillars and beams and grand classical facades, are still encircled by the original third- and fourth-century **Gallo-Roman walls**, which are among the best-preserved in Europe and run for several hundred metres. Their shape, and the elaborate geometric details set into their pink brick, are best viewed from the river, which can be accessed by steep steps from the south side of place du Cardinal Grente.

Local crafts and history are showcased at the **Musée de la Reine Bérengère**, rue de la Reine-Bérengère (May–Sept daily 10.30am–12.30pm & 2–6.30pm; Oct–April Tues–Sun 2–6pm; €2.80, or €5.20 with Musée de Tessé), which is named after Queen Bérengère of Navarre, the wife of Richard the Lionheart. The museum is dull, but the house is a beautiful fifteenth-century construction, one of many such on the street. The **Maison des Deux-Amis**, opposite, gets its name for the carving of two men (the "two friends") supporting a coat of arms between the doors of numbers 18 and 20. Heading away from the cathedral, you enter the equally ancient **Grande Rue**. Further down on the left, just off place St-Pierre, a sixteenth-century apothecary's shop known as the **Maison d'Adam et Eve** is superbly carved, the pair of original sinners apparently contemplating a gigantic toffee apple.

In the 1850s a road was tunnelled under the quarter – a slum at the time – helping to preserve its self-contained unity. The road tunnel comes out on the south side, by an impressive **monument to Wilbur Wright** – who tested an early flying machine in Le Mans – and into place des Jacobins, the vantage point for the St-Julien apse. From here, you can walk east through the park to the **Musée de Tessé** (July & Aug Tues–Sun 10.30am–12.30pm & 2–6.30pm; Sept–June Tues–Sat 9am–noon & 2–6pm, Sun 10–noon & 2–6pm; €4, or €5.20 with Musée de la Reine Bérengère), where the highlight is an exquisite enamel portrait of Geoffroi le Bel, which was originally part of his tomb in the cathedral. Otherwise it's a very mixed bag of paintings, furnishings and sculptures, while in the basement there's a full-scale reconstruction of the ancient Egyptian tomb of Queen Nefertari.

Le Mans' associations with automobiles began early, when local bell-founder Amadée Bollée built the world's first car in 1873 – though it was steam-powered, as Gottlieb Daimler's internal combustion engine only appeared in 1887. Over a century later, Le Mans has a huge Renault factory operating in its southwest suburbs, and the **24 Heures** race is a giant of the racing calendar, attended by a quarter of a million petrolheads – 80,000 of them British.

The first big race at Le Mans was the Grand Prix de l'Automobile Club de l'Ouest in 1906. Two years later **Wilbur Wright** took off in his prototype aeroplane, alongside what is now the fastest stretch of the racetrack, remaining in the air for a record-breaking one hour and 31.5 minutes. 1923 saw the first 24-hour car race, run on the present 13.6-kilometre circuit, with average speeds of 92kph (57mph). It established the classic rule – that all drivers must make repairs on the circuit. The original suicidal start, which saw drivers running to their cars from a standing line-up, was only abolished in 1970, the year Porsche began their legendary winning streak. In 1979, the actor Paul Newman finished second; the following year a Frenchman, Jean Rondeau, won in a car he had built himself. These days, expensively backed professional teams dominate – in 2003, the race was won by a British team, Bentley, the first time they had taken the chequered flag since 1930. The drivers had covered some 5000km (3000 miles) in the 24 hours, averaging around 210kph (130mph).

The racetrack and car museum

The **Sarthe circuit**, on which the world-renowned **24 Heures du Mans** car race takes place each year, stretches south from the outskirts of the city, along ordinary roads. The simplest way to get a taste of the track is just to take the main road south of the city towards Tours, a stretch of ordinary highway which follows the infamous **Mulsanne straight** for 5.7km – a distance that saw race cars reach speeds of up to 375kph (230mph), until two chicanes were introduced in 1989, bringing the revs down a few notches. You can follow the straight down to the Mulsanne corner, turn along the D140 towards Indianapolis and the Arnage corner, then follow the D139 to the Ford corner, at the entrance to the Bugatti circuit – the dedicated race-track section of the 24-hour route.

Races

Entrance to the actual **24 Heures** race, in mid-June, costs from around €30 to €60, depending on the level of access. Tickets can be bought direct from the organisers at Ⓦwww.lemans.org, but be sure to book well in advance. Many enthusiasts' clubs and ticket agencies offer packages including accommodation – difficult to find at race times – and the crucial parking passes; try Ⓦwww.clubarnage.com or Ⓦwww.motorracingtours.com, or look through the adverts in a local motor-sports magazine. At other times of the year you can attend the **Le Mans Classic**, in September, and the bikers' **24 Heures Moto**, in early April, among other races.

Musée de l'Automobile

The **Musée de l'Automobile** (daily: June–Sept 10am–7pm; Oct–Dec & March–May 10am–6pm; €6) is on the edge of the Bugatti circuit, the dedicated track section of the main Sarthe circuit. As a stunning parade of some 150 vehicles, ranging from the humble 2CV to classic Lotus and Porsche race cars,

THE NORTHERN APPROACHES | Le Mans

the museum speaks for itself, but there's also a good attempt to document the early history of car racing, including automobile anatomy and automated assembly. The visit ends with audio-visual displays examining the world of car racing, including a simulated high-speed track.

The Abbaye de l'Epau

If car racing holds no romance, there's another outing from Le Mans of a much more contemplative nature, to the Cistercian **abbaye de l'Epau** (daily 9.30am–noon & 2–5.30pm; opening hours may vary in summer to accommodate exhibitions; ☎02.43.84.22.29; €2.80), 4km out of town, off the Chartres–Paris road. If you haven't got your own transport, take bus #14 from place de la République in Le Mans to the "Pologne" stop, from where it's a five-minute walk. The abbey was founded in 1229 by **Bérengère**, or Berengaria of Navarre, the wife of Richard the Lionheart – though they rarely saw each other, and never had children, perhaps because of Richard's probable homosexuality. In fact, Richard repeatedly spurned her, and formally repudiated her in 1196, after which she retired to Anjou and then, after fighting John for a share of the rapidly diminishing Plantagenêt territories in France, to Le Mans.

The abbey stands in the Cistercian's favoured rural setting, and has remained more or less unaltered since its early fifteenth-century restoration after a fire. You can visit the huge dormitory under its wooden barrel vault, and the typically plain abbey church, but more interesting is the **chapterhouse**, whose four columns support a web of ribbed vaulting protecting Bérengère's original **tomb**. Her slightly outsized effigy clutches a book, representing her "life story".

Eating and drinking

In the centre of town, the **cafés** and **brasseries** on place de la République stay open till late, while on nearby place l'Eperon there's a very good, if pricey, traditional French **restaurant**, *Le Grenier à Sel* (☎02.43.23.26.30; closed Sat lunch & Sun; *menus* from €19). The most atmospheric restaurants, however, are located in the labyrinthine streets of the old town. The *Auberge des 7 Plats*, 79 Grande-Rue (closed Sun & Mon), does a good range of inexpensive *plats* and a good-value *menu* at €14. For a special occasion make for the rustic *Le Flambadou*, 14bis rue St-Flaceau (☎02.43.24.88.38; closed Sun), which offers a very meaty *menu* from Périgord and the Landes from around €30. Nearby on place St-Pierre, *Le Fontainebleu* (☎02.43.14.25.74; closed Tues) has pleasant outside seating facing the Hôtel de Ville and serves classic French cuisine, with *menus* from €15.

There's a daily **market** in the covered halls on place du Marché, plus a bric-a-brac market on Wednesday, Friday and Sunday mornings on place du Jet-d'Eau, below the cathedral on the new town side.

The Sarthe valley

The **River Sarthe** begins its course some 30km north of Le Mans, from where it winds southwest through the heart of the historic Maine region before joining the Mayenne just north of Angers. The most beautiful stretch of river lies between Le Mans and the border with Anjou, a picturesque backwater corner of France made up principally of *bocage* – an English-style landscape of small fields, orchards and patches of woodland criss-crossed by hedgerows and streams. You can picnic at picturesque villages such as **Asnières-sur-Vègre** and **St-Denis-d'Anjou**, and visit the ceramics centre of **Malicorne-sur-Sarthe**, but most fascinating of all is the Benedictine monastery at **Solesmes**, whose abbey church houses two extraordinary sculptural groups.

Malicorne-sur-Sarthe

Follow signs off the Le Mans ring road towards Allones and you'll quickly find yourself on the D23, one of the more attractive roads leading southwest towards Anjou. After 35km you'll arrive at **MALICORNE-SUR-SARTHE**, a centre of pottery production since Roman times, and of fine faïence since 1747. Two faïence workshops are still in business, while the entire history of local ceramics is displayed at the **Espace Faïence**, 24 rue Victor-Hugo (April–Sept daily 10am–7pm; Oct–Dec & March Mon & Wed–Sun 10am–noon & 2.30–6.30pm; €6), a large, modern gallery and museum stacked with ceramics ranging from beautifully glazed eighteenth-century pieces to contemporary art works. If you want to explore further, Malicorne's **tourist office**, 3 place du Guesclin, beside the bridge (☎02.43.94.74.45, ⊛www.ville-malicorne.fr) can help arrange visits to the two active faïence workshops. It also rents out **boats**, kayaks and pedalos for paddling about on the river – the centre of the village overlooks a broad, attractive stretch with weirs, watermills and a small island. There's little else to do apart from visit the plain but very old **église St-Sylvestre**, an eleventh-century structure housing the fifteenth-century tomb effigy of local lord Guy de Chaource.

La Petite Auberge, 5 place du Guesclin (☎02.43.94.80.52; *menus* from €15; closed Mon; Oct–March closed Mon–Fri & Sun evening) is an excellent place for a **restaurant** meal, serving up gourmet dishes, with an emphasis on fish, at a sunny terrace overlooking the river. The riverbank **campsite** *Le Port Ste-Marie* (☎02.43.94.80.14; closed Nov–March) is close at hand.

Asnières-sur-Vègre

From Malicorne-sur-Sarthe, the D8 leads to **Parcé-sur-Sarthe**, 10km west, a picturesque riverside village with a number of rustic eighteenth-century houses. Prettier still is **ASNIÈRES-SUR-VÈGRE**, 7km north of Parcé – to get there you'll have to cross back over the Sarthe, as if heading east, then turn immediately left on the D57 through Avoise. Asnières is entirely constructed in the golden-coloured local stone and is centred on a twelfth-century humpback bridge over the River Vègre, a tributary of the Sarthe. Signposts point out various ancient houses and other local landmarks such as the **manoir de la Cour**, a large shell of a thirteenth-century manor house, and the **église St-Hilaire**, a simple parish church with a Gothic choir and Romanesque nave, the latter decorated with beautiful wall-paintings that were only discovered underneath the whitewash in 1950. It's a pleasant stroll across the bridge and up the hill to the elegant, eighteenth-century **château de Moulin Vieux**, though the château is private and the grounds only sporadically open for visits.

The **restaurant** *Le Pavillon*, in the centre of the village, is usually open for snacks and simple meals, but this is perfect picnic territory. If you want to stay locally, there are two excellent if pricey **chambres d'hôtes** in the nearby countryside, both set in fifteenth-century buildings on the Vègre and well signposted from the centre. The atmospheric but relatively modest *Manoir des*

Claies, 2km northwest of the village (☎02.43.92.40.50, 🖷02.43.92.65.72; ❺; closed Nov–Easter), offers three welcoming and sympathetically decorated rooms, and a swimming pool in the summer months, while the *Château de Dobert*, on the minor road towards Avoise, the C4 (☎02.43.92.01.52; ❻; closed July & Nov–April), is a grander place extended in the eighteenth century, with three elegant, antique-furnished bedrooms.

Juigné-sur-Sarthe and Solesmes

The D22, an attractive back road heading southwest from Asnières towards Sablé-sur-Sarthe, reaches the river just below **JUIGNE-SUR-SARTHE**, 6km away, a medieval hilltop village with a thirteenth-century church and a fine view downriver. Below in **Port-de-Juigné**, a local enthusiast has opened **l'Amusant Musée** (Sat, Sun & school holidays 2.30–7pm; €5, children under 16 €4), a private toy museum crammed into two tiny rooms. The owner will engagingly demonstrate many of his two thousand or so old-fashioned and contemporary toys for you, and let you discover others for yourself – most visitors seem to find some forgotten treasure from their own era.

Just over 1km west of Juigné, the **abbaye de St-Pierre** (ⓦwww.solesmes.com) at **SOLESMES** dominates the valley bottom. The bulk of the castle-like monastic buildings are the work of the reforming Dom Guéranger, who refounded the Benedictine monastery in 1833, some forty years after it had been broken up in the Revolution. There are now over sixty brothers, following St Benedict's original rule of poverty, chastity and obedience, and doing research – theoretical and practical – into Gregorian chant. The monks welcome visitors to their sung services at 10am (High Mass), 1pm (Sext), 1.50pm (None), 5pm (Vespers) and 8.30pm (Compline), and young men are received freely as guests on retreat.

Most visitors, however come to visit not the monks but the extraordinary **saints de Solesmes**, two monumental groups of statues in the transepts of the abbey church – the nave of which dates back to the first priory, founded here in 1010. The extraordinarily naturalistic *Entombment* group in the **south transept** dates from around 1500. It is framed by an arch that drops down at the centre into a stone case inscribed with the words *factus in pace loc eius* ("his place having been made in peace"). Once a year, on Easter Monday, this reliquary displays the **Holy Thorn**, a relic from Jesus' crown brought back from the Crusades in the twelfth century by the local lord of Sablé.

In the 1530s, the monks decided to outdo the work in the south transept by filling the **northern side** with some hundred figures of saints and biblical scenes. The statues themselves are similar in style to the earlier group, apparently caught in motion, but the architectural framing is in the full grip of the Renaissance, crawling with columns, medallions and floral and scallop-shell motifs. The main scene shows the burial of Mary, while above is her Assumption into heaven.

Practicalities

If you want to **stay**, the *Grand Hôtel de Solesmes*, 16 place Dom-Guéranger (☎02.43.95.22.26, 🖂grandhotelsolesmes@wanadoo.fr; ❻), has a superb location immediately opposite the abbey, and a three-star rating for its room sizes, sauna and modern facilities, but the actual rooms are in an ugly modern block and not half as swish as you'd think from the building's facade and reception. The restaurant is rather overpriced, with *menus* starting at €25, but it's reliable enough.

Sablé-sur-Sarthe and around

Three kilometres downstream of Solesmes, the small, semi-industrialized town of **SABLÉ-SUR-SARTHE** doesn't have much to recommend it – a poultry slaughterhouse is one of its biggest employers – except perhaps the little river port at its heart, the local biscuits known as *sablés* and the usual facilities of a fair-sized town, as well as good TGV connections to Le Mans and Angers and a helpful **tourist office** on the central place Raphël-Elizé (Mon–Sat 10am–noon & 2–5.30pm; ☎02.43.95.00.60, ⊛www.sable-sur-sarthe.com). Sablé's handful of hotels is uninspiring, but the **restaurant** *Le Saint Martin*, 3 rue Haute St-Martin, just off the main square (☎02.43.95.00.03; closed Wed evening, Sun evening & Mon), serves excellent traditional French cuisine, with lots of reasonably priced à la carte options.

Fourteen kilometres south of Sablé-sur-Sarthe, a short drive beyond **Précigné**, the *Manoir de la Tigrenière* (☎02.43.92.74.20, ⊛http://manoirtigre-niere.free.fr; ❺–❻) offers two beautifully done-up **chambres d'hôtes** in a grand sixteenth-century farmhouse, and a suite whose exposed stone walls, earthenware-tiled floor, roof beams and four-poster bed are particularly enticing. To get there, take the D24 southeast of the village and turn north after 3km up the D254; it's signposted after a short distance.

St-Denis-d'Anjou

Eleven kilometres beyond Sablé-sur-Sarthe along the D309, **ST-DENIS-D'ANJOU** is one of the most beguiling of the region's little villages. At its heart is the **église St-Denis**, a chaotically constructed mongrel building whose most interesting feature is the set of rustically sketched sixteenth-century wall-paintings that brighten the nave. The rest of the village repays a wander. Rue des Halles leads behind the church, across the stream, past some lovely old houses and a slate *pissoir*, and onto **place des Halles**, where the large, timber-roofed market hall dates from 1509. You can turn left to return via the smithy and fifteenth-century **manoir**, or continue round via **rue du Puits Morin**, one of the best-preserved medieval streets.

Despite its modest size, the village has a number of excellent places to eat and stay. The part-fifteenth-century *Auberge du Roi René* (☎02.43.70.52.30, ⊛www.roi-rene.fr; ❹), managed exuberantly and with a definite personal touch by a husband-and-wife team, has four characterful yet homely **chambres d'hôtes**, and an atmospherically decorated **restaurant** offering sometimes inventive, sometimes hearty dishes, with *menus* from €20 to €40. Set in an old post-house, the *Hostellerie La Calèche*, rte d'Angers (☎02.43.70.61.00, ⓔhostellerielacaleche@wanadoo.fr; ❸), is more of a conventional provincial **hotel** – welcoming, family-run and with just seven modern, bright and unfussy rooms and a traditional, inexpensive restaurant (closed Sun evening & Mon). *Le Logis du Ray* (☎02.43.70.64.10, ⓔecoleattelageduray@laposte.net) runs some attractive chambres d'hôtes as a sideline from its horse-and-carriage business, while deep in the countryside near **Varennes**, a pretty hamlet on the Sarthe, 5km southeast of St-Denis, the organic farm *La Morlière* (☎ & ⓕ02.43.70.91.65; ❸) offers a welcoming "ecologîte" – everything is built and runs in a sustainable way – and two simple but cosy chambres d'hôtes in a restored farm outbuilding.

Travel details

Trains

Chartres to: Le Mans (11 daily; 1hr 15min–1hr 45min); Paris Montparnasse (at least hourly; 1hr); Tours (usually requires change; 4–6 daily; 2hr 10min–3hr 20min).

Le Mans to: Angers (17 daily; 40min–1hr 20min); Paris (hourly; 1hr); Tours (7 daily; 1hr).

Sablé-sur-Sarthe to: Angers (6–11 daily; 20–35min); Le Mans (6–11 daily; 20–30min).

Vendôme to: Châteaudun (2 daily; 35min); Tours (11 daily; 30min–1hr).

Buses

Chartres to: Châteaudun (4 daily; 1hr); Orléans (9 daily; 1hr 10min–1hr 45min); Tours (2 daily; 1hr 40min).

Le Mans to: Baugé (2 daily; 1hr 15min); Saumur (1–2 daily; 2hr).

Vendôme to: Blois (5–6 daily; 1hr–1hr 35min); Châteaudun (4 daily; 45min–1hr).

Contexts

Contexts

History

T he role of the Loire region in French history has been rather like the river itself: generally sleepy and placid, though its easy flow has at times been disrupted by violent floods. Chief among these disruptive episodes were the Plantagenêt era in the twelfth century; the last years of the Hundred Years War, when Joan of Arc roused the French to victory in 1429; and the late fifteenth and early sixteenth centuries, when the Loire was in the vanguard of the French Renaissance. Since then, the region's political and commercial influence has steadily dwindled even as the river has silted up, and it has now settled into a comfortable provincial existence.

Prehistory

The Atlantic Ocean has come and gone many times over the terrain that now makes up the Loire, like a vast tide in geological time. The deposits it repeatedly left behind now form the **Bassin Parisien**, which extends across much of northern France towards Paris. Most of the region's typically soft, chalky rock, known as *tuffeau blanc*, or **tufa**, was laid down towards the end of the Upper Cretaceous period, roughly 90 million years ago, during the era geologists have called the Turonian, after Touraine. In the Miocene era, between 15 million and 9 million years ago, the sea invaded up the Loire as far the site of modern-day Blois, creating the Mer des Faluns, named after the **faluns**, or fossilized shells, that characterize the rock. From around this time, the Alps began to be pushed upwards, causing the River Loire to change its course from the north – it once flowed into the Seine – to the west.

The earliest peoples in the Loire may have arrived as early as 10,000 BC, but little is known about them other than that they used flint and bone tools. The age of **megaliths** lasted for roughly a thousand years, from around 2500 BC to 1500 BC, during which time hundreds of dolmens (burial chambers) and menhirs (single standing stones) were erected all over the Loire – roughly 150 have been found in the region, with a particularly high concentration in the Saumurois. It is impossible to reconstruct more than a fragmentary picture of **Stone Age** life, but it seems that a thriving trade followed the rivers, flints from Anjou being transported up the Loire across to the Rhône and down to the Mediterranean – archeologists have turned up goods from as far away as Greece. The land between the rivers was heavily forested, as is recalled by the many place names ending in *-euil*, such as Bourgueil and Montreuil, which comes from the Gallic word *ialos*, meaning "clearing".

Celts and Romans

When Julius Caesar began his conquest of Gaul in 58 BC he found a sophisticated Iron Age people living in fortified villages and loosely gathered into tribes: the Turones from what is now Touraine; the Carnutes, from between Chartres and the Orléanais; the Andecavi from Anjou; and the Bituriges from Bourges – whose name means "kings of the world". These **Celtic** tribes had probably arrived in the region from the east in around 500 BC and presumably settled alongside the earlier peoples. Caesar's account of his campaign, the *Conquest of Gaul*, refers to a great druidic meeting in the Forest of the Carnutes, probably held in the vicinity of modern St-Benoît-sur-Loire, in what was called the *omphalos*, or navel, of the country. Valuable material evidence of this druidic culture was found near Orléans in 1861, when the Treasure of Neuvy-en-Sullias was discovered, its sophisticated cast bronze animals and figurines indicating some kind of veneration of forest creatures. Caesar found the Carnutes particularly hard to subdue, and they were among the leaders in the Gaulish uprising of 52 BC. Caesar responded by razing their capital, Cenabum, on the site of modern-day Orléans, in the same year as he conquered Vercingetorix at Alésia.

Roman rule brought the well-known benefits: order, straight roads, aqueducts, trade with the empire, country villas, wine and towns. The chief cities of the Loire were all founded in this era – albeit probably on Celtic sites – from Juliomagus (Angers), Caesarodunum (Tours) and Vindinium (Le Mans), to Vindocinum (Vendôme), Avaricum (Bourges) and Aurelianum (Orléans). Le Mans and, to a lesser extent, Tours, still preserve their Gallo-Roman walls, and near Luynes you can see a stretch of the aqueduct that once supplied Tours with water.

The Franks

From the third century, Gaul began to be invaded by waves of warlike pagans from the east, at much the same time as Christianity started to pervade the empire. The bishop St Gatien is known to have preached in Tours in around 250, but Christianity only became established at the end of the fourth century, with the arrival of **St Martin** (see box on p.69). In the early fifth century, the **Franks** fought the Visigoths for control of Touraine, while Attila's Huns attacked Orléans, only to be repulsed by troops rallied by another early bishop, St Aignan. By 485, the Franks, under Clovis, had finally crossed the Loire and won control of Gaul, establishing the **Merovingian** dynasty. As described by the chronicler Gregory of Tours, Clovis converted to Christianity and summoned a council of bishops to Orléans, where they drew up the **Lex Salica**, the legal code of the Franks, which established the rule that daughters could not inherit land – this "salic law" was to become very significant in the dynastic struggles that ensued.

Years of vicious and fratricidal power struggles followed, until the palace mayor Charles Pepin, known as Charles Martel, "the Hammer", usurped his Merovingian overlords. He defeated the invading Arab armies in 732, the battle taking place somewhere on the plateau between southern Touraine and northern Poitou. Local legend claims that the prisoners were settled in the **Pays du Véron**, the spit of land between the Loire and Vienne, and that the local population is still darker skinned than in neighbouring *communes*.

Martel's grandson, **Charlemagne** (747–814) presided over a massive expansion of the Frankish territories well beyond the boundaries of modern-day France. Sadly, little remains of this miniature renaissance, other than a few scraps of decorative fragments on the church at Azay-le-Rideau and the oratory chapel near St-Benoît built by Theodulf, Charlemagne's counsellor and bishop of Orléans. Of the great centre of learning established by **Alcuin of York** at

Tours, nothing remains except Carolingian minuscule, the superbly readable script – it invented spaces between words, for one thing – on which the exact shapes of all modern European letters are based.

Capets and Plantagenêts

From the end of the eighth century, **Viking** raiders began to make incursions up the Loire, besieging Tours in 843, sacking Angers in 854 and taking control of Normandy, to the north of the Loire region, in the early tenth century. The ensuing chaos hastened the final collapse of the Carolingian empire, ushering in an era of highly militarized local lords. The area between Orléans and Paris belonged to the Robertians, who under Hugues le Grand became the most powerful family in France. Le Grand's son, **Hugues Capet** – named after the famous cape of the local patron St Martin (see box on p.69) – was eventually elected king of the Franks in Ste-Croix cathedral, in Orléans, in 987, thus beginning the **Capetian** dynasty. The coronation only gave him notional overlordship over his feudal vassals, however, and he had little power outside his own territories in the Orléanais and Ile de France.

Over to the west, the counts of Anjou and Blois fought it out over Touraine. Under **Foulque Nerra** (972–1040), the "Black Falcon" of Anjou, the Angevins (the people from Anjou) won decisively, and protected their enlarged territories with a string of fortified keeps, a number of which – Loches and Langeais, in particular – still survive. Nerra went on to conquer Maine and the Vendômois, establishing Anjou as one of the most powerful counties in France.

The Plantagenêt empire

In the early twelfth century, the Angevin count Geoffroi le Bel – called "**Plantagenêt**" for his habit of wearing a sprig of broom (*genêt* in French) in his hat – made two moves which significantly extended the territories belonging to Anjou. In 1110 he married Matilda, the daughter and heir of Henry I of England, and he later conquered Normandy in 1144. His son, Henri Plantagenêt, did even better, marrying **Eleanor of Aquitaine** (see box on p.235) and inheriting the English throne as **Henry II**, which made him master of a miniature empire stretching from the Scottish border to the Pyrenees, and incorporating roughly a third of France – a far larger territory than that controlled by the Capetian king, Louis VII.

War between the Capets and Plantagenêts was almost inevitable, especially as Eleanor had previously been Louis' wife; the sporadic clashes that ensued were named the "**First Hundred Years War**". By 1189, the rebellion of Henry's elder sons forced him to sue for peace, and he died in Chinon a broken man (see box on p.93). In the first years of the thirteenth century, his youngest son, John "Lackland", lost most of the empire to Philippe-Auguste, the martial son of Louis.

The Loire now lay wholly in Capetian hands, and under Louis VIII it was parcelled up and given to the royal children in appanage, meaning it could be held as a semi-autonomous territory under the Crown. The main purpose of the system was to provide the royal children with an independent source of income. Louis' youngest son was given Anjou and Maine, becoming **Charles I d'Anjou** (numerals being used for scions of powerful families as well as kings). His eldest son, **Louis IX**, signed the Treaty of Paris in 1259, officially ending the First Hundred Years War. Under its terms, all that remained of the Plantagenêts' continental territories was Guyenne, in Aquitaine. It soon proved to be a contentious bit of land.

Charles I used his Angevin power-base to launch the conquest of Naples and Sicily between 1265 and 1268 – the twin kingdoms whose titles he had been granted by the pope. He didn't hold onto the territories for long, but the claim to their titles passed down to his descendants – along with the title to king of Jerusalem, which Charles bought in 1277.

The origins of the Valois kings

The last Capetian monarch, Charles IV, died in 1328 without a male heir. Two nobles came forward to claim the throne. One was **Philippe de Valois**, a descendant of Charles I d'Anjou and nephew of Philippe IV. The other was Edward III of England, who based his title on being the grandson of Philippe IV through his daughter Isabelle. The salic law clearly ruled out Edward's claim, and in 1328 **Philippe VI** was duly crowned at Reims. He was the first of the Valois line, the dynasty that so favoured the Loire over the next two hundred years.

In 1341 Philippe applied the **gabelle** – the salt tax on which royal revenue was based – to the whole of France. Much of France's salt came up the Loire from Brittany, and the tax began to be applied rigorously along its length. Soon afterwards, the boatmen who worked on the Loire formed a **guild** to protect themselves against rapacious tolls levied by the land-owning aristocrats on either bank. It was one of the first signs of the rising confidence of local trades-men, an early hint of the Loire-based rise of the bourgeoisie.

The Hundred Years War

Edward III had initially done homage to Philippe VI as feudal overlord of the remaining English provinces in Aquitaine, but in 1337 he repudiated his oath and launched what became known as the **Hundred Years War**. The English landed in France in 1346 with the dual aims of making Edward III's claim to the French throne a reality and recapturing the lost Plantagenêt territories of Anjou, Aquitaine and Normandy. At **Crécy**, in northern France, the English won a decisive battle, decimating the French cavalry. They almost immediately signed a truce. Thus began a succession of brief conflicts followed by periods of peace, forming a pattern which lasted for 116 years. English armies and merce-nary bands roamed throughout northern and western France, alternately gain-ing, losing and simply terrorizing the lands they passed through, which often included the Loire. The wars were a tragedy for the peasantry, in particular, as their lives became steadily more brutish and insecure. The arrival of the **Black Death** in 1348 decimated the Loire region along with the rest of France, killing as much as a third of the population.

A second major French defeat, at **Poitiers** in 1356, led to the imprisonment in England of Philippe's son, Jean le Bon. Jean's elder son succeeded him as Charles V, pursuing a more successful policy of gradually chipping away at the territories held by the English in northern and southwestern France until, in 1369, he seized all of Aquitaine. Meanwhile, Charles V's brothers – the dukes of Anjou, Berry (see box on p.208) and Burgundy – ruled their allotted provinces in appanage, growing rich and powerful, especially after they became regents for the child king Charles VI, from 1380. Over in England, the dethronement of Richard II in 1399 and his subsequent death brought an end to the Plantagenêt line there.

Joan and the Dauphin

The wars between France and England received new impetus when the Burgundian duke **Jean sans Peur** ("the Fearless"), son of Philippe le Hardi, threw in his lot with the English in 1414. In 1415 the English armies arrived under the warlike Henry V, defeating the French at **Agincourt** on October 25 and taking control of most of northern France over the next four years. In 1418 the Burgundians occupied Paris, and in 1420 Charles VI was forced to sign the **Treaty of Troyes**, which disinherited his son and heir, the **Dauphin Charles**, in favour of Henry V of England. The Dauphin fled to the Loire and the territories he had inherited from his uncle, Jean de Berry, moving frequently between his châteaux in Bourges, Mehun-sur-Yèvre, Chinon and Loches.

In 1421 the battle of **Baugé**, in northern Anjou, stemmed the English advance. The following year Charles had himself proclaimed king of France at Mehun-sur-Yèvre, although he controlled no more than a fraction of the country – his enemies mockingly calling him the "little king of Bourges". Advisers such as **Georges de la Trémoïlle**, from Sully-sur-Loire, advised him to follow a pacifying, diplomatic solution, while others such as **Dunois**, of Châteaudun and Beaugency, wanted confrontation. The Loire became the front line. In 1426 Charles won a minor battle at Montargis, north of Orléans, but two years later the English were able to lay siege to Orléans, threatening Charles's heartlands. The situation was parlous, and might well have ended in complete defeat had it not been for the arrival at court, in 1429, of **Joan of Arc** (see box on p.174), a peasant girl who galvanized Charles into action with promises of divine support. The English were driven back, the Dauphin crowned as Charles VII at Reims in July 1429, and Joan burnt at the stake in 1431.

The royal Loire

Over the next twenty years, **Charles VII** drove the English out of all France except for a pocket around Calais; Paris was retaken in 1436, Le Mans in 1448. The Loire was now no longer an island of vulnerable French territory, but the heartland of a kingdom rapidly growing in wealth, population and confidence. From the 1450s, the court embarked on an era of luxury centred on the Loire valley. Aside from Charles's personal knowledge of the region, earned during the hard times of the war, the valley's attractions were obvious. Its climate was excellent, the forests provided good hunting, the vines produced excellent **wine** and there was a pre-existing network of fine châteaux between which the court – still itinerant at this time – could move. The Loire also had the advantage of being politically reliable, having backed the Crown during the wars – unlike Paris. Charles installed his mistress, **Agnès Sorel** (see p.118), in Loches and indulged in hunting, jousting and other chivalric pursuits with his sophisticated relative, **René d'Anjou** (see box on p.255), who had his own miniature court to the west. In Blois, the poet-duke **Charles d'Orléans** set up a third, relatively modest court, which later grew famous as the site of the **Concours de Blois**, a poetry contest held in the late 1550s (see p.132).

The later Valois kings

Charles VI	1380–1422	Louis XII	1498–1515
Charles VII	1422–1461	François I	1515–1547
Louis XI	1461–1483	Henri II	1547–1559
Charles VIII	1483–1498	François II	1559–1560

For the court, it was a time of prosperity and ease, and even for the local **peasantry** life grew less hard. The threats of war and plague steadily receded, and, from 1450, the harvests did not fail for an unbroken period of seventy years. Populations began to grow again, especially in the towns of the Loire where there was new employment on the fringes of the court circle. In the countryside, a kind of peasant aristocracy took shape in the form of the small-holder *fermiers*, or *coqs de village*, who acted as intermediaries between journey-men peasants, and merchants and the local *seigneur*, or lord. In the towns, the *aisés*, or well-to-do merchants and artisans, began to form the basis of what became the bourgeoisie. The **Loire**, as ever, formed a crucial trade artery, its shallow-drafted sailing vessels carrying goods from the Atlantic ports deep into the centre of France, from where they were shipped across to Paris or over into the Rhône valley, for access to the Mediterranean.

In 1461 **Louis XI** came to the throne, making Tours the home of the court in preference to Paris. He established a major silk industry in the city, and set about uniting the various territories of France, inheriting Anjou, Maine and Provence after the death of René in 1481, and winning control of Burgundy and Picardy a year later. During his reign, the merchant classes grew steadily more powerful. The most powerful families were all intermarried and financially intertwined, and in 1465 the Beaunes, Briçonnets and Berthelots formed a powerful syndicate, pro-tected by Jean Bourré, who built Langeais and Le Plessis-Bourré.

In the last years of his life, Louis succumbed to paranoia, barricading himself into his château at **Plessis**, just outside Tours. In 1483 he was succeeded by his 13-year-old son **Charles VIII**, though the kingdom was effectively run for the next seven years by **Ann de Beaujeu** from her seat in Gien. She had to fight both Brittany and domestic rebels. The malcontents – **Louis d'Orléans**, son of the poet Charles, and François I d'Orléans-Longueville, son of Dunois – were defeated at Beaugency in 1485, and later banished, while the skirmishes with Brittany were resolved by the forced marriage of Charles to the duchess of Brittany, Anne, at Langeais in 1491 (see box on p.89).

Charles VIII

By the close of the fifteenth century, the Loire had become the centre of a rich, large and well-ordered kingdom. After scarcely fifty years of peace, the French now turned their attention beyond their borders, to **Italy**, where Ferdi-nand of Naples had just died. Re-invoking the Angevin claim to the throne, Charles VIII invaded in August 1494 and conquered Naples by February 1495, his swift victory partly due to the new invention of iron cannon balls and part-ly to the age-old technique of treating the opponent with extreme cruelty – such that the murder, rape and firestorm left in the army's wake was known as the *furia francese*. By July 1495, however, Charles was forced to retreat across the Alps, and he had lost all his gains by December.

The French brought back two things that changed the shape of French his-tory. The first was **syphilis**, which the French called the "Neapolitan sickness"

CONTEXTS | History

(the Neapolitans, by contrast, called it the "French disease"). The second was a taste for Italianate architecture which soon mushroomed into a full-blooded passion for all things Italian, ushering in the rediscovery of Classical learning and taste in the **French Renaissance**. Charles began elaborate works on his château at Amboise, but in 1498 hit his head on a doorway while on his way to watch a game of tennis (see p.78) and died, suddenly, without heirs.

Louis XII

Under the salic law, the heir to the throne had to be traced through the male line, which meant Louis d'Orléans, the son of the poet Charles and great nephew of Charles VI. He duly ascended the throne as **Louis XII** in 1498, and quickly set about getting rid of his infertile wife, **Jeanne de France**, whom he had married in 1476 under the orders of her father Louis XI – ironically, in an attempt to ensure the termination of the rival Orléans line. An infamous annulment was quickly granted in Tours. Jeanne founded an order of nuns in Bourges and later took the veil herself. Louis was now free to secure Brittany by marrying Charles's widow, Anne de Bretagne, which he did in 1499.

Louis made **Blois** his capital, bringing the merchant classes fully within the circle of power for the first time in French history and relying increasingly on their financial acumen and resources. He continued the **Italian wars**, his Loire-based captain Charles II d'Amboise (see p.152) helping conquer Milan. The French brought back the Milanese duke Ludovico Sforza as a prisoner and held him captive in Loches (see p.119). More significant in the long term was the arrival of Italian artists and craftsmen, who were set to work decorating proto-Renaissance châteaux such as **Chaumont** and the Louis XII wing at **Blois**.

François I and the Renaissance

François I, a cousin of Louis XII, became king through yet another failure in the male line. According to an English chronicler, was "a goodly prince, stately of countenance, merry of chere, brown coloured, great eyes, high nosed, big lipped, fair breasted and shoulders, small legs and long feet". He was also six foot tall, courageous, charming and well educated: a true Renaissance prince. During his reign the fortunes of the Loire valley reached their zenith. The importation of Italian artists and Renaissance ideas continued to gather pace, and the king built fabulous new lodgings at **Amboise** – where he had been brought up and to which he later invited **Leonardo da Vinci** (see box on p.80) – and **Blois**, as well as a vast new château at **Chambord**.

The turning point came in 1525, when François I was defeated at **Pavia** while prosecuting yet another futile and aggrandizing military campaign in Italy. The king was made prisoner by Charles V of Spain: "all is lost", he said, "except my honour and my life." When he returned to France, in 1526, he found his **finances** in dire need of attention. Huge loans had been required for châteaux construction, the Italian wars and the king's ransom of two million gold écus, and the daily expenditure on a court of some 10,000 people was vast. Initially, the necessary income had been supplied by the same group of *haut bourgeois* families that had begun to grow wealthy under Louis XI, but the whole financial system collapsed in the great accounting scandals of the late 1520s. In 1527 the arch-financier **Jacques de Beaune-Semblançay** was hanged at the age of eighty – more because the king owed him millions than because of any wrongdoing – and many of his cronies and relations were brought down with him. As the royal investigations progressed, the hitherto suspiciously hasty construction of two of the newest and most sumptuous country residences – Gilles Berthelot's **Azay-le-Rideau**, and **Chenonceau**, built by Thomas de Bohier and Catherine Briçonnet – was brought to an abrupt halt. Berthelot fled the country in 1527, while the Bohiers were forced to give Chenonceau to the Crown in 1533.

It was the end of the Loire's golden age. François steadily abandoned the region for Paris and his new palaces at the Louvre and Fontainebleau, and turned his attention to fighting the new menace to the kingdom's unity: Protestantism.

The Wars of Religion

On October 18, 1534 placards appeared in Paris and Amboise, entitled: *True articles on the horrible, great and insufferable abuses of the papal mass*. One was even found on the door of the king's bedchamber. It was the first murmuring of an impending civil war of bewildering complexity, known as the **Wars of Religion**. For a while, however, civil war seemed a distant prospect. During the reign of Henri II, who succeeded François I in 1547, and his wife **Catherine de Médicis**, from the powerful Medici clan of Florence, the court continued its life of peripatetic luxury. Thousands of people would move lock, stock and barrel from one Loire château to another, living a life dedicated to pleasure and giving balls of legendary decadence – most famously in the **château de Chenonceau** (see p.83). On the back of this elaborate court culture, literature reached a new peak with the creation of the **Pléiade**, a group of seven writers who aimed to reinvent French poetry following Classical and Italian models; chief among them were locally born **Pierre de Ronsard** (see p.328) and **Joachim du Bellay** (see p.327). Meanwhile, **François Rabelais** from Chinon wrote his landmark tales *Gargantua* and *Pantagruel* (see p.329).

It was only after Henri died in a jousting accident in 1559 – a splinter from a broken lance lodged in his eye – that the simmering religious tensions boiled over. In 1560 came the **Tumult of Amboise** (see p.79), swiftly followed by François de Guise's massacre of Huguenot worshippers in 1562. From this time, the name of **Guise**, belonging to the powerful dukes of Lorraine, became inextricably associated with an ultra-Catholic faction pitted against the Protestant **Huguenots**. The Guises were determined to make the Crown enforce religious unity, while the Huguenot leaders sought guarantees of religious toleration. Catherine de Médicis – who became sometime regent and influential powerbroker for the next thirty years during the reigns of her three sons François II, Charles IX and Henri III – attempted to hold the balance of power. At first she pursued a policy of moderate (by sixteenth-century standards) toleration, but neither Guises nor Huguenots could ever be satisfied. Immediately after the massacre of 1562, the Huguenot leader, the prince de Condé, seized **Orléans**, followed by other cities along the Loire. Protestantism was particularly strong in the Loire, where it had found favour among the burgeoning middle classes; **Saumur**, in particular, became a Huguenot stronghold, as was **Sancerre**, at the opposite end of the region. Huguenots rampaged through the region's cathedrals and churches in an iconoclastic fury, and for much of the next twenty years civil war raged right across France. For once, ordinary people were willing participants.

In Paris, the **St Bartholomew's Day Massacre** of August 24, 1572 saw Protestants murdered in the streets by mobs or agents of the Guises, and the violence spread rapidly; hundreds, perhaps thousands were murdered in the towns of the Loire; the attacks in Bourges, Saumur and Angers were particularly vicious. In 1574 Henri III came to the throne, and in 1576 Henri de Guise formed the radical **Catholic League**, after which the conflict deepened. The next stage of the wars acquired the name of the **War of the Three Henrys**, after Henri III, Henri, duc de Guise, and Henri de Navarre, the leader of the Protestant cause and the heir to the throne. In May 1588 the king was forced to abandon Paris by rampaging supporters of the Catholic League. He fled to Tours, where he made peace with Henri de Navarre; their joint armies defeated the troops of the League just outside the city. In December, in an attempt to resolve the crisis definitively, the king summoned the French parliament, the Etats Généraux, to Blois, where he had Henri de Guise murdered (see box on p.135). Catherine died a few days later, and Henri III himself was assassinated by a fanatical Catholic the following year.

The Bourbons

From 1589 Henri de Navarre ruled as **Henri IV**, taking the name of his father, Antoine de Bourbon, as the name of his dynasty. It was to be the last. Henri's coronation had to take place at **Chartres**, as Reims was still in the hostile hands of the Catholic League, but after renouncing Protestantism, he swiftly pacified his kingdom. The 1598 Edict of Nantes allowed a degree of religious freedom. Not all French Catholics were reconciled, however, and the king was assassinated by a radical Catholic in 1610. He was succeeded by his 8-year-old son, Louis XIII, whose mother, **Marie de Médicis**, acted as regent.

Under Henri IV, a Protestant academy had been set up in Saumur, but the Bourbon court was now firmly established in Paris, and the Loire was forgotten by the main stream of national affairs. The populations of the main towns fell throughout the seventeenth century and the region steadily became little more than another provincial backwater. As early as 1617 **Blois** was considered far enough from court to be a suitable place of exile for Marie de Médicis, sent there by the newly assertive Louis XIII to keep her out of state affairs. She escaped in 1619, but was soon replaced at Blois by Louis' rebellious brother, **Gaston d'Orléans**, who devoted himself to building the fourth and last of the château's wings. In the 1630s **Cardinal Richelieu**, Louis XIII's chief minister, attempted to promote a revival by planning a new town in southern Touraine, modestly called Richelieu, but few investors were interested. The main economic activity took place along the rivers, which carried ever-increasing amounts of trade to Paris, a route facilitated by the building of a **canal** linking the Seine and the Loire in the mid-seventeenth century.

Louis XIV may have briefly sheltered in Gien during the tax revolts of the **Fronde** in 1652, and he later enjoyed summer sojourns in **Chambord** – where **Molière** performed the première of the *Bourgeois Gentilhomme* – but he did nothing to promote the region. In fact, his **revocation of the Edict of Nantes** in 1685 seriously undermined the Loire's prospects. Thousands of Protestants, many of them from the prosperous middle classes, fled renewed religious persecution. Tours and Saumur were particularly hard hit, while Orléans rode out the crisis on the strength of its thriving river trade and burgeoning vinegar industry, and Angers and Blois maintained brisk business in wine and spirits. During the eighteenth century, Angers also laid down the foundations of its fruit and market-gardening industries, and opened up large-scale slate mines. In the countryside, however, peasant life remained a matter of bleak subsistence.

The Revolution and the nineteenth century

The **Revolution** of 1789 and the proclamation of the Republic in 1792 affected the Loire less than other French regions. The church lost all its extensive landholdings, which were redistributed among the peasantry, but the nobility mainly kept their châteaux and attached lands. Both governing classes and peasantry largely accepted the decrees from Paris, and only in the southwest of the region was there serious trouble, when the "Whites", or Royalist, Catholic conservatives of the Vendée and western Anjou, mobilized against revolutionary troops in 1793. Saumur and Angers suffered under the revolutionary backlash, but the murderous "Terror" of 1793–4 left the Loire largely untouched. The fluctuating price of grain seemed to be the peasantry's chief concern and later, under Napoleon, the threat of conscription.

During the **nineteenth century**, technology slowly revolutionized society. Agriculture became more productive and potentially profitable, and for the first time the countryside started to boom in comparison with the towns. Steamboats, introduced in the 1830s, briefly invigorated the river trade by cutting journey times by more than half – it used to take the **mariners** just under a week to sail from Orléans to Angers, and up to three times that in the opposite direction. But the **train line** between Orléans and Tours was completed in 1845, and the Paris–Orléans route just one year later. Trade quickly shifted from the capricious, weather- and season-dependent Loire to the reliable trains instead. With the end of channel-dredging, the river's navigable channels quickly silted up. Steadily, cities and towns turned their backs on the river, building new civic squares and landmark buildings inland, beside the train stations. In just a few years, the once-vibrant quays were abandoned.

Napoleon III's disastrous **Franco–Prussian war** of 1870 was quickly followed by the siege of Paris and the fall of the Second Empire. On October 7, the Minister of the Interior, **Léon Gambetta**, fled in a hot air balloon, landing at Tours where he briefly formed a government – the first time the region had tasted anything approaching national significance since the Etats Généraux of 1588. The only French victory in the entire sorry affair occurred at Coulmiers, just west of Orléans, in November 1870, though the victorious Armée de la Loire lost three times as many troops as the Prussians and, in any case, the battle had almost no effect on the progress of the war. As the politicians jockeyed for power in the new Third Republic, the **comte de Chambord** (see box on p.144) was approached with a view to establishing a constitutional monarchy, but his uncompromising **White Flag Manifesto** of 1871 effectively scotched Bourbon chances. The region's wine industries were devastated by the depredations of the **phylloxera beetle** between 1876 and 1883. In the later nineteenth and the early twentieth century, the Loire again lapsed into provincial obscurity, though the foundations of later growth were laid down with the establishment of Orléans' pharmaceutical industry.

The World Wars

The fighting of **World War I** killed tens of thousands of the region's young men, one of them being the author **Alain-Fournier**, who died defending Paris in September 1914 during the desperate battle of the Marne. The trenches lay hundreds of kilometres to the north, but the Loire was close enough and safe enough to receive train- after train-load of the injured and mutilated. In the winter of 1918–19 the **Spanish influenza** killed yet more people, including the elderly and women and children weakened by four years of malnourishment.

In the aftermath of the war, rural areas all over France suffered, and the Loire was no exception. Grain prices – still a major concern – collapsed, unemployment was rife, and the economic benefits of the peace were slow to filter through. Socialism grew in popularity, though the Loire region remained relatively conservative, cut off from affairs in Paris, let alone elsewhere in Europe. Germany, certainly, seemed very far away.

World War II

The German invasion at the beginning of **World War II** was sudden, fast and devastatingly effective. On June 10, 1940 the government fled south from Paris towards **Tours**, quartering itself in various nearby châteaux – most of them not connected by telephone. When **Winston Churchill** arrived at the Préfecture, the offices of the regional government, on June 13, he found the place deserted. He eventually tracked down the errant national government later that day, but could do nothing to persuade it to fight. The same night the Germans bombed Tours and then occupied Paris the next day, even as the French government fled south again, to Bordeaux. Meanwhile, millions of **refugees** and leaderless soldiers streamed south across the bridges of the Loire. The Germans savagely strafed and bombed the riverside quarters of the Loire towns, causing the partial destruction of many of the loveliest among them – notably Orléans, Tours, Blois and Gien. The French destroyed their own bridges. On June 17, **Marshal Pétain** broadcast his call for an armistice; the next day **Général de Gaulle** delivered his radio-call for resistance from London. Most mayors responded to this murder and destruction by declaring their towns "open", stating that they would not resist the Occupation. Only in Saumur was the Loire successfully held against the advancing Germans – astonishingly, by mere cadets (see box on p.229). But their resistance lasted just three days. On June 22 the **armistice** was signed, dividing France into occupied and unoccupied sectors.

The armistice split Touraine in two. The new border ran along the Cher east of Tours – right through **Chenonceau** – then turned southwest. Chinon and everywhere west lay under German control, while Loches, southeastern Touraine and most of the Berry formed part of the new **Vichy France**. On October 24, at the railway station of **Montoire-sur-Loir**, Hitler and Pétain met to agree the official policy of collaboration.

Other than a few sporadic episodes of genuine heroism – such as the stance taken by **Jean Moulin**, the prefect of Chartres (see p.283) – the experience of the Loire was typically mixed. Collaboration, both reluctant and enthusiastic, could be found alongside passive or active resistance, and profiteering went hand in hand with severe deprivation. Rivalries and hatreds established at this time are still a matter of passionate debate, a situation fomented by a recent spate of books naming names in the wake of the recent release of official records. At the time, most of the peasantry just put up with the Germans as best as they could. Thousands of young agricultural workers were sent away to work the fields in Germany, while the deportation of Jews, homosexuals and dissidents began in 1942. On November 11 the same year, the Germans completed the occupation of France. The regime grew harsher and resistance stiffer.

British and American troops stormed the **Normandy beaches** on June 6, 1944, but it wasn't until mid-August that the Allied armies reached the Loire. The Liberation was tinged with sadness. Allied bombing in the prior weeks had completed the destructive work begun by the Germans in 1940, and many towns lay partially in ruins, especially along the riverbanks.

The Loire since 1945

At the end of World War II the Loire was still a deeply traditional region. Peasants – not an insulting term in France – still wore clogs and worked the soil, often by hand, while aristocrats still occupied their châteaux and the middle classes confined themselves to the towns. Many rural people lived largely on what they grew themselves, and market day was the highlight of the week. Much of that is still true today, though a good deal has changed.

Cars and tractors replaced horses in the 1950s, at the same time as the economic growth of the cities sucked thousands in from the countryside. Bombed-out quarters were rebuilt, at first rapidly and carelessly, later with more concern for aesthetics. From the 1960s, state spending increased dramatically. In 1964 the first of four **nuclear power stations** was built on the Loire, at Avoine, near Chinon, and market gardens were established using the warm – and supposedly radiation-free – water from the cooling towers. River pollution grew steadily – mostly due to over-use of fertilizers rather than heavy industry – and hydroelectricity dams upstream led to **salmon** numbers plummeting from hundreds of thousands to mere hundreds; fishing for salmon, once the symbol of the Loire, is still banned today. Public **universities** were set up in Orléans, Tours and Angers in the late 1960s and early 1970s, and at around the same time the **wine industry** regenerated itself: *appellations* were re-established, vineyards re-planted and quality more tightly controlled. Tourism, too, grew exponentially with the help of government backing and a new entrepreneurial spirit among the region's private château owners – faced with giant tax bills, there was little else they could do. In 1990 the high-speed **TGV**, or *train à grande vitesse*, arrived in Vendôme from Paris. As it has steadily spread its electrified tentacles south and west into the heart of the region, it has brought with it thousands of buyers of **second homes**, at first from the Paris region – many people even commute – and later from southeast England. Certain pockets of the Loire, are particularly popular with *les Anglais*, notably the Maine *département*, north of Angers, and the region around Chinon. Comparisons are often made locally with the Plantagenêt days.

The rediscovery of tradition

Despite the many social and technological changes, the Loire remains a quietly conservative region. The **old customs** are maintained in subtle ways: small vegetable plots can be seen everywhere, for example, tiny scraps of country vineyard provide wine for many town tables, and hunting is practised with passion by rich and poor alike – rich and poor men, that is. Church-going is no more prevalent than elsewhere in republican France, but Sundays are respected as days for visiting the family or eating out in a restaurant. Family-owned businesses from *charcuteries* to shoe shops still hold out against the multinationals, and even supermarkets source much of their food products locally. Most obviously, the cooking in homes and restaurants alike is resolutely regional, with few concessions to even Parisian fads, let alone foreign styles of cooking.

If anything, the Loire has become *more* traditional in recent years. The **heritage industry** has helped ignite a powerful kind of local patriotism that encompasses anything from rebuilding the old wooden boats used by the Loire mariners to rediscovering ingredients and dishes enjoyed in the Middle Ages. In such an atmosphere, tourism is not so much voyeurism as a matter of taking part in the region's rediscovery of itself. Increasingly, the Loire is the chief object of both local and tourist attention. Every village and town has plans to redevelop the quays, to put boats back on the river and to outdo the river festivities of neighbouring *communes*. Everywhere there is evidence of a desire to somehow turn back to where it all began: the Loire itself.

The château

There's no English translation for "château". It can mean anything from a ruined castle in the middle of a town to an exquisitely furnished, eighteenth-century country mansion. What all châteaux had in common was a noble owner who derived his status from the building itself – and many still do today. The heart of any château was its tower, or keep. More than just a defensive device, more even than a feudal symbol, it legally confirmed the nobility of its owner, almost like a written document (curiously, dovecotes had similar status – see box on p.147). Old keeps were rarely demolished in later years, even when the rest of a château was wholly rebuilt in a Classical style. Some commentators have even described the tower as the central idea driving all French secular architecture, creating a distinctive emphasis on vertical thrust rather than smooth horizontal lines.

Donjons to châteaux

The earliest châteaux in the Loire region are powerful, foursquare **donjons** – these are keeps, not dungeons – built in the eleventh and twelfth centuries. The most ancient, as at **Langeais** and **Loches**, date back to Foulque Nerra, the belligerent eleventh-century count of Anjou, while later examples can be seen at **Beaugency** and **Montrichard**. From the early thirteenth century onwards, **Crusader** techniques began to be influential, and giant curtain walls were constructed at strategic sites such as **Chinon** and **Angers**.

Walls increasingly enclosed the entirety of the *basse-cour*, a wide open space at the château gates that was typically used for trading, games and farm work. This courtyard was flanked on two or more sides by the *communs*, or outbuildings, originally used for labourers, though in many cases they later became almost as elaborate as the châteaux themselves – as at **Le Plessis-Macé**, in Anjou. Even where no curtain wall existed, a gate would guard the approach to the *basse-cour*, often fortified with two **poivrières**, or pepper-pot towers.

The **medieval château** itself was reserved for the **seigneur**, his feudal entourage or household, his servants and his garrison, the latter usually made up of paid mercenaries. Life focused on the **grande salle**, a large room usually on the first floor used for anything from law-giving to feasting and accommodation for guests. The servants ate and congregated in a separate *salle basse* on the floor below. Ordinary meals could be taken anywhere, with trestle tables being brought in whenever and wherever required, including in the **chambre**, or bedroom, which was usually shared. Furniture was sparse, partly because most households moved regularly between a number of different châteaux. Chests and trunks could double up as beds, if covered with a few blankets, and the bare walls could be covered and insulated with huge tapestries. Privacy as we know it did not exist, as is evident from the lack of corridors – the main rooms were as much public thoroughfares as defined spaces.

Gothic castles

In the fourteenth and fifteenth centuries, **Gothic** stone-carving was applied with increasing finesse to doors and windows, and roofscapes began to come alive with fine balustrades, elaborately sculpted gables and exquisite leadwork finials and ridges. In this way, the old keeps were slowly transformed into relatively sophisticated structures. Louis d'Anjou's late fourteenth-century chivalric castle at **Saumur** has lost many of its more fantastical features, but it is still very obviously much more than just a plain fortress. A little later, moats came into fashion, as at **Sully**, constructed in around 1400.

Unbridled experimentation in luxury had to wait until the 1450s, however, after the end of the Hundred Years War. The early châteaux of this era still look defensive, but only superficially. Among those built in the 1460s and 1470s by Louis XI's treasurer, Jean Bourré, **Le Plessis-Bourré** has stout walls, a wide moat and a drawbridge, while **Langeais** is buttressed by towers and ringed by a machicolated *chemin-de-ronde*, or guard-walk. Look more closely, however, and you'll notice large, elaborately carved windows – of little use for defence.

In the course of the fourteenth century, life inside the château changed subtly but significantly. Courts and households were still itinerant, capping the amount of attention spent on internal decoration or design, but new types of structure such as the **logis** were slowly developed. This "lodging" was more sophisticated than a mere adapted keep, and for the first time incorporated private rooms. The chief occupant would usually live in a suite of rooms on a single floor. There would be two or more *chambres*: the outer room, known as the **chambre d'apparat** or *chambre de parement*, was used for public audiences, while the inner **chambre de retrait** or *chambre de gîte* was used for sleeping and more private conversations. Off it lay a *garderobe*, or latrine, and sometimes a private oratory or study. The basic layout can be seen in châteaux all over the region, but is best preserved in the Vieux Logis at **Loches**.

Renaissance palaces

A new style arrived along with some two dozen Italian craftsmen in the entourage of Charles VIII (see p.78). At **Chaumont** and **Amboise** they worked on decorative, Classically inspired motifs not seen in France since Romanesque times, and buildings were planned with new attention to symmetry and aesthetic balance. The fashion for all things Italian gathered momentum during the reign of **Louis XII**, under whom brick became a fashionable medium, especially in the eastern part of the region (where it was already traditional). **Gien**, **Blois** and the **château du Moulin** are exceptional examples of the elaborately patterned brickwork of the time.

The Renaissance proper is usually held to begin with François I, whose new wing at **Blois** established the key design features of **early Renaissance** architecture, most of it borrowed from the Classical world by way of fifteenth-century Italy. Stone windows were framed by pilasters topped by Classically themed carved capitals; decorative panels of marble (or locally available slate) were set into the stone for contrast; shallow-carved motifs of shells, putti, scrolls and flowers proliferated; regularly spaced window openings were alternated with plain stone walls divided by "string courses", or horizontal bands of stone. The flamboyance of the treatment, however, owed as much to local skills and the soft, easily worked local stone, called **tufa**.

The new architectural fashions quickly spread across the region, influencing the construction of many *hôtels* (private town mansions) and châteaux, notably at **Azay-le-Rideau** and **Chenonceau**. Delight in symmetry and decorative flair spilled over into **garden design**, and many châteaux were surrounded by elaborately planted terraces – as superbly recreated at **Villandry** – divided into the *parterre*, or raised flower-beds, and the *potager*, the vegetable garden. Both were geometrically arranged and surrounded by trellises, vines and fruit trees.

A key development in château design was the slow transformation of the **staircase**. These were particularly significant as they lay at the heart of the château's social life, as front door, great hall and feudal symbol rolled into one. Medieval château employed defensible, turret-enclosed spirals tacked onto the outside of the main structure. At first, the form was preserved, as at Blois, even if the decoration changed. But gradually, the idea of using a series of straight flights divided by landings became popular, and they could be easily incorporated into the body of the building. Early, open examples still preserve the look of towers, as at **Châteaudun** and Azay-le-Rideau. In typically half-Gothic, half-Renaissance style, François I's **Chambord** keeps the spiral form of the staircase, but brings it inside the body of the château, forming a strange kind of central staircase-tower – and one that is all the stranger for following a double-helix form.

In the 1530s François I quit the Loire for Paris and Fontainebleau. A modified architectural style emerged from the north, applying Classical principles with ever increasing strictness and sobriety. The Loire was no longer the origin of taste.

Classical to modern

The new Classicism flourished in the latter half of the sixteenth century, during the **Second Renaissance**, with elegant, superbly planned châteaux such as **Beauregard** and the bridge section of **Chenonceau**. Both have long **galleries** and exquisite **cabinets**, or small rooms for business and private study. These rooms already existed in medieval times – astonishingly, despite all the developments in architectural design, the internal arrangements of châteaux had scarcely changed since the Middle Ages – but their use was new. They were private. The *cabinet*, in particular, was used for entertaining intimate friends – itself a radically new social concept.

In the **seventeenth century** the basic arrangement of the medieval *logis* still persisted. Floors were divided into *appartements*, with a succession of rooms of various degrees of privacy. The public **salon** became the lynchpin of social life, the home of polite "conversation" – another French invention of the era. Leading off the *salon* was the *antechambre*, then the *chambre*, which usually had an alcove for the bed, and finally the private *cabinet*.

The architectural fashion of the time was for *œil-de-bœuf* (bull's eye) and "French" windows. The former brought light into the topmost floors, which started to be occupied by servants, while the latter allowed the salon to flow into the gardens. In the Loire, serene, horizontally organized facades were built in the local white tufa and topped by smooth slate roofs. An element of verticality remained, however, with most châteaux divided up into discernible segments, or pavilions. Superb examples are **Cheverny** and the Gaston d'Orléans wing at **Blois**, both from the first half of the seventeenth century. Sadly, **Richelieu**'s vast château in Touraine has been destroyed, though much of his new town survives. The visual effect of the approach to the château became ever more important, the *basse-cour* being replaced by a symmetrically arranged *avant-cour*, with formal gardens flanked by miniature moats and elegant pavilions, often used as stable blocks. **La Ferté-St-Aubin**, south of Orléans, is a beautiful example.

In the eighteenth century picturesque landscapes became the thing. Gardens were turned over to grass and trees in the "English" style, and at **Chaumont**, **Villandry** and **Ussé**, whole wings were torn down in order to open up the internal courtyard to the view. There was little new building out in what had become the sticks, though the exquisite **Montgeoffroy** is a notable exception, and the fashionably Oriental **Pagode de Chanteloup**, outside Amboise, has survived the destruction of its associated château. **Nineteenth-century** châteaux tend to ape the designs of the past, often on a vast scale, and often with an admixture of stuffy Englishness. Scores were built all over the Sologne and in Anjou, but almost all remain in private hands and can't be visited.

In both the nineteenth and twentieth centuries **restoration** has been the keynote, both inside and out. France has traditionally followed a policy of returning monuments to their "original" condition, rather than merely arresting decay. Nineteenth-century restorers have brutalized more stone-carving than the heritage industry cares to admit, and even today you can see whole areas of facade gleaming with new-cut white tufa – in fact, this stone is so soft that almost any surface that has been exposed to the weather must have been recut at some point in its life. Nowadays, any building designated a "**National Monument**" is subject to strict regulation, with rules to stipulate even which officially licensed craftspeople may work on them.

Books

There's a big discrepancy between the large amount of fiction set in the Loire and the small number of non-fiction books about the region – in English at least. In non-fiction, the Loire tends to feature only as background to its historical celebrities, of which the three most notable are, unusually, women: Eleanor of Aquitaine, Joan of Arc and Catherine de Médicis. For more on local literature, see Writers of the Loire (p.324).

History and biography

Robert Gildea *Marianne in Chains: In Search of the German Occupation 1940–45*. This controversial work of war history is really an intimate biography of Chinon, a town chosen largely for its ordinariness. Rejecting the heroic view of the Occupation as Resistance versus collaborators, Gildea depicts the compromises and everyday hardships of life under the Nazis.

Mary Gordon *Joan of Arc*. Gordon's simple and moving retelling of Joan's story places the woman herself at the forefront.

Gregory of Tours *History of the Franks*. This sixth-century chronicle by a bishop of Tours won't be everyone's favourite bedtime reading, though some fascinating and occasionally scurrilous tales lurk among the drier passages.

★ **J.H. Huizinga** *The Waning of the Middle Ages*. This book makes for superb reading, creating a detailed and fascinating portrait of life in the fourteenth and fifteenth centuries. Focuses on Burgundy, but also has plenty of material on the French court in general.

R.J. Knecht *The Rise and Fall of Renaissance France, 1483–1610*. Unimpeachably accurate and detailed, though as you might expect from an academic historian, there's little attempt to create atmosphere. Still, the subject matter of this 500-page tome – focusing mostly on François I and the Wars of Religion – is exciting enough to help keep the pace up.

R.J. Knecht *Catherine de' Medici*. Knecht puts the final nail in the coffin of the "Black Legend" of the *Reine Margot* in this serious, historical portrait of a powerful Renaissance queen fighting for her family interests in the face of religious warfare and national chaos.

Ian Littlewood *Rough Guide History of France*. If you're feeling a bit lost in French history, try this pocket-sized guide, which offers a handy chronology plus background snippets on cultural movements and key historical figures.

Marion Meade *Eleanor of Aquitaine*. This chatty, journalistic biography tries to focus directly on Eleanor in order to conjure up a picture of her as a woman. As a result, it sometimes strays into embarrassing emotional speculation and lacks the necessary breadth of historical context. Readable, nonetheless.

Régine Pernoud and **Marie-Véronique Clin** *Joan of Arc*. Fascinating biography of Joan, including detailed biographies of all the historical figures involved in the last phase of the Hundred Years War.

★ **Marina Warner** *Joan of Arc*. The most illuminating and erudite of all the books on Joan, placing her within the spiritual and intellectual traditions of her time. Beautifully written, too.

★ **Alison Weir** *Eleanor of Aquitaine: By the Wrath of God, Queen of England*. Despite the title,

Weir's scholarly biography focuses just as much on Eleanor as a French ruler as an English queen, while a wealth of contextual detail makes this as much a history of the life and times of the Plantagenêt empire as of Eleanor herself.

Fiction

Honoré de Balzac *Eugénie Grandet*. This masterful, taut novella is one of Balzac's masterpieces. Set entirely in bourgeois, nineteenth-century Saumur, it exists in a claustrophobic world of half-strangled emotion, bitter irony and defiant hope. The detail is intensely naturalistic, while the plot and the characters – the miser Grandet, his daughter Eugénie and her flashy cousin Charles – could almost come from a fairy tale. See p.330.

Honoré de Balzac *The Lily of the Valley*. Not one of Balzac's best efforts, with an irritatingly sentimental, semi-autobiographical hero and a meandering plot revolving around his idealized mistress's marriage to a monster. The descriptions of the landscape around Azay-le-Rideau, however, are beautiful. See p.331.

Alain-Fournier *Le Grand Meaulnes*. Widely available in English, and sometimes translated as *The Wanderer* or *The Lost Domain*, this early twentieth-century classic is at once a coming-of-age novel, a wistful love story and a gentle hymn to youthful idealism. It draws heavily on the author's own childhood in the Sologne. See p.331.

Joanne Harris *Five Quarters of the Orange*. The author behind the successful film *Chocolat* spins a moving yarn about a middle-aged woman who returns to the Loire village where she grew up during the war. She sets up a restaurant, using her mother's recipe-book for inspiration, but the traumas of the past slowly resurface.

J.-K. Huysmans *The Cathedral*. This rich novel, the third of a trilogy, was published towards the end of Huysmans' life, in 1898. It ostensibly continues the spiritual journey of the ex-Satanist hero, Durtal, but the chief protagonist is really Chartres cathedral, whose Catholic symbolism is described in learned and mesmerizing detail.

François Rabelais *Gargantua and Pantagruel*. This outrageous parody of a sixteenth-century epic is extravagantly inventive, savagely satirical, filthy, erudite, drink-sodden and, after nearly five hundred years, still very funny. The first book tells the life story of the giant Gargantua and his mock-heroic exploits in the Chinonais. It takes some time to get used to the prose style and the breath-taking, piss-taking erudition, but it's well worth persevering. See p.329.

George Bernard Shaw *Saint Joan*. Shaw may be out of fashion, but this was one of his most successful dramas. The Joan he creates is sassy, provocative and lovable, and he depicts the corrupt political world encircling her with a very modern kind of satirical absurdity.

Emile Zola *The Earth*. This dark, elemental tale of brutish peasant life was Zola's favourite among his own novels. It is set in the 1860s on the plain of the Beauce, between Vendôme and Châteaudun. As the title suggests, the real hero is *la terre* itself.

Poetry

Joachim du Bellay You'll have to look hard to find translations of du Bellay on his own, but if you're willing to pay the extra, go for *Lyrics of the French Renaissance*, a beautiful edition of Marot, du Bellay and Ronsard from Yale University Press, with skilful verse translations by American academic Norman R. Shapiro. See p.327.

Guillaume de Lorris and **Jean de Meun** *The Romance of the Rose*. This long, thirteenth-century poem is really two works: Lorris's poem is a highly allegorical dream vision of love, while Meun adds on an extended, theoretical commentary on medieval life. At the time of writing, two good prose translations of the *Romaunt de la Rose* were available in paperback, from OUP and

Princeton University Press. See p.324.

★ **Pierre de Ronsard** Various translations and collections of Ronsard's work are available, but Penguin's *Selected Poems* is particularly good as it supplies the original French along with a straightforward prose translation. Otherwise, you could opt for Yale's edition of Renaissance lyric poets (see under Joachim du Bellay, above). See p.328.

François Villon *The Legacy and the Testament*. Villon isn't widely translated into English, though Anvil Press Poetry recently published an excellent and affordable bilingual edition, including all of *The Testament*, with bold verse translations by poet Peter Dale. See p.325.

Art and architecture

★ **André Chastel** *French Art: the Renaissance 1430–1620*. The great French art historian tries to define what is distinctively French about French art in this, the second book of his three-volume work. Insightful and superbly illustrated.

Ivan Cloulas and **Michèle Bimbenet-Privat** *Treasures of the French Renaissance: Architecture, Sculpture, Paintings and Drawings*. Excellent commentaries by two French scholars make this beautifully produced, glossy art book a good guide to the wider artistic context of the Loire châteaux.

★ **Mark Girouard** *Life in the French Country House*. Girouard meticulously recreates the social and domestic life of the French châteaux, starting with the great halls of early

castles and ending with the commercial marriage venues of the twentieth century. Fascinating background reading.

Robert Polidori and **Jean-Marie Pérouse de Montclos** *Châteaux of the Loire Valley*. Relatively original photography makes this one of the better "château of the Loire" coffee-table books. The text is reasonably accurate and peppered with interesting quotations.

Lillian Schacherl *Très Riches Heures: Behind the Gothic Masterpiece*. The colour reproductions of Jean de Berry's illuminated prayer book are excellent, but the text is rather awkwardly written. Nevertheless, it does attempt to explain the meaning behind the exquisite images.

Miscellaneous

John Ardagh *France in the New Century: Portrait of a Changing Society.* This overview of contemporary France concentrates on the last twenty years in Paris and the regions, with an emphasis on politics. Nothing in particular on the Loire, but good background nonetheless.

Henry James *A Little Tour in France.* James spends a healthy proportion of his "little tour" poking his nose around the great Loire towns and châteaux, and commenting on them with a characteristic mix of snootiness and penetrating observation.

Hugh Palmer *The Most Beautiful Villages of the Loire.* This solid coffeetable book has thin text but wonderful photographs that, for once, don't focus exclusively on the châteaux.

Judy Smith *Holiday Walks in the Loire Valley.* Details 32 walks in the Loire valley, most ranging from 5km to 15km. The area covered ranges from the source of the Loire to its Atlantic mouth, but most of the walks are in the classic "Val de Loire". Useful maps included.

Roger Voss *The Wines of the Loire.* This book is an odd combination of lots of technical facts and statistics with very personal accounts of visits to wine-makers in their vineyards. It is out of print, and the vintage tables are out of date unless you're buying older wines, but there's plenty of guidance on how to find the betterregarded vineyards.

Theodore Zeldin *The French.* Nothing about the Loire here, but well worth reading as an original and inspiring portrait of a nation as told through the everyday lives of real people.

Writers of the Loire

L
iterature and the Loire have been intertwined since the medieval era, when Guillaume de Lorris and Jean de Meun, both from the Orléanais, wrote the *Romance of the Rose*. The fifteenth-century poet François Villon spent time in the region – much of it in prison – but it was in the Renaissance that the Loire came to the forefront. Three of the greatest writers of the epoch were born in the region: François Rabelais, near Chinon, Pierre de Ronsard, in the Vendômois, and Joachim du Bellay, in Anjou. *La Belle au bois dormant*, the most famous of Charles Perrault's seventeenth-century fairy tales, was supposedly inspired by the château d'Ussé, but the Loire only became prominent again in the nineteenth century, notably through the work of Honoré de Balzac, who was born in Tours and based a number of his novels in Touraine; Alexandre Dumas and Alfred de Vigny also successfully exploited the region's rich past in their historical novels *La Dame de Montsoreau* and *Cinq Mars*. The regions surrounding the Loire valley proper have also been fertile ground for fiction: the Beauce region, just north of the Loire, is the setting for Emile Zola's powerful evocation of peasant life, *La Terre*; J.-K. Huysmans' *La Cathédrale* celebrates Chartres; while Marcel Proust's *A la récherche du temps perdu* opens in the author's childhood home in Combray (Illiers), just southwest of Chartres. South of the Loire, the rustic life of the Berry is portrayed in fine, naturalistic detail in Georges Sand's *Le Meunier d'Angibault, Jeanne* and *La Mare au diable*, while the atmosphere of the Sologne is superbly conjured in Maurice Genevoix's *Raboliot* and Alain-Fournier's *Le Grand Meaulnes*. For reviews of books available in translation, see p.321.

Guillaume de Lorris

Very little is known about the two authors of the *Romance of the Rose*, but their names indicate that they both came from the Loire region: Guillaume de Lorris, from the village of the same name in the Forêt d'Orléans, and Jean de Meun from Meung-sur-Loire. Guillaume probably wrote the original 4000-line poem in the 1230s, Jean de Meun adding his 18,000 lines some forty years later. In its final form, the *Romance* was a medieval bestseller, reproduced in hundreds of beautifully illuminated manuscripts, and influencing generations of poets, including Geoffrey Chaucer. It takes the form of a dream vision and allegorical tale about a Lover's journey towards his Rose, variously helped and thwarted on the way by such figures as Pleasure, Courtesy, Rebuff and Jealousy. Guillaume de Lorris's part is a relatively straightforward coded account of the progression of a love affair, containing, as he put it "the whole art of love . . . anyone who aspires to love should pay attention".

The dream begins, from the *Romance of the Rose*

In this delightful month, when Love excites
All things, one night I, sleeping, had this dream.
Methought that it was full daylight. I rose
In haste, put on my shoes and washed my hands,
Then took a silver needle from its case,

Dainty and neat, and threaded it with silk.
I yearned to wander far outside the town
To hear what songs the birds were singing there
In every bush, to welcome the new year.
Basting my sleeves in zigzags as I went
I pleased myself, in spite of solitude,
Listening to the birds that took such pains
To chant among the new-bloom-laden boughs.
Jolly and gay and full of happiness
I neared a rippling river which I loved;
For I no nicer thing than that stream knew.
From out a hillside close thereby it flowed,
Descending full and free and clear and cold
As water from a fountain or well.
Though it was somewhat lesser than the Seine,
More broad it spread; a fairer ne'er I saw.
Upon the bank I sat, the scene to scan,
And with the view delight myself, and lave
My face in the refreshing water there;
And, as I bent, I saw the river floor
All paved and covered with bright gravel stones.
The wide fair mead reached to the water's edge.
Calm and serene and temperate and clear
The morning was. I rose; and through the grass
Coasting along the bank I followed the stream.

Translated by Harry W. Robbins
(Syracuse University Press, 2002)

François Villon

More is known about the life of François Villon than most medieval poets, mostly because he was continually in trouble with the law. Born in 1431, he studied at Paris in the 1450s, where he burgled the Collège de Navarre and managed to kill a priest during a riot. He seems to have fled Paris, and attended Charles d'Orléans' poetry contest at Blois (see p.132), which required all the poets attending to compose a ballad beginning with a first line written by Charles himself; all the subsequent lines had to contain antitheses. Villon was later imprisoned by the Bishop of Orléans at Meung-sur-Loire (see p.183) – a sentence railed against with superb spleen in his most famous poem, a brilliant and rebelliously spirited mock will entitled *Le Testament* ("The Will"). Back in Paris, he was arrested again in 1462 and seems to have been sentenced to death or banishment – whereupon he disappears from the record.

From the Ballad, written for the contest at Blois

Je meurs de seuf auprès de la fontaine,
Chault comme fer, et tremble dent a dent;
En mon païs suis en terre loingtaine,
Lez ung brasier frissonne tout ardent;

Nu comme ung ver, vestu en president,
Je ris en pleurs et attens sans espoir;
Confort reprens en triste desespoir;
Je m' esjouÿs et n'ay plaisir aucun;
Puissant je suis sans force et sans povoir,
Bien recueully, debouté de chascun.

Rien ne m'est seur que la chose incertaine;
Obscur fors ce qui est tout evident;
Doubte je ne fais, fors en chose certaine;
Science tiens a soudain accident;
Je gaigne tout et demeure perdent;
Au point du jour dis: "Dieu vous doint bon soir!"
Gisant envers, j'ay grant paour de cheoir;
J'ay bien de quoy et si n'en ay pas ung;
Eschoitte attens et d'omme ne suis hoir,
Bien recueully, debouté de chascun.

[...]

Prince clement, or vous plaise sçavoir:
Que j'entens moult et n'ay sens ne sçavoir.
Parcial suis, a toutes loys commun.
Que sais je plus? Quoy? Les gaiges ravoir!
Bien recueully, debouté de chascun.

I die of thirst beside the fountainhead;
I chatter, tooth on tooth, as hot as fire.
A foreigner in my own land I tread;
Ardently shivering, by the brazier perspire.
Bare as a worm, in presidential attire,
I laugh in tears and hope without a hope;
I take more comfort in despair to mope;
Enjoy myself with no pleasure under the sun;
Forceful with no strength or power to cope,
So well received, thrown out by everyone.

I'm certain of uncertainty ahead;
Since everything's so clear, confused as mire;
Doubt nothing but what's certain, taken as read;
An accident all knowledge I acquire.
I always win yet stay a loser, sure-fire;
Bid folk good night as daybreak spreads its scope.
And, lying down, fear falling off the rope.
Legacy await, though neither heir nor son,
And, rolling in it, without a bean I lope,
So well received, thrown out by everyone.

[...]

Merciful Prince, please believe the scope
Of what I grasp, an ignorant, senseless dope.
Your party man, commoner in law I run.

Taken from Poems of François Villon, *translated by Peter Dale (Anvil Press Poetry, 2001)*

Joachim du Bellay

Joachim du Bellay was born in around 1522 into a noble family from Liré, a village beside the Loire in the far west of Anjou. As part of the coterie of poets around the poet Pierre de Ronsard, the Pléiade, du Bellay took on the newly discovered models of Classical and Italian poetry while writing in his native language. In 1553 he went to Rome, where he seems to have fallen in love and been bitterly disappointed – at least, if the emotions described in his two greatest collections, *Les Antiquitez de Rome* and *Les Regrets*, both published in 1558, are to be trusted. As he put it, "I did not find Rome in Rome". The two sequences, however, are among the finest written in French, at once deeply personal and highly accomplished, pushing forward the possibilities both for poetry and the French language. He died in 1560, and is buried in Paris's Notre-Dame cathedral.

Sonnet from *Les Regrets*

Heureux qui, comme Ulysse, a fait un beau voyage,
Ou comme cestuy là qui conquit la toison,
Et puis est retourné, plein d'usage & raison,
Vivre entre ses parents le reste de son aage!
Quand revoiray-je, helas, de mon petit village
Fumer la cheminee, & en quelle saison,
Revoiray-je le clos de ma pauvre maison,
Qui m'est une province, & beaucoup d'avantage?
Plus me plaist le sejour qu'on basty mes ayeux,
Que des palais Romains le front audacieux,
Plus que le marbre dur me plaist l'ardoise fine:
Plus mon Loyre Gaulois que le Tybre Latin,
Plus mon petit Lyré, que le mont Palatin,
Et plus que l'air marin la douceur Angevine.

Happy the man who, like Ulysses, went
Sailing afar; or him who won the fleece,
Then, wise and worldly grown, returned to Greece,
Amongst his own, to live and die content.
Alas! When shall I end my banishment,
To see my village rooftops smoke, to cease
My wandering, see my humble home, in peace,
More grand to me than realm magnificent?
More do I love the home my fathers made
Than Rome's bold palaces, in pride arrayed:
More do I love fine slate than marble rare;
More than their Tiber do I love my Loire;

Their Palatine, more my Liré by far;
And more than sea's salt breeze, Anjou's soft air.

Taken from Lyrics of the French Renaissance: Marot, du Bellay, Ronsard, *with English versions by Norman R. Shapiro (Yale University Press, 2002)*

Pierre de Ronsard

Pierre de Ronsard was born at La Possonnière (see p.289 in 1524. Educated at the Collège de Navarre – as burgled by François Villon – he became the foremost of a group of seven lyric poets known as the Pléiade, after the stars of that constellation, which aimed to revive French literature by emulating the poets of Greece, Rome and Renaissance Italy; five of the group were from the Loire region. In 1552 Ronsard published his greatest collections, the *Second Livre d'Amours* and the *Amours de Cassandre*. His poems were immediately recognized as masterpieces, and still reach a wide audience – partly because of their obsession with roses, used as symbols of beauty and mortality. In later life, Ronsard lived between Paris and Vendôme; he died in 1585 at St-Cosme, where he had been nominated prior.

Sonnet from *Le Second Livre d'Amours*

Comme on voit sur la branche au mois de May la rose
En sa belle jeunesse, en sa premiere fleur
Rendre le ciel jaloux de sa vive couleur,
Quand l'Aube de ses pleurs au poinct du jour l'arrose:
La grace dans sa fueille, et l'amour se repose
Embasmant les jardins et les arbres d'odeur:
Mais batue ou de pluye ou d'excessif ardeur
Languissante elle meurt fueille à fueille déclose.
Ainsi en ta premiere et jeune nouveauté
Quand la terre et le ciel honoroient ta beauté,
La Parque t'a tuee, et cendre tu reposes.
Pour obseques reçoy mes larmes et mes pleurs,
Ce vase plein de laict, ce panier plein de fleurs,
Afin que vif et mort ton corps ne soit que roses.

Just as, upon the branch, one sees the rose's
Bud bloom in May, young blossom newly spread
Before the sky, jealous of its bright red,
As Dawn, sprinkling her tears, the morn discloses;
Beauty lies in its leaf, and love reposes,
Wafting its scent on tree, bush, flowerbed:
But, lashed by rain or torrid heat, soon dead,
Leaf after leaf its fragile grace exposes.
So too, blooming with youth, as earth and heaven
Honoured your beauty, to Fate was it given
To slay your flesh, which now in ash reposes.
Take thus these tears that I, in tribute, shed,

This jug of milk, these blossoms heaped, outspread,
So that in death, as life, that flesh be roses.

Taken from Lyrics of the French Renaissance: Marot, du Bellay, Ronsard, *with*
English versions by Norman R. Shapiro (Yale University Press, 2002)

François Rabelais

François Rabelais was born near Chinon in around 1494, an episode
"described" in typically Rabelaisian manner in the extract below. He trained
first as a monk and later studied medicine. In 1532 he published *Pantagruel*, a
heady mix of serious humanistic learning, satire and earthily exuberant come-
dy. The book was almost immediately condemned as obscene by the Sorbonne.
In 1533 came the prequel, *Gargantua*, and in 1537 he became attached to the
court of François I, later visiting Italy as part of the retinue of Cardinal Jean
du Bellay, the cousin of the poet Joachim. The Third Book was drier and safer,
but the scurrilously antipapal content of the Fourth Book lost him his position
and may even have landed him in prison. Rabelais died in Paris soon after, in
1553.

Gargantua's birth, from *Gargantua*

Whilst they were pleasantly tattling on the subject of drinking, Gargamelle
began to feel disturbed in her lower parts. Whereupon Grandgousier got up
from the grass, and comforted her kindly, thinking that these were birth-pangs
and telling her that since she had been resting under the willows she would
soon be in a good state. She ought to take new heart, he said, at the coming of
her new baby. For although the pains would be somewhat severe, they would
nevertheless be quickly over, and the joy which would follow after would ban-
ish all her pain, so that only the memory of it would be left. [...]

A little while later she began to groan and wail and shout. Then suddenly
swarms of midwives came up from every side, and feeling her underneath
found some rather ill-smelling excrescences, which they thought were the
child; but it was her fundament slipping out, because of the softening of her
right intestine – which you call the bum-gut – owing to her having eaten too
much tripe, as has been stated above.

At this point a dirty old hag of the company, who had the reputation of being
a good she-doctor and had come from Brizepaille, near Saint Genou, sixty
years before, made her an astringent, so horrible that all her sphincter muscles
were stopped and constricted. Indeed you could hardly have relaxed them with
your teeth – which is a most horrible thought – even if you had copied the
method of the devil at the Mass of St Martin, when he wrote down the chatter of two local girls and stretched his parchment by tugging with his teeth.

By this misfortune the cotyledons of the matrix were loosened at the top, and
the child leapt up through them to enter the hollow vein. Then, climbing
through the diaphragm to a point above the shoulders where this vein divides
in two, he took the left fork and came out by the left ear.

As soon as he was born he cried out, not like other children: "Mies! Mies!"
but "Drink! Drink! Drink!", as if inviting the whole world to drink, and so
loud that he was heard through all the lands of Booze and Bibulous.

I doubt whether you will truly believe in this strange nativity. I don't care if you don't. But an honest man, a man of good sense, always believes what he is told and what he finds written down. Is this a violation of our law or our faith? Is it against reason or against Holy Scripture? For my part I find nothing written in the Holy Bible which contradicts it. If this had been the will of God, would you say that he could not have performed it? For goodness' sake do not obfuscate your brains with such an idle thought. For I say to you that to God nothing is impossible. If it had been His will women would have produced their children in that way, by the ear, for ever afterwards.

Was not Bacchus begotten by Jupiter's thigh? Was not Rocquetaillade born from his mother's heel, and Crocquemouche from his nurse's slipper? Was not Minerva born from Jupiter's brain by way of his ear, and Adonis from the bark of a myrrh-tree, and Castor and Pollux from the shell of an egg laid and hatched by Leda? But you would be even more flabbergasted if I were now to expound to you the whole chapter of Pliny in which he speaks of strange and unnatural births; and anyhow, I am not such a barefaced liar as he was. Read Chapter three of the seventh book of his *Natural History*, and don't tease my brain any more on the subject.

Taken from Gargantua and Pantagruel, *translated by J.M. Cohen (Penguin)*

Honoré de Balzac

Honoré de Balzac, the giant of nineteenth-century "realism", was born in Tours in 1799. Despite being sent away to school in Vendôme, and then moving to Paris, Touraine remained the novelist's spiritual home, the only place where he could rest and recover his creative powers – he described the sensation of returning to the region as like being "buried up to the neck in foie gras". Balzac wrote a number of his novels in Saché, at the house of Jean de Margonne, the father of his illegitimate brother, and later in life considered buying the château de Moncontour, near Vouvray. Most of the ninety novels of his great sequence, *La Comédie humaine,* are Paris-based, but a few are set in the Loire: most evocatively, *Le Lys dans la vallée,* a tale of troubled young love with the countryside around Azay-le-Rideau as a spectacular backdrop; *Eugénie Grandet,* an unflinching story about frustrated love set in provincial Saumur; *Louis Lambert,* which draws heavily on Balzac's own experiences in Vendôme; and *Le Curé de Tours,* a novella about petty ambition and rivalry in the shadow of Tours' cathedral.

M Grandet's house, from *Eugénie Grandet*

Two pillars supported the arch above the doorway, and for these, as also for the building of the house itself, a porous crumbling stone peculiar to the district along the banks of the Loire had been employed, a kind of tufa so soft that at most it scarcely lasts for two hundred years. Rain and frost had gnawed numerous irregular holes in the surface, with a curious effect; the piers and the voussoirs looked as though they were composed of the vermicular stones often met with in French architecture. The doorway might have been the portal of a jail. Above the arch there was a long sculptured bas-relief of harder stone, representing the four seasons, four forlorn figures, aged, blackened and weatherworn. Above the bas-relief there was a projecting ledge of masonry where some chance-sown plants had taken root; yellow pellitory, bindweed, a plantain or two, and a little cherry tree, that even now had reached a fair height.

The massive door itself was of dark oak, shrunk and warped and full of cracks; but, feeble as it looked, it was firmly held together by a series of iron nails, with huge heads, driven into the wood in a symmetrical design. In the middle there was a small square grating covered with rusty iron bars, which served as an excuse for a door knocker which hung there from a ring, and struck upon the menacing head of a great iron bolt. The knocker itself, oblong in shape, was of the kind that our ancestors used to call a "jaquemart", and not unlike a huge note of exclamation. If an antiquary had examined it carefully, he might have found some traces of the grotesque human head that it once represented, but the features of the typical clown had long since been effaced by constant wear. The little grating had been made in past times of civil war, so that the household might recognize their friends without before admitting them, but now it afforded to inquisitive eyes a view of a dank and gloomy archway, and a flight of broken steps leading to a not unpicturesque garden shut in by thick walls through which the damp was oozing, and a hedge of sickly-looking shrubs. The walls were part of the old fortifications, and up above upon the ramparts there were yet other gardens belonging to some of the neighbouring houses.

Taken from Eugénie Grandet, *translated by Ellen Marriage (Everyman's Library)*

The Indre valley, from *Le Lys dans la vallée*

With no other sustenance than a dimly seen object that filled my soul, I found infinite love written in the long ribbon of water streaming in the sun between two green banks, in the rows of poplars adorning this vale of love with their flickering lace-work, in the oak trees rising between the vineyards on the ever-changing slopes that the river rounds off, and in the shadowy horizons shifting athwart each other. If you want to see nature in the beauty and purity of a betrothed, go there on a spring day; if you want to soothe the bleeding wounds of your heart, return there during the last days of autumn. There, in springtime, Love flutters his wings in mid air; there, in autumn, one thinks of those who are no more. There the sick lungs inhale a kindly freshness, and the eye reposes upon golden copses that impart their peaceful sweetness to the soul.

At this moment, the mills situated on the falls of the Indre were giving voice to this quivering valley, the poplars were swaying in their glee, there was not a cloud in the sky, birds were singing, grasshoppers chirping, everything there was melody. Do not ask me again why I love Touraine; I do not love it as one does one's birthplace, or as one loves an oasis in the desert; I love it as an artist loves art; I love it less than I do you; but, without Touraine, maybe I might not now be living.

Alain-Fournier

Alain-Fournier was born Henri Alban at La Chapelle-d'Angillon, in the Sologne, in 1886. Much like the watchful and forlorn narrator of *Le Grand Meaulnes*, he was the son of a country schoolteacher – the atmosphere of the provincial schoolroom, and of the Sologne in general, suffuses the novel. *Le Grand Meaulnes* was published in 1912, drawing heavily on the author's unrequited love for a woman he had met by chance in Paris. In 1914 he began his second novel, but was forced to join the army in August that year. He was killed within a month, during fighting on the Meuse.

Meaulnes' journey, from *Le Grand Meaulnes*

At daybreak he set out again. But his knee had swollen and was hurting him. So sharp indeed was the pain that he was forced to stop and rest every few minutes. In the whole of the Sologne it would have been hard to find a more desolate spot than the region in which he now found himself. Throughout the morning he saw no one but a shepherdess guiding her flock some distance away. He called out, and attempted to run, but she disappeared without having heard him.

He limped on in the direction she had taken but his progress was disheartingly slow ... Not a roof, not a living soul, not even the cry of a curlew from the reeds of the marshes. And over all this desolation streamed the thin and frigid light of a December sun.

It must have been getting on for three in the afternoon when he at last saw the spire of a turret above a large grove of fir trees.

"Some forsaken old manor," he surmised. "Some deserted pigeon-house ..."

But he kept wearily to his course. At a corner of the wood he came upon two white posts marking the entrance to an avenue. He turned into it and had not gone far when he was brought to a halt in surprise and stood there, stirred by an emotion he could not have defined. Then he pushed on with the same dragging steps. His lips were cracked by the wind which at moments almost took his breath away. And yet he was now sustained by an extraordinary sense of well-being, an almost intoxicating serenity, by the certitude that the goal was in sight, that he had nothing but happiness to look forward to. It reminded him of days gone by when he would nearly faint with delight on the eve of the midsummer fête, when out in the village street they would be setting up fir trees and his bedroom window was obstructed by branches.

Then he scoffed at himself for rejoicing at the prospect of "a tumble-down pigeon-house full of owls and draughts ..."

Disgruntled, he paused, half inclined to turn back and walk on till he came to a village. As he stood trying to make up his mind, his eyes fixed on the ground, he noticed that the avenue had been swept in wide symmetrical circles, as on very special occasions at home. It was like the high street at La Ferté on the morning of Assumption ... He could not have been more surprised had he come upon a group of holiday-makers stirring up a cloud of dust as if it were June ...

"And yet," he mused, "of all places for a fête – this wilderness!"

Taken from Le Grand Meaulnes, *translated by Frank Davison (Penguin)*

Wine

The Loire is the kid sister of French wine regions: lively, charming, fresh-faced, full of promise and usually not taken seriously by friends of her rich older brothers, Bordeaux and Burgundy. As a wine region, the geographical area covered by the Loire is unusually large, extending almost 400km from Sancerre, in the very centre of France, to Nantes, on the Atlantic coast. The soil and climate are particularly varied, as are the wines. There are two dozen different *appellations* to discover, ranging from crisp, white Sancerre to honeyed Bonnezeaux, and from a zesty, youthful Touraine *primeur* to a heady old Chinon red. The Loire is subdivided into four main wine regions: **Centre**, which means Sancerre and the wines of the Haut Berry; **Touraine**, which also includes the region around Blois; **Anjou–Saumur**; and, over the border in Brittany, **Nantes**.

This following is only an introduction to the main wine styles of the Loire. Wine buyers can find incredibly detailed information available free at tourist offices in all wine areas, including maps of the well-signposted **wine roads**, or *routes des vignobles*, lists of addresses of wine *caves* and advice on finding growers who speak English, if need be. Due to the northerly climate, **vintages** are particularly important in the Loire, especially for red wines, as the grapes only ripen properly in sunnier, drier years. Of course, the weather in some years is better than others, but it's impossible to generalize any further, as different regions and even different winemakers can produce wines of higher or lower quality in any given year. For serious research, try to get hold of a copy of Jacqueline Friedrich's opinionated *Wine and Food Guide to the Loire* or Roger Voss's charming *Wines of the Loire* (unfortunately, both are out of print). Some recommendations on partnering **food and wine** are given below, but for more on the cuisine of the Loire, see Basics (p.31).

Touraine wines

Most of the Touraine wine you can buy outside the region is the standard, white Apellation d'Origine Contrôlée (AOC) **Touraine**, much of it pretty ordinary stuff with an unfortunate astringency resulting from not-quite-ripe Sauvignon Blanc grapes. The better-quality wines can be appealing, however, with a good balance of acidity and sweetness and a heady floral nose. **Vouvray** has its own separate and very well-known *appellation*, while the tiny **Touraine Azay-le-Rideau** AOC is starting to produce some good Chenin Blanc whites. Red AOC **Touraine** wine is less commonly seen, and not much missed, though some interesting reds are being produced under the more tightly controlled **Touraine Amboise** and **Touraine Mesland** *appellations*, which allow a blend of Gamay with smaller amounts of Cabernet Franc and Côt. The former is sold everywhere in and around Amboise, east of Tours, while the latter is centred around the Blésois villages of Monteaux and Mesland, on the right bank of the Loire opposite Chaumont.

Vouvray and Montlouis

Some of the best wines in the Loire are born in the chalky uplands of **Vouvray**, which slope back from the Loire just east of Tours, but there's still a fair

The great grape of the white wines of Touraine and Anjou is **Chenin Blanc**, known locally as **Pineau de la Loire**. It is increasingly planted in California and South Africa, but only achieves its potential in the Loire valley. Wines made with the Pineau are typically redolent of honey, quince, grilled almonds and lime leaves, often with a distinctive smell of wet wool or musty stone – not unlike the limestone *caves* in which it often matures. It is capable of producing a bewildering range of wine styles ranging from sweet to dry, as well as sparkling, and notorious for having a "closed" period – wines made with the Chenin Blanc tend to be drinkable young but then lose the best of their flavour for a period of anything from five to ten years. You'll need to find an all-too-rare older wine to discover the best of the grape. **Sauvignon Blanc** is the staple of Sancerre, Pouilly-Fumé and ordinary Touraine. It thrives in a cool climate, producing superbly crisp, grassy, smoky-perfumed wines at its best. At its worst, it can make an astringently acidic wine whose smell has been described as "cat's pee on a gooseberry bush".

amount of sulphurous rubbish too. The trick is to follow a local recommendation and avoid buying blind, as all too often you can't tell from the label what's inside. Vouvray is always white but it can be *sec* (dry), *tendre* (half-dry) or *demi-sec* (slightly sweet), and in good years when the noble rot sets in, it can be *moelleux* (sweet) and even *doux* or *liquoreux* (very sweet). Sparkling wines are covered on p.339. Vouvray's character varies enormously, but basically, it's the classic expression of the Chenin Blanc grape (see box above) on its classic Loire soils – either *aubuis*, which is chalky Loire tufa, or *perruches*, which is a flinty silex. The latter produces a more severe, mineral-flavoured wine, but the former is a true Loire Chenin, with a smoky dampness in the nose, an apricot or apple fruitiness on the palate and a firm acidity to hold all the flavours together. It goes perfectly with fish. The most famous Vouvray wines include Le Haut Lieu, Domaine des Aubuisières, Château Gaudrelle, Clos Baudoin and Clos Naudin – all in Vouvray itself. Of the two cooperatives, the Cave des Producteurs du Vouvray, in Vouvray's Vallée Coquette, is the higher rated.

Montlouis, across the river, makes very similar wines that tend to age a little faster and cost a little less. There's an excellent Cave Cooperative in Montlouis itself, but if you want to follow the wine roads, make for the villages of Husseau, on the Loire, and St-Martin-le-Beau, at the far side of the *appellation*, on the Cher. At the former, look for the *caves* of Dominique Moyer, Claude Levasseur and Yves et François Chidaine; at the latter, make for G&G Deletang.

Chinon and Bourgueil

Facing each other across the Loire are the two great red wine *appellations* of Touraine: **Bourgueil**, on the north bank, and **Chinon**, on the south. Both rely almost solely on the Cabernet Franc grape, as grown in Bordeaux – which means they risk comparison with their more famous southern cousin. A good bottle can silence claret-loving detractors, maturing for up to thirty or forty years and offering up rich spicy, truffle-like flavours in age. An indifferent bottle, however, can be a little thin and unrewarding, and is best enjoyed young, lightly chilled and without fuss. Between the two extremes, a more typical Chinon or Bourgeuil should be aged for at least five years. If you're expecting a classic wine like a Burgundy or an old Bordeaux, or a loud, super-fruity New

World offering, you'll be disappointed. These wines are typically light on the palate, gently laced with warm earthiness and the lingering taste of summer fruits, and sometimes perfumed with violets. Top wine-makers include Charles Joguet, in Sazilly, and Couly-Dutheil and Château de la Grille, on the edges of Chinon itself. There are also rich pickings around the village of Cravant-les-Côteaux.

It's hard to pick out differences between the two. Chinon, which catches a little more sunshine, is perhaps bigger and more rounded, while Bourgueil is sometimes rougher-edged, with more tannin – qualities particularly pronounced in **St-Nicolas-de-Bourgueil**, a separate appellation just west of Bourgueil itself. If you know the origin of the wine, it's more helpful to talk about the different types of soil, as all three appellations share the same basic types. The gravelly, sandy soil of the valley bottoms produces a fast-maturing, rustic wine best suited to drinking young, while the chalky limestone-clay of the plateaux produces the smoother, more serious, longer-maturing wines. The wines are often used locally in rich meat sauces, and tend to go well with meat and game in general. Their fruitiness also makes them an excellent partner for cheese, especially goat's cheese. Even if you're not serving them chilled, they shouldn't be too warm, perhaps three or four degrees below room temperature. For excellent Bourgueil wines, look for Domaine de la Lande and Domaine de la Coudraye, in Bourgueil, and Pierre-Jacques Druet, in the Hameau de la Croix-Rouge, just outside Benais. In the St-Nicolas *appellation*, try the Domaine Joël Taluau.

Jasnières

Fashionable Parisian restaurants and wine-sellers started a trend for this previously obscure wine a few years back, pushing **Jasnières** into the national wine consciousness. The main drawback for this *appellation* is its northern latitude – Jasnières is closer to Le Mans than Tours, situated in the Loir valley near Vendôme. Yields are kept very low to ensure only the ripest grapes get through, but in colder, wetter years the acidity can be intolerably high, producing a poor, tight-lipped wine. A good vintage can be exceptional, however, especially if you can wait six or seven years for the Chenin Blanc flavour to really open up. The leading wine-maker is Joël Gigou, based in La Chartre-sur-le-Loir.

Red wine grapes

The classic red wine grape of the Loire is the **Cabernet Franc**, locally called the **Breton**, probably because it arrived here from Brittany. The grape is best known for its use in Bordeaux, mostly as a junior partner in the blend, though it plays a bigger role in Pomerol and St-Emilion, with their limestone soils and damper climate. Its finest expression, however, is in the Loire, where its popularity partly stems from its ability to ripen early and resist cold winters. It produces wonderfully silky, summery reds, smooth, pungent and with a distinctive taste of raspberries. It is often drunk young, but the better wines should be laid down. The traditional local grape is the **Grolleau**, or Groslot, a robust grape now best served by its use in rosé. As in Beaujolais, **Gamay** is popular as a **primeur** – made for drinking very young. Less common are **Cabernet Sauvignon**, the classic grape of Bordeaux, Burgundy's **Pinot Noir** – used for red Sancerre – and the plummy **Malbec**, known locally as the **Côt**.

Anjou and Saumur wines

Even by Loire standards, Anjou makes an extraordinary variety of white wines, especially if you include those of the Saumurois, with which they are normally grouped. By volume, rosé is the leading wine, but there are significant amounts of usually unexceptional **AOC Anjou** and **AOC Saumur** – names which can refer to both white wines made with the Chenin Blanc grape and red wines made with a mixture of Cabernet Franc and Cabernet Sauvignon. The more interesting red wines come under the **Anjou-Villages, Anjou-Villages-Brissac** and **Saumur-Champigny** *appellations*, while **Savennières** is the elite *appellation* for dry whites. There's also a fair amount of **Anjou Gamay**, which has seen passing trends as an alternative *primeur* to the ubiquitous Beaujolais. But the most extraordinary wines produced in this region are the exquisite sweet wines of the **Côteaux du Layon** and, to a lesser extent, the **Côteaux de l'Aubance**.

C

Rosé d'Anjou

Anjou's reputation suffers from the glut of bargain-priced rosé wines that dominate the market. **Rosé d'Anjou** can make pleasant summer drinking, but more typically it's over-sweet and dull. The drier, more aromatic **Rosé de Loire** appellation tends to be superior. Both are made with varying mixtures of the Cabernet Franc, Cabernet Sauvignon, Côt, Gamay, Grolleau and local Pineau d'Aunis grapes, but Rosé d'Anjou relies primarily on the Grolleau. The **Cabernet d'Anjou** and much rarer **Cabernet de Saumur** rosé *appellations* both restrict themselves to just the two Cabernet grapes, but they're very different in style. The former is fruity and semi-sweet, making a good dessert wine, while the latter is dry, lively and highly floral, and perfect with grilled and spiced meats.

Savennières

The white wines of **Savennières** are in a class of their own. The unusually steep, south-facing slopes around this small western Anjou village are made of volcanic schist, which soaks up every available ray of sunshine. Yields are kept tiny, and the local techniques are highly rarified. Many producers follow complex variations on organic growing methods that are designed to express the character of the local *terroir* to the greatest possible degree. The wine itself is equally unusual – deep golden in colour, ageing superbly up to thirty years, but almost exclusively dry. One wine writer has described Savennières as having "the distant beauty of an ice maiden". The grape variety is Chenin Blanc, which offers up some surprising flavours in this context: white peaches, minerals, jasmine and, later in life, dried fruit, beeswax and honey. It's a classic served alongside fish in a *beurre blanc*, especially the Loire favourites, *sandre* and salmon. A Savennières should only be very lightly chilled, certainly not lower than 10°C. The top-rated vineyards are Roche-aux-Moines and Coulée de Serrant – the latter so small as to be exclusively owned by one wine-maker, the philosophical Nicolas Joly, who follows the "biodynamic" theory of wine-making. Other great Savennières wines include Clos de Colaine, Château d'Epiré and Domaine du Closel.

Côteaux du Layon

The Layon valley and the slopes, or *côteaux*, that surround it, is one of the few areas in France where climate and topography come together to allow the autumnal growth of a fungus called *botrytis cinerea*. Morning mist and hot afternoon sunshine allow this "**noble rot**" to develop, weakening the skin of the grape so that it shrivels and dehydrates, causing the sugars inside to concentrate. Growers have to make many *tries*, or passes through the vineyard, to handpick the grapes where noble rot has set in to the required extent. The result is one of the finest sweet wines in France, a serious rival to the internationally better-known Sauternes, though made with the Loire's Chenin Blanc grape rather than Bordeaux's Sémillon. The main flavour of a Côteaux du Layon is honey, but the sweetness is balanced by herby notes and fruity acidity – you might detect apricot, citrus zest and figs, and it's easy to imagine oversweet grapes bursting in the late-year, late-afternoon sun. The top wines can last a lifetime, and slowly become more and more pungent with spices, delicate and yet muscular at the same time. The idea of "dessert wine" is anathema to the French, and these wines should be drunk as an apéritif or paired with foie gras and other liver pâtés. Alternatively, they can partner sauced fish, and make a superb match for blue cheese – especially Roquefort. Serve cool, at around 8–10°C.

The *appellation* **Côteaux du Layon** extends along the length of the Layon valley, from near Doué-la-Fontaine to Chalonnes-sur-Loire. Within that stretch are two elite mini-*appellations* – **Quarts de Chaume**, near Rochefort-sur-Loire, and **Bonnezeaux**, around Thouarcé. At both, the slopes face south to southwest, allowing the maximum afternoon sunshine to reach the grapes. Highly rated Bonnezeaux wines include Domaine de la Sansonnière and Château de Fesles, both based in Thouarcé, while for Quarts de Chaume the top end of the market is dominated by Château de Bellerive and Domaines Baumard, both in Rochefort-sur-Loire.

Saumur-Champigny

The name "Champigny" supposedly comes from the Latin *campus ignis*, meaning "field of fire", and refers to the sunny microclimate that favours this sheltered corner of the Saumurois. It is this warm weather that allows the region to produce top-quality red wines, all of which are dubbed **Saumur-Champigny** to distinguish them from the local white wines. Like its great rival, Chinon, the *cépage* is Cabernet Franc, and the flavours are similar: raspberry, strawberry, cherry, sometimes vanilla, with distinctive violet notes.

The area is well defined, stretching back from the south bank of the Loire between Saumur and the border with Touraine. The principal wine town is St-Cyr-en-Bourg, in the southwestern corner of the *appellation*, but you'll find growers in all the villages along the Loire too: Montsoreau, Turquant, Parnay and Dampierre.

Centre wines

Unlike the rest of the Loire region, the **Sauvignon Blanc** – a relative of the Cabernet Sauvignon, which originally came from Bordeaux – is the chief grape variety for white wines from the Centre region. One name dominates:

Sancerre. Its dry whites are exported all over the world, and sold at high prices relative to other Loire wines. Explore a little further afield, however, and you'll find subtly different offerings at **Menetou-Salon**, a few kilometres west of Sancerre, where the whites are more forgiving and floral than Sancerre, and can be better value, and at **Pouilly-Fumé**, on the east bank of the river, where the wines lean in the opposite direction, towards flinty austerity. **Pouilly-sur-Loire** comes from the same area as the Fumé, but is made with the frankly inferior Chasselas grape. Less well known than any of these are the tiny *appellations* of **Reuilly** and **Quincy**, isolated on the left bank of the Cher, west of Bourges. In the **Côteaux du Giennois**, north of Sancerre down the Loire, they make a straightforward, lightweight red from a mix of the Gamay and Pinot Noir grapes, and a white that often tastes like a rather slight Pouilly-Fumé.

Reuilly and Quincy

The twin vineyards of **Reuilly** and **Quincy** are minuscule, together covering scarcely a tenth of the area of Sancerre, and for years they were scarcely known outside the region. The popularity of Sauvignon Blanc has galvanized the local producers in the last decade or so, however, and the wines are now gaining a reputation as a quirky, insider's alternative to Sancerre – as promoted in the restaurants of Paris. A good bottle of either can be wonderfully aromatic, slightly tart with the flavour of gooseberries. Reuilly also comes in rosé, made with Pinot Noir and Pinot Gris, and in good years it can be very interesting: soft, fresh and perfumed with red fruits. The red Reuilly wines, made with Pinot Noir, are not highly regarded.

Sancerre

Sancerre is one of the few Loire regions with a serious international reputation. Made with the **Sauvignon Blanc** grape, the white wines are traditionally dry, crisp and acid – you could almost describe the flavour as green. Increasingly, however, wine-growers are using New World techniques to get as much fruity, floral flavour as possible out of the grape. It's unusually difficult to get to know the wines of Sancerre, as most growers' holdings are very small, and often split up into tiny parcels on a number of different vineyards. What's more, the growers aren't allowed to name the vineyard or origin on the label, even if there is only one; instead they have to put their own name to it, or resort to *cuvée* names that hint slyly at the vineyard of origin. And there are three very different types of **soil**. On the western hilltops are the *terres blanches*, or Kimmeridgean chalk soils, which produce the classic Sancerre, especially when combined with wines from the drier *caillottes*, or pebbly limestones (on their own, wines grown on the *caillottes* are more suitable for younger, easier drinking). Just a fifth of the territory is *silex*, the flint-clay soil which many believe makes the finest Sancerre whites of all – complex, steely, powerful and best drunk aged a few years. All can be drunk as apéritifs, but they also go well with white meats and creamy dishes, the acidity cutting through the fat. The big names are Mellot and Vacheron in Sancerre itself; Lucien Crochet, in Bué; and Henri Bourgeois, in Chavignol, but it's well worth trying out smaller wine-makers.

Red Sancerre is much harder to find outside the region, but it can be exceptional in a good year. Like red Burgundy, which is geographically quite close, it is made with the **Pinot Noir** grape, which can produce a surprisingly pale, thin-looking wine that browns quite quickly. Some drinkers find it off-putting, and the nose is even more extraordinary, a composty smell that some describe as like raw meat or rotting fruit. The flavour is less heavy and full-bodied than Burgundy, but can be just as complex, rich with spicy, earthy flavours; it goes well with game, duck and meaty fish dishes. It can be very enjoyable when drunk young and lightly chilled. Sancerre's soft, fruity **rosé** enjoyed a brief fashion in the 1970s, but is relatively uninteresting.

Pouilly-Fumé

Not to be confused with Burgundy's Pouilly-Fuissé, the wines of Pouilly-Fumé are twinned with Sancerre and, as such, fall definitively within the Loire wine region. In terms of geography, however, Pouilly lies on the east bank, in Burgundy, and you won't, therefore, find it in this guidebook. This needn't deter wine buyers, who need only drive across the bridge from St-Satur, and turn right onto the D553 for **Tracy-sur-Loire**, one of the main wine *communes*, situated on a delightful stretch of the Loire. You can then continue to the main village of **Pouilly-sur-Loire**, as well as nearby St-Andelain and Les Berthiers, just off the A77/N7.

Pouilly-Fumé is, if anything, even more serious than Sancerre: gun-metal flinty, mineral-flavoured and sometimes severe. Roger Voss, writing in *Wines of the Loire*, claims that the wines "express the character of the Sauvignon Blanc in complete simplicity". Top wine-makers include Château de Nozet, just north of Pouilly; Château de Tracy, close to the river; and the Dagueneau brothers: Jean-Claude, in Les Berthiers, and Didier, in St-Andelain.

Sparkling wines

The sparkling wines of the Loire are made in exactly the same way as champagne, and indeed they called themselves that before the wine-growers of the actual Champagne region started to object. **Méthode traditionelle** is now added to the label to denote a serious sparkling wine made in the traditional way. The Loire's sparklers are, on the whole, excellent value – a good sparkling Vouvray or Saumur typically costs roughly half the price of an inferior bottle of champagne, where you're paying for the brand. If you're in Saumur or Vouvray, a visit to the rock-cut *caves*, where thousands of racked-up bottles take advantage of the ideal cool conditions to mature, is a must. If you're not, a glass or two as an apéritif is just as obligatory – in France, sparkling wines are not restricted to celebrations.

Saumur

The longest-established Loire sparkling wine is **Saumur** *mousseux*, often marketed as Saumur Brut. Saumur was the first town in the Loire to use the champagne technique, and some of the great houses are still owned by champagne-makers: Gratien & Meyer is part of Alfred Gratien Champagne, while Bouvet-Ladubay is owned by Taittinger, and Langlois-Château by Bollinger. The local giants – whose budget-priced wines may be relatively disappointing – are Ackerman-Laurance and Veuve Amiot. Saumur mostly relies on the local Chenin Blanc, but with various admixtures of Cabernet Franc and Champagne's Chardonnay grape to moderate any acid hardness in the Brut. *Demi-secs* can be packed with honeyed flavour, especially when aged, and Gratien & Meyer even make a sparkling red.

Vouvray

Connoisseurs are particularly keen on **Vouvray**, an *appellation* just east of Tours which makes around half of its wines into sparklers, depending on the year. Most common is the full-pressure *mousseux*, usually known as Vouvray Brut, which is crisper and less heady than champagne, the acidity and quince or apple-like fruitiness of the Chenin Blanc grape balancing any creamy sweetness. Some people prefer it to champagne, but it has to be said that an inferior Vouvray can be rather thin. Don't ignore the honeyed *demi-secs* and the gently fizzing *pétillant* wines, which can be superb. **Montlouis**, just across the Loire from Vouvray, makes similar, often slightly lighter sparkling wines.

Crémant de la Loire

One sparkling wine to watch out for is Crémant de la Loire, although it's still somewhat scarce. Unusually, these are blended wines from across Touraine and Anjou, but the quality is assured by regulations insisting on very low grape yields, hand-harvesting and bottle ageing for at least a year. The wine is usually made with 60 percent Chenin Blanc and 25 percent Cabernet Franc, with the champagne grape Chardonnay (15 percent) adding a familiar creamy richness.

Language

Language

French

rench can be a deceptively familiar language because of the number of words and structures it shares with English. Despite this, it's far from easy, though the bare essentials are not difficult to master and can make all the difference. Even just saying "Bonjour madame/monsieur" and then gesticulating will usually get you a smile and helpful service. People working in tourist offices, hotels and so on, almost always speak English and tend to use it when you're struggling to speak French – be grateful, not insulted.

Pronunciation

One easy rule to remember is that **consonants** at the ends of words are usually silent: Tours is thus pronounced "toor", Orléans is "or-lay-on" and Angers "on-jay". Otherwise they are much as in English, except that: *ch* is always "sh", *c* is "s", *h* is silent, *th* is the same as "t", *ll* is like the "y" in yes, *w* is "v", and *r* is growled (or rolled). **Vowels** are the hardest sounds to get exactly right, but they rarely differ enough from English to make comprehension a problem – though note that *au* sounds like the "o" in "over", as in *aujourd'hui* ("oh-jor-dwi") *oi* becomes "wa", as in Blois ("Blwa") and adding "m" or "n" to a vowel, as in *en* or *un*, adds a nasal sound, as if you said just the vowel with a cold.

Basic words and phrases

French nouns are divided into masculine and feminine. This causes difficulties with adjectives, whose endings have to change to suit the nouns they qualify – you can talk about *un château blanc* (a white castle), for example, but *une tour blanche* (a white tower). If you're not sure, stick to the simpler masculine form – as used in this glossary.

yes **oui**	later **plus tard**
no **non**	at one o'clock **à une heure**
please **s'il vous plaît**	at three o'clock **à trois heures**
thank you **merci**	at ten-thirty **à dix heures et demie**
sorry **pardon/Je m'excuse**	at midday **à midi**
excuse me **pardon**	man **un homme**
OK/agreed **d'accord**	woman **une femme** (pronounced "fam")
hello **bonjour**	here **ici**
goodbye **au revoir**	there **là**
good morning/afternoon **bonjour**	this one **ceci**
good evening **bonsoir**	that one **cela**
good night **bonne nuit**	open **ouvert**
help! **au secours!**	closed **fermé**
today **aujourd'hui**	entrance **entrée**
yesterday **hier**	exit **sortie**
tomorrow **demain**	big **grand**
in the morning **le matin**	small **petit**
in the afternoon **l'après-midi**	more **plus**
in the evening **le soir**	less **moins**
now **maintenant**	a little **un peu**

a lot **beaucoup**	hot **chaud**
cheap **bon marché/pas cher**	cold **froid**
expensive **cher**	with **avec**
good **bon**	without **sans**
bad **mauvais**	

Numbers

1 **un**	21 **vingt-et-un**
2 **deux**	22 **vingt-deux**
3 **trois**	30 **trente**
4 **quatre**	40 **quarante**
5 **cinq**	50 **cinquante**
6 **six**	60 **soixante**
7 **sept**	70 **soixante-dix**
8 **huit**	75 **soixante-quinze**
9 **neuf**	80 **quatre-vingts**
10 **dix**	90 **quatre-vingt-dix**
11 **onze**	95 **quatre-vingt-quinze**
12 **douze**	100 **cent**
13 **treize**	101 **cent-et-un**
14 **quatorze**	200 **deux cents**
15 **quinze**	300 **trois cents**
16 **seize**	500 **cinq cents**
17 **dix-sept**	1000 **mille**
18 **dix-huit**	2000 **deux milles**
19 **dix-neuf**	1,000,000 **un million**
20 **vingt**	

Days and dates

January **janvier**	Monday **lundi**
February **février**	Tuesday **mardi**
March **mars**	Wednesday **mercredi**
April **avril**	Thursday **jeudi**
May **mai**	Friday **vendredi**
June **juin**	Saturday **samedi**
July **juillet**	Sunday **dimanche**
August **août** (pronounced "oot")	
September **septembre**	August 1 **le premier août**
October **octobre**	March 2 **le deux mars**
November **novembre**	July 14 **le quatorze juillet**
December **décembre**	2005 **deux mille cinq**

Talking to people

When addressing people a simple **bonjour** is not enough; you should always use **Monsieur** ("muh-syuh") for a man, **Madame** for a woman, **Mademoiselle** ("mam-zelle") for a young woman or girl. This isn't as formal as it seems, and it has its uses when you've forgotten someone's name or want to attract someone's attention. **Bonjour** can be used well into the afternoon, and people may start saying **bonsoir** surprisingly early in the evening, often as a way of saying goodbye.

Do you speak English? **Parlez-vous anglais?**	What's your name? **Comment vous appelez-vous?**
How do you say it in French? **Comment ça se dit en français?**	My name is… **Je m'appelle…**

I'm… **Je suis…**
…English …**anglais[e]**
…Irish …**irlandais[e]**
…Scottish …**écossais[e]**
…Welsh …**gallois[e]**
…American …**américain[e]**
…Australian …**australien[ne]**
…Canadian …**canadien[ne]**
…a New Zealander …**néo-zélandais[e]**
…Dutch … **néerlandais[e]**
I understand **Je comprends**
I don't understand **Je ne comprends pas**

Can you speak slower? **S'il vous plaît, parlez moins vite**
How are you? **Comment allez-vous?/Ça va?**
Fine, thanks **Très bien, merci**
I don't know **Je ne sais pas**
Let's go **Allons-y**
See you tomorrow **A demain**
See you soon **A bientôt**
Leave me alone **Fichez-moi la paix!** (aggressive)
Please help me **Aidez-moi, s'il vous plaît**

The simplest way of asking a question is to start with **s'il vous plaît** (please), then name the thing you want in an interrogative tone of voice. For example:

Where is there a bakery? **S'il vous plaît, la boulangerie?**
Which way is it to the château? **S'il vous plaît, la route pour le château?**
Similarly with requests:
We'd like a room for two? **S'il vous plaît, une chambre pour deux?**
Can I have a kilo of oranges? **S'il vous plaît, un kilo d'oranges?**

where? **où?**
how? **comment?**
how many/how much? **combien?**
how much is it? **c'est combien?**
when? **quand?**
why? **pourquoi?**
at what time? **à quelle heure?**
what is/which is? **quel est?**

Getting around

bus **autobus/bus/car**
bus station **gare routière**
bus stop **arrêt**
car **voiture**
train/taxi/ferry **train/taxi/ferry**
boat **bâteau**
plane **avion**
shuttle **navette**
train station **gare (SNCF)**
platform **quai**
What time does it leave? **Il part à quelle heure?**
What time does it arrive? **Il arrive à quelle heure?**
a ticket to… **un billet pour…**
single ticket **aller simple**
return ticket **aller retour**
validate your ticket **compostez votre billet**
ticket office **vente de billets**
how many kilometres? **combien de kilomètres?**
how many hours? **combien d'heures?**
hitchhiking **autostop**

on foot **à pied**
Where are you going? **Vous allez où?**
I'm going to… **Je vais à …**
I want to get off at… **Je voudrais descendre à …**
the road to… **la route pour…**
near **près/pas loin**
far **loin**
left **à gauche**
right **à droite**
straight on **tout droit**
on the other side of **à l'autre côté de**
next to **à côté de**
behind **derrière**
in front of **devant**
before **avant**
after **après**
under **sous**
to cross **traverser**
bridge **pont**
town centre **centre ville**
old town **vieille ville**

Cars

to park the car **garer la voiture**
car park **le parking**
no parking **défense de stationner/stationnement interdit**

fuel **essence**
4-star petrol/gas **super**
unleaded **sans plomb**
diesel **gas-oil**

fill it up! **faites le plein!**
oil **huile**
petrol station **station-service**
service station **garage**

put air in the tyres **gonfler les pneus**
to break down **tomber en panne**
insurance **assurance**

Cycling

I'd like to hire **je voudrais louer un…**
bicycle **vélo**
mountain bike **VTT** ("vay-tay-tay")
brakes **freins**
cassé **broken**
chain **chaîne**
gears **les vitesses**
inflate **gonfler**

inner tube **chambre à l'air**
pump **pompe**
puncture **crevaison**
repair **réparer**
spanner **clef**
spoke **rayon**
tyre **pneu**
wheel **roue**

Accommodation

I'd like to reserve/book **je voudrais réserver**
a room for one/two persons **une chambre pour une/deux personne(s)**
with a double bed **avec un grand lit**
with two singles **avec deux lits**
with a shower **avec douche**
with a bath **avec salle de bain**
with a sink **avec lavabo**
with a shared bathroom **avec WC dans le palier**
for one/two/three nights **pour une/deux/trois nuits**
Can I see it? **Je peux la voir?**
a room on the courtyard **une chambre sur la cour**
a room over the street **une chambre sur la rue**
first floor **premier étage**
second floor **deuxième étage**
with a view **avec vue**
key **clef**

to iron **repasser**
do laundry **faire la lessive**
sheets **draps**
blankets **couvertures**
hot water **eau chaude**
cold water **eau froide**
Is breakfast included? **Est-ce que le petit déjeuner est compris?**
I would like breakfast **Je voudrais prendre le petit déjeuner**
I don't want breakfast **Je ne veux pas de petit déjeuner**
bed and breakfast **chambres d'hôtes**
evening meal at a B&B **table d'hôte**
Can we camp here? **On peut camper ici?**
campsite **camping**
tent **tente**
tent space **un emplacement**
hostel **foyer**
youth hostel **auberge de jeunesse**

Health

doctor **médecin**
chemist **pharmacie**
hospital **hôpital**
I don't feel well **Je ne me sens pas bien**
medicines **médicaments**
prescription **ordonnance**
I feel sick **Je suis malade**

I have a headache **J'ai mal à la tête**
stomach ache **mal à l'estomac**
pain **douleur**
it hurts **ça fait mal**
condom **préservatif**
morning-after pill **pilule du lendemain**

Other needs

stamps **timbres**
bank **banque**
money **argent**

toilets **toilettes**
police **police**
telephone **téléphone**

Food and drink terms

Basic words and phrases

lunch **déjeuner**
dinner **dîner**
set menu **menu**
individually priced dishes **à la carte**
starters **entrées**
main courses **les plats**
a carafe of water **une carafe d'eau**
mineral water **eau minérale**
fizzy water **eau gazeuse**
still water **eau plate**
wine list **carte des vins**
a quarter/half-litre of red/white house wine **un quart/demi de rouge/blanc**
a glass of white/red wine **un (verre de) rouge/blanc**

I'd like to reserve a table **Je voudrais réserver une table**
for two people, at eight thirty **pour deux personnes, à vingt heures et demie**
I'm having the €15 set menu **Je prendrai le menu à quinze euros**
Waiter! **monsieur/madame!**
the bill/check please **l'addition, s'il vous plait**
a glass of beer **une pression**
coffee (espresso) **un café**
white coffee **un crème**
big bowl of milky breakfast coffee **un café au lait**

Cooking terms

bio or **biologique** organic
cru raw
cuit cooked
fumé smoked

pimenté spicy
salé salted/savoury
sucré sweet

Essentials

beurre butter
bouteille bottle
couteau knife
cuillère spoon
à emporter takeaway
formule lunchtime set menu
fourchette fork
huile oil
lait milk
moutarde mustard

œuf egg
pain bread
plat main course
poivre pepper
sel salt
sucre sugar
table table
verre glass
vinaigre vinegar

Snacks

un sandwich/une baguette a sandwich
croque-monsieur grilled cheese and ham sandwich
panini toasted Italian sandwich
tartine buttered bread or open sandwich
crêpe pancake
galette buckwheat pancake

omelette omelette
...nature plain
...aux fines herbes with herbs
...au fromage with cheese
salade de tomates tomato salad
salade vert green salad

Soups (soupes) and starters (hors d'œuvres)

assiette anglaise plate of cold meats
assiette composée mixed salad plate, usually cold meat and vegetables
bisque shellfish soup
bourride thick fish soup

consommé clear soup
crudités raw vegetables with dressings
hors d'œuvres combination of the above plus cold meats
potage thick vegetable soup

349

soupe à l'oignon onion soup with rich cheese topping

velouté thick soup, usually fish or poultry

alose shad
anchois anchovies
anguilles eels
barbue brill
bigourneau periwinkle
brème bream
brochet pike
cabillaud cod
calmar squid
carrelet plaice
colin hake
congre conger eel
coques cockles
coquilles St-Jacques scallops
crabe crab
crevettes grises shrimps
crevettes roses prawns
daurade sea bream
éperlan smelt or whitebait
escargots snails
flétan halibut
friture assorted fried fish
gardons roach
goujons gudgeon
hareng herring
homard lobster
huîtres oysters
lamproie river lamprey
langouste spiny lobster
langoustines saltwater crayfish (scampi)
limande lemon sole
lotte de mer monkfish
loup de mer sea bass

maquereau mackerel
merlan whiting
moules (marinière) mussels (with shallots in white wine sauce)
palourdes clams
raie skate
rouget red mullet
sandre pike-perch or zander
saumon salmon
sole sole
thon tuna
truite trout
turbot turbot
Fish dishes and terms
arête fish bone
assiette de pêcheur assorted fish
beignet fritter
darne fillet or steak
en matelote in a red-wine stew
en beurre blanc in a butter, shallot and white-wine sauce
friture deep-fried small fish
fumé smoked
fumet fish stock
gigot de mer large fish baked whole
grillé grilled
hollandaise butter and vinegar sauce
à la meunière in a butter, lemon and parsley sauce
mousse/mousseline mousse
pané breaded
quenelles light dumplings

agneau lamb
andouille pork sausage
andouillette tripe sausage
bavette French cut of beef equivalent to flank
bifteck steak
bœuf beef
boudin blanc sausage of white meats
boudin noir black pudding
caille quail
canard duck
caneton duckling
contrefilet sirloin roast
dinde/dindon turkey
entrecôte rib steak
faisan pheasant
faux filet sirloin steak

foie liver
foie gras pâté of force-fed duck/goose liver
gibier game
gigot (d'agneau) leg (of lamb)
grenouilles (cuisses de) frogs (legs)
grillade grilled meats
hâchis chopped meat or mince hamburger
langue tongue
lapin/lapereau rabbit/young rabbit
lard/lardons bacon/diced bacon
lièvre hare
mouton mutton
museau de veau calf's muzzle
oie goose
onglet French cut of steak
os bone

pâté au biquion pâté of pork, veal and goat
pintade guinea fowl
porc pork
poulet chicken
poussin baby chicken
rillettes pork mashed with lard and liver
rillons cubes of fatty pork
ris sweetbreads
rognons kidneys

rognons blancs testicles
sanglier wild boar
tête de veau calf's head (in jelly)
tournedos thick slices of fillet
tripes tripe
tripoux mutton tripe
veau veal
venaison venison

Meat and poultry dishes and terms

aile wing
blanquette, daube, estouffade, hochepôt, navarin, ragoût types of stew
blanquette de veau veal in cream and mushroom sauce
bœuf bourguignon beef stew with Burgundy, onions and mushrooms
carré best end of neck, chop or cutlet
cassoulet casserole of beans, sausages and duck/goose
choucroute pickled cabbage with peppercorns, sausages, bacon and salami
civet game stew
confit meat preserve
côte chop, cutlet or rib
cou neck
coq au vin chicken slow-cooked with wine, onions and mushrooms
cuisse thigh or leg

épaule shoulder
en croûte in pastry
farci stuffed
au feu de bois cooked over wood fire
au four baked
garni with vegetables
gésier gizzard
grillade grilled meat
grillé grilled
magret de canard duck breast
marmite casserole
médaillon round piece
mijoté stewed
pavé thick slice
poêlé pan-fried
râble saddle
rôti roast
sauté lightly fried in butter
viennoise fried in egg and breadcrumbs

Terms for steaks

bleu almost raw
saignant rare
à point medium rare

bien cuit well done
très bien cuit very well done
brochette kebab

Garnishes and sauces

auvergnat with cabbage, sausage and bacon
béarnaise sauce of egg yolks, white wine, shallots and vinegar
bonne femme with mushroom, bacon, potato and onions
bordelaise in a red wine, shallot and bone-marrow sauce
boulangère baked with potatoes and onions
bourgeoise with carrots, onions, bacon, celery and braised lettuce
chasseur white wine, mushrooms and shallots

châtelaine with artichoke hearts and chestnut purée
diable strong mustard seasoning
forestière with bacon and mushroom
fricassée rich, creamy sauce
mornay cheese sauce
pays d'auge cream and cider
périgourdine with foie gras and possibly truffles
piquante gherkins or capers, vinegar and shallots
provençale tomatoes, garlic, olive oil and herbs
savoyarde with gruyère cheese

Vegetables (légumes), herbs (herbes) and spices (épices)

ail garlic
anis aniseed

artichaut artichoke
asperge asparagus

avocat avocado
basilic basil
betterave beetroot
blette/bette Swiss chard
cannelle cinnamon
capre caper
cardon cardoon, a beet related to artichoke
carotte carrot
céleri celery
cèpes ceps/edible boletus
champignons (de Paris) mushrooms
chou (rouge) (red) cabbage
choufleur cauliflower
concombre cucumber
cornichon gherkin
echalotes shallots
endive chicory
épinard spinach
estragon tarragon
fenouil fennel
fèves broad beans
flageolets flageolet beans
gingembre ginger
girolles chanterelles
haricots haricot beans (French/string)
  verts string beans
  rouges kidney beans
  beurres yellow snap beans
laurier bay leaf

lentilles (vertes) (green) lentils
maïs maize (corn)
menthe mint
moutarde mustard
oignon onion
panais parsnip
pélandron type of string bean
pâte pasta or pastry
persil parsley
petits pois peas
pieds bleu/jaune blue/yellow-foot mushrooms
pignons pine nuts
piment (rouge/vert) (red/green) chilli pepper
pleurotes oyster mushrooms
pois chiche chick peas
pois mange-tout snow peas
poireau leek
poivron (vert/rouge) (green/red) sweet
  pepper
pommes de terre potatoes
primeurs spring vegetables
radis radish
riz rice
safran saffron
salade verte green salad
sarrasin buckwheat
tomate tomato
trompettes de la mort horns of plenty
truffes truffles

Vegetable dishes and terms

beignet fritter
duxelles fried mushrooms and shallots with cream
farci stuffed
feuille leaf
fines herbes mixture of tarragon, parsley and
  chives
gratiné browned with cheese or butter
à la grecque cooked in oil and lemon

jardinière with mixed diced vegetables
mousseline mashed potato with cream and eggs
parmentier with potatoes
petits farcis stuffed tomatoes, aubergines,
  courgettes and peppers
râpée grated or shredded
à la vapeur steamed
en verdure garnished with green vegetables

Fruit (fruit) and nuts (noix)

abricot apricot
acajou cashew nut
amande almond
ananas pineapple
banane banana
brugnon, nectarine nectarine
cacahouète peanut
cassis blackcurrant
cérise cherry
citron lemon
citron vert lime
datte date
figue fig

fraise (de bois) strawberry (wild)
framboise raspberry
fruit de la passion passion fruit
grenade pomegranate
groseille redcurrant
marron chestnut
melon melon
mirabelle small yellow plum
myrtille bilberry
noisette hazelnut
noix walnuts or nuts in general
orange orange
pamplemousse grapefruit

pêche peach
pistache pistachio
poire pear
pomme apple

prune plum
pruneau prune
raisin grape
reine-claude greengage

Fruit dishes and terms

agrumes citrus fruits
beignet fritter
compôte stewed fruit
coulis sauce of puréed fruit

crème de marrons chestnut purée
flambé set aflame in alcohol
frappé iced
tapée dried (local apples and pears)

Desserts (desserts or entremets) and pastries (pâtisserie)

brioche sweet, high-yeast breakfast roll
clafoutis heavy custard and fruit tart
crème Chantilly vanilla-flavoured and sweetened whipped cream
crème fraîche sour cream
crème pâtissière thick, eggy pastry-filling
crêpe suzette thin pancake with orange juice and liqueur
fromage blanc cream cheese
gaufre waffle
glace ice cream

macaron macaroon
madeleine small sponge cake
mousse au chocolat chocolate mousse
parfait frozen mousse, sometimes ice cream
petit-suisse a smooth mixture of cream and curds
petits fours bite-sized cakes/pastries
poires belle hélène pears and ice cream in chocolate sauce
tarte Tatin upside-down apple tart
yaourt/yogourt yoghurt

Cheese

assiette de fromage plate of selected cheeses
cendré dusted with ash
chèvre goat's cheese

fermier farm-produced
frais fresh/unmatured
sec dry (strong)

Glossary

alimentation food

Angevin/Angevine from Anjou; a man/woman from Anjou

appellation (d'origine) contrôlée government certification guaranteeing the quality of a French wine; often written AOC

autoroute motorway/freeway

Berrichon/Berrichonne from the Berry region; a man/woman from the Berry

boulangerie baker's

centre ville town centre

chambres d'hôtes B&B accommodation in a private house

charcuterie sells cold meats and other prepared foods

département administrative division of France, roughly equivalent to a English county

dégustation tasting, as in wine tasting

église church

étang a marshy pond or small lake

fief land held under the feudal system

foyer residential hostel for young workers and students

fromagerie cheese shop

gare routière bus station

gare SNCF train station

gîte (d'étape) privately rented, government-regulated accommodation

halles market

hôtel particulier mansion or townhouse

Hôtel de Ville town hall (in a city)

Mairie town hall

marché market

patisserie cakeshop

plats du jour daily specials

pont bridge

quartier district in a town or city

rue street

seigneur the lord of a château

Solognot/Solognote from the Sologne; a man/woman from the Sologne

tabac tobacconist's, also selling bus/metro tickets and phone cards

table d'hôte a communal dining table in a home or restaurant

Tourangeau/Tourangelle from Touraine; a man/woman from Touraine

traiteur delicatessen

Architectural terms

These are either terms you'll come across in the *Guide*, or come up against while travelling around.

abbaye abbey

ambulatory passage round the outer edge of the choir of a church, behind the high altar

apse semicircular termination at the east end of a church

arcade series of arches; in a church, the bottom-most of usually two or three well-defined horizontal sections, below the triforium

Baroque largely seventeenth-century style of art and architecture distinguished by dynamism and extreme ornateness

beaux-arts fine arts

capital top of a column, often carved

Carolingian dynasty (and art, sculpture, etc) named after Charlemagne; mid-eighth to early tenth centuries

chancel part of a church containing the altar and sanctuary

château mansion, country house, castle

château fort castle

choir the part of a church between the altar and nave, used by the choir and clergy

chevet east end of a church

Classical architectural style incorporating Greek and Roman elements: pillars, domes, colonnades, etc; dominant in France from the seventeenth century

clerestory upper storey of a church, incorporating the windows

collégiale collegiate church (run by canons)

communs the outbuildings of a château, often with stables

cornice decorative line dividing the facade from the roof

crypt area of a church usually under the choir, sometimes used for burial

cul-de-lampe decorated base of a corbel or projecting bit of masonry

donjon castle keep

dormer upright window projecting from a sloping roof

échauguette bartizan, or overhanging corner turret

église church

First Renaissance from the early sixteenth century

Flamboyant late style of Gothic architecture (c.1450–1540) characterized by elaborate, "flame-like" stone-carving

Gallo-Roman from the Roman era in France

hôtel (particulier) mansion or town house

loggia open gallery or arcade

logis noble wing of a château, often a dedicated building

machicolation openings pierced in a parapet for dropping stones etc on attackers

Merovingian dynasty (and art, etc), ruling France and parts of Germany from sixth to mid-eighth centuries

misericord shelf under a choir seat for leaning against, often carved

narthex entrance hall or porch of a church

nave main body of a church, usually at the west end and flanked by aisles

œil-de-bœuf small, circular "bull's-eye" window, often set into the roof

porte gateway

Rayonnant mid-period style of Gothic architecture (c.1340–1450) characterized by chapels radiating from the apse

Renaissance in architecture, a Classically-influenced, rationally planned style developed in fifteenth-century Italy and imported to France in the early sixteenth century

retable altarpiece

Roman Romanesque (easily confused with Romain – Roman)

Romanesque early medieval architecture (eleventh to thirteenth centuries) distinguished by rounded arches and naive sculpture; called Norman in Britain.

stringcourse horizontal band of stone dividing a facade

stucco heavy limestone plaster used for decoration

tour tower

transept transverse arms of a church

triforium wall-passage at middle-level of a church, between the arcade at the lowest level and the clerestory above

trompe-l'oeil artistic effect that deceives the eye, usually with the illusion of depth

tufa creamy, crumbly limestone typical of the Loire region

tympanum sculpted panel above a church door

voussoir wedge of stone around an arch

Rough
Guides

advertiser

Rough Guides travel...

ROUGH GUIDES ADVERTISER

UK & Ireland
Britain
Devon & Cornwall
Dublin
Edinburgh
England
Ireland
Lake District
London
London mini guide
London Restaurants
London & SE England,
  Walks in
Scotland
Scottish Highlands &
  Islands
Wales

Europe
Algarve
Amsterdam
Andalucía
Austria
Baltic States
Barcelona
Belgium & Luxembourg
Berlin
Brittany & Normandy
Bruges & Ghent
Brussels
Budapest
Bulgaria
Copenhagen
Corfu
Corsica
Costa Brava
Crete
Croatia
Cyprus
Czech & Slovak
  Republics
Dodecanese & East
  Aegean
Dordogne & The Lot
Europe
First-Time Europe
Florence
France

Germany
Greece
Greek Islands
Hungary
Ibiza & Formentera
Iceland
Ionian Islands
Italy
Languedoc & Roussillon
Lisbon
The Loire
Madeira
Madrid
Mallorca
Malta & Gozo
Menorca
Moscow
Netherlands
Norway
Paris
Paris Mini Guide
Poland
Portugal
Prague
Provence & the Côte
  d'Azur
Pyrenees
Romania
Rome
Sardinia
Scandinavia
Sicily
Slovenia
Spain
St Petersburg
Sweden
Switzerland
Tenerife & La Gomera
Turkey
Tuscany & Umbria
Venice & The Veneto
Vienna

Asia
Bali & Lombok
Bangkok
Beijing

Cambodia
China
First-Time Asia
Goa
Hong Kong & Macau
India
Indonesia
Japan
Laos
Malaysia, Singapore &
  Brunei
Nepal
Philippines
Singapore
South India
Southeast Asia
Thailand
Thailand Beaches &
  Islands
Tokyo
Vietnam

Australasia
Australia
Gay & Lesbian Australia
Melbourne
New Zealand
Sydney

North America
Alaska
Baltic States
Big Island of Hawaii
Boston
California
Canada
Chicago
Florida
Grand Canyon
Hawaii
Honolulu
Las Vegas
Los Angeles
Maui
Miami & the Florida
  Keys
Montréal

New England
New Orleans
New York City
New York City Mini
  Guide
New York Restaurants
Pacific Northwest
Rocky Mountains
San Francisco
San Francisco
  Restaurants
Seattle
Skiing & Snowboarding
  in North America
Southwest USA
Toronto
USA
Vancouver
Washington DC
Yosemite

**Caribbean
& Latin America**
Antigua & Barbuda
Argentina
Bahamas
Barbados
Belize
Bolivia
Brazil
Caribbean
Central America
Chile
Costa Rica
Cuba
Dominican Republic
Ecuador
First-Time Latin
  America
Guatemala
Jamaica
Maya World
Mexico
Peru
St Lucia
South America
Trinidad & Tobago

358

Rough Guides are available from good bookstores worldwide. New titles are
published every month. Check www.roughguides.com for the latest news.

...music & reference

Africa & Middle East
Cape Town
Egypt
The Gambia
Jerusalem
Jordan
Kenya
Morocco
South Africa, Lesotho
& Swaziland
Syria
Tanzania
Tunisia
West Africa
Zanzibar
Zimbabwe

Travel Theme guides
First-Time Around the
World
First-Time Asia
First-Time Europe
First-Time Latin
America
Gay & Lesbian
Australia
Skiing & Snowboarding
in North America
Travel Online
Travel Health
Walks in London & SE
England
Women Travel

Restaurant guides
French Hotels &
Restaurants
London
New York
San Francisco

Maps
Algarve
Amsterdam
Andalucia & Costa del Sol
Argentina
Athens

Australia
Baja California
Barcelona
Boston
Brittany
Brussels
Chicago
Crete
Croatia
Cuba
Cyprus
Czech Republic
Dominican Republic
Dublin
Egypt
Florence & Siena
Frankfurt
Greece
Guatemala & Belize
Iceland
Ireland
Lisbon
London
Los Angeles
Mexico
Miami & Key West
Morocco
New York City
New Zealand
Northern Spain
Paris
Portugal
Prague
Rome
San Francisco
Sicily
South Africa
Sri Lanka
Tenerife
Thailand
Toronto
Trinidad & Tobago
Tuscany
Venice
Washington DC
Yucatán Peninsula

**Dictionary
Phrasebooks**
Czech
Dutch
Egyptian Arabic
European
French
German
Greek
Hindi & Urdu
Hungarian
Indonesian
Italian
Japanese
Mandarin Chinese
Mexican Spanish
Polish
Portuguese
Russian
Spanish
Swahili
Thai
Turkish
Vietnamese

Music Guides
The Beatles
Cult Pop
Classical Music
Country Music
Cuban Music
Drum'n'bass
Elvis
House
Irish Music
Jazz
Music USA
Opera
Reggae
Rock
Techno
World Music (2 vols)

**100 Essential CDs
series**
Country
Latin

Opera
Rock
Soul
World Music

History Guides
China
Egypt
England
France
Greece
India
Ireland
Islam
Italy
Spain
USA

Reference Guides
Books for Teenagers
Children's Books, 0–5
Children's Books, 5–11
Cult Football
Cult Movies
Cult TV
Digital Stuff
Formula 1
The Internet
Internet Radio
James Bond
Lord of the Rings
Man Utd
Personal Computers
Pregnancy & Birth
Shopping Online
Travel Health
Travel Online
Unexplained
Phenomena
The Universe
Videogaming
Weather
Website Directory

Also! More than 120 Rough Guide music CDs are available from all
good book and record stores. Listen in at www.worldmusic.net

ROUGH GUIDES ADVERTISER

Rough Guides maps

Rough Guide Maps, printed on waterproof
and rip-proof Yupo™ paper, offer an
unbeatable combination of practicality,
clarity of design and amazing value.

CITY MAPS

Amsterdam · Barcelona · Berlin · Boston · Brussels · Dublin
Florence & Siena · Frankfurt · London · Los Angeles
Miami · New York · Paris · Prague · Rome
San Francisco · Venice · Washington DC and more...

COUNTRY & REGIONAL MAPS

Andalucía · Argentina · Australia · Baja California · Cuba
Cyprus · Dominican Republic · Egypt · Greece
Guatemala & Belize · Ireland · Mexico · Morocco
New Zealand · South Africa · Sri Lanka · Tenerife · Thailand
Trinidad & Tobago Yucatán Peninsula · and more...

360

US$9.99   Can$13.99   £5.99

ROUGH GUIDES ADVERTISER

Visit us online
roughguides.com

Information on over 25,000 destinations around the world

- **Read** Rough Guides' trusted travel info
- **Share** journals, photos and travel advice with other readers
- Get exclusive Rough Guide **discounts** and travel **deals**
- Earn membership points every time you contribute to the
  Rough Guide **community** and get **free** books, flights and trips
- Browse thousands of CD reviews and artists in our **music** area

361

ROUGH GUIDES ADVERTISER

Athens
DIRECTIONS

1843533146

Lisbon
DIRECTIONS

1843533154

London
DIRECTIONS

1843533162

Paris
DIRECTIONS

1843533170

San Francisco
DIRECTIONS

1843533189

Venice
DIRECTIONS

1843533537

PUBLISHED AUGUST 2004

Amsterdam
DIRECTIONS

1843533065

Antigua & Barbuda
DIRECTIONS

1843533197

Barbados
DIRECTIONS

1843533200

Marrakesh
DIRECTIONS

1843533219

New York City
DIRECTIONS

1843533227

Tenerife & La Gomera
DIRECTIONS

1843533225

DIRECTIONS

362

US$10.99 · Can$15.99 · £6.99

MUSIC ROUGH GUIDE

Rough Guides To
A World Of Music

'stick to the reliable Rough Guide series' *The Guardian (UK)*

'Over the past few years the Rough Guide CDs, with their stylish covers, have distinguished themselves as approachable and well-chosen introductions to the music of the countries concerned. They have been consistently well-reviewed and, like the guidebooks themselves, stand out as an obvious first choice for journeys in world music'
Simon Broughton, Editor Songlines

Hear sound samples at WWW.WORLDMUSIC.NET

Available from book and record shops worldwide or order direct from World Music Network, 6 Abbeville Mews, 88 Clapham Park Road, London SW4 7BX, UK
T. 020 7498 5252 F. 020 7498 5353 E. post@worldmusic.net

ROUGH GUIDES ADVERTISER

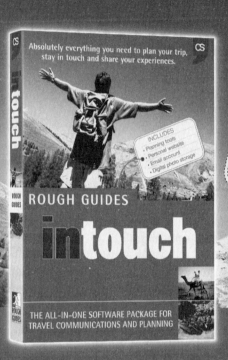

Absolutely everything you need to plan your trip, stay in touch and share your experiences.

INCLUDES
• Planning tools
• Personal website
• Email account
• Digital photo storage

ROUGH GUIDES

intouch

THE ALL-IN-ONE SOFTWARE PACKAGE FOR TRAVEL COMMUNICATIONS AND PLANNING

ROUGH GUIDES

A NEW CONCEPT IN TRAVEL

ROUGH GUIDES SOFTWARE
Share your adventures on the move

Rough Guides have launched **intouch**, a new all in one software package for planning your trip and staying in touch with people back home before, during and after your travels.

Create an itinerary and budget using on-screen information and maps, and take advantage of the diary to keep family and friends informed of your whereabouts.

The diary can be linked to your mobile phone so that you can send a text message, **intouch** will automatically send an email or cheap SMS to those listed on your account.

You can also post photos and diary entries online and then download them to make a journal on your return.

Rough Guides **intouch** is easy to install and you don't need to take anything with you – just hit the synchronize button and then use it from any internet café in the world.

Rough Guides **intouch** includes:
Planning tools
Free email address
Free personal website
Digital photo storage   And much more.....

£5 OFF your purchase of Rough Guides **intouch** if you buy online at
www.roughguidesintouch.com reference code: Rough Guide Books

Recommended retail price £24.99 available through leading retailers e.g. WH Smith, Waterstones and PC World

364

450 BRANCHES WORLDWIDE

SPECIALISTS IN TRAVEL FOR STUDENTS & YOUNG PEOPLE

LOW COST FLIGHTS > OVERLAND & ADVENTURE TOURS
ACCOMMODATION > TRAVEL INSURANCE > CAR HIRE
CITY & CLUBBING BREAKS > ROUND THE WORLD > GAP YEAR
SKI & SNOWBOARD > TRAVEL HELP > WELL TRAVELLED STAFF

STA TRAVEL LTD

ABTA
99209

3206
AVOL
PROTECTED

0870 160 6070
www.statravel.co.uk

ROUGH GUIDES ADVERTISER

STANF♦RDS
EXPLORE DISCOVER INSPIRE

The world's finest map and travel bookshops

Explore   **Discover**   **Inspire**

Maps

Travel Guides

Illustrated Books

Travel Literature

World Atlases

Globes

World Wall Maps

Climbing Maps & Books

Maritime Maps & Books

Historical Maps

Instruments

Children's

**Stanfords Flagship Store
12-14 Long Acre
Covent Garden
London
WC2 9LP
(T) 020 7836 1321**

**39 Spring Gardens
Manchester
M2 2BG
(T) 0161 831 0250**

**29 Corn Street
Bristol
BS1 1HT
(T) 0117 929 9966**

**International Mail Order
Department
+44 (0)20 7836 1321**

www.stanfords.co.uk

Inspiring exploration and discovery for 150 years

372

Miles better for France

Wherever you live in the UK, wherever you're heading for in France, there's a Brittany Ferries' route to save you miles of unnecessary driving. Sail by day or overnight from Portsmouth, Poole or Plymouth and enjoy award-winning service.

New for 2004
Portsmouth to Cherbourg route
Additional overnight Portsmouth to St Malo sailings

Call now to book
0870 366 6283

CORK

PLYMOUTH POOLE PORTSMOUTH

CHERBOURG
CAEN
ROSCOFF ST MALO

SANTANDER

Brittany Ferries

www.brittanyferries.com

373

Don't bury your head in the sand!

Take cover!

with Rough Guide Travel Insurance

Worldwide cover, for Rough Guide readers worldwide

UK Freefone **0800 015 09 06**
Worldwide **(+44) 1392 314 665**
Check the web at
www.roughguides.com/insurance

ROUGH GUIDES

Insurance organized by Torribles Insurance Brokers Ltd, 21 Prince Street, Bristol, BS1 4PH, England

ROUGH GUIDES ADVERTISER

374

Index
+ small print

Twenty years of Rough Guides

In the summer of 1981, Mark Ellingham, Rough Guides' founder, knocked out the first guide on a typewriter, with a group of friends. Mark had been travelling in Greece after university, and couldn't find a guidebook that really answered his needs.There were heavyweight cultural guides on the one hand – good on museums and classical sites but not on beaches and tavernas – and on the other hand student manuals that were so caught up with how to save money that they lost sight of the country's significance beyond its role as a place for a cool vacation. None of the guides began to address Greece as a country, with its natural and human environment, its politics and its contemporary life.

Having no urgent reason to return home, Mark decided to write his own guide. It was a guide to Greece that tried to combine some erudition and insight with a thoroughly practical approach to travellers' needs. Scrupulously researched listings of places to stay, eat and drink were matched by careful attention to detail on everything from Homer to Greek music, from classical sites to national parks and from nude beaches to monasteries. Back in London, Mark and his friends got their Rough Guide accepted by a farsighted commissioning editor at the publisher Routledge and it came out in 1982.

The Rough Guide to Greece was a student scheme that became a publishing phenomenon. The immediate success of the book – shortlisted for the Thomas Cook award – spawned a series that rapidly covered dozens of countries. The Rough Guides found a ready market among backpackers and budget travellers, but soon acquired a much broader readership that included older and less impecunious visitors. Readers relished the guides' wit and inquisitiveness as much as the enthusiastic, critical approach that acknowledges everyone wants value for money – but not at any price.

Rough Guides soon began supplementing the "rougher" information – the hostel and low-budget listings – with the kind of detail that independent-minded travellers on any budget might expect. These days, the guides – distributed worldwide by the Penguin group – include recommendations spanning the range from shoestring to luxury, and cover more than 200 destinations around the globe. Our growing team of authors, many of whom come to Rough Guides initially as outstandingly good letter-writers telling us about their travels, is spread all over the world, particularly in Europe, the USA and Australia. As well as the travel guides, Rough Guides publishes a series of dictionary phrasebooks covering two dozen major languages, an acclaimed series of music guides running the gamut from Classical to World Music, a series of music CDs in association with World Music Network, and a range of reference books on topics as diverse as the Internet, Pregnancy and Unexplained Phenomena. Visit **www.roughguides.com** to see what's cooking.

SMALL PRINT

Rough Guide credits

Editors: Claire Saunders and Gavin Thomas
Layout: Link Hall and Dan May
Cartography: Ed Wright, Miles Irving and the Delhi team
Picture research: Jj Luck, Louise Boulton
Proofreader: Jennifer Speake

....

Editorial: London Martin Dunford, Kate Berens, Helena Smith, Claire Saunders, Geoff Howard, Ruth Blackmore, Gavin Thomas, Polly Thomas, Richard Lim, Lucy Ratcliffe, Clifton Wilkinson, Alison Murchie, Fran Sandham, Sally Schafer, Alexander Mark Rogers, Karoline Densley, Andy Turner, Ella O'Donnell, Keith Drew, Andrew Lockett, Joe Staines, Duncan Clark, Peter Buckley, Matthew Milton; **New York** Andrew Rosenberg, Richard Koss, Yuki Takagaki, Hunter Slaton, Chris Barsanti, Thomas Kohnstamm, Steven Horak
Design & Layout: London Dan May, Diana Jarvis; **Delhi** Madhulita Mohapatra, Umesh Aggarwal, Ajay Verma

Production: Julia Bovis, John McKay, Sophie Hewat
Cartography: London Maxine Repath, Ed Wright, Katie Lloyd-Jones, Miles Irving; **Delhi** Manish Chandra, Rajesh Chhibber, Jai Prakesh Mishra, Ashutosh Bharti, Rajesh Mishra, Animesh Pathak
Cover art direction: Louise Boulton
Picture research: Sharon Martins, Mark Thomas, Jj Luck
Online: New York Jennifer Gold, Cree Lawson, Suzanne Welles; **Delhi** Manik Chauhan, Amarjyoti Dutta, Narender Kumar
Marketing & Publicity: London Richard Trillo, Niki Smith, David Wearn, Chloë Roberts, Demelza Dallow, Christina Pentland; **New York** Geoff Colquitt, David Wechsler, Megan Kennedy
Finance: Gary Singh
Manager India: Punita Singh
Series editor: Mark Ellingham
PA to Managing Director: Julie Sanderson
Managing Director: Kevin Fitzgerald

Publishing Information

This first edition published May 2004 by **Rough Guides Ltd**,
80 Strand, London WC2R 0RL.
345 Hudson St, 4th Floor,
New York, NY 10014, USA.
Distributed by the Penguin Group
Penguin Books Ltd,
80 Strand, London WC2R 0RL
Penguin Putnam, Inc.
375 Hudson Street, NY 10014, USA
Penguin Books Australia Ltd,
487 Maroondah Highway, PO Box 257,
Ringwood, Victoria 3134, Australia
Penguin Books Canada Ltd,
10 Alcorn Avenue, Toronto, Ontario,
Canada M4V 1E4
Penguin Books (NZ) Ltd,
182–190 Wairau Road, Auckland 10,
New Zealand
Typeset in Bembo and Helvetica to an original design by Henry Iles.

Printed in Italy by LegoPrint S.p.A

© James McConnachie

No part of this book may be reproduced in any form without permission from the publisher except for the quotation of brief passages in reviews.

400pp includes index
A catalogue record for this book is available from the British Library

ISBN 1-84353-257-3

The publishers and authors have done their best to ensure the accuracy and currency of all the information in **The Rough Guide to the Loire**, however, they can accept no responsibility for any loss, injury, or inconvenience sustained by any traveller as a result of information or advice contained in the guide.

1   3   5   7   9   8   6   4   2

Help us update

We've gone to a lot of effort to ensure that the first edition of **The Rough Guide to the Loire** is accurate and up to date. However, things change – places get "discovered", opening hours are notoriously fickle, restaurants and rooms raise prices or lower standards. If you feel we've got it wrong or left something out, we'd like to know, and if you can remember the address, the price, the time, the phone number, so much the better.

We'll credit all contributions, and send a copy of the next editio

Guide if you prefer) for the best letters. Everyone who writes to us and isn't already a subscriber will receive a copy of our full-colour thrice-yearly newsletter. Please mark letters: "**Rough Guide Loire Update**" and send to: Rough Guides, 80 Strand, London WC2R 0RL, or Rough Guides, 4th Floor, 345 Hudson St, New York, NY 10014. Or send an email to **mail@roughguides.com**

Have your questions answered and tell others about your trip at
......atinfopop.com

3 1327 00428 5474

Acknowledgements

I'd like to say a special thank you to my parents, Robin and Gwen McConnachie, for their expert advice and for introducing me to the Loire in the first place; to Jonathan Buckley, for his encouragement and inspiration; and to Alice Hunt, for all her support. I'd also like to thank everyone at Rough Guides, especially Kate Berens and Martin Dunford, and my admirable editor, Claire Saunders. This guide couldn't have been written without the help of the many enthusiastic and engaging staff at tourist offices and tourist boards, and the passionate owners and diligent guides who have welcomed me to their châteaux, museum, vineyard or balloon basket; my sincere thanks to all. Finally, thanks also to Anne-Sophie Ascher, Sarah Barnes, Samuel Buchwalder, Sofia Dyson, Tom Dyson, Dominique Dumet, Monsieur et Madame Dumet, Didier Gea, Jerry Goodman, Jane Janvier, Sally Jones, Philip Macgregor, Charlie Marshall, Monsieur et Madame Mercier, Marc Metay, Evelyne de Pontbriand, Natalie Robinson, Pierre Sabouraud, Richard Scholar, Anita Silvestre, Matthew Teller, Gavin Thomas, Stephen Tuckwell, Colin Tudge, Greg Ward and Clifton Wilkinson.

SMALL PRINT

Photo Credits

Cover Credits
Main front: Chambord ©Alamy
Small front top picture: Chenonceau ©Alamy
Small front lower picture: Tours ©Alamy
Back top picture: Villandry fountain ©James
    McConnachie
Back lower picture: Cathédrale Ste-Croix,
    Orléans ©Alamy

Colour introduction section
The Loire from the Grande Levée ©James
    McConnachie
Architectural evolution, Châteaudun ©James
    McConnachie
Sign ©Lourens Smak/Alamy
Picnic near the château of Saumur ©Giruad
    Philippe/CORBIS
Vine terraces at Villandry ©James
    McConnachie
West front of St-Gatien, Tours ©James
    McConnachie
Late summer on the Loire ©James
    McConnachie
Joan stained glass at Ste-Croix, Orléans
    ©James McConnachie
Café at Chinon square ©Michael Juno/Alamy

Things not to miss
01 Garden of Love, Villandry ©James
    McConnachie
02 Poplars by the river, Montreuil-Bellay
    ©James McConnachie
03 Geese outside château, La Ferté-St-
    Aubin ©James McConnachie
04 St-Etienne, Bourges, by night ©James
    McConnachie
05 Dining out in Place Plum', Tours
    ©James McConnachie
06 King's bedchamber, château de Blois
    ©James McConnachie
07 Staying at the château des Réaux
    ©James McConnachie
08 Yvan Thibaudat's canoe descents,
    Sancerre ©James McConnachie
09 Tomb of Agnès Sorel, Loches ©James
    McConnachie
10 Angel vault at St-Julien, Le Mans
    ©James McConnachie
11 Boats under the arches, Chenonceau
    ©James McConnachie
12 Richard Rak's troglodyte house,
    Coutures ©James McConnachie
13 Meadows of Montrésor ©James
    McConnachie
14 Compagnon's secret, Dénezé-sous-
    Doué ©James McConnachie

15 Wisteria at Montgeoffroy ©James
    McConnachie
16 Bourgueil market ©James
    McConnachie
17 Cycling ©Bo Zaundrs/CORBIS
18 Tapestry of the Apocalypse, Angers
    ©James McConnachie
19 The river façade, Chambord ©James
    McConnachie
20 Plantagenet tombs, Fontevraud
    ©James McConnachie
21 Common tern ©Mike Lane/Alamy
22 Sparkling bottles in the caves, Saumur
    ©James McConnachie
23 Rose garden, Prieuré de St-Cosme
    ©James McConnachie
24 Château overlooking the Loire,
    Montsoreau ©James McConnachie
25 Blue Virgin window, Chartres ©James
    McConnachie
26 Azay-le-Rideau son-et-lumière
    ©James McConnachie

Black and white images
p.54 Bridge at Amboise ©James
    McConnachie
p.66 Towers of St-Gatien, Tours ©James
    McConnachie
p.110 The old town and the Vienne, Chinon
    ©James McConnachie
p.126 Château de Cheverny ©James
    McConnachie
p.149 François I staircase, château de Blois
    ©James McConnachie
p.166 Summer flowers at château de Sully
    ©James McConnachie
p.173 Statue of Joan of Arc at Hôtel
    Groslot, Orléans ©James
    McConnachie
p.202 Street facade of Palais Jacques-Cœur,
    Bourges ©James McConnachie
p.211 Cul-de-lampe at Hôtel Lallemant,
    Bourges ©James McConnachie
p.222 Riverbank and château, Saumur
    ©James McConnachie
p.236 Cloister, Fontevraud ©James
    McConnachie
p.248 Gatehouse at Le Plessis-Bourré
    ©James McConnachie
p.270 Gates, Montgeoffroy ©James
    McConnachie
p.276 Ronsard's motto, La Possonnière
    ©James McConnachie
p.281 Twin spires, Chartres ©James
    McConnachie

SMALL PRINT

Index

Map entries are in colour

Map symbols

maps are listed in the full index using coloured text

-----	Chapter division boundary
--·--·--	Departmental boundary
▬▬	Motorway
▮ ▮ ▮ ▮	Motorway under construction
═══	Main road
──	Minor road
ⲙⲙⲙⲙ	Steps
▬▬	Pedestrianized street (town maps)
▄▄▄▄▄	City wall/fortifications
⊢⊢⊢⊢	Railway
──	River
✈	Airport
♦	Point of interest
∴	Ruin/prehistoric site

🏛	Château
♜	Castle
⌂	Abbey
⊙	Statue/memorial
⊠–⊠	Gate
⚔	Campsite
ⓘ	Tourist office
⊠	Post office
⊞	Hospital
⊜	Swimming pool
▬	Building
➕	Church (town maps)
▦	Park
░	Forest

BOOK SALE WITHDRAWN